PRAISE FOR HUMAN BEHAVIOR: A CELL TO SOCIETY APPROACH

"*Human Behavior: A Cell to Society Approach* represents the most contemporary knowledge about the role both biology and technology play in human development and behavior. The material is represented in a way that is intellectually challenging yet accessible, and the use of the case studies, spotlight topics, and expert's corner keep the reader interested and engaged."

Rachel A. Fusco, Assistant Professor
University of Pittsburgh, School of Social Work

"The authors provide social workers with an essential tool to navigate the new cross-disciplinary environment. Their take on HBSE content will enable students to communicate with researchers and practitioners across disciplines about the complex factors impacting health and well-being in today's world."

Sarah Gehlert, PhD
E. Desmond Lee Professor of Racial and
Ethnic Diversity at the Brown School of Social Work,
Washington University

"*Human Behavior: A Cell to Society Approach* provides social workers in training with foundational knowledge about human adaptation to the social environment from neurobiological through psychosocial perspectives across the life-cycle. Information and illustrations are well organized and clearly communicated, derived from classic and cutting-edge theory and research, and include case vignettes and attention to technology. This knowledge broadens reader understanding of client, family and community, and social problems, and prompts consideration of multiple congruent intervention approaches."

Kurt C. Organista, PhD, Professor,
University of California, Berkeley, School of Social Welfare

"This bold new approach brings Human Behavior in the Social Environment into the 21st Century. Highly recommended."

Paul T. Shattuck, PhD
Associate Professor
Brown School of Social Work,
Washington University

HUMAN BEHAVIOR

HUMAN BEHAVIOR
A Cell to Society Approach

Michael G. Vaughn
Matt DeLisi
Holly C. Matto

This book is printed on acid-free paper.∞

Copyright © 2014 by John Wiley & Sons, Inc. All rights reserved.

Published by John Wiley & Sons, Inc., Hoboken, New Jersey.
Published simultaneously in Canada.

For general information on our other products and services please contact our Customer Care Department within the United States at (800) 762-2974, outside the United States at (317) 572-3993 or fax (317) 572-4002.

Wiley publishes in a variety of print and electronic formats and by print-on-demand. Some material included with standard print versions of this book may not be included in e-books or in print-on-demand. If this book refers to media such as a CD or DVD that is not included in the version you purchased, you may download this material at http://booksupport.wiley.com. For more information about Wiley products, visit www.wiley.com.

Library of Congress Cataloging-in-Publication Data:

Vaughn, Michael G.
  Human behavior: a cell to society approach / Michael G. Vaughn, Matt DeLisi, Holly C. Matto.
     pages cm
  Includes bibliographical references and index.
  ISBN 978-1-118-12154-2 (pbk.)
  ISBN 978-1-118-63968-9 (ebk.)
  ISBN 978-1-118-41625-9 (ebk.)
  ISBN 978-1-118-41896-3 (ebk.)
  1. Human behavior. 2. Human behavior—Physiological aspects. I. DeLisi, Matt. II. Matto, Holly C. III. Title.
  BF199.V38 2014
     150—dc23
                                                                        2013001788

Printed in the United States of America
10 9 8 7 6 5 4 3 2 1

BRIEF CONTENTS

DETAILED CONTENTS

CHAPTER 14
BELIEF SYSTEMS AND IDEOLOGY   283

We feel there is a need for an evolution, if not revolution, in the human behavior and the social environment (HBSE) curriculum. Despite the widespread acceptance of the person-in-environment conceptualization, there are few advanced approaches that can truly delineate this overall metaphor in a cutting-edge transdisciplinary scientific framework. We propose a new integrative perspective, a *cell to society approach*, which represents a leap forward in the advancement of human behavior for the helping professions.

Specifically, a cell to society approach to HBSE advances an integrative understanding of human behavior from the cellular level to global institutions, and across human history (e.g., Bowles, Choi, & Hopfensitz, 2002; Fuentes, 2009). The transdisciplinary and historical appreciation of human life experience cultivates an intellectual understanding of behavior beyond what has typically been put forth. Indeed, we know that human behavior is influenced by myriad factors, spanning from communication among neurons that influence brain structure and behavioral regulation to the ways in which structural and environmental conditions and socioeconomic life changes shape life course trajectories over time (e.g., Spear, 2010; Turrell, Lynch, Leite, Raghunathan, & Kaplan, 2007). The cell to society approach can account for complex, multilevel processes that shape human development and well-being. For instance, we can use the approach to reach across disciplines to consider how relationally based self-regulation capacity in infancy, as influenced by institutional and structural conditions, can lead to differential developmental trajectories. The cell to society approach also can enable the understanding of the social networking structure of human service organizations and its impact on persons and populations, as well as geospatial disparities in health and well-being. Although many schools and departments of social work often split the HBSE course sequence into two courses reflecting micro or individual-level orientation and a macro or systemic societal focus, we take a decidedly integrative, biosocial, multiple-level-of-influence approach that allows students to appreciate the transactional forces that shape life course opportunities and challenges among diverse populations in the United States and around the world. Our perspective allows us both to connect students to the roots and principles of the profession and simultaneously to move them forward into the transdisciplinary scientific landscape, where integrative and dynamic modeling of health and well-being of the human condition will transform the ways in which social work professionals work with clients and client systems.

Although a developmental lens is important as a guiding framework for understanding client systems, our current HBSE curricula often have relied solely on this approach at the expense of integrating a more holistic person-environment perspective that is more compatible with our profession's unique principles. Thus, students' criticism has largely been that they already know this information from their undergraduate social sciences classes. What typically follows, then, becomes either earnest attempts to be waived out of the class or to otherwise petition to get out of taking the sequence. However, we see HBSE foundation coursework as an essential core of the MSW curriculum—in fact, one of the most important parts of the curriculum in social work education. It is a place where micro, meso, and macro dimensions can be truly integrated. We see HBSE as a forum and opportunity for students to become transformational thinkers and leaders in the profession. The result is a stronger intellectuality and credibility for the profession as a whole.

We have tremendous respect for those who teach human behavior and HBSE courses. The sheer magnitude of material that is potentially involved could literally encompass multiple courses. Indeed, many of us spend our entire academic careers on these topics yet often feel like we have hardly scratched the surface of all there is to know. Thus, we recognize that there is a tension between being comprehensive and achieving depth. Our goal was to accomplish both. However, we do so not within a conventional textbook style, but one that is meant to be read. Although we cover the Educational Policy and Accreditation Standard (EPAS) competencies and include figures, tables, and informational inserts such as spotlight topics in each chapter, the emphasis is more on engaging concepts and translating research. Our signature Expert's Corner in each chapter highlights the key scholars in a respective discipline on a human behavior topic, bringing together a transdisciplinary network of experts from across the biological and social sciences.

Although this book advances a theoretical perspective, it is ultimately rooted in the principles of empirical science and the evidence-based paradigm. Throughout we review research studies from leading scientific journals to firmly tie cell to society rubrics to leading-edge data. The cell to society perspective is predicated upon a viewpoint of scientific research consisting of empirical and conceptual aims. Empirical aims seek to gather data or facts and to link theoretical constructs with them in a cycle of exchange toward greater interpretation, intervention, and renewed data collection. Conceptual aims relate to implicit or explicit worldviews, assumptions, and strategic commitments that occur prior to theoretical construction and empirical discovery. In science, conceptual aims are usually neglected, either unconsciously or consciously. However, these underlying concepts or ideas still remain to influence scientific findings and theories. As such, rendering them explicitly increases overall clarity for the benefit of others.

Paradigms are essentially worldviews that set forth rules that govern the conduct of knowledge acquisition. They help people in particular arenas solve problems and interpret the world. Can the cell to society approach be evaluated given that it is more of a paradigm? Comparisons and evaluations of paradigms can be performed based on criteria such as logical structure and internal consistency, scope, parsimony, novelty and innovation, and empirical tests or outcomes of scientific theories that emanate from them. Further, paradigms can be examined to the extent they show where and how to intervene and help others and organize preexisting data (Magnarella, 1993). From the outset we believe it is important to clearly render the major assumptions that guide this book. The following five assumptions and strategies serve as a starting point for elaborating the cell to society approach: (a) human behavior and social life are too complex to efficiently understand without a coherent outline or conceptual framework, (b) human behavior is both determined and allows for choice and agency, (c) it is advantageous for helping professionals to utilize scientific models aimed at ameliorating human problems, (d) some paradigms can explain and direct interventions better than others, and (e) human social problems are shaped largely by the practical problems imposed by collective survival.

In our view, social work perspectives and values are compatible with the aims of the cell to society approach. This compatibility is based upon a consistent theme of scientifically understanding the origins of individual and social phenomena within the boundaries or constraints imposed by biology, environment, human institutions, and ideas. Such understanding is cultivated not only for the sake of knowledge, but also to increase human happiness, decrease human suffering, and promote social justice. The lesson is that scientifically credible knowledge can guide more effective solutions. Our hope is that the cell to society approach elaborated in this book provides a foundation for helping professionals to be sophisticated, credible, and (most important) effective agents of social welfare and social change.

ACKNOWLEDGMENTS

There are a number of people we would like to thank for seeing this book to its completion. First, we would like to thank the team at Wiley, including Rachel Livsey and Amanda Orenstein. They were a pleasure to work with from beginning to end. We would also like to thank research assistants Kristen Peters, for her hard work on several tedious tasks, and Davina Abujudeh, for her input on case studies. Finally, we appreciate the many reviewers who gave their time to read and make numerous thoughtful comments, including Rachel Fusco, Kurt Organista, Carmen Ortiz-Hendricks, Emily Nicklett, Paul Shattuck, Sarah Gehlert, Christy Sarteschi, Brandy Maynard, Christopher Salas-Wright, Michael Mancini, and Shannon Cooper-Sadlo. The book is far better because of their input.

HUMAN BEHAVIOR *AND THE CORE COMPETENCIES (EPAS)*

At the outset we would like to note that this book provides coverage of the 10 core competencies in the Educational Policy and Accreditation Standards, with special emphasis on knowledge of human behavior in the social environment (see Item 7). However, this book exceeds and transcends these core competencies by using the innovative and cutting-edge cell to society approach. The grid at the end displays the 10 competencies and their coverage across the 14 chapters.

10 Core Competencies (CSWE Educational Policy & Accreditation Standards)

1. Identify as a professional social worker and conduct oneself accordingly. (Competency 2.1.1)

2. Apply social work ethical principles to guide professional practice. (Competency 2.1.2)

3. Apply critical thinking to inform and communicate professional judgments. (Competency 2.1.3)

4. Engage diversity and difference in practice. (Competency 2.1.4)

5. Advance human rights and social and economic justice. (Competency 2.1.5)

6. Engage in research-informed practice and practice-informed research. (Competency 2.1.6)

7. **Apply knowledge of human behavior and the social environment. (Competency 2.1.7)**

8. Engage in policy practice to advance social and economic well-being and to deliver effective social work services. (Competency 2.1.8)

9. Respond to contexts that shape practice. (Competency 2.1.9)

10. Engage, assess, intervene, and evaluate with individuals, families, groups, organizations, and communities. (Competency 2.1.10a–d)

Chapter 1: Introducing the Cell to Society Framework

Chapter 1 covers all 10 of the EPAS core competencies, with attention to distinguishing, appraising, and integrating multiple sources of knowledge for use in professional decision making to advance the goals of the profession. The chapter helps readers critically analyze the complexities of how culture and socioenvironmental factors shape life-course development. It draws on the empirical, theoretical, and practice literature to help readers comprehensively understand the needs of social work populations.

Chapter 2: Genes and Behavior

Chapter 2 focuses on EPAS Competencies 1, 2, 3, 6, 7, and 9, with specific attention to using knowledge from the biological and behavioral/social sciences to guide assessment and ethical reasoning in social work practice.

Chapter 3: Stress and Adaptation

Chapter 3 focuses on EPAS Competencies 1, 3, 4, 5, 6, 7, 9, and 10, with attention to the role of oppression and marginalization on developmental opportunities across the life course. It emphasizes the detrimental effects of economic and social injustice on human development.

Chapter 4: Emotion

Chapter 4 focuses on EPAS Competencies 1, 3, 6, 7, 9, and 10, with attention to the use of evidence-based practice to guide assessment, and on judiciously using theories from the biological, behavioral, and social sciences to understand the developmental challenges and opportunities of client populations.

Chapter 5: Executive Functions

Chapter 5 focuses on EPAS Competencies 1, 3, 5, 6, 7, 9, and 10, with attention to using the scientific knowledge base to shape the effective delivery of services.

Chapter 6: Temperament

Chapter 6 focuses on EPAS Competencies 1, 2, 3, 4, 6, 7, 9, and 10, with attention to the importance of developing culturally informed skills that promote equity and social inclusion.

Chapter 7: Personality

Chapter 7 focuses on EPAS Competencies 1, 3, 4, 6, 7, 8, 9, and 10, with attention to differential diagnosis and a focus on the interpersonal dynamics and contextual factors that shape professional relationship development.

Chapter 8: Cognition and Learning

Chapter 8 focuses on EPAS Competencies 1, 3, 6, 7, 8, 9, and 10, with attention to applying the scientific knowledge base to guide assessment and service delivery for diverse social work populations. It emphasizes contextual influences on human development and learning potential.

Chapter 9: Social Exchange and Cooperation

Chapter 9 focuses on EPAS Competencies 1, 3, 4, 5, 6, 7, 8, and 9, with attention to examining how power and privilege impact social work practice across systems; and on identifying how oppression and discrimination influence client-system behavioral functioning.

Chapter 10: Social Networks and Psychosocial Relations

Chapter 10 focuses on EPAS Competencies 1, 3, 5, 6, 7, 8, 9, and 10, with attention to understanding current human development and family formation trends across practice contexts, and implications for social work practice.

Chapter 11: Technology

Chapter 11 focuses on EPAS Competencies 1, 3, 4, 6, 7, 8, 9, and 10, with attention to applying relevant scientific and technological processes to work with client populations. It also develops critical assessment skills to effectively meet the changing needs of diverse social work populations.

Chapter 12: The Physical Environment

Chapter 12 focuses on EPAS Competencies 1, 3, 4, 5, 6, 7, 8, and 9, with attention to understanding community development trends across contexts and the implications for developing and evaluating programs and policies.

Chapter 13: Institutions

Chapter 13 focuses on EPAS Competencies 1, 3, 5, 6, 7, 8, and 9, with attention to understanding how laws, policies, and governing agreements influence social work clients' life course trajectories. Attention is focused on identifying and engaging relevant institutional stakeholders to advocate for social and economic well-being.

Chapter 14: Belief Systems and Ideology

Chapter 14 focuses on EPAS Competencies 1, 2, 3, 4, 5, 6, 7, 8, and 9, with attention to how the political process and social ideologies contribute to advancing or impeding human development. Attention is focused on evaluating the strengths and weaknesses of theoretical perspectives applied in macro practice.

The Cell to Society Perspective and EPAS Core Competencies

Chapter	EP 2.1.1 Identify as professional social worker	EP 2.1.2 Ethical principles	EP 2.1.3 Critical thinking	EP 2.1.4 Diversity in practice	EP 2.1.5 Advance human rights and justice	EP 2.1.6 Research-informed practice	EP 2.1.7 Knowledge of human behavior	EP 2.1.8 Engage in policy practice	EP 2.1.9 Contexts that shape practice	EP 2.1.10a–d Engage, assess, intervene, and evaluate
1	X	X	X	X	X	X	X	X	X	X
2	X	X	X			X	X		X	
3	X		X	X	X	X	X		X	X
4	X		X			X	X		X	X
5	X		X		X	X	X		X	X
6	X	X	X	X		X	X		X	X
7	X		X	X		X	X		X	X
8	X		X			X	X		X	
9	X		X	X	X	X	X	X	X	
10	X		X		X	X	X	X	X	
11	X		X			X	X	X	X	X
12	X		X	X	X	X	X	X	X	X
13	X		X		X	X	X	X	X	
14	X	X	X	X	X	X	X	X	X	

ABOUT THE AUTHORS

Michael G. Vaughn is Professor in the School of Social Work at Saint Louis University. A practitioner for many years in the areas of youth development and delinquency prevention, homelessness, and economic self-sufficiency, he continues to provide consultation and service to numerous community and government agencies. His transdisciplinary research, composed of more than 200 peer-reviewed articles, books, and book chapters, has been published across outlets in numerous fields including social work, psychology, psychiatry, criminology, epidemiology, medicine, and general social science.

Matt DeLisi is Professor and Coordinator of Criminal Justice Studies and Affiliate with the Center for the Study of Violence at Iowa State University. Professor DeLisi has nearly 20 years of practitioner and consultant experience in the fields of criminal justice, juvenile justice, and social/human services. A Fellow of the Academy of Criminal Justice Sciences, Professor DeLisi has authored more than 200 scholarly publications across several fields in the social and behavioral sciences. A reviewer for nearly 100 journals, Dr. DeLisi is Editor-in-Chief of *The Journal of Criminal Justice*.

Holly C. Matto, Associate Professor, received her MSW from the University of Michigan and her PhD from the University of Maryland. Since 2000, Dr. Matto has taught theories of human behavior, direct practice, and research methods in social work master's and doctoral programs. Dr. Matto has more than 15 years of research and clinical social work practice experience in the addictions field. Her research focuses on both assessment practices and interdisciplinary treatment interventions with diverse substance abuse populations. She is currently conducting a clinical trial with Inova Fairfax Hospital and Georgetown University that uses neuroimaging technology to examine functional and structural brain change associated with behavioral health interventions for substance-dependent adults.

CHAPTER 1

INTRODUCING THE CELL TO SOCIETY FRAMEWORK

Solving major social problems and making positive changes in the lives of individuals, groups, communities, and societies is a complex task. Humans are a highly social species whose behavior is impacted by biological, psychological, and broad environmental factors. People in the helping professions have the enormously difficult task of intervening across a multitude of levels through a range of practices and policies. To do so effectively, social workers, counselors, public health workers, and other helping professionals require a deep understanding and appreciation of human behavior. Although it has been recognized in social work and related professions that human behavior is a biopsychosocial phenomenon and that people interact within environments, a stronger elaboration of these principles for the benefit of social work is needed. We use the term *cell to society* to denote that human behavior is impacted by processes ranging from those occurring at the smallest levels of biological organization to the largest levels of social and physical environmental systems. Concomitant with this task is the need to root these theoretical principles in the best scientifically available data. This book combines these two major tasks within an overarching framework to advance the overall effectiveness of helping others.

Many years ago, esteemed scholar Kurt Lewin (1936) wrote a simple equation, $B = f(I, E)$, that simply means behavior (B) is a function (f) of the interaction between the individual (I) and the environment (E). Although the equation is simple, what it entails about the individual and the environment is not. There are many layers to

the individual (e.g., biological and psychological) and environment (e.g., climate and political) that are very difficult to apprehend without a map or blueprint to guide the effort. The cell to society framework demonstrates how multiple units of analysis and disciplinary perspectives can be brought to bear for understanding and intervening in human behavior across levels of analysis. From molecular genetics to neuropsychological functioning to psychological traits and conditions to behavior within the modifying effects of technology and environment, the cell to society approach incorporates research from the natural and biological sciences and the social sciences to produce a comprehensive and scientifically accurate account of empirical phenomena for the helping professions.

The cell to society framework is broad and expansive, beginning with genes and moving to larger levels of physiological organization that impact human behavior such as stress, emotion, and executive functions in the human brain. We order these domains to reflect their evolutionary development. For example, emotional centers of the human brain evolved prior to development of rational thinking areas (MacLean, 1990; Massey, 2002). These biologically based domains influence the development of temperament, personality and micro-level social exchanges. However, it should be kept in mind that human development and behavior are plastic, meaning that external input from the environment molds and shapes us in myriad ways. Therefore, the cell to society framework goes beyond individual, biologically based domains to address successive levels of macro-level environmental influences that surround the individual. These levels include the nature of exchange and cooperation between individuals, social networks and psychosocial relations, technology, the physical environment, and belief systems and ideologies. These components are very necessary for collective survival, as every society must produce for itself (and reproduce itself), doing so using technology, institutions, and associated belief systems and ideologies that interact with specific environments.

The cell to society framework we are proposing is justified by virtue of the multidimensional nature of human behavior and the need for a general synthesis that incorporates biological and sociocultural science in a coherent fashion. The cell to society approach is therefore a conceptual strategy designed to integrate cutting-edge developments from multiple disciplines within a biological and cultural evolutionary framework

for guiding and advancing knowledge for the helping professions (e.g., social work and public health). As a synthesis, the cell to society framework is ultimately based on seminal research and numerous empirical studies drawn from such diverse fields as anthropology, behavior genetics, neurobiology, cultural geography, economics, psychology, primatology, and macrosociology. The cell to society framework begins at smaller units at the person level (e.g., genes) and builds outward to larger units such as the physical environment and institutions (see Figure 1.1). Unlike many models, the cell to society approach is of broad scope and can inform clinical, individual, community, and global level frameworks.

In this chapter, we delineate the major conceptual and theoretical underpinnings of the cell to society framework. Namely, we discuss the importance of employing theories and research from multiple disciplines, incorporating biological and cultural evolution, embracing systems

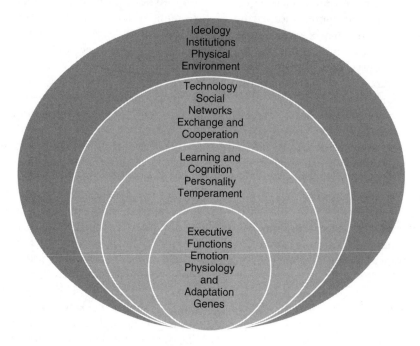

FIGURE 1.1   Major Domains in the Cell to Society Approach

thinking and complexity, utilizing science and the scientific method, and taking a life-course perspective. We then provide an overview of the domains that represent the major areas of the cell to society approach, which will be the focus of subsequent chapters: genes and behavior, stress and adaptation, emotion, executive functions, temperament, personality, cognition and learning, exchange and cooperation, social networks and psychosocial relations, technology, the physical environment, and belief systems and ideology.

CASE STUDY: MALIA'S DIFFERENT ABILITIES

Malia is 52 years old and has a spinal cord injury—well, technically, amyotrophic lateral sclerosis (ALS), or Lou Gehrig's disease.[1] All Malia really cares about, though, is walking normally again (without so much tripping and stumbling), and ceasing to be such a burden to her family. Although Malia's speech is becoming slurred and she is progressively finding it difficult to swallow, frequent visits to her nutritionist have helped her by adjusting her diet. She does find the muscle weakness and cramps, fatigue, and pain intolerable at times, but her care team works together to help her when she has flare-ups like this. Although she has difficulty managing the small motor movements required for getting dressed, she winnowed out her wardrobe, retaining only the easiest styles. She has replaced the fancier garments of her recent past, those with buttons, zippers, or fancy fasteners, with simple pull-on shirts and sweaters that help her maintain independence in dressing herself, at least for now. So far, Malia has not lost any cognitive functioning; she is aware of everything that is going on with her bodily functions and has not suffered any memory deterioration or thinking problems. However, when you ask her how she's feeling, she will tell you that she feels increasingly isolated and "down" much of the time. She is not sure if it is depression, but she knows her motivation has decreased and her sense of pleasure in life and relationships is not as full as it once was. At one point recently, when she returned home from a doctor's visit, she expressed the frustration and disappointment of her progressive illness like this: "I feel like I'm the manager of a losing baseball team. You have to show up, but you know you're going to lose." Some days just mustering the motivation to get up and out of bed can be almost too much for her to bear. Other days, she says, she has a "sunnier disposition" and better perspective on managing her illness.

What helps her, you might ask? Malia says it helps to avoid thinking about the tube feeding and respiratory failure that's bound to come, and to "distract herself from the inevitability" of this incurable illness. She also says lots and lots of support has been very helpful. And she doesn't mean the kind of support that well-intentioned people often give her: help with the door, sympathetic looks, trying to talk for her as she slurs her speech, or underestimating and overlooking the functional capacities she still has. The kind of support that Malia says really helps her is the genuine, silent patience that comes from those friends who slow down and take their time with her. Malia likes best the kind of support that does not underestimate her functional capacity, but does not overlook her functional limitations, either; the kind that balances both, takes time for the relational connections, not just the tasks at hand, and appreciates her continued contributions as a partner in the friendship, as opposed to a dependent to be pitied and cared for. Of course, other, more concrete and tangible levels of support that come from her multidisciplinary care team, like medication to help control her pain, and a computer-based communication aid to help when her speech becomes increasingly difficult to manage, are also helpful to her. Malia has experienced some physical and mental success (muscle management and improved nighttime sleep, respectively) by engaging in physical therapy–directed exercises, such as simple walking and swimming regimens and range of motion and stretching exercises. She has authorized the occupational therapist to make some limited structural alterations to her home, such as a ramp to her door in anticipation of the day she will become reliant on a wheelchair for her mobility, but she is reluctant to do much more than that right now, to keep the environment as a space that reminds her of her independence and, as she puts it, so that the place doesn't end up looking like "the home of a dying disabled person!"

Malia says the social workers she has come in contact with have been very helpful. They have helped her and her family members better understand the medical, emotional, and financial dimensions of the disease, and as she says, they have helped her plan for her future while still helping her live in the moment, day to day, with dignity and purpose. She said her social workers constantly work with her toward her goal of living interdependently and taking what she needs from those who can help, while acknowledging and maximizing what she still has control over. Her social workers have worked with legal counsel in helping her draft a durable power of attorney and a living will, and have located ALS support groups for her caregivers. Her care team has told her about complex rehabilitation technology (CRT): medically necessary customized technology, typically customized mobility devices and services used by people with disabilities, which often require continuous technology assessment, evaluation, and adjustment to tailor the products to individual needs. These are the type of mobility devices she will need in the near future, and they are different than other types of standard medical devices in their specialization and individualized fit requirements. The customized process of product alignment, assessment, continuous evaluation, and adjustment will be done by her interdisciplinary team, which includes a rehab technology professional certified by the Rehabilitation Engineering and Assistive Technology Society of North America. Her social workers have told her that professional groups like these are encouraging policy makers to make Medicare changes that would offer unique coverage for CRTs to better meet the needs of people requiring these devices, as part of the Ensuring Access to Quality Complex Rehabilitation Technology Act of 2012. Advocacy efforts like Roll on Capitol Hill, the United Spinal Association's annual legislative advocacy event, address issues like this that impact the independence and well-being of those living with spinal cord injury and disease.

Malia's doctors have told her that scientists are not certain of the origins of ALS, but some scientific hypotheses are currently being explored: too great an accumulation of free radicals, autoimmune response, or too much glutamate in the bloodstream. Other scientists, like Dr. Moses Chao, professor of cell biology, physiology, neuroscience, and psychiatry at the NYU School of Medicine and past president of the Society for Neuroscience, suggest that important new cutting-edge neuroscientific studies are showing successful stimulation of the spinal cord through electrical, chemical, and physical (treadmill) interventions. Dr. Chao believes that such interventions "stimulate the neurons in the spinal cord" in a way that facilitates locomotion and activates the motor system. Malia knows she doesn't have much time, according to current statistics. She hopes these scientific discoveries can be advanced in a timely manner so she might benefit from them. But if she ends up dying before that time, her only hope is that she can live out her final months, weeks, and days in dignity and with those she loves most.

In this case example, we saw how Malia's physical health affected her thinking patterns around what it means to be independent, her emotions and ensuing struggle with mild depression, and her interpersonal relationships as she worked with her professional care team and informal caretakers to try to maintain positive supporters in her life who could help her with the emotional and instrumental aid she needed to get through each day. As Malia's social workers can attest, existential and spiritual questions will continue to emerge as end-of-life care (hospice services) are introduced when Malia's degenerative condition progresses to its final stage. We saw how technological advancements, such as customized rehab technologies that include individually tailored mobility and communication devices, can enhance and prolong independence for those who need such assistance. And we saw how legislative advocacy, such as the United Spinal Association's annual Roll on Capitol Hill, can increase awareness and bring about policy changes, such as advocating for a new Medicare benefit category for conditions that require these customized products and services.

We have also seen a lot of systems at work. We have seen that the human body is a system where the physical outcomes associated with a medical condition can influence the person's psychological response (mood and emotion); and how a person's mood can, in turn, influence the behavioral motivation to make decisions about one's health condition. We have seen other systems at work as well. Malia is part of a family system, some members of whom have taken on the caretaking role to help Malia manage her illness. The strain of caregiving may lead such family members to seek support for themselves, by engaging in an ALS support group where they may receive educational, emotional, and interpersonal support for their care of Malia. The social workers working with Malia are also part of a multidisciplinary care team, a system made up of helping professionals from unique and specialized disciplines organized to help with Malia's physical, psychological, familial, and financial needs. Understanding the patterns of interactions within this system (e.g., the way members from each discipline communicate information and ideas to the rest of the team) will help members influence the way in which the care plan is developed and enacted. Malia also is indirectly affected by the political system. Because Malia is struggling with ALS in 2012, she benefits from the Americans With Disabilities Act of 1990. But because Malia is struggling with ALS in 2012, she currently is not a beneficiary of a separate Medicare benefit for CRT, a change currently on the legislative advocacy agenda of groups such as the United Spinal Association.

Critical Thinking Questions:

- Think about our social institutions (e.g., health care, family, economy/labor market, etc.). How do you think they relate to people with disabilities? In what ways do they promote or hinder the opportunity for people with disabilities to be fully included in and full contributors to our society?

- Think about the built environment: the physical space you occupy each and every day (your home, neighborhood, community roads and buildings, etc.). What noticeable accommodations have been made in your built environment to promote navigation and accessibility for those with functional limitations? Where could improvements be made? How would you advocate for such improvements?

- Reflect on Malia's case example. What do you think Malia might be struggling with in relation to identity? How about in terms of interpersonal relationships?

- As a social worker working with Malia, how might you help her develop a shift in identity to accommodate new statuses and roles? How might you assess her receptivity to and her interface with assistive technologies to support functioning? What would you specifically want to find out about her relationship to her assistive technologies?

[1]According to the National Institute of Neurological Disorders and Stroke (2012). "Amyotrophic lateral sclerosis (ALS), sometimes called Lou Gehrig's disease, is a rapidly progressive, invariably fatal neurological disease that attacks the nerve cells (neurons) responsible for controlling voluntary muscles. The disease belongs to a group of disorders known as motor neuron diseases, which are characterized by the gradual degeneration and death of motor neurons. Eventually, all muscles under voluntary control are affected, and patients lose their strength and the ability to move their arms, legs, and body. When muscles in the diaphragm and chest wall fail, patients lose the ability to breathe without ventilatory support. Most people with ALS die from respiratory failure, usually within 3 to 5 years from the onset of symptoms. However, about 10 percent of ALS patients survive for 10 or more years."

ON THE IMPORTANCE OF TRANSDISCIPLINARY APPROACHES

In 1974, the late anthropologist Marvin Harris, commenting on the need to traverse and transcend multiple disciplinary fields to understand the puzzles of human behavior, wrote, "Nothing in nature is quite so separate as two mounds of expertise" (Preface, p. vii). By this, Harris was referring to the tendency of scientific disciplines to develop bodies of knowledge and understanding that are often all but entirely independent of the knowledge of other disciplines. For instance, what psychology has to say about child or adolescent development may be markedly distinct from the perspectives arising from sociology or anthropology. In developing the cell to society framework in this book, we draw from the insights of Harris and other scholars who advocate the utility of an approach that draws from multiple disciplines. We ignore disciplinary boundaries quite simply because human behavior involves processes that are influenced by genetic, physiological, psychological, political, economic, and environmental factors. The history of the study of human behavior is replete with a broad literature strongly supporting the notion that factors exist that occur at multiple levels of analysis (i.e., genetic, cellular, hormonal, individual, family, community, nation). Because the study of human behavior is multidimensional in nature, its understanding necessarily will involve a host of disciplines (e.g., genetics, neuroscience, endocrinology, psychology, sociology, geography). This joining together and transcendence of disciplines toward a common understanding of complex phenomena can be termed *transdisciplinary*.

Transdisciplinary approaches imply a wider swath of knowledge than the term *interdisciplinary* and are gaining ascendancy across scientific fields because of their potential ability to solve problems that cut across multiple domains. Indeed, the Office of Behavioral and Social Sciences Research (OBSSR) has the mission of integrating behavioral and social science research across the many institutes of the National Institutes of Health, the largest funder of scientific research in the United States. The OBSSR uses a framework that organizes well-being across a continuum of biological and social factors that occur over the life course. Levels of organization range from the genomic to the global economic, with such domains as organ and community levels in between. One example of employing a transdisciplinary approach on a large scale is the funding of 17 mind-body centers in health. Such mind-body centers focus on fostering wellness and treating disease within a framework that takes seriously the connections between our psychological, social, and vocational wellness and our overall health and well-being. This effort involves the National Cancer Institute, the National Institute on Aging, the National Institute of Drug Abuse, and several other national institutes with research centers at several universities, including Columbia University, University of California at Berkeley, University of Utah, University of Pittsburgh, and many others, each with a focused investigative topic and ongoing information sharing.

What are the consequences of not using a transdisciplinary approach? Just as Harris has pointed out that nothing in nature is quite as separate as two mounds of expertise, one of the consequences of not using transdisciplinary reasoning is the myopic state of explaining human behavior strictly in terms of a unidisciplinary focus (e.g., just sociology). For instance, trying to understand a complex phenomenon such as interpersonal violence exclusively from a sociological perspective can lead to conclusions that fail to capture the entire problem. Simultaneously considering the nature of violence from the perspectives of behavioral genetics, psychology, anthropology, and even history can facilitate a much more nuanced and multifaceted understanding of why human beings

sometimes hurt one another. Additional consequences include a lack of person–environment integration, which prevents isolated studies from being linked together, limits use of new methods, and keeps theories arising from various fields of knowledge fields from communicating with one another. Such communication breakdowns bring to mind the image of two ships passing in the night, both laboring strenuously to advance in their desired direction but entirely unaware of one another's presence and the benefits their communication—and collaboration—might yield. Although scholars often acknowledge the necessity for transdisciplinary approaches for comprehending and intervening in complex human problems (e.g., Caspi & Moffitt, 2006; Laub, 2006), overly narrow disciplinary training and indoctrination often hampers the effective execution of transdisciplinary knowledge gathering, which in turn inhibits theory development and testing. This is not to state that some disciplinary fields have not made major contributions on their own or that any solution is merely the sum of viewpoints from different fields. For some problems, certain disciplines may have more to offer. Despite the dominance of discipline-specific socialization and the tendency to view human behavior from a "strictly sociological," "psychological," or "biological" point of view, there is a growing realization that singular perspectives, although useful, are ultimately stagnant and limited.

With respect to social work and the helping professions, a cell to society conceptual framework that can begin to organize theories and research in productive ways is needed to account for individuals' biological structure and dynamics across successive levels of context. This framework also ought to be able to form links across disciplines and identify points of intervention at both the individual and population levels. Although individuals in the helping professions may not be able to intervene across the many levels needed, possessing a fuller understanding and appreciation of human behavior as a transdisciplinary experience allows helping professionals to look beyond their areas of expertise to see new possibilities and collaborations for effecting change at various levels.

CHANGE AND ADAPTATION: BIOLOGICAL AND CULTURAL EVOLUTION

Evolution can be an intimidating concept and often a controversial one when invoked in the study of human behavior. Most people typically think of biology when they see or hear the term *evolution*. But the word itself refers to change and adaptation over time (more commonly large swaths of time). Historical change and adaptation in human societies, particularly around major changes such as the Industrial Revolution, can be thought of as cultural evolution (Harris, 1979; Sanderson, 1990). For instance, in Western Europe in the 17th, 18th, and 19th centuries, as mechanical production and other technological advancements drew more and more individuals away from traditional agricultural communities and into rapidly expanding urban centers, a tremendous amount of cultural change or so-called "evolution" took place. For people of that era, a profound social evolution transformed the ways they thought about their experiences and how they engaged in work, family and community life, and politics (see Table 1.1). When such changes occur, human behavior adaptations follow. In this way, evolutionary principles can be applied to human behavior vis-à-vis its relations with a given environment.

Similar to biological evolution with its emphasis on natural selection as a driving force, cultural evolution relies on selection processes, too. An additional component in evolution is chance, which can often be accounted for by mutation or other unidentified factors (Mayr, 1976). Change and adaptation is composed of the tandem of chance and selection processes. As always, behavior cannot be accounted for by a single gene (Greenspan, 1999) and as such each gene can or

does participate in a multitude of developmental processes. This failure to identify single genes capable of explaining specific behaviors is in large part due to the impact that socialization and cultural influences have on the developing person. Studies conducted in less complex organisms such as fruit flies indicate that many genes contribute to specific behaviors (Greenspan, 1999). Many selective forces or agents exist naturally in our environments, and some of these agents are a product of human industry. For example, pollution as a byproduct of industrial activity has been shown to contribute to disease, yet the susceptibility to contaminants is variable in humans (Birdsell, 1999).

The study of primate behavior, of which humans are a part due to our genetic, morphological (i.e., outward appearance and internal structure), and behavioral similarities, helps shed light on the origins and contours of human behavior. For instance, recent research synthesizing African field site studies of chimpanzees (*Pan troglodytes*) shows evidence of nongenetic transmission of behavior or, in simpler terms, chimpanzee "culture." For instance, chimpanzee communities in certain regions of Africa regularly use tree leaves as napkins or sponges, whereas chimps in different regions do not do so. Similar differences can be observed in terms of chimpanzees using tools to crack nuts and other profoundly useful behaviors. These examples and countless others highlight the fact that primates, although certainly influenced by their genetic makeup, are also profoundly influenced by social and environmental factors. Research on a lesser-known ape, the bonobo (*Pan paniscus*), shows additional variability between primate species. For instance, bonobo communities are decidedly different from those of chimpanzees. In contrast to the male-dominated chimpanzee culture, bonobos are a profoundly female-centered species that is quick to use sexual behavior to defuse potential conflicts between groups (de Waal, 1995). Although the fascinating details of primate research could fill a textbook, two takeaway points are particularly important for our understanding.

Table 1.1   Examples of Key Variables That Influence Societal Evolution

Infrastructure Variables: Production

Technological advancements	Road transportation
Food manufacturing	Trail transportation
Textile manufacturing	Water transportation
Chemical manufacturing	Air transportation
Metals manufacturing	Rail transportation
Machinery manufacturing	Fossil fuel reserves
Lumber manufacturing	Crude petroleum
Electrical manufacturing	Coal
Crop production	Natural gas
Farmlands	Animal waste
Livestock production	Geothermal heat
Mineral resources	Hydroelectric power
Territorial size	Climate
Soils and vegetation	Supply and utilization of water
Pollution and deforestation	

Infrastructure Variables: Reproduction

Morbidity rates	Population characteristics (age, sex, ethnicity)
Immigration	Fertility
Population density	Disease
Urban/rural	Nurturing of infants
Suicide	Mating patterns
Mortality rates	Migration
Medical control of demographic pattern (conception, abortion, infanticide)	

Structural–Institutional Variables

Family composition	Political organizations, clubs, associations, parties	Corporate structure (leadership, compensation, hierarchies)
Family wealth	Government structure (leadership, compensation processes)	Interest rates
Family debt		Inflation
Personal wealth	National division of labor	Gross domestic product
Personal debt	Taxation	Gross national product
Domestic hierarchies	Income stratification	Foreign aid
Domestic division of	War	Banking
labor	Police	Government regulations of business
Family socialization	Criminal justice	Budgets
Social sanctions	Law/crime rates	Employment rates and processes
Age and sex roles	(political/corporate crime)	(unemployment)
Expenditures	Tribute	Voting patterns
Rates of consumption		

Ideational Variables

Art forms (aesthetics)	Electronic media	Class ideologies
Music	Print media	Educational values and ideologies
Sports	Literature	Taboos
Recreational activities	Marketing and advertising	Magic
Folklore	Religious practice and ideologies	Superstitions
Myths	Political ideologies	Racial and ethnic ideologies
Rituals	Ethical ideologies	

Note: Adapted and expanded from Harris (1979).

First, primatological research reveals an astounding degree of plasticity and cultural flexibility among primates; second, such research also reveals that change and adaptation do take place among primates and that certain behaviors and social problems are not inevitable or fixed.

One of the key points of contention in the study of evolution involves the difference between acknowledging a role for biology and biological determinism. In 1975, Harvard University biologist Edward Wilson, noted for his studies of ants, published a seminal and controversial book titled *"Sociobiology: The New Synthesis."* The goal of sociobiology was to explain human behavior by using principles derived from biological evolution. It was viewed as an approach that was aimed toward reducing or absorbing the social sciences into biology and its overarching paradigm of natural selection. Although sociobiology affords culture an important role (Wilson, 1975), it seemingly does so as a reflex of biology. Sociobiology and Edward Wilson personally were attacked for a variety of reasons. One of the major reasons was that the implication of sociobiology is that the status quo in society is a biologically mandated inevitability. Although Wilson (1975) cautioned against falling into this ethical trap, his work nevertheless contributes to this notion, which of course has real political effects (Sussman, 1999). Wilson has recently written a book on the social conquest of the planet that relies on the relationship between biology and culture (Wilson, 2012). It is certainly the case that reducing human behavior to biological inevitability is simplistic and an easy trap to fall into. On the other hand, determinism can apply both ways, as most social scientists tend to be environmentalists or social determinists. Moving beyond tired, ideological nature-versus-nurture debates and comprehending the rich tapestry of human behavior in ways that can lead to productive outcomes for the helping professions is badly needed.

As previously alluded, societies must produce and capture energy from an environment to survive. We take for granted all the modern conveniences that technology has to offer, but just think about how problematic it is when electricity goes off, water stops running, or one runs out of food and doesn't have sufficient money to buy any. We cannot escape these basic material necessities, upon which contemporary social life depends. Thus, societal evolution is built on these biologically programmed basic survival needs. Examples include sex drive; hunger; thirst; sleep; language; requirements for affective nurturance; nutritional and metabolic processes; and vulnerability to mental and physical disease and to stress from darkness, cold, heat, altitude, moisture, lack of oxygen, and other ecological endangerments (Harris, 1979, 1999). These basic survival needs can be thought of as biopsychological constants of human nature. They are constants because they have always been with us as human beings and are likely always to be with us in the future. Therefore, theories of human behavior that focus strictly on social factors must confront the inescapable importance of these fundamental biological and psychological factors. As such, the necessity for understanding the psychobiological complex that comprises the individual in relation to behavior and environment (social and natural environment) is critical to a comprehensive understanding of human behaviors and human societies. How humans and their culture meet these needs over time via various behavioral adaptations can be thought of as societal or cultural evolution and in many ways is analogous in principle to biological evolution.

SYSTEMS THINKING AND COMPLEXITY

Broadly defined, a *system* is any set of interrelated elements that influence each other over time (Roberts, Andersen, Deal, Garet, & Shaffer, 1983; Senge, Kleiner, Roberts, Ross, & Smith, 1994). But how do we know something is a system rather than "just a bunch of stuff"? Donella Meadows (2008) posed four questions to help determine whether or not something is a system: (a) Can you identify parts? (b) Do the parts affect each other? (c) Do the parts produce an effect that is different than the effect of each part on its own? (d) Does the effect persist in a variety of circumstances? If the answer is yes to all four questions, then the "bunch of stuff" meets criteria as a system. Although all systems have these characteristics in common, systems are ubiquitous and exist in many forms and sizes. Examples of systems include but are not limited to: the solar system, the human body, a community, a hospital, a football team, a river or stream, and so forth. Exchanges between humans are another kind of system. People interact with each other, for example, in a manner that gives rise to dynamic processes, such as pressures to conform to rules and social situations, decision-making biases, attitudes and changes in attitude, power, and ambition and resulting influence, et cetera. These interactions are often quite complex (Thelen & Smith, 1998). It is important to recognize that individuals behave within a system of successive levels of context and constraint imposed by biological, political-economic, and cultural processes (see Matsumoto, 2007; Peck, 2007; Vaughn, 2007).

The study of systems is guided by a variety of general theoretical approaches (e.g., general systems theory, cybernetics, and system dynamics) that fall under the general rubric called *systems theory*. They all share the idea that the behavior of systems is generated by its underlying "structure," or the pattern of interrelationships that constitute the system. An understanding of system structures always presupposes explanations of the dynamic process of interacting parts.

Systems theory is composed of several key concepts that are important to understanding systems. Two of these are positive and negative feedback. *Negative feedback* refers to any system-maintaining innovation that modifies a change or divergence that preserves the fundamental characteristics of the system. For instance, a simple example of negative feedback is a thermostat, which is designed to regulate a base temperature by turning off a heating system when a house becomes too warm or turning it on if a house becomes too cold. Whereas negative feedback serves to maintain system homeostasis, *positive feedback* denotes system-changing innovations. Applying the concept to human societies, policies that change the status quo can be thought of as positive feedback. Although the term "*positive*" seems to imply something that is good, positive feedback in the context of systems theory simply means that the system has changed; the change could be detrimental to the system itself. Although certain innovations in some aspects of a system may result in changing the whole system more than others (e.g., changes in technology or how societies produce energy, food, and water), it is difficult to predict the consequences of these innovations.

Contingency and emergence are two fundamental processes that influence the understanding of complex systems. *Contingency* means that something occurs as a result of something else. When there are many interactive parts in a system, the contingencies become very complex. *Emergent properties* are those that appear in complex systems as a result of nonlinearity; that is, they do not appear at any lower level of interactive parts and are a result of complex interactions. Contingency and emergence have to do with the whole being more than the sum of its parts. A classic example is when a sudden severe storm emerges as a result of a number of changing weather conditions such as wind, temperature, moisture, and other environmental pressures, all of which can vary dramatically. As such, both can be thought of as a counterpoint to reductionism in complex systems (Gould, 2003). Science has relied on reductionism to explain complexity by understanding the regularities that govern the parts. Interactions that can be predicted from the knowledge of the parts can be said to be linear in that direct, one-to-one relations or patterns can be observed. Reductionism is inadequate if these emergent properties are necessary to explain any higher order phenomena. Contingency refers to historical events, idiographic cases, and inherent particularism in a given system under study.

These cases or events can occur by chance or accident. They are not observable regularities. Approaches that study complex, higher order systems need to confront both emergence and contingencies. Although we tend to think of complex systems as reflective of societies, states, or cities, they can also include psychological traits such as personality and character. According to research by Cloninger and colleagues (Cloninger, 1999, 2004; Cloninger, Svrakic, & Pryzbeck, 1993; Cloninger, Svrakic, & Svrakic, 1997), the relations between temperament and character traits are nonlinear, meaning that more than one configuration can give rise to several character combinations and vice versa. In fact, this research has demonstrated that personality development can follow the nonlinear form of a complex adaptive system. Other basic terms and processes are important in systems thinking. These include *transactions* (the exchange of information and behavioral interactions among people in their environment), *inputs* and *outputs* (the flow of energy—i.e., stimuli—into a person or system is input; the flow outward is output), *interface* (the point of interaction or target of change), *adaptation* (the capacity to adjust to changes in the environment), *interdependence* (mutual reliance between actors in a system and habitat, similar to symbiosis), *differentiation* (change toward greater complexity in a system), *equifinality* (many different means to achieve the same end), and *multifinality* (one starting point leading to many different outcomes).

There is a growing consensus that to intervene in behavioral and social problems (e.g., poverty, development, health and disease, violence), a greater understanding of how various factors occurring at multiple levels influence human behavior is needed (e.g., Galea, Riddle, & Kaplan, 2010; Glass & McAtee, 2008). Most human phenomena are not caused by single factors. In this book we conceptualize human behavior in the social and physical environment in an explicit way to fully view the multiple levels that influence human behaviors over the life course. The cell to society framework is consistent with systems thinking; however, it attempts to move beyond just describing system parts by incorporating scientific findings into each major domain that constitutes the approach. New discoveries in complex systems are fully compatible with the cell to society approach.

SCIENCE AND SCIENTIFIC METHODS

As Kirk and Reid (2002) have pointed out, social work has used science to deliver rational and structured services and to use scientific evidence as a means to inform social work practice. The dangers for the helping professions of not using science are a loss of credibility and professional standing and a great potential for ineffectiveness. *Science* is a way of knowing about the world that is based on empiricism and testing. In science, ideas or claims are subject to empirical testing, in which data are gathered and a hypothesis formulated that is subject to falsification. In science, we are trying to disprove rather than prove something is true. Because we will never know the absolute truth, knowledge gained under scientific principles is always tentative and subject to revision. As a process, science consists of deduction and induction. *Deduction* is when we have an idea or theory about something and then gather data to assess how valid the theory is. *Induction* works in the opposite direction; we observe facts and form a theory capable of explaining or making sense of our observations.

This is not to suggest that the process of science is free of social or psychological factors, such as power or ambition; only that the procedures of science help us to understand the world better than other ways of knowing. Certainly science can be thought of as a form of ideology like any other, but with at least one major caveat that differentiates it from other ideologies. That is, science is the only way of knowing that, at its very core, doubts the findings and results gained under its procedures; unlike other practitioners of various ideologies, scientists do not attempt to "prove," per se, without empirical testing. This relentless skepticism can protect us from the vast array of unsubstantiated claims that pervade the helping professions (e.g., Gambrill, 2012). So, despite science being part of a human context of susceptibility to power and ambition and other intrusions that shape the validity of knowledge, we are committed to its principles until something better comes along.

Pseudoscience and the Human Condition

Another reason why science is important to the helping professions is that it protects from pseudoscience and nonscientific claims about how to help people. In the helping professions, it is important first to remember not to do any harm. Some interventions can harm people or, at the very least, waste money and resources that could have been better spent elsewhere. Pseudoscience uses persuasion and misinformation in support of cherished claims and avoids empirical tests, rigorous external review, and self-correction (Lohr, Devilly, Lilienfeld, & Olatunji, 2006). As such, a pseudoscience approach is more closed minded than the open-minded yet skeptical approach of science. However, it is often difficult for people to differentiate science from pseudoscience because advocates of pseudoscientific approaches cloak the validity of their claims in scientific rhetoric. There are several examples of the dangers of pseudoscience (see Makgoba, 2002). Health policy in sub-Saharan Africa, which has been influenced by the unfounded notion that HIV does not cause AIDS, has done tremendous harm. Early eugenics movements aimed at eradicating so-called "genetic inferiors" are another example. In these situations, ideology and pseudoscience were substituted for rigorous empirical science. Well-intentioned social workers and counselors have fallen prey to strongly marketed therapies that have little to no scientific support. This is understandable as social workers and counselors have a strong desire to help and find many therapies to be very seductive; however, they can be potentially harmful and waste time and resources. For this reason, many skeptical scientists have developed baloney detection kits (e.g., Sagan, 1997) and other criteria to protect from bogus pseudoscience and junk-science claims (see Spotlight Topic).

SPOTLIGHT TOPIC: "BALONEY DETECTION"

To protect ourselves from bogus knowledge claims about human behavior that can harm, scientists such as Carl Sagan have drawn together a toolkit based on scientific principles to be used to evaluate a variety of these claims. Carl Sagan called this the *baloney detection toolkit*. These tools include:

- Encourage substantive debate on the evidence by knowledgeable proponents of all points of view.
- Arguments from authority carry little weight (in science there are no so-called "authorities").
- Spin more than one hypothesis; don't simply run with the first idea that caught your fancy.
- Try not to get overly attached to a hypothesis just because it's yours.
- Quantify wherever possible.
- If there is a chain of argument, every link in the chain must work.
- Apply "Occam's razor": If there are two hypotheses that explain the data equally well, choose the simpler one.

- Ask whether the hypothesis can, at least in principle, be falsified (i.e., shown to be false by some unambiguous test). In other words, it is testable? Can others duplicate the study or experiment and get the same result?

  In addition, there are several common fallacies of logic and rhetoric to pay attention to:

- Ad hominem (attacking the arguer and not the argument).
- Argument from "authority" (the director of the institute believes this intervention is effective, so it must be true).
- Ecological fallacy (findings about a population must apply to specific individuals—not true!).
- Appeal to ignorance (absence of evidence is not evidence of absence).
- Observational selection (counting the hits and forgetting the misses).
- Statistics of small numbers (such as drawing conclusions from inadequate sample sizes).
- Misunderstanding the nature of statistics (e.g., a president or prime minister expressing astonishment and alarm on discovering that fully half of all Americans have below average intelligence!)

For Reflection

Pick a sensational claim about which you feel it is appropriate to be skeptical. Next, apply baloney detection principles and try to uncover the mistakes in reasoning that occur.
In addition, pick a social issue that is receiving significant political attention and examine the various viewpoints political candidates have expressed in the media. Identify the various fallacies in their arguments.

THE CELL TO SOCIETY FRAMEWORK AND THE LIFE COURSE

From the maternal milieu to older adulthood, a complexity of interactions occur over the life course, ranging in involvement from the smallest units inside the body (e.g., neurons) to the largest aggregations (e.g., the worldwide system). For example, due to technological changes, resource depletions, or political strife, the price of energy can fluctuate dramatically; when it does, it affects households around the globe that depend on energy sources such as electricity and gasoline for automobiles. Households, in turn, experience greater levels of psychological and biological stress when gasoline prices are high or electricity is out. This is one of many ways that environment "gets under the skin" and impedes or enhances development. Developmental science has its own life course and in many ways is still in its infancy. Researchers are attempting to comprehend the ways in which the many levels within and beyond us as humans intersect across the life course. One thing for certain is that social science, neurobiology, genetics, and behavioral and cognitive science have joined to produce significant advances in understanding how children, adolescents, and adults suffer adversity, adapt, and thrive. Successive chapters of this book review this research; here we introduce the major developmental milestones and theories and highlight their cell to society basis.

Major Developmental Milestones

As shown in Table 1.2, several notable developmental milestones over the life course involve the unfolding of biology sculpted by environmental

Table 1.2   Major Developmental Milestones

Milestones	Period
Transformation of single-celled organism to human organism ready for growth and development	Conception to birth
Rapid changes to physiology, central nervous system, and social receptiveness	Infancy
Gross and fine motor skills are developed, and language and thought flower	Early childhood
Attendance at school, making friends, sense of self, development of morality	Middle to late childhood
Puberty and sexual activity, growing autonomy and value system, stronger reliance on peers, and formation of social identity	Adolescence
Independence, career and work, marriage or intimate partnership, child rearing	Early adulthood
Greater mastery and leadership, sense of one's own mortality, helping children and others reach independence and success	Middle adulthood
Adapting to diminished physical capacity, loss of life partner, life reflection, new ways to occupy time	Late adulthood

experiences. In the earliest stages of gestation and at birth, human growth and development are rapid, and these changes continue with greater central nervous system development in infancy. Children are "pre-wired" for emotional responses and learning. The human brain is highly plastic, meaning that it changes based on experience and as such is highly adaptable. In fact, children have an overabundance of synaptic pathways; those that are most stimulated are retained and those that are understimulated are eliminated, a process commonly termed *synaptic pruning* (Kolb, 1999). Thus, stimulation and enriched environments are critically important for a functional and adaptive developing brain. The social experiences, attention, and nurturance given during infancy and early childhood are an important part of the development of thought, language, and temperament. From childhood through adulthood, contact with the social environment expands. One important point to bear in mind is culture and context. For example, most of what is known and studied about development has been derived from North American and European samples. Therefore, some social-developmental milestones may differ somewhat in samples from other places and contexts. We tend to think of the teenage years in the American context as being tempestuous

and full of upheaval. Yet cross-cultural research findings indicate that many cultures do not have a demarcated period known as adolescence, and the problems associated with adolescence in the United States are not replicable (Schlegel & Barry, 1991). Still, there do appear to be many universal features; for instance, brain plasticity and adapting to diminished capacity as we grow older are two of many such features.

Major Theoretical Perspectives

As shown in Table 1.3, the cell to society approach is more expansive yet congruent with various aspects of developmental perspectives, and also surmounts some of the disadvantages of these viewpoints. Historically, perspectives on development have changed, with different schools of thought holding sway at various times. Psychoanalytic and *psychodynamic theories*, which emphasized internal states and drives, were highly influential during the first half of the 20th century but were later supplanted by *behaviorism*, which emphasized actual behaviors and the factors in the environment that shape them, and the *cognitive perspective*, that demonstrated the importance of thought and information processing from the external environment. Although many components of these

Table 1.3 Major Developmental Theoretical Perspectives and Their Cell to Society Basis

Psychodynamic Theory

Description: Psychodynamic theory posits that development takes place in a series of discrete stages driven by innate sexual impulses and early experiences. The early forms of this theory put forth by Freud were modified significantly by Erickson with less of an emphasis on biology and internal drives and more emphasis on external psychosocial relations.

Cell to society: Psychodynamic theory is biosocial and interactive, involving the cell to society domains of emotion, temperament, personality, and cognition and learning. Genes, stress, and physiological adaptations and executive functions, although likely involved, are not specified. Macrosocial context is largely ignored, although Freud extended the perspective to civilization (society) and Erickson to major societally contingent life stages such as career and employment.

Behaviorism

Description: Environmental input shapes behavior of the organism. Many of these environmental inputs involve social learning via reinforcement. Thus, development is a sum of learning experiences based on specific environmental conditions. Behaviorists do not deny existence of important biological factors, but they emphasize environmental contingencies. Later modifications to behaviorism involved incorporations of thoughts (cognitions).

Cell to society: Although born out of physiology, limited genetic and neuroscience input is evident. Far more emphasis is placed on nurture as opposed to nature in this theory. Although larger social structures such as institutions (as well as broad societal factors like technology) can be linked to behavioral changes, very little study of these linkages has been undertaken.

Cognitive Perspective

Description: Departing from earlier psychodynamic and behaviorist positions, the cognitive revolution in developmental studies was led by Piaget. This viewpoint focused attention on the frame of reference or schemas that humans are born with. We need to have this structure to process information from our external environment. Humans assimilate this information in stages. Recent cognitive theories of development focus on attention, memory, and reasoning.

Cell to society: There is strong input from biology, but it is not a focus of study. Emphasis is on cognition and learning and, to some extent, executive functions and belief systems. However, limited roles are specified for temperament and personality as well as institutions and technology.

Evolutionary Approaches and Gene–Environment Interplay

Description: Heredity plays an important role in development, but this hereditary factor is not destiny and the environment has great impact on the human genotype. As such, humans must adapt to environments, but this adaptation is partly influenced by genetic factors. Thus, some people respond differently to the same environment. Environmental factors vary over different periods (e.g., adolescence), just as they do in other developmental theories. In these theories, not only does environment act upon humans, but individuals often select environments (and change them) consistent with their genotype.

Cell to society: There is strong emphasis on genetics, but also upon executive functions, stress and adaptation, temperament, personality, and cognition and learning. Similar to other major developmental perspectives, the role of larger social aggregates is neglected.

Ecological Systems Theory

Description: The individual interacts with multiple levels of the environment (i.e., micro, meso, and macro) to influence behavior and development across time in complex ways. Concepts such as equifinality and multifinality are prominent. This theoretical perspective is very systems oriented and, unlike early theories, does not posit discrete changes or place substantial emphasis on early experiences.

Cell to society: Biology is somewhat deemphasized, as well as temperament and personality. Social factors—even macro ones like institutions and communities—are given substantial weight. Successive levels of context surround the individual.

theories still thrive, contemporary perspectives on development appear to be moving toward conceptualizing development as a consequence of both biology and environment and their reciprocal exchanges (metaphorically acting as dance partners). Most major developmental theoretical perspectives focus attention at the individual level. This is completely understandable given that most of these theories have been generated from the field of developmental psychology, a science of individual behavior. However, factors that influence developmental processes are wide and involve multiple levels. This can be seen in research on resilience in maltreated children, where some maltreated children bounce back from adversity due to a combination of genetic and environmental stress (Cicchetti & Blender, 2004). An even wider number of levels are involved in the effects of lead on the behavior of children, which are conjointly influenced by political economy via the regulation of solvents and paints, the physical environment as expressed in older housing in disadvantaged neighborhoods, and neurobiology by lead affecting important areas of the brain (Wright et al., 2008). The cell to society approach serves as an organizing framework that indicates how context and interaction matter.

EXPERT'S CORNER: JOHN BREKKE

John Brekke is Frances G. Larson Professor of Social Work Research at the University of Southern California (USC). Brekke embodies the cell to society approach. His research on serious mental illness has transcended narrow disciplinary research by testing biosocial models of schizophrenia, community risk associated with that disorder such as criminal victimization and arrest, and cross-cultural validations.

Brekke and fellow researchers at USC were among the first to study the interrelations between the neuropsychology and psychophysiological correlates of psychosocial functioning in people diagnosed with schizophrenia in 1997. In a 2005 study, Brekke, Kay, Kee, and Green tested a biosocial model of functional outcomes (work, relationships, independent living) among a sample of 139 people diagnosed with schizophrenia and residing in the Los Angeles area. It was theorized that neurocognition (e.g., attention and focus, verbal skills) would be causally associated with social cognition, which would lead to increases in social support and social competence, which in turn would be directly associated with the aforementioned functional outcomes. Results found good support for the theorized model, suggesting that interventions for these individuals may be more effective if neurocognitive skills are targeted rather than simply attending to social-cognitive factors and psychosocial needs. In a study (Brekke & Barrio, 1997) comparing symptoms among White, Black, and Latino people diagnosed with schizophrenia, Brekke and his research team found support for the ethnic culture hypothesis, which essentially asserts that cultural and ethnic identity serves as a protective factor and lowers risk severity.

Brekke is also committed to advancing the science of social work. He has argued for social work to have a stronger scientific identity. In fact, he has

(Continued)

Photo of John Brekke
Courtesy of Brian Goodman,
on behalf of USC School of
Social Work

suggested a set of five goals adapted from those elaborated for engineers (Brekke, 2012, p. 8):

1. To be multidisciplinary and interdisciplinary. This is something that social work has always strived for, but it has not been done from a position of a well-defined scientific identity.

2. To advance the frontiers of science and social work. These frontiers are contained in the development of the identity of social work, the refinement of the science, and the impact it will have on the social domains we seek to understand and change.

3. To develop the theoretical underpinnings of scientific phenomena and their social work applications. It is clear that social work will be able to contribute to knowledge building in many sciences, and we will continue to translate that work into specific social work applications.

4. To lead in anticipating and pioneering the human service technologies of the future and to transfer leading-edge human service technologies for use in furthering the public health and eliminating disparities for marginalized and disenfranchised people. The values of social work will always direct its scientific activity toward human change and social justice.

5. To create new paradigms for the delivery and dissemination of social work science education. Our science will propel us to create new frameworks for training our practitioners and for educating new generations of social work scientists. Perhaps this will become the signature activity for defining our profession across generations.

The cell to society approach is part of this movement to gain for social work and the helping professions a stronger scientific basis, not only for the credibility of the profession but also for the well-being of those whom these professionals serve.

COMPONENTS OF THE CELL TO SOCIETY FRAMEWORK

The following is an overview (and preview) of the domains that represent major areas of the cell to society approach. As described previously, we begin with key biological domains and move outward toward the macro environment.

Genes and Behavior

Even today, there are research communities in the social sciences and social work field that advocate a nature-or-nurture approach to understanding behavior. This contrasts with the synergistic nature-and-nurture perspective that has been in place in developmental science. The importance of gene–environment integration is that it matches empirical reality: Behavior represents the unfolding of etiological influences from within and outside the individual. Although genes produce proteins and not behaviors, they do have a role to play in human behavior, and the helping professions benefit from a stronger understanding of genetics. Specific examples of the nature–nurture approach are discussed to illustrate how person and environmental factors are mutually reinforcing.

Stress and Adaptation

The ways that individuals experience stress and adapt their behavior to environmental conditions are a cornerstone of the study of typical and atypical development and conventional and maladaptive behaviors. This chapter provides an overview of the neurological, endocrine, and hormonal systems involved in the experiencing of stress in both adaptive and maladaptive ways.

Emotion

Emotional reactions precede rational thought and represent powerful internal states that influence human behavior. Core emotions such as fear, joy, and anger are causally related to a range of behavioral phenotypes. In this chapter we emphasize the understanding of the evolutionary roots and contemporary nexus of emotions and social environment to wellness and maladaptation over the life course.

Executive Functions

Executive functions—the higher order cognitive processes involved in decision making, behavioral modulation, planning, sustaining attention, the inhibition of socially inappropriate responses, and related processes—have been implicated in important clinical disorders and are essential for day-to-day functioning in society. This chapter explores the executive functions and delineates the major concepts that reveal their importance for social work.

Temperament

Temperament is broadly defined as the usual way that an individual regulates his or her thoughts and behaviors and reacts to environmental conditions, and is considered the biological forerunner of personality. This chapter explores typologies of temperament and the ways that specific temperamental styles and their goodness of fit to environments manifest in both prosocial and maladaptive forms of behavior.

Personality

Personality is a set of individual characteristics arising from a complex interchange of biological and social inputs that influence how one responds to the social environment. This chapter examines theories of personality and developmental psychopathology and their etiologic underpinnings. Practice strategies for intervening in personality problems and personality over the life course are also considered.

Cognition and Learning

Cognitive processes are an important individual-level construct that are associated with successful functioning in society. In the face of other individual-level risk factors, cognitive strength can mediate the liabilities posed by other risk factors, whereas cognitive deficits can interact with underlying liabilities to increase risk for maladaptive outcomes. Learning represents a dynamic and reciprocal interaction of biological and personal factors, behavior, and environment. Learning also represents the individual as an active agent able to acquire information from its surroundings. The process of learning manifests as a rich set of interrelationships whereby the impact on behavior is conditional in nature. Consistent with the cell to society framework, learning is a result of individual attributes, behavior, and proximal and distal contextual factors. This chapter explores the place of cognition and learning for individual human development and adaption to the environment.

Social Exchange and Cooperation

The evolution of human social behavior and the resulting formation of larger structures are predicated to a large extent on the nature of exchange and cooperation between individual actors. This chapter will examine what is currently understood about these concepts and demonstrate the many ways in which they are expressed across diverse settings.

Social Networks and Psychosocial Relations

Humans are a highly social species and are enmeshed in a number of dense social networks over the life course. Family and friends are examples of important social networks that vary in influence over time. In this chapter, the fundamental components of the web of psychosocial relations and interactions will be described and their impact assessed.

Technology

Basic biological needs such as food, water, energy, sex, and shelter are part and parcel of how a given society produces and reproduces itself within a particular habitat. Doing so requires the use of technology. This chapter focuses on the role of technology in human behavior and the aggregate effects of technology in relation to daily life.

The Physical Environment

Physical landscapes influence and are influenced by human behavior in myriad ways. The importance of environment and sustainability in placing large-scale constraints on human behavior is examined. Specific effects of the natural and built environments and associated spatial determinants on the ability to pursue well-being in an individual and collective sense are delineated in this chapter.

Institutions

Previously examined micro-level exchange and cooperation processes are aggregated into basic formal institutions of political economy, governance, and associated organizational features, and in turn are influenced by these structures. In the long view, technology and physical environment have important effects on the ways in which political economy and societal institutions are expressed. The constraints placed on individuals operating under varying institutional arrangements are examined in this chapter.

Belief Systems and Ideology

The origins and expressions of ideologies from a biological, psychological, and social perspective have important effects in both the short term and long term. The individual and collective commitments to various forms of ideology and belief that weigh heavily on human social life are considered in this chapter. Key concepts such as confirmatory bias and social change within the context of these ideologies are explored.

■ ■ ■

The cell to society framework can be used to organize knowledge for practice, policy, or research. In our view, research, practice, and policy are highly intertwined and their continued separation conceptually and operationally hampers efforts to prevent and intervene in human affairs for the better.

SUMMARY

Helping professionals are faced with extremely complex and difficult tasks. Overall, social workers, counselors, public health, and related professionals can benefit from a more comprehensive understanding of human behavior. In this chapter, the basic elements and strategic commitment of the cell to society approach were delineated. Successive chapters focus on each of the core components of this perspective. The cell to society approach has several key points:

• A broad literature strongly supports the notion that an understanding of human behavior includes factors that occur at multiple levels such as genetic, hormonal, cognitive, family, community, and nation. Involving and transcending a host of disciplines (e.g., neuroscience, endocrinology, psychology, sociology, geography) toward a common understanding of complex phenomena can be termed *transdisciplinary*.

• Change and adaptation over time is fundamental to the study of human behavior. This can occur at the biological, individual, and cultural levels. When changes occur, adaptations in human behavior also follow, which initiate further change. In this way, evolutionary principles can be applied to human behavior vis-à-vis its relations with a given environment.

• Systems thinking is an important ingredient in the cell to society framework. Examples of the ubiquity of systems include the human body, a community, a hospital, a football team, climate, and even interactions between groups of people. It is important to recognize that individuals behave within systems that are constrained by biology, environment, and culture.

• Science is a way of knowing about the world that is based on empiricism and testing. Knowledge gained using scientific methods is never absolute but is always subject to revisions and improvements. Social work relies on science to deliver rational and effective services and to use scientific evidence to inform social policies and practices. Not using science has many pitfalls, including ineffectiveness and reduced credibility and professional standing. Science provides tools to increase our skepticism and the ability to detect and protect social workers from bogus claims and using approaches that may harm clients.

• There is a tremendous complexity of interactions that occur over the life course that range in involvement from the smallest units inside the body (e.g., neurons) to the largest aggregations (e.g., worldwide systems). Humans are highly plastic and depend on the social environment for experiences that stimulate healthy brain development. Development is embedded in our biological heritage and cultural context. Although humans have much in common with one another, biological and cultural variation molds and endows us and provides us with uniqueness as well.

KEY TERMS

Adaptation	Interdependence
Behaviorism	Interface
Cell to society	Multifinality
Cognitive perspective	Outputs
Deduction	Psychodynamic theory
Differentiation	Science
Equifinality	Transactions
Induction	Transdisciplinary
Inputs	

CHAPTER 2

GENES AND BEHAVIOR

It has long been understood that forces of nature and nurture, of the person and the environment, and of the individual and the context work together to produce behavior. There are features of an individual's personality and behavior that emerge early and present so consistently that it seems they are innate. Similarly, there are attitudes and behaviors that appear to be entirely dependent upon context to emerge. In this way, it is generally acknowledged that both forces are important. According to conventional wisdom, this is known as the nature-and-nurture debate. In the social sciences, it is known as the *diathesis-stress model*, in which persons who are at genetic risk for some disorder or condition are most sensitive to the stressors that environmental risk creates (see Figure 2.1).

Social work practitioners also face the independent and interactive effects of nature and nurture each day in the course of their professional duties. Pervasive developmental disorders such as autism are among the most heritable disorders in psychiatry. Upwards of 90% of the causal variance of autism is attributable to genetic factors. However, early intervention and intensive treatment—environmental factors under the control of social work and other helping professionals—can dramatically reduce the problem symptoms of autism. Moreover, clients with actively involved parents and strong family and community supports constitute additional environmental strengths that can surmount various disabilities. In other words, social workers have a host of clients who, they sense, present with some balance of biological,

genetic, or neurological risks (and assets) coupled with environmental risks (and assets).

In the case of substance-abusing clients, social workers have a general idea that some of their clients have drug problems that appear to be environmentally based, such as clients who only use substances when with specific drug-using peers. When those negative influences are absent, these clients maintain sobriety, employment, and adult functioning fairly well. Other clients abuse drugs regardless of their peer networks or environmental context, and have dependency issues that are more pernicious. Still other clients respond quickly and affirmatively to supervision and desist from drug use completely. All of these examples relate to the variance that typifies human behavior and the apparent ease with which interventions can change behavior.

On a broader scale, in the 21st century, understanding about the relative contribution of personal and environmental factors has advanced to an extraordinary scientific level, as studies using brain imaging and/or methodologies in which measured genes and environments are analyzed together have produced knowledge about human behavior. Each week, more than 2.5 million queries of major genome data servers are made (Lander, 2011). Each day it seems scholars are producing startling insights into the genetic underpinnings of complex human behaviors and constructs, such as sex and gender differences (Fine, 2010; Jordan-Young, 2010), morality (Churchland, 2011), war (Potts & Hayden, 2008), and evil (Baron-Cohen, 2011). Consider this brief sampling of fascinating

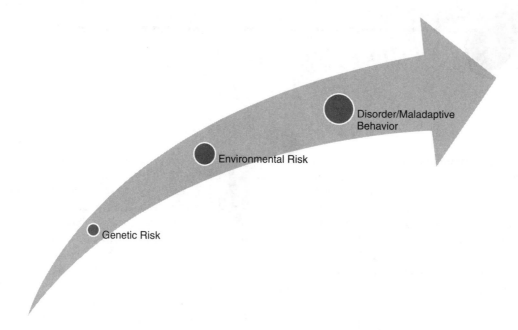

FIGURE 2.1 Diathesis-Stress Model

insights about the ways that genes, the brain, and the environment interact:

• Neuroscientists using functional magnetic resonance imaging (fMRI) methods found that living in a city negatively affects the neural mechanisms for managing social stress. Urban upbringing affected the perigenual anterior cingulate cortex, a brain region responsible for the regulation of limbic activity and the processing of negative affect and stress (Lederbogen et al., 2011). It has long been recognized that the size, crowding, noise, and pollution of large cities is stress inducing, and this recent research articulates precisely how those urban conditions affect the brain's ability to deal with stress in a healthy manner.

• The linkages between socioeconomic status and intelligence, and the roles that genes play in the relationship, have recently been clarified. Psychologists found that among 750 pairs of twins, genes accounted for little variance in mental ability at age 10 months. However, at follow-up at age 2 years, genes accounted for nearly 60% of variance in mental ability among children reared in more affluent homes, but less than 5% of variance in mental ability among children reared in homes of low socioeconomic status (Tucker-Drob, Rhemtulla, Harden, Turkheimer, & Fask, 2011). The study speaks to the importance of how environment and genetic factors work in tandem to explain behavioral outcomes. Moreover, the findings of this study show that 95% of the variance in mental ability among children in poorer conditions is environmental, which offers opportunities for intervention.

• Each day, social work practitioners see the damaging effects of child abuse and other early-life traumas on the development of children. A host of research labs worldwide have studied the gene–environment interactions between a polymorphism known as monoamine oxidase A (MAOA) and abuse. The gene encodes the MAOA enzyme that is responsible for metabolizing neurotransmitters in the brain such as norepinephrine, serotonin, and dopamine. Children who were abused and had the low-activity allele of MAOA are at significant risk for conduct problems, crime, violence, and criminal justice system involvement (Caspi et al., 2002; Frazzetto et al., 2007; Prom-Wormley et al., 2009). Similar gene–environment interplay is found among children who are resilient to early-life deprivation such as poverty, in which nearly 50% of cognitive resilience and 70% of behavioral resilience is attributable to genetic factors (Kim-Cohen, Moffitt, Caspi, & Taylor, 2004).

• How does parental attachment insulate children at genetic risk for conduct problems? Psychologists have recently explored gene–environment interactions responsible for children's self-regulation. Kochanska, Philibert, and Barry (2009) examined the polymorphism in the serotonin transporter gene (5-*HTTLPR*) and its interaction with maternal attachment at age 15 months on self-regulation at 25, 38, and 52 months. Children at genetic risk who were insecurely attached had poor regulatory capacities, whereas children at genetic risk who were securely attached had normal self-regulatory capacity (Kochanska et al., 2009). In other words, a healthy, secure attachment mutes the genetic risk factor.

• Neuropsychologists recently demonstrated the damaging effects of environmental pathogens over and above the role of genetic risk. Using data from a longitudinal sample of twins, researchers found that children who were maltreated by adults were more than 3 times likely, and children who were bullied by peers were nearly 2.5 times more likely, to display psychotic symptoms at age 12 than children who did not incur these abuses. Importantly, these environmental risks persisted even when controlling for genetic vulnerabilities relating to a composite measure of genetic risk for psychosis and maternal history of psychosis (Arseneault et al., 2011).

• Impulsivity generally diminishes with age because of protracted development of the prefrontal cortex. Because impulsivity is central to multiple behavioral disorders, it is important to determine neural commonalities and differences across disorders. Rubia et al. (2008) conducted an event-related fMRI study that compared brain activation of 13 boys with pure conduct disorder (CD), 20 boys with pure attention-deficit/hyperactivity disorder (ADHD), and 20 boys without a disorder. The boys were scanned while doing a stop task that measures the neural substrates of inhibition and stopping failure. They found that boys with ADHD and CD had distinct brain abnormality patterns during inhibitory control. Boys with ADHD, however, displayed differences in prefrontal regions whereas boys with CD had differences in the posterior temporal parietal lobe. The importance of their study is that the disorders—which are often comorbid—have distinct underlying neural abnormalities despite the commonality of inhibition as a symptom.

Rubia et al.'s (2008) findings point to interesting social work practice implications, suggesting the necessity of tailored and individualized intervention strategies in children who may be given similar "externalizing disorder" diagnoses. For example, perhaps children with ADHD would benefit more from cognitive-based techniques that shore up the prefrontal cortex executive functioning area of the brain and that focus on planning protocols, enhancing concentration, and strengthening goal-directed decision making. Children with CD, by contrast, might benefit more from techniques that bolster the emotional centers of the brain and focus on social information processing and emotional (implicit) self-regulation strategies, perhaps to include meditation and mind–body interventions.

These exciting examples are a scant few of the hundreds and perhaps thousands of new research findings produced each year toward a cell to society understanding of human behavior. Unfortunately, exploration of cell biology and genetics is not the usual subject matter for the social sciences generally and social work specifically, and many prospective and current social work practitioners might fret about the complexities of human genetics. This chapter explores basic issues in molecular biology and explains ways that genes can differ across individuals, and how these changes can produce incremental but important susceptibility to adaptive and maladaptive behaviors. Although this chapter is very technical in places, we did not want to short-change the helping professions of a comprehensive overview of genes and behavior. We promise that careful reading will be rewarding.

In addition to the challenges of learning an altogether different field, such as behavioral genetics, social work students also might have potential ideological concerns about the role of genetic factors toward understanding behavior. As explored in Chapter 1, the essence of a biosocial, cell to society approach is to acknowledge and respect the important roles of environment and individual factors in explaining behavior. This respect includes understanding the role of genes. Renowned psychiatrists Kenneth Kendler and Carol Prescott (2006) captured this sentiment well: "It is critical to emphasize that, although the magnitude of genetic effects for common psychiatric and substance use disorders is not overwhelming, neither is it trivial. It is too large to be ignored by anyone who wants to truly understand the etiology of these disorders. . . . This is a brute fact of our world. It will not be changed by whether it does or does not fit our ideological, philosophical, or religious views about the nature of personhood" (p. 340). With that, this chapter explores the fascinating role of genes and human behavior.

CASE STUDY: CORY

"Cory, you've defied the odds!" rejoiced my mother as she read my nearly flawless report card. There are many people in the world, past and present, who have defied the odds, whatever those odds may be. Many of those people are distinguished for their success at overcoming their hindrances, but most are not as well known. Everyday people who happen to have autism are among those unsung heroes. I'm one of them.

When I was three years old I was diagnosed with pervasive developmental disorder, which was later refined to being Asperger's syndrome. In the early 1990s, a diagnosis of autism meant a doomed life for many kids and parents. Nobody knew how to treat autism at the time, but many parents, including mine, did their best to provide the best. I recall being sent to numerous schools as a toddler, some exceedingly far away, as a result of my mother's efforts at trying to find a place where I could be properly "handled." I observed similar types of peculiarities in my classmates even as I jumped from school to school, and I too was guilty of many if not most of these actions: hand-flapping, "rocking," perseverating (over toys, routines, ideas, and transitions), violent tantrums, being unresponsive, and general inappropriate behavior. The fascinating part of this is while I was aware that I exhibited many of these behaviors and was grouped with the "special kids," I adamantly believed that I was not part of any of it and made it known to my mother. That was the spark of her new crusade to help me become mainstream.

Middle school was a very tumultuous time for me. The expectations were higher than in elementary school, both academically and socially, and I was very ill equipped. If there was any sort of workload that seemed daunting to me, I wouldn't even try it. My grades were C average at best throughout my middle school experience; my mind always an obstacle to success. In order to combat that belief, I was required to be in a Special Needs class in middle school, which was basically a time for me to study and recoup. There was a pivotal point in my life in seventh grade when after one of my outbursts, the Special Needs teacher calmly asked me to join her outside the classroom, where she disclosed to me that I was autistic. No one had ever labeled me this way. For the first time in my life I knew why I acted the way I did. From then on, I began to develop an acute awareness of myself and my peers, both normal and handicapped, a characteristic that today still defines who I am.

Something changed in high school—many call it maturation, I call it a revelation. My first year in high school was better than any in middle school, for I began to get As, which was an impossible feat for me beforehand. It was in 10th grade, though, that I experienced a revelation when I decided to take on the challenge of reading *Atlas Shrugged* by Ayn Rand. Her book immeasurably impacted my life. *Atlas Shrugged* became a catalyst for seeing life in a new way. Up until then, I saw myself as I assumed others saw me: the socially awkward boy. After finishing *Atlas Shrugged*, I learned that it was perfectly fine to be who I was all along. I have gained the confidence to advance into a completely mainstream curriculum, place out of a speech requirement, and become an honor roll student, all while preserving and cherishing my eccentricities.

Although I acknowledge my Asperger's, that's not how I define myself. I've learned not to allow my Asperger's dictate who I am or what I can achieve. I have become a better critical thinker, and I utilize this ability along with my quirky perspectives to create a unique point of view. Looking back at it all, I am very proud of myself and all the odds I've defied. I aspire to defy even more odds in college where I can accomplish more and nurture my interests for my awaiting future.

[Cory graduated from high school and started college in the fall of 2010.]

What can we, as social workers, learn from Cory's life experiences? Cory's story illuminates the mutually reinforcing and transactional interdependency of environmental forces and individual genetic predispositions and characteristics. He gives us a glimpse into his own growth and development through his interactions within various social institutions. Cory reminds us of the importance to focus on biological and environmental assets, in addition to recognizing functional deficits. This may be ever more challenging for social workers who work within educational settings where the institutional climate is focused on learning outcomes and identifying barriers to the learning process. Strengths can remain hidden behind missed, delayed, or inaccurate diagnoses that lead to delayed access to appropriate environmental resources that might enhance individual functioning.

Critical Thinking Questions:

- How can we as social workers promote successful adaptation given a particular genetic risk profile? Give an example.

- Within what settings and working with which populations might you anticipate controversy in employing a biosocial or genetic–environmental approach in your social work practice? Explain.

- Within what settings and with which populations might this approach work best? Why?

DISTAL CONTEXT

Principles of Human Evolution

In 1859, Charles Darwin published *On the Origin of Species by Means of Natural Selection, or the Preservation of Favoured Races in the Struggle for Life*, which advanced his theory of evolution and natural selection as the unified scientific explanation for survival, adaptation, and change in the human population over thousands of generations. Darwin's theory of evolution is on the short list of the greatest and most influential contributions in the history of science. The essence of *natural selection* is that characteristics that facilitate the survival and reproductive success of an organism persist, whereas characteristics that do not facilitate the survival of the species desist. Natural selection occurs when there is variance in characteristics of the organism, the variance is heritable (i.e., attributable to genetic factors), and there is variance in reproductive success among the organisms. It is important to note that natural selection operates on observed characteristics or behaviors, but the genetic basis that gives rise to adaptive traits will become more common over time.

Darwin's notion of natural selection is an action-oriented theory whereby the environment hones the value of human traits over time. Another monumental evolutionary idea is that humans evolve according to random, neutral processes that affect our genes. In a landmark paper, geneticist Motoo Kimura (1968) calculated that the rate of evolution of nucleotide substitutions was so high that many of the mutations occurred neutrally and not as the result of some adaptive advantage during the course of natural selection. In other words, a considerable amount of genetic evolution is random in nature, an idea known as *genetic drift*. Subsequent geneticists have supported Kimura's theory that a significant portion of genetic evolution is random. For example, a study of 100 DNA polymorphisms (discussed later in this chapter) from five populations selected from four continents found that 63% of the polymorphisms were selectively neutral

(Bowcock et al., 1991). Thus, both forces of natural selection and neutral mutation are at work on modifying the human genome.

The dual ideas of active natural selection and neutral genetic drift are important to think about when considering the effects of genes on behavior. Genes can have big, dramatic effects on human conditions, especially in the case of catastrophic disease. An inherited condition caused by a single genetic mutation is known as a *Mendelian disorder*, named from Gregor Mendel's famous pea plant hybridization experiments during the 1850s and 1860s. Mendelian disorders are also called simple inheritance disorders because a single gene inherited from the mother or father causes the condition.

Heritability

The study of human genetics involves language such as *inheritance*, *heredity*, and *heritable*, terms that social work students commonly use in normal conversation. Some behaviors, such as temperamental features and other core constitutional factors, appear to run in families. This is accurate, as these constructs are strongly heritable. Ranging between 0.0 and 1.0, *heritability* (usually indicated by the symbol h^2) is a population statistic indicating the proportion of variance in a phenotypic (or outcome) trait in a population that is attributable to genetic factors. Heritability captures the biological contribution to variance in human behaviors and characteristics. Behavioral geneticists usually organize the variance in behaviors along three dimensions. Heritability encompasses the first, the biological or genetic contribution. The remaining two sources of variation are environmental in nature. One relates to common environmental exposure that relates usually to within-family characteristics. This is known as the *shared environment*, commonly expressed with the notation c^2. The other source of environmental variation relates to circumstances that are unique to the individual, even within the same family. This type is known as the *nonshared environment*, commonly expressed as e^2

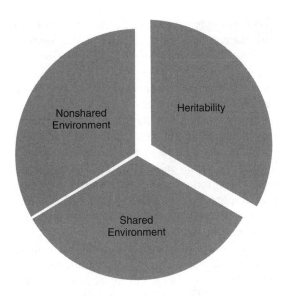

FIGURE 2.2 Sources of Variance in Human Behaviors/Phenotypes

(see Figure 2.2). Using data from twins, behavioral geneticists can model the correlations for twin type where identical twins are commonly referred to as monozygotic or MZ twins, and their genetic correlation is $r = 1.0$, whereas fraternal twins are commonly referred to as dizygotic or DZ twins, and their genetic correlation is $r = .5$.

Heritability estimates vary depending on environmental conditions; thus different heritability estimates are produced for the same sample if analyzed at different points of time and under different circumstances (e.g., childhood, adolescence, or late adulthood). There is also not a static heritability for a specific phenotype. Different researchers using different samples will likely arrive at different estimates of the role of genetic factors. For example, five relatively recent meta-analytic or summary studies are helpful in obtaining a general sense of the degree to which antisocial traits and behaviors are influenced by genes and environment:

1. Mason and Frick (1994) published a meta-analysis of 12 twin and 3 adoption studies with a total sample size of over 4,000 that provided 21 estimates of the heritability of antisocial behavior. The overall effect size for h^2 was .48, meaning that 48% of the variance was attributable to genetic factors.

2. Miles and Carey (1997) published a meta-analysis of 24 studies of human aggression and found that genes accounted for 50% of the variance.

3. Similarly, Rhee and Waldman (2002) published a meta-analysis of 51 twin and adoption studies of antisocial behavior and found that genes accounted for 41% of the variance, nonshared environmental factors accounted for 43% of the variance, and shared environmental factors accounted for 16% of the variance in antisocial behaviors.

4. Moffitt's (2005) exhaustive review of the literature indicated that genes influenced 50% of the population variation in antisocial behavior, with the nonshared environment accounting for between 20 and 30% and shared (family) influences accounting for about 20%.

5. Ferguson (2010) conducted a meta-analysis of 38 studies, comprising 53 separate observations published from 1996 to 2006 with a combined sample size of nearly 97,000. He reported that 56% of the variance in antisocial personality and behavior was attributable to genes, 31% to the nonshared environment, and 13% to the shared environment. In other words, genes, family environments, and unique environments all contribute to the cause of antisocial behavior.

Behavioral genetic designs allow researchers to understand the relative roles of nature and nurture in contributing to various human behaviors. For example, Vinkhuyzen, van der Sluis, Posthuman, and Boomsma (2009) examined the heritability of aptitude and exceptional talent across a range of domains among 1,685 twin pairs between ages 12 and 24 years, derived from the Netherlands Twin Register. They were interested in the contribution of genetics to self-reported giftedness in art, knowledge, language, mathematics, memory, music, sports, and writing. The highest additive genetic effects were found for music ($h^2 = .92$), mathematics ($h^2 = .87$), sports ($h^2 = .85$), and writing ($h^2 = .83$). Moderate additive genetic effects were observed for language ($h^2 = .50$), art ($h^2 = .56$), memory ($h^2 = .56$), and knowledge ($h^2 = .62$). With the exception of sports, the preponderance of the remaining variance was accounted for by nonshared environmental factors. They concluded "that high heritability does not mean environmental influences are unimportant. To reach exceptional levels of ability, deliberate practice is indispensible even for people with a genetic predisposition to develop a talent. This study does, however, show that differences in genetic make-up control individual differences in self-reported aptitude and talent" (p. 10).

Despite the apparently high heritability estimates for many characteristics and behaviors, human traits and behaviors are not inherited in a Mendelian way, unfortunately. As Meyer-Lindenberg and Weinberger (2006) observed, "almost by definition, the more behavioral the phenotype, the less directly it will be predicted by a genotype" (p. 818). In fact, there are several important differences between Mendelian disorders and *multifactorial phenotypes*—phenomena caused by genes, environments, and their interaction, such as psychopathology and externalizing behaviors. Recall that Mendelian disorders are caused by rare allelic mutations that produce catastrophic effects, such as Huntington's disease, which in 1983 became the first single-gene disorder linked to genetic markers on a chromosome (Plomin & Caspi, 1998). Other single-gene disorders include cystic fibrosis, sickle-cell anemia, and hemophilia. Mendelian disorders are rare because catastrophic mutations are weeded out via natural selection. However, they persist due to mutation-selection balance, the process by which new mutations at the disease locus are introduced into the population at a low frequency (Cannon & Keller, 2006).

In contrast, behaviors and psychiatric conditions are *polygenic*—caused by many genes—and *pleiotropic*—where individual genes are associated with many behaviors. These risk alleles produce smaller, incremental effects that affect traits (e.g., aggressiveness or impulsivity) in quantitative ways. Compared to rare Mendelian disorders, personality traits are significantly more common because according to mutation-selection balance, they have higher trait-level mutation rates and the selection against each mutation is much lower. As Cannon and Keller (2006) noted, "the relative commonality of certain mental disorders may simply reflect the much larger number of environmental and genetic factors that contribute to these disorders" (p. 272).

Understanding human evolution is a central goal of contemporary human evolutionary genetics, and a major scientific goal of society. For example, The 1000 Genomes Project began in 2008 with the goal of creating a database that captures the genetic diversity of the human population. The design of The 1000 Genomes Project includes whole-genome sequencing, array-based genotyping, and deep targeted sequencing of all coding regions in 2,500 individuals from across the world. This includes five population samples of 100 individuals with ancestry from Europe, East Asia, South Asia, and West Africa and seven populations totaling 500 individuals from North and South America. This sampling design was used to increase the likelihood of detecting low-frequency genetic variants, known as *alleles* (The 1000 Genomes Project Consortium, 2010). The 1000 Genomes Project Consortium has thus identified 95% of genes that have different forms (within a population these are known as *genetic polymorphisms*) where there is a single nucleotide difference (single nucleotide polymorphisms [SNPs], pronounced "snips"). There are about 11 million SNPs and 3 million short insertions or deletions. The Consortium also recently found that on average, each person carries between 250 and 300 loss-of-function genetic variants and 50 to 100 genetic variants that have previously been implicated in inherited disorders (The 1000 Genomes Project Consortium, 2010).

SPOTLIGHT TOPIC: NATURE AND NURTURE MEANS BOTH

No serious scholar believes that either forces of nature or forces of nurture are solely responsible for explaining human behavior. Of course, some of the variance in outcomes is attributable to genes, some to shared environmental factors, and some to nonshared environmental factors. Nevertheless, some social scientists continue to assert that biologically oriented research of human behavior is somehow dangerous and should be subjected to special ethical treatment. Consider this recent study by Males (2009), who expressed concern about research on neurodevelopmental issues and adolescents:

> Biodeterminist claims are the most profound and potentially dangerous that scientists can make about human beings. They posit a group as innately limited by unalterable biology. They obligate the state to take custodial measures to protect society and the inferior group by restricting the freedoms and behaviors of those pronounced inherently incapable of controlling themselves. When groups labeled by scientists as biologically limited are also publicly feared and politically powerless—as they always seem to be before brain scientists appear on the scene—legal and social repressions can be serious and long-lasting. For these reasons, biological claims should be subjected to the strictest levels of scientific skepticism, ethics, and scrutiny. (p. 5)

In response, the Biosocial Criminology Research Group (see DeLisi, Wright, Vaughn, & Beaver, 2010) briefly reviewed several examples that demonstrate a unified nature and nurture perspective toward studying and conceptualizing human behavior. Moreover, a biosocial, cell to society approach can yield progressive outcomes, such as the categorical exemption of juveniles from capital punishment (*Roper v. Simmons*, 2005) based on neurodevelopmental evidence about the adolescent brain.

This concern is not new, and once characterized more mature academic disciplines such as psychiatry, which is today substantially biological in scope. "The change from antipathy to acceptance of genetic factors in the behavioral sciences has occurred so rapidly and thoroughly, especially in psychiatry, that a reminder is warranted about how environmentalistic the behavioral sciences were, even in the 1960s, for example, the major explanation for schizophrenia was abnormal parenting" (Plomin, Owen, & McGuffin, 1994, p. 1733).

For Reflection

In what ways have biology and environment joined together to make you the person you are today?

PROXIMAL MECHANISMS

A Molecular Biology Primer for the Social Work Practitioner

The foundation of a cell to society approach is literally in our cells. In all of the approximately 100 trillion cells in the human body, with the exception of red blood cells, exists our genome. A *genome* is the complete genetic map of an organism. Before the human genome was sequenced or mapped, it was believed that it contained 100,000 genes. That estimate was conventionally reduced to 25,000 to 30,000.

More accurate data indicate that the human genome consists of about 20,500 genes (National Human Genome Research Institute, 2011). The genetic code is written in deoxyribonucleic acid, or more famously, *DNA*. About 6 feet of DNA are packed into 46 chromosomes within each cell. Twenty-three chromosomes are inherited from our mother and 23 chromosomes are inherited from our father. An important point that is emphasized throughout this text is that more than half of the genes in the human genome relate to functions in the brain, which speaks to the incalculable importance of the brain for understanding human behavior.

DNA has four major functions. First, DNA contains the blueprint or code for making proteins and enzymes. Second, it regulates how and when proteins and enzymes are made. Third, DNA carries this information when cells divide. Fourth, DNA transmits this information from parental organisms to their biological children. The "thing" that is a product of the DNA code is a *gene*, which is a distinct section of DNA in a cell's chromosome that contains the codes for producing specific proteins involved in brain and bodily functions (Balog, 2006; Carey, 2003).

As shown in Figure 2.3, DNA has a unique double helix appearance similar to a ladder that is twisted continuously. The sides of the double helix are made up of sugars and phosphates. The "rungs" of the double helix are composed of two chemicals (composed of atoms of carbon, hydrogen, oxygen, nitrogen, and phosphorous) called *nucleotides* or *base pairs*. There are four base pairs in DNA: adenine (abbreviated as A), thymine (T), guanine (G), and cytosine (C). A always pairs with T and G always pairs with C. This principle, called *complementary base pairing*, is important because if one sequence of nucleotides is known, so is the other. For instance, if the double helix were split vertically in half so that one side included ATGCTC, we know that the other side is TACGAG. Moreover, the principle of complementary base pairing is essential for understanding the ways that DNA becomes protein (Carey, 2003).

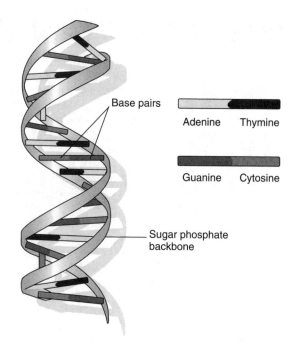

FIGURE 2.3 The DNA Double Helix
Source: National Institutes of Health.

The way that DNA becomes a protein is known as the *central dogma of molecular biology* (Figure 2.4). Formally advanced by Francis Crick (co-discoverer of the structure of DNA, for which he shared the Nobel Prize in Physiology or Medicine), this principle describes the process by which DNA is transcribed and then translated during protein synthesis (Crick, 1970). The process is:

- *Transcription*: This phase could be thought of as the photocopying stage. The double helix of DNA is split by an enzyme, so that the strands of the DNA ladder separate (technically, enzymes cut the hydrogen bonds, which causes the separation). Here the complementary base pairing plays a role again, as RNA, or ribonucleic acid, is synthesized from the single strand of DNA. RNA is very similar to DNA except that RNA is single stranded, uses the nucleotide uracil (U) instead of thymine, and possesses additional differences that are beyond the scope

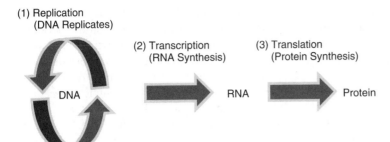

(1) Replication
(DNA Replicates)

(2) Transcription
(RNA Synthesis)

(3) Translation
(Protein Synthesis)

DNA   RNA   Protein

FIGURE 2.4   The Central Dogma of Molecular Biology

of this chapter. Approximately 10 to 15% of DNA is actually transcribed in an area called the promoter region.

• *Posttranscriptional modification*: This phase could be thought of as the editing stage because sections of nonuseful or junk RNA called *introns* are cut out and sections of useful RNA called *exons* are spliced together. Three general types of information are important during this stage. The first is the exons, which contain the blueprint for the synthesis of protein. The second piece of information is the "punctuation marks" that start or stop the process, and the third is the introns. There can be many exons and introns in a single molecule of transcribed RNA. The exons that are spliced together are known as messenger RNA (mRNA). Three adjacent mRNA nucleotides that contain the message for a specific amino acid are known as a *codon*. Different amino acids are produced from slight codon changes, and these changes can in turn contribute to real behavioral effects.

• *Transportation*: mRNA leaves the cell nucleus, enters the cytoplasm, and attaches to a ribosome. The ribosome is basically a protein factory where polypeptide chains or series of amino acids that are linked together are produced.

• *Translation*: A codon of mRNA enters a reading frame in the ribosome, where a molecule of transfer RNA (tRNA) with a complementary triplet of nucleotides, known as an anticodon, binds to the codon. The amino acid carried by the tRNA attaches to the polypeptide chain, which is a series of amino acids linked together.

• *Posttranslational modification*: This could be thought of as the final assembly stage, where the polypeptide chain folds on itself to take a three-dimensional form.

Genetic Variation and Neural Substrates

Admittedly, molecular biology seems like an alphabet soup of base pairs such as A, T, G, C, and when RNA is involved, U. The importance of these strands of base pairs is that small and often subtle changes during protein synthesis can give rise to both catastrophic and mundane changes in genetic expression. James Watson, who shared the 1962 Nobel Prize for Medicine and Physiology with Francis Crick and Maurice Wilkins, offered insight about genetic variation in his personal account of the discovery of the structure of DNA.

> So in building models we would postulate that the sugar-phosphate backbone was very regular, and the order of the bases of necessity was irregular. If the base sequences were always the same, all DNA molecules would be identical and there would not exist the variability that must distinguish one gene from another. (Watson, 1968/1996, p. 52)

What is essential to recognize is that apparently mundane changes differentiating one codon from another can have important implications for human behavior. A codon consists of three adjacent mRNA nucleotides that contain the message for a specific amino acid. For example, the amino acid tryptophan is composed of the mRNA nucleotides UGC. Recently, behavioral geneticists discovered a stop codon in the Q20 allele of the HTR2B gene that is relatively common but exclusive to people of Finnish descent. The HTR2B stop codon predisposes people to severe impulsivity, such as that displayed by violent criminal offenders (Bevilacqua et al., 2010).

Of course, most genetic variation is not limited to a single population, such as the Finnish example, but instead extends to most of the human population. Likewise, most genetic effects are not catastrophic single-gene Mendelian disorders, but are instead more subtle. Consider the example of sensation or novelty seeking: the tendency to actively obtain stimulation from the environment. Sensation/novelty seeking is strongly heritable; Hur and Bouchard (1997) found that between 40 and 55% of assorted facets of sensation seeking was heritable. Moreover, 55% of the variation between sensation seeking and impulsivity had a shared genetic etiology.

Genetic mutations occur and give rise to differences in brain pathways, often called *neural substrates*, that in turn affect neuropsychological functioning. Thus, although all humans are more than 99% identical in terms of their genome, the subtle differences that exist genetically form the raw material for susceptibility to various conditions. To some, it is controversial to suggest that exceptional ability or intelligence is heritable despite the scientific evidence. But it is important to note that the very physical architecture of the brain is itself similarly heritable. Chiang et al. (2009) conducted the first study to analyze genetic and environmental factors that affect brain fiber architecture (e.g., white matter) and its linkage with cognitive functioning in a sample of 92 twin pairs. They produced three main findings. First, genetic factors accounted for almost 80% of the variance in white-matter integrity. Second, white-matter integrity was significantly correlated ($r \sim .40$)

with IQ. Third, they found that some of the same genes mediated the correlation between IQ and white-matter integrity, which suggests a common physiological mechanism for both.

More than half of human genes are expressed in the brain; thus the subtle genetic differences that have been explored in this chapter give rise to different types of brain functioning among individuals. This logic is seen in television advertisements for medications that treat anxiety and depression. These medications, known as selective serotonin reuptake inhibitors, seek to maintain a more optimal level of serotonin in the brain. More evidence for the links between genes and neural substrates is seen in behavioral genetic evidence about major brain-based disorders (see Table 2.1).

Remember that genetic variation is only part of the equation. The environment is also important, as is the interaction between genetic expression and environmental conditions. One way that genetic differences occur is DNA

Table 2.1 Heritability and Twin Concordance Estimates for Psychiatric Disorders

Diagnosis	Heritability Range	Twin Concordance
ADHD	60–90%	MZ: 60% DZ: 21%
Alcohol dependence	50–60%	MZ: 40% DZ: 10%
Anxiety (panic) disorder	40–50%	MZ: 23–73% DZ: 0–17%
Autism	90%	MZ: 36–82% DZ: 6%
Major depression	40%	MZ: 46% DZ: 20%
Manic depression	60–85%	MZ: 70% DZ: 19%
Schizophrenia	70–85%	MZ: 40–50% DZ: 14%

Note: ADHD = attention-deficit/hyperactivity disorder, MZ = monozygotic twins, DZ = dizygotic twins.
Source: Adapted from "Psychiatric Genetics: Progress amid Controversy," by M. Burmeister, M. G. McInnis, and S. Zöllner, 2008, *Nature Reviews Genetics, 9*, pp. 527–540.

methylation, a gene modification process that deactivates a gene's expression but does not alter the genetic code. It is an example of an epigenetic phenomenon where environmental conditions affect gene expression (Ma et al., 2010). Technically, DNA methylation occurs at cytosine bases when a methyl group is added to the 5′ position on the pyrimidine ring (Day & Sweatt, 2010). What does this mean? For example, prolonged periods of starvation that occur prenatally, as occurred during the Great Chinese Famine from 1958 to 1961 and the Dutch *Hongerwinter* (hunger winter) famine during World War II (Ahmed, 2010), have been found to be associated with later life problems, such as obesity and schizophrenia. The environmental adversities that malnutrition caused for these developing children affected the expression of genes.

The dopaminergic system, an important neurotransmitter system that is involved in reward, has been shown to be associated with persistence in psychiatric conditions that are associated with problem behaviors. For instance, Langley et al.'s (2009) study of 151 children aged 6 to 12 years who met diagnostic criteria for ADHD were reinterviewed 5 years later. The 7R allele of *DRD4* and *DRD5* CA(n) microsatellite 148 bp markers was related to persistent ADHD symptoms (Langley et al., 2009). Similarly, Barkley, Smith, Fischer, and Navia (2006) found that the homozygous DBH Taq1 A2 allele was associated with greater hyperactivity during childhood and pervasive behavioral problems during adolescence among respondents from a Milwaukee longitudinal study of hyperactive and normal-activity children. Significant effects were also found for the dopamine transporter *DAT1* but not *DRD4* (Barkley et al., 2006). Based on data from 188 ADHD cases and 166 controls selected from the Northern Finland Birth Cohort 1986, Nyman et al. (2007) found that the DBH SNP (rs2073837) minor allele conferred fivefold increased odds for ADHD (DBH is an enzyme that catalyzes the conversion of dopamine to norepinephrine). In a summary of research, Li, Sham, Owen, and He (2006) conducted a meta-analysis of 73 studies that examined linkages between dopamine polymorphisms and ADHD and found consistent strong effects for *DRD4* and *DRD5*.

Another condition, Parkinson's disease, is a movement disorder caused by dopamine deficiency in the brain, specifically the striatum. The classic Parkinsonian personality is described as introverted, rigid, slow tempered, and displaying temperance. Driven by reduced dopamine, the Parkinsonian personality is the polar extreme of the addictive personality (Dagher & Robbins, 2009). The reason why substance abuse and addiction are associated with the dopamine system is that large amounts of it are released after ingestion of an illicit substance and is thus involved in the high that is achieved.

Serotonin is an inhibitory neurotransmitter that stabilizes information processing in neural systems. High levels of serotonin are associated with excessive restraint, anxiety, and cognitive inflexibility, whereas low levels are associated with behavioral disinhibition. Most serotonin is located in the brainstem; forebrain serotonin is produced almost entirely by neurons located in the raphe nuclei of the midbrain (Jacobs & Azmitia, 1992). Van Goozen, Fairchild, Snock, and Harold (2007) suggest that a reduced serotonergic functioning and stress-regulating system, such as the hypothalamic-pituitary-adrenal (HPA) axis and the autonomic nervous system, interacts with early-childhood adverse environments to increase susceptibility to severe, persistent antisocial behavior. Children with these deficits do not understand dangerous settings and do not display appropriate emotional response to them. As a result, they do not physiologically experience the threat of dangerous settings via autonomic or endocrine stress response. This leads to a vicious cycle of selection of dangerous settings and a muted response to the dangers therein. They are incapable of normal stress responses to situations that typically bring upon anger, embarrassment, and most importantly, fear (van Goozen et al., 2007).

GENES AND BEHAVIOR OVER THE LIFE COURSE

Thus far some fairly complicated evolutionary and genetics research has been covered. Some of this information is very general and some of it is extraordinarily specific. However, several common-sense summary points should be understood prior to delving into gene–environment interplay over the life course. First, evolutionary processes span thousands of millennia and random, rapid periods from one generation to the next. In some ways, the human genome reflects the advantages of natural selection whereby traits and behaviors that ensure survival and reproductive success persist. In other ways, the human genome reflects random and neutral mutations where very small changes in genetic variants—sometimes affecting a single nucleotide—produce large consequences.

Second, by exploring the molecular biology of the gene, students can understand that seeming genetic differences between individuals are not dramatic. Indeed, as mentioned, 99% of all humans share the same genes. Genetic variation is instead incremental and often reflects random insertions, deletions, and repeats. Thus, a sequence for most people that looks like this:

ATT   ATC   ATC   TTT   GGT   GTT   TCC

may look like this in other individuals:

ATT   ATC   TTT   GGT   GTT   TCC

Notice that these sequences are identical except that the third codon is deleted. People who have the deleted codon develop cystic fibrosis (Balog, 2006).

Fortunately, most genetic mutations do not produce such catastrophic health problems as cystic fibrosis. Instead, most result in efficiencies in the brain that relate to communications between neurons (i.e., neurotransmission) and other important cognitive processes. These differences in turn relate to quantitative differences between people. Thus, people vary in terms of their temperamental characteristics, personality traits, and cognitive abilities. Social work practitioners already know this, as their client list represents a broad distribution of traits, such as impulsivity, temper, agreeableness, conscientiousness, work ethic, and aggression. Their clients range from low to high on all of these traits in idiosyncratic combinations that make all individuals slightly different and unique.

Last, heritable conditions are only part of the story; an individual's underlying genetic, neurological, or (more broadly speaking) biological susceptibility to a disorder or behavior interacts with the environment. The next section explores fascinating ways that the gene–environment interplay unfolds over the life course.

Fetal Environment and Infancy

Imagine two pregnant women on a standard social work caseload. The first regularly sees her obstetrician, lives a healthy lifestyle, has ample spousal and family support, and eagerly awaits the birth of her child. The second client has only been to the doctor once and is reluctant to return because she is ashamed of her alcoholism, a condition that has worsened during her pregnancy. These clients are polar opposites in terms of their likelihood of success. But another important difference relates to the damage that alcohol is causing to the developing child and, more specifically, the neural pathways in the child's brain.

Maternal substance use is a direct, pernicious way that parents can cause neurological problems for their children. Environmental risks, or pathogens, also exist in indirect broader contexts as well. For example, many toxins found in the environment have been shown to affect brain development and behavior. One of the most damaging pathogens is lead. In a landmark study, Wright et al. (2008) examined the effects of prenatal and infant exposure to lead and its effects on behavior during adulthood. They found that higher levels of fetal and infant lead exposure were associated with higher levels of criminal activity and violent arrests during adulthood, even while controlling for important correlates of offending, such as the mother and child's demographic characteristics. A reason for the prospective link between lead exposure and crime is that lead reduces MAOA activity and interferes with synapse formation. Among the most replicated findings in molecular genetic association studies, MAOA activity has consistently been associated with various forms of antisocial behavior including gang membership and weapons use (Beaver, DeLisi, Vaughn, & Barnes, 2010).

The gene–environment interplay can also be seen in the neuroregulatory behaviors among neonates. For instance, Auerbach et al. (2005) assessed 158 healthy male infants, some of whom were at familial risk for ADHD based on paternal symptoms of the disorder (i.e., their parents likely had ADHD). They found that children at risk for ADHD had state organization and regulation difficulties pertaining to irritability, state lability, and self-quieting ability. These neuroregulatory problems were also seen when children were assessed at age 7 months. Susceptibility to satisfying immediate desires emerges early in life. For instance, Judith Auerbach and her colleagues (2001) studied the effects of *DRD4* and *5-HTT* on sustained attention abilities among a sample of sixty-four 1-year-old infants. They found that during structured play situations and on an information-processing task, infants with the 7R allele of *DRD4* displayed less sustained attention. Those with risk alleles for *DRD4* and *5-HTT* also demonstrated reduced sustained attention, which was characterized by latency to first look away, duration of looking at and manipulating toys, and facial indications of interest. Auerbach et al. (2005) concluded that allelic variation in *DRD4* is a possible developmental link to ADHD based on early sustained attention and information processing. Because the dopaminergic system is involved in motivational or seeking behaviors, it has clear theoretical links to impulsive action. A recent meta-analysis indicated that *DRD4* was associated with not only impulsivity but also novelty seeking (Munafò, Yalcin, Willis-Owen, & Flint, 2008).

Childhood

A number of potential genes are involved in typical and atypical development during childhood. The catechol-O-methyltransferase gene, known as *COMT*, is an important candidate gene for antisocial and other problem behaviors due to the major role the enzyme plays in modulating dopamine levels in the prefrontal cortex, the area of the brain that controls executive cognitive functioning. The *COMT* gene has a cytogenic location of 22q11 (this means it is located on chromosome 22) and contains a valine/methionine polymorphism at codon 158 (Val^{158}Met), which is associated with a 40% reduction in prefrontal enzymatic activity (Chen et al., 2004). As a consequence, there are higher levels of dopamine in the prefrontal cortex and excess brain dopamine is associated with externalizing disorders.

Caspi et al. (2008) examined the association between *COMT* Val^{158}Met and antisocial behavior among three samples of children with ADHD. Children were selected from three data sources. The first is the Cardiff ADHD Genetic Study, which is a sample of 376 White British children selected from child psychiatry and pediatric clinics in England and Wales between 1997 and 2003. The second is the Environmental Risk (E-Risk) Study, which is a birth cohort of 2,232 British children drawn from the 1994–1995 birth registry in England and Wales, and the third is the Dunedin Longitudinal Study, a prospective birth cohort study of 1,037 children born in Dunedin, New Zealand, in 1972–1973. Caspi et al. found across the three samples that children with the valine/valine (Val/Val) homozygotes had more symptoms of conduct disorder, were more aggressive, and were more likely to be convicted of crimes than methionine carriers (Met/Met or Val/Met).

It is important to note that heritable conditions are not exclusively related to antisocial behaviors, but also to other forms of maladaptive or unhealthy behaviors, such as obesity. For instance, Seeyave et al. (2009) surveyed 805 children who were participants in the National Institute of Child Health and Human Development Study of Early Child Care and Youth Development, along with their mothers. They found that children who were unable to delay gratification at age 4 years were significantly more likely than children who could delay gratification to be overweight at age 11. This relationship withstood controls for the child's body mass index at age 4, maternal expectations of the child's ability to delay gratification for food, and mother's weight status, although the last was also an important variable.

Adolescence

Adolescence is a time of rapid change; as such, much research of adolescents has focused on risk taking. Adolescent risk taking appears to be the outcome of the unequal development of the prefrontal cortex vis-à-vis the limbic system. According to their model, impulsivity wanes over time because the prefrontal cortex develops in a linear fashion. Emotional centers of the brain such as the limbic system, specifically the accumbens and amygdala, develop by adolescence. However, the previously mentioned control centers, such as the prefrontal cortex, are not. This results in a prefrontal cortical brain that is not sufficiently developed to override the risky impulses emanating from subcortical regions. The result—and the reason that adolescence is characterized as a period of risky choices and behaviors—is the mature limbic system overrides its immature prefrontal region.

The unequal development of these brain regions is useful for understanding developmental patterns of risk-taking behavior. According to Casey, Jones, and Hare (2008):

> During adolescence, relative to childhood or adulthood, an immature ventral prefrontal

cortex may not provide sufficient top-down control of robustly activated reward and affect processing regions (e.g., accumbens and amygdala). This imbalance in development of these regions and relative top-down control results in less influences of prefrontal systems (orbitofrontal cortex) relative to the accumbens and amygdala in reward valuation and emotional reactivity. (p. 118)

The A1 allele of the dopamine *D2* receptor gene (*DRD2*) has also been linked to impulsivity-based endophenotypes. Esposito-Smythers, Spirito, Rizzo, McGeary, and Knopik (2009) examined 104 adolescents who had been hospitalized for psychiatric problems and found that carriers of the *DRD2* A1 allele and who were diagnosed with conduct disorder reported higher levels of problem drinking and more severe problem drug use than noncarriers. Their findings suggested an interrelationship among impulsivity, externalizing disorders, and *DRD2*.

Adulthood

Although the prefrontal cortex is more fully developed by adulthood, there are other neural systems that are coded for by important genes that impact behavioral functioning. For example, White, Morris, Lawford, and Young (2008) examined the A1 allele of the *ANKK1* TaqIA polymorphism, which is associated with reduced dopamine receptor density in the striatum and implicated in addiction. In their study, 72 healthy young adults were randomly assigned to either a relaxation-induction condition or an acute stress condition. Behavioral phenotypes of impulsivity were measured using a card-sorting index of reinforcement sensitivity and computerized response inhibition and delay discounting tasks. Those with the A1 *ANKK1* allele displayed deficits relating to reinforcement learned and evinced an impulsive behavioral style compared to those with the A2 allele. Moreover, these genetic effects were independent of stress.

Not only are there neural differences in the brains of violent offenders, but also between types of violent offenders. It is likely that brain differences differentiate predatory, instrumental, or cold-blooded violent offenders from emotional, reactive, or hot-blooded offenders. The main difference is the ability of the prefrontal cortex to modulate basic impulses from the limbic system. A study by Raine et al. (1998) speaks directly to this. They examined glucose metabolism in the brain using positron emission tomography on 15 predatory murderers, 9 affective or reactive murderers, and 41 controls. They found that affective or reactive murderers had reduced prefrontal activity and increased subcortical (limbic) activity compared to controls. Predatory murderers had similar prefrontal activity to controls but excessive subcortical activity. These findings suggest that cold-blooded killers are able to exercise neurocognitive control of their instincts despite excessive limbic activity, whereas hot-blooded killers are not.

EXPERT'S CORNER: TERRIE E. MOFFITT

Terrie E. Moffitt, the Knut Schmidt Nielsen Professor in the Department of Psychology and Neuroscience at Duke University, is among the most accomplished social scientists in the world. Her vanguard leadership dominates an array of fields including psychology, neuroscience, and criminology. Moffitt has offered several summary statements about gene–environment interplay; these comments helpfully summarize the content of this chapter:

Photo of Terrie E. Moffitt
Courtesy of Terrie Moffitt

- The main or direct effects of environmental and genetic risks are generally small, but the interaction of these risks produces larger behavioral effects.
- Gene–environment interplay provides an authenticity to research toward understanding and explaining human behavior.
- Longitudinal research using gene–environment designs can explain the continuity of behavior—prosocial and antisocial—over the life course.
- Research should focus on pathological or extreme forms of behavior.
- Gene–environment studies are helpful for determining the traits and conditions (intermediate constructs that, in genetics, are known as endophenotypes) that give rise to human behavior.
- Gene–environment research can inform intervention efforts and thus has direct policy relevance.
- This type of research must include both geneticists/neuroscientists and social scientists to understand the ways that nature and nurture interact over time.

SUMMARY

Virtually everyone has commented about a certain trait, feature, or behavior about themselves, their parents, or their children that appears to be genetic in terms of its causality. This chapter provided an overview of basic concepts and terminology in the study of human genetics. Although it is admittedly complex material, it is clear to see how subtle differences included in genetic polymorphisms partially engender human differences. Except for rare Mendelian disorders that are largely weeded out via natural selection, most genetic differences are small and depend upon the environment to be exacerbated or muffled. This is the very essence of the biosocial framework that dominates the current scientific study of human behavior. Several key points examined in this chapter include the following:

• The diathesis-stress model asserts that genetic risks are most sensitive to environmental risks for disorders and maladaptive behaviors.

• A cell to society approach advances a biosocial framework, where nature, nurture, and their interaction produce behavior.

• Natural selection and neutral, random mutation are responsible for evolutionary changes in the human genome.

• An inherited condition caused by a single genetic mutation is a Mendelian disorder, and these follow the laws of simple inheritance.

• Variance in behavior is attributable to three sources: heritability, shared environment, and nonshared environment.

• Behaviors that are caused by genes, environments, and their interaction are known as multifactorial phenotypes.

• The central dogma of molecular biology articulates the ways that DNA is transcribed into RNA and ultimately translated into proteins and enzymes.

• Genetic polymorphism produces genes that have different forms within a population; the individual variants are called alleles.

• More than half of human genes are expressed in the brain, and genetic variation gives rise to variance in neural substrates or pathways that relate to cognitive and behavioral functioning.

• Gene–environment interactions occurring during gestation, infancy, childhood, adolescence, and adulthood shape human behavior.

KEY TERMS

Alleles

Central dogma of molecular biology

Codon

Complementary base pairing

Diathesis-stress model

DNA

Gene

Genetic polymorphisms

Genome

Genetic drift

Heritability (h^2)

Mendelian disorder

Multifactorial phenotypes

Natural selection

Neural substrates

Nonshared environment (e^2)

Nucleotides (base pairs)

Pleiotropic

Polygenic

Posttranscriptional modification

Posttranslational modification

Shared environment (c^2)

Transcription

Translation

Transportation

CHAPTER 3

STRESS AND ADAPTATION

The title of this chapter is fitting in that *stress* and *adaptation* are two words that accurately describe the world of social work and the challenges faced by many of the clients with whom social workers interact and to whom they provide services. A central focus among many social work practitioners' client populations centers on the unique stresses of their diagnoses, legal status, and socioeconomic functioning, and the positive and negative ways they respond to them. Consider these examples:

- Families who are characterized by child abuse, child neglect, and ongoing criminal behavior are at risk of losing their children to the foster care system. In many cases, the negative behaviors that parents perpetuate reflect a general inability to handle the stressors and responsibilities of raising children. Family preservation programs are an example of a policy designed to provide services to parents to be better able to process the stresses of parenting in an adaptive, not maladaptive, way (Tyuse, Hong, & Stretch, 2010). When intact families are preserved, children are also spared the stress of foster care placement.

- Families with special-needs children face financial costs that are exponentially higher than those faced by families without special-needs children (not to mention the emotional and physical challenges that special-needs children also present). These costs take a heavy toll on families in terms of stress, but there are few evidence-based interventions that help families with special-needs and/or chronically ill children (Anderson & Davis, 2011).

- Children with disabilities are more likely to have insecure attachments to parents and caregivers due to the challenges of the disability and the parent's difficulty in handling those challenges. When working with families who have children with disabilities, social work practitioners should cultivate social support for the family, provide accurate and realistic information about the child's disability and the treatment interventions that are available, help parents and siblings resolve traumatic issues relating to the disability, and help parents develop more secure attachments to their child (Howe, 2006).

- Many social work occupations require significant exposure to individuals in distress. This can result in *secondary traumatic stress* where practitioners display symptoms of chronic stress exposure due to their frequent interaction with persons in need (Bride, Jones, & Macmaster, 2007). Certain factors increase the likelihood that a social work practitioner will experience secondary traumatic stress, including work characteristics (e.g., case load size and administrative support) and personal characteristics (e.g., friendship networks, social support, and personal history of traumatic experiences).

- Childhood trauma is a well-known risk factor for maladjustment, and sexual abuse victimization is among the most severe forms of trauma. Research on youth in confinement facilities has shown that sexual-abuse victimization is significantly associated with externalizing symptoms (e.g., delinquency), internalizing symptoms (e.g., anxiety and depression), and suicidal behaviors. Witnessing traumatic events is also related to these outcomes, although at lower levels. Youth who both experienced and witnessed sexual abuse and traumatic incidents are most likely to manifest behavioral problems, psychiatric problems, and suicidal ideation and attempts (Coleman, 2005).

• A major problem among individuals who suffered various childhood traumas is that the memories of the experience are never appropriately dealt with. Instead, childhood traumas are often denied, repressed, or allowed to directly contribute to maladaptive behaviors such as substance abuse. In terms of social work practice, patients who revisit the emotional pain of their trauma and then go through a reappraisal process are more likely to get better emotionally (Littrell, 2009). Allowing clients to reflect on their traumatic experiences provides insights on how best to develop interventions that will allow them to overcome the trauma.

For social work practitioners, the frequent exposure to people in distress can lead to *compassion fatigue*, which is a state of tension and preoccupation with the suffering of those being helped to the degree that it is traumatizing for the helper. Compassion fatigue contributes to several maladaptive characteristics including increased work stress and work anxiety, and reduced efficacy and work productivity. Unfortunately, stress, compassion fatigue, and maladaptive responses are common in social work and human services professions. A recent study of genetic counselors found that half of those studied experience compassion fatigue and more than 26% consider leaving their job because of it (Injeyan et al., 2011). Consistent with material on temperament (Chapter 6), counselors with more optimistic dispositions and an internal locus of control (the feeling that one determines one's life) were more likely to avoid compassion fatigue and the attendant distress of their work. On the other hand, counselors with a less sunny disposition and/or those with an external locus of control (the feeling that others determine one's life) were more likely to experience compassion fatigue. The key conclusion from this study is that stress is not experienced equally and can alternately lead to healthy adaptations or unhealthy, maladaptive responses. The variation in responses that individuals and groups have to stressful conditions also suggests that social work interventions can be tailored to some extent for different people. Social workers must remember that before they can adequately help others they must take steps to care for self. This chapter explores the role of stress in human behavior, and the ways that biological, psychological, and social factors contribute to responses to stress.

CASE STUDY: JUAN CARLOS—PROFILE OF ADAPTATION IN UNPREDICTABLE AND UNCERTAIN TIMES

The housing crisis and economic recession of 2008 hit Juan Carlos particularly hard. Juan Carlos immigrated from El Salvador at the age of 12, coming to the United States legally under the U.S. asylum program at the time. He immigrated with his mother and younger brother, leaving the rest of his aunts, uncles, cousins, and grandparents back in his home country. Juan Carlos successfully completed his secondary education in the United States, thanks to his own motivation and the commitment of a spirited guidance counselor. Upon graduation, Juan Carlos enrolled in a local community college; however, he quickly met a girl from El Salvador and they soon learned she was pregnant. Seventeen years old like his girlfriend, and with a baby on the way, Juan Carlos put his community college course ambitions on hold, but "only temporarily," as he justified it.

He was immediately able to become gainfully employed full time at a neighborhood foreign auto-parts and service shop, doing odds and ends, but mostly just making sure the place was clean for customers. He quickly moved up to become a mechanic's assistant at the auto shop, and soon moved up again to working on cars himself. The business was always busy and the owners seemed to admire his work ethic and the rapport he had with the customers. That did not surprise Juan Carlos, as he had always been told he was a "people person." He worked 7 A.M. to 9 P.M. 6 days a week, loved his work, and was able to put away a good amount of his paycheck each week in savings. In time Juan Carlos and his girlfriend had another baby, and they needed to move out of their small rental. With their savings and his steady full-time job, the family was able to afford a small starter house, with an adjustable mortgage rate. They were proud to be able to move into a place of their own and were the first in their families to be homeowners.

Then, in 2009, the family-owned auto mechanic shop where Juan Carlos worked slowed down. The owners reluctantly cut Juan Carlos's hours, which was better than letting him go as they had to do with their other employees. Now instead of working 70- to 80-hour work weeks, Juan Carlos could barely squeeze 15 to 20 hours out of his schedule. His girlfriend was now trying to find a job to help make ends meet. She knew that without finishing high school and with two young children at home it would be challenging, but with relatives in the area who could help watch the boys, she thought it was worthwhile to pursue employment, if even part time. She finally found employment in a local restaurant, but all of her shifts were at night. Her oldest son, who was now 8, often came with her to the restaurant after school and stayed there into the night; relatives helped take care of their younger son. Despite trying to cobble together part-time positions, and having relatives to provide the commodity of time in caring for their children, Juan Carlos and his girlfriend could not keep up with the payments on their home, especially now with the newly adjusted higher interest rate. The owners of the business liked Juan Carlos and wanted to give him more hours, but business was slow, and eventually his hours dropped to only a few a week. Juan Carlos and his family just recently learned that they will lose their house to foreclosure. But they are keeping their spirits high, and Juan Carlos says he will not give up on his dream to give his sons a better life than he has had. And he will keep his promise . . . he has worked too hard to give up now. And, anyway, it's not his personality to give up—just ask anyone who knows him.

Critical Thinking Questions:

- As you think about Juan Carlos and his family's experience, does a story of hope and resilience, or stress and deprivation, come to mind first? What do you think makes Juan Carlos's story different than other similar experiences?

- How do you think our social and economic institutions facilitate or inhibit adaptation in our most vulnerable populations? How might we, as a society, do a better job at helping people adapt to adverse circumstances? Are our educational institutions a gateway to our economic institutions? In what ways?

- Despite the constant wear and tear on the body that comes from living in marginal and unpredictable economic circumstances, Juan Carlos was able to keep the motivation to do better by his family and for his children. What do you think helped him keep his faith in being able to provide a better future for his children? What are your concerns about what the family needs to do now for their children to help them develop adequate coping responses in the midst of the current stressors?

DISTAL CONTEXT

What Is Stress and What Does It Have to Do With Human Behavior?

Although it can be defined variously, *stress* is a challenge, change, or threat to an individual's internal feeling of balance and well-being (generally referred to as *homeostasis*). Feelings of stress upset a person's homeostasis both physiologically and psychologically. The specific events, people, places, or situations that cause stress are called *stressors*. Although it has a negative connotation, stress is a perfectly natural phenomenon that people deal with and effectively process throughout each day. There are countless examples. A blaring alarm clock jolts us from sleep and signals the start of another school- or workday. Despite the short-term allure of sleeping in, people get out of bed, shrug off their fatigue, and prepare themselves and their families for their responsibilities. During traffic, work meetings, visits with clients, and even mundane tasks, an assortment of stress-producing events arise that people usually overcome quickly, efficiently, and with finality. When a person overcomes a stressor, they have displayed successful *adaptation*, the ability to handle stress in a healthy, effective, and prosocial way (see Figure 3.1).

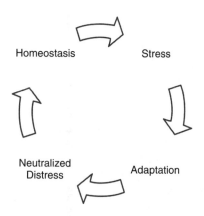

FIGURE 3.1   Homeostasis, Stress, and Adaptation

Unfortunately, people are sometimes unable to overcome stress in their lives and return themselves to a state of homeostasis. As a result, they continue to experience the aversive, negative emotional state. This is known as *distress*. Distress can be a short-term or chronic condition, but whatever its duration, it is unpleasant and damaging both psychologically and physiologically. As a result, individuals often attempt to cope with the distress in counterproductive, unhealthy ways, such as acting out against others aggressively or numbing themselves with drugs and alcohol. Negative responses to stress and distress are known as maladaptation, or more commonly, *maladaptive behavior*. For example, a common type of negative response to stress is *rumination*, which is the repetitive thinking about or rehashing of the negative features of a stressful incident. Because it entails fixation on negativity and stress, rumination is associated with anxiety and depression. Overall, the negative consequences of maladaptive responses to stress include posttraumatic stress disorder (PTSD); depression; anxiety; sleep disorders; aggression; delinquency; substance use; and family, school, and work dysfunction.

Of course, there is significant individual-level variation in how people not only experience stressful conditions, but also how they respond to them. Social work practitioners see this variation each day among the clients on their caseload. Some individuals seemingly crumble at the slightest inconvenience, whereas most are able to surmount day-to-day distress. Some individuals appear almost immune to stress. The process whereby individuals are able to successfully adapt despite considerable environmental stress is known as *resilience*. Even within the same family, there can be different ways of experiencing and handling the same family problem. This chapter will explore the many biological, psychological, and sociological factors that influence stress and adaptation as well as prominent theoretical explanations of stress-response systems.

Principles of Human Evolution

Within the human body, there are several systems that control the vital functions. The central nervous system consists of the brain and spinal cord, and the peripheral nervous system is the nerves and connections from the central nervous system to the rest of the body. Within most biological systems, there are subsystems, and a subsystem of the peripheral nervous system is the autonomic nervous system. The autonomic nervous system controls the involuntary functions (e.g., respiration and digestion) that allow people to survive. In turn, one of the subsystems of the autonomic nervous system is the *sympathetic nervous system*, which controls the response to stress and initiates the "fight or flight" response to it. In terms of evolutionary history, environmental stress triggered multiple, instantaneous responses to threats, during which humans could either try to overcome the threat by force or flee it.

Stress and adaptations to stress are essential for human behavior, have evolved across history, and have played a part in natural selection (see Kobak, Cassidy, Lyons-Ruth, & Ziv, 2006). In prehistoric times, basic environmental stress caused by hunger, cold, danger from animals, and competition with other humans served to motivate individuals to adapt to their environment in such a way that survival was possible, or to migrate to a more hospitable environment, or else they perished. When considered in an evolutionary framework, stress can be appreciated for its motivating nature, which helps to contribute to the reproductive success of the individual, and in turn, the species.

In this sense, stress and adaptations to it are examples of what evolutionary psychologists refer to as *adaptive phenotypic plasticity*, which is the capacity of genetic factors to support a range of phenotypes or behaviors depending on the environmental context in which they occurred. Ellis and Boyce (2008) suggested that extreme responses to stress are not necessarily vestiges of prehistoric responses to environmental threat (e.g., hunger, cold, danger), but can be adaptive given the correct environmental conditions. Their evolution-based account of stress and adaptation, called *biological sensitivity to context*, has three principles.

- Acute childhood stress exposure up-regulates stress reactivity, which increases the capacity of individuals to detect and respond to environmental threats and danger.

- Exposure to very supportive childhood environments also up-regulates stress reactivity, which increases susceptibility to social resources and social support.

- Exposure to mundane childhood environments down-regulates stress reactivity, which buffers individuals from a world that is similarly often mundane (i.e., neither extremely adverse nor supportive).

Stressful conditions also serve to "toughen" the individual to be better equipped to handle environmental adversity. Persons who successfully overcome stressful situations increase their self-efficacy (sense of mastery and effectiveness) and thus are likely to cope with stress successfully in the future. Recent research indicates, for instance, that experiencing stress or adversity is in some respects more beneficial than never experiencing adversity. Seery (2011) examined the relationships between general distress, functional impairment, life satisfaction, and PTSD symptoms and how these constructs were affected by lifetime adversity. The results were interesting and demonstrated the value of stress and successful adaptations to it. Persons who had experienced some adversity in life had better mental health, greater well-being, and less distress when faced with painful conditions compared to those who had never experienced adversity and those who had experienced high levels of adversity. This suggests that stress is good in small doses as it sharpens the ability to cope psychologically and physiologically.

One of the most influential accounts of the behavioral importance of stress and adaptation is John Bowlby's (1969, 1973, 1980) work on attachment. Bowlby focused on the attachments that develop between mothers and their children, and how problematic attachment can lead to psychological distress and behavioral problems. Bowlby achieved great notoriety for "Maternal Care and Mental Health" (1951), a report on the welfare of homeless children commissioned by the World Health Organization. The report showed developmental problems among children living in institutions who had no maternal care. These early deficits had long-term negative consequences. For instance, compared to a control group of children who were not raised in an institution, those who spent their first 3 years of life in an institution without maternal care had significantly lower intelligence, poorer cognitive skills, more speech problems, less social maturity, greater conduct problems, reduced capacity for guilt upon breaking rules, and reduced capacity for relationships. Children who did not attach to their mother were significantly unpopular with other children, were prone to restlessness and hyperactivity, had self-regulation problems, and had poor school achievement. In his concluding remarks, Bowlby noted that the early-life deprivation and the lack of a caregiver bond creates an affectionless or psychopathic character in children. *Attachment theory* suggests that the enduring affective bond between child and caregiver (usually parents) is importantly related to child development and the ability of the child to adapt to and overcome stress across life.

Three general patterns of attachment are seen. *Secure attachment* is the normative response and occurs in approximately 70% of children. Secure attachment means that children feel that their emotional needs will be met by their caregivers/parents because their parents have been responsive previously. These children are able to go about playing after reuniting with their parent following a brief separation (stressor). *Insecure/avoidant attachment* occurs in about 20% of children, where they ignore or avoid their parent after reuniting with them following a brief separation (stressor). Avoidant attachment is more likely to occur when there is maternal lack of

emotion or maternal inconsistency in responding to the needs of her infant. Because of this, infants with avoidant attachment tend to minimize their expression of negative emotions in front of their parent because of the prior rejection of their emotions. *Insecure/ambivalent attachment* occurs in approximately 10% of children who display closeness to their parent and are not able to separate from them after reuniting following a brief separation (stressor). Mothers who inconsistently respond to the attachment signals of their infants are likely to produce an ambivalent (sometimes called resistant) attachment. As a result, ambivalently attached infants display high levels of negative emotions and attachment behaviors in an effort to get the attention of the generally lackadaisical parent.

Research on maltreated children produced evidence of a fourth type of attachment, the one that is likely most germane to social work practice: disorganized attachment. *Disorganized attachment* is characterized by a breakdown in the attachment process where the child lacks a consistent strategy for organizing responses to needs for comfort and security during periods of distress. Van Ijzendoorn, Schuengel, and Bakermans-Kranenburg (1999) characterized the creation of disorganized attachment in an eloquent way:

> Maltreating parents, for example, are supposed to create disorganized attachment in their infants because they confront their infants with a pervasive paradox: they are potentially the only source of comfort for their children, whereas at the same time they frighten their children through their unpredictable abusive behavior. The parent is thought to be a source of fear for the child and at the same time the only attachment figure who can provide relief from distress. The incompatible behaviors of flight and proximity seeking are proposed to lead to temporary breakdown of organized attachment behavior. (pp. 226–227)

The numerous negative consequences of disorganized attachment are explored later in this chapter.

Another important feature of Bowlby's work is that it drew on ethology, or the study of animal behavior. As Rutter (2010) noted, Bowlby's work "was remarkable in its bringing together of quite diverse sources of evidence, both human and animal, and quite diverse theoretical perspectives. It alerted the world to the importance of the development of children's selective attachments in early life and the ways in which they provided the basis for later social relationships of all kinds" (p. 690). This suggests that early life attachments between mothers and their offspring provide the various resources and wherewithal for the offspring to survive, and thrive. Threats to that bond that occur early in life contribute to the unfolding of maladaptation across life.

SPOTLIGHT TOPIC: POSTTRAUMATIC STRESS DISORDER

One of the most challenging stress-based disorders that social workers face is PTSD. According to formal diagnostic criteria for PTSD (American Psychiatric Association, 2000, pp. 467–468), the individual experienced, witnessed, or was confronted with an event that involved actual or threatened death or serious injury, or a threat to the physical integrity of self or others, and the response involved intense fear, helplessness, or horror. This event sets into motion a network of negative effects. First, the traumatic event is reexperienced in multiple ways:

- Recurrent and intrusive recollections of the event
- Recurrent distressing dreams of the event
- Feeling as if the event were reoccuring
- Intense psychological distress to cues that remind the individual of the event
- Physiological reactivity to cues that remind the individual of or resemble the event

Second, the individual persistently avoids stimuli that are associated with the trauma, and there is a numbing of responsiveness. This is characterized by:

- Efforts to avoid thoughts, feelings, or conversations relating to the trauma
- Efforts to avoid activities, places, or people that recall the trauma
- Inability to recall a specific aspect of the trauma
- Markedly diminished interest and participation in significant activities
- Attachment and estrangement from others
- Restricted range of affect
- Sense of shortened future

The third aspect of PTSD relates to persistent feelings of increased arousal that were not present before the trauma. These include sleep problems, anger and irritability, difficulty concentrating, hypervigilance, and exaggerated startle response. These symptoms persist for at least 1 month and impair functioning in multiple areas, such as family, work, or school responsibilities. Although the prevalence of PTSD in the United States is 8%, the burden of the disorder is high (Ozer, Best, Lipsey, & Weiss, 2003). PTSD is highest among Blacks (at nearly 9%), moderate among Hispanics (7.4%) and Whites (7%), and lowest among Asian Americans (4%). Despite these differences, all groups are less likely to seek treatment for PTSD than Whites (Roberts, Gilman, Breslau, Breslau, & Koenen, 2011). If left untreated, PTSD contributes to a deterioration of mental health and is significantly associated with suicide.

Fortunately, there are effective coping strategies for persons with PTSD. A meta-analysis of 103 studies found that religious coping and positive reappraisal were the strongest predictors of psychological improvement following the onset of PTSD. Moderate effects were also found for social support, spirituality, and optimism (Prati & Pietrantoni, 2009). Overall, individuals with greater social supports and person-specific resilience characteristics, such as an optimistic worldview and the capacity to reappraise negative events in a positive way, seem particularly likely to surmount the distress associated with their traumatic event. Social work practitioners should target these resilience factors for optimal recovery.

For Reflection

Think about how living in poverty might exacerbate symptoms of PTSD. What kinds of factors might be most problematic?

PROXIMAL MECHANISMS

Neural Substrates and Stress

Stress sets into motion a series of brain and body processes that serve to bring the individual back into homeostasis. As all social work practitioners can attest, an individual who is experiencing distress and is having difficulty adapting to it is recognizable by behaviors that suggest several problems, including social cognitive ones. For example, clients who ruminate about a recent negative event, clients who are hypervigilant in the wake of a recent victimization, and clients who withdraw from their daily responsibilities collectively represent altered decision-making and social-cognitive deficits in response to stress. From a treatment perspective, these clients need assistance slowing down their understanding and responses to stress in order to overcome them. In other words, even a non-neuroscientist recognizes the essential role of the brain and neurological functions in adapting to stress.

One of the most comprehensive models of the neural responses to stress is the Adaptive Calibration Model of stress responsivity (Del Giudice, Ellis, & Shirtcliff, 2011). It suggests that adaptation to stress represents three broad neural functions. First, the brain coordinates the response to various physical and psychosocial threats or challenges. Second, the brain encodes

and filters information about the environment to understand the meaning of environmental inputs. Third, the brain regulates the physiological and behavioral responses to the environment, which include defensive behaviors, attachment, learning, affiliation, competition, and reproductive functioning.

Perhaps nothing better conveys the biosocial nature of behavior than the plasticity of the brain. In early life, neural connections are molded and pruned according to experiences and environmental circumstances. Chronic exposure to stress is one example of the environmental conditions that can modify brain structure and function. For example, there is evidence that chronic stress reduces dopaminergic functioning in the central nervous system. In addition, brain regions that are implicated in self-regulation have been shown to have hypoactive dopamine levels (Mead, Beauchaine, & Shannon, 2010). Thus, impulsivity and hyperactivity can in part be the outcome of the brain's exposure to chronic stress.

The interplay among the brain, the environment, and the ways that both respond to stress sheds light on the difficulties that clinical social work clients sometimes face. According to Susman (2006):

Plasticity in the developing brain represents a window of opportunity for healthy growth in optimal child rearing circumstances but a period of vulnerability in non-optimal rearing environments. Early brain development is especially vulnerable to the effects of environmental stressors. If trauma or inconsistent parenting is experienced then the result can have negative implications or later development including memory, dreams, and emotional impairments. If the experience of care giving is noncontingently responsive, if pain or distress is an unpredictable or frequent occurrence, the brain, specifically the hypothalamic/ANS stress system, is proposed to adapt in a manner that is inconsistent with optimal cortical development. (p. 382)

From this perspective, every time a social worker or juvenile justice practitioner reduces the incidence of child abuse, child neglect, parental discord, or another family-based stressor, that professional is enhancing the neurological and ultimately psychosocial growth of children and adolescents.

Endocrine System and Function

The *hypothalamic-pituitary-adrenal (HPA) axis* is the major neurological-endocrine response system to stress (e.g., the fight or flight syndrome) and is intimately connected to the limbic system, which is involved in emotion, long-term memory, and motivation. In very stressful conditions requiring a fight or flight response, corticotrophin-releasing factor is released from the hypothalamus, which in turn stimulates the release of the adrenocorticotropin hormone from the pituitary gland. This in turn prompts the adrenal glands to release cortisol. Cortisol is a hormone involved in energy mobilization, memory formation, attention, and behavioral vigilance (see Figure 3.2). ,

There are costs to chronic activation of stress hormones. Chronic and acute stress damages the HPA axis (stress is particularly detrimental to the hippocampus, where memories are stored) and results in dysfunctional response to stressful conditions. Mead et al. (2010) articulated that, "Acutely, physical threat leads to a cascade

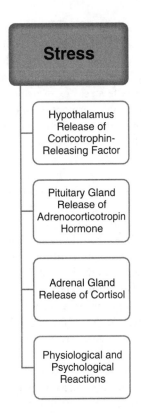

FIGURE 3.2 The HPA Axis

of neuroendocrine responses that prepare an organism to either escape the situation or stay and defend itself. In such a moment, the primary objective is immediate survival. Accordingly, the body prepares for action via attentional allocation and behavioral arousal" (p. 10).

The endocrine consequences of stress exposure figure in an array of works. From a general behavioral theory perspective, Gray's (1982) influential Behavioral Activation System (BAS) and Behavioral Inhibition System (BIS) theory implicates the dopaminergic system that innervates the limbic system and the hippocampus and septum, respectively. The BIS/BAS theory seeks to explain both behavioral restraint/inhibition and approach and has clear implications for both internalizing and externalizing conditions. Depending on the individual, chronic stress exposure differentially affects the BAS and BIS, which has clear implications for adaptive behavior. For example, patients with dysthymia and depression who incur early-life stress are more likely than similarly depressed patients without early-life stress exposure to suffer from relapses following treatment. In addition, depressive symptoms are more chronic among those with early-life stress (Gillespie & Nemeroff, 2007).

As noted later in Chapter 6, van Goozen, Fairchild, Snock, and Harold (2007) suggest that a reduced stress regulating system, such as the HPA axis and the autonomic nervous system, interacts with early childhood adverse environments to increase susceptibility to severe, persistent antisocial behavior. Children with these deficits neither understand dangerous settings nor display appropriate emotional response to these settings. As a result, they do not physiologically experience the threat of dangerous settings via autonomic or endocrine stress response. This leads to a vicious cycle of selection of dangerous settings and a muted response to the dangers therein. They are incapable of normal stress responses to situations that typically bring upon anger, embarrassment, and most importantly, fear. In fact, underarousal from stress is a core physiological feature of antisocial children, adolescents, and adults. A variety of samples, including habitual criminals, children with behavioral disorders, institutionalized delinquents, and violent prisoners display lower cortisol levels than their peers in control groups (see Susman, 2006).

How do stress and the HPA axis work together in a cell to society way? An example is the corticotropin-releasing hormone receptor 1 gene (*CRHR1*), which plays an important role in the regulation of the HPA axis in response to stressful events and influencing anxiety-related behaviors in response to stress. Variants of the *CRHR1* gene have been shown to buffer individuals who were maltreated as children from experiencing depression during adulthood (Polanczyk et al., 2009). The primary way this occurs is by

controlling memory consolidation that centers on emotionally arousing experiences.

Stress, Inflammation, and Biomarkers

Another by-product of the wear and tear on our physiology resulting from chronic stress is inflammation. Inflammation is a bodily reaction designed to protect itself from harm, and it can be acute and chronic. The redness seen in response to an insect bite is an example of acute inflammation. Prolonged stress and the chronic release of stress hormones from difficult environmental triggers results in inflammation processes that in turn increases the vulnerability to high blood pressure, heart disease, and even cancer. Environmental stress varies by individuals and racial and ethnic groups, some of whom are experiencing distress due to difficult living conditions, resulting in heightened susceptibility to inflammation and health problems. As such, many health disparities in social groups are tied to the nexus of environmental stress and inflammation. The indicators of these various states and forms of inflammation can be identified by a biomarker such as cortisol that can be accessed via collection of saliva. Biomarkers are important for social work because they facilitate interventions that are better specified to individuals and groups who have them. Biomarkers are also important because they show clear evidence of the results of how the environment, such as living in a disadvantaged neighborhood, literally can get under our skin and cause substantial physiological stress that leads to inflammation.

Environmental Triggers

As indicated at the beginning of this chapter, the opportunities for stress in daily life are ubiquitous. No one can avoid stressful situations. A bevy of environmental factors have been shown to be particularly distressing and lead to maladaptive responses. In terms of attachment-related traumas, for example, four major types have been identified, including the following:

1. Attachment disruption occurs when there is a protracted period of separation between child and caregiver. Family dissolution is a major societal problem and a common background feature in the lives of children, adolescents, and adults who display conduct problems and related mental health problems.

2. Physical victimization by an attachment figure, when the caregiver is simultaneously the person expected to provide safety and the victimizer. A major challenge in social work practice is providing services to families where one or more family members are also abusers because the number one concern is the health and safety of one's clients.

3. Loss of an attachment figure through death or another event, such as incarceration. In communities characterized by high levels of crime, there is a commensurate high prevalence of resident involvement in the criminal justice system. Criminal justice supervision produces many challenges for social workers in terms of providing services for clients involved in the correctional system as well as considering the service needs of the children of incarcerated adults.

4. Attachment injuries where the child is abandoned during a stressful time of need (Kobak et al., 2006).

Each of these types impairs secure attachment and reduces the child's ability to regulate stress in an appropriate, adaptive way. Even in research beyond an attachment theory approach, there is strong evidence that family conflict serves to negatively affect the ability of children to appropriately respond to stress (El-Sheikh & Erath, 2011; Susman, 2006).

Within psychology, human services, and social work, emotional security theory is prominent. *Emotional security theory* suggests that parental discord (e.g., arguing, fighting, engaging in destructive behavior) increases children's vulnerability to psychopathology by disrupting the sense of safety, security, and protection that children receive from parents (Davies & Cummings, 1994). According to the theory, parental discord forces children to constantly walk on eggshells out of fear of upsetting their parents. This produces stressful hypervigilance and feelings of subjective distress. As indicated by the discussion of the effects of stress on the neuroendocrine system, emotional security theory suggests that parental discord impairs children's self-regulation, reasoning, problem-solving capacities, and emotional regulation—all of which detract from their well-being.

For example, ostracism is a negative social situation where an individual is excluded from peer interactions. Recent research demonstrates that being ostracized activates the same regions in the brain that are associated with physical pain. Moreover, to avoid this "social pain," ostracized individuals will engage in desperate behaviors in an attempt to garner social attention from those who have ostracized them (Williams & Nida, 2011). Thus, social isolation and marginalization creates a multitude of negative feelings that can bring about negative behaviors.

A host of environmental factors also serve as buffers from the negative effects of stress and facilitate adaptive as opposed to maladaptive responses. For instance, social support is the material and emotional support that family members, friends, community groups, and others provide. Social support helps to facilitate healthy responses to stress in two ways: directly by providing support to individuals in need, and indirectly by functioning as an available support system for the individual (Cohen & Wills, 1985). In other words, simply knowing that friends, family, and others are there to help and furnish support goes a long way toward handling stress.

Indeed, a central goal in working with any social work client is to identify and involve the client's social supports. Drawing on data from a nationally representative survey of American youth, Wright, Cullen, and Miller (2001) found that family social support was positively related to moral beliefs, time spent studying, and grades, and negatively related to having delinquent friends. In addition, adolescents with strong family support were also significantly likely to exercise, maintain a healthy lifestyle, and be committed to their jobs and were less likely to have deviant friends or use drugs. In a study of participants from the National Longitudinal Study of Adolescent Health, social support was also significantly associated with mental health status, as youth with reduced social support were more likely to experience depression (Cornwell, 2003).

Childhood Stress Caused by Structural Violence

As mentioned briefly in this section, many children in our nation suffer extreme stress caused by structural violence. This includes aspects of our society such as oppression, poverty, and institutional racism that keep a particular group of people in a position of inferiority to the dominant group in that society. Children growing up in poverty, whose parents may both work multiple jobs or may be receiving welfare benefits (and living with the stigma of being a family receiving those benefits), whose parents may be undocumented immigrants living with the fear of being deported and having their family separated, who may go to a school that delivers below-par education and where their teachers seem to not care—these children deal with unimaginable stress on a daily basis. This stress is different from other types of stress caused by cases of child abuse because the cause of this stress is not as easily identifiable. Additionally, this type of stress largely has been accepted by our society as a normal feature of living in poverty. As social workers, it is our job not to accept it as reality. We believe that every child, regardless of their socioeconomic status, has a right to a happy, minimally stressful childhood experience that contributes to healthy development and promotes positive growth. But as a social worker, how can you work toward this?

SPOTLIGHT TOPIC: HOW ENVIRONMENTAL STRESS GETS UNDER THE SKIN

One of the most fascinating empirical developments in recent years is the increased understanding of how environmental stress gets under the skin, so to speak, and affects genetic expression, endocrine functioning, psychological health, and most importantly, behavior. There are many examples of this exciting research:

- The neuropeptide *oxytocin* plays an important role in social behavior and is involved in the regulation of stress. Oxytocin is both a hormone and a neurotransmitter. It is produced in the hypothalamus (the relay station of the brain) and released in both the brain and the bloodstream. Oxytocin is sometimes used in treating persons with autism because it enhances responsiveness to others and sociability, which is a core deficit of autism. In addition, ingesting oxytocin via inhalation results in reduced reaction to stress. Neuroscientists recently studied a variant in the oxytocin receptor gene (*OXTR*) and found that carriers of the G allele of a polymorphism of the gene who received social support showed lower cortisol responses to stress. Carriers of this genetic "buffer" who did not receive social support nevertheless showed elevated cortisol responses (Chen et al., 2011). This shows that variants in the *OXTR* gene, coupled with emotional support from a friend, can get under the skin to reduce stress reactivity.

- A related construct to stress reactivity is empathy, or the degree of emotional relatedness and the capacity to share in another person's emotional responses. In a study of the aforementioned *OXTR* gene, neuroscientists found that compared to persons with the G allele, those with one or two copies of the A allele of the *OXTR* gene exhibit lower behavioral and dispositional empathy (Rodrigues, Saslow, Garcia, John, & Keltner, 2009). Carriers of the

A allele also showed greater dispositional and physiological reactivity to stress than G allele carriers.

- Poverty is a major stressor. It has long been recognized that poverty denotes many health risks, including morbidity relating to stress. Recent research found that compared to persons reared in higher socioeconomic strata, those raised in poverty in early life showed elevated cortisol levels in daily life and were prone to inflammation stemming from overreactivity to stress (Miller et al., 2009). Moreover, these negative effects were seen decades later. This suggests that poverty serves as a stress-inducing condition that programs the body to respond to the threats that impoverishment poses. Over time, however, the chronic activation of stress contributes to health problems associated with the chronic conditions of aging.

- The notion that a pregnant women's emotional health has some impact on her child's temperament, development, and adaptability is widespread. The serotonin transporter polymorphism 5-*HTTLPR* has been studied for its role in moderating negative emotions in the face of life stress. Pluess et al. (2011) recently found that women who experienced greater anxiety during pregnancy were prone to have children who displayed higher levels of negative emotionality, a disposition that is associated with maladaptive responses to stress. Carriers of two short alleles of 5-*HTTLPR* (the risk allele) had the strongest effect between maternal anxiety and infant negative emotionality, whereas carriers of two long alleles (the protective allele) displayed the weakest effect. This suggests that stressful circumstances during pregnancy that increase maternal anxiety are likely to differentially and negatively influence the temperament of the developing child.

Not only do disadvantaged environmental contexts get under the skin, but also advantageous ones. For instance, despite the effects of poverty on stress reactivity and inflammation over the life course, there is evidence these damaging effects are neutralized by maternal nurturance. Based on data from the Midlife in the United States Study, poor children who were raised with high levels of maternal nurturance (e.g., involvement in child's life, awareness of child's emotions and problems, amount of time and attention allocated to the child) were resilient to the health problems associated with it during adulthood (Miller et al., 2011). In fact, 50% of individuals avoided health-related problems attributed to child poverty due to maternal nurturance. These findings show the power of tender loving care from parents, specifically mothers, at undoing the effects of stress.

For Reflection:

How does this understanding help the social work practitioner? Does it suggest that differential responses to treatment may exist? Keep in mind that the failure to respond to treatment is not necessarily a willful violation by the client or a failure of the treatment program, but could reflect gene–environment interactions that occurred earlier in the client's life.

STRESS AND ADAPTATION OVER THE LIFE COURSE

Over the life course, environments vary in terms of their stress content. At the lowest level is an environment with little stress. This is a safe environment that Bowlby referred to as a *secure base*. Most environments have moderate levels of stress. At the next level are environments that are unpredictable and dangerous, which represent high levels of stress. Last, traumatic environments present the highest level of stress.

How individuals respond to these various environmental contexts depends on a host of factors, including their temperament, attachment security, autonomic functioning, experiences, family and friendship networks, socioeconomic status, and other factors. One of the most clever ways to conceptualize stress and adaptation over the life course is to use the hawk and dove profiles. Korte, Koolhaas, Wingfield, and McEwen (2005) theorized two archetypal ways that individuals experience and adapt to stress. The *hawk profile* describes an individual who reacts to stress in a fight or flight way and whose dominant autonomic nervous system is the sympathetic nervous system. The hawk has a high activity level, a dominant negative affect, is bold and approach oriented, and is at risk for externalizing behaviors.

Conversely, the *dove profile* describes an individual who reacts to stress in a hide-and-freeze way and whose dominant autonomic nervous system is the parasympathetic nervous system, which encompasses the body at rest. The dove has a low activity level, a vulnerable negative affect, is inhibited and withdrawn, and it at risk for internalizing behaviors. Hawks have diminished HPA axis reactivity, whereas doves have elevated HPA axis reactivity. In many respects, the hawk and dove models are consistent with Jerome Kagan's uninhibited and inhibited temperament profiles (Chapter 6).

Examples of stress and adaptation to it over the life course are examined next, along with interventions that have proven helpful for increasing healthy coping.

Fetal Environment and Infancy

Because many traits are moderately heritable, there is frequently a correlation between parents' stress and reactivity profiles and those of their children. Parents who experience depressive symptoms and who display maladaptive behaviors toward their children are likely to have children with similar profiles. For instance, a recent study found that preschool children whose parents had a history of depression exhibited higher cortisol levels than peers who parents did not have depression (Dougherty, Klein, Rose, & Laptook, 2011).

Studies of infants and their mothers' reactions to anger show its negative consequences for adaptive responses. Moore (2009) studied the physiological responses to anger among a sample of 6-month-old infants and found that anger exposure sensitizes them to stress, increasing their need for physiological regulation. In addition, anger exposure challenges mothers' self-regulation, which in turn compromises their ability to provide support to their children. A troubling conclusion from that study is that anger is a universal emotion, and one that is common when caring for infants. The study suggests that anger is not just a short-term negative interaction between parent and child, but that it sets into motion an impaired ability to respond to stressful situations.

In a test of the hawk and dove profile, Sturge-Apple, Davies, Martin, Cicchetti, and Hentges (2012) found that harsh parenting differentially manifested in internalizing symptoms, externalizing symptoms, cortisol levels, and autonomic nervous system reactivity. Infants and toddlers who fit the hawk profile were prone to respond to harsh parenting by acting out, whereas those who fit the dove profile were prone to respond to harsh parenting by withdrawing.

Given the role of negative emotions in modifying the stress adaptation of toddlers, it is a relatively easy area to target with behavioral interventions. For instance, emotional availability coaching is a program administered to child care workers to improve the emotional connection and attachment to the children they supervise. A recent evaluation of emotional availability coaching focused on caregiver sensitivity to children, caregiver structuring of interactions, caregiver nonhostility, and caregiver nonintrusiveness to avoid coercive, stressful interactions with children. After the coaching intervention, caregivers displayed improved care on all measures. Moreover, children displayed higher levels of security, more supportive behavior, less detachment, and lower hostility (Biringen et al., 2012). These findings are consistent with similar research that indicated that a few training sessions on better caregiving can result in healthier interactions between caregivers and children, more secure attachments, less stress for adults and children, and fewer maladaptive behaviors.

Early Childhood and Childhood

A host of conceptual areas demonstrate the biosocial interaction among person-specific factors, environmental conditions, and social interactions as determinants of behavior. This is particularly true in studies of stress and adaptations to it. Consider the broad example of childhood psychopathology and the conduct problems that children with behavioral disorders can present. Conduct problems not only severely impair the social development of children, but also compromise prosocial interactions with parents, teachers, and peers. Children with conduct problems, such as those with diagnoses for oppositional defiant disorder, CD, ADHD (combined type), and others are prevalent on social work caseloads.

In addition to conduct problems, maladaptive responses to stress are characteristic of children with externalizing and internalizing disorders. For example, children with anxiety disorders such as social phobia are characterized by extreme feelings of distress and hyperreactivity to stress. A recent study of 8- to 12-year-old children with social phobia disorder found that compared to controls, they showed heightened reactivity to a subjective anxiety task and showed chronically elevated heart rate levels throughout the laboratory session. Children with social phobia showed a sixfold higher number of anxiety symptoms in addition to significantly higher levels of internalizing and externalizing symptoms (Krämer et al., 2012). Among children who are maltreated and/or bullied, there is evidence

of blunted cortisol responses to stress, and this HPA axis difficulty is associated with pervasive social and behavioral problems (Ouellet-Morin et al., 2011).

Bakermans-Kranenburg, van Ijzendoorn, and Juffer (2003) conducted a meta-analysis of 88 interventions involving over 9,000 participants that sought to increase parental sensitivity to their children and infant attachment security. They found that programs with a moderate number of sessions and a focus on behavioral issues were most effective, and overall effect sizes were modest yet significant. Interventions can help parents become more attuned and sensitive to the attachment needs of their children, and this greater sensitivity improved the parent–child attachment. Unfortunately, attachment problems are often not caught in time, and children display negative behaviors that must be addressed therapeutically.

Fortunately, there are interventions that have demonstrated effectiveness at helping parents overcome the stressors created by their children's misbehavior. An example is the Behavioral Parent Training (BPT) component of Carolyn Webster-Stratton's The Incredible Years intervention. The BPT consists of two components: the BASIC component, which addresses praise and rewards, limit setting, handling misbehavior, and appropriate play; and the ADVANCE component, which includes coping strategies for depression and upsetting thoughts, communication skills, and problem solving. Overall, parents are taught to be less critical of their children, to be more consistent and inductive (as opposed to inconsistent and harsh) in their disciplining, and generally to be more positive in responding to their child's behavior. A recent evaluation of the program involving 4-year-olds with CD in the Netherlands found program effects 2 years after the end of the intervention. Parents were more likely to respond to their child's stressful conduct with appropriate discipline and praise and less likely to use coercive parenting. In addition, the children displayed fewer conduct problems compared to controls.

Adolescence

Many of the same lessons about effective adaptations to stress in childhood spill over into adolescence. Unfortunately, many adolescents in the human services and juvenile justice domains suffer from a range of risk factors, including neighborhood violence, poverty, gangs, and substance use. However, supportive home environments can reduce the pernicious effects of various exposures to violence. For example, a recent study of Black adolescents living in urban public housing projects found that social cohesion—supportive home environments where parents inculcated appropriate adaptations to stress and adversity—resulted in lower levels of substance abuse (Nebbitt, Lombe, Yu, Vaughn, & Stokes, 2012). Moreover, social cohesion served as a buffer against drug abuse even when domestic violence exposure, witnessing community violence, and experiencing community violence were high.

Beyond home environments, culturally sensitive interventions are another opportunity to provide healthy stress adaptations to populations that are disproportionately served by social work and juvenile justice practitioners. For instance, programs that are steeped in Hispanic culture and applied to Latino youth have been shown to be effective at reducing externalizing symptoms and improving health coping (Hodge, Jackson, & Vaughn, 2010).

Given the stressful nature of life during adolescence, there is pressing need for policy interventions. Sometimes merely thinking about a stressful event in more positive terms can help youth better cope with stress. A recent experimental study is illustrative. A sample of adolescents was instructed to think about a recent stressful event in their life (the most common ones were a fight and the death of a relative). They were assigned to four treatment conditions: some ruminated about the event, some engaged in positive reappraisal, some merely accepted it, and others distanced themselves from the stressor (Rood, Roelofs, Bogels, & Arntz, 2012). Adolescents who engaged in positive reappraisal, in which they contemplated the personal growth and positive aspects of the stressful situation, experienced more positive affect and less negative affect than those in the other three conditions.

Corrective attachment therapy seeks to provide the conditions of secure attachment to children and adolescents who engage in aggressive and antisocial forms of behavior. Effective corrective attachment therapy includes the following:

- *Structure*, in which the therapist provides boundaries, rules, and limits to the child to reflect clear and consistent guidelines for the therapy;

- *Attunement*, where the therapist understands what the child needs to feel safe and provides that sense of safety;

- *Empathy*, in which the therapist conveys caring for the child and reacts to even negative behaviors in a compassionate, empathic way;

- *Positive affect*, where the therapist engages in positive ways, even when the child presents defiant or problem behaviors;

- *Support*, in which the therapy is tailored to the development needs and abilities of the child, and later on to the child's successes during treatment, for maintenance;

- *Reciprocity*, where the therapist guides the child toward a reciprocally supporting relationship based on mutual respect and sensitivity; and

- *Love*, in which the therapist provides a sense of caring and commitment (Levy & Orlans, 2000).

Adolescence is a challenging life stage where individuals variously develop from child to adult in a variety of contexts relating to increased responsibilities, autonomy, civic rights, and uncertainty. When teens have a secure base, these stressors are dealt with in healthy ways. In the face of multiple risk factors, adolescents are more likely to respond to the stressors of adolescence in unhealthy ways that can follow them through adulthood.

Adulthood

The true power of stress and adaptations to it is seen during the latter stages of the life course. It is during adulthood where the long-term consequences of distress and negative coping with it manifest in an assortment of behavioral outcomes. For instance, in a meta-analysis of 233 reports of 119 longitudinal studies, including more than 3,100 participants, Derzon (2010) found that family stress occurring during childhood was associated with problem behaviors into adulthood, criminal behavior occurring in adulthood, and violent behavior during adulthood. In many respects, early life adaptations to stress serve as schemas that forecast how these individuals will respond to adversity later in life. An important example is the university experience, one that is filled with exciting opportunities but also a host of stressors associated with increased adult independence and responsibilities. In a recent study of university students in Spain, Camara and Calvete (2012) found that students with early life schemas that one's emotional needs were unlikely to be met and perceptions that others are unstable were associated with depressive symptoms. Students with recurrent schemas that led them to believe they would not be able to handle daily responsibilities, and those who were fearful of imminent threats, were significantly likely to display anxiety symptoms.

Of course, adult-onset coping with stress is a central problem that social work clients face. There are many examples of this. Women living in shelters who have experienced domestic violence endure incredibly high stress levels that negatively affect their future relationships. A recent comparative study found that battered women in shelters displayed more anxiety symptoms, more avoidant behaviors, and reduced subsequent warm/romantic emotions in relationships than a control group of women (Shecory, 2012). Battered women were also more likely to utilize more pragmatic, problem-focused strategies than emotionally focused methods for responding to stress.

Despite the limitations of their disorders, many patients with anxiety and depression symptoms maintain a functional place in society. Nevertheless, they still benefit from minimal guidance from mental health or social work counselors. An example is guided self-help, where clinicians provide input and assistance to patients with difficulty handling the stressors of daily life. There is evidence that guided self-help is effective in helping patients cope with feelings of anxiety in the face of distress (Coull & Morris, 2011).

Last, a potentially valuable social work treatment for adults is mindfulness meditation, which has been shown to improve well-being and reduce stress-related symptoms. Mindfulness meditation specifically targets attention regulation, body awareness, and emotional regulation and is helpful for allowing patients to reappraise their experiences without being negatively affected by those experiences internally. As Hölzel et al. (2011) noted, there is evidence of neurological change among adults who participate in mindfulness meditation. This suggests that the biosocial interactions relating to adaptations to stress are not limited to early life, but occur across the life course.

Sex Differences

Despite some commonality, there is evidence that men and women experience stress in different ways across the life course. That they do not experience stress identically reflects both biologically and culturally mediated gender differences. For example, men show greater HPA axis reactivity to achievement-related tasks than women, which is consistent with men's status motivations. Similarly, women show greater HPA reactivity to emotional connections, such as social rejection (Del Giudice et al., 2011). In contexts where the environment is unpredictable or even dangerous, both men and women are likely to respond in a vigilant manner. However, men are more likely to be agonistic or aggressive, whereas women are more likely to be withdrawn.

In environments where there is severe traumatic stress, women are still more likely to withdraw, whereas men are more likely to behave in unemotional, antisocial ways.

There are several examples of sex differences in adaptations to stress. For example, men are prone to riskier decision making during periods of stress, whereas women display less risk taking during stressful events (Mather & Lighthall, 2012). In a recent study of childhood neglect and the serotonin transporter gene (one that is extensively covered in molecular genetics and behavioral studies; see Chapter 2), Vaske, Newsome, and Wright (2012) found that women with the risk alleles for this gene were more likely to experience child neglect than those who did not have the genetic risk factor. In addition, women with the genetic risk and who were neglected were more likely to use marijuana as a coping strategy. None of these effects were observed for men, based on data from the National Longitudinal Study of Adolescent Health.

There are also sex differences among court-ordered social work clients. For instance, male criminal offenders are characterized by work-related problems, substance abuse, and criminal justice system noncompliance. Comparatively, female offenders are disproportionately characterized by relationship problems, depression, suicide, and poorer physical health (Moffitt, Caspi, Rutter, & Silva, 2001). For adjudicated adolescents or adults, these trends suggest different target areas in terms of the most likely sources of stress and areas of adaptation.

EXPERT'S CORNER: BRUCE S. McEWEN, ROCKEFELLER UNIVERSITY

One of the towering figures in the study of stress and adaptation is Bruce McEwen. The author of nearly 1,000 scientific papers and the recipient of numerous international and national awards, Professor McEwen has pioneered the study of stress, the effects of stress on brain functioning and structure, and how the brain shapes adaptive and maladaptive responses to stress. His work has included animal and human studies and has produced many important contributions, including several covered in this chapter. For instance, he showed that glucocorticoid hormones that are released in the brain in response to stress serve to damage the ability of the brain to regulate their release.

Another of his important contributions centers on the study of allostasis, which means "achieving stability through change." Normally, the physiological response to stress occurs quickly, and then the person quickly recovers as the requirements to successfully respond to the stressor are met. When homeostasis is not achieved, one explanation is the existence of *allostatic load*, or the wear and tear on the body and brain resulting from chronic over- or underarousal of the stress response system (McEwen, 2007). Four categories of stress and adaptation contribute to allostatic load. These are:

1. Repeated normal responses stemming from environments characterized by multiple stressors;

2. Lack of adaptation, where the normal physiological response to stress is reduced over time;

Photo of Bruce S. McEwen
Courtesy of Bruce S. McEwen

3. Prolonged response due to a delayed shutdown; and

4. Inadequate response, where other hormonal systems compensate for problems in normal stress response.

Taken as a whole, the concept of allostatic load is useful for understanding the various and at times extreme sources of stress that social work clients encounter each day. High-risk social work clients, such as those with PTSD, extensive victimization histories, and extensive criminal records, face pathologically high levels of day-to-day stress. In turn, these stressors contribute to the maladaptive responses that human-services clients often display. Although the social work professional is aware of allostatic load in practice, Dr. Bruce McEwen has been largely responsible for producing the science behind it.

SUMMARY

In sum, stress and adaptation are salient to social work professionals because so many clients and their families whom they serve display variable coping skills. Helping clients respond to stress in a healthy manner goes a long way to facilitating adaptive responses and better psychosocial functioning. Additional principles to bear in mind include:

• Stress and adaptation are normal human processes that have evolved over time to allow individuals to adapt to environmental conditions.

• There is significant individual-level variation in terms of the degree to which one experiences stress and the ways that one copes with it.

• Resilience is the ability of people to adapt in a healthy, prosocial way despite environmental conditions that usually manifest in maladaptive behavior.

• John Bowlby advanced attachment theory, which suggests that children and caregivers/parents develop an emotional bond that serves as the basis for the ways that the individual will respond to stress over the life course.

• The hypothalamic-pituitary-adrenal (HPA) axis is the major neurological-endocrine response system to stress.

• The fight or flight response is associated with the sympathetic nervous system.

• The root of many forms of maladaptive behavior stem from biosocial interactions involving childhood characteristics, parent characteristics, and harsh/antisocial parenting.

• Social work practitioners can display secondary traumatic stress, which appears as symptoms of chronic stress exposure due to their chronic interaction with persons in need.

• Compassion fatigue is a state of tension and preoccupation with the suffering of those being helped to the degree that it is traumatizing for a helper, such as a social work practitioner.

• Due to the plasticity of the brain, a variety of treatment options and program interventions can address the neurological and endocrine system responses to stress.

• Stress is experienced across the life span, and negative coping with stress is associated with a range of externalizing and internalizing conditions.

KEY TERMS

Adaptation

Adaptive phenotypic plasticity

Allostatic load

Attachment theory

Compassion fatigue

Corrective attachment therapy

Disorganized attachment

Distress

Emotional security theory

Homeostasis

Hypothalamic-pituitary-adrenal (HPA) axis

Insecure/ambivalent attachment

Insecure/avoidant attachment

Maladaptive behavior

Oxytocin

Resilience

Secondary traumatic stress

Secure attachment

Stress

Stressors

Sympathetic nervous system

CHAPTER 4

EMOTION

Emotion is central to human behavior, and indeed to life. It is often the case that many social work clients (e.g., persons with major depressive disorder, bipolar disorder, dysthymia, autism, oppositional defiant disorder [ODD], CD, antisocial personality disorder, and others) have deficits in processing, reacting to, and regulating their emotions. Emotional regulation problems in turn contribute to maladaptive behaviors and make getting along with others—whether within one's family, at school, at work, in therapy, at treatment, or in custody—more challenging. Although many constructs contribute to psychosocial functioning, a failure to handle and regulate one's emotions is a significant risk factor.

In a recent review, Dolan (2002) artfully conveyed the importance of emotion to behavior:

> Emotion provides the principal currency in human relationships as well as the motivational force for what is best and worst in human behavior. Emotion exerts a powerful influence on reason and, in ways neither understood nor systematically researched, contributes to the fixation of belief. A lack of emotional equilibrium underpins most human unhappiness and is a common denominator across the entire range of mental disorders from neuroses to psychoses. (p. 1191)

This quotation likely rings true for the social work practitioner. Due to the developmental importance of emotional disorders, treatments and other interventions in social work-related fields, human services, juvenile justice, and criminal justice are dedicated to helping children and adolescents with emotional problems. A national assessment (Bradley, Henderson, & Monfore, 2004) of strategies to support those with emotional disorders and related conduct problems found that, among school districts in the United States:

- Nearly 70% of districts use a community mental health agency,
- More than 65% of districts work with local police departments,
- Nearly 64% of districts coordinate with Head Start,
- Nearly 63% of districts engage the juvenile justice system,
- About 55% of districts network with health and human service agencies,
- Nearly 54% of districts are partnered with child protective services,
- About 50% of districts network with substance abuse clinics, and
- More than 33% of districts have contacts with a crisis intervention center.

Thus, emotional problems constitute a considerable focus of social service organizations. Of course, not all populations to which social work professionals provide services have emotion regulation problems, but all must deal with emotion at some level. There are many examples. Social work students often intern at children's clinics, providing therapy and services to children with emotional and behavioral disorders, including autism, ADHD, and other conditions. There they assist children in more appropriately and functionally processing their emotions and relating to others. Social work staff members often accompany students and their families at Individualized Education Program/Plan meetings to facilitate the utilization and receipt of school services. Whether working with homeless families, individuals in substance abuse treatment, families with special-needs children, or victims of bullying, a major thrust of social work is to provide social support to help people manage emotions in a way that is productive and helpful. This chapter explores emotion, delves into its important behavioral properties, and examines how emotional experiences evolve over the life course and influence behavior in multiple ways.

Before getting into the chapter content, brief insight into recent research will be illustrative because it touches on an emotion that is unfortunately difficult for many people to attain: happiness. Across cultures, *happiness*—a state of well-being characterized by high positive emotion and low negative emotion—is a central part of psychological and even physical health. Like other types of positive emotion, happiness facilitates goal-motivated behavior, stimulates creativity, enhances attention, and generally boosts cognitive processes. There appears to be no downside to happiness.

However, Gruber, Mauss, and Tamir (2011) suggest that there is a dark side to happiness that carries potentially damaging behavioral consequences. They argue that too much happiness is consistent with the clinical condition of mania, in which patients experience persistently elevated mood. Among individuals with bipolar disorder, this extreme positive mood has been characterized as positive emotion persistence (Gruber, 2011). The prolonged "high" of a manic episode, during which patients report feeling extreme happiness, can impair their ability to experience other emotions and contribute to risky behaviors, such as sexual promiscuity, substance use, and the neglect of threats that could result in criminal victimization (and offending). Extreme positive emotion is associated with more intense forms of mania and worse symptoms.

In other words, even the best emotions have negative features to them when they are not counterbalanced with other emotional states (see Spotlight Topic). This raises two themes that guide this chapter. First, emotion is a much deeper concept than its lay conceptualization. Emotion serves as both a guide and feedback process for behavior. Second, emotion is variably experienced, processed, and regulated by individuals in society. Whereas most individuals are generally competent in the ways they process emotions, others are not and can display emotional disorders that are associated with maladaptive behaviors.

SPOTLIGHT TOPIC: EMOTIONAL VALENCE AND AFFECT

Life is characterized by a relative mix of emotional experiences ranging from negative to positive. The characterization of an emotion as positive or negative is known as *valence*, which captures how good or bad, attractive or aversive, a specific emotion is. The manner in which individuals present their emotions is commonly known as *affect*. It too ranges from negative to positive. Negative affect includes states such as anger, fear, scorn, revulsion, guilt, self-dissatisfaction, rejection, and sadness and is behaviorally associated with lethargy and withdrawal. Positive affect includes states such as happiness, joy, pride, satisfaction, enthusiasm, interest, and strength and is behaviorally associated with high energy, full concentration, and pleasurable engagement (Watson & Clark, 1984; Watson, Clark, & Tellegen, 1988).

In healthy individuals, emotional experiences include all of these emotions in an appropriate response to environmental conditions and behavioral demands. Regardless of an individual's personality, the death of a close relative is likely to produce great negative emotion, just as the birth of a child is likely to produce great positive emotion. As these experiences wane, so too does the emotional experience.

In unhealthy individuals, there are deficits in the experiencing and regulation of emotion and a general proneness toward negative emotionality, known as *severe mood dysregulation* (SMD). It is characterized by abnormal mood involving irritability, anger, and/or sadness that is noticeable to others and present most of the time. It also involves hyperarousal including insomnia, racing thoughts, pressured speech, and increased reactivity to negative emotional stimuli. Recent epidemiological research on severe mood dysregulation has shown that it is a potent predictor of emotional problems and related conduct problems. For instance:

- The lifetime prevalence of SMD is 3.3%. Of children who had SMD, about one in four also had ADHD, ODD, or CD.
- Children with SMD were twice as likely to develop any psychiatric diagnosis, emotional disorder, or behavioral disorder as children without it.
- Children with SMD were more than 7 times more likely to develop any depressive disorder.

Given this comorbidity, SMD and disorders characterized by negative emotion and affect generally are major emphases in prevention, social work treatment, and juvenile justice interventions. For instance, one model program is *Multisystemic Therapy (MST)*, which is an intensive family- and community-based treatment that addresses the multiple needs of serious, violent, and chronic juvenile delinquents. Within the context of support and skill building, MST therapists help parents and teachers by placing developmentally appropriate demands on the adolescents and his or her family for responsible, prosocial behavior. For a usual duration of 60 contact hours over a 4-month span, MST interventions can include strategic family therapy, structural family therapy, behavioral parent training, and cognitive behavior therapies. MST has been shown to reduce problem behaviors, juvenile justice system involvement, emotional problems, and other mental health problems while increasing social competence and functioning (Borduin & Schaeffer, 2001; Burns, Schoenwald, Burchard, Faw, & Santos, 2000; Henggeler, Mihalic, Rone, Thomas, & Timmons-Mitchell, 1998).

For Reflection

What affective states do you experience when seeing children misbehave? Do your emotions help you to effectively understand and empathize?

CASE STUDY: TAMIKA

Tamika Johnson is 13 years old. She has been in the therapeutic foster care program in Chicago for 4 years, and in and out of foster care for most of her childhood. When you ask her what she loves most, Tamika's large dark brown eyes glow with delight—it's her writing. Yes, she does have a special fondness for her younger foster brother, Raphael, too, but mostly what gets her going each day and what gets her through most nights is her writing. Tamika is a poet. She's always had a muse inside her, she says. But lately, it's her poetry that tells her story. And Tamika has a story to tell. Tamika does not know her father, Tony, and of course it's better that way, as her biological mother had said. Tony was absorbed in running a street corner gambling ring for nearly a decade before

Tamika was born, successfully directing the flow of money and other goods through the hands and pockets of his network. Tony commanded a great deal of respect from the runners, lookouts, and corner captains in the neighborhood who worked under him, until one day when a longtime corner captain discovered that Tony was pocketing more than his fair share of the money. A trusted friend, the corner captain lured Tony into a local bar one night and stabbed him to death in the back bathroom. Tamika was only 14 months old.

Tamika's mother, Janice, was a single mom with two other children, a 14-year-old son and a 16-year-old daughter, who had a different biological father. Janice received Temporary Assistance for Needy Families, but her time was running out and she needed to find a job. And so when Tamika was a toddler, Janice found a job as a store stocker, but it was a nighttime position that required taking a string of buses for over an hour to the suburbs. Janice was desperate, so she accepted the position. The new arrangement meant that she was mostly absent from the home, leaving Tamika primarily in the care of her now 19-year-old daughter, Stephanie. And if you ask Tamika, this is when the trouble began.

Stephanie invited her friends over often, and many boys and young men circled in and out of the house at all hours of the day and night. Drug use was prevalent and the house became known in the neighborhood as the "dug-out dig"—code for a drug dealing den. The police would come on occasion, but an informal "neighborhood watch," set up by the network of dealers, would alert the house members in a timely manner, so that the police presence rarely posed any real barrier to drug runs and use. As the house itself quickly deteriorated into a domestic wasteland of strewn beer cans, rolling papers, fast food wrappers (some with and some without week-old food still inside), hair clips, pill bottles, syringes, and lighters and pipes, interpersonal relationships deteriorated at equal speed and intensity. Violence became commonplace, resulting from bad deals, damaged loyalties, or bad decisions while high. Assaults and sexual and physical abuse were frequent. Tamika was caught in the middle of the devastation. Ultimately, the lifestyle could not be sustained, and Child Protective Services removed 5-year-old Tamika from her mother's home to ensure a safer environment for the child.

Tamika was placed in three different foster homes by the time she was 11, and now attends an alternative school across town where, as Tamika says, "all the peeps who don't have peeps" go. Tamika accepts that fact that, in her words, she "does not have a real family," and she acknowledges that she never was very good at making friends. She internalizes the world around her and tries her best to make it on her own. Tamika says there's one thing you don't have to worry about with her—drug use. She vows to never so much as touch a drug. She says she's seen too much of the destruction it causes, and that she wants no part of it. And so far, she's kept her promise to herself.

What has helped Tamika in the past to cope? Tamika's answer: cutting. Tamika was a cutter. When she cut herself, she felt better. Release; relief; sustained relief. She can't really explain it. But when she tries, she says it just made her "brain feel better." One other thing that she knows also helps her brain feel better is her writing. Tamika has compiled four notebooks of poems over her short life. And she shares them readily with those who are interested and will listen—and Tamika can tell who those people are. She also has started a weekly support group in her therapeutic foster care program for other foster youth who are interested in writing; she said she lets the therapist sit in to learn something, too. In addition, she has allowed the agency to put one of her poem books on display in the waiting room, so that others who might be nervous about first appointments can read her story. So far Tamika says she is making it. And for her, writing poetry has been a great way to help her "brain feel better" along the way.

Critical Thinking Questions:

- What kinds of emotional self-regulation strategies did Tamika use? How were they different or similar in their effects on brain and emotional regulation/coping response?

- What would you hypothesize about the parts of Tamika's brain that might have needed "retraining" or clinical attention?

- What might you speculate to be the parts of Tamika's brain that might be the focus of therapy?

- How did environmental conditions and interpersonal relationship experiences shape Tamika's emotional-regulation capacity across her childhood?

- What strategies might you use with Tamika to help her improve her emotional awareness, emotional acceptance, and emotional versatility?

DISTAL CONTEXT

In everyday discourse and social work practice, *emotion* is a term used to describe the internal feeling states of individuals. From this perspective, emotions such as happiness and sadness reflect simply how a person is feeling. To understand human behavior, a functionalist definition of emotion, which points to the behavioral, motivational, and interactional properties of emotion, is useful. From a functionalist perspective, *emotion* is defined as a person's attempt to establish, maintain, or change the relation between the person and his or her changing circumstances on matters that are of significance to that person (Saarni, Campos, Camras, & Witherington, 2006, p. 227). In this way, emotions are not superficial indicators of how people are feeling, but signals to motivate behavior.

Emotions have evolved to serve specific goals and adaptive functions and are accompanied by specific physiological reactions that have been environmentally honed throughout evolutionary time. In *The Expression of Emotion in Man and Animals*, Darwin (1872/2005) theorized that emotion expressions (nonverbal facial gestures) evolved to prepare humans and animals to respond adaptively to environmental stimuli and to communicate important social information. Over time, emotional expressions evolved from voluntary gestures to convey a particular emotion to involuntary gestures that were automatically expressed. More recently, Ekman's (1992) landmark research provided evidence for *basic emotions*—anger, disgust, fear, happiness, sadness, and surprise—that are universally expressed emotions found across cultures and epochs and theorized to be hardwired into brain circuits by evolution. Ekman suggested (1992), "If emotions are viewed as having evolved to deal with fundamental life-tasks in ways which have been adaptive phylogenetically, then it is logically consistent to expect that there will be some common elements in the contexts in which emotions are found to occur" (p. 183).

As shown in Figure 4.1, two broad strategies have evolved: reappraisal and suppression (Canli, Ferri, & Duman, 2009). *Emotional reappraisal* is the strategy of changing one's interpretation of situations that may elicit strong/negative emotion in a way that reduces the emotional experience. Reappraisal can occur involuntarily or voluntarily and is the internal component of dealing with strong emotions, which usually are negative in valence. *Emotional suppression* is the strategy of inhibiting the behavioral (usually facial) expression of one's emotional experience. It is the external component of dealing with strong emotions, such as putting on a "brave face" to hide how one is feeling. Suppression contributes to increased sympathetic activation of the cardiovascular system because it does not reduce the feeling of the emotion, but only reduces the behavioral expression of it. Of the two, suppression is a less adaptive and healthy way to control emotion.

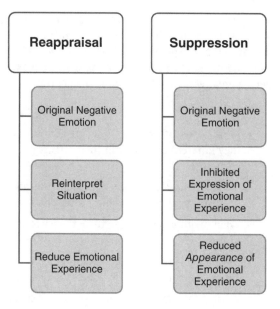

FIGURE 4.1 Emotional Reappraisal and Suppression

REFLECTION: SOCIAL WORK INTERN IN THE EMERGENCY ROOM

During my time as a social work intern in the emergency room of a local hospital, I was confronted with individuals dealing with extremely emotional issues, including the deaths of family members, sometimes children. As an emergency room social worker, you are usually the first point of contact a family has upon learning of the death and occasionally you are in the room with a family when the doctor announces that a loved one has passed away or will likely be passing away soon. Obviously in this position you are confronted with a lot of raw and incredibly intense emotion. Something I struggled with throughout my time there was how to deal with my emotional reactions to grieving families. What was the "appropriate" role for me as a social worker? How would my emotional reaction impact the family and their experience of one of the most significant moments in their lives?

I've heard a couple of different answers to this question from professional social workers who worked in the hospital. The one thing everyone agreed on is the fact that, despite whatever professional or educational credentials you have, you will always be a human and with that comes the fact that you have emotions that can be difficult to control when confronted with a situation like that. Where the division of opinions came, however, is in how to deal with those emotions. Some social workers felt that the display of emotional reaction to a grieving family is disrespectful to the family and delegitimizes your role as a professional who is there to offer them strength, support, and empathy. You are not the one who just lost someone close to you—they are. And they may not appreciate your show of emotions for something that they are experiencing. Aren't they the ones who need comforting? How can you comfort them if you are also emotional? Additionally, you never know how someone will react in this highly emotional state, and you must be prepared for anything. Letting your emotions take over or making yourself vulnerable by showing your emotions can potentially put you and others at risk.

On the other hand, some social workers saw the value in displaying emotion and encouraged it. For one, you are human and part of your job is to create real, human connections to help people deal with the emotional trauma they're experiencing. What will best help people going through this process: a room full of seemingly cold, emotionally withdrawn professionals or sincere, open individuals who show genuine concern and emotional response to your situation? What is most needed by people in this situation is to feel emotionally supported, and by showing that you are also feeling pain, you are creating an emotional connection to them and helping them feel more at ease in showing how they are feeling.

As with any other work with people, it is important to remember that what is most important is not what you think is right, but what the client wants you to do for them. It's okay to ask how you can be helpful to someone going through this. They may want to be left alone, or they may want you to hold their hand and cry with them.

—Davina Abujudeh

The physiological reactions to emotional experiences can be seen in common emotional experiences. For instance, *anger* involves active movement to eliminate obstacles that prevent the attainment of goals. In addition, anger facilitates the communication of power or dominance. Anger produces increases in heart rate, increases in skin temperature, and facial flushing. Another emotion, *fear*, involves flight or active withdrawal from dangerous stimuli. Fear also motivates learning about dangerous stimuli to avoid in the future. Physiologically, fear produces a high heart rate, low skin temperature, and gasping respiration. *Sadness* involves disengagement from stimuli and withdrawal. Sadness serves an adaptive function of conserving energy until new information can be gained to improve the emotion or the nurturance of others is provided. Sadness reduces heart rate, and lowers skin temperature and skin resistance. *Disgust* involves the active rejection of a stimulus that can cause harm or illness. Disgust also involves learning to avoid whatever the contaminating stimuli is, and produces reduced heart rate, lowered skin temperature, and increased skin resistance. *Guilt* motivates outward behavior to repair social relations and punish oneself for a transgression. An adaptive function of guilt is to mold prosocial behavior and moral development.

Physiologically, guilt produces high heart rate, high skin conductance, and irregular respiration. *Shame* involves withdrawal to avoid others and repair one's self-esteem. Adaptive functions of shame include the motivation toward prosocial behavior and social interaction/communication. Shame produces a lower heart rate and increased skin temperature.

Emotions are also intimately related to the environment. The places where we live and work influence our emotions and emotional reactivity. For example, Graham and Shier (2010) surveyed about 700 social work practitioners to examine the correlates of practitioner happiness, which was characterized in the study as subjective well-being. They then interviewed the 13 social work practitioners with the highest scores of subjective well-being. A variety of factors were associated with high subjective well-being, including greater perceived autonomy at work, high workplace flexibility, positive impact on others and clients, task significance and task variety, teamwork, social support, and low organizational constraints. Importantly, nearly all correlates of happiness among social work practitioners were work-related characteristics. This demonstrates how environmental conditions influence one's emotions.

PROXIMAL MECHANISMS

Prefrontal Cortex

As Chapter 5, "Executive Functioning," makes clear, the *prefrontal cortex* is involved in a range of processes that deal with modulating emotional signals and regulating behavior. In a prominent theory of emotional regulation, Davidson and colleagues (Davidson, 2001, 2003; Davidson, Putnam, & Larson, 2000) suggest that the prefrontal cortex is responsible for modulating negative emotional stimuli that are projected from the limbic system of the brain. According to this theory, the left prefrontal cortex is primarily involved in approach-related thoughts or the pursuit of appetitive goals, whereas the right prefrontal cortex is primarily involved in withdrawal-related or inhibited behaviors. Both frontal regions are responding to negative emotions such as fear and uncertainty emanating from the amygdala. However, this brain circuit is dysfunctional in individuals who display impulsive behaviors. This neural circuit explains why antisocial persons are characterized by negative emotions/affect and the hasty reactions to that negativity. According to Davidson (2001), "Individuals who report greater dispositional negative affect and who show increased reactivity to stressful events are more likely to be those individuals who have difficulty regulating negative affect and specifically in modulating the intensity of negative affect once it has been achieved" (p. 662).

The prefrontal cortex serves to manage emotions in interesting ways. The right side of the prefrontal cortex manages negative emotions, whereas the left side manages positive emotions. As such, people with dominant left brains are more likely to be optimistic, happy, confident, enthused, and relatively free of stress. When they encounter depressing events, they are able to get through them and recover quickly. Conversely, people with dominant right brains are more anxious, pessimistic, and prone to depression (Ackerman, 2004).

Evidence for the prefrontal role in emotional regulation is seen in disorders such as ADHD. In addition to attention and conduct problems, children with ADHD have deficits at modulating their emotions, which often exacerbates the other problems. However, positive emotional nurturing can help youth with ADHD to better regulate their conduct and emotions. Sonuga-Barke et al. (2009) found that children and adolescents with ADHD whose mothers spoke with positive emotions about them were more likely to regulate their emotions appropriately. In this way, expressed emotions from a parent help to boost emotional control in children.

The prefrontal cortex is also an important brain region for understanding addiction and the emotional factors that guard against it. Positive emotionality has been shown to be associated with dopamine activity in the prefrontal cortex, striatum, and cingulate cortex—regions that process natural rewards and rewards in drug abuse. Volkow et al. (2011) recently found that positive emotionality was associated with brain glucose metabolism in the orbitofrontal cortex and other reward regions. The importance of this is that positive emotions, such as well-being, achievement striving, and motivation guard against substance use disorders. Conversely, dysfunction in the prefrontal cortex (and other brain regions) is a common risk factor for developing substance use problems.

Limbic System

The emotional signals that the prefrontal cortex must handle come from the *limbic system*: the emotional seat of the brain, responsible for processing basic emotions (most notably fear) and storing memory. The limbic system is extensively studied for its role in emotion and behavior, especially among populations with poor regulation of emotion and behavior, namely criminal offenders. Consider this artful passage by DeLisi (2011):

> At its core, criminal behavior could be viewed as the triumph of emotion over reason. Murder is frequently borne from mundane

circumstances involving interpersonal conflicts with a person with whom we have close emotional connections, and the primary motivators for these conflicts are anger, vengeance, lust, and other deadly sins. Other types of crimes, such as shoplifting, drug use, or drunk driving involve fleeting decisions to take what we want, and to do what we want. Freud referred to these primal drives that are able to overcome thought and reason as a component of the personality called the id. More generally, these primal, visceral emotions originate from the region of the brain known as the limbic system. The limbic system is involved in autonomic or involuntary and somatic or voluntary behavioral activities relating to emotion and emotional memory. (p. 167)

The limbic system, in other words, provides the emotional raw material that must be handled by the prefrontal cortex to produce appropriate behavior. Metaphorically, the circuitry between the limbic system and the prefrontal cortex represents the symbiotic relationship between emotion and behavior.

The limbic system has important behavioral and societal implications. For example, the capacity to punish is an essential part of life and a major structure of the criminal law and criminal justice system. Brain imaging research has shown that the emotional desire to punish is created in the limbic system of the brain. In a novel study, Gospic et al. (2011) conducted brain scans and administered a placebo or a tranquilizer to participants who were playing the Ultimatum Game. The Ultimatum Game involves punishing other players' unfair behavior despite receiving an economic loss for doing so. Using fMRI, they were able to measure limbic activity during decision-making points in the Ultimatum Game, while also considering that some participants had taken a drug that reduces emotional responses and limbic activity. They found that amygdala activity was associated with the desire to impose punishment, and that the pharmacological treatment reduced punishing behavior and activity in the amygdala/limbic area.

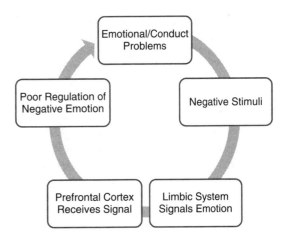

FIGURE 4.2 The Prefrontal-Limbic Circuit of Emotion Regulation

Of course, the prefrontal (or cortical) and limbic (or subcortical) regions should not be learned in isolation from each other, but together, given their connectivity (see Figure 4.2). Recent neuroimaging research on deception demonstrates how these brain systems are compatible. Baumgartner, Fischbacher, Feierabend, Lutz, and Fehr (2009) explored the neural systems involved in making and then breaking a promise. Their brain scan data indicated that when individuals broke a promise that they had earlier made, there was increased brain activity in the frontal cortex (specifically the dorsolateral prefrontal cortex) and in the limbic system (specifically the amygdala). The emotional conflict of breaking a promise could be seen in the connectivity between these two regions. Interestingly, neuroimaging research of deception and brain activity among persons with psychopathic traits found some significant differences in the brain activation patterns that occur when lying (Fullam, McKie, & Dolan, 2009). This suggests that psychopathic individuals find it easier to lie and be deceptive, and even recruit different neural pathways when doing so.

With this neural framework in mind, it is important to think about emotional regulation and the ways that it influences behavior in social contexts. This relationship is captured with social information processing theory.

Social Information Processing

Social information processing theory suggests there are individual differences in the ways that people read or encode, interpret, respond to, and evaluate social contexts and interactions. In healthy individuals, social information is viewed as positive or, more commonly, neutral in its connotation. This allows people to interact with others without imputing harm or negativity to those interactions. Consequently, healthy individuals read, interpret, and respond to the emotions of others and their own emotions in a straightforward, uncontroversial way.

On the other hand, persons with deficits in processing emotion have a much harder time in social interactions. A major problem that can occur relating to emotional processing is *hostile attribution bias*, which is the tendency to believe that others have hostile intentions toward them. Persons with hostile attribution bias experience high levels of negative emotions such as anger, and often low levels of other negative emotions such as fear. Children and adolescents with this bias are susceptible to serious relationship difficulties and conduct problems. For instance, a comparative study examined nonaggressive adolescents, severely violent adolescents, and moderately aggressive adolescents from a sample of nearly 300 boys in Grades 4 and 7 (Lochman & Dodge, 1994). They found that the most aggressive boys displayed poor interpersonal cue recall, had fewer help-seeking solutions to interpersonal conflicts, and more hostile attributions. Violent boys also had lower overall self-worth. In similar research, Crick and Dodge (1994, 1996) reported that schoolchildren with social information processing deficits are more prone to be reactively aggressive, proactively aggressive, or display both forms of aggression compared to control groups of peers. More disturbingly, they found that proactively aggressive children reported more positive outcome expectations and greater self-efficacy from aggressive behavior.

Broadly speaking, when emotion is regulated too little or too much, there is an increased risk for aversive social interactions and maladaptive behavior. For instance, individuals who have deficits in cognitively controlling emotions, especially anger, resentment, jealousy, and other self-conscious emotions, are more likely to respond to social situations with aggression to avoid uncomfortable emotional states. On the other hand, persons who overregulate their emotions are at risk for increased negative affect, increased physiological arousal, impaired decision making, and other factors that contribute to aggressive behavior. Roberton, Daffern, and Bucks (2012) suggest that three emotional regulation skills help people appropriately process social information and social interactions, and control their behavior. First, *emotional awareness* is the understanding of one's emotions, how they relate to their behavior, and how both affect others. People with high levels of emotional awareness are able to tolerate and contain negative emotional states, such as anger or frustration, and persevere to complete social and behavioral goals. At a clinical level, *alexithymia* is a condition characterized by an inability to articulate one's emotional experiences. Second, *emotional acceptance* is the value-free acknowledgement of emotions without experiencing negative reactions to those emotions if appropriate. In other words, individuals who acknowledge that social interaction involves both positive and negative emotional experiences, and who are able to deal with that reality, have reached emotional acceptance. Third, *emotional versatility* is the use of and access to a variety of emotional regulation strategies that individuals utilize to control their emotions to achieve behavioral goals. Most of this control relates to cognitive appraisals of situations and developing appropriate ways to emotionally respond or not respond.

SPOTLIGHT TOPIC: EMPATHY

A large part of emotionality and social behavior relates to the ability of an individual to understand, appreciate, and even "feel" the emotions of others. *Empathy*, the capacity to vicariously experience the emotions, feelings, or thoughts of other people, is one of the core skills of emotional competence. Moreover, empathy allows us to connect to others in important ways. For instance, people are able to join into the happiness and pride of another person who accomplishes a goal (e.g., making a goal in soccer, performing well on a math test, successfully giving a public lecture, or passing a driving test) because they understand and have felt those emotions themselves and realize the integration of behavior (i.e., the performances just described) with its emotional response.

Social work practitioners are also familiar with another group of people who have severe deficits in empathy, namely those with psychopathic personality. Researchers have shown that individuals who are highly callous, shallow in their emotional responses, and lacking empathy are likely to display psychopathic features and commit crime. The reason is straightforward. Because psychopathic individuals lack an emotional connection or sharing with others, they do not experience the distress that results from victimizing others (Patrick, Fowles, & Krueger, 2009). Without empathy, it is harder to feel others' pain and suffering.

Like virtually all constructs relating to human behavior, empathy is produced by a mixture of biological, social, and biosocial processes. Processes that occur during childhood, such as the development of joint attention, parent–child bonding, secure attachment, and even simple acts such as taking turns during game play, help to cultivate empathic understanding (see Kochanska & Murray, 2000; Zahn-Waxler, 1991). Empathy is also partly genetic in origin. When empathy scores are in the extreme range, such as among psychopathic individuals who commit crime, there is evidence that they are mostly genetic in origin. For example, Viding, Jones, Frick, Moffitt, and Plomin (2008) examined the heritability of callous-unemotional traits and antisocial behavior among 9-year-olds selected from 2,570 twin pairs who are part of the Twins Early Development Study, a large population-based longitudinal study of twins born in England and Wales. Viding et al. found the highest heritability estimates when callous-unemotional traits and severe antisocial behaviors were co-occurring. In fact, 71% of the shared variance between low empathy–unemotional traits and conduct problems was attributable to genetic factors.

In the brain, empathy is facilitated by a neuropeptide called oxytocin (discussed in Chapter 3) that is produced in the hypothalamus. Oxytocin has been shown to be associated with social attachment and other affiliation-related behaviors. Interestingly, researchers have found that administering oxytocin via nasal inhaler contributes to greater levels of trust and connectedness to others (Kosfeld, Heinrichs, Zak, Fischbacher, & Fehr, 2005). This raises interesting treatment possibilities for helping individuals with empathy deficits better relate to their fellow people.

For Reflection

Is it possible to form an effective therapeutic alliance with another person without feeling what they feel? If not, why?

In addition to these emotional regulation skills, it is important to recall from the temperament and personality chapters that there is tremendous variance in the ways that people are equipped to deal with various emotional stimuli in social life. Whereas healthy people process social information in a generally positive or even benign way, others do not (Hertel & Mathews, 2011). Persons who are prone to negative emotions, such as anxiety and depression for instance, are more likely to attend to negative cues (e.g., becoming upset over trivial negative events), interpret even ambiguous events in negative ways (e.g., "That person must not like me"), and remember the negative features of events (e.g., "The delayed flight ruined my entire vacation"). Conversely, a person who processes social information in healthy ways does not even notice such trivial events, interprets people as busy and not meaning any harm, and remembers the big picture of events where the many positive episodes far outweigh the few inconveniences. Social information processing provides a framework for understanding how one's emotional repertoire frames behavior and how one cognitively reflects on their behavior.

EMOTIONAL DEVELOPMENT AND PSYCHOSOCIAL RELATIONS OVER THE LIFE COURSE

Research from an array of disciplines makes clear that emotions, emotional regulation, and emotional disorders are attributable to a complex mix of genetic and environmental sources. Although the general liability for a particular type of emotional problem is often strongly heritable, it is also the case that more specific emotional disorders within the general problem area are less so. So what does this mean? A prevalent problem among various social work clients, such as youth receiving mental health counseling, their families who are also often in counseling, juvenile justice clients, and patients with pervasive developmental disorders such as autism, relates

to negative emotionality (see Chapter 6, "Temperament"). A large-scale study of twins found that the overall heritance for anxiety disorders was about 54%, meaning that more than half of variance in anxiety problems is genetic in origin (Tambs et al., 2009). However, specific emotional problems within the broader anxiety framework, such as panic disorder, generalized anxiety disorder, phobias, obsessive-compulsive disorder, and PTSD, were less heritable and more environmental in their etiology. This is helpful for social workers on two fronts. First is the recognition that many emotionally based problems (e.g., those relating to anxiety) are genetic and often run in families, emerge early, and can be difficult to treat. However, there are also many environmental causes of these disorders, which serve as target areas for treatment.

Given the importance of emotional disturbance among many social work clients, a major goal for social work practitioners is to assist clients in reaching *emotional competence*: the achievement of self-efficacy (competence) during social interactions that often create emotional challenges. In other words, a healthy, prosocial child, adolescent, or adult who is stable and able to handle himself or herself during emotionally challenging situations is more likely to similarly behave in healthy, prosocial ways. On the other hand, individuals who do not effectively achieve emotional competence have deficits in dealing with others, are prone to respond in emotionally inappropriate ways, and (most important) engage in inappropriate or maladaptive behavior.

As shown in Figure 4.3, emotional competence develops over the life course and consists of several skills (for a review, see Saarni, 1999; Saarni et al., 2006). First, an individual must be aware of his or her emotional state and recognize that it can include overlapping emotions, conflicting emotions, and emotions that are both conscious and unconscious. Second, a person must be able to read others' emotions based on their behavior, expressions, and other cues. Third, a person must employ vocabulary and expressions that convey emotion. Fourth, an

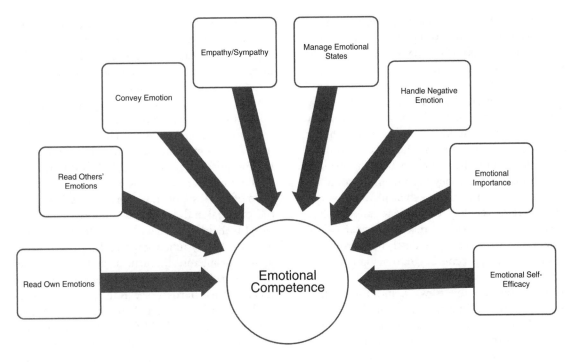

FIGURE 4.3 Emotional Competence

individual must have the capacity to empathize and sympathize with the emotions of others (see Spotlight Topic).

Fifth, individuals must learn to manage their internal emotional states with their external emotional expression. Many times in life, one must modulate his or her true emotional content to successfully adapt in social settings. Indeed, a hallmark of emotional disorders is the inability to appropriately modulate emotional impulses. A sixth and related skill is the ability to handle aversive or negative emotions with self-regulation. Seventh, one must be aware that emotions matter in terms of maintaining relationships and that a large part of social relations centers on emotional communication. The eighth and final point for emotional competence is that the individual is comfortable with his or her emotional experiences; this state of *emotional self-efficacy* contributes to a sense of emotional homeostasis.

Although all people work toward emotional competence, some either do not achieve it or achieve it at different ages across the life course. The next section examines how emotional development contributes to behavior from infancy to late adulthood.

Fetal Environment and Infancy

As examined in the Temperament chapter, there are important individual-level differences in the ways that people regulate themselves and react to the environment. These differences exist at birth and are apparent in the earliest days of childhood. This means that some infants display a mostly cheerful disposition that suggests they experience a wealth of positive emotions relative to negative emotions. On the other hand, other infants have a more negative disposition that suggests a greater experiencing of negative emotions relative to positive ones (Kagan, 1994). The importance of these baseline temperamental differences and emotion profiles is that parents respond differentially to infants based upon their presentation of positive and negative emotions.

During infant development, events such as crawling and walking are not only motor milestones but also significant changes in individuals' emotional life. Prior to having any real sense of locomotion, infants are mostly docile, and parents do not attribute tremendous emotional complexity to them. At this point, children cry when they are hungry or need their diaper changed. In other words, they are driven by basic physical needs. As infants begin to explore the world, however, they become more sophisticated in terms of exploring their physical world. Infants are more likely to experience anger (when a particular toy is out of reach) and fear (when they place themselves in modestly dangerous positions). In turn, parents begin to recognize these emotional displays. A similar progression occurs once toddlers are able to walk, and, for the first time, defy what their parents want them to do (e.g., do not walk into the kitchen when the burners on the stove are on). Overall, "motor milestones such as walking and crawling fundamentally alter the infant, her social world, and her relation to that world and in the process reorganize her emotional life and the emotional climate in which she lives" (Saarni et al., 2006, p. 235).

During infancy and toddlerhood, children also increase their understanding of emotions and the behavioral implications of emotions. For example, *referential specificity* is the understanding that emotional expressions are specifically directed toward objects in the environment (e.g., other people) and not randomly directed. Another skill that develops during this time is *affect specificity*, which is the child's ability to make distinctions among emotions that are similar or have the same valence, such as understanding the differences between fear and anger. These skills set the stage for continued development, behavior, and social interaction during childhood.

Early Childhood and Childhood

Given the interplay between a child's emotional style, emotional regulation, and the ways that parents, caregivers, and others respond to it,

much research funding and many social service interventions are devoted to providing social support to caregivers of young children. One interesting initiative is the Consortium of Longitudinal Studies of Child Abuse and Neglect (LONGSCAN), which is a group of longitudinal studies designed to study the risk factors and consequences of child maltreatment (http://www.iprc.unc.edu/longscan). A recurrent finding in research based on LONGSCAN data is the importance of positive emotion in the form of social support. Generally, *social support—* the material and emotional support that is provided to help other people—has been shown to improve family functioning and reduce psychological problems. In turn, social support contributes to less child maltreatment and reduced social service burden (see Kang, 2012; Lindsey et al., 2012; Thompson, 2010; Thompson et al., 2007). Moreover, LONGSCAN demonstrates the central role that emotion and management of emotions among children and their caregivers play in prosocial and maladaptive behaviors.

In addition to the emotional experiences that occur during childhood, how a child regulates emotions has important predictive validity for later life outcomes. For instance, recent research found that infant attachment security at age 1 year and peer competence at ages 6 to 8 years were associated with friendship security at age 16 years, and use of negative emotions in romantic relationships at ages 20 and 21 years (Simpson, Collins, & Salvatore, 2011). Securely attached infants had greater social competence across the life course and were better able to resolve emotional conflicts with their romantic partners during adulthood. More impressively, the enduring effects of early childhood emotional stability predicted adult emotional functioning in romantic relationships even while controlling for characteristics of the adult relationship such as quality and functioning.

Adolescence

Emotional competence is probably most difficult to achieve during adolescence because of the many developmental changes that coincide with this part of the life course. The transition from child to adult involves myriad social, biological, and neurological changes that create ambiguity in status. In some respects, adolescents are viewed as adults and achieve adult-related responsibilities relating to driving rights, voting rights, legal rights, purchasing rights, and access to tobacco and alcohol at various stages. In other respects, adolescents are viewed as "less than" adults, and this role ambiguity is theorized to explain the sudden increase in externalizing behaviors during late adolescence (Moffitt, 1993).

In terms of emotional development, a variety of skills are developed during adolescence (Lee & Hoaken, 2007). These include:

- Regulating intense emotions
- Modulating rapidly vacillating emotions
- Achieving awareness of one's emotions
- Attending to one's emotions
- Handling one's emotions without being overwhelmed by them
- Distinguishing emotions from facts
- Increasing cognitive reasoning as opposed to emotional reasoning
- Maintaining interpersonal relationships that often involve strong emotions

Unfortunately, it is during adolescence that some youth fail to successfully develop these skills, and as such are at risk for emotional and behavioral disorders. This risk is heightened when adolescents have incurred abuse and neglect during childhood.

In many communities, adolescent emotional problems constitute a major proportion of the caseload of many social work practitioners. This is particularly true for youth whose emotional and conduct problems have resulted in juvenile justice system involvement. Adolescents who have been adjudicated and placed in out-of-home settings have significantly worse problems

with substance use, alcohol use, suicidal behavior and self-harm, externalizing behaviors, and emotional dysregulation (Vaughn, Howard, Foster, Dayton, & Zelner, 2005). In addition, adolescent psychosocial functioning that relates to how they regulate emotion is a key target for treatment (Vaughn & Howard, 2004).

Adulthood

There is evidence that emotional regulation is relatively stable across the life course into adulthood. The reason for this stability in emotion and behavior is attributable to genetic and environmental factors. This is known as the *set-point hypothesis*, which suggests that genetic and environmental factors produce a baseline level of a specific emotional response to which people will return after specific events. This means that a very happy person is prone to return to a happy state even after an unhappy event. Similarly, a generally unhappy person is prone to resume being unhappy even after a happy event. A recent study of more than 12,000 twins followed across nearly 60 years of data collection is illustrative. Kendler and his colleagues (2011) found that negative emotions such as anxiety and depression persisted within individuals across life, and that depressing environmental situations that are faced in midlife are not transitory events, but instead contribute to further stability. This is consistent with temperament research that has also shown that early life emotionality, especially negative forms such as depression, are persistent across life.

Emotions are an important part of the lives of adults who are current or former social work clients. A recent study of adults with mental health needs who formerly were foster care youth found that emotion was a strong determinant and barrier to service use (Munson, Scott, Smalling, Kim, & Floersch, 2011). Some adults feared the perceived complexities of the treatment system and thus were reluctant to take advantage of opportunities to help themselves. Others feared behavioral problems associated with their psychiatric problems, such as drug relapse, and utilized services. There is also evidence that adults with various emotional assets are also able to overcome situations that contribute to negative behaviors generally. One of those emotional assets is agreeableness, which is a personality construct in which high scorers are warm and friendly, and low scorers are cold and prone to conflict. Experimental research has shown that when highly agreeable people are exposed to aggression-related stimuli, they are able to engage in prosocial thoughts that buffer against situations that commonly promote aggression (Meier, Robinson, & Wilkowski, 2006).

Although there is relative stability in emotion and emotional regulation, this does not suggest that adulthood is free from emotional experiences and their effects. An interesting example of this is seen with envy, a negative emotion associated with social comparisons to others of real or perceived higher status. Unlike other emotions that carry clear facial expressions, envy is hidden and instead involves negative internal emotional states of resentment, indignation, and inferiority. Experimental research has shown that envy carries significant cognitive consequences (Hill, DelPriore, & Vaughn, 2011). Envy requires significant resources relating to attention and memory, and this resource expenditure depletes self-regulation skill. Millions of people sit at work each day quietly envying their colleagues, and this research shows that such emotional activity not only wastes time, but also precious cognitive resources.

In sum, emotion and emotional regulation play important parts in behavior across the life course. Emotion is a major contributor to social interactions, and plays an important role in facilitating conventional behavior and—when there are deficits—contributing to problem behaviors.

Sex Differences

Social work practitioners are quite aware of sex differences in emotional regulation in their daily work. The overall trends, in which men are susceptible to externalizing symptoms (e.g., the use of aggression) and women are susceptible to internalizing symptoms (e.g., rumination and emotional resignation), directly bear on sex differences in emotions. On this issue, Kret and De Gelder (2012) suggested:

> Research indicates that men and women possess different skills related to the sending and receiving of emotional messages. In general, women are more emotionally expressive, whereas men conceal or control their emotional displays [reference omitted]. In addition to their encoding ability, women tend to express emotion through facial expression and interpersonal communication, whereas men generally express emotion through actions such as engaging in aggressive behavior. (p. 1)

Many biosocial reasons explain gender differences in emotional regulation and expression. These include

- cultural norms and socialization that are differentiated by gender,

- sex-differentiated hormones,

- chromosomal and genetic factors,

- sex differences in brain structure and functioning, and

- sex differences in brain laterality and connectivity between the two hemispheres.

Taken together, these differences contribute to advantages for women in the areas of recognizing emotion and emotional expression and in the area of underresponse to threatening cues. In addition, men are further disadvantaged (in terms of antisocial behavior) because they show greater emotional responses to threatening stimuli relating to dominance, violence, and aggression (Kret & De Gelder, 2012; Whittle, Yücel, Yap, & Allen, 2011).

Neuroimaging research has added scientific rigor to experimental and survey research showing sex differences in emotional processing. In a review of studies, Whittle et al. (2011) found that women and men utilize different brain regions during emotion perception, which contributes to greater emotional perception among females. They also reported sex differences in the neural correlates of automatic or unconscious and effortful or conscious emotion regulation processes. Overall, despite some gender commonalities, there are significant brain sex differences in terms of emotion perception, reactivity, experience, and regulation.

Sex differences in emotion and in the neural substrates that produce them suggest genetic differences as well. For example, geneticists have studied a functional polymorphism in the gene that encodes the MAOA enzyme and various environmental triggers that produce problems with emotional regulation and antisocial conduct (Taylor & Kim-Cohen, 2007). A recent study examined a sample of adolescents and their mothers, some of whom had smoked cigarettes during their pregnancy (Wakschlag et al., 2010). They found that male carriers of the low-activity MAOA genotype (which has been shown to be a genetic risk factor for conduct problems) who had been exposed to prenatal cigarettes were prone to CD, which is characterized by poor emotional regulation. In contrast, girls who had been exposed to prenatal cigarettes and were carriers of the high-activity genotype were likely to display CD symptoms, poor emotional regulation, and hostile attribution bias.

EXPERT'S CORNER: JEANNE TSAI, STANFORD UNIVERSITY

Jeanne Tsai has asked a simple yet important question: How does culture shape emotion? The reasons why this is profound are twofold. First, we know that individuals around the world are greatly influenced by the cultures in which they are embedded. Second, most mental health problems are characterized by emotional discomfort. Therefore, a better understanding of the intersection between culture and emotions may enhance treatments for mental health problems in cross-cultural context.

One of the key distinctions that needs to be made, according to Tsai, is between how people actually feel and how they want to feel. Tsai has developed a theory based on these distinctions between actual and ideal affect. Tsai points out that people do a host of different things to regulate their emotions, such as going to sporting events, visiting with friends, or spending some time alone reading a good novel. However, what people choose to do to feel good is impacted by the cultural context in which they reside. The behavioral options available to everyday Americans who have high levels of income, for example, may be entirely different than those available to people in other countries. There are also within-nation variations based on culture. For example, European Americans may be more inclined to do certain activities compared to Asian or Latino Americans. Admittedly, there is additional variation within these general ethnic categories as well.

Tsai has developed a measure of ideal affect termed the Affect Valuation Index. In several studies designed to better measure and understand ideal affect and how culture impacts this distinction, Tsai has found that among persons of different cultures and religious traditions, people want to feel more positively than they actually do. So in essence, people feel a disconnect between how they actually feel and want to feel. Culture appears to affect the way in which they want to feel. For example,

(Continued)

Photo of Jeanne Tsai
Courtesy of Mark Estes
Photography

in studies comparing European American college students and Chinese students from Hong Kong who grew up amid Chinese culture, Tsai and her colleagues (2000) found that feeling happy was associated with excitement among European American college students and serenity among the Chinese students. Tsai and colleagues also found among children age 3–5 years that European American children associated happiness with excited smiles more so than Taiwanese and Chinese students, suggesting cultural differences in ideal affect states. This research indicates that affect is at least partly tied to culture and that helping professionals may be able to harness this in ways that increase their effectiveness.

SUMMARY

Emotion is a powerful part of the human experience, and more profoundly related to behavior than is likely commonly believed. Emotions are not merely internal feeling states, but powerful motivators of conduct that have been refined over evolutionary history. Perhaps equally important to emotion are the ways that it is regulated. Emotional regulation involves interplay between the limbic system and the prefrontal cortex. It is the prefrontal cortex that is explored next in Chapter 5 with a focus on executive functions. Several major summary points regarding emotion include:

• Emotions involve a person's attempt to change their relation to others and environmental contexts and thus are important determinants of behavior.

• The existence of basic emotions across wildly different cultures and among primates suggests that emotions have evolved to serve important behavioral and communicative functions.

• Emotions range from negative to positive in terms of their valence, affect, and behavioral correlates.

• People modify their emotions by reappraising and suppressing their emotions in the face of environmental contexts.

• Many behavioral disorders are associated with experiencing mostly negative emotions, difficulties regulating emotions, or both.

• Emotional competence is the achievement of self-efficacy or general satisfaction with one's emotional experiences and regulation.

• Emotional development occurs across the life course and is associated with the development of conventional and maladaptive behaviors.

• Emotion is regulated in a circuit involving the limbic system and prefrontal cortex. Dysfunction in this neural circuitry is associated with impulsivity, aggression, and diverse externalizing behaviors.

KEY TERMS

Affect

Affect specificity

Alexithymia

Basic emotions

Emotion

Emotional acceptance

Emotional awareness

Emotional competence

Emotional reappraisal

Emotional self-efficacy

Emotional suppression

Emotional versatility

Empathy

Happiness

Hostile attribution bias

Limbic system

Multisystemic Therapy (MST)

Prefrontal cortex

Referential specificity

Set-point hypothesis

Severe mood dysregulation (SMD)

Social information processing theory

Social support

Valence

CHAPTER 5

EXECUTIVE FUNCTIONS

Although intelligence receives most of the attention, the concept that is more importantly related to how well an individual gets along and functions in school settings, occupational settings, and relationships is the focus of the current chapter: executive functions. Although executive functions represent complex neuroscience, they also are apparent even in mundane behaviors. Consider this interesting passage:

> The traffic light turns from green to yellow. With just one car between you and the intersection, your brain sprints into action, calculating distances and relative velocities; checking for hurried pedestrians; simulating the mental processes of the driver in front of you; and readying every muscle in preparation for a split-second decision that could literally change your life: Which pedal? So many of our mental processes, at any given moment, rely upon this constant, "high stakes" computation involving powerful impulses on one hand and inhibitory control on the other. This balancing act of neuronal signals is at the core of complex human behaviors and thus, its malfunction could have a range of adverse medical and social consequences. (Volkow & Baler, 2012, p. 546)

Many of the behaviors of daily life involve executive functions. How well one pays attention, focuses, listens, and follows through on instructions are basic skills of life, and carry broad implications for functioning at school, at work, at home, in relationships, and in other settings. Making careless errors, failing to keep track of things, forgetting things, and leading a sloppy and disorganized life are common indicators of suboptimal executive functioning. Among

children, how well they can sit still, stay seated, settle down, rest, keep quiet, wait their turn, and interact with others are prime behavioral indicators of functions that occur in the prefrontal section of their brains.

Executive functions are exceedingly important not only for understanding the etiology of behavior, but also for understanding the tremendous diversity of performance in human behaviors, including intelligence and cognitive performance (Coyle, Pillow, Snyder, & Kochunov, 2011), personality (Unsworth et al., 2009), addiction (Berkman, Falk, & Lieberman, 2011), wealth accumulation and eminence (Rindermann & Thompson, 2011), work performance (Parasuraman, 2011), antisocial behaviors (Séguin, 2004), psychopathic personality (DeLisi, Vaughn, Beaver, & Wright, 2010), and many others. In other words, understanding cognition, emotion, personality, internal dialogue, and external behavior is not possible without considering executive functions. Moreover, this knowledge has tremendous implications for social work practice. We agree with Matto and Strolin-Goltzman (2010), who suggest that "it is critical that social workers become integrally involved in making use of and advancing the social neuroscience literature for social work education, practitioner training, and new treatment model development" (p. 154).

In addition, many social work clients present with conditions that relate broadly or specifically to executive functions and deficits in executive processing. The clearest example, and one that is covered extensively in this chapter, is ADHD. Other conditions that social workers routinely also encounter are importantly related to executive functions. Autism is one such example.

Although autism is characterized by communication deficits, social deficits, and stereotypy in behaviors, many of the specific features of the disorder suggest global impairments in executive functioning. As Ozonoff, Pennington, and Rogers (1991) noted, "Their cognition often seems to lack executive functions; autistic individuals do not appear future-oriented, do not anticipate long-term consequences of behavior well, and have great difficulty self-reflecting and self-monitoring. They frequently appear impulsive, as if unable to delay or inhibit responses" (p. 1083). Other conditions, such as Tourette's syndrome, reflect motor inhibition and self-regulation problems. Finally, conduct-related problems are in part caused by deficits in the prefrontal areas of the brain that regulate emotional and reward drives (as examined in Chapter 4). In short, social workers, particularly those working in clinical settings, are likely to interact regularly with clients who display problems with executive functioning.

CASE STUDY: CORPORAL WAGNER

Like Tamika in Chapter 4, U.S. Marine Corporal Jonathan Wagner III is doing some writing too. Corporal Wagner also has a story to tell. He wanted to be in the military for as long as he can remember. It was not only a family tradition, but also was something he could be proud of and that excited him. He wanted to serve his country, and it was important to him that he make his family and community proud. Wagner was hardworking and determined. In fact, his work ethic was what almost everyone thought to be most remarkable about him. Wagner never gave up, no matter what happened. He was a very social child, and emerged as an outgoing and exceptionally reliable young adult. Everyone could count on Wagner, and that's the way Wagner liked it. He persevered not just for himself, but for everyone he knew who depended on him.

The day he entered the Marine Corps, he recalls, was the best day of his life. The day he was sent home—December, 12, 2011—was the worst day of his life. Like numerous service members serving in the wars in Iraq and Afghanistan, Corporal Wagner sustained a serious head injury resulting from the explosion of an improvised explosive device (IED) that targeted the vehicle he was riding in. As he looks back now, the physical trauma and burns he experienced that day were not nearly as bad as being sent home with what he considered to be "invisible wounds." He remembers feeling intense, almost immobilizing guilt and despondency in "abandoning" his unit, without the "honorable wounds" that someone sent home would have sustained. Specifically, Corporal Wagner explains it like this: "When you lose an arm, everyone can see that. They know your limitation. When you tell someone you have a TBI [traumatic brain injury] or PTSD, they don't see it. They don't understand your limitation. It's harder to understand." What don't they understand? Corporal Wagner says he is just not himself most days. He experiences a great deal of anxiety just trying to manage the tasks of daily living; he has short-term memory problems, saying that he is more forgetful than he ever used to be. He's not so sure people could or should rely on him much anymore. He also finds himself irritable for "no reason," is easily angered, and says he just "can't think right" anymore. These are not the characteristics that someone from high school would have used to describe him. This is not how Corporal Wagner would like to describe himself now. He admits he needs help.

What happens when a brain disorder, like a TBI or PTSD, compromises our executive functions and impairs our ability to perform critical decisions and judgments—like those critical decisions and judgments required of military personnel in combat arenas? Along with pharmacotherapy and neurological testing and treatments, Corporal Wagner also participated in a holistic mental health program, which included creative writing and expressive art therapy protocols, to allow him to begin expressing and coping with the emotional consequences of his injuries. Wagner was able to express his emotions and tell his story through his writing—and when he found he didn't have the words for what he felt, he used clay, paints, and chalk to communicate his narrative. One day he created a sculpture of a frozen hand emerging from an icy terrain, outstretched in angst but reaching for help. The image, he said, embodied his desire to make a connection and reach out to get the help he needs, but it also communicated that he felt as vulnerable as he was determined. Wagner talked of the strain he experienced in trying to keep "pushing through" and the disconnect he often felt from his unit, his family, and himself—he spoke of a "disjointedness" or disintegration within his body, mind and relationships.

Through experiential processing treatment methods, like expressive art therapy and creative writing, veterans like Corporal Wagner are learning to access traumatic experiences that have been encoded in the limbic system and in cognitively inaccessible parts of the emotional brain, in order to express the range of intense emotions attached to the trauma experience. For example, the National Intrepid Center of Excellence, in Bethesda, Maryland, is a new interdisciplinary assessment and treatment facility that includes expressive therapy and creative writing in their medical protocols, for veterans of Operations Enduring Freedom and Iraqi Freedom who are suffering from PTSD and/or TBI and their family members. Therapeutic protocols include creative writing, storytelling, and art. As Ron Capps, veteran and founder of the Veterans Writing Project, explains, they helped him because "I had a lot of memories that I had to work through. By writing, I was able to shape each of those and get control of them so that they were not just festering in the back of my mind."

Critical Thinking Questions:

- How must social workers adapt treatment when working with a client who has impaired executive functioning?
- When an individual experiences both a physically and emotionally traumatic experience, what symptoms should be targeted first to help the client properly cope with the trauma?

DISTAL CONTEXT

Executive functions is an umbrella term that is meant to characterize the interrelated cluster of higher order cognitive functions that assist individuals in modulating their emotional and behavioral responses to the environment through problem solving, planning, attention, verbal reasoning, and related tasks. Neurologically, executive functioning occurs in the prefrontal cortex, also sometimes referred to as the cortical section of the brain.

All constructs in this text include a small section on the role that human evolution played in their development. In the case of executive functions, it could be argued that its development is largely responsible for the adaptive success of humans. For instance, Coolidge and Wynn (2001) utilize an archeological perspective to provide evidence for the development of what we now call executive functions. For example, during the Neolithic era, loom weaving and ceramic manufacturing were common, which is evidence of sequential memory. Inhibition or gratification delay is seen in the European Mesolithic era based on agricultural tasks such as cultivation, planting, storage, and others. Also interesting is the Paleolithic evidence of organization and planning based on early forms of colonization that occurred in Australia and other Pacific islands. Coolidge and Wynn suggest that the aforementioned executive skills were a major evolutionary acquisition that led to modern human thinking, cognition, and self-regulation.

In an influential thesis, Barkley (2001, 2012) theorized that the executive functions are a biological adaptation that shifted the control of behavior from the immediate context, other people, and the temporal present to self-regulation by internal representations of the hypothetical social future (see Figure 5.1). In other words, Barkley suggests that executive functions allowed humans to internalize action into thought and have an internal dialogue that allowed them to understand the world and behave accordingly.

Barkley also asserts that executive functions evolved to allow humans to adapt in a variety of ways. These adaptations included the ability to engage in social exchange or reciprocal altruism, imitation, vicarious learning, self-regulation, gestural communication, and private behavioral rehearsal, among others.

According to Barkley, viewing executive functions as an adaptive advantage that allowed humans to develop their superior cognitive abilities is a better conceptual model than any approach that simply views executive functions as computer-like cognitions. For instance:

> The brain-as-computer framework is of limited value for it is devoid of history, detached from human motives, and sanitized of the general selection pressures to which all life must answer (genetic replication and its attendant adaptive problems). It is decoupled from the specific niche-related adaptive problems with which human ancestors had to contend. (Barkley, 2001, p. 27)

In sum, executive functions developed over time for the purpose of helping individuals get along socially and to manage their emotions and behaviors. The phrase "check your tongue" is instructive. Some people have difficulty inhibiting their true thoughts about particular topics or other people, and thus state aloud what they are thinking. Many times, this unfiltered behavior creates controversy, hurts other people's feelings, or creates social conflict. An individual who is able to "check themselves" and refrain from making inappropriate comments embodies the executive functions, and the vital ways in which they contribute to self-regulation.

PROXIMAL MECHANISMS

One of the challenges of learning about executive functions is that there is not a consensus about the exact processes that comprise them. As reviewed by Kalbfleisch and Loughan (2012, p. 391), all of the following are definitions and/or components of executive functions:

- skills related to planning, monitoring, and regulating behavior;

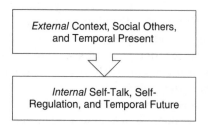

FIGURE 5.1 Evolution of Executive Functions

- ability to maintain adequate problem solving over time for the purpose of attaining future goals;

- multiple processes that include planning, decision making, judgment, and self-perception;

- metacognition, which resembles executive functions and includes monitoring, planning, organization, coordinating knowledge and resources, and self-regulation;

- skills that are requisite for goal-directed and purposeful activity, volition, planning, purposeful action, and effective performance;

- goal-directed behaviors;

- a set of general-purpose control processes that regulate one's thoughts and behaviors;

- and many others.

Although scholars disagree on the precise set of executive functions, there are several that appear in multiple conceptual models. Some of these are examined here. *Working memory* is the ability to maintain mental representations that are in active memory and manipulate them for behavioral purposes. *Attentional control* is the ability to focus on environmental demands in the face of distractions, irrelevant information, and habitual or overlearned behaviors. *Updating* is the ability to constantly monitor and rapidly add or delete information from working memory. *Planning* is the ability to manage current and future-oriented task demands. *Inhibitory control* is the ability to modulate unwanted thoughts, emotions, and actions and stop one's behavior. *Emotional control* is the modulation of emotional responses to the environment. *Mental flexibility* or *set shifting* is the ability to move from one stimulus to another as environmental circumstances demand. *Performance monitoring* is the ability to self-evaluate one's work or performance. *Concept formation* is the ability to begin tasks and devise problem-solving strategies. *Effortful control* is the subordination of a dominant or prepotent impulse in favor of a subdominant but socially appropriate one.

It is insightful for readers to review the aforementioned list of executive functions and to think about their own level of functioning. In virtually every case, an individual will be strong in one or multiple areas of executive functioning but have difficulties in other areas. That is normal and expected. No one is perfect with regard to the performance of their executive functioning; everyone has strengths and weaknesses. However, an individual who has pervasive deficits in multiple areas may be experiencing executive dysfunction and thus will likely have problems regulating their emotions and behavior. It is these individuals—those who experience problems regulating their emotions and behavior—who are likely to need the assistance of social work professionals. The inability to self-regulate one's emotions and behavior contributes to problems with social functioning, substance use, antisocial behaviors, and in many cases leads to involvement in social services and the criminal justice system.

A complicating aspect of executive functions is that they are overlapping and coordinated processes. Because the main purpose of executive functions is to regulate behavior, the proximal mechanisms that influence executive functions relate to emotion, rewards, and relationships. These areas are examined next.

Emotion, Rewards, and Relationships

As examined in Chapter 4, a major role of the prefrontal cortex involves modulating emotions. As shown in Figure 5.2, executive functions that relate to cognitive processes are known as *cold executive functions* whereas those that relate to affective/emotional processes are known as *hot executive functions*. The cold/hot metaphor suggests that cognitive processes have less emotional valence whereas hot functions have high emotional valence.

The differences between cold and hot executive functions are both metaphorical and

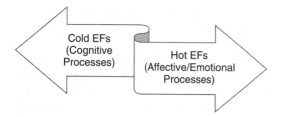

FIGURE 5.2 Cold and Hot Executive Functions (EFs)

neurological. People with disorders such as ADHD, which are characterized by cold processes, including inhibition, attention, and cognitive timing, show abnormalities in brain regions involved in these tasks. In contrast, disorders, such as CD, that are characterized by hot processes that regulate affect and motivation show abnormalities in regions of the brain that regulate these tasks (Rubia, 2011).

Experimental research has shown that hot and cold executive functions produce different behavioral outcomes in the face of situational inducements, or temptation. In one study, people in a cold, nonaroused state used cognitive factors to support self-control when presented with tempting stimuli. Those in a hot, aroused state used cognitive factors to commit impulsive behavior, such as staring at an attractive woman or smoking a cigarette (Nordgren & Chou, 2011).

The same hot/cold metaphor is useful for understanding how individuals relate to others, especially when their relationships include negative experiences. For example, experimental research has shown that when people think about a time in their life when they perceive themselves to have been rejected, the emotional response to that rejection depends on their attentional control. Persons who attended to the physiological and emotional aspects of their rejection were likely to have increased anger, hostility, and negative affect. On the other hand, persons who attended to aspects of the rejection that distracted or distanced themselves from it manifested less negative emotion (Ayduk, Mischel, & Downey,

2002). In other words, attending to cold aspects of a social experience, even if it is negative, allows one to regulate oneself in a healthier, more positive way. Attending to hot features of it in turn produces similarly hot negative emotions. The larger conclusion is that attentional control is an essential way for individuals to regulate their behavior in productive ways.

Emotion, rewards, and relationships have differential value and importance depending on an individual's age. Teenagers, for example, are notorious for their unpredictable decision making and apparent deficits in executive functioning. This reflects neurological development over the life course. Cohen et al. (2010) insightfully explained this concept:

> Adolescence is a unique period in psychological development that is characterized by increased risky choices and actions as compared with children and adults. This may reflect the relatively early functional development of limbic affective and reward systems in comparison with prefrontal cortex, causing adolescents to make poor decisions and risky choices more often than both children (who are not yet fully sensitive to rewards) and adults (who are sensitive to rewards, but have the ability to exert control over reward-driven urges). (p. 669)

From that perspective, the well-known increase in antisocial behavior during adolescence reflects the difficulty that frontal areas of the brain have in modulating reward and emotional impulses from subcortical areas.

When executive functions are unable to modulate emotion and reward-based motivations, the result is *behavioral disinhibition*, which is a general behavioral tendency characterized by failure to inhibit antisocial behaviors because of susceptibility to emotional impulses and rewards, such as substance use. Behavioral disinhibition subsumes delinquent behavior and substance use, and research has shown that much of the variance in it stems from genetic factors. For example, Krueger et al. (2002) analyzed data on 1,048 male and female 17-year-old twins selected from the Minnesota Twin Family Study, which is a birth-record-based epidemiological study of twins born in Minnesota. Krueger et al. used variance decomposition modeling to explore the degree to which externalizing behaviors that subsumed adolescent antisocial behavior, CD, alcohol dependence, and drug dependence had its origins in heritability and environmental forces. They estimated that the heritability of externalizing behaviors was .81. In a similar study based on different data, Young, Stallings, Corley, Krauter, and Hewitt (2000) examined 172 MZ and 162 DZ twin pairs recruited through the Colorado Twin Registry and the Colorado Longitudinal Twin Study. They examined a composite measure of behavioral disinhibition that contained symptoms of CD and ADHD, drug use, and novelty seeking and found that 84% of the variance in this general antisocial trait was accounted for by genes.

In a study of the overlap between ADHD symptoms, ODD, and subsequent CD, Lahey et al. (2009) found that genetic factors accounted for 57% of the variance in CD and 31% of the variance in ODD. Moreover, ODD and ADHD symptoms at ages 4 to 7 years predicted conduct problems at ages 8 to 13 years. That finding was based on a large sample of 6,466 youth from the children in the National Longitudinal Survey of Youth study.

If deficits at managing emotion and reward are mostly genetic in etiology, how can social work professionals effectively intervene? There are many interventions that target executive functions, including cognitive behavioral therapy, cognitive restructuring, and related modalities that are designed to help individuals (particularly drug users) change the way they think, process their emotions, and respond to behavioral drives. For instance, dual processing interventions help substance users to manage social cues and emotional self-regulation. The goals of dual processing interventions are to help addicts develop multiple responses to internal feelings: restructuring their beliefs; developing cognitive coping responses, especially in high-risk settings; and generating healthy emotional and behavioral responses. Matto, Strolin, and Mogro-Wilson (2008) found that this approach is helpful in reducing drug cravings and boosting self-efficacy.

One of the main goals of social work professionals is to assist clients in developing healthy psychological ways of thinking and behaving. Gaining these skills will positively impact a client's general psychosocial functioning and overall well-being. For instance, persons with low self-esteem often have greater histories of rejection and social exclusion, and thus are likely to focus their attentional control on these negative experiences, which can lead to low self-esteem. However, researchers have shown that high attentional control can assist individuals with low self-esteem in overcoming their reactions to rejection, thus improving their psychological health (Gyurak & Ayduk, 2007). In other words, an executive function—attentional control—can overcome psychological deficits to produce greater psychological health. Social workers who utilize this knowledge have the potential to effectively reverse their client's negative life experiences.

SPOTLIGHT TOPIC: ADHD

Social worker professionals and forensic social workers often have extensive contact with individuals with *attention-deficit/hyperactivity disorder (ADHD)*. What is today known as ADHD was once referred to as "defect of moral conduct," "defect of moral control," "post-encephalitic behavior disorder," "hyperkinetic disease of infancy," "minimal brain damage," "minimal brain dysfunction," and others. There are three types of ADHD: one that relates predominantly to impulsivity, one that relates predominantly to hyperactivity-impulsivity, and a combined type that includes both. The criteria for ADHD read like a list of executive dysfunctions. According to the American Psychiatric Association (2000, pp. 92–93), the symptom list for inattention includes:

- often fails to give close attention to details or makes careless mistakes in schoolwork, work, or other activities;
- often has difficulty sustaining attention in tasks or play activities;
- often does not seem to listen when spoken to directly;
- often does not follow through on instructions and fails to finish work;
- often has difficulty organizing tasks and activities;
- often avoids, dislikes, or is reluctant to engage in tasks requiring sustained mental effort;
- often loses things necessary for tasks or activities;
- is often easily distracted by extraneous stimuli; and
- is often forgetful in daily activities;

The symptom list for hyperactivity and impulsivity includes:

- often fidgets with hands/feet or squirms in seat,
- often leaves seat in classroom,
- often runs about or climbs excessively,
- often has difficulty playing or engaging in leisure activities quietly,
- is often on the go as if driven by a motor,
- often talks excessively,
- often blurts out answers before questions have been completed,
- often has difficulty awaiting turn, and
- often interrupts or intrudes on others.

These symptoms must be present prior to age 7 years and there must be evidence of impairment in two or more settings such as home, school, or other.

There is ample evidence that ADHD is effectively a disorder of the executive functions. A meta-analysis of 83 studies including nearly 4,000 participants with ADHD and nearly 3,000 without it found that people with ADHD have significantly worse executive functioning. Specifically, people with ADHD displayed impairments in response inhibition, vigilance, working memory, and planning compared to those without the disorder (Willcutt, Doyle, Nigg, Faraone, & Pennington, 2005). These deficits compromise social development and functioning across the life course. Many individuals with ADHD manage the disorder with treatment and medication.

One of the best ways that social work professionals can help children and adolescents with ADHD and their families is to help parents get involved in their child's treatment. The executive function deficits that children with ADHD have contribute to a range of issues that can impair the entire family, including overall family functioning. Meta-analytic research found that parents who get involved in their child's treatment are likely to positively impact child internalizing symptoms and child academic problems (Corcoran & Dattalo, 2006). These improvements contribute to greater family functioning and better relations between parents, children, and siblings. Moreover, these interventions are grounds for optimism at treating children with ADHD and improving their social functioning.

For Reflection

What are some specific ways that family members can get involved to facilitate improved treatment outcomes for children with ADHD?

EXECUTIVE FUNCTIONS AND PSYCHOSOCIAL RELATIONS OVER THE LIFE COURSE

The assorted executive functions are strongly heritable, which means that variance in these outcomes is attributable to genetic factors. For example, researchers at the Institute for Behavioral Genetics at the University of Colorado examined sources of variance in three executive functions: response inhibition, updating working memory representations, and set shifting, a function similar to multitasking. They found these executive functions are influenced by a common factor that is 99% heritable, making executive functioning among the most heritable psychological constructs (Friedman et al., 2008). This means that much of the variance in executive functions in the population is attributable to genes and the neural pathways that develop from them. Just as intelligence is strongly based in genetic factors, so too are executive functions.

As shown in Figure 5.3, in addition to these neurogenetic factors, a host of environmental factors are also associated with executive functions and attendant neuropsychological deficits. Drawing on nationally representative data from the National Longitudinal Study of Adolescent Health, Beaver, Vaughn, DeLisi, and Higgins (2010) found that a variety of biosocial, socialization, and demographic factors explained variance in neuropsychological deficits. Specifically, prenatal exposure to cigarette smoke, breastfeeding duration, maternal involvement, household income, and race were significant predictors of executive function deficits. Social work practitioners will likely notice that many of these predictors of neuropsychological deficits are entirely preventable. By understanding neuropsychological deficits, social work professionals can impart this knowledge to their clients, positively improving the executive functioning of their children and thus improving the health, lifestyle, and parenting practices of young families.

Fetal Environment and Infancy

The first months of life is a time of tremendous development with regard to executive

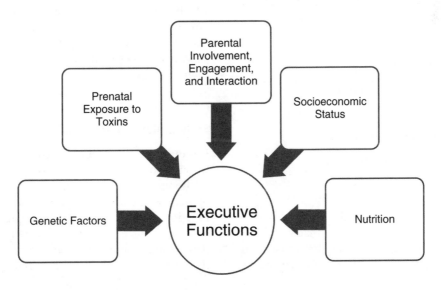

FIGURE 5.3 Etiological Factors in Executive Functions

functioning and the infant's ability to regulate himself or herself and to interact with the environment. Similar to Barkley's theory about the evolutionary development of executive functions from external to internal, developmental psychologists (e.g., Kopp, 2002; Munakata, Snyder, & Chatham, 2012) have shown that children's brains begin to understand that behavior can be goal directed, and increase their capacity for memory and for proactive in addition to reactive behavior. For example, infants:

- develop alertness by focusing on caregiver faces,

- engage in eye contact,

- develop emotional responses to the sight of a caregiver's face,

- distract themselves by orienting to a new stimulus,

- discriminate between objects and subjects in their environment,

- attend to novel stimuli,

- remember goal-based stimuli,

- coordinate visual attention with fine-motor skills,

- look toward sounds,

- engage in joint attention,

- begin to gesture to caregivers,

- point,

- imitate environmental stimuli,

- attend to objects and others, and

- perform many other tasks.

These are some of the skills that are seen in healthy infant development and that reflect an explosion of connections in the brain. It is also during infancy that pathological impairments in executive functioning can be seen. For example, children with autism commonly display deficits in these areas, especially eye contact and joint attention due to their inward focus. Joint attention is when there is shared focus with another individual such as looking at a picture or reading a story together.

Another area where early-occurring deficits potentially portend a behavioral disorder is ADHD. In an ingenious study, Auerbach et al. (2005) examined 158 healthy male infants, some of whom were at familial risk for ADHD based on paternal symptoms of the disorder. They found that children at risk for ADHD had executive deficits in terms of their self-regulation skills. Infants whose parents displayed features of ADHD were more emotionally reactive, labile, and irritable, and were less efficient at self-quieting ability. These neuroregulatory problems were also seen when children were examined again at age 7 months. Their conclusion was fully compatible with the biosocial, cell to society theme of this text: "Behavioral markers of vulnerability to ADHD may be present in the neonatal period. There is also the possibility that these markers are nonspecific, that is, they are indicative of risk for psychopathology, but which type of pathology will be primarily determined by the caretaking environment" (Auerbach et al., 2005, p. 223). Moreover, these findings support the notion that executive processes are strongly neurogenetic in their etiology.

Early Childhood and Childhood

It is during early childhood, when children transition from being at home to spending 30 to 40 hours per week at school, that the developmental course and implications of executive functions become clear. School imposes on children a set of expectations and responsibilities that require emotional, behavior, and cognitive control. The bulk of children are able to negotiate the transition from home to school well and their sociocognitive skills are sufficiently developed and developing to handle the new stressors and opportunities of school. For reasons that relate to their executive functioning, other children struggle to regulate themselves and are at risk for problems and maladaptive behavior.

A fascinating way to examine the emotional and behavioral health of children, and by proxy, their executive governance is to study what they draw. For instance, the Draw A Person test involves children drawing a picture of a man, a woman, and of themselves, and provides insight into psychopathology in a noninvasive way. Matto and her colleagues (Matto, 2002; Matto, Naglieri, & Clausen, 2005) have shown that human figure drawing is able to predict internalizing symptoms net the effects of other correlates of those symptoms. In addition, drawing is useful for nonverbal children, such as those with apraxia or severe autism, and thus can provide information for social workers who work with nonverbal clients.

An umbrella term that typifies how well a child's executive functions are developed is self-control. Children who are high in self-control are poised to perform adequately to well in school and social settings. Children with impairments in self-control face a different pathway. Research has shown how importantly executive deficits relate to behavioral regulation. For example, drawing on data from the Early Childhood Longitudinal Study, Kindergarten Class of 1998–1999 (ECLS-K), Beaver, Wright, and DeLisi (2007) found that executive functioning as measured by fine and gross motor skills was significantly related to childhood self-control, even while controlling for the effects of parental involvement, parental withdrawal, parental affection, family rules, physical punishment, neighborhood disadvantage, sex, race, and prior self-control. Children with poorer executive functioning had lower self-control, which is

essential for self-regulation and conduct problems. In the event that executive functions are impaired, there is significant risk for impaired behavioral health later in life. For example, psychologists have found that a childhood diagnosis of ADHD is among the strongest predictors of life-course-persistent criminal offending (Odgers et al., 2007).

Social workers often work in school settings and are asked to assess the behavioral problems of students. They often play a vital role in addressing the needs of children and their families. Despite the problems that deficits in executive functions cause for children, there is ample evidence that social services, education, and treatment programs are effective at helping them (Diamond & Lee, 2011). Important takeaway points are:

1. Children with the greatest executive function deficits show the greatest gains from education programs. In this way, executive function training goes a long way to reduce the cognitive and behavioral gaps that exist between controls and children with executive dysfunction, such as those with ADHD.

2. The greatest improvements in child executive functioning are seen from intensive, demanding programs.

3. Executive function training can be cost-effectively accomplished in regular classrooms, and its use in public school curricula provides the greatest promise for large-scale improvements. Programs that combine executive function training with exercise (e.g., martial arts) tend to show better effects among older children.

4. Effective programs reduce classroom stress, improve child self-confidence and self-efficacy, and increase bonding with prosocial peers. These factors are in turn associated with improved executive functioning and academic achievement.

SPOTLIGHT TOPIC: PSYCHOTROPIC DRUG TREATMENT

Many social work clients, such as persons with autism, anxiety, depression, and ADHD, take medication to alleviate their symptoms relating to executive dysfunction, emotional regulation, and related behavioral regulation. The use of psychotropic medication for children and adolescents is controversial. Although many medications have helped to reduce problem behaviors and sharpen the focus of youth with neuropsychological deficits, there is nevertheless concern about the long-term consequences of these drugs on the developing brain.

How do social work professionals feel about psychotropic drug treatment? Moses and Kirk (2006) examined this question using survey data from members of the National Association of Social Workers. Their findings showed the multifaceted ways that social workers feel about the use of psychotropic drug treatment for youth. For instance:

- 81% felt that psychotropic medication was a necessary treatment for many emotional disorders.
- 60% felt that the benefits of medication far outweigh the costs.
- Only 9% felt that medication was the best way to get adolescents' behavior under control.
- 89% felt that medication should always be accompanied by other forms of therapy.
- Nearly 81% felt that medication without other therapy left unchanged the basic problems that youth have.
- 68% felt that all other treatment options should be explored before using medication.
- 67% felt that medication was used as a substitute for other treatments.
- Nearly 41% felt that medication was often given to youth because of their parents' poor parenting.
- Nearly 16% felt that medication could make youth even more disturbed.

Overall these results indicate a remarkable balance between polar positions where psychotropic medication is seen as a panacea and where any form of medication is viewed as harmful and unnecessary. Social workers see the potential in medication, and recognize that it is one component of an effective and efficacious service plan.

Adolescence

Beginning in childhood and continuing through adolescence, executive functioning of children has important cascading effects on their parents, their own conduct, and the dynamics between them. A large-scale study of 26,000 4th through 12th graders in Sweden is telling. Glatz, Stattin, and Kerr (2011) analyzed a subsample of more than 700 youth who displayed behavioral indicators of executive dysfunction including inattention, hyperactivity, and impulsivity. They found that these characteristics tended to cluster within youth who displayed all of these deficits—this is essentially the profile of combined-type ADHD. The executive dysfunctions contributed to self-regulation problems and unresponsiveness to correction and discipline. These problems lead parents to believe that they are powerless to control their children. This sense of powerlessness results in parents investing less in their children in terms of talking with them and discussing their schoolwork and other activities.

Instead, parents tend to focus almost exclusively on control-based parenting practices that, by their own admission, are unlikely to work given the executive and behavioral deficits that their children display.

Adolescents with ADHD perform worse on delay discounting, which is the time one must wait in order to receive a reward, compared to peers without ADHD. In addition, there is evidence that adolescents with ADHD rate themselves as more impulsive than their peers without the disorder. Both of these findings are significantly predicted by dopamine genes responsible for innervation of the prefrontal cortex (Paloyelis, Asherson, Mehta, Faraone, & Kuntsi, 2010). Delay discounting has obvious implications for school performance and functioning, where many rewards are only achieved after extensive gratification delay. In addition, if teens with ADHD view themselves as simply more impulsive than others, it could set into motion a self-fulfilling prophecy even if treatment or medication has reduced their impulsivity.

Taken together, the network of problems relating to executive deficits provides interlocking opportunities for social work professionals to intervene and to provide treatment. Competent intervention by social work professionals could make the difference in the psychological development of children. Such interventions would positively impact individuals, families, and the systems with which they interact. Providing interventions to bolster deficits relating to attention, impulsivity, emotional regulation, and decision making is the first step in the intervention process. Involving parents in the intervention process helps both the parents and the child understand how executive improvements will contribute to improved behavior and relationship functioning. When executive deficits are reduced or controlled via programs, medication, or both, the aversive effects of the deficits are also reduced. This helps parent and child see each other in a new light, and presumably increases opportunities for meaningful communication and sharing.

Unfortunately, interventions sometimes are not successful or are ignored, and the problems relating to executive dysfunction persist. In a broad perspective, deficits in executive functions contribute to maladaptive and antisocial forms of behavior. A large body of literature demonstrates that executive functioning is a central part of antisocial behavior. For example, Morgan and Lilienfeld (2000) conducted a meta-analysis of 39 studies that encompassed 4,589 participants and found that antisocial groups performed 0.62 standard deviation units worse on executive functioning tests than their control groups. This is a medium to large effect size. Participants included those with antisocial personality disorder, CD, psychopathy, delinquent status, or offender status. The effect sizes were largest for groups whose criminal behavior had attracted the attention of the criminal justice system and resulted in a correctional or judicial status.

Recently, Ogilvie, Stewart, Chan, and Shum (2011) conducted a significantly larger meta-analysis of studies that explored the linkages between neuropsychological deficits, executive functioning, and antisocial behavior. Building on the work by Morgan and Lilienfeld (2000), Ogilvie et al. examined 126 studies that involved 14,784 participants. They reported a medium-grand mean effect size, indicating that antisocial individuals have greater neuropsychological deficits than their conventional peers. Additionally, largest effects were found when comparing criminality and externalizing behavior disorders. In criminology, these deficits in executive functioning are often called *neuropsychological deficits*, defined as brain-based deficits in social cognitive processes that are risk factors for conduct problems and related maladaptive behaviors, such as unhealthy habits and school, relationship, and work problems.

An important way that social work practitioners can assist children and adolescents with executive dysfunction and similar disorders is to provide counseling and services at school. School social workers can complement the treatment that children receive in the community and at home, and serve as a social support to bolster children's mental, behavioral, emotional, and academic health. Franklin, Kim, and Tripodi (2009) conducted a meta-analysis of school social work practices and found they significantly reduce externalizing and internalizing problems among youth. School social work interventions also contribute to greater academic success, especially among students with better school attendance and grades.

Adulthood

Executive functions continue to exert an important influence on the general psychosocial functioning in adulthood. A lighthearted example will be illustrative. A common stereotype is that much older adults have worse driving skills than younger drivers in part because of declines in their mental sharpness. Recent research compared older drivers to younger drivers in controlled settings using a driving simulator and in naturalistic settings of actual road driving. In both settings, older drivers performed significantly worse on scanning and attention tasks at intersections—the types of mistakes that often contribute to traffic accidents (Pollatsek, Romoser, & Fisher, 2012). However, a training program using head-mounted cameras to show the older drivers their lack of scanning and attention resulted in improvements in their driving performance. In short, a simple training intervention largely rectified the problem, which in part suggests executive deficits.

Another important area showing the relevance of executive functioning is financial health. The executive functioning deficits that contribute to threats to physical and mental health (e.g., overeating and obesity, smoking, substance use, alcohol use, gambling, etc.) also relate to one's creditworthiness. A recent study examined the relationship between gratification delay or time discounting and credit score (Meier & Sprenger, 2012). They found that adults with better gratification delay had significantly higher credit scores, and this relationship withstood the effects of income, education, age, sex, race, and total borrowing history. Specifically, persons in the lowest quartile of time discounting had a credit score of about 590. Those in the highest quartile of time discounting had a credit score of about 620. The 30-point difference has important implications for the terms and conditions of borrowing money for important investments, such as home ownership.

Adults with deficits in executive functioning that relate to ADHD show a wide range of impairments relative to their peers without ADHD. A large-scale study using an epidemiological sample of more than 43,000 participants found that adults with ADHD are at an elevated risk for a multitude of psychiatric problems, including bipolar disorder, several personality disorders, generalized anxiety disorder, PTSD, and others (Bernardi et al., 2012). In addition, adults with ADHD display significant deficiencies in inhibitory control, as evidenced by gambling, spending problems, and reckless driving. They also show worse planning, indicated by quitting a job without knowing what to do next and making sudden changes in career or personal goals. Adults with ADHD also have significantly more lifetime traumas, lower social functioning, worse mental health, lower emotional health, and poor physical health than peers without ADHD. Despite the toll that ADHD wreaks on adults, fewer than half ever seek treatment for the disorder (Bernardi et al., 2012).

SPOTLIGHT TOPIC: IMPROVING EXECUTIVE FUNCTIONS

Given the genetic and neural basis of executive functions, it is commonly though incorrectly assumed that little can be done to improve an individual's functioning and subsequent behavior. Fortunately, that is not true and there are a range of interesting programs that have been shown to improve executive functions among diverse participants. Computerized cognitive training to improve executive functions have shown promising results among the elderly, children with ADHD, and adults with schizophrenia, and there is emerging evidence for this approach among persons with autism, anxiety disorders, mood disorders, and TBI (Vinogradov, Fisher, & de Villers-Sidani, 2012). A sampling of some interesting and effective approaches includes:

Interactive computerized training programs using music have been shown to improve scores on verbal intelligence tests among preschoolers. The 20-day training led to improved functioning among 90% of the sample, and IQ score was positively correlated with brain plasticity during an executive function task (Moreno et al., 2011). Interestingly, only the music training worked; a similar protocol that used art did not result in the improvements.

The *Tools of the Mind* curriculum targets inhibitory control, working memory, and cognitive flexibility among at-risk preschool children. The curriculum consists of 40 activities that are designed to promote lower order executive functioning, including dramatic play, memory and attention tasks, and self-regulatory private speech, which involves telling oneself out loud what the appropriate behavior is. A recent evaluation indicated that children who are placed in the Tools of the Mind program demonstrated improved functioning compared to peers who were not in the program. Indeed, program involvement accounted for more variance in neuropsychological skills than age or sex (Diamond, Barnett, Thomas, & Munro, 2007).

Behavioral parent training is a behavioral modification program based on learning theory that teaches parents to identify and manipulate the causes and consequences of behavior. Commonly used for children with deficits in executive functioning and conduct problems, it involves daily behavior checklists and report cards, establishing and enforcing rules, developing time-out procedures, and developing problem-solving techniques that help parents mold their child's conduct. It has been shown to be effective at improving the parent–child relationship, the psychosocial functioning of children with attention and behavior problems, and reducing delinquency and related problem behaviors (Chronis, Chacko, Fabiano, Wymbs, & Pelham, 2004).

Researchers in the Netherlands examined the effect of working-memory training, which enhances the ability to maintain and manipulate goal-relevant information on alcohol use among a sample of middle-age adults who were problem drinkers. They found that 1 month of working-memory training contributed to declines in drinking, and that the effects lasted more than 1 month after the end of the intervention (Houben, Wiers, & Jansen, 2011). Overall, the training led to better control over impulses to drink alcohol.

One of the main correlates of cognitive and memory decline is aging; thus interventions are often targeted toward adults to improve their executive functioning. For example, Lutz et al. (2009) evaluated the effects of a 3-month intensive training course in focused-attention meditation among adult respondents. They found that the program increased the stability of attention, reduced the effort required to sustain attention, and sharpened brain responses (as measured by electroencephalography) to task-related sensory inputs.

Mindfulness training involves the use of meditation to become aware of and accept mental and emotional realities. The approach is theorized to enhance well-being; increase relaxation while decreasing stress; improve self-awareness; and enhance behavioral, cognitive, and emotional regulation. Research has shown that brief-meditation mindfulness training improves executive functions relating to self-regulation among incarcerated juvenile delinquents (Himelstein, Hastings, Shapiro, & Heery, 2012).

Sex Differences

Social work practitioners with clinical experience may be aware of anecdotal sex differences in behavior among their clients. Probably the clearest difference is the disproportionate link between externalizing symptoms among boys and men and internalizing symptoms among girls and women. Although behavior and psychopathology suggest universality in some respects, it also suggests clear sex differences. This is particularly apparent in executive functions. Consider this powerful summary:

> Differences favoring males are seen on the mental rotation test, spatial navigation including map reading, targeting, and the embedded figures test although there are conflicting studies regarding the latter. Males are also more likely to play with mechanical toys as children, and as adults, they score higher on engineering and physics problems. In contrast, females score higher on tests of emotion recognition, social sensitivity, and verbal fluency. They start to talk earlier than boys do and are more likely to play with dolls as children. (Baron-Cohen, Knickmeyer, & Belmonte, 2005, p. 819)

In addition to these overall trends, a recent study of psychosocial functioning, antisocial personality, and reading comprehension highlights the sex differences in executive functioning. DeLisi et al. (2011) used a statistical technique that finds unobserved or latent groups of similar individuals among a sample of 432 middle school students. They found evidence of four groups or classes. Class 1 contained nearly 72% of the sample and characterized children who were healthy in terms of their executive functions. They displayed few if any problems relating to inattention and hyperactivity, and had the highest reading comprehension scores. In other words, this group, which was 52% female and 48% male, served as a normative control group. Class 2 contained less than 12% of the sample and contained youth who displayed features consistent with ADHD, predominantly inattentive type. This group had a male to female ratio of nearly 3:1.

Class 3 was 7% of the sample and contained youth who displayed features consistent with ADHD, predominantly hyperactive/impulsive type. It was more than 56% male and nearly 44% female. Class 4 was 9.5% of the total sample and contained youth whose executive functioning resembled ADHD, combined type. The youth in Class 4 were the most psychopathic and the least accomplished scholastically. The male to female ratio for this severe group was nearly 4:1.

Disorders that relate to executive functioning—whether ADHD, autism, CD, or psychopathy—show marked sex differences, in which men are much more affected than women. Baron-Cohen (2003) has suggested that sheer brain differences reflect different executive strengths and weaknesses for men and women.

According to this theory, women's brain circuitry is advantaged for *empathizing*, which involves inferring the mental states of others and responding in emotional ways. Conversely, men's brain circuitry is advantaged for *systemizing*, which is the capacity to analyze input-operation-output relations and inferring rules that govern such systems. To support his model, Baron-Cohen argues that autism reflects an "extreme male brain" characterized by enhanced systemizing and impaired empathizing.

Although debates about core brain differences as a major explanation for sex differences in behavior are far from settled, there is little doubt of significant sex differences in executive functions. Depending on the particular function or skill, some favor women whereas others favor men.

EXPERT'S CORNER: RUSSELL A. BARKLEY, PROFESSOR OF PSYCHIATRY AND BEHAVIORAL SCIENCES, SUNY UPSTATE MEDICAL UNIVERSITY

Russell Barkley is perhaps the leading scholar-practitioner in the area of ADHD in the United States. He conducts workshops on ADHD around the world and has been instrumental in advancing the scientific understanding of this disorder and executive dysfunction generally (see http://www.russellbarkley.org). A central idea of his about executive functions and ADHD surrounds the idea of the internalization of cognitive and behavioral factors that were once external. What does this mean? Developing children often talk incessantly (especially to their parents) about topics that interest them, environmental stimuli, and their thoughts. As children progress through the preschool years, they learn to internalize much of this activity and engage in "self-talk" as a way to modulate their thoughts and actions.

Barkley (1997a, 1997b, 2001) suggests that four executive functions are related to behavioral inhibition. These are:

- Nonverbal working memory, which involves covert, self-directed sensing of visual and auditory stimuli.

- Verbal working memory, which is the self-speech related to reflection, problem-solving, and self-questioning.

- Self-regulation of affect, motivation, and arousal, which serves as the basis or capacity to support goal-motivated behavior. This self-regulation is essentially willpower.

- Reconstitution involves the flexibility to analyze social situations and devise behavior that is appropriate given the context.

Children with deficits in these areas are less able to internalize their speech, cognition, and behavior and thus present with the common features of executive deficits and even ADHD. The importance of internal self-dialogue is seen in the treatment literature, where a major goal is to help youth stop, think, and internalize their thoughts and words before articulating them. In doing so, children are better able to avoid harmful and unproductive behaviors.

SUMMARY

In sum, executive functions are an example of complex brain science that manifest in simple daily cognitions and behavior. How we think, plan, decide, organize, regulate, and behave largely reflect executive functions and the interplay between cortical and subcortical regions of the brain. Executive dysfunctions are relatively stable and largely genetic in origin; however, a range of modalities have shown success at improving executive functions in children, adolescents, and adults. This is promising because severe impairments in executive functioning are found in populations that are commonly seen by social work practitioners, clinical social workers, and juvenile justice practitioners. Key chapter summary points are as follows:

• Executive functions are a set of cognitive functions that broadly involve emotional and behavioral regulation, planning, decision making, and related tasks.

• The evolution of executive functioning enabled human development and broadened humans' intellectual capacity.

• Barkley's model suggests that executive functions reflect the internalization of speech, emotion, and conduct and a future orientation compared to external constraints that cause behavior.

• Cold executive functions involve cognitive processes and distinct neural circuits, whereas hot executive functions involve affective/emotional processes and other neural circuits.

• A host of disorders, especially ADHD and autism, involve impairments in executive functioning.

• Although executive functions are largely genetic in origin, a range of treatment modalities and interventions have shown success in improving these functions among children, adolescents, and adults.

• Social work practice often involves cognitive restructuring, emotional training, and decision-making tasks that broadly serve to improve executive performance.

• Neuropsychological deficits are a strong correlate of antisocial behavior in large part because they reflect impairments in cortical control of emotional impulses and rewards.

• ADHD is among the most common neurobehavioral disorders and reflects impulsivity, activity, and deficits in attention.

KEY TERMS

Attention-deficit/
hyperactivity disorder (ADHD)

Attentional control

Behavioral disinhibition

Behavioral parent training

Cold executive functions

Concept formation

Effortful control

Emotional control

Empathizing

Executive functions

Hot executive functions

Inhibitory control

Mental flexibility or set shifting

Neuropsychological deficits

Performance monitoring

Planning

Systemizing

Tools of the Mind

Updating

Working memory

CHAPTER 6

TEMPERAMENT

Social work practitioners work with an array of clients. Each client brings (hopefully) some protective factors, and unfortunately some risk factors, that serve to facilitate or complicate their treatment. Some clients are relatively easy, whereas others are more of a challenge to service providers. Consider some of these examples:

• A case worker who assists treatment and counseling staff serving juvenile delinquents on probation has a client who seems to be wound up like a toy. The 17-year-old boy is in constant motion, talks excessively in all situations even when it is not appropriate, and likes to "be where the action is." He feels that he "must" go out seven nights per week to any party in town, where he often finds substance-using peers and gets into trouble.

• The same caseworker has another 15-year-old female client who appears to be the polar opposite of the boy just mentioned. She always prefers to be by herself and withdraws from interaction with others. She rarely attends school because of the social networks and perceived social pressures there, and has difficulty in treatment because she is unwilling to open up and talk with treatment staff.

• A human services caseworker assists a family whose daughter is severely autistic and has a range of sensory problems. Despite her cognitive and social deficits, the young girl has an irrepressibly positive spirit and is almost always in a good mood. In turn, the girl's mother and father have responded to her condition with a ferocious advocacy that has resulted in many strides in her development.

• A social worker attends home visits with her client's parole officer. The client was recently released from prison after serving time for armed robbery, and is attempting to reenter society and resume his relationships with his wife and two sons. The sons (ages 11 and 13 years) have responded to their dad's return in very different ways. The younger son is cold and aloof, and appears unemotional not only about his father's return but also about most interpersonal matters in general. The older son is having a greater difficulty responding to the transition, and his characteristic moodiness, anger, and negativity have worsened.

These profiles present a host of constructs that are meaningful to understanding variance in positive and antisocial forms of behavior. Client 1 relates to activity level, extraversion, and an approach-oriented interpersonal style. Client 2 relates to introversion and a withdrawal-oriented interpersonal style. Client 3 shows (as we explored in Chapter 2) the myriad ways that environmental factors can blunt the effects of biological risks and demonstrates the power of positive emotionality. Client 4 has children with very different constitutions: One is characterized by callousness and unemotionality whereas the other is characterized by negative emotionality. In other words, the engine driving these constructs and the behavioral styles that unfold are temperament.

The idea that a person's temperament, personality, or more broadly their constitution is associated with their behavior is not new. Although its precise origin is unknown, the scientific study of temperament is attributed to Hippocrates,

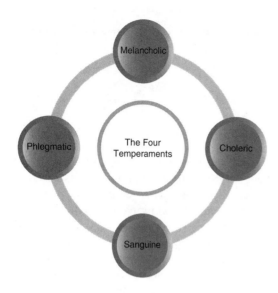

FIGURE 6.1 The Four Temperaments

who was born approximately 460 B.C.E. In the Greco-Roman typology of temperament based on body humors, there were four classifications of persons (Figure 6.1). The *melancholic* person was described as moody and anxious with a predominance of black bile. The *sanguine* person was described as cheerful, spirited, and good natured with a predominance of blood. The *choleric* person was angry and irritable with a predominance of yellow bile, and the *phlegmatic* person was slow to arouse with predominance of phlegm. These descriptions had important implications for individuals' emotions and self-regulatory abilities. Sanguine persons were sociable and had positive affect whereas phlegmatic persons were slow, stoical, even withdrawn. Melancholic persons were fearful and sad; choleric persons were aggressive, angry, and irritable.

In the second century, the physician *Galen* expanded the Hippocratic model of temperament and developed a conceptual model that would last nearly until modern times. A Roman physician of Greek ethnicity, he is also commonly known as Galen of Pergamon, which is modern-day Turkey. He is considered the leading Greco-Roman scholar in the study of temperament.

According to Galen, the four archetypal temperaments represented less than ideal types, where one bodily fluid represented an imbalance with natural elements and qualities of those elements. The natural elements were water, earth, fire, and air, and the qualities of those elements were cold, dry, moist, and hot. The phlegmatic person corresponded to water, north, and winter. The sanguine person corresponded to air, east, and spring. The choleric person corresponded to fire, south, and summer. The melancholic person corresponded to earth, west, and autumn. In other words, Galen's conceptualization of temperament drew many linkages that are consistent with a biosocial model of behavior. He pointed to the importance of weather, seasonality, environmental conditions, and most importantly, person–environment balance for understanding behavior. In addition, Galen's model advanced archetypal ways to understand different "types" of people (Arikha, 2007; Kagan, 1998; Stelmack & Stalikas, 1991).

Galen's approach to temperament was influential for centuries. Philosopher Immanuel Kant suggested, "To assign a man the title of a particular class we do not need to know beforehand what chemical composition of the blood entitles us to name a certain characteristic property of temperament; we need to know, rather, what feelings and inclinations we have observed in him (Kant, 1798/1974, p. 157). Indeed, Kant was so convinced of the relevance of temperament and the differential capacity that people had to experience guilt and other emotions, that he based his ideas on morality in rationality and reason (Kagan, 1998). Other influential social scientists ranging from Ivan Pavlov to Sigmund Freud to Michael Rutter similarly conducted temperament research in part inspired by Galen's methods.

In addition to its timeless scholarly history, temperament has been shown to transcend culture, language, and geography. For example, recent research found cross-national invariance for broad temperamental features among children sampled from Australia, China, Costa Rica, the Philippines, the United States, and

Zimbabwe (Benson, Oakland, & Shermis, 2009), suggesting it is a core feature of humanity. In short, temperament is relevant to ancient civilizations and contemporary social workers in that it provides a sound basis for understanding human behavior and its etiological bases. The next section explores major theories of temperament.

CASE STUDY: GLORIA

Gloria Munoz emigrated from El Salvador to Jersey City 10 years ago, at the urging of her husband, Jose Sr., who had emigrated 2 years before her to find work there. At the time of her departure, Gloria left behind a 3-year-old son, Jose Jr., and a 7-year-old daughter, Esmeralda, both of whom stayed in their rural Salvadoran-countryside home and were raised by Gloria's mother, Rose, and several aunts and uncles who lived nearby. In the United States, Gloria works cleaning houses and her husband, Jose Sr. works in construction. Two years ago, Gloria became pregnant again, with a daughter named Ana. Ana is now 2, Jose Jr. is 13, and Esmeralda is 17. Gloria works tirelessly cleaning homes and Jose Sr. has moved up to a supervisory position with his construction company and takes on additional overtime at every chance he gets, so the couple can save enough money to bring both of her children permanently to the United States.

Gloria's dream has always been to have her entire family reunited. Although Gloria and Jose Sr. talk to their son and daughter in El Salvador often by phone, they have rarely had the opportunity over the past 10 years to visit them in their home country. This has made both parents very sad, and they can hardly believe how much both have grown over the decade when they see pictures. Gloria knows that her son is having many motivational challenges at home; he is not currently employed and is not in school. Jose Jr. is very quiet, tends to keep to himself much of the time, and has limited contact with friends. He does like to work with his hands and has even built a bicycle out of used parts he collected. Esmeralda, by contrast, is in school but is not doing well academically. She hangs out with her friends both in and out of school, but Rose is concerned that she has been hanging out with a "bad crowd." Esmeralda admits to drinking and staying out late, but she says everyone she knows does the same and there's not much else to do anyway. Ana is a sweet, sociable, gregarious 2-year-old, and not worrisome to her parents because of her fearlessness and never-ending energy. Several months ago, Gloria and Jose Sr. found themselves in a Jersey City emergency room after Ana toppled off a bathroom window sill that she climbed onto after her bath when Gloria left the room briefly to get a towel from the apartment laundry room. Sometimes Gloria says she can't keep up with Ana during the day, and that her daughter can barely stay focused for more than a few minutes even to eat a meal. She does not know how much longer she can take Ana with her when she cleans houses, or how much longer she can keep up the energy level Ana requires.

Critical Thinking Questions:

- Based on the temperament literature, what are the three children's risk and strength profiles at their current ages? What do you think might have contributed to these profiles? How can the concept of goodness of fit, as discussed later in this chapter, be applied to the Munoz family?

- As a social worker, how might you come to better understand the attachment systems and differential developmental attachment processes that have occurred over time in the Munoz family? How might this exploration help you in understanding the children's unique dispositions and behavioral opportunities and challenges?

- Imagine that Gloria and Jose Sr. are able to bring Jose Jr. and Esmeralda to the United States next year. What do you anticipate as being challenges to the transition for the two children? Who do you think might adapt more successfully? What kinds of social work services or interventions might be considered for each child, based on their anticipated needs?

- Change one cultural artifact of this story. How might your assessment and intervention as a social worker working with this family be different? How might these temperaments and behavioral dispositions be interpreted differently, given your change in cultural context?

DISTAL CONTEXT

What Is Temperament?

Temperament is an interesting concept that has utility in conventional wisdom, popular culture, science, and social work application. To the layperson and even the clinical practitioner, temperament describes the fundamental nature of an individual's usual behavior, way of interacting with others, and way of responding to environmental situations. Unfortunately, within the literature, there are many nonidentical definitions. Famed personality researcher Gordon Allport (1961) defined temperament as "the characteristic phenomena of an individual's nature, including his susceptibility to emotional stimulation, his customary strength and speed of response, the quality of his prevailing mood, and all the peculiarities of fluctuation and intensity of mood, these being phenomena regarded as dependent on constitutional make-up, and therefore largely hereditary in origin" (p. 34). Bates (1989) defined temperament as "biologically rooted individual differences in behavior tendencies that are present early in life and are relatively stable across various kinds of situations and over the course of time" (p. 4).

Personality scientists Robert McCrae, Paul Costa, and their collaborators (McRae et al.,

2000) suggest that "personality traits, like temperaments, are endogenous dispositions that follow intrinsic paths of development essentially independent of environmental influences" (p. 173). Rothbart (2011) offers a more comprehensive definition:

> We have defined temperament as relatively stable, primarily biologically-based individual differences in reactivity and self-regulation [references omitted]. By reactivity, we mean the excitability or arousability of behavioral, endocrine, autonomic, and central nervous system response, as assessed through response parameters of threshold, latency, intensity, rise time, and recovery time. By self-regulation, we mean processes, such as attention, approach, avoidance, and inhibition; that serve to modulate (enhance or inhibit) reactivity. Behaviorally, temperament can be observed at all ages as individual differences in patterns of emotionality, activity, and attention. Phenomenologically, it is experienced as feelings of energy, interest, and affect. (p. 510)

Although these definitions are different, they obviously capture the same general set of ideas to describe a person. For the purposes of this text, *temperament* is the stable, largely inborn tendency with which an individual experiences the environment and regulates his or her responses to the environment.

THEORIES OF TEMPERAMENT

Alexander Thomas and Stella Chess

The pioneers of the contemporary study of temperament are *Alexander Thomas* and *Stella Chess*. Their New York Longitudinal Study examined 141 infants over a period of 6 years and utilized a reciprocal understanding of temperament in which infant reaction patterns, which were assumed to be innate or biologically driven, interacted with environmental conditions, such as the responses from their parents. Based on their observations, Thomas and Chess identified nine dimensions of infant temperament that were believed to have strong implications for their psychological and social development. Their nine dimensions were:

1. *Activity level* is the motor component a child displays and his or her general balance of active and inactive periods.

2. *Rhythmicity* is the child's regularity in terms of eating, sleeping, and elimination and relates to his or her general predictability.

3. *Adaptability* is characterized by responses to changes in children's environment and to new situations.

4. *Responses to novelty*, which can be either positive or approach oriented or negative or withdrawal oriented.

5. *Responsiveness threshold* is the intensity level of stimulation that is necessary to evoke a response.

6. *Intensity of reaction* to others is the energy level of this response.

7. *Mood quality* is the child's amount of pleasant, joyful, friendly behavior compared to its unpleasant, crying, and unfriendly behavior.

8. *Distractability* is the effectiveness of extraneous environmental stimuli in interfering with current behavior.

9. *Task persistence* relates to the child's attention span and persistence in continuing with an activity in the face of obstacles to maintaining the activity.

In their seminal work, Thomas and Chess (1977; Chess & Thomas, 1996; Thomas, Chess, Birch, Hertzig, & Korn, 1963) suggested three general types of children with relatively coherent temperamental profiles. *Easy children* were well-adjusted, *difficult children* were prone to conduct problems and externalizing conditions, and *slow-to-warm children* were more cautious and inhibited but still prosocial. Decades later the same three profiles were observed, although using sophisticated latent-profile analyses that locate unobserved groupings in data. Researchers in the Netherlands, for example, found a well-adjusted "typical" group, an "expressive" group with increased externalizing problems, and a "fearful" group at risk for internalizing problems (van den Akker, Dekovic, Prinzie, & Asscher, 2010). Although more sophisticated taxometric analyses indicate that temperamental types are more different in degree than in kind (Walters, 2011), the content areas of child temperament in Thomas and Chess's work are still relevant today.

The other seminal contribution from Thomas and Chess centered on what today would be understood as the biosocial interaction between child temperament and their early home environment, such as the relationship with parents. Chess and Thomas (1999) called this interaction goodness of fit. According to them:

> Goodness of fit results when the properties of the environment and its expectations and demands are in accord with the organism's own capacities, characteristics, and style of behaving. When consonance between organism and environment is present, optimal development in a progressive direction is possible. Conversely, poorness of fit involves discrepancies and dissonances between environmental opportunities and demands and the capacities of the organism, so that distorted development and maladaptive functioning occur. (p. 3)

In other words, *goodness of fit* is the match between child temperament and parenting strategies that produces the best opportunities for prosocial development and behavior.

Jerome Kagan

Jerome Kagan has enjoyed a lengthy career studying child development and temperament and has made numerous contributions to the field. The cardinal feature of his temperament research centers on persons characterized as either high reactive or low reactive (see Figure 6.2). Both groups display clear physiological and psychological temperamental styles during early childhood (e.g., infancy), and these temperamental features often extend into adulthood. Indeed, inhibition to novel or unfamiliar stimuli is among the most heritable temperamental constructs (Emde et al., 1992).

High-reactive children are individuals with high activity levels and who respond with distress to unfamiliar stimuli, including other people and social situations. According to Kagan's (1998, 2003) research, about 20% of infants display a high-reactive temperament. They are prone to be shy, timid, and fearful when exposed to

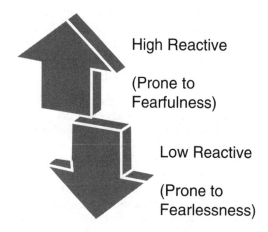

FIGURE 6.2 Kagan's Reactivity Temperament Model

unfamiliar events during toddlerhood. Of children who are high reactive, about one third become very fearful and display general inhibition. This characterization is not exclusive to Kagan's work, as other developmental psychologists have found that, beginning in toddlerhood, extremely uninhibited children remain so through middle adulthood (Pfeifer, Goldsmith, Davidson, & Rickman, 2002).

Low-reactive children are individuals who display lower levels of motor activity and minimal distress to novelty. About 40% of infants in most samples are low reactive. These children are prone to be sociable and relatively fearless. Among this group, about one third are extremely low reactive and are called *uninhibited*. In addition, there are physiological differences between low-reactive and high-reactive children, particularly among those who are inhibited. *Inhibited* children have higher baseline and accelerated heart rates and reduced heart rate variability, which points to the arousal connections in temperament.

Kagan explains these different temperamental styles by pointing to the limbic system, the part of the brain that processes emotional reactivity, and more specifically to the amygdala. High-reactive children have hyperreactive amygdalar responses to novelty, whereas low-reactive children have hyporeactive amygdalar responses to novelty. The *amygdala* is important because it is not only responsible for processing fear but also for processing uncertainty. In Kagan's work, inhibition is not necessarily proneness for fear, but is instead intolerance of uncertainty. For example, in a recent study (Schwartz et al., 2010), adults who were low reactive as infants and thus more likely to become uninhibited showed greater thickness in the left orbitofrontal cortex, which is implicated in the suppression of unpleasant feelings. On the other hand, those who were high reactive as infants and more likely to become inhibited showed greater thickness in the right orbitofrontal cortex.

Mary Rothbart

Mary Rothbart and her colleagues have studied infant temperament for decades, and have identified several important temperamental domains, including approach/positive affect (which is essentially extraversion), fear, irritability and anger, effortful control, and duration of orienting or sustained attention. These constructs are apparent in infancy and are stable based on her longitudinal study of children and their families. For instance, Rothbart, Ahadi, and Evans (2000) found that fear assessments at ages 3, 6, and 13 months predicted a child's fearfulness (or fearlessness) at age 7 years. Similar predictive continuity was found for anger/frustration occurring between infancy and age 7 years. In other words, like other temperament scholars, Rothbart demonstrated the continuity in child temperament from the earliest months of development.

Among her many contributions, Rothbart (1981) developed the Infant Behavior Questionnaire-Revised, which is an important instrument for assessing temperamental constructs during infancy. It contains 14 subscales for approach, vocal reactivity, high-intensity pleasure, smile and laughter, activity level, perceptual sensitivity, sadness, distress to limitations, fear, recovery from distress, low-intensity pleasure,

cuddliness, duration of orienting, and soothability. Factor analysis (a quantitative technique that reduces data into core components or factors) conducted on these subscales produced three broad temperamental dimensions: surgency/extraversion, negative affectivity, and orienting/regulation (Gartstein & Rothbart, 2003; Rothbart, 2007) and are explored in detail next.

As mentioned earlier, although Rothbart's (2007) research demonstrates the importance of an array of temperamental constructs, the essence of her work centers on three broad dimensions of temperament (see Figure 6.3). The first, *effortful control*, relates to a general sense of self-control and includes four subcomponents. *Attention control* is the capacity to focus and shift attention when desired. *Inhibitory control* is the capacity to plan future action and suppress inappropriate responses. *Perceptual sensitivity* is the awareness of slight, low-intensity stimuli in the environment. *Low-intensity pleasure* is the pleasure derived from stimuli involving low intensity, complexity, novelty, and incongruity.

The second dimension in Rothbart's work is negative affectivity. *Negative affectivity* is the frequency of negative mood based upon experiencing negative emotions. *Frustration* is the

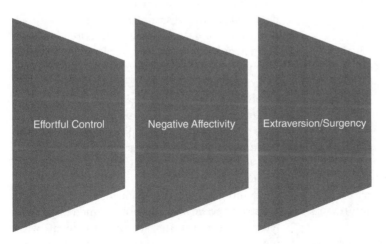

FIGURE 6.3 Rothbart's Temperament Model

Effortful Control   Negative Affectivity   Extraversion/Surgency negative affect stemming from the interruption of ongoing tasks or goal blocking. *Fear* is the negative affect associated with the anticipation of distress. *Discomfort* is the negative affect related to sensory qualities of stimulation including light, movement, sound, and texture. *Sadness* is the negative affect and lowered mood and energy related to exposure to suffering, disappointment, and object loss. *Soothability* is the rate of recovery from peak distress, excitement, or general arousal.

The third dimension in Rothbart's (2007) temperament model is *extraversion/surgency*, which is the tendency to approach stimuli in an excitatory as opposed to inhibitory way. An easy way to think of this dimension is that extraverted people tend to "surge" toward social interaction. There are seven subdimensions of extraversion/surgency. *Activity* is the level of gross motor activity that the person displays. *Low-shyness* is the behavioral inhibition to novelty and challenge, especially when it is of a social nature. *High-intensity pleasure* is the pleasure derived from activities involving high intensity or novelty. *Smiling and laughter* is a positive affect in response to stimuli. *Impulsivity* is the speed of response initiation. *Positive anticipation* is positive excitement and anticipation of expected pleasurable activities. *Affiliation* is the desire for warmth and closeness to others.

Robert Cloninger

One of the influential models of temperament and personality is the biosocial approach of Robert Cloninger and colleagues. According to Cloninger (1987), temperament forms the emotional core of personality and is theorized to involve heritable neurobiological dispositions to emotions and their corresponding automatic behavioral reactions. Temperamental traits are thus heritable biases in the ways that individuals respond to danger, novelty, and reward (Figure 6.4).

The brilliance of Cloninger's theoretical model is that it explicitly links temperamental

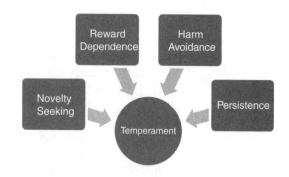

FIGURE 6.4   Cloninger's Temperament Model

constructs to neurotransmitter systems (Cloninger, 1987; Cloninger, Svrakic, & Przybeck, 1993). *Novelty seeking* is characterized by a heritable tendency of frequent exploratory activity and intense feelings of joy/satisfaction in response to novel or appetitive stimuli (other conceptual models refer to it as *sensation seeking*). Dopaminergic pathways are believed to underlie novelty seeking. Individuals who score highly on novelty seeking are impulsive, irritable, exploratory, and extravagant. Low scorers are deliberate, reserved, thrifty, and stoical.

Harm avoidance is characterized by a heritable tendency of intense avoidant or inhibitory responses to stimuli. Serotonergic pathways underlie harm avoidance, which can be understood as the restraint-oriented opposite of novelty seeking. Individuals who score highly on harm avoidance are pessimistic, fearful, shy, and fatigable. Low scorers are optimistic, daring, outgoing, and energetic. *Reward dependence* is involved in behavioral maintenance involving conditioned responses to reward and the avoidance of punishment. Norepinephrine is believed to underlie it. Highly reward-dependent people are sentimental, open, warm, and appreciative, whereas low scorers are detached, reserved, cold, and independent. A fourth temperamental construct, *persistence*, was not assigned an underlying neurotransmitter system. Individuals with high scores on persistence are industrious, determined, enthusiastic, and perfectionistic. Low scorers are inert, spoiled, underachieving, and pragmatic.

Cloninger's model has served as a useful guide toward understanding the genetic architecture of personality. Heath, Cloninger, and Martin (1994) compared the personality systems of Cloninger, which include harm avoidance (theorized to be associated with serotonin neurotransmission), novelty seeking (theorized to be associated with dopamine neurotransmission), and reward dependence (theorized to be associated with norepinephrine neurotransmission) with those of Hans Eysenck, which include extraversion, neuroticism, social conformity, and toughmindedness. Genetic factors accounted for between 54 and 61% of the stable variation in these traits (Heath et al., 1994).

Arnold Buss and Robert Plomin

Arnold Buss and Robert Plomin (1975) were more vocal about the genetic underpinnings of temperament. In their view, temperamental traits needed to satisfy five basic conditions: (a) heritability, (b) stability across childhood, (c) retention into adulthood, (d) being adaptive, and (e) being present in other species. Many of these conditions will sound familiar from topics explored in Chapter 2. Buss and Plomin's conceptualization is deeply rooted in behavioral genetics and an evolution-based understanding of human behavior.

Like most temperament researchers, Buss and Plomin tended to focus on specific components of temperament in their model. They developed a tripartite EAS model, which represents emotionality (E), activity (A), and sociability (S), that together embodied the ways that an individual regulated his or her feelings and emotions, the ways that he or she acted and behaved, and the ways that he or she engaged the social world. Based on the focus on the stability of temperamental dimensions, Buss and Plomin viewed temperament as the forerunner of adult personality.

There is profound evidence for the view that temperament and personality constructs are under considerable genetic influence. For instance, Plomin (1990)—among the most eminent behavioral scientists in the world—noted that personality dimensions yield heritability estimates ranging from 20 to 50% based on a multinational study of over 30,000 twin pairs. Recall that this means environmental factors are responsible for between 50 and 80% of the variance in personality. However, some parts of temperament were more strongly heritable. For example, Plomin found that both neuroticism and extraversion were about 50% heritable. In another comprehensive review, Thomas Bouchard and John Loehlin (2001) reported that about 50% of variance in personality traits was heritable for all of the Big Five domains.

Even in middle childhood, temperament is largely under genetic control. For instance, heritability estimates for negative emotionality and self-regulation capacity are comparable to those observed in infancy (Mullineaux, Deater-Deckard, Petrill, Thompson, & DeThorne, 2009). It is also stable. Broad dimensions such as positive emotionality, negative emotionality, and constraint have been shown to be significantly stable from toddlerhood (in one study, ages 18–29 months), and middle childhood (ages 6–10 years; Neppl et al., 2010). Consistent with Buss and Plomin's conceptualization, the relative stability of temperamental features speaks to their important biological and biosocial bases.

Central Nervous System and Evolutionary Underpinnings

Pet owners and livestock farmers often readily understand the study of temperament for good reason: They can see temperamental variation in their animals. There are many examples of this. Within a species, some animals will have an easygoing demeanor, whereas other animals will be more challenging to feed and care for. Some dogs appear to be highly neurotic and find it difficult to relax, whereas other dogs appear completely nonneurotic and relax easily. The former type is useful for protection, because his or her system is more tightly wound, more perceptive to environmental stimuli, and more aroused overall. The latter type is useful for being a play companion for children because of his or her calm, relaxed temperament. Indeed, particular breeds of dogs are bred for the express purpose of having a pet with specific temperamental or demeanor traits.

The evolutionary underpinnings of temperament reflect the processes of natural selection, in which physiological processes, such as the ability to be fearful of threatening stimuli, provide a protective feature to human behavior. Recall from Chapter 2 that a large part of evolutionary history also involves random, neutral genetic mutations that in turn contribute to differential neural substrates in the brain. This in turn relates to differential autonomic, endocrine, and other system differences found in the variance of temperament (Buckingham, 2002). For example, introverts have greater tonic (or baseline) brain activity than extraverts. As such, introverts have

an optimal level of arousal at lower levels of stimulation and thus do not require additional or excessive stimulation. In contrast, extraverts have suboptimal arousal, which necessitates seeking out additional stimulation to achieve homeostasis. This simple difference helps to explain the association between extraversion/introversion and behavior. To illustrate, self-regulation reflects the degree to which an individual can regulate or control themselves generally and in the midst of environmental situations. Self-regulation involves the inhibition of what we want to do in favor of what is appropriate given the situation. It encompasses involuntary reactions that are largely driven by fear and voluntary reactions that require effort. It is often used interchangeably with self-control and effortful control. In this way, introverts with strong self-regulation are seemingly disposed against opportunities for problem behavior, whereas extraverts with weak self-regulation are seemingly disposed toward opportunities for problem behavior.

SPOTLIGHT TOPIC: THE CRIMINOLOGY OF THE AMYGDALA

An advantage of using temperament to understand the biosocial nature of behavior is that it is directly linked to neurological functioning and the physiological processes that stem from it. Neuroscientists and even criminologists have particularly focused on the amygdala, a central part of the brain's limbic system. The main function of the amygdala is to detect stimuli in the environment that could be threatening to the individual. When stimuli are novel or unknown, or when the brain has already memorized a stimulus as threatening (a function performed by the hippocampus), the amygdala produces signs of fear in the autonomic, somatic, and endocrine systems. In other words, those instantaneous feelings of fear that arise during extremely scary, dangerous situations are the product of the amygdala.

The amygdala is central to a prominent theory of psychopathy developed by Blair, Mitchell, and Blair (2005). According to the theory, psychopaths display a variety of deficits relating to fear induction, or learning what stimuli should generate an appropriate fear response. Reduced responses include neural responses to threatening stimuli, aversive conditioning, emotional responses in anticipation of punishment, emotional responses to imagined threatening events, startle reflex to aversive stimuli, and others. These deficits cause impairments not only in distinguishing right from wrong but also in learning from punishment. Given the amount of antisocial behavior that psychopaths commit, it has been suggested that the amygdala is an essential brain region for criminology (DeLisi, Umphress, & Vaughn, 2009).

Of course, as Kagan's work makes clear, the amygdala and the construct of fear are not only pertinent to the fearless behavior displayed by psychopathic individuals, but also to the fearful behavior displayed by individuals with high-reactive temperament styles (e.g., infants who cry vigorously in response to unfamiliar sights, sounds, and smells, and individuals who develop anxiety-related disorders). In other words, among persons characterized as fearful, the amygdala is overreactive to novelty in the environment. Among persons characterized as fearless, the amygdala is underreactive to novelty in the environment, among other things. Thus, temperament and neural substrates that mediate temperament relate to both externalizing and internalizing conditions and related behaviors.

For Reflection

What are some of the advantages and disadvantages of a fearless temperament?

Over the years, a range of explanatory models (in addition to Cloninger's temperament model) have been developed to explain the phylogenetic development of the arousal systems associated with temperamental variation. In terms of a general behavioral theory, Gray's (1982) influential BIS/BAS theory, as described in Chapter 3, seeks to explain both behavioral restraint/inhibition and approach (in addition to the fight or flight system, which controls sympathetic nervous system responses to stressful environmental stimuli). Gray's system has clear implications for temperamental contributions to both internalizing and externalizing conditions, and demonstrates the ways that psychological traits are rooted in a deeper neural and hormonal basis.

More recently, van Goozen, Fairchild, Snock, and Harold (2007) suggest that reduced serotonergic functioning and stress regulating system, such as the HPA axis and the autonomic nervous system, interacts with adverse early-childhood environments to increase susceptibility to severe, persistent antisocial behavior. Children with these deficits neither understand dangerous settings nor display appropriate emotional response to these settings. As a result, they do not physiologically experience the threat of dangerous settings via autonomic or endocrine stress response. This leads to a vicious cycle of selecting dangerous settings and a muted response to the dangers therein. They are incapable of normal stress responses to situations that typically cause anger, embarrassment, and most importantly, fear.

PROXIMAL MECHANISMS

Prefrontal Cortex and Executive Governance

Many of the neuropsychological deficits that social work clients display generally relate to liabilities in executive governance and the appropriate inhibition of inappropriate behavioral responses—or in plain language, *self-control*. Self-control is extraordinarily important toward the understanding of both conventional and deviant behavior. As Moffitt et al. (2011) assessed, "The need to delay gratification, control impulses, and modulate emotional expression is the earliest and most ubiquitous demand that societies place on their children, and success at many life tasks depends critically on children's mastery of such self-control" (p. 2693). The lasting effects are made clearer when considering the implications of high self-control. For instance, Tangney, Baumeister, and Boone (2004) examined the effects of self-control on an array of outcomes among 351 undergraduates. Students with high levels of self-control had higher grades, higher self-esteem, fewer psychiatric symptoms, drank less, ate better, had better interpersonal skills, enjoyed better relationships, and were more emotionally healthy. In fact, there were no negative effects from having high self-control, such as feeling overly controlled.

In his work on emotional regulation, Davidson and colleagues (Davidson, 2001, 2003; Davidson,

Putnam, & Larson, 2000) describe the important interplay between *prefrontal or cortical* and *limbic or subcortical* regions in the appropriate ability to regulate negative emotion and conduct. According to his theory, the left prefrontal cortex is primarily involved in approach-related thoughts or the pursuit of appetitive goals, whereas the right prefrontal cortex is primarily involved in withdrawal-related or inhibited behaviors. Both frontal regions are responding to negative emotions such as fear and uncertainty emanating from the amygdala. This neural circuit explains why antisocial persons are characterized by negative emotions/affect and the reaction to that negativity. According to Davidson (2001), "Individuals who report greater dispositional negative affect and who show increased reactivity to stressful events are more likely to be those individuals who have difficulty regulating negative affect and specifically in modulating the intensity of negative affect once it has been achieved" (p. 662).

In short, the prefrontal area of the brain is essential for understanding behavior, but the interplay between these regions and other areas of the brain is needed to fully understand the neural bases of behavior. One of those important regions, the limbic system, is explored next.

The Limbic System, the Amygdala, and Emotional Processing

The limbic system (*limbic* meaning on the edge, margin, or border of the cerebral hemisphere), was purportedly discovered by and attributed to Paul Broca in 1878. But it was not until the 1930s and 1940s that the contemporary understanding of the limbic system and its role in memory, emotional learning, and fear conditioning was established, most famously in work by Papez (1937) and MacLean (1949, 1955). Papez was seminal in articulating the role of emotional processing in the limbic system, but focused mostly on the hippocampus. In MacLean's (1949, 1955, 1990) influential *triune brain hypothesis*, the limbic system was referred

to as the paleomammalian component of the brain—phylogenetically younger than the reptilian brain, which controlled the most basic instinctual behaviors involved in the survival of the species, but older than the neomammalian brain, which controlled the most evolutionarily advanced (and thus human) behaviors centering on language, cognition, and executive functioning.

Two broad points are important to understand. First, the structures of the limbic system are important for processing emotional stimuli and influencing responses in the endocrine and autonomic nervous systems. Indeed, MacLean referred to the limbic system as the "visceral brain," suggesting that it was the anatomical seat of powerful emotions. Second, the limbic system is intimately connected via the thalamus to the frontal or cortical regions, where emotional information is modulated and controlled.

When the amygdala is under- or overresponsive to environmental threats, there are negative consequences in terms of emotional processing and often behavior. If the limbic system is too busy inferring threats from the environment, the individual is governed by the negative emotions that result from it. The result is the experiencing of acute fear and anxiety, even when those responses are not appropriate. If the limbic system is limited in detecting fear, the result is a fearless disposition, which can contribute to impulsive, poorly contemplated action.

Neurological Deficits

Neuropsychological functions broadly refer to cognitive and self-regulation processes, such as concentration, motor and cognitive planning, attention, goal formulation, self-awareness, self-monitoring of behavior, and perhaps most importantly, the suppression or modulation of cognitive and behavioral impulses. As explored in Chapter 5, executive governance problems are often discussed in the social sciences as relating to self-control or self-regulation. Children who have lower self-regulation often display neurological deficits, and there is synergy among neurological deficits, executive functioning, and antisocial behavior. For example, Morgan and Lilienfeld (2000) conducted a meta-analysis of 39 studies including 4,589 participants and found that antisocial persons performed 0.62 *SD* worse on executive functioning tests than comparison groups, which is a medium to large effect size.

Indeed a host of investigators link self-control to executive functions, neuropsychological deficits, and related constructs. Drawing on data from 325 individuals selected from the Pittsburgh Youth Survey, Raine et al. (2005) found that boys on the life-course-persistent pathway had significantly greater neuropsychological deficits compared to those in behaviorally less-severe comparison groups. Specifically, life-course-persistent offenders scored significantly worse on four measures of intelligence, two measures of spatial memory, and one measure of executive functioning. The life-course-persistent group also had a higher prevalence of ADHD diagnosis, higher child abuse victimization, higher child neglect victimization, more extreme family poverty, and had sustained a greater number of head injuries that resulted in unconsciousness.

Similarly, Beaver, Wright, and DeLisi (2007) reformulated self-control as an executive function and speculated that children with neuropsychological deficits would also have low self-control. Based on data from the ECLS-K, they found that neuropsychological deficits did predict self-control net the effects of parental socialization measures. Using data from the National Survey of Children, Ratchford and Beaver (2009) found that neuropsychological deficits predicted parent and teacher reports of self-control and a composite measure despite the competing effects of birth complications, low birth weight, parental punishment, family rules, neighborhood disadvantage, sex, race, and age.

In a longitudinal designed study with nationally representative data, Beaver, DeLisi, Vaughn, and Wright (2010) found that deficits in verbal skills were predictive of delinquency, violent delinquency, and low self-control across two waves of data that extended through adolescence. In a latent class analysis of data from the ECLS-K, Vaughn, DeLisi, Beaver, and Wright (2009) found that just over 9% of kindergartners comprise a severe impairment group characterized by deficits in verbal skills and attendant problems with higher impulsivity, higher externalizing behaviors, reduced self-regulation, reduced cognitive abilities, and greater classroom difficulties. In short, research on executive governance, particularly among children and adolescents who display neurological deficits, presents a profile that is consistent with temperamental constructs, including fearlessness, negative emotionality, and activity level.

Attachment and Neural Function

An important concept from Thomas and Chess's research is goodness of fit, which speaks to the match between a child's temperament and his or her parents' ability to supervise the child. When children are easy, they are, of course, relatively easy to parent. But when children have a more aversive temperament, they are likely to have more frequently negative interactions with their parents. Over time, this can complicate the parent–child bond and lead to less attachment between them. Ultimately, a poor fit between a child's temperament and his or her parents' ability to deal with that temperament contributes to family problems, the type that social work practitioners often must address.

A variety of scenarios bear on child attachment vis-à-vis temperamental constructs. According to Kochanska, Barry, Aksan, and Boldt (2008), "children's conscience, a complex system encompassing moral emotions, conduct, cognition, and self, is critical for mental health in that it is perhaps the most powerful factor that prevents disruptive, callous, and antisocial conduct" (p. 1220). In their longitudinal studies, maternal responsiveness to the child during the first year of life engenders a reciprocal responsive stance in the child that is observable by age 2 years. This responsiveness to others becomes enduring and generalized by age 52 months or so and constitutes the intact beginnings of the child's conscience. Disruptive behaviors at age 6 are more likely among children with deficits in their conscience. Importantly, conscience development occurs among children with diverse temperaments. For instance, fearless children—a correlate of externalizing behavioral risk—develop conscience in part due to secure attachment and maternal responsiveness (Kochanska, 1997; Kochanska, Aksan, Knaack, & Rhines, 2004; Kochanska & Murray, 2000).

Kochanska, DeVet, Goldman, Murray, and Putnam (1994) have shown that by age 3, conscience becomes more nuanced and includes affective discomfort, which encompasses feelings of guilt, apology, empathy, and concern with "making good" with parents after wrongdoing. Another facet of conscience is active moral regulation or vigilance, which includes confession and reparation following acts of wrongdoing, concern about others' wrongdoing, and internalization of codes of conduct—in other words, self-regulation (Kochanska et al., 1994).

Another way parents can steer the temperaments (and deficits) of their children centers on attention. Attention is critical for self-regulation both positively (e.g., shifting attention toward a positive stimulus to maintain appropriate arousal and emotion) and negatively (e.g., shifting away from a negative stimulus that alters arousal and emotion). Thus, mastering attention is crucial for children to modulate their arousal and emotion in specific settings, and to regulate their behavior to be appropriate to those settings (Derryberry & Rothbart, 1988). Parents should assist their children by modifying their environments to minimize negative stimuli and facilitate opportunities to attend to positive stimuli. For instance, Auerbach, Benjamin, Faroy, Geller, and Ebstein (2001) studied the effects of the *DRD4* (a dopamine receptor) and *5-HTT* (serotonin transporter) genes on sustained attention abilities among a sample of 64 1-year-old infants. They found that during structured play situations and on an information-processing task, infants with the 7R allele of *DRD4* displayed less sustained attention. Those with risk alleles for *DRD4* and *5-HTT* also demonstrated reduced sustained attention, which was characterized by latency to first look away, duration of looking at and manipulating toys, and facial indications of interest. Auerbach and her colleagues (2005) concluded that allelic variation in *DRD4* is a possible developmental link to ADHD based on early sustained attention and information processing. Because the dopaminergic system is involved in motivational or seeking behaviors, it has clear theoretical links to impulsive action. A recent meta-analysis indicated that *DRD4* was associated with not only impulsivity but also novelty seeking (Munafò, Yalcin, Willis-Owen, & Flint, 2008).

To summarize, children and adolescents who have neuropsychological deficits present with a range of problems relating to verbal skills, receptive language, sustaining attention, memory, response inhibition, and self-control. In school settings, these deficits create a host of problems for the child whose cognitive deficits and the maladaptive behavioral responses to those cognitive problems set into motion a dynamic, negative process whereby the youth becomes estranged from school and conventional peers. This cascade of negative interactions between the neuropsychological deficits and the responses to them also occurs at home and in other social settings, and contributes to aversive, often punitive responses from adults (DeLisi & Vaughn, 2011). The next section explores various psychiatric disorders that clearly implicate temperamental constructs.

DISORDERS RELATED TO TEMPERAMENT

Temperament is essential to psychiatric disorders and overall psychological functioning. The general logic around ancient civilizations' beliefs about temperamental humors relating to a person's overall mental health is still relevant today. Each day, we interact with people who appear to differ, and differ fundamentally, in terms of their predominant mood, level of activity, need to interact with others, ability to be alone, and the degree to which they can regulate their conduct. The mix of temperamental traits in our social work clients produces an interesting set of challenges that is unique to each caseload. Some clients are relatively easy to serve, whereas others are more challenging. As Thomas and Chess described, the most appropriate fit of staff skills and resources to the client's individual temperament provides the best opportunity for a good service outcome.

Broadly speaking, there are important linkages among temperamental constructs, psychiatric conditions, and behavior (Krueger, 1999; Whittle, Allen, Lubman, & Yücel, 2006). For example:

- Negative affectivity that relates generally to anxiety has clear relevance for major depression, dysthymia, and generalized anxiety disorder.

- Negative affectivity that relates generally to fear has clear relevance for panic disorder, social phobia, and specific phobia.

- Positive affectivity is negatively associated with major depression, dysthymia, and generalized anxiety disorder.

- Constraint has a strong, negative association with alcohol dependence, drug dependence, and antisocial personality disorder.

The consequences of maladaptive temperamental traits are enormously costly to society. For example, a recent population study of over 5,000 individuals in the Netherlands found that the annual costs of neuroticism were approximately $1.4 billion and were more than two and a half times as costly as other mental disorders (Cuijpers et al., 2010). Perhaps the clearest linkage between temperament and behavior is

seen in the criminological sciences. The more pronounced an individual's criminal propensity, often measured by their criminal career, the more intractable their behavior appears to be. As Loeber (1991) noted, "The behavior is particularly virulent; once in full bloom, it is difficult to eliminate through current available intervention techniques. In that sense, disruptive behavior is very enduring; it is also changeable, however, especially in the first 12 or so years of life" (p. 396).

To what type of conduct was Loeber referring? The following study is illustrative. Keenan and Wakschlag (2000) examined a sample of clinic-referred preschoolers from low-income neighborhoods. In this group, a bevy of disturbing behaviors were already present. More than 40% of these children blamed others, were easily annoyed, purposely annoyed others, argued with adults, defied adults' rules, and frequently lost their temper. Moreover, more than 40% started fights and bullied other children. As preschoolers, a handful of boys were involved in burglary, fire setting, theft with confrontation, and even forced sexual activity. These are the type of children who are expelled from preschool (Keenan & Wakschlag, 2000).

As shown in Figure 6.5, distinct neural pathways are shown to be associated with disorders that relate to high negative affect (seen in Pane a), high positive affect (Pane b), and constraint (Pane c). In disorders that are characterized by high levels of negative emotionality—what Galen would have called melancholic or choleric temperaments—there are neural connections between the hippocampus, the right side of the dorsolateral prefrontal cortex, and dorsal anterior cingulate cortex to subcortical regions including the amygdala and ventral anterior cingulate cortex.

For disorders that are characterized by high levels of positive emotionality (e.g., extraversion, sensation seeking, novelty seeking), there is a similar neural pathway that involves the left side of the dorsolateral prefrontal cortex and the dorsal anterior cingulate cortex to subcortical

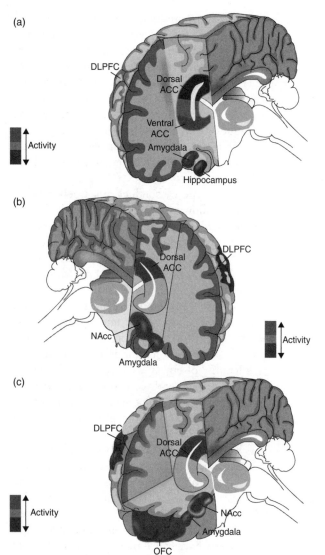

FIGURE 6.5 Brain Regions and Temperament

Source: Reprinted from "The Neurobiological Basis of Temperament: Towards a Better Understanding of Psychopathology," by S. Whittle, N. B. Allen, D. I. Lubman, and M. Yücel, 2006, *Neuroscience and Biobehavioral Reviews, 30*, 511–525, with permission from Elsevier.

DLPFC = dorsolateral prefrontal cortex
ACC = anterior cingulate cortex
NAcc = nucleus accumbens
OFC = orbitofrontal cortex

areas including the amygdala. Last, constraint involves a network linking the orbitofrontal cortex, dorsolateral prefrontal cortex, and dorsal anterior cingulate cortex to the amygdala and nucleus accumbens (Whittle et al., 2006). These neural pathways—the outcome of brain imaging research—demonstrate the commonality in temperament for allied disorders.

SPOTLIGHT TOPIC: PSYCHOPATHY

Few behavioral disorders capture the public imagination like psychopathy. Psychopathy is a clinical construct usually referred to as a personality disorder defined by a constellation of interpersonal, affective, lifestyle, and behavioral characteristics that manifest in wide-ranging antisocial behaviors (Hare & Neumann, 2008). On the interpersonal domain, it is characterized by glib or superficial charm, narcissism or grandiose self-worth, pathological lying, and conning/manipulation. In terms of affect, psychopathic personality is characterized by callousness and lack of empathy, failure to accept responsibility, shallow emotion, and lack of guilt or remorse. For the lifestyle dimension, psychopaths lack realistic life goals; have a parasitic orientation; and are globally irresponsible, impulsive, and stimulation seeking. On the antisocial dimension, psychopaths have poor behavioral control, evince early behavior problems, engage in juvenile delinquency, are criminally versatile, and have records of noncompliance/revocation of conditional release. In short, the theory of psychopathy describes a person who is selfish, self-centered, and self-motivated to secure his or her self-interest. This pursuit of self-interest is achieved through manipulation or force with little to no concern for the other person. In fact, the lack of concern for others is noteworthy because it occurs without guilt, remorse, or the most basic empathic notion that another person is being victimized (DeLisi, 2009).

An interesting literature has translated psychopathy into information that is relevant to the study of temperament, or more specifically, personality. For instance, according to Lynam and Widiger (2007), the core elements of psychopathy include extremely high interpersonal antagonism, pan-impulsivity, the absence of negative self-directed affect, the presence of angry hostility, and interpersonal assertiveness. What makes psychopathy such a fascinating disorder is that there are high levels of negative emotions that are all deflected outward. Pure psychopaths are noteworthy for their lack of anxiety and internalizing conditions, which explains why they feel nothing for their victims and appear to be without conscience.

Not surprisingly, psychopathic individuals display similar neural pathways as other antisocial persons discussed in this chapter. For example, in their review of brain abnormalities in antisocial persons, Yang, Glenn, and Raine (2008) concluded:

> In the frontal region, deficits in the prefrontal and anterior cingulated cortex may contribute to impulsivity, irresponsibility, poor decision-making, and deficient emotional information processing in antisocial individuals. In the temporal regions, the amygdala-hippocampal and superior temporal impairments may predispose to antisocial features such as inability to follow social rules, deficiency in moral judgment, and failure to avoid punishment. (p. 74)

Thus, temperament shows its versatility by virtue of its relevance to conventional behavior displayed by the majority of individuals, and extreme antisocial behavior displayed by psychopaths.

For Reflection

Consider the ways in which the psychopathy label should be used with caution. Should youth be designated psychopathic?

TEMPERAMENT OVER THE LIFE COURSE

Fetal Environment and Infancy

As discussed in Chapter 2, biosocial development occurs very early in life during gestation (even a generation earlier in the case of epigenetic effects) and exposure to healthy and pathogenic environments are associated in turn with prosocial development and maladaptive development. It is an incredibly important period of the life course because it reflects not only the true nature of an individual's temperament—before the environment has much time to affect it—but also the critical early phases of child development. In 1885, author Samuel Taylor Coleridge artfully captured this idea: "The history of man for the nine months preceding his birth would, probably, be far more interesting and contain events of greater moment than all the three score and ten years that follow it" (cited in DiPietro, Ghera, & Costigan, 2008).

An intriguing literature examines the fetal development of infant temperament. DiPietro, Hodgson, Costigan, and Johnson (1996) conducted a study of 31 fetuses at six gestational ages between 20 and 39 weeks and also gathered data on mother reports of the infant's apparent temperament at ages 3 and 6 months. They found that fetal neurobehavior accounted for between 22 and 60% of variance in the prediction of temperament scores. More specifically, higher fetal heart rate was associated with lower emotional tone, lower activity level, and unpredictability. Even more fascinating, more active fetuses were more difficult, active, and had greater difficulty adapting as infants.

A conceptually similar study examined the effects of maternal emotional activation during pregnancy on fetal response, and whether that fetal response had enduring predictive power on infant temperament at 6 weeks. Fetuses with greater intensity in their reaction to their mother watching a birth video, particularly the birth scene, demonstrated greater irritability during their 6-week developmental pediatric exam (DiPietro et al., 2008).

Drawing on data from neonates (ages 3–5 days), researchers in Taiwan compared the pain cries occurring before and after receiving a hepatitis B virus vaccine with mother-rated temperament at 1 month of age. They found that neonates with a more positive mood or disposition gave louder cries than negative neonates. Moreover, negative neonates—who cried with less intensity—showed poorer regulation. Their study suggested that cry acoustics could be an early marker of mood quality, activity, and adaptability (Jong et al., 2010). The early signs of temperament make sense given their heritability. For instance, in their behavioral genetic analyses of infant temperament, Goldsmith, Lemery, Buss, and Campos (1999) found varying heritability estimates for temperamental dimensions. For instance, soothability was 0% heritable and based entirely on shared and nonshared environment. However, other dimensions including negative affect ($h^2 = .64$), distress to novelty ($h^2 = .58$), activity level ($h^2 = .55$), distress to limitations ($h^2 = .66$), and duration of orienting ($h^2 = .45$) were moderately heritable (Goldsmith et al., 1999).

An array of fascinating findings on early temperament has been found. Crockenberg, Leerkes, and Barrig Jo (2008) noted that children who witness frustrating events, such as the removal of a toy, at age 6 months are more likely to be aggressive at age 2.5 years. Moreover, infants who shift attention away from frustrating events are more likely to be less aggressive. Research also suggests that mothers who do not help high-reactive infants shift attention away from frustration are also more aggressive later (Crockenberg et al. 2008). Similar to Thomas and Chess's goodness of fit idea, maternal behavior can exacerbate aggression in infancy. Using data from German mother–infant pairs, maternal assessments of their infant's distress response to novelty at age 4 months was associated with the child's behavioral inhibition at 14 months (Marysko, Finke, Wiebel, Resch, & Moehler, 2009).

Another novel way to access temperamental style is to measure anticipatory looking. Infants who can visually orient themselves tend to have greater self-regulation as indicated by a more cautious behavioral approach to novel situations. The importance of executive functioning among 6-month-olds is that it relates to the ability of infants to regulate themselves as they interact with the environment (Sheese, Rothbart, Posner, White, & Fraundorf, 2008). Auerbach et al. (2005) assessed 158 healthy male infants at 7 months of age, some of whom were at familial risk for ADHD based on paternal symptoms of the disorder. They found that children at risk for ADHD had regulation difficulties pertaining to irritability, state lability, and self-quieting ability.

The seeds of important behavioral disorders, such as ADHD, can also be seen during infancy. Children with the combined-type form of ADHD display developmental patterns characterized by extreme levels of positive approach to novel stimuli coupled with permissive socialization. In other words, infants constantly approach things that they want while rarely having their impulsive desires thwarted by parents or other caregivers. Between ages 6 to 18 months, this routine contributes to problems with regulation development. During infancy, children with ADHD display significantly greater activity levels during waiting situations where there is not a stimulus that is shown to be causing the active response (Ilott, Saudino, Wood, & Asherson, 2010).

In sum, it is during the first year of life that the temperamental seeds of both positive and negative behaviors are seen. It is also during the first year of life that parents respond to the temperamental cues from their infants, and adjust their parenting behaviors accordingly. Infants who are agreeable, unfussy, and predictable in their behaviors—suggesting self-regulation—are at very low risk for problem behaviors later in life. Such children are also relatively easy to parent because caregiving is so facile an experience. On the other hand, infants who are fussy and more difficult to predict in terms of their day-to-day behavior are more challenging. Far from being a facile experience, parenting a child with a more difficult temperament leads to aversive parent–child interactions and sets into motion the coercive family dynamics that are linked to problem behaviors occurring up to age 13 years in a recent study of nearly 2,000 children (Lahey et al., 2008).

Childhood

Based on the evidence presented thus far, it is perhaps surprising but nonetheless true to note the strength with which temperamental constructs affect behavior. Fortunately, the majority of children display a temperament that is mostly positive and allows children to appropriately respond to situations, interactions, and environmental conditions in an age-appropriate way. In other words, the bulk of children are compliant and display rare and often trivial forms of misbehavior. For other children, the biosocial interplay between their temperament and environmental conditions, such as interactions with parents, teachers, and peers, is more problematic. A large literature has explored the development of antisocial conduct very early in life. At this point in the life course, temperamental features can help steer a child along both prosocial and antisocial pathways. For example, 2-year-olds whose parents and teachers describe as "aggressive and rough" in their play are prone to continued problem behaviors in preschool and kindergarten (Keane & Calkins, 2004). Children who are exuberant at age 2 are more positive, less shy, and show greater interest in novel situations. However, if they lack appropriate effortful control, they are also prone to problem behaviors throughout the preschool period (Stifter, Putnam, & Jahromi, 2008).

At age 2, problems with emotional regulation and inattention strongly predict externalizing problems as children enter kindergarten. Indeed, one study found that a 1-SD increase in inattention increased the likelihood of a chronic, clinical behavioral problem 18-fold (Hill, Deg-nan, Calkins, & Keane, 2006). Keenan and Wakschlag (2000) reported that preschoolers as young as 30 months present symptoms that are consistent with serious behavioral disorders, such as ADHD, ODD, and CD. In their study of 79 clinic-referred preschool children ages 2.5 to 5.5 years, nearly 50% met criteria for CD and 75% met criteria for ODD. Nearly 27% met diag-nostic criteria for all three disorders. Some of these children were so aggressive and uncon-trollable that they were expelled from preschool. Susan Campbell and Linda Ewing (1990) found that 67% of children who were rated as hard to manage at age 3 years met diagnostic crite-ria for externalizing disorders at age 9, and the diagnostic data were validated by maternal and teacher reports. Hard-to-manage preschoolers display a troubling set of characteristics that lend themselves to prolonged antisocial conduct and compromised prosocial development. Mothers, fathers, and teachers report that hard-to-manage children as young as age 3 are noteworthy for their poor impulse control, oppositional tenden-cies, poorly developed social skills, inattention, and school problems (Campbell, 1994).

Temperamental constructs such as self-control, approach, and sluggishness can endure across periods of childhood. In a sample of 800 children from a New Zealand birth cohort, lack of control at age 3 years was significantly corre-lated with problem behaviors at age 15. Boys who lacked control at 3 years old were likely to have internalizing problems during late childhood and adolescence, to have externalizing and conduct problems during late childhood and adolescence, and to be less socially competent during ado-lescence. Similar effects were found for girls, although the correlation between age-3 lack of control and age-15 lack of social competence was even stronger (Caspi, Henry, McGee, Moffitt, & Silva, 1995).

Last, Raine, Reynolds, Venables, Mednick, and Farrington (1998) prospectively examined the interrelationships between fearlessness, stim-ulation seeking, and large body size among a sample of 1,130 male and female Indian and Creole children from the island of Mauritius. Children characterized as highly stimulation seeking at age 3 years were significantly likely to be highly aggressive at age 11, suggesting that toddler stimulation seeking is an important precursor of childhood aggression.

Adolescence

Drawing on data from the National Institute of Child Health and Human Development's Early Child Care Research Network Study of Early Child Care, a recent study examined the stability of self-control over a 10-year period when the children were ages 4.5 to 10.5 years. Over a period that began during the preschool years and extended toward the end of elementary school, they found considerable stability in self-control. Preschoolers who were characterized by very low levels of self-control (measured as 1 SD below the mean) remained that way throughout the study period. More importantly, by age 10.5, they were most discrepant from their peers. Similarly, children who were average and those who were above average (measured as 1 SD above the mean) were stable across the 6 years. Self-control also strongly covaried with deviance (Vazsonyi & Huang, 2010).

In a study of children ages 2, 4, and 6 years who had temperamental dispositions reflective of behavioral disinhibition showed strong as-sociations with behavioral disorders (Hirshfeld-Becker et al., 2002). Disinhibited children were about 2.5 times more likely than controls and 4.5 times more likely than inhibited children to develop a disruptive behavior disorder. The disparities for ADHD and ODD were similarly large. Other studies have found that the emo-tional regulation of frustration caused by delay of gratification is predicted by vagal tone and temperament among children as young as age 4. Children with low vagal tone and those with more irritable temperaments are less able to handle frustration (Santucci et al., 2008).

Caspi and Silva (1995) tracked a birth cohort from Dunedin, New Zealand, and explored their personality and temperamental paths from age 3 to 21 years. They found three types that were consistent with those developed by Thomas and Chess. The well-adjusted type included children who were capable of self-control, were adequately self-confident, and were generally fine when faced with new situations or upon meeting new people. The inhibited type included children who were fearful, socially reticent, and easily upset by strangers. The undercontrolled type included children who were impulsive, restless, negativistic or disagreeable, and emotionally labile. These were their characteristics at age 3.

Between ages 5 and 11, the undercontrolled children were consistently and significantly rated by parents and teachers to have externalizing problems. By ages 13 to 15, children undercontrolled at age 3 continued to be noteworthy for their externalizing behaviors in addition to internalizing problems. By 18, undercontrolled children had low constraint, were admittedly reckless and careless, enjoyed dangerous and exciting activities, scored high on negative emotionality, were aggressive, and felt alienated and mistreated by others. At 21, formerly undercontrolled children reported employment difficulties and conflicts with family and romantic partners. They were described as conflict prone, unreliable, and untrustworthy. They had problems with alcohol and often had extensive criminal records. Similar continuity was observed for the other two groups. Inhibited children developed into lives characterized as depressive, lacking agency and social connection, and prone to internalizing problems and the well-adjusted type who developed into normal young adults (Caspi, 2000; Caspi & Silva, 1995).

Other researchers have found that behavioral observations made at age 3 years significantly predict adult outcomes. For instance, Caspi and his colleagues (1995, 1996) conducted a longitudinal-epidemiological study in which 3-year-old children were classified into groups based on their behavioral disposition and re-assessed at age 21. Those who were described as undercontrolled or impulsive at age 3 were 2.9 times more likely than nonimpulsive children were to be diagnosed with antisocial personality disorder at age 21. Moreover, they were 2.2 times as likely to be repeat offenders and 4.5 times more likely to be convicted of a violent crime. Compared to a control group, formerly impulsive children were also more likely to attempt suicide and have alcohol problems. In this sense, serious adult psychopathology was the outcome of readily observable impulsivity problems at age 3. These effects were also seen at age 26.

In a classic study, Caspi, Elder, and Bem (1987) examined longitudinal data spanning 30 years on boys and girls ages 8 to 10 years who had frequent temper tantrums. Were temper tantrums merely a passing phase of late childhood or did they have enduring meaning? The results were alarming. They found that the explosive, poorly tempered outbursts of childhood similarly emerged in adult contexts when people had to subordinate themselves such as in work and school settings. Having a bad temper as a child predicted middle-adulthood occupational mobility (i.e., frequent job changes due to quitting or firing), educational attainment, and divorce, and these effects were similar for men and women.

A large-scale longitudinal study (Tracking Adolescents' Individual Lives Survey, or TRAILS) of Dutch adolescents shows that good parenting practices and higher socioeconomic status can moderate temperamental risks such as frustration (or general negative emotionality) and fearfulness. Teens at risk for delinquency and other externalizing behaviors remained crime free when buffered by parents who provided emotional warmth and higher socioeconomic status (Sentse, Veenstra, Lindenberg, Verhulst, & Ormel, 2009). These parent and socioeconomic effects are important because left unchecked, temperamental profiles clearly distinguish adolescents with externalizing problems. Specifically, youth with high levels of negative affect and low levels of effortful control are significantly at risk for problem behaviors (Oldehinkel, Hartman, De Winter, Veenstra, & Ormel, 2004).

Adulthood

The "long shadow" of temperament, as Kagan and Snidman (2004) called it, extends through adulthood. Indeed, its enduring effects in some cases are strongest for prosocial behaviors. For example, researchers in the Czech Republic assessed 83 participants and rated their temperament between ages 12 and 30 months. Three factors of temperament emerged: positive affectivity, negative affectivity, and disinhibition. The latter factors predicted extraversion and self-efficacy 40 years later. None of the other factors were associated with adult functioning (Blatny, Jelinek, & Osecka, 2007). In other words, who

we are during infancy in many respects portends who we are decades later.

There is even evidence to suggest that temperament contributes to longevity. In a longitudinal study of over 2,000 participants followed over 5 decades, there was ample evidence of a link between temperament and length of life. Activity level, emotional stability (or low neuroticism), and conscientiousness were associated with lower risk of death net the effects of other correlates of mortality. Specifically, every 1-SD increase in activity, emotional stability, and conscientiousness was associated with a 13%, 15%, and 27% risk reduction, respectively (Terracciano, Lockenhoff, Zonderman, Ferruci, & Costa, 2008). Conscientious people are disciplined, organized, resourceful, adaptive, and well-behaved. These features made them relatively easy to care for as children, and help them tend to avoid risky lifestyles and settings as adults.

EXPERT'S CORNER: JEROME KAGAN

In his long career, Kagan's academic work has hoped to bring popular attention to temperament and its implications. In many respects, temperament is the ideal construct to show how individual-level factors, mostly innate in origin, give rise to biosocial interaction. According to Kagan (1998), "The idea of temperament is not socially dangerous, even though the concept of inherent temperamental differences, like a speck of dirt on a fresh snow field, mars the democratic ideal by implying that some children are lightly burdened before the race of life begins, while others start with a tiny unfair advantage" (p. 18). One of these tiny advantages that has mostly interested Kagan is inhibition, and his research has produced exciting findings about the continuity and course of infants who are either inhibited or disinhibited.

Photo of Jerome Kagan
Courtesy of Jerome Kagan

During infancy, some children are timid to approach novel people, objects, and situations, whereas others spontaneously approach. Schwartz, Wright, Shin, Kagan, and Rauch (2003) conducted an fMRI study of adults who had been categorized as inhibited or uninhibited. They found significant amygdala responses to novelty, with the formerly inhibited children showing greater activation when shown novel faces. Two of the adults had been diagnosed with generalized social phobia, both of whom were inhibited during infancy.

Infants who are extreme in restraint or spontaneity to novelty also display significant physiological differences. In a landmark study, Kagan, Reznick, and Snidman (1988) found that inhibited children have lower thresholds for limbic-hypothalmic arousal to novelty and unexpected changes in the environment. The result is a range of outcomes, including childhood shyness to extreme forms of social avoidance. As they observed, "A frequent scene during the play sessions was a cluster of three or four children playing close to each other, often talking, and one or two children standing or playing alone one to several meters from the center of social activity. These isolated, quiet children were typically those who had classified as inhibited 5 or 6 years earlier." (p. 168)

Kagan's fascinating work has even pointed to the value of smiling. Four-month-olds who spontaneously smiled and interacted with the examiner of their sessions with smiles were significantly more likely to be low reactive, and this was seen even when respondents were age 15 years! In addition, Kagan and colleagues found that high-reactive children were less likely to smile than low-reactive children at every point of assessment and data collection—a period that spanned age 4 months to 15 years. In short, few temperament researchers have done more to demonstrate the enduring power of its features than Jerome Kagan.

Sources: Kagan, J. (1998). *Galen's prophecy: Temperament in human nature.* Boulder, CO: Westview; Kagan, J., Reznick, J. S., & Snidman, N. (1988). Biological bases of childhood shyness. *Science, 240,* 167–171; Schwartz, C. E., Wright, C. I., Shin, L. M., Kagan, J., & Rauch, S. L. (2003). Inhibited and uninhibited infants "grown up": Adult amygdalar response to novelty. *Science, 300,* 1952–1953; Kagan, J. (2010). *The temperamental thread: How genes, culture, time, and luck make us who we are.* New York: Dana Press.

SUMMARY

Temperament encompasses psychological and physiological characteristics that give rise to the typical ways that an individual experiences the environment and regulates his or her responses to it. Temperament is an important concept for social workers and helping professionals in general. Several highlights about temperament from this chapter follow.

• Temperament has been studied for thousands of years from Hippocrates and Galen in the Greco-Roman tradition.

• The four humors or temperaments are melancholic (moody and anxious) sanguine (cheerful, spirited, good-natured), choleric (angry and irritable), and phlegmatic (slow to arouse).

• Alexander Thomas and Stella Chess resurrected the study of temperament in the mid-1950s and presented three archetypal temperament profiles in children: easy, difficult, and slow to warm.

• The goodness of fit concept is essentially a biosocial interaction between child temperament and parenting behaviors/early home environment.

• Although several major temperament models exist, the common themes center on self-control/regulation, positive/negative emotionality, and approach/withdrawal-oriented styles.

• The frontal or cortical regions of the brain perform higher order cognitive and emotional functions that serve to modulate visceral emotional impulses from limbic or subcortical regions.

• Temperament is intimately related to a variety of psychiatric and behavioral disorders relating to mood, affective style, and antisocial behavior.

KEY TERMS

Amygdala

Chess, Stella

Choleric

Difficult children

Easy children

Effortful control

Extraversion

Galen

Goodness of fit

Harm avoidance

High reactive

Limbic/subcortical

Low reactive

Melancholic

Negative affectivity

Novelty seeking

Persistence

Phlegmatic

Prefrontal/cortical

Reward dependence

Sanguine

Self-control

Slow-to-warm children

Surgency

Temperament

Thomas, Alexander

Triune brain hypothesis

CHAPTER 7

PERSONALITY

The concept that most captures an individual's essential attributes is personality. Understanding the concept of personality is a crucial element in the study of human behavior and behavioral performance in life domains. Personality is intrinsically linked to behavior and it may, in some instances, be a matter of life and death. Case in point: A recent epidemiological study compared the relative effects of personality and socioeconomic status (SES) on mortality in the United States, and found that those in the 25th percentile of SES had a 43% greater chance of mortality than persons in the 75th percentile of SES (Chapman, Fiscella, Kawachi, & Duberstein, 2010). Essentially, individuals who had more money were found to be healthier and had a lower risk of death than those with less money. Interestingly, trends were uncovered for specific personality features. Individuals in the 75th percentile on the Neuroticism dimension had a 38% greater chance of mortality than individuals at the 25th percentile. That finding suggests that more worry and negative emotionality are unhealthy personality traits. Those at the 75th percentile on the Conscientiousness dimension had a 37% reduced likelihood of mortality than those at the 25th percentile. Overall, it was found that personality explained 20% of the mortality, whereas SES only explained 8% of personality risk. All of these effects were adjusted for demographic and lifestyle characteristics, also thought to influence mortality.

Conscientiousness is an important element of personality that deserves further discussion. It can be defined as taking greater care and attention in tasks and being governed by a strong sense of right and wrong. A major reason for the enduring link between conscientiousness and health factors is that conscientious people simply avoid behaviors that pose a risk to their well-being. Research on the personality profiles of drug users—a common type of client on many social worker caseloads—clearly shows this. Drawing on data from over 1,100 participants from the Epidemiologic Catchment Area program in Baltimore, Maryland (average age of participant was 57 years), Terracciano, Löckenhoff, Crum, Bienvenu, and Costa (2008) found marked differences in conscientiousness. Individuals who abstained from drug use had the highest levels of conscientiousness, whereas those who smoked cigarettes and used marijuana displayed much lower levels of conscientiousness. Those who were using cocaine and/or heroin displayed the lowest levels of conscientiousness among all participants. In fact, those who abstained from any drug use (including smoking) had significantly higher levels of conscientiousness compared to various smokers and substance users.

In a related study using the same data, Terracciano, Löckenhoff, Zonderman, Ferrucci, and Costa (2008) found that three personality traits were significant predictors of longevity: activity level, emotional stability, and conscientiousness. Of the three, conscientiousness was associated with the greatest health benefit. For every 1-SD increase in conscientiousness, there was a 27% reduction in mortality risk. It seems that conscientious people live longer.

In a meta-analytic review of 194 studies on conscientiousness and health-related behaviors, Bogg and Roberts (2004) found strong evidence that conscientiousness is associated with self-control behaviors. Specifically, individuals who are more conscientious were less likely to drink alcohol to excess, use drugs, have unhealthy eating habits, engage in risky driving or sexual behaviors, be suicidal, use tobacco, and commit violent crime.

The aforementioned research has clear implications for social work professionals. As a social worker, it is essential to understand all aspects of a client's personality. Often, social workers help clients to identify maladaptive personality characteristics that may be interfering with their lives. In such scenarios, social work professionals are ultimately tasked with facilitating the development of healthy psychological behavior to improve the quality of their clients' lives. In many respects, the various personality deficits examined in earlier chapters (e.g., adaptation to stress, emotional regulation, executive functioning, and most explicitly, temperament) manifest in personality. This chapter examines personality with particular focus on the Five Factor Model of Personality, the predominant conceptual model of human personality. This chapter also explores disorders of personality, and investigates the relationship between personality and behavioral and social functioning over the life course.

CASE STUDY: THE SALDAGO TWINS

The first question most people ask the Saldago sisters is if they are identical twins. The second question that most people ask, once they get to know them, is how twin sisters could possibly be so different. It is Saturday night, and it is the evening of the twins' coming-of-age *quinceañera* party, and so you'll soon see why people ask. The two 15-year-olds, Camille and Carmen, both outwardly radiate their excitement while they awkwardly negotiate the room in floor-length soft-orange taffeta gowns, complete with embroidered edging around the bodices and costume jewels that line the gowns' sweeping perimeter, showing off the handiwork of their maternal grandmother. Their tiaras sparkle against their long, dark, wavy hair. The celebration is a mix of bright colors, flavorful food, loud music, dancing, and ceremony. Aunts, uncles, cousins, grandparents, and cherished community members all pile into the community center's large banquet hall to help mark Camille and Carmen's special transition from childhood to maturity.

But transitions have not always been easy for the twins—especially not for Camille. In infancy and early childhood Camille was a handful. Mrs. Saldago said it sometimes took her mother and aunt hours to calm her cries, taking turns cradling and gently rocking her, before she would exhaust herself and sleep. And given Camille's fussy temperament, sleep was at a premium for everyone in the house during those early years—except for Carmen. Carmen, on the other hand, has always been an "easy child." If you ask Mrs. Saldago, she will tell you that ever since birth, Carmen has had an easy disposition and was never a problem to console. In fact, she consoled herself quite often. She rarely minded being left alone, which occurred frequently as an infant twin, but Carmen always seemed able to soothe herself after only a couple minutes of crying. Rarely did Mrs. Saldago have to worry about her. In fact, she recalls one time Carmen was so quiet playing in her crib alone in the other room that Mrs. Saldago forgot all about her for several hours, and when she realized she was gone, she looked about the house desperately trying to find her.

Research shows that personality at age 5 years can influence teacher bonding and investment at age 12. And Mr. and Mrs. Saldago sure know that. In kindergarten Carmen was already proving to be a very conscientious, hardworking, and ambitious student. Carmen was an early reader, extraverted and "very sociable," and that seemed to garner special attention in her kindergarten classroom. She became a role model for other kids in the class, and she took that role seriously, helping other students at her table with their worksheets. Camille, on the other hand, had few close friends, but tended to be more shy than Carmen, which teachers tended to interpret as "not trying very hard." Camille's kindergarten teacher noted how Camille tended to "need a lot of attention" to be able to complete her work. When the teacher left her side, she retreated into her own little world. And even today, Camille's teachers note that they are concerned she is "smarter than what she puts forth in effort" and that they worry she does not have a lot of friends. Carmen, on the other hand, is an officer in student government, and her teachers consistently recommend her for various service and academic awards.

Physically, it's hard to tell Camille and Carmen apart. But once you get to know them, they delight the curious-minded over how such physically similar sisters, raised in the same household, could indeed be so different in personality. It is likely that these individually unique personality traits will endure as they age into young adulthood, and everyone waits with anticipation to see how each will fare in their educational, occupational, and family formation pursuits. It will be interesting to talk to Camille and Carmen in 10 years to see how alike and how different they are then.

The literature suggests that children from low-income immigrant Latino families are at higher risk for school dropout and teen pregnancy, as compared to White children and children from families with higher SES. As we have seen with Camille and Carmen, personality traits, though relatively stable across childhood, influence and are influenced by experiences in the social environment. Thus, children growing up in vulnerable families who are particularly at risk for developing behavioral health problems should be of concern to helping professionals. One such program was developed to target low-income Latino immigrant families, and seeks to expand upon the cultural assets and strengths brought out through their Latino traditions to enhance the life-course opportunities for adolescent girls as they ready themselves for adulthood transitions. In Prince George's County, Maryland, the county-run program Mis Quince Años is composed of workshops designed to help Latina girls communicate better with their parents, troubleshoot challenges, and gain support from other families. The program provides help with filling out college applications and making campus visits, and offers opportunities for girls to interface with Latina professionals in the community. Other program goals include helping girls develop self-esteem and pride in their cultural identity through celebration of Hispanic traditions such as dance and etiquette. Most of the parents are low-income immigrants with low-wage jobs and limited English proficiency. The girls participate in the workshops along with other girls their same age, and the 10-week program ends with a *quinceañera* party (http://www.pgxtremeteens.com/Hot_Happenings/Programs/Mis_Quince_A_os.htm).

Critical Thinking Questions:

- Using the Five Factor Model of Personality, what are the personality differences between Camille and Carmen?
- As a school social worker, how could you work with Camille and Carmen's teachers to ensure both girls are receiving the adequate attention needed?
- Keeping in mind the girls' unique personalities, what type of support will each girl need from teachers to succeed?

DISTAL CONTEXT

What Is Personality?

Personality is a collection of the traits that generally typify a person and the ways in which he or she behaves. A trait is a "neuropsychic structure having the capacity to render many stimuli functionally equivalent, and to initiate and guide equivalent or meaningfully consistent forms of adaptive and expressive behavior" (Allport, 1961, p. 347). In many respects, personality is a general presentation of an individual based on the concepts that have been discussed in earlier chapters. The cognitive and emotional regulation styles, adaptive flexibility, and temperament of a person appear in everyday life as an individual's personality. In this way, *personality* relates to the relatively consistent and stable ways in which an individual behaves, thinks, and feels.

Personality psychologists have identified a variety of important aspects about personality. For instance, McAdams and Olson (2010, pp. 536–537) summarized personality development over the life course focusing on evidence that suggests two important elements: that personality is mostly stable and that personality is susceptible to change. The summary points suggest the following:

• Personality is a constellation of dispositional traits (the person as actor), characteristic adaptations (the person as agent), and integrative life stories (the person as author) situated in time and culture.

• Early temperamental dimensions gradually develop into the dispositional traits observed in adulthood through complex, dynamic, and multilevel interactions between genes and environments over time.

• Temporal stability for individual differences in traits increases over the life course and reaches impressively high levels in middle adulthood.

• Cross-sectional and longitudinal studies show that average scores for conscientiousness

and agreeableness increase and neuroticism decreases from adolescence through late middle age.

• Motives, goals, and other adaptations emerge as important features of personality development in middle adulthood, and the content, structure, organization, and pursuit of goals may change according to the needs of daily life.

• In late adolescence and early adulthood, people begin to reconstruct their autobiographical past and imagine the future to develop an internalizing life story that provides their life with meaning and purpose. In terms of personality development, the life stories are layered over goals and motives that are in turn layered over dispositional traits.

• As dispositional traits mature from adolescence to middle adulthood, goals and narratives show increasing concern with commitments to family, civic involvement, and productive activities aimed at promoting the next generation.

• From late midlife through old age, personality development plateaus and eventually descends as trait scores show some negative reversals, goals shift to maintenance of the self and coping with loss, and life narratives show an inexorable decline in the power of self-authorship.

In short, personality is relatively stable but also shows plasticity as individuals respond to various life stages and environmental situations.

Central Nervous System and Evolutionary Underpinnings

Recall from Chapter 6 that the evolutionary underpinnings of temperament reflect the processes of natural selection, in which physiological processes, such as the ability to be fearful of threatening stimuli, provide a protective feature to human behavior. A large part of evolutionary history also involves random, neutral genetic mutations that contribute to differential neural substrates in the brain. This in turn relates to differential autonomic, endocrine, and other system differences found in the variance of temperament. In many respects, temperament is the physiological foundation on which personality rests. For example, introverts have greater tonic (or baseline) brain activity than extraverts. As such, introverts require less stimulation than extraverts. Because extraverts require more stimulation than introverts, they need to seek out additional stimulation to achieve homeostasis. That simple difference helps to explain the association between extraversion/introversion and various aspects of behavior. In this example, an individual's personality traits (being extraverted or introverted) are an extension of the core, physiological, temperamental basis.

The Five Factor Model of Personality

Over the years, psychologists have devised many systematic ways to conceptualize and measure personality, which are known as *structural models of personality*. Several structural models of personality exist, and despite differences in terminology across models, there is consistency among the constructs that are employed. Major structural

models of personality contain some measure of neuroticism, or a general tendency toward negative emotionality. Extraversion or positive emotionality is also common across models. Depending on the author, there may also be constructs relating to sensation seeking, novelty seeking, drive, or appetitive behaviors.

One of the most influential and empirically examined structural models of personality is the *Five Factor Model of Personality* as shown in Figure 7.1. The Five Factor Model is a structural model of personality that contains five dimensions: Openness to Experience, Conscientiousness, Extraversion, Agreeableness, and Neuroticism (the acronym OCEAN is commonly used to recall them). These five dimensions are often referred to as the *Big Five*.

Beginning in the 1930s, with research that examined adjectives used to describe personality traits, many psychologists contributed to the development of the Five Factor Model. It became a more formal structural model in the late 1980s and early 1990s (for a history, see Digman, 2002). Although multiple instruments are used to measure the constructs in the Five Factor Model, the predominant is the NEO-PI (Costa

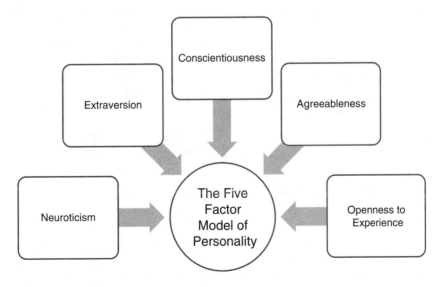

FIGURE 7.1 The Five Factor Model of Personality

& McRae, 1985) and the newer NEO-PI-R (Costa & McRae, 1992). The five dimensions of personality with descriptions of high, medium, and low scorers are:

• *Neuroticism* refers to the chronic level of emotional adjustment and instability. It includes facet scales for anxiety, angry hostility, depression, self-consciousness, impulsiveness, and vulnerability. Persons who score high on Neuroticism are prone to psychological distress, emotional, sensitive, and easily upset. Medium scorers sometimes experience negative emotions but are able to adapt to them and deal with stress. Low scorers are calm, relaxed, "cool under pressure," and rarely appear upset.

• *Extraversion* refers to the quantity and intensity of preferred interpersonal interactions, activity level, need for stimulation, and capacity for joy. It includes facet scales for warmth, gregariousness, assertiveness, activity, excitement seeking, and positive emotions. High scorers are known as *extraverts* and are outgoing, energetic, and enjoy being around other people. Medium scorers are known as *ambiverts*, are more moderate in activity and enthusiasm, and prefer a balance of privacy and the company of others. Low scorers, known as *introverts*, are generally reserved, serious, and prefer to be alone or with only close friends.

• *Openness to Experience* involves the appreciation and seeking of experiences. It includes facet scales for fantasy, aesthetics, feelings, actions, ideas, and values. Open individuals are characterized as curious, imaginative, willing to have novel experiences, and open to varied emotional experiences. Medium scorers are practical and consider old and new approaches and ideas. Closed individuals are characterized as conventional, conservative, dogmatic, rigid, and behaviorally set in their ways.

• *Agreeableness* refers to the kinds of interactions a person has along a continuum from compassion to antagonism. It includes facet scales for trust, straightforwardness, altruism, compliance, modesty, and tender-mindedness. High scorers on Agreeableness are good natured, trusting, soft hearted, helping, and altruistic. Medium scorers are generally warm and get along with others, but can also be competitive and occasionally stubborn. Low scorers tend to be cynical, rude, uncooperative, irritable, and manipulative.

• *Conscientiousness* captures the degree of organization, persistence, control, and motivation in goal-directed behavior. It includes facet scales for competence, order, dutifulness, achievement striving, self-discipline, and deliberation. High scorers are organized, reliable, hardworking, self-directed, ambitious, and persevering. Medium scorers are dependable and generally well-organized, but not as driven. Low scorers are aimless, unreliable, lazy, careless, negligent, and hedonistic.

Everyone's personality can be measured with the Five Factor Model of Personality, and indeed there are many so-called personality tests using it or similar measures freely available on the Internet. It is important to note that there are no right or wrong personalities per se, because various personality features are functional or not functional depending on context and other environmental factors. However, it is also important to note that some personality features, especially when displayed in combination with other traits, increase the likelihood for psychopathology and maladaptive behavior. These issues are examined later in the chapter.

PROXIMAL MECHANISMS

Neural Substrates

The neural substrates of personality are in many respects the same neural pathways discussed in other chapters in this text relating to emotion, temperament, cognition, and executive functions. Dysfunction in various neural substrates and the neurotransmitter systems associated with them contribute to problems with personality functioning. Consider a commonly discussed topic prevalent among many clinical social work clients: the so-called addictive personality. This can be understood neurobiologically as a dysfunction in the reward pathway in the brain known as the *mesolimbic reward system*. It provides positive reinforcement for eating, drinking, sex, and other functions that are basic to survival and rooted in our evolutionary past, but it can be corrupted. For instance, if a person engages in substance abuse, the mesolimbic reward system essentially floods the brain with the neurotransmitter dopamine to levels that far exceed the normal rewards produced by basic behaviors such as eating, drinking, and having sex. These extra rewards can lead to compulsive substance use for the purpose of achieving the supernormal levels of reward, which overwhelm the inhibitory mechanisms (i.e., it stops them) in the brain that normally regulate such behavior (Vaughn & Perron, 2011). In other words, what is called an addictive personality is not simply an excuse or a rationalization for compulsive behavior, but an accurate portrayal of what is happening inside the brains of addicted people.

Various neural systems and pathways are also important to understanding personality disorders. Recently, Siever and Weinstein (2009) identified key neural substrate and neurotransmitter connections to personality disorders. First, a low threshold for impulsive aggression, as seen among individuals with borderline personality disorder and antisocial personality disorder, is associated with excessive amygdala reactivity, reduced prefrontal inhibition, and diminished serotonin connections between limbic and prefrontal areas. Second, excessive limbic activity relating to glutamate, GABA, and acetylcholine circuits results in increased sensitivity to emotional stimuli and manifests in the affective instability that is seen in Cluster B personality disorders. Third, frontal disturbances in cognitive organization and information processing contribute to cognitive distortions, detachment, and incompatibility with the environment, as seen in Cluster A personality disorders. Fourth,

excessive anxiety and serotonin functioning are associated with the fearful and anxious nature of Cluster C personality disorders.

Genetic Underpinnings

There is an undeniable genetic basis to personality. For example, Heath, Cloninger, and Martin (1994) compared the personality systems of Robert Cloninger and Hans Eysenck and found that genetic factors accounted for 54 to 61% of the stability in traits. In a landmark article published in the prestigious journal *Science*, Plomin (1990) found that personality dimensions yielded heritability estimates ranging from 20 to 50%. In another instance, a multinational study of over 30,000 twin pairs indicated that both neuroticism and extraversion were about 50% heritable. In a comprehensive review by Bouchard and Loehlin (2001), it was reported that about 50% of variance in personality traits was heritable for all of the Big Five domains. Indeed, many personality features and even apparently environmentally based contexts relating to personality are genetic in origin. Kandler, Bleidorn, Riemann, Angleitner, and Spinath (2012) noted that "while common sense suggests that life events reflect external influences on an individual, behavioral genetic research has shown heritability for most measures of life events suggesting that individual differences in the experience of life events can at least partly be explained by genetic differences" (p. 57).

The genetic underpinnings of personality are even more pronounced when considering antisocial personality features. For instance, disregard for rules is a common trait associated with several personality and/or behavioral disorders. In a study of nearly 600 twin pairs ranging in age from 20 to 64 months, genetic factors accounted for much of the stability in disregard for rules across this developmental period (Petitclerc, Boivin, Dionne, Pérusse, & Tremblay, 2011).

It is important to note that although personality is partly inherited, environmental factors are also influential. A recent behavioral genetic study of personality in childhood illustrates that assertion. Spengler, Gottschling, and Spinath (2012) found that the components of the Five Factor Model were variously influenced by genetic, shared environmental, and nonshared environmental sources at two points in time. For example, Conscientiousness varied by measurement time point. At the first point of measurement, it was 31% genetic, 30% shared, and 39% nonshared. At the second point of measurement, it was 2% genetic, 67% shared, and 31% nonshared.

The same logic applies to components of personality disorder. To illustrate, Kendler, Aggen, and Patrick (2012) recently studied the genetic and environmental sources of antisocial personality disorder among nearly 4,300 twins selected from the Virginia Adult Twin Studies of Psychiatric and Substance Use Disorders. They found two underlying genetic factors. The first—an aggressive-disregard factor—was associated with risk for CD, early-onset and severe alcohol use, and low educational status. The other factor—disinhibition—was strongly correlated with young age, novelty seeking, and major depression. Kendler et al. also found that various criteria for antisocial personality disorder derived exclusively from either genetic or nonshared environmental sources (shared environment such as family factors had no effect). These included not conforming (57% genetic, 43% environmental), deceitfulness (32% genetic, 68% environmental), failure to plan (47% genetic, 53% environmental), irritability and repeated fights (50% genetic, 50% environmental), reckless disregard (43% genetic, 57% environmental), irresponsibility (33% genetic, 67% environmental), and lacks remorse (12% genetic, 88% environmental).

In sum, personality features and various psychopathological traits relating to personality are caused to some extent by genetic factors. We concur with Kendler and Prescott (2006) who concluded,

> It is critical to emphasize that, although the magnitude of genetic effects for common

psychiatric and substance use disorders is not overwhelming, neither is it trivial. It is too large to be ignored by anyone who wants to truly understand the etiology of these disorders.... This is a brute fact of our world. It will not be changed by whether it does or does not fit our ideological, philosophical, or religious views about the nature of personhood. (p. 340)

Environmental Contexts

What are some of the environmental contexts that modify personality traits? A host of factors, including parental warmth, abuse, and neglect, among others, have been shown to affect the development and expression of personality traits. There is generally an interaction between personality traits and the environment. This essentially means that negative environmental conditions, such as abuse, interact with negative personality features and produce negative behavioral outcomes. Similarly, positive environments can interact with positive personality traits to produce positive behavioral outcomes.

To illustrate the interaction between personality traits and the environment, a recent meta-analysis of 30 studies, which included nearly 6,000 parent–child dyads, examined the role of personality traits and behavior among parents (Prinzie, Stams, Dekovic, Reijntjes, & Belsky, 2009). They found that parental warmth and parental behavioral control were associated with parent extraversion, agreeableness, conscientiousness, and openness, and were negatively associated with neuroticism. Parental autonomy support was more likely among parents who were agreeable, open to new experiences, and had lower neuroticism. Overall, these parenting behaviors set the stage for more prosocial parenting and positive child-rearing environments.

Social institutions can also influence an individual's personality. For instance, the military is an important social institution that provides educational and vocational experiences, public service, and national security. A debate exists about whether certain personality characteristics drive an individual to choose to enter the military, or if being involved in the military changes an individual's personality. There is evidence to support both sides. Recent research has found that high school students who score low on personality traits such as agreeableness, neuroticism, and openness to experience are more likely to enter the military after graduating high school (Jackson, Thoemmes, Jonkmann, Lüdtke, & Trautwein, 2012). It was also found that military training caused reductions in the personality trait of agreeableness. The decreased levels of agreeableness persisted for 5 years after military service, even when participants entered college or gained employment.

SPOTLIGHT TOPIC: PERSONALITY AND THE SOCIAL WORK PROFESSION

The personality of a social work professional is an important factor in how well they perform their duties, how well they adapt to the issues a challenging caseload raises, and whether they thrive and persist in their duties, suffer burnout, or leave the profession. Several studies have examined the relationship between a practitioner's personality and their emotional and occupational health at work. As a general rule of thumb, the "ideal" set of personality features for a social worker would involve low neuroticism, high extraversion, high agreeableness, high conscientiousness, and high openness to experience. These personality features are associated with lower burnout, greater job stability, and better performance at work (Acker, 1999; Bakker, Van Der Zee, Lewig, & Dollard, 2006; Barak, Nissly, & Levin, 2001; Ben-Zur & Michael, 2007).

A study of the personality–work stress link in another helping profession—health care—demonstrated how specific personality features are associated with various components of work burnout. For instance, Zellars, Perrewe, and Hochwarter (2000) found that emotional exhaustion at work was predicted by neuroticism. Depersonalization, which can be common in social work, was predicted by low extraversion, low openness to experience, and low agreeableness. Diminished personal control at work was predicted by low extraversion and low openness to experience. All of these personality effects withstood controls for hours worked, number of persons supervised, work experience, age, number of children, role conflict, role ambiguity, and work role overload.

It is critical to understanding personality functioning among social work professionals given the various ways that negative personality features can impair job performance, engagement, and satisfaction. For example, a recent survey of social work undergraduates found that 50% were at or above a clinical cutoff on a measure of depression (Ting, 2011), which in personality parlance would suggest high neuroticism and perhaps low agreeableness. These students are precisely those at risk for negative work outcomes given prior research on their personality traits, and how they impact social worker performance.

For Reflection

Should agencies require helping professionals to assess their own personality traits for self-discovery and perhaps aid them in improving job performance and forestall burnout? What are the advantages of doing so? What are the limitations?

Personality Disorders

Social work professionals may encounter clients whose personality characteristics create difficulties in important major areas of functioning including interpersonal relations and school or work settings. Pervasive and inflexible personality difficulties might signify that an individual has a personality disorder. A *personality disorder* is an enduring pattern of inner experience and behavior that deviates markedly from the expectations of the individual's culture. Individuals with personality disorders often experience considerable life distress. Untreated personality disorder symptoms might lead to the breakup of family relationships or intimate partnerships, the inability to maintain a steady career and thus economic stability, and in extreme cases, the loss of one's freedom.

Consider this example: Kim has been described by friends as "difficult to get along with." She expresses intense anger in situations in which most people would react with relatively little anger or none at all. She can be sarcastic and feels bitter toward people who she considers better than her. When interacting with such individuals, she purposefully focuses on their negative qualities and attempts to present these individuals in a negative light. In her mind she's attempting to humble them, but from the perspective of others, it is perceived as jealousy or a form of manipulation. In relationships, Kim constantly feels slighted by friends. For instance, Kim becomes very upset when a friend does not call her back at the exact time at which they said they would. In such situations, Kim considers such a mistake to be a personal affront or a rejection of her. She is hypersensitive to criticism and is even suspect of personal compliments. Kim's social interaction style, in which she easily feels abandoned and rejected by friends and reacts accordingly, makes the development of deep and meaningful relationships difficult.

Kim's inability to develop relationships would likely significantly hinder her happiness and thus her overall psychological well-being. Friends and family may not be willing to tolerate her style of interaction for very long and thus attempt to end the relationship. A concrete way in which social workers could assist Kim is to identify and highlight the ways in which Kim's behavior or personality may be negatively impacting her ability to develop and maintain relationships. In doing so, the goal of the social worker would be to facilitate the development of new, more agreeable personality traits, which would ultimately serve to improve the quality of her relationships and her life.

There is a general belief that because temperamental facets are relatively stable and enduring, they will manifest in adulthood. Recently, De Pauw and Mervielde (2010) merged childhood temperament models with the Five Factor Model of Personality in an attempt to explain internalizing (e.g., depression) and externalizing (e.g., aggression) disorders. Individuals with anxiety disorders would have high scores on Neuroticism, characterized by high levels of fear and anxiety. They would have low scores on Extraversion, evidenced by high levels of social inhibition, and low scores on Conscientiousness, based on low levels of attentional control. For externalizing disorders, similar translations can be made. For example, ADHD is characterized by high Extraversion scores based on hyperactivity levels and low Conscientiousness scores based on reduced attentional and inhibitory control. Antisocial conduct characterized by reactive aggression would be captured by high Extraversion scores (e.g., high activity level), low Conscientiousness scores (e.g., low inhibitory control), and low Agreeableness (e.g., high anger and high antagonism). This represents the general temperamental risk profile for antisocial youth. Antisocial conduct characterized by proactive aggression would be captured by very low Neuroticism scores (e.g., reduced fear) and very low Agreeableness scores (e.g., very low empathy). This represents the general personality risk profile for psychopathic youth.

Criminological epidemiologists recently examined the social welfare burden of personality disorders in the United States. They utilized data from the National Epidemiologic Survey on Alcohol and Related Conditions, which is a nationally representative sample of more than 43,000 adults (Vaughn et al., 2010). It was found that diagnoses for any personality disorder predicted whether an individual was a recipient of Medicaid, Supplemental Security Income (SSI), and Supplemental Nutrition Assistance Program aid (SNAP; formerly food stamps). Moreover, individuals who were diagnosed with antisocial personality disorder—the personality disorder that most directly corresponds to a criminal personality—were significantly likely to receive Medicaid, SNAP, and Women, Infants, and Children assistance. Serious criminal offenders, particularly those with personality disorders, increase the monetary burden on society.

According to the fourth (revised) edition of the *Diagnostic and Statistical Manual of Mental Health Disorders* (DSM-IV-TR), there are three types of personality disorders, which are grouped into clusters. *Cluster A personality disorders* are characterized by odd or eccentric thinking. Individuals with these disorders are often detached from others and prefer to be alone. The three disorders within Cluster A are paranoid personality disorder, schizoid personality disorder, and schizotypal personality disorder. *Paranoid personality disorder* is characterized by a pervasive pattern of distrust and suspiciousness of others. An individual with paranoid personality disorder might believe that the motives of others are suspect and may interpret them as being malevolent. *Schizoid personality disorder* is characterized by a pervasive pattern of detachment from social relationships. Individuals with schizoid personality disorder are often restricted in their ability to properly express emotions in interpersonal settings. *Schizotypal personality disorder* is characterized by a pervasive pattern of social and interpersonal deficits, marked by acute discomfort with and significant difficulty with engaging in close relationships. Those diagnosed with schizotypal personality disorder also experience cognitive or perceptual distortions

and eccentricities in behavior (American Psychiatric Association, 2000). The following sections expand upon the symptoms of the Cluster A disorders just described.

Paranoid Personality Disorder

Individuals with this disorder:

- Suspect, without sufficient basis, that others are attempting to exploit, harm, or deceive them;
- Doubt others' loyalty or trustworthiness;
- Are reluctant to confide in others; they fear that the information told to others will be used against them;
- Believe that there is hidden or demeaning intent in benign remarks or events;
- Hold grudges (i.e., are unforgiving of insults, injuries, or slights);
- Perceive others to be attacking their character or reputation and are quick to react or counterattack with anger; or
- Have recurrent suspicions of their spouse or partner's sexual infidelity (American Psychiatric Association, 2000, p. 694).

Schizoid Personality Disorder

Individuals with this disorder:

- Lack a desire for intimacy, seem indifferent to developing close relationships, and do not derive much satisfaction from being part of a family or social group;
- Almost always choose solitary activities over those that would include interaction with others;
- Have little, if any, interest in having a sexual relationship with another person;
- Take pleasure in few, if any, activities;

- Lack close friends or confidants other than immediate relatives;

- Appear indifferent to the praise or criticism of others; or

- Show emotional coldness, detachment, or flattened affectivity (American Psychiatric Association, 2000, p. 697).

Schizotypal Personality Disorder

Individuals with this disorder:

- Incorrectly interpret casual incidents and external events as having a particular and unusual relevance to them;

- Are superstitious or preoccupied with paranormal phenomena outside the norm of their subculture (in children, bizarre fantasies; in adults, belief in clairvoyance or telepathy);

- Have unusual perceptual experiences, including bodily illusions;

- Exhibit odd thinking and speech (i.e., vague, circumstantial, or metaphorical);

- Exhibit suspicious or paranoid ideation;

- Have inappropriate or constricted affect during interaction (i.e., stiff or constricted in mannerisms);

- Display behavior or appearance that is odd, eccentric, or peculiar;

- Lack close friends or confidants other than first-degree family members; or

- Show excessive social anxiety that does not diminish with familiarity and tends to be associated with paranoid fears rather than negative judgments about the self (American Psychiatric Association, 2000, p. 701).

Cluster B personality disorders are those that are viewed as being dramatic or emotional. There are four types of personality disorders within Cluster B. *Antisocial personality disorder* is characterized by a pervasive pattern of disregard for

and violation of the rights of others. *Borderline personality disorder* is characterized by a pervasive pattern of instability of interpersonal relationships, self-image, affect, and marked impulsivity. *Histrionic personality disorder* is characterized by a pervasive pattern of excessive emotionality and attention seeking. *Narcissistic personality disorder* is characterized by a pervasive pattern of grandiosity in fantasy and behavior, need for admiration, and lack of empathy. Specific symptoms of Cluster B disorders are described in the following sections.

Antisocial Personality Disorder

Individuals with this disorder exhibit:

- Failure to conform to social norms with respect to lawful behaviors, as indicated by repeatedly performing acts that are grounds for arrest;

- Deceitfulness, as indicated by repeated lying, use of aliases, or conning others for personal profit or pleasure;

- Impulsivity, marked by failure to plan ahead;

- Irritability and aggressiveness, as indicated by repeated physical fights or assaults;

- Reckless disregard for safety of self or others;

- Consistent irresponsibility, as indicated by repeated failure to sustain consistent work behavior or honor financial obligations; or

- Lack of remorse, as indicated by being indifferent to or rationalizing having hurt, mistreated, or stolen from another (American Psychiatric Association, 2000, p. 706).

Borderline Personality Disorder

Individuals with this disorder exhibit:

- Frantic efforts to avoid real or imagined abandonment;

- A pattern of unstable and intense interpersonal relationships characterized by alternating between extremes of idealization and devaluation;

- Identity disturbances, creating a markedly and persistently unstable self-image or sense of self;

- Impulsivity in at least two areas that are potentially self-damaging, such as spending, sex, substance abuse, reckless driving, or binge eating;

- Recurrent suicidal behavior, gestures, or threats, or self-mutilating behavior;

- Affective instability due to a marked reactivity of mood, such as intense episodic dysphoria, irritability, or anxiety usually lasting a few hours and rarely more than a few days;

- Chronic feelings of emptiness;

- Inappropriate, intense anger or difficulty controlling anger, such as frequent displays of temper, constant anger, or recurrent physical fights; or

- Transient, stress-related paranoid ideation or severe dissociative symptoms (American Psychiatric Association, 2000, p. 710).

Histrionic Personality Disorder

Individuals with this disorder:

- Are uncomfortable in situations where he or she is not the center of the attention;

- Interact with others in ways often characterized by inappropriate, sexually seductive, or provocative behavior;

- Display rapidly shifting and shallow expressions of emotions;

- Consistently use physical appearance to draw attention to oneself;

- Have a style of speech that is excessively impressionistic and lacking in detail;

- Show self-dramatization, theatricality, and exaggerated expression of emotion;

- Are suggestible or easily influenced by others; or

- Consider relationships to be more intimate than they actually are (American Psychiatric Association, 2000, p. 714).

Narcissistic Personality Disorder

Individuals with this disorder:

- Have a grandiose sense of self-importance (i.e., exaggerate their achievements);

- Are preoccupied with fantasies of unlimited success, power, brilliance, beauty, or ideal love;

- Believe that they are "special" and unique and can only be understood by, or associate with, other special or high-status people (or institutions);

- Require excessive admiration;

- Have a sense of entitlement (i.e., unreasonable expectations of especially favorable treatment);

- Are interpersonally exploitative (i.e., take advantage of others to achieve their own ends);

- Lack empathy; are unwilling to recognize or identify with the feelings of others;

- Are often envious of others or believe that others are envious of them; or

- Show arrogant, haughty behaviors or attitudes (American Psychiatric Association, 2000, p. 717).

Individuals with narcissistic personality disorder can also exhibit antisocial and aggressive behaviors. Twenge and Campbell (2003) found that narcissists had higher levels of anger, fewer internalized negative emotions, and greater direct and indirect levels of aggression than individuals without narcissistic personality disorder. Narcissists were particularly sensitive to social rejection and would respond with aggression to both the individual who rejected them and to an innocent third party. In another study conducted in New Zealand, Donnellan, Trzesniewski, Robins,

Moffitt, and Caspi (2005) found that narcissism was significantly correlated with anger, hostility, verbal aggression, and physical aggression.

Cluster C personality disorders are those that are viewed as anxious or fearful. There are three disorders within this cluster. *Avoidant personality disorder* is characterized by a pervasive pattern of social inhibition, feelings of inadequacy, and hypersensitivity to negative evaluation. *Dependent personality disorder* is characterized by a pervasive and excessive need to be taken care of that leads to submissive and clinging behavior and fears of separation. *Obsessive-compulsive personality disorder* is characterized by a pervasive pattern of preoccupation with orderliness, perfectionism, and mental and interpersonal control at the expense of flexibility, openness, and efficiency. The specific symptoms of Cluster C disorders are detailed in the following sections.

Avoidant Personality Disorder

Individuals with this disorder:

- Avoid occupational activities that involve significant interpersonal contact, because of fear of criticism, disapproval, or rejection;

- Are unwilling to get involved with people unless certain of being liked;

- Show restraint within intimate relationships because of fear of being shamed or ridiculed;

- Are preoccupied with being criticized or rejected in social situations;

- Are inhibited in new interpersonal situations because of feelings of inadequacy;

- View themselves as socially inept, personally unappealing, or inferior to others; or

- Are unusually reluctant to take personal risks or engage in any new activities because they may prove embarrassing (American Psychiatric Association, 2000, p. 721).

Dependent Personality Disorder

Individuals with this disorder:

- Have difficulty making decisions without an excessive amount of advice and reassurance from others;

- Need others to assume responsibility for most major areas of their lives;

- Have difficulty expressing disagreement with others because they fear losing support or approval;

- Have difficulty initiating projects or doing things on their own because they lack confidence;

- Go to excessive lengths to obtain nurturance and support from others, to the point of volunteering to do things that are unpleasant;

- Feel uncomfortable or helpless when alone because of exaggerated fears of being unable to care for themselves;

- Urgently seek another relationship as a source of care and support when a close relationship ends; or

- Are unrealistically preoccupied with fears of being left to take care of himself or herself (American Psychiatric Association, 2000, p. 725).

Obsessive-Compulsive Personality Disorder

Individuals with this disorder:

- Are preoccupied with details, rules, lists, order, organization, or schedules to the extent that the major point of the activity is lost;

- Show perfectionism that interferes with task completion;

- Are excessively devoted to work and productivity to the exclusion of leisure activities and friendships;

- Are overly conscientious, scrupulous, and inflexible about matters of morality, ethics, or values;

- Are unable to discard worn-out or worthless objects even when they have no sentimental value;

- Are reluctant to delegate tasks or to work with others unless they submit to exactly their way of doing things;

- Adopt a miserly spending style toward themselves and others; money is viewed as something to be hoarded for future catastrophes; or

- Show rigid stubbornness (American Psychiatric Association, 2000, p. 729).

CLIENTS AND PERSONALITY FUNCTIONING

Clinical social workers' clients commonly display an array of emotional, behavioral, and personality disorders, and nowhere is this clearer than among clients who have been adjudicated by the juvenile and criminal justice systems. Several meta-analyses have been conducted to identify the particular personality features that are associated with aggressive and antisocial forms of conduct. For example, Miller and Lynam (2001) examined four structural models of personality among 59 studies and found the strongest evidence linking low Agreeableness and low Conscientiousness to crime.

In their meta-analysis, Samuel and Widiger (2008) investigated the Five Factor Model and its facets among the personality disorders using data from 16 samples. Although there were many significant effects among the personality disorders, the most pertinent, as expected, were for antisocial personality disorder. It is characterized most strongly by low levels of Agreeableness and Conscientiousness. Jones, Miller, and Lynam (2011) reviewed 53 studies to explore the association between the Five Factor Model and outcome measures for antisocial behavior and aggression. Overall, effect sizes for three of the five factors were significantly associated with antisocial behavior. There was a positive link between Neuroticism and antisocial behavior, indicating that people who experience greater levels of negative emotionality, such as anger and hostility, are more likely to commit crime. Larger effect sizes were found for Agreeableness and Conscientiousness, with more antagonistic and less conscientious domains associated with antisocial behavior. All five factors were significantly associated with aggression. The direction for Neuroticism, Agreeableness, and Conscientiousness was the same for aggression. In addition, Extraversion and Openness to Experience were negatively correlated with aggression.

More recent research examined how personality features influence various forms of aggression, which is essentially the raw material component of crime. Bartlett and Anderson (2012) found that different types of aggression (e.g., aggressive emotions, aggressive attitudes, physical aggression, and violent behavior) are differentially predicted by personality as measured by the Five Factor Model. Extraversion was only associated with physical aggression. Openness to Experience was positively associated with physical aggression and negatively associated with aggressive attitudes. Agreeableness was negatively associated with aggressive emotions, aggressive attitudes, and physical aggression. Neuroticism was positively associated with aggressive emotions, but negatively associated with physical aggression. Conscientiousness was not correlated with any measure of aggression in this study.

Unfortunately, interventions for serious criminal offenders with personality disorders are costly and not particularly cost effective. A recent evaluation of a program for dangerous severe personality disorder in the United Kingdom found that the cost per serious offense prevented was over £2 million, and the authors concluded that there is little evidence to support the cost effectiveness of such programs (Barrett & Byford, 2012).

SPOTLIGHT TOPIC: BORDERLINE PERSONALITY DISORDERS AND DIALECTICAL BEHAVIOR THERAPY

Borderline personality disorder (BPD) is a challenging diagnosis for social work clients and the professionals who provide them services. It is characterized by pervasive instability in affect, mood, self-image, interpersonal relationships, and often, impulsive behaviors. According to the American Psychiatric Association, BPD is diagnosed mostly (about 75%) in women. Common behaviors they display are self-harming, self-mutilation, and suicidal attempts. Newhill, Vaughn, and DeLisi (2010) examined 221 patients with BPD selected from the MacArthur Violence Risk Assessment Study and found high comorbidity with other personality disorders and psychopathy. At a lower level, patients often present with severe deficits at emotional regulation and processing of negative affect (Newhill, Mulvey, & Pilkonis, 2004).

One approach to treating social work clients with BPD is *dialectical behavior therapy (DBT)*, which is a cognitive behavioral treatment that helps patients to validate their feelings and experiences while changing their emotional expression and behavior responses to environmental stimuli that previously produced conflicts. In other words, patients learn ways to stabilize their affect and mood, which in turn (it is hoped) will normalize their social relationships and behavioral responses. Evaluation research has shown that DBT helps to reduce impulsive behaviors, self-mutilation, and self-damaging behaviors among women with BPD when compared to usual treatment approaches (Verheul et al., 2003). In addition, DBT appears particularly helpful among women with extensive histories of self-mutilation. To be sure, personality disorders impose a significant aggregate burden on society and are catastrophic to the lives of patients who live with them. Fortunately, social work professionals are there to assist them and provide efficacious therapies to reduce their symptoms.

For Reflection

Why are personality disorders often considered difficult to treat? In what ways do personality problems compromise social relationships?

PERSONALITY OVER THE LIFE COURSE

Given the relative stability of personality features, positive personality traits such as agreeableness, extraversion, and conscientiousness increase the likelihood of adaptive, functional outcomes over the life span. Likewise, negative personality traits and personality disorders can negatively influence an individual's life, which can be especially problematic when symptoms associated with personality disorders go untreated. The next section explores the various ways in which personality impacts one's life, from birth and beyond.

Fetal Environment and Infancy

Personality and temperamental traits are apparent in the earliest stages of life. For example, during infancy some children are too timid to approach new people, objects, and situations, whereas others spontaneously approach them. Infants who have been described as being extreme in restraint or spontaneity to novelty also display significant physiological differences. Kagan, Reznick, and Snidman (1988) found that inhibited children have a lower threshold for limbic-hypothalmic arousal to novelty and unexpected changes in the environment, which can result in childhood shyness or extreme forms of social avoidance. As discussed in the previous chapter, Kagan et al. observed "A frequent scene during the play sessions was a cluster of three or four children playing close to each other, often talking, and one or two children standing or playing alone one to several meters from the center of social activity. These isolated, quiet children were typically those who had classified as inhibited 5 or 6 years earlier" (p. 168). Similarly, Schwartz, Wright, Shin, Kagan, and Rauch (2003) conducted an fMRI study of adults who had been categorized as inhibited or uninhibited as children. When shown novel faces, they found significant amygdala responses showing greater activation among the formerly inhibited children. Interestingly, two adults in their study had been diagnosed with generalized social phobia and would have been considered "inhibited" during infancy.

The interplay among personality, behavior, and the neural bases of the personality–behavior link has also been shown in case studies. The case of "PF1" is particularly illustrative of the profound impact of neural functioning on behavior. PF1 is a 14-month-old boy who sustained focal damage to the right inferior dorsolateral prefrontal cortex following a surgical procedure on his third day of life. PF1 recovered well from the surgery and developed normally, based on his mother's assessments of his communication abilities and social, motor, and daily living skills. PF1 was compared to 50 boys his age who did not have a neurological history. The children participated in structured and unstructured situations that were designed to elicit positive and negative emotions and that would place demands on their attention. Compared to his peers, PF1 demonstrated significant difficulties in regulating his emotions, which included the expression of high positive affectivity and low restraint. He was unable to restrain his behavior when he wanted a particular object and was told "no." When kept from his particular object of desire, he expressed a high, atypical level of anger. PF1 also demonstrated impairments in attention during a problem-solving task (Anderson et al., 2007).

Early Childhood and Childhood

Retrospective studies have shown the profound implications of childhood personality on later life functioning. In a classic New Zealand study Caspi, Elder, and Bem (1987) examined longitudinal data spanning 30 years from boys and girls ages 8 to 10 years who had frequent temper tantrums. They wondered if temper tantrums were a passing phase of late childhood or if they had enduring meaning. The results were alarming. Capsi and his colleagues found that children who exhibited explosive, poorly tempered outbursts in childhood also acted similarly as adults, particularly when placed in subordinate roles, such as in work or school settings.

Having a bad temper as a child predicted frequent middle adulthood occupational mobility, such as frequent job changes due to quitting or firing, educational attainment, and divorce. These effects were similar for men and women.

Other studies have shown similar results. For instance, Goodman, Joyce, and Smith (2011) examined the longitudinal consequences of early-life psychological functioning of nearly 18,000 children born in England during March 1958. They found that children with more negative personality features and generally lower psychological functioning continued to experience those same problems as adults. These findings have wide-ranging implications. Individuals with more negative personality features and lower psychological functioning as children had greater employment problems, less wealth, and reduced social mobility as adults. In fact, childhood personality and psychological deficits were found to have accounted for nearly a 30% reduction in earnings by age 50. They also struggled with a host of additional problems, including marital instability, lower agreeableness, lower conscientiousness, more emotional instability, and reduced self-efficacy.

An essential feature of childhood is education. How well a child functions in a school setting can affect whether he or she has a conventional or a maladaptive adolescence and adulthood. A child's personality features can significantly affect how he or she is perceived by a teacher. For instance, a recent study examined children's personality features and whether they affected a teacher's effort toward the child, such as providing encouragement, helping the child to attend school, curbing disruptive behavior, making work rewarding, and engaging in one-on-one interaction (Houts, Caspi, Pianta, Arseneault, & Moffitt, 2010). They found that a child's personality at age 5 years predicted teacher effort toward that same child at age 12. Children with personalities characterized by negative affect and irritability were viewed as being more aversive, which resulted in a weaker bond with the teacher. That finding suggests that when a child has a personality that is considered negative, it can limit the amount of time and effort teachers are willing to provide.

Adolescence

Personality features appear to be particularly important during adolescence. Adolescence is a period of unprecedented physiological and psychological change. Adolescence is also a risky period for the onset of problem behaviors (Moffitt, 1993). For example, adolescents who are prone to seeking thrills and adventures, boys especially, are significantly likely to commit delinquent behaviors during this time. Sensation seeking is also associated with a range of risky behaviors, including reckless driving, having unprotected sex, drug use, and engaging in impulsive and delinquent acts such as vandalism (Arnett, 1996). The obvious downside to a high sensation/novelty-seeking behavioral pattern is the risk associated with these behaviors. In fact, adolescents' attraction to sensation-seeking behaviors is a main reason they are overrepresented in the criminal justice system.

Neuroscientists have suggested that emotional responses to prior behavioral consequences essentially become guides to decision making in uncertain and risky situations (Damasio, 1994).

Individuals with emotional impairments are unable to generate or recall the negative consequences associated with their prior engagement in risky behaviors and repeatedly make the same mistakes in judgment.

Another problematic personality feature is self-centeredness, also known as narcissism. To explore its association with antisocial conduct, this personality trait has been studied in a variety of contexts and samples of the population. In a study of individuals in the general population, Thomaes, Bushman, Stegge, and Olthof (2008) conducted an experiment with 163 preteens and adolescents to examine the interrelationships among narcissism, self-esteem, shame, and aggression. In the experiment, participants purposely lost to an opponent on a competitive task. Individuals assigned to the shame condition were told that their opponent was no good and the participants could see their own name at the bottom of a ranking list. Neither of these occurred in the control condition. Aggression was measured by allowing study participants to blast their opponents with noise. The study revealed that narcissistic children were more aggressive but only after they were shamed. Interestingly, it was also found that narcissistic children with high self-esteem were extraordinarily aggressive toward their peers.

We have described the potentially problematic aspects of adolescence with regard to their personality development but it is important to highlight the many positive aspects of personality development. The large-scale longitudinal TRAILS study of Dutch adolescents showed that good parenting practices and higher socioeconomic status can decrease the risk for frustration and fearfulness. Teens who were at risk for delinquency and other externalizing behaviors remained crime free when their parents provided emotional warmth and had a higher socioeconomic status (Sentse, Veenstra, Lindenberg, Verhulst, & Ormel, 2009). These parental and socioeconomic effects are important to understand because certain temperamental profiles among adolescents have been linked to externalizing problems. Specifically, adolescents with high levels of negative affect and low levels of control are significantly at risk for problem behaviors (Oldehinkel, Hartman, De Winter, Veenstra, & Ormel, 2004).

Adulthood

In the literature of adult personality functioning, there are two conflicting lines of research. One suggests that an individual's personality remains largely unchanged from childhood to adulthood. The other suggests that environmental factors can affect an individual's personality and, based on the evidence, that change is possible. Roberts, Harms, Caspi, and Moffitt (2007) provided evidence for both positions in a 23-year follow-up study of personality among individuals they tracked from birth. They found that individuals who were diagnosed with CD during adolescence were significantly likely to be a so-called counterproductive employee as an adult. Counterproductive work behaviors included being late for work or absent, having conflicts with coworkers, committing work-based crimes including theft and substance abuse, and being fired, among others. Their findings are important because they demonstrate how criminality-based personality traits can negatively impact various aspects of an individual's life.

Overall, positive personality features tend to predict adaptive, functional outcomes, whereas negative personality traits and personality disorders are associated with problematic behavioral outcomes. The college years are a particularly important developmental period in emerging adulthood, and certain personality features are significantly associated with student lifestyle and behavioral outcomes. For example, students who have greater impulse control are more likely to maintain a healthy lifestyle, more likely to attend to their physical health, less likely to use drugs and alcohol, less accident prone, and have fewer traffic violations (Edmonds, Bogg, & Roberts, 2009).

In middle and late adulthood, certain personality features have been shown to moderate serious health problems. For instance, a study by Boyce and Wood (2011) of nearly 12,000 individuals, more than 300 of whom were disabled, found that individuals with moderate scores on agreeableness were able to regain healthy life satisfaction levels faster than less agreeable individuals. The study also found that those who were described as being more agreeable had levels of life satisfaction that were nearly .5 SD higher than those of individuals considered disagreeable.

As examined in Chapter 6, the enduring effects of temperament are strongest for prosocial behaviors in some cases. Researchers in the Czech Republic rated the temperaments of 83 children between the ages of 12 and 30 months. Three specific elements of temperament emerged: positive affectivity, negative affectivity, and disinhibition. The last factor predicted whether or not an individual would be extroverted or self-effectual 40 years later. None of the other factors were associated with adult functioning (Blatny, Jelinek, & Osecka, 2007).

Sex Differences

Social work professionals may agree that there are similarities and differences with regard to personality functioning and personality disorders among their male and female clients. Some personality disorders (e.g., antisocial personality disorder) are more prevalent among men and contribute to their disproportionate involvement in the criminal justice system. Other disorders, such as borderline personality disorder, are more prevalent among women and contribute to problems relating to self-harm, relationship difficulties, and impulsivity. In some cases, perceptions about sex differences in personality are anecdotal and perhaps not empirically supported. In other cases, the stereotypes are entirely supported by research.

Consider this assessment: "The idea that there are only minor differences between the personality profiles of males and females should be rejected as based on inadequate methodology" (Del Guidice, Booth, & Irwing, 2012, p. 1). That bold statement is from a study of more than 10,000 participants in the United States that uncovered significant and large sex differences in personality features. In the study, personality distributions for women and men overlapped by only 10%, suggesting that with regard to personality, they are very different.

Naturally, the sex differences in personality suggest that there are also sex differences in personality disorders. In a large-scale study of more than 18,000 British adults, Furnham and Trickey (2011) examined sex differences in personality disorders and found several differences. Women displayed significantly more symptoms of borderline, avoidant, and dependent personality disorders, and of passive aggressiveness, a trait not associated with these personality disorders. Men displayed significantly more symptoms of paranoid, schizoid, narcissistic, antisocial,

histrionic, and schizotypal personality disorders. The only disorder in which sex differences were not evident was obsessive-compulsive personality disorder.

To summarize, personality is the totality of an individual's personal traits and characteristics. On the elemental level personality is how an individual thinks, feels, and behaves. Most of an individual's traits and characteristics remain relatively consistent throughout their lives, but they may possibly change in the later stages of the life course. Importantly, certain personality characteristics can determine how well an individual functions in life and can even affect how long a person will live. There is no correct or incorrect blend of personality traits, but there are enduring patterns of inner experience and behavior that deviate markedly from the expectations of an individual's culture; these are known to social workers and related professionals as personality disorders.

EXPERT'S CORNER: PAUL COSTA

One of the leading scholars in the area of personality is Paul Costa, who along with Robert McCrae devised the dominant measure of the Five Factor Model of Personality. For nearly 30 years, Dr. Costa has been the Chief of the Laboratory of Personality and Cognition at the Gerontology Research Center of the National Institute on Aging (part of the National Institutes of Health). Over a six-decade publishing career, Costa has shown that personality features are associated with virtually every aspect of human behavior and he has been a widely cited scholar in many areas of human behavior.

In recent years, Costa, often together with Robert McCrae (see, McCrae & Costa, 2010) devised the Five Factor Theory of Personality, which uses the expansive empirical literature about the relevance of extraversion, neuroticism, agreeableness, conscientiousness, and openness to experience and frames the life-course continuity of personality functioning. The basic principles of the Five Factor Theory of Personality are that

- all adults can be characterized by their differential standing on a series of personality traits that influence patterns of thoughts, feelings, and actions;

- personality traits are endogenous basic tendencies that can be altered by exogenous interventions, processes, or events that affect their biological bases; and

- the development of personality traits matures in the first third of life but continues across life.

Personality molds the ways that individuals adapt to life circumstances, the ways that individuals see themselves, and the ways that individuals interface with the environment. Costa's work has been instrumental in showing the enduring power of traits as predictors of all behavior, whether antisocial and maladaptive or conventional and functional.

SUMMARY

Personality describes the relatively consistent and stable ways in which an individual behaves, thinks, and feels. Personality is related to behavior, and is a determinant of mortality and overall life functioning. Although there is neither a correct nor incorrect blend of personality traits, there are enduring patterns of inner experience and behavior that can deviate markedly from the expectations of the individual's culture. These are known as personality disorders, and are the type of psychopathology that is commonly seen by clinical social workers, juvenile justice officials, and related human services professionals. To summarize:

• The Five Factor Model of Personality is the dominant structural model of personality. It contains five dimensions: Openness to Experience, Conscientiousness, Extraversion, Agreeableness, and Neuroticism.

• In many respects, personality is the psychological extension of temperament, which is physiologically based.

• Personality disorders create significant impairments in multiple areas of life.

• Cluster A personality disorders are odd and eccentric in nature and include paranoid, schizoid, and schizotypal personality disorders.

• Cluster B personality disorders are emotional and dramatic in nature and include antisocial, borderline, histrionic, and narcissistic personality disorders.

• Cluster C personality disorders are anxious and fearful in nature and include avoidant, dependent, and obsessive-compulsive personality disorders.

• Personality features impact behavioral outcomes across the life course.

• There are substantial sex differences in personality.

KEY TERMS

Agreeableness

Ambiverts

Antisocial personality disorder

Avoidant personality disorder

Borderline personality disorders

Cluster A personality disorders

Cluster B personality disorders

Cluster C personality disorders

Conscientiousness

Dependent personality disorder

Dialectical behavior therapy (DBT)

Extraversion

Extraverts

Five Factor Model of Personality

Histrionic personality disorder

Introverts

Mesolimbic reward system

Narcissistic personality disorder

Neuroticism

Obsessive-compulsive personality disorder

Openness to experience

Paranoid personality disorder

Personality

Personality disorder

Schizoid personality disorder

Schizotypal personality disorder

Structural model of personality

CHAPTER 8

COGNITION AND LEARNING

Our cognitive processes are very much related to our emotional capacities, and enhanced functioning of our neurocognitive systems is associated with increased self-regulation. Environmental conditions and socioeconomic status can profoundly influence the shaping of the mind, learning opportunities, and academic success, through their impact on brain development and its related socioemotional outcomes. We know that enriched environments and enriching, nurturing relationships can enhance the development of these neurocognitive systems, and can be even more important for children living in distressed or economically disadvantaged communities. The brain's remarkable capacity for growth and change across the life course (i.e., neuroplasticity) holds promise for those who help to shape and change developmental trajectories, and underscores how important it is to craft effective prevention and intervention programs that help people learn new skills.

This chapter provides an overview of how the mind develops over the life course, its capacity for making sense of the world around us, its influence on learning and self-regulation, and the impact that our life experiences and environment have on these developmental processes. Our anatomical cognitive workspace allows us to self-reflect, perceive and attend to stimuli, and judge and decide on a course of action, in big and small ways, each day of our lives. As humans, we have different levels of "access" to the contents of this workspace, based on how the information is processed, encoded, and retrieved across our life course. This cognitively conscious (explicit) and unconscious (implicit) information forms our memories and sense of self and in turn influences our identity.

DISTAL CONTEXT

Conscious and Unconscious Mind

The mind is only capable of managing a limited amount of information at any single moment in time; thus, it processes information at different levels of awareness, making only a limited amount of information available to us at any given point in time. *Subliminal* processing is undetectable even with focused attention, whereas *preconscious* processing can be retrieved with effortful attention to suppress the distractions that mask conscious awareness (Dehaene & Changeux, 2011). But what is attention and how does it relate to consciousness? William James (1890; in Dehaene & Changeux, 2011) first described *attention* as "the taking possession by the mind, in clear and vivid form, of one out of what seems several simultaneously possible objects or trains of thought" (p. 201). This, we now know from experimental work, includes the ability to inhibit distraction, selectively focus, and consciously process incoming data. The range of this capacity is easy to see in the kindergarten classroom, where some children sit with eyes transfixed on the story reader, hands in their laps and mouths open in awe and anticipation, whereas other heads turn wildly toward the latecomer at the door, the garbage truck's beeping near the classroom window, or the incessant itch on the back of the neck.

Research on the human brain conducted in the social and biological sciences over the past several decades has significantly advanced our understanding of how humans attend to information, think, and learn. Technological innovations such as neuroimaging capabilities have allowed scientists the opportunity to build and empirically test theoretical models of the mind. For example, Hester and Garavan (2009) examined the executive functioning (attention) capacity of 16 active cocaine users in a functional magnetic resonance imaging (fMRI) scanner when presented with drug and neutral stimuli. Participants showed decreased attentional control when presented with background cocaine images, and were "distracted" by the drug-related stimuli, which affected their ability to focus on the high-demand cognitive task in the scanner.

In contrast to earlier vertical models of conscious processing (e.g., top down, bottom up), Dehaene and Changeux (2011) proposed a Global Neuronal Workspace model that conceptualizes a cognitive workspace that engages and "broadcasts" projections from perceptual, motor, memory, and evaluative areas of the brain, via long-distance axons. They describe this as a "horizontal workspace" where global network information, across all processing areas of the brain, is circulated throughout this workspace and becomes what we then experience as consciousness. The anatomical architecture in the human prefrontal cortex is particularly adaptable to cell input from these long-distance communication projections; this conceptual model and accompanying empirical findings suggest, therefore, that this space is our seat of our consciousness. Abnormal conscious processing, as seen in disorders like multiple sclerosis and schizophrenia, are characterized by impairment of these long-distance excitatory axon connections (Dehaene & Changeux, 2011).

In our professional social work practice, we help clients increase their conscious awareness to accomplish agreed-upon treatment goals, so that clients can choose better behavioral alternatives. We often encounter the client who says, "I don't know why I did what I did. It just happened." In practice, such unaccounted-for behavior represents a hiccup in the "thinking" part of the situational sequence from event (e.g., boy bumps into another boy in line) to behavior (second boy shoves first boy to the ground). Our goal in working with clients is to restore this "thinking" part—to slow down the thought–emotion–behavior sequence of events—so that our clients develop a greater repertoire of behavioral choice (i.e., behavioral flexibility) from which to respond. In time, their choices hopefully will become more consistent with their treatment goals. Another way of thinking about this is that, in practice, we hope to strengthen the regulatory top-down connections in our clients' brains; to help them harness the cognitive/thinking part when they need it most, often in the presence of intensely emotional situations.

CASE STUDY: JACK

Jack is 12 years old and lives in a family with three other children: a younger biological sister who is 5 years old, an older biological brother who is 15 years old, and a 2-year-old foster child named Ava who came to live with Jack's family 8 months ago. Child Protective Services took Ava from her biological father's home due to a substantiated report of child sexual abuse. Jack's mother, Dionne, is a single parent whose husband of 10 years died suddenly of a heart attack only 2 years ago. Dionne has a boyfriend who is in and out of the home and contributes financially, but not much emotionally, to the stability of the household. Dionne has a good-paying full-time job in a 24-hour daycare center in the city, and often works nontraditional shifts. Currently her schedule is 3 P.M. to 11 P.M.

Monday through Friday. Dionne has an associate's degree in early childhood education from the local community college. She is happy with her current employer, but hopes one day to open her own daycare center. Jack goes to school regularly, is in good health, and has many friends at the neighborhood public school he attends. He has been diagnosed with a learning disability but is getting the educational services and support he needs to succeed in his academic work. Jack also loves basketball. He plays on the community recreation league and is a leader on the team. Dionne knows he took his father's death very hard, but she also knows that it has been 2 years and he seems to be doing okay. She never required him to get counseling because she said it would have been too hard for her to have him "relive the loss" with someone whom he does not know.

One day, all four children were home alone on a Saturday when Dionne had to attend an all-day training and take a test for her job. Jack told the police he just does not know what happened. He does not remember the details, but he does know in his heart he did not mean to harm Ava. He cannot even recall the circumstances of the incident. He said he was not angry; he was just trying to help teach her a lesson and to get her to stop crying. Jack's 15-year-old brother called 911 and the paramedics came and took Ava to Children's Hospital. That is all Jack said he could remember. From there everything is "kind of real confusing" to him, he says. Ava died 2 days later of blunt-force trauma to the head and chest.

When the charges were read, the judge asked, "Do you understand the charges against you?"

Jack replied, "Yes. I mean not really. I don't know, Sir."

Currently Jack is residing in a youth detention facility in his home state. Jack may spend his days in a correctional facility until his early 20s.

Critical Thinking Questions:

- Should sentencing policy take into consideration youth's cognitive development and "mental age" during the adjudication process? If so, how should such developmental information be used in fair sentencing?

- What can you speculate might have been Jack's undiagnosed or unattended needs in his childhood and early adolescent years?

- What areas of Jack's development and the family's life cycle development would you want to examine in more detail to better understand the circumstances of his behavior?

- Where were the points in the system that could have and should have been more responsive to the family's, and Jack's, needs?

Components of consciousness that we focus on include self-awareness, perception, attention, and reflection. Self-awareness depends on the ability to retrieve memories that define the self. Damasio and Meyer (2009) explain how memories contribute to defining the self, suggesting that *core consciousness* results from the integration of new sensory information with a subjective sense of self to create a conscious self-representation, whereas *expanded consciousness* occurs when this integrated self-representation is modified to include past memories. The memories that are available to us at a cognitively conscious level are called *explicit* memories; others reside at a nonverbal, or *implicit*, level of awareness. Explicit memories include facts, episodes, and autobiographical memories, whereas implicit memories are nonverbal, sensory based, and procedural in nature (e.g., like learning how to ride a bike; Aamodt & Wang, 2011). The way in which we retrieve and process memories is determined by the neuronal architecture that underlies memory encoding. For example, Childress et al. (2008) at the University of Pennsylvania found that cocaine-related images trigger parts of the brain at an unconscious level in cocaine-dependent adults. Flash images of drug cues, presented at a speed not detectable at the conscious level of awareness, triggered activity in brain centers associated with emotion and reward and were linked to craving response.

New research is now finding a genetic link to our memory systems. Working at the National Institutes of Health, Uhl (2008) found that 21 of 89 genes whose variants are implicated in substance abuse and mental health disorders are found to be "cell adhesion" genes that affect the implicit memory system. For example, these specific genes may affect drug addiction in that the drug effect may be stored deep in the implicit memory system, where it exerts a strong influence on behavior. "Implicit memory plays a more important role than euphoria in the long-term story of a drug addiction" (Uhl, p. 8). Memories from stressful events are particularly likely to be encoded in this unconscious or implicit memory system because stress increases the release of hormones and neurotransmitters that increase amygdala excitability (Carter, 2010). Stress hormones function to increase consolidation of memories, thereby strengthening the synaptic connections and our memory. A most interesting recent study suggests that drugs designed to block NMDA-type glutamate receptors before drug-association memory activation may reduce drug-seeking behavior even up to

1 month after administration (Milton, Lee, Butler, Gardner, & Everitt, 2008).

Memories are created when messages are sent across synapses among cells; genes can also enhance or inhibit memory formation and strength by turning on or off the protein production that strengthens synaptic connections (LeDoux, 2002). As Carter (2010) wrote:

> A memory is not, in fact, a recollection of an experience but the recollection of the last time you recalled that experience. Hence our memories are constantly changing and redeveloping.... Each time we recall something, it is changed a little because it becomes mixed up with things that are happening in the present. Reconsolidation is a process by which this slightly altered memory effectively replaces the previous one, writing over it.... (p. 165)

In other words, we *are* our memories.

Therefore, some information about our past, our experiences, and our selves is not always consciously available to us, and cannot always be accessed through talking about it. Emotional and sensory-based experiences are necessary to activate those memories that are encoded at an implicit or cognitively unconscious level. This is why the smell of boiled cabbage in your university residence-hall dining facility might remind you of Sunday dinners and the accompanying cabbage rolls at your late grandmother's house back in Pennsylvania two decades ago. Indeed, visual, olfactory, and other sensory-based information can trigger access to and retrieval of prior experiences that are not in an individual's immediate cognitively conscious control (see Figure 8.1).

What is the emotional currency attached to a memory and how does that affect retrieval and subsequent behavioral action? Nobel Laureate and Princeton Professor Daniel Kahneman's work in behavioral economics shows how the neuronal architecture of the mind shapes cognition and behavioral decision making. People are prone to the simple message and a quick

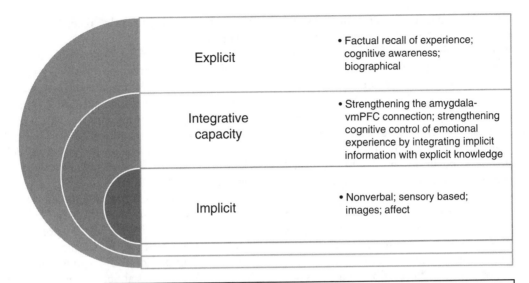

Explicit	• Factual recall of experience; cognitive awareness; biographical
Integrative capacity	• Strengthening the amygdala-vmPFC connection; strengthening cognitive control of emotional experience by integrating implicit information with explicit knowledge
Implicit	• Nonverbal; sensory based; images; affect

A goal of treatment is to bring into conscious awareness the implicitly stored experiences that guide behavioral decision making, and to integrate that with explicit cognitively conscious information so that clients gain greater control of their actions.

FIGURE 8.1   Integrating Implicit and Explicit Cognitive Processing

Note: vmPFC = ventromedial prefrontal cortex.

assessment of incoming information, even if such quick assessments are subject to inherent logical errors and message inconsistencies. Kahneman (2011) discusses our "System 1" and "System 2" information processing systems and the different ways in which they respond to information. System 1 is based on a fast, reflexive, impulsive response system, characterized by heightened amygdala excitation and "fast-tracking" of response to incoming stimuli. It is inherently prone to confirmation biases and snap judgments. System 2 is highly reflective, discerning, and takes a slower, more analytic path to evaluation and conclusions. Perhaps because of the additional energy System 2 takes to reflect on, evaluate, and make judgments from incoming information, it has become, over time and across evolution, the "lazier" of the two systems—as Kahneman (2011) comments, we have are predisposed to take "thinking short-cuts." Therefore, a consequence is that our mind may, at times, trick us into believing truth in information where we should exercise suspicion. For example, participate in this thought experiment. Write down the first thoughts that come to your mind after reading this sentence: "Jamal is 18 years old, lives in South Side Chicago, and was pulled over the by police." Why was he pulled over by the police? Now write down your immediate thoughts about this sentence: "Jimmy is 18 years old and drives a pickup truck in rural Georgia. He was pulled over by the police." Why was he pulled over by the police? Contrast your answers. What about the context of the sentence mattered in your thought processes? What biases or assumptions informed your conclusions? Did you notice a difference in your immediate thoughts between the two scenarios? What do you think caused those immediate conclusions?

Judgment in decision making is influenced by how available information is to us and the ease with which it can be retrieved.

Availability and retrieval are determined by the *frequency* (repetition) and *fluency* (emotional intensity) of the information (Kahneman, 2011). Salient and vivid stories are those we will likely remember best because their fluency is higher. Behavioral economics helps us understand public policy decision, preferences, and support. For example, news media coverage that creates an emotional charge may lead to additional, similar coverage, resulting in an "availability cascade" that appeals to emotion (System 1) rather than systematic discernment (System 2; Kahneman, 2011). We have learned that cognitive ease can bias beliefs/judgment. Familiarity with one part of a statement may bias one to accept the entire statement as true, via this cognitive ease mechanism. Similarly, the "halo effect" suggests we have a tendency to jump to a generalized conclusion after our first impression of one piece of information, without appropriate evaluative evidence for the other pieces of information. Further, repetition or frequency of a message tends to increase favorable disposition to the information and increases believability of the content. Kahneman (2011) discusses human error of "ignoring ignorance of limited information" that favors forming a quick coherent narrative out of incomplete information and that trumps caution and speculation in believing such a narrative. "The tendency to revise the history of one's beliefs in light of what actually happened produces a robust cognitive illusion" (p. 203). It's like 4-year-old Owen who, when asked the question, "Who lives in the White House?," quickly and smugly smiled with certainty and said, "Santa!"—confidently remembering last Christmas season when he visited Santa in the white house located in his hometown, while simultaneously forgetting that he knew that Barack Obama is the president of the United States and lives in *the* White House located 15 miles east of the other white house where Santa came to visit. Research shows this can happen to all of us regardless of our position in the life course, where we tend to maximize one part of the information we receive and jump to a conclusion without

rationally weighing the other pieces of contextual data provided.

Knowing these tricks of the mind can be beneficial to the advertising and social marketing industries as well as to other businesses that either rely on persuasion and quick consumer decision making or attempt to capitalize on the subjugation of the discerning mind to the impulsive one. Let's take, for example, politicians and the persuasive capacity needed to craft and sell public policy for political and legislative adoption. How might knowledge of Kahneman's System 1 and System 2 help in crafting and advocating for housing policy? Consider for a moment the following social policy issue. In Fairfax County, Virginia, an affluent inner suburb located about 15 miles outside of Washington, DC, the county's recent Bridging Affordability Program, part of the its Housing Blueprint, seeks to prioritize spending on affordable housing targeted to the county's most vulnerable populations: low-income and working poor families. The Bridging Affordability Program, operating through the collaboration of nine nonprofit organizations, would enable the economically neediest families in the county to receive subsidized housing aid for 2 years. Toward its goal of helping families gain housing permanency with what they call an emphasis on "workforce housing," employment aid would also be part of the service plan for working families. There has been resistance from some Fairfax County constituency groups about the plan, arguing that the county has not considered the cost of lost revenue from businesses in the area that will have to curtail their real estate footprint (and therefore the tax base) to make way for local affordable housing structures. Imagine you are on the advisory council for the Bridging Affordability Program (from Kunkle, 2012). How would you craft your planning strategy to engage as many county constituency groups as possible to support this program? How might Kahneman's behavioral economics information be useful to you in crafting your public engagement and communication strategies?

INTELLIGENCE

How do we define and measure intelligence? What cognitive processes are involved in IQ? It has been said that intelligence is what intelligence tests measure. That is to say, there has been great debate over the past century in defining and operationalizing the construct of intelligence. The neuroscientific literature shows a neuroanatomical correlation with intelligence, where neuronal dendritic branches and brain connectivity, specifically the pathway among the prefrontal cortex, anterior cingulate cortex, and parietal cortex, are associated with intelligence (Aamodt & Wang, 2011).

Generally speaking there is consensus to date that our IQ is composed of a variety of types of intelligences. Howard Gardner, a professor of cognitive and educational sciences at Harvard University, developed the theory of *multiple intelligences* (1983, 2006), comprising seven core intelligences of the human mind: (a) linguistic (words/language), (b) logical-mathematical (logic and numbers), (c) musical (rhythm, music, sound), (d) bodily-kinesthetic (movement) (e) spatial-visual (images, finding one's way through physical environment), (f) interpersonal (relationships with others and knowing others' emotions), and (g) intrapersonal (self-awareness). There are three additional intelligences that Gardner currently proposes for consideration: (h) naturalist (relationship with natural environment), (i) spiritual/existential (religion and relationship with higher power), and (j) moral (ethics, humanity, and valuing life). Gardner recently wrote another book, *Five Minds for the Future* (2009), that anticipates the five capacities of the mind that will be necessary for successful employment and workforce development in coming years and decades: (a) the disciplinary mind (master of craft and content), (b) the synthesizing mind (ability to integrate interdisciplinary ideas and content and to communicate such integrated discoveries effectively), (c) the creating mind (capacity to identify and conceptualize new problems and ideas), (d) the respectful mind (appreciation for difference among human groups), and (e) the ethical mind (ability to fulfill obligations as a worker and citizen; taking stock and action). Other researchers have identified a part of our IQ called *crystallized* intelligence, characterized by knowledge and remembering facts, which tends to increase as we get older; and *fluid intelligence*, characterized by logical reasoning and analysis, which tends to decrease in efficiency and processing speed as we age (Aamodt & Wang, 2011).

SES seems to have an effect on the relationship between genetic heritability and IQ. In impoverished environments, there is little to no correlation between IQ and inherited genes, with researchers hypothesizing that disadvantaged environments do not provide a sufficiently rich or stimulating environment to interact with gene potential (Aamodt & Wang, p. 192). In comparison, there tends to be a 30% inheritability for middle-class populations in childhood, which increases to a 70–80% genetic contribution to IQ in adolescence and adulthood for this population (Aamodt & Wang, 2011, p. 192).

LEARNING

Learning changes the brain. Experience is learning. Therefore, experience, of all kinds, changes the brain. In fact, your brain has changed since you started reading this chapter. You have probably encountered some familiar concepts that you glossed over, then came to some unfamiliar concepts that your mind quickly tried to fit with familiar constructs from your repertoire of stored experiences. Perhaps your mind was able to find something it recognized—like the word *unconscious*—that you know you have heard before. That word is now retrieved in a new context, and in an undetectably short amount of time your mind is attempting to assimilate that new word to its new contextual meaning. Learning is contextual.

Social workers have always held a deep commitment to and belief in humans' capacity for growth and change. We have remained close to our conviction and core values that guide our work and that encourages us to maintain optimism that, with help, people have the capacity to alter life-course trajectories in favor of more promising developmental outcomes. The rapidly expanding scientific literature supports these core values. Neuroplasticity, or the brain's ability to grow neurons and form new neuronal connections throughout the life course as a result of experience and relationships, gives compelling empirical evidence to the ways in which psychosocial factors shape what the human mind can do. Therefore, although there are key developmentally sensitive periods of time in the life course for specific milestones to occur, there is inspiration from the bench sciences that we are not merely products of our early life experiences, nor are we constrained by them; rather, we are the active agents in a dynamic, interactive process throughout the life course. The promise of developmental plasticity across our life leaves us with the optimism that, indeed, change happens.

Experiences can change cell function by altering protein production and, thus, gene expression and regulation dynamics, which leads to behavioral action (Francis, 2011). Cozolino (2002) discusses learning as the "modification of neural networks," where synapses are changed when (a) we encounter new information, (b) we have new experiences, and (c) when memories are reprocessed. As Cozolino (2002) describes, psychotherapy itself is a learning process. The neuroscience of psychotherapy consistently demonstrates the importance of cognitive-emotional integration to facilitate behavioral judgments (actions) that are in line with treatment goals. "The organization of autobiographical memory in a manner that includes processing from multiple neural networks enhances self-awareness, increases the ability to problem solve, and allows us to cope with stress and regulate affect" (p. 232). Therefore, best practice advises that

psychotherapeutic treatment models should be designed in a way that facilitates communication and processing of information across all areas of the brain—left–right and top–down (cognitive-emotional)—to accomplish this goal.

Stress experiences can hijack top-down (cognitive) capacity and impair judgment. Resilient individuals are those who show sufficient medial prefrontal cortex capacity (part of the cognitively conscious brain) necessary to dampen excitation of the amygdala (the emotional and cognitively unconscious part of the brain) after stress exposure (Charney, 2004). "More neural traffic rises up from the limbic system than down from the cortex. This means the emotional part of our brain has more power to influence behavior than the rational part" (Carter, 2010, p. 98). For example, states of intense or chronic distress and the resulting increased cortisol levels lead to poor verbal learning and memory in substance-dependent individuals (Sinha & Li, 2007). Stress activates similar neural structures to the ones that drugs do, and may lead to impaired prefrontal functioning (cognitive functioning) and poor behavioral decision making (Brewer & Potenza, 2008).

Memories and learning consolidate during sleep, demonstrating its importance on learning and academic achievement. Children who are chronically sleep deprived or who grow up in noisy environments are at risk for delays in reading achievement, attention problems, and struggles with long-term memory (Aamodt & Wang, 2011). Babies' hearing is most vulnerable to loud noises in the third trimester and first 6 months of life (Aamodt & Wang, 2011). Long-term, cumulative exposure to stress hormones can impair hippocampal functioning (the structure associated with autobiographical memory and learning potential) through decreasing the volume in this brain structure over time (in Aamodt & Wang, p. 235, citing Sapolsky et al., 1990). Therefore, stressful environments can affect learning potential. During stress response, glucocorticoids attach to receptors in the hippocampus, which triggers corticotrophin-releasing hormone to shut down glucocorticoid production. Elevated glucocorticoid levels over a long period of time can lead to impaired memory processing, which affects learning, but they can also cause high blood pressure, decreased immune functioning, and other diseases, so it is important to look at the restorative capacity of the stress response system. Enriched environments and enriching relationships can facilitate resiliency in stress response by increasing the number of glucocorticoid receptors, allowing for more stressors to be taken and still trigger shutdown of glucocorticoid production. Whereas deprivation and abuse decrease the number of receptors and leave cortisol in the brain and body, nurturing environments and relationships increase these important receptors (Cozolino, 2002).

Also, over time stress can cause dendrites in prefrontal cortex to atrophy, compromising executive functioning. Other studies (e.g., Aamodt & Wang, p. 260) have shown that low SES is significantly related to poor executive functioning, specifically compromising the medial prefrontal and anterior cingulate cortices. Therefore, stressful environments and low SES can contribute to changes in health and learning potential, all of which can affect academic achievement. And research shows that SES matters most in early childhood. "In general, people whose SES improves later in life gain less advantage from the change than people whose SES improves in childhood" (p. 263).

Learning Challenges

We have seen already that environmental and socioeconomic conditions can have a profound effect on differentially shaping learning opportunities, achievement, and other developmental outcomes. Noble, Tottenham, and Casey (2005) identify cognitive control, learning and memory, and reading as the essential neurocognitive systems associated with school readiness. These systems are influenced by children's early life experience, which can enhance or compromise their structure and function. Noble et al. (2005) found that living in an orphanage early in life, as well as chronic childhood abuse, have deleterious effects on these systems, and they propose targeting educational interventions aimed at changing the brain structures underlying these systems to improve school readiness for these populations. Structured play, which includes activities such as imaginative play and pretending, is associated with behavioral flexibility and reduction in stress cortisol levels. Risk taking that occurs naturally during social play experiences can facilitate interpersonal boundaries and in vivo practice opportunities for self-inhibition and taking other perspectives (Aamodt & Wang, 2011). Tools of the Mind is an example of an evidence-based preschool curriculum that uses relationships as a context for helping children from disadvantaged communities to build interdependent skills, and enhance cognitive control and social and emotional regulation, through structured play opportunities.

SPOTLIGHT TOPIC: TOOLS OF THE MIND

Drs. Elena Bodrova and Deborah Leong began the Tools of the Mind preschool program in 1993 (Bodrova & Leong, 2007). Based on Dr. Lev Vygotsky's classic cultural historical approach to early childhood education, Tools of the Mind helps teach self-regulation and executive functioning skills to students from disadvantaged communities. Relationships serve as the scaffolding platform from which these socioemotional and neurocognitive skills develop, and through which children are able to realize their full potential. Decades of evidence-based evaluation have shown that the program increases cognitive control and strengthens social and emotional regulation. Specifically, the curriculum focuses on helping children develop inhibitory control, working memory, and cognitive flexibility. Through structured play, children learn to replace reactive behavior with intentional behavior by strengthening attention and shoring up their ability to ignore distractions and maintain focus. The curriculum helps children become more reflective thinkers, which requires working memory and the ability to hold information in the mind to see how new patterns or association emerge, to sequence information from a story, and to develop narrative comprehension. Other curricular activities help children to adjust levels of attention to classroom conditions, bring behavioral alternatives to mind when needed, to take the perspective of the other, and filter out distractions in the environment to make good behavioral decisions.

For Reflection

Think about some of the reasons and barriers as to why these program principles have not been adopted and diffused on a national level.

MOTIVATION

"I don't want drugs at all; but sometimes it runs through my mind but I never act on it."
(Opiate user in her late 30s)

Prochaska and DiClemente's (2005) transtheoretical model of change offers an empirically tested five-stage sequential model of behavioral motivation. The five stages of change are precontemplation, contemplation, determination, action, and maintenance. Clients in the *precontemplation* stage exhibit no intention to change behavior anytime soon and demonstrate limited awareness of the problem. When clients move into *contemplation*, they do so because of increased awareness of the problem, but they are still not ready to make a commitment to change. In the *determination* stage, ambivalence favors action and typically clients are ready to make a change within the next month. The *action* stage is characterized by actual behavioral changes and observable commitment to making progress toward goals. In the *maintenance* stage, clients try to sustain desired results and actively maintain a focus on doing what they need to do to stay on track with their goals and with the changes already made. Of course the context under which a behavioral decision is made matters, and *relative utility*, or comparative value of the decisions based on context,

needs to be understood. Context and conditions frame the parameters under which people make a current decision. People are, generally speaking, loss averse—that is, more sensitive to the losses in a decision than to the gains—and therefore will often favor no change if perceived losses are high relative to perceived gains (see Table 8.1 for an example of decisional framing exercise; Kahneman, 2011). One's past experiences and current reference point influence behavioral change decisions and motivation for action.

Brief interventions, such as *motivational interviewing (MI)* and *motivational enhancement therapy (MET)*, are evidence-based practices commonly used with clients to shore up their motivation in a relational, collaborative manner. MI relies on client autonomy in treatment decision making, and invites clients to explore perceived discrepancies between their own values, goals, and problem behaviors (Miller & Rollnick, 2002). Brief motivational interventions can be used in diverse settings, such as outpatient primary care settings and in the schools. MET is similar in focus to MI, and focuses on the FRAMES model: providing *Feedback* to the client; helping clients take *Responsibility* for change; offering *Advice* and encouragement; compiling, with the client, a *Menu* of options for change; using *Empathic* rapport; and working to *Support* client self-efficacy (Miller & Rollnick, 2002).

Table 8.1   Cognitive Priming and Framing of Scenarios

The following example, presented in Daniel Kahneman's 2011 book, *Thinking, Fast and Slow*, illustrates the importance of context and framing on interpretation, even when presented with the exact same information.

Imagine that the United States is preparing for the outbreak of an unusual Asian disease, which is expected to kill 600 people. Two alternative programs to combat the disease have been proposed. Assume that the exact same scientific estimates of the consequences of the programs are as follows:

- If program A is adopted, 200 people will be saved.
- If program B is adopted, there is a one-third probability that 600 people will be saved and a two-thirds probability that no people will be saved.

Which would you choose?
Now consider:

- If program A′ is adopted, 400 people will die.
- If program B′ is adopted, there is a one-third probability that nobody will die and a two-thirds probability that 600 people will die.

Which would you choose? (p. 368)

Why do the majority of people choose to save the 200 people in the first scenario, but choose to gamble on the outcomes, rather than save 200 people for certain, in the second scenario? Kahneman points out that when the choices are framed with negative outcomes, people prefer the risk over sure thing; when framed with positive outcomes as anchor, people prefer the safe bet over taking risk. People are generally more affected by threat of loss than they are to the emotional reaction of potential gain, so will often make decisions to avoid risk rather than gain reward when they have to choose. Indeed, when I presented this scenario to my advanced MSW research class, the results were in line with these other studies: 19 students chose program A versus 3 who chose program B; whereas only 10 chose program A′ and 10 chose program B′ (with 2 students opting out of having to make a decision in the second scenario).

In addition to the conscious processing of change that Prochaska and DiClemente (2005) propose an individual goes through in making behavioral change decisions, behavioral motivation can be influenced by unconscious processes. Basic drives, urges, and desires that motivate behavior come from the unconscious brain and operate as reflexive, automatic responses to environmental stimuli (Carter, 2010, p. 197). Empirical studies have shown visual stimuli can present at a cognitively unconscious level and can have a subliminal priming effect with profound influence on emotion and action. For example, subliminal monetary incentives have been shown to increase motivation in an experimental task (Pessiglione et al., 2007). But we might wonder, how does this play out in our work with clients and client systems? Slovic, Finucane, Peters, and MacGregor's (2002) affect heuristic model suggests that

implicit information influences behavior directly and indirectly by influencing the assessment of potential risk and benefit, thereby biasing judgment in decision making. We know from the substance-abuse literature that drugs of abuse hijack the brain's natural reward system, which explains the motivational struggle people with addiction undergo when trying to abstain from using substances (Volkow, Fowler, & Wang, 2004). Findings show that individuals in early recovery are often unsuccessful in being able to substitute other reinforcers (e.g., food, social interactions, positive recreational activities) for drug and alcohol use because the neurobiological reward effects for these new stimuli are blunted while the reward effects from drug and alcohol cues are significantly and simultaneously increased (Di Chiara, 2002; Di Chiara & Bassareo, 2007). So seemingly rational decision making is undermined by a dysregulated reward system that favors drug use over recovery-related substitutes.

Behavior, and the accompanying motivation to alter behavior, is influenced by two information processing systems, according to dual process theories of cognition (Rooke & Hine, 2011): the explicit cognitive system (Wiers, Rinck, Kordts, Houben, & Strack, 2010) and the implicit cognitive system. Results from Rooke and Hine (2011) showed that implicit cognition may have a stronger effect on adolescent risk-taking behavior as compared to adults. In their study, implicit cognition showed a stronger association with binge-drinking episodes for adolescents versus adults. Therefore, the authors suggest that risk-reducing and health-promoting prevention and intervention programs should target both implicit and explicit cognitions, especially for adolescent populations, and that such interventions should focus on emotions, impulses, memory associations, and cues, in addition to providing educational/factual information. Other fMRI studies support these recommendations by providing neurobiological evidence that adolescent decision making does not occur in the frontal lobes (rational centers) as adult decision making more typically does (Blakemore, den Ouden, Choudhury, & Frith, 2007). In summary, fMRI studies implicate the following core brain regions with behavioral motivation states:

- The anterior cingulate cortex and medial prefrontal cortex are responsible for attention and memory processes and encode motivational value of stimuli (Grüsser et al., 2004; Heinz et al., 2004; Myrick et al., 2004; Tapert, Brown, Baratta, & Brown, 2004).

- The orbitofrontal cortex is responsible for the evaluation of stimuli and confers reward value that enhances a motivational state (Myrick et al., 2004; Wrase et al., 2002);

- The ventral striatum (nucleus accumbens) is associated with stimuli motivation and motor reactions (Wrase et al., 2007)

Self-Regulation and Cognitive Control

Self-regulation, which includes emotional control and behavioral inhibition, is the cornerstone for successful social and psychological functioning and academic achievement, even into adulthood. Academic achievement is related to social competence, and social rejection is associated with decreased self-control and subsequent poor performance on reasoning tasks. Self-control can be developed through social play and is associated with later academic success. Improvement in self-control can be gained through structured goal-directed play activities, like those used in the evidence-based Tools of the Mind program (2007), which build impulse inhibition skills through imaginative play.

Perlman and Pelphrey (2011) discuss two types of executive functioning, "cool" and "hot," and describe their relationship to self-control. Cool executive functioning is associated with more rational analytic processes, and hot with emotional regulation and motivation. Cool executive processes are primarily governed by the dorsolateral prefrontal cortex, whereas hot executive functioning is influenced by the ventral and medial prefrontal cortices. Perlman and Pelphrey used fMRI to examine the brain mechanisms implicated in the development of affective regulation in children ages 5 to 11 years, and found increased connectivity between the anterior cingulate cortex and amygdala when emotional regulation capacity was marshaled during a task, with the pattern of neural connectivity increasing with age. "Our study implicates increased connectivity as a neural mechanism for the development of affective self-regulation" (Perlman & Pelphrey, 2011, p. 618). Similarly, Ochsner, Bunge, Gross, and Gabrieli's (2002) fMRI study found decreased negative emotion in adult patients was associated with increased anterior cingulate cortex activation, implicating it as a structure that regulates emotion. Other researchers have found similar findings with child participants (Levesque et al. 2004), where increased activation of prefrontal and anterior cingulate cortices were associated with suppressing emotion in response to sad images.

What are other ways we can help clients enhance self-regulation capacity in the service of tipping the behavioral decision-making scale in favor of health promotion? Houben, Schoenmakers, and Wiers (2010) discuss an evaluative conditioning approach as a treatment technique designed to change the affective value associated with a risk behavior in order to decrease the behavioral impulse. The authors call this a "counterconditioning" effect, where the introduction of new affective association with the risk behavior decreases the value of the behavior and subsequently decreases its frequency. For example, in their experimental condition, pictures of beer (conditioned stimulus) were paired with negative International Affective Picture Scheme (IAPS) pictures (unconditioned stimulus) or negative adjectives; water pictures were paired with positive IAPS pictures or positive adjectives. The control condition in the study was shown the same pictures but not temporally paired. Results showed the experimental condition held more negative attitudes toward alcohol compared to the control; there was less beer craving in the experimental condition; and those in the experimental condition consumed less beer during the week after the experiment.

INTERPERSONAL NEUROBIOLOGY

Daniel Siegel, in his work on interpersonal neurobiology and his book, *The Developing Mind* (1999), describes the science behind how the brain is built and rebuilt via social relationships. Secure attachment with nurturing, warm, supportive caregivers protects the hippocampus from stress by increasing glucocorticoid receptors in the brain, and protects working memory and learning potential. Social bonding processes activate neural plasticity necessary for quality learning experiences, and early social interactions facilitate the development of mirror neurons that allow attunement with a caregiver and emotional regulation. "Alienated/isolated shame-ridden people die" (Cozolino, 2002). Positive parent–child behaviors and contingent communication are important for later moral development; sensitive and warm parenting leads to social competence, and poor emotional regulation predicts poor social adjustment across life span (Aamodt & Wang, 2011). So, relationships matter tremendously over the long run. We know from the literature that early childhood relationships provide the neurobiological template and secure base for later cognitive, social, and emotional regulation capacity, and are key in opening up learning potential by facilitating healthy mental-skill development such as high-functioning working memory and the capacity to attend to a topic and filter out distracting information. We know that this early start can have lasting consequences on later development, keeping in mind that our knowledge of brain plasticity offers hope that nurturing relationships introduced at other points in the life course can alter the neurobiological trajectory and developmental outcomes.

Therefore, we must ask ourselves: Do our interventions build on or undermine these implications drawn from the cognitive sciences? For example, recently in Virginia, several legislators in the General Assembly have begun questioning the impact of segregated, solitary confinement on prisoners housed in maximum security correctional facilities in the state. Certainly the interpersonal neurobiology literature base strongly suggests that segregated confinement with scarce human contact, sometimes for years on end, would not be the optimal rehabilitation intervention for prison inmates, and would undermine successful outcomes in community transitioning upon release. In fact, some states across the country are beginning to introduce legislation to reduce the length of segregation time for inmates, particularly for inmates with serious mental illness for whom the absence of human contact might compound existing developmental deficits. Human contact is essential to survival. Without contact, humanity is lost. It is time we turned a critical eye to how our social institutions and systems restore or undermine human development.

> Lydia Alturo is mother to a 1-month-old baby boy and two girls, ages 10 and 6 years, who both attend the neighborhood elementary school. Recently, Ms. Alturo was pulled over by the police for failing to come to a complete stop at a crosswalk stop sign, as she was on her way to her job cleaning houses. During the routine traffic stop it was found that she was driving with a suspended license and it was noted that she had entered the country twice without proper documentation. She crossed the Texas border in 2000 after spending 2 months traveling on buses and on foot from Guatemala to the United States. Ms. Alturo is now required to wear a tracking device on her ankle and is eagerly awaiting the results of her deportation appeal. She is hoping for a 6-month stay of removal. But she has a backup plan if she does not obtain the stay and is deported to Guatemala. She has one relative in her home country, whom she does not know well but with whom she could initially stay, should she be deported. She would decide not to take her children with her because it has always been her dream for them to grow up in the United States, and she has indeed already risked so much and worked so hard to get them to their current legal status in the United States. So she has a plan. Her 1-month-old baby would stay in America with Ms. Alturo's father, a permanent resident; and the two older girls would stay in the United States with their grandmother. As you ponder Ms. Alturo's plan and the potential consequences of her choices, think about how the interpersonal neurobiology literature could be used to understand the impending challenges this family faces if the attachment system between parent and children is disrupted as a result of parental deportation. How might you use this information to advocate for this family in legal or policy arenas?

We know that SES (defined here as the resources available to a family relative to others in their society) and status or privilege in society are correlated with health and well-being (Sapolsky, 2005). But what do we know of social hierarchy, loss of status that is often the case when immigrating to the United States, and neurobiological functioning? Zink et al. (2008) examined the neural representation of social hierarchy status, using fMRI technology to identify the neural mechanisms that undergird superiority and inferiority status, both in stable and unstable social hierarchies. When viewing a superior player in a stable hierarchy (vs. viewing an inferior player), the following regions showed greater activation: bilateral occipital/parietal cortex, ventral striatum, parahippocampal cortex (which is associated with contextual/associative processing),

and dorsolateral prefrontal cortex (see Table 8.2 for information on brain structures). Regional activation was similar in the unstable hierarchy, but unique to viewing a superior player in an unstable hierarchy were activations in the bilateral thalamus, right amygdala, posterior cingulate cortex, medial prefrontal cortex, primary motor cortex, somatosensory cortex, and supplementary motor area. Status loss was correlated with activity in the bilateral occipital/parietal cortex and ventral striatum (these two regions associated with perceptual/attentional processing), midbrain/thalamus, and anterior insula (Zink et al., p. 276). When there was a positive hierarchical outcome (superior lost), the following brain regions were significantly activated: dorsal striatum, midbrain/thalamus, medial prefrontal cortex, dorsal premotor cortex, pre-supplementary

Table 8.2   Important Brain Structures and their Functions

Ventral tegmental area: This area of the brain contains the reward circuitry and includes structures such as the nucleus accumbens and amygdala.

Dorsolateral prefrontal cortex: The executive center, with focus on planning; making decisions to act in one way over another; and helping us to shift our thinking to avoid intrusive thoughts. Poor decision making has been linked to decreased activation of the right dorsolateral prefrontal and medial prefrontal cortices.

Orbitofrontal cortex: This structure lies between the frontal cortex (cognitive area of the brain) and the limbic system (emotional areas of the brain), so it has functions in both areas. It helps us gain regulatory control over our emotions, inhibits inappropriate actions, defers immediate rewards in favor of long-term advantages, and is developed and strengthened via social interactions and through our relationships with others.

Insula: The "visceral" (emotional) self; helps us monitor body boundaries and information from our internal organs.

Anterior cingulate cortex: Connects higher cognitive areas of the brain to the limbic system. Contributes to behavioral agency. Information passing through this area contains wordless memories, urges, and drives. Focuses attention to be able to attend to one's own thoughts; helps in monitoring internal states. It is particularly active when people assess their actions in social contexts. Structure is active when measuring actions against goals, and provides a feedback mechanism so people can alter their actions.

Ventromedial prefrontal cortex: When emotions are experienced, this structure helps assign them meaning based on our perceptions; it helps us to make decisions to avoid negative consequences.

Note: Adapted from *Mapping the Mind: Revised and Updated Edition*, by R. Carter, 2010, p. 182.

motor area. "Viewing a superior player compared with an inferior player activated the [dorsolateral prefrontal cortex], amygdala, thalamus, posterior cingulate, and [medial prefrontal cortex] in the social (not computerized) situation only" (Zink et al., 2008, p. 276). The research can be summarized by the following:

- Dynamic, changeable hierarchies are more stressful due to fear of loss of competitive edge and lack of access to resources.

- The dorsolateral prefrontal cortex plays a role in social judgments and assessing social status and social norm compliance.

- The amygdala is highly activated in unstable social hierarchy contexts, and is associated with social anxiety.

- Motivation to compare the self upward with superiors can lead to negative affect via activation of neural mechanisms responsible for making social comparisons, such as the medial prefrontal cortex.

How do you think Ms. Alturo's current social environment and undocumented status might be contributing to her emotional and motivational state? How might the stress of living in an unstable social situation affect Ms. Alturo's elementary school children, their attachment to their school system, their peer comparisons and self-evaluations, and their learning potential at school?

TECHNOLOGICAL ADVANCES TO UNDERSTAND THE MIND

Technological advancements in neuroimaging have amplified our ability to peer into the mind and examine the brain's influence on behavior. In this area, there are four directions that will empirically advance our understanding of interactive brain–environment–behavior processes: (a) real-time fMRI, (b) using fMRI to individualize treatment sequencing, (c) discovery of neural connectivity profiles associated with resiliency, and (d) examining the influence of social processes on brain–behavior change.

Real-Time fMRI

Real-time fMRI provides clients with in-scanner visual feedback on how their brains change in response to the application of specific treatment techniques or strategies learned in the treatment sessions. Clients are able to see how their brains react to stressors they might encounter in their environment after they leave treatment. Specifically, clients are given the opportunity to practice strategies learned in treatment for emotional regulation and cognitive control while the scanner flashes drug stressor cues. The participant receives immediate visual feedback from a thermometer bar on the scanner computer screen that shows the magnitude of functional activity in brain regions while he or she employs the treatment strategy.

Training clients to down-regulate (decrease activation) or up-regulate (increase activity) target brain regions to control specific emotional and behavioral responses linked to identified treatment goals (e.g., pain management or emotional regulation) for a population or problem of interest offers unique, individualized treatment opportunities. Data could be systematically collected over time and across clients in a focused problem area that links specific treatment goals, in-session therapeutic strategies, and in-scanner client training protocols, with associated functional changes in targeted brain areas.

For example, patients in our recent study (Matto, Strolin-Goltzman, Hadjiyane, Kost, Minter, & Wiley, in press) viewed drug stressor and neutral images, presented in random order in the scanner, and were prompted to either passively "watch" or to "use what you know to reduce your discomfort" preceding each drug stressor image. One patient in the study described experiencing emotional and physiological changes when employing cognitive strategies during the scanner task (i.e., looking away, imagining the image as part of a theatrical event, attending to the humor in the drug color and to the artistic stylization of how the drug image was assembled, etc.). The scanner experience became a learning environment for the patient to apply a set of therapeutic cognitive strategies to the presentation of a drug stressor image, and to experience, in the moment, the subsequent visceral-response change associated with technique application.

Individualizing Treatment Sequencing

fMRI can also be used to calibrate treatment sequencing to individual client need. Clients may differentially benefit from the available evidence-based treatments in any given practice area; they may respond to various combinations of treatment protocols at different times and at different dosage levels. fMRI can be used as a clinical decision-making tool, along with other clinical assessment criteria, to identify when a client might be most responsive to a particular evidence-based treatment approach or when they may have reached a plateau where a new treatment approach should be introduced. In addition, treatment-sequence designs that include a cost-analysis component can examine how calibrating individual client treatment response to outcomes over time might lead to a more cost-effective, efficient course of treatment.

Neural Profiles of Resiliency

Although there is a significant and compelling body of neuroscience research based on the neural profiles that emerge from extreme stress disorders and socially toxic environments, to date there is scant empirical attention to the neurobiology of resiliency. For example, in working with people struggling with various stages of addiction, we could examine efficiency ratios in brain regions of interest to estimate utilization by length of time in recovery. Effortful control may decrease in the anterior cingulate cortex over time in treatment, as recruitment of this region is less necessary for gaining the same impact in self-regulation capacity—a significant treatment effect on brain-region response efficiency that could be benchmarked to time in recovery. In addition, examining how behavioral health treatments influence neural circuit pathways and pattern change among distributed networks, rather than just region-of-interest magnitude change, is an important area for future intervention research. There is strong empirical evidence to suggest that the integration of affective-cognitive processing (e.g., among amygdala, anterior cingulate cortex, and anterior insular cortex) are indicative of treatment progress. Treatment-related neural connectivity profiling is an important area for further study to understand how therapeutic learning changes the brain and subsequent behavior. For example, in our recent neuroimaging study (Matto, Strolin-Goltzman, Hadjiyane, Kost, Minter, & Wiley, in press) that examined how brain reactivity and cognitive control capacity changes as a result of participation in a 10-week, 20-session, experientially based relapse-prevention protocol (the dual-processing intervention that integrates art therapy methods with cognitive-behavioral verbal processing protocol), we found that regions associated with cognitive control capacity did indeed increase functional activity at the end of the 10 weeks in response to drug stressor images presented in the scanner. Our research team's next direction is to identify cues and triggers for recovery that might be identified and introduced into treatment protocols to strengthen the neural connectivity patterns in the brain that enhance motivation for enacting recovery-related behaviors. The stress-vulnerability model of addiction has helped us understand the significance of unconscious processing on emotions, motivation, and behavioral response, and we anticipate that expanding that model to extend understanding of the neural correlates of recovery, and the cognitive-emotional neural connectivity patterns that prompt activation of recovery behaviors, will provide important scientific evidence that can guide the strategic development and refinement of behavioral health treatment interventions to maximize treatment outcomes with substance abuse populations. As social workers who work with substance abuse populations, we need to understand how drug cues impact a person's recovery trajectory; but it is equally imperative that we begin to understand how recovery-related cues to which clients are exposed and that they develop from treatment experiences can shape the brain and behavior in favor of sustained recovery trajectories posttreatment.

Social Process Influence on Brain–Behavior Change

Examining how engagement in support networks impact region-of-interest functioning and neural circuitry communication—such as how utilization of sober supports impacts the orbitofrontal-amygdalar neural pathway in favor of enhancing emotional regulation capacity—is an innovative and important area for further study. Integrating the neurosciences with a social processes approach to understanding healing trajectories can help guide treatment decisions, particularly helping clients plan for postinstitution community transitioning. Brain and behavior must be understood within a larger sociocultural context that includes social interactions and community-level engagement.

A combination of these empirical applications using fMRI technology can lead us to a better understanding of how participation in behavioral health treatment programs restores capacity in brain regions and strengthens neural pathways that impact treatment goals—specifically, how social process mechanisms (e.g., participation in support networks) impact healing trajectories.

EXPERT'S CORNER: FRANK KRUEGER

Frank Krueger, PhD, is Assistant Professor of Social Cognitive Neuroscience at George Mason University, Chief of the Evolutionary Cognitive Neuroscience (ECON) Lab at the Krasnow Institute, and Co-Director of the Center for the Study of Neuroeconomics

(Continued)

at George Mason University. He is Lead Investigator of the Warfighter Head Injury Study, which is a comprehensive, longitudinal, and multidisciplinary study that examines brain neuroplasticity in war veterans who have suffered TBI. Dr. Krueger's research examines the role of the prefrontal cortex in behavioral decision making and its influence on our emotional and social lives. He is particularly interested in the neuroplasticity of the human brain, particularly its executive functioning capacity after experiencing adverse events.

Krueger et al. (2009) have examined the executive functioning capacity of Vietnam veterans with TBI and compared them to a control veteran sample (no TBI) using clinical, neuropsychological, and fMRI assessments. Their study findings show that damage to the ventromedial prefrontal cortex leads to diminished ability to regulate and manage emotional information, whereas damage to the dorsolateral prefrontal cortex leads to diminished ability to perceive and integrate emotional information. Without the ability to process incoming emotional information and reconcile it with one's thoughts, the ability of those with TBI to enact goal-directed behavior may be compromised. Krueger et al. state, "The [dorsolateral prefrontal cortex] is closely interconnected with the sensory neocortex receiving converging visual, somatosensory, and auditory information from the occipital, temporal, and parietal cortices, which make it well suited to perceive and use emotionally relevant information" (p. 22488). Their findings support the significance of cognitive processing areas (prefrontal region) on emotional intelligence (effectively understanding and managing emotional information). At the Center for Neuroscience and Regenerative Medicine, Krueger et al. (2011) are also examining how the brains of veterans from the Iraq and Afghanistan wars, particularly those with PTSD and mild TBI, change over the course of 1 year. In addition to researching the structural and functional capacity of the frontal lobe, Krueger has examined the molecular factors that influence recovery in executive functioning for those who have experienced traumatic brain injury. In a recent study (Krueger et al., 2011), he found that war veterans with frontal lobe lesions who had the Met66 allele of the brain-derived neurotrophic factor (*BDNF*) gene (which is significantly related to brain neuroplasticity) showed executive functioning capacity comparable to a control group. This allele accounted for 6.2% of the variation in executive functioning, suggesting this Met66 allele is associated with neural recovery. For a more in-depth read of Krueger's studies, please see Krueger et al. (2009, 2011).

COGNITIVE DEVELOPMENT ACROSS THE LIFE COURSE

First you have brown hair.
Then you have black hair.
Then you have white hair.
Then you shrink.
Then you die.

—Carter, age 6

Early Brain Maturation

What is the current thinking about how cognition develops across the life course?

Let's take a look at how the brain develops, how neurons communicate, and how the mind emerges across the life course. The neural tube becomes the brain and spinal cord and closes by the fourth week after conception. Segmentation or division of this neural tube into regions occurs by the sixth week (Aamodt & Wang, 2011). One of the greatest risks to fetal development is malnutrition, and the third trimester is a particularly vulnerable time for fetal brain growth. Brain maturation occurs from back of brain to front. Glial cells help guide neurons to their correct place in the brain's pathways. Neuronal axons are long, thin fibers that extend from the brain to various places in the body. The brainstem controls the autonomic functioning like heart rate, breathing, sleep, and digestion. Sensory information enters the body and travels to the thalamus, which passes on information to the four lobes of the cortex. A synapse is the gap between neurons where electrical and chemical messaging occurs. The first 3 years of life is the time when neurons form the majority of their axons and dendrites; communication between neurons and strengthening or weakening of these synaptic pathways occurs across the life span. By 10 months, infants are able to selectively attend to environmental stimuli to self-soothe; at 27 to 30 months, they show effortful control and the ability to follow rules and change behavior (Aamodt & Wang, 2011). Environmental influences (experiences) enter the brain through the senses and cause biochemical changes that modify gene expression and protein production. "When DNA is copied during cell division, the pattern of epigenetic modification is copied as well, so that all descendants of the cell maintain the information" (Aamodt & Wang, 2011, p. 34). Early social stressors can modify later behavior by changing particular genes. For example, "prenatal and early postnatal nutrition can influence the adult risk of heart disease, type 2 diabetes, obesity, and cancer in people" (p. 34). Chemical alternation caused by experience can turn off certain genes in certain cells forever. For instance, children whose mothers experienced a natural disaster, especially during the fifth through ninth months of pregnancy, showed lower IQ and language ability and greater risk of autism.

Childhood and Adolescence

The gray matter of the neocortex is where the neurons, dendrites, and synapses exist, and reaches peak volume by age 9–11 years; between ages 3–8, children's brains (measured in gray matter area) uses twice as much energy as adult brain tissue. The temporal cortex achieves maximum volume at age 14; the optimal development of the frontal cortex follows. White matter, which is responsible for connecting different parts of the brain, consists of myelinated axons that carry information between neurons. They reach 85% of adult size in adolescence and continue to grow into middle adulthood. "If the experience required to complete an early developmental process is not available, the sensitive period is normally extended for a while, resulting in delayed maturation of that brain circuit and all the others that depend on it. Eventually, though, the window of opportunity closes, and any resulting damage may become permanent" (Aamodt & Wang, 2011, p. 47).

Piaget's cognitive development stage of concrete operations (ages 7–11 years) suggests that children begin moving from imaginative play and symbolic focus to increased logical reasoning and enhanced problem-solving capacity during these early elementary school years. To illustrate the beginnings of this concrete operations stage, we offer a 7-year-old's perspective on a widely accepted societal practice: funeral burial in modern Western society. Take note of the problem-solving capacity involved when the child processes information that is inconsistent with an existing schema of experience; rather than accepting the information as fact, he changes the outcome to fit a more acceptable construct of funeral practice.

Upon driving by a cemetery, the 7-year old asked, "What are those stones for?" Astounded by the burial explanation, he incredulously barked, "They put people in the ground?"

His older brother retorted, "Yes, but they are dead."

"But there are worms and all kinds of things down there," observed the 7-year-old.

"Yes, but people are dead," the older brother restated.

Problem-solving an answer that would be more consistent with his personalized schema of funeral practice, the 7-year-old suggested, "Can you just put stones around me instead?"

A second round of pruning synapses to increase the brain's energy efficiency occurs in adolescence. Adolescence is a period of sensation seeking at the same time that the judgment and executive functioning areas of the brain—key to self-regulation and behavioral inhibition—are not fully developed. Early maturation of subcortical regions responsible for reward and emotion, combined with later maturing areas in the frontal cortex that are responsible for reason and inhibition, can lead to risky behaviors in adolescence. Adolescents, therefore, may not fully understand the consequences of their actions. The orbitofrontal cortex is also a late-maturing region that connects emotion and good judgment; damage to the orbitofrontal cortex results in making bad decisions (Aamodt & Wang, 2011). However, there is also an increase in self-reflection and cognitive flexibility in adolescence, and Scarborough, Lewis, and Kulkarni (2010) offer pragmatic activities (e.g., client goal-setting processes) that can promote executive functioning and social cognitive skills in adolescence.

Spatial skills in boys' brains are developed through active play opportunities; children living in deprived environments show decreased spatial ability (Aamodt & Wang, 2011). In one study cited in Aamodt and Wang (2011), boys from low-SES families scored lower on mental rotation tests than boys from middle- and high-SES families. First-graders from poor areas score lower than middle-class first-graders in reading and math (Aamodt & Wang, 2011). Sleep loss reduces neural plasticity by reducing the opportunity to consolidate information learned into memory storage. Some school systems are beginning to revise educational start times for students in light of this sleep research, with some middle and high schools changing to a later morning time, given the research that shows adolescents have a different sleep pattern (later to bed and later to awaken) than young children, while still requiring at least 9 hours of sleep at night for adequate cognitive functioning and learning potential.

Cognitive Functioning and Decline in Adulthood

Knudsen, Heckman, Cameron, and Shonkoff (2006) warn that with rising income inequality in the United States and wage stagnation over the past 30 years, a greater proportion of individuals will be growing up in socioeconomically disadvantaged communities. They point to the research that suggests early childhood experiences impact cognitive and social developmental opportunities, which impacts the availability of human capital for later workforce success, particularly in these disadvantaged communities. They propose that because of the hierarchical nature of brain maturation and skill development (i.e., subsequent developmental outcomes depend upon preceding developmental opportunities), early childhood should be the life-stage target of intervention and investment to maximize positive developmental outcomes later in life. Inevitably, our national workforce and economic stability will be enhanced or inhibited as a result. This is particularly relevant given the recent economic recession, rising income inequality, and the growing cost of higher education in the United States for the foreseeable future. For example, although we are currently seeing increased corporate "in-sourcing" with manufacturing and factory jobs coming back to the United States, the employable skills necessary to land these relatively good middle-class jobs require advanced technical skills and the aptitude for operating, programming, and maintaining computerized factory machinery. Called computer numerically controlled (CNC) machines, they require workers to learn the technical programming language to operate them and to ensure accuracy in their output productivity, sometimes to the precision of a thousandth of an inch. Currently there is a shortage of workers with these necessary specialized skills to fill such jobs. Community colleges are starting to respond to the skills gap, offering classes with names like "Mechatronics," that teach CNC programming languages in their associate degree programs (Whoriskey, 2012). Ultimately, machinists will need to program the machines, not just push buttons, and even on the factory floor, workers will increasingly need specialized skill sets that require high cognitive demand, cognitive flexibility, and creative problem-solving capacity.

In older adulthood, although the type of intellectual capabilities may change over time (e.g., we saw that fluid intelligence decreases and crystallized intelligence increases as we age), for the most part intellectual functioning remains strong in healthy aging adults. Although some age-related changes in short-term memory are associated with normal aging, significant cognitive decline in our later years is not part of normal aging, and could be indicative of brain disease or disorder. For example, Alzheimer's disease, a neurodegenerative brain disease with severe cognitive impairment, can affect even young and middle-age adults, but its onset is generally seen in later adulthood. The disease affects neurobiological processes that lead to atrophy and cognitive decline, resulting from a buildup of proteins (amyloids) in the brain. New neuroimaging research is working to identify the neurobiological causes that lead to its onset, but currently, our etiological understanding and treatment interventions are limited, and ultimately the course of decline is progressive and without cure (Fjell & Walhovd, 2012). Although memory lapses are a normal part of aging, and are not necessarily suggestive of dementia, risk of dementia does go up with age, with about a 50% chance of getting Alzheimer's at age 85 (Fishman, 2010, p. 133). However, a person with a healthy brain can anticipate lifelong learning opportunities and having an active neural network that functions well into later adulthood.

SUMMARY

This chapter emphasized that behavioral decisions are influenced by more than conscious choice. Underlying processes such as implicit memories have an impact on our life choices and how we act on them. The ability to attend to information, despite the presence of distracting unconscious memories and urges or interfering environmental stimuli, increases the opportunity for academic success resulting from strengthened self-, social, and emotional regulation systems. Cognitive functioning therefore impacts emotional regulation capacity. The research suggests the following:

• Prevention and intervention efforts should be particularly targeted to high-stress, socioeconomically disadvantaged, and resource-limited environments.

• Unstable social hierarchies and high-daily-stress experiences can impair brain structures associated with working memory and sensory reactivity.

• These systems can then influence learning potential and may disproportionally disadvantage those who live in high-stress environments.

• Approaches that use nurturing human relationships as the medium through which children can learn self-regulation skills seem to be most promising for strengthening the neurocognitive systems associated with academic success.

• Neuroplasticity, or the brain's capacity to grow and change over the life course, allows us the promise of intervening at all points in a person's development to help strengthen and build those skills that enhance functional capacity and well-being.

KEY TERMS

Action stage

Contemplation stage

Core consciousness

Determination stage

Expanded consciousness

Explicit

Fluency

Frequency

Fluid intelligence

Implicit

Maintenance stage

Motivational enhancement therapy (MET)

Motivational interviewing (MI)

Multiple intelligences

Preconscious

Precontemplation stage

Real-time fMRI

Subliminal

CHAPTER 9

SOCIAL EXCHANGE AND COOPERATION

Human beings need each other to satisfy basic needs necessary for survival. To ensure survival, humans are interdependent on one another. As such, humans are social creatures who exchange a wide variety of things with one another, including material goods, services, and friendships. Exchange is found in every culture. Cooperation and sometimes conflict are part and parcel of these exchanges. The evolution of human social behavior and the formation of larger social and economic structures are predicated to a large extent on the nature of social exchange and cooperation. These elementary forms of social behavior exhibited in social exchange are thus the building blocks for the chapters that follow. This chapter examines what is currently understood about these concepts and demonstrates the many ways in which they are expressed across diverse settings and in experiments and game scenarios.

One of the major scholars noted for their work on social exchange theory is sociologist Peter Blau, who believed that the main influences on human behavior were the situational and personal factors that are related to the choices that people make, and the external conditions that constrain or facilitate those choices (Allan, 2007). Situational and personal factors impacting individuals' behavioral choices might include an individual's temperament, intelligence, or sociodemographic factors such as their age, race/ethnicity, or gender. Similarly, external conditions that shape the realm of possibility in terms of choices include factors such as local culture, level of economic development, and prescribed rules around gender or other components of identity. Figure 9.1 depicts an exchange between two actors that relies upon situational conditions. Thus, for Blau (and many others), the connection or tension between the individual and society is ever present. Consistent with our cell to society perspective, biological and psychological factors that influence individual behaviors take place within a set of conditions that include structural and collective factors that are external to the individual. *Social exchange and cooperation* is a way to conceptualize the way in which humans primarily interact with one another to meet and optimize their well-being. We move beyond narrow disciplinary boundaries and define social exchange in a broad sense that also includes economic exchange. Exchange is an important link between the individual-level factors acting on human behavior that we have studied thus far and the larger units in the cell to society framework that follow.

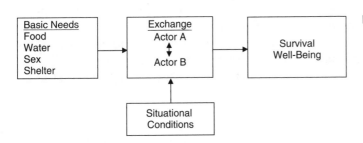

FIGURE 9.1   Basic Model of Social Exchange

CASE STUDY: FOOD COOPERATIVES

The Park Slope Food Coop (short for *cooperative*) is a Brooklyn, New York–based example of a new mode of social exchange within a community. The way food and groceries cooperatives work is as follows: Only members can shop at the cooperative; anyone, regardless of where they live or any other characteristic, is eligible to become a member. Being a member means that you must dedicate a certain number of hours a month (the Park Slope Food Coop requires 2 hours and 45 minutes) to working at the cooperative without being paid. In exchange, you get to shop at the coop, which is able to keep its prices very low because it does not have to pay for 75% of its labor costs.

The social exchange that happens at the Park Slope Food Coop and other cooperatives like it around the country is mutually beneficial to both the store as well as its members. It benefits the community because it is able to provide less expensive food to its members in exchange for their voluntary work commitments, which is why it can sell the food more cheaply than most other grocery stores.

This exchange is an example of people within a community working together to identify a need (inexpensive food) and finding a way to mutually provide that need for anyone who would like to participate. The Park Slope Food Coop does not exclude anyone from its membership. Members can be from any location (even out of state), any gender, any race, have any sexual orientation—it doesn't matter. The only thing the cooperative asks of its members is that they respect the rules of the cooperative, pay a startup and investment fee, and provide 2 hours and 45 minutes of free labor per month. They provide lower fees for members who cannot pay the investment or startup costs, and have jobs readily available for members who are not physically able to perform certain tasks.

This type of social exchange is not altruism—there is clearly something to be gained on both sides of the exchange. The cooperative receives free labor in exchange for providing low prices on its goods to the same people providing the free labor. However, it is still a successful and creative way to meet a community need through social exchange. As mentioned, there are food cooperatives all over the country, following a similar construct to provide inexpensive food to communities. Especially in times like those we face today, when people have fewer and fewer financial resources to pull from, it is essential to be able to have another resource—our time and ability to provide labor—to be able to put food on our tables.

Another example of social exchange is microfinance banks. These types of banks are set up in rural areas of developing nations and provide small loans, expected to be paid back with interest, to locals. The purpose of these loans is for villagers to begin small businesses within the community and eventually hire other villagers to work for them, thereby stimulating the local economy.

Critical Thinking Questions:

- Can you think of any other examples of social exchanges in your community or beyond that are working to promote community interests?
- Can you think of any that don't yet exist but that could be beneficial?
- Do you see a connection between these exchanges and social work?
- Do you consider food cooperatives and microfinance banks to be forms of social activism?

DISTAL CONTEXT

The formal study of social exchange and co-operation is rooted in the evolution of social behavior and, intellectually, in classical utilitarianism. Thus, social exchange plays a central role in the ongoing relationships that people have with each other. An understanding of social exchange in its evolutionary and philosophical context permits a stronger appreciation of its fundamental nature in both practice and policy applications.

Evolution and Social Exchange

In their computational theory of social exchange, Cosmides and Tooby (1989) argue that there are certain boundaries or constraints under which social exchange can evolve. They make the case that across the evolution of humanity, the behavioral ecology necessary for social exchange has been present for thousands of years. Given certain conditions, humans confront several issues that are a prerequisite for social exchange. Some of these conditions involve protection and self-defense from predators, which was a driving force for early humans (as well as other primates) to form coalitions. Even as early humans hunted other species, they quickly realized that without the protection of other cooperative humans, they would be easy prey for more physically powerful animals. Other conditions include sharing of resources such as meat. This is based on the notion that sharing a resource, particularly when there is more than what one individual needs, can lead to a credit of sorts where the receiver "owes" the giver something. Thus, these are cognitive adaptations to solving problems in the natural and social environment. These adaptations reflect areas in the brain that have been selected for over time because they have guided thought and behavior in a functionally adaptive way (Cosmides & Tooby, 1992). Although these basic needs around protection and meat sharing may seem distant at first glance, they are alive and well

in contemporary social relationships occurring across different settings, whether in urban America or rural India. For instance, such functionally adaptive behavior can be seen when individuals in a community come together to form a neighborhood watch group, to become members of a community-supported agriculture program, or to take part in a wide variety of other activities that benefit individual survival and sustenance by means of collective collaboration. Social workers and human service professionals can benefit from identifying important exchanges in the lives of their individual clients and also those that are a part of political advocacy or community practice.

GAME THEORY

Much of the empirical evidence and validation of social exchange and altruistic theories and hypotheses have come from using experimental games. Conceptually and empirically, game theory is derived from and has made a major impact upon fields such as economics, biology, political science, and logic. The objective behind game theory is to uncover the reasons why people make decisions, whether they are seemingly rational or irrational. Game theory states that no matter who you are, your life involves interactions with others, and the strategies and decisions these interactions require can be modeled using games, because the outcomes that we need or desire are also being pursued by other people. As Barash (2003) has pointed out, animals also play games, such as when two males want to mate with a female and the outcome depends upon what each male does and the decision that the female makes. Likewise, our actions associated with a goal are not always under our control. The outcome is based in part on the combined behavior of two or more individuals. This is true even among the simplest of events. Barash nicely explains this in what he calls the interrupted telephone call-back game, in which two friends are talking to each other and the dial tone is interrupted. Do you wait for the other person to call?

Or do you return the call knowing that the other person may be calling you at the same time, and therefore the line will be busy? Thus, there are gamelike moves that need to be made, and the decisions made can lead to different outcomes. These everyday life scenarios are the grist of game theory. Obviously, many of these scenarios take on greater importance than just a friendly telephone conversation. A more philosophically oriented decision scenario is based on Pascal's wager. Blaise Pascal (1623–1662) was a famous French philosopher who argued that everyone should believe in God based on the following gamelike scenario: God exists or does not exist, and people can freely choose to believe or not believe, but what do you get if you don't believe and you're right, versus choosing to believe and being right? For Pascal, it was a poor decision not to believe because nothing was gained. At least if you did believe and you were right there would be the theoretical payoff of going to heaven.

Researchers use all types of games to explore human behavior outcomes (Camerer, 2003). Some of the more common ones are the ultimatum game, the public goods game, and the classic prisoner's dilemma (described later). Games are chosen depending on what hypothesis about human behavior is being tested. For example, if one is interested in fairness in bargaining and negotiating, then the ultimatum game can be useful, because in this game two players or sides must divide a limited sum of money, and offers are rejected or accepted (e.g., Gintis, Bowles, Boyd, & Fehr, 2003). If trust is being investigated, then the prisoner's dilemma is often appropriate.

Prisoner's Dilemma

Arguably, the most classic of all games in game theory's arsenal is the prisoner's dilemma (see Figure 9.2). The prisoner's dilemma game is so compelling because players attempt to achieve the best possible outcome for themselves during a difficult situation. Here is how it works: Suppose the police arrest two people for robbing a bank. The police and the prosecutor place both prisoners in different cells. Their objective is to get both suspected bank robbers to confess, and so both would be guilty. For the police and prosecutor's office, this is the best outcome. The prisoners' best outcome is to be released and gain their freedom. The prosecutor offers them a deal. He tells them both that he does not have enough evidence to convict them both, but if they don't talk he can convict them of a lesser charge and they will spend a year in jail. Their other choice is cooperating with the prosecutor, pleading guilty, and implicating their partner. In this option, the prisoner will go free for cooperating with the government's case and his partner will receive the maximum penalty of 30 years. However, if both plead guilty and in effect rat on each other, they will both receive 10 years in prison. This is a very difficult situation for the player. If you and your partner keep quiet, you'll both spend only 1 year in jail; but if you keep quiet and your partner confesses, you will spend 30 years in jail. If you talk, the most you will receive is 10 years. What do you do?

Fully developed by Princeton University mathematician Albert Tucker based on

Options	Person A: Does not confess (i.e., maintains silence)	Person A: Cooperates with prosecutor (i.e., "rats" on partner)
Person B: Does not confess (i.e., maintains silence)	Both Persons A & B receive 1 year in jail	Person A goes free; Person B gets 30 years
Person B: Cooperates with prosecutor (i.e., "rats" on partner)	Person B goes free; Person A gets 30 years	Both Persons A & B receive 10 years in jail

FIGURE 9.2 Possible Scenarios for the "Prisoner's Dilemma"

preliminary work by the RAND Corporation, and unveiled during a seminar taking place in 1950 at Stanford University (Barash, 2003), the prisoner's dilemma has inspired substantial research into human behavior and the nature of trust and cooperation. It also reflects real-life scenarios where decisions can result in serious consequences and the decision is partly dependent on what another person decides. The prisoner's dilemma scenario is also played out among nations as part of decisions related to war and peace, trade and economics, energy and transportation issues, and other situations that involve high-stakes relations among governments. Research on the prisoner's dilemma is usually carried out in experiments or simulations where the game is played out many times. One of the most illuminating is the iterative prisoner's dilemma, which involves the same players going through the prisoner's dilemma scenario numerous times. In a strict sense, the correct or best method for playing the game usually involves talking (defecting); however, this depends on the opponents and how the iterated game is to be played. In tournaments, the tit-for-tat approach is often the winner. This strategy involves cooperation first (keeping quiet) and then doing whatever the opponent does.

COOPERATION

Until 50 years ago, cooperation has traditionally taken a backseat in evolutionary thought. Perhaps the main reason for this is that cooperation often seemed counterproductive in light of evolution being more about selfish behavior and all-out competition. But as Axelrod and Hamilton (1981) have pointed out, individuals undoubtedly benefit from being cooperative with each other. Axelrod and Hamilton were among the early pioneers of using game theory (specifically the prisoner's dilemma game) to test how Darwinian principles play out. Developing a theory of cooperation based on when and how humans cooperate and with whom has enormous

implications. Nowak (2006) showed that cooperation was essential for the development of new levels of organization across biological and social systems. Nowak defines *cooperation* as paying some sort of cost for another to receive a benefit. A literal example of paying a cost would be the payment of taxes, in which individuals give their personal money to the government for the benefit of other individuals and the society as a whole. A more personal example would be getting out of bed in the middle of the night to help a friend whose car broke down and who needs a ride—you pay the cost of forgoing sleep to benefit the safety and well-being of your friend. By "new levels of organization," Nowak means new patterns of complexity that evolve from or subsume the lower levels. So, for example, human societies began as hunter-gatherer groups (lower level), but agriculture and resulting increases in population facilitated larger and increasingly complex levels of organization such as towns and cities (higher level). Nowak identified five mechanisms by which cooperation is essential: kin selection (genetic relatedness), direct reciprocity (increases probability of another exchange), indirect reciprocity (social acquaintances), networks of reciprocity (increased number of neighbors), and group selection (things that act to increase or decrease the well-being and power of a group). The dynamics of interaction occurring via these mechanisms of cooperation are catalysts that drive the organization of new levels of organizational complexity. Paying a cost can vary in terms of magnitude and across mechanisms. It is believed that people will, on average, pay a higher cost for another to benefit if that other person is related to them. This is why people are often willing to sacrifice dearly for family members but not as much for strangers.

Government Shutdowns Due to Lack of Congressional Cooperation

In the United States, during one of the worst recessions in decades, a deeply divided Congress has come far too close too many times to putting our country through a government shutdown, or closure of multiple governmental institutions. One of the biggest reasons for this is the lack of cooperation in Congress. Democrats and Republicans have very different ideas about how much money our government should be spending and how to spend it. Both sides believe strongly in their positions and are seemingly unwilling to compromise, which has brought our nation frighteningly close to a shutdown several times already.

Although believing in something without wavering is often seen as a positive quality, especially when one is fighting for social-justice issues, it is sometimes necessary to compromise, especially if the result of not doing so may be detrimental to others. This is true on the national scale, such as the example of our current Congress, as well as on international, state, family, and individual levels. Compromising does not always mean we are compromising our values. Sometimes it means putting the needs of others before our own opinions.

Placing exchange and cooperation into an updated and broader view of the evolution of human social behavior is beneficial for the social and behavior sciences and the applications it has for social work and related professions. Anthropologist Augustin Fuentes (2009) has developed a framework that is instructive for doing so. The framework principles include (a) seeing human behavior as an ongoing system of evolving; (b) understanding that humans modify their surroundings (niche construction) as opposed to the idea that humans are only acted upon by their surroundings; (c) ecological and social inheritance (humans exist in places where other humans already were); (d) information transfer via communication; (e) feedback loops are common (not everything is a direct linear relationship; i.e., A influences B, but B also influences A); (f) processes that change behavior occur across multiple levels (e.g., the cell to society approach); and (g) behavior changes do not always result in maximizing or optimizing

gains (humans are flexible). Interestingly, we can insert cooperation into any of these principles and see how it potentially can be an important aspect. For example, niche construction will typically require cooperation, as in the case of human beings working together to find supportive housing or raise money to establish a community health center. The same can be said in terms of feedback loops in which, for example, a clinical social worker influences the well-being of her client, which helps the social worker grow as a practitioner and as a person due to the therapeutic relationship. Helping professionals often attempt to facilitate positive niche construction for individual clients and communities they serve by using information and connecting people to groups that clients previously had no knowledge about (new levels). Humans are fundamentally equipped to cooperate because cooperation is often a highly effective strategy.

The adaptations necessary to be effective in social exchange require the intellectual capacity to do so effectively. Cosmides, Barrett, and Tooby (2010) cogently argue (and experimentally test) the proposition that humans evolved their cognitive structure in the face of several specific challenges, such as acquiring adequate food and tools, which are tied to social exchange relations occurring in a survival context. Hence, natural selection processes favored the mental calculations necessary to succeed in facing these problems. One of the calculations involves exchange and cooperation, because humans benefit from trading things of value with one another. Thus, the computational capacity or wiring humans developed is very sensitive to social exchange. Cosmides et al. (2010, p. 9008) state the conditional rule of exchange as follows: "If you accept benefit B from me, then you must satisfy my requirement, R" (e.g., "If I give you a ride to work, then you must buy me a coffee later in the day"). Accordingly, if the conditional rule is violated (e.g., the rider purchases no coffee) or exchanges are explicitly unfair ("If I give you a ride to work, then you buy me a car"), our sense of being cheated will be high. Cheating in social exchanges is an adaptive problem because the mutual benefit gained by social exchange and cooperation breaks down if cheating is present. This does not mean that innocent mistakes do not happen, and in fact humans are able to make distinctions between exchange violations. Experimental tests of cheater detection in simulated games reveal that humans perform well in games where violations (and thus the cheater) could be identified. Thus, human intelligence is connected to the behavior stream of the past by being highly attuned or adapted to the detection of when basic rules of fairness are violated in social exchanges.

SPOTLIGHT TOPIC: THE "BIG MAN" THEORY

The term *big man* was developed by anthropologists whose field research among tribes, bands, and villages showed that some individuals were able to centrally place themselves in competitive exchanges in such a way that persons became indebted to them; thus, the big man was able to reap rewards and status from social exchange (Sahlins, 1972). Much of this work has been traced to anthropologist Marshall Sahlins's work in Melanesia, where he studied leadership and political hierarchy as well as many other cultural features. Essentially, big men are able to manipulate resources and give away the surplus of production during redistribution celebrations, which are common among small societies such as band and village cultures (Roscoe, 1988). The act of giving away surplus and resources such as pigs and kava (a plant root drunk for its calming properties) in effect accrues a debt to the big man (Lindstrom, 1984). Using redistribution in a strategic manner increases the number of ranks and contributes, as some have argued, to the development of hierarchies and inequalities (Harris, 1989). The process of redistribution occurs when members of bands and villages turn in surpluses. Small-group societies such as bands pool resources. Someone has to decide what to do with these surpluses, and that is usually the big man. Typically, when groups from neighboring villages meet up with their surpluses, they have a feast of celebration, followed by redistribution. Initially, some leader would generously give away the surpluses and take little for themselves. This person is extolled for their hard work and virtue, but also accumulates favors, debt service, and a network of supporters that can be brought to bear later. This is the path to becoming a big man.

It is natural to ask: Can a big man be dethroned? The answer is yes. Harris (1989) tells the story of how this works based on the field research of anthropologist Douglas Oliver among the Siuai of the Solomon Islands in the South Pacific. During the celebration, one leader challenges the big man by giving away more pigs, sago-almond puddings, and other desirables than the big man has. If the present big man cannot give away more at the next celebration, he is essentially overthrown. In some respects, this is analogous to politicians in contemporary Western cultures who promise the citizens more than other politicians and are then more likely to be voted into office. This big-man lesson also shows us how one can provide more than others in a social exchange as a way to indebt as many people as possible to oneself.

For Reflection

Think of specific persons in your life who were able to dominate social exchanges. How did they do it? What were the techniques they used?

Utilitarianism and Social Exchange Theory

Although human groups such as hunter-gatherers have practiced social exchange for thousands of years, the intellectual idea and formulation of social exchange theories have their roots in the concept of utilitarianism as expressed in the work of philosopher John Stuart Mill (1806–1873). For Mill, the development of a utilitarian philosophy was firmly rooted in a moral theoretical tradition. This perspective views human behavior from a rationalist stand-point, meaning that it begins with the assumption that human beings attempt to calculate the costs and benefits of their options, presumably toward increasing gratification and decreasing suffering. Mill wished to maximize happiness, which he defined as pleasure. He did so because he felt that happiness was the bedrock of morality, and that decisions and behaviors should be guided by whether happiness was increased or decreased. To Mill, criteria needed to be developed for making judgments about morality, and the happiness or pleasure principle was the standard. Mill also argued that people would not be happy if they pursued pleasure in such a way as to merely satisfy primitive urges; rather, happiness involved higher order thinking and quality of life. Despite the critiques of utilitarian philosophy (too rational and too many cost–benefit calculations), the basic premise that maximizing the good and minimizing the bad does seem to play a part in common decision making. Human beings will behave in ways that are most rewarding. The key factor in the genesis of exchange theory is that people make rational calculations in an effort to maximize their return of value as they perceive it. The analysis of these exchanges can occur at multiple levels, including between two people (dyads), groups, organizations, and nation-states.

Conflict Resolution for Personal Gain

In the field of conflict resolution, one issue that comes up frequently is that of the means versus the ends. If the goal in a conflict situation is the resolution or transformation of that conflict into something more positive, do the means to that end matter? For example, consider a developing nation that has been engrossed in civil war for a decade. The war is beginning to garner more international attention, thanks to the efforts of nongovernmental organizations and brave citizens willing to share their stories with the media. This new attention has cast a very negative image of the country's president, who has benefited from the war and has ruled over the country as a brutal dictator, rigging elections since first winning office over a decade ago.

Due to intense international advocacy and pressure, several influential nations have decided to sanction the country, and large lending organizations are considering options to cease funding to the country. The president now sees the immense wealth he has enjoyed potentially slipping away from him. He suddenly has an interest in ending the war and pursuing peace with the rebels he has fought against all these years. The rebels are willing to pursue a peace option; it has always been the president who has declined to participate in a peace process because it was never beneficial to him.

If the president does go ahead and initiate a peace process with the rebels, thus ending the war, the atrocities, and the sanctions on the country and continuing the funding the country receives from lending institutions—but only does so out of his own personal, greedy interest—is it still a good thing that the conflict is over? What if the president receives international acclaim and credit for ending the conflict? What if he is awarded a Nobel Peace Prize? What is more important, the means or the ends? Was it more important that he ended the conflict or that he acted in a way that only benefited him?

HOMANS'S ELEMENTARY FORMS OF SOCIAL BEHAVIOR

According to influential sociologist and exchange theorist George Homans (1958), no matter the size of the social exchange structure, its elementary forms lie in the basics of social behavior. Homans (1958) defined *social behavior* as "an exchange of goods but also non-material ones, such as the symbols of approval or prestige," going on to note that "persons that give much to others try to get much from them, and persons that get much from others are under pressure to give much to them" (p. 606). As is evident, this theory is fundamentally rooted in the rationality principle—that is, the principle that individuals assess the logic of situations in an attempt to reach their personal goals. In contrast to the prevailing beliefs of the times, Homans believed that for the understanding of social exchange to advance, it was important that field observations of human social exchanges be consistent with laboratory evidence done under experimental conditions. Homans also emphasized that propositions derived from the convergence of field and experimental research would need to be tested on larger levels of complexities, such as larger groups and organizations. One of Homans's hopes was that exchange theory would draw sociology and economics closer together. But one can readily envision behaviorist psychology also being included in this duo of disciplines, given its focus on rewards and contingencies (if this, then that). Homans, however, believed that behavioral psychology and its principles of operant conditioning were merely the beginning for establishing an exchange theory of social behavior. Many scholars have criticized the Homans model of social behavior for being so formal and not taking into account irrational behaviors. Although sometimes it is easy to view certain exchanges between people as not making rational sense from the outside, having a fuller understanding of the dynamics of the situation allows us to gain insight into why particular human actors behave in a particular manner.

EMOTION AND SOCIAL EXCHANGE

One of the criticisms of social exchange theory is its reliance on rationally based and seemingly mechanical and nonemotional elements. But as Lawler and Thye (1999) articulate, social exchanges also involve relationships based on affection (e.g., friends and family members), fear, and anger. The outcomes of social exchanges also involve key emotions such as contentment, excitement, and guilt, which have been found in other studies (e.g., Lawler & Yoon, 1996). Lawler and Thye theorize that emotions are important outcome factors across the exchange context and exchange process. The *exchange context* is guided by emotion norms that are derived from social interactions and guided by scripts, or prescribed ways of displaying emotions, based on prevailing norms. In other words, people may feel a strong emotion internally, but social norms govern the outward expression of that emotion. For example, social workers may have encounters with clients that are upsetting or even offensive, but rather than simply reacting with argumentative words, they strive to maintain a stance of professionalism and emotional regulation to facilitate the therapeutic growth of the client. In short, it is certainly acceptable for the client to become upset, but social work professionals are expected to maintain their composure and to work collaboratively with the client (even as they directly address the client's upsetting or offensive behavior).

Additional context issues involve power and status, which are well-known generators of strong emotions and have important implications within the social worker–client relationship. *Exchange processes* involve the information derived from emotion-sharing interactions. This also involves information about oneself that is gained by an awareness of feelings during exchange processes. The learning gleaned from a clinical social worker's awareness of countertransferential thoughts or feelings toward a particular client is an example of an exchange process. Importantly, there is empirical support that these processes may be universal, as research has found support for their cross-cultural existence (Heise, 1966). During exchanges, some results are successful; some have their goals blocked, and sadness or anger ensues; and others involve elation and shame. For example, a social worker can work to obtain housing for a client and experience intense emotions of happiness and joy due to the successful outcome. Lawler and Thye (1999) make an important contribution by revealing the salience of emotions in social exchanges. As such, they show that social exchange theory and research, often criticized as assuming an almost robotic rational calculus (e.g., Zafirovski, 2005), is entirely commensurate with what is known about emotions in social interactions.

Taking a long view can reveal the central importance of incorporating emotion into social exchange. In his presidential address to the American Sociological Association, Massey (2002) pointed out the importance of combining emotionality and rationality into social theorizing. Massey marshaled evidence on human evolution and showed how emotions were refined and used as social intelligence prior to a full development of rationality, and how the vast majority of our time on earth as a species has involved the interplay of emotions and rationality, with emotions preceding the latter. Moreover, neuroscience data shows that the order of perception from the external environment passes first to the emotional centers of the brain before it reaches the rational centers (LeDoux, 1996). Simply put, emotion undoubtedly plays an important role in human perception, decision making, and ultimately in social exchange.

EXPERIMENTS INVOLVING SOCIAL EXCHANGE

A number of experimental tests of social exchange theory have been conducted with the goal of elucidating one or more components of the overall theory. One of these major components involves trust in exchange relationships. In a test of commitment and trust in a sample of undergraduate students, Kollock (1994) used two experimental conditions: knowing the quality of a product before purchasing (certainty) and knowing the quality after purchase (uncertainty), with buyers

and sellers (the exchange relationship) randomized to each condition. Findings showed that to a large degree trust was dependent upon sticking with a partner despite a superior offer (i.e., commitment). Results also showed very sophisticated and nuanced strategies. As Kollock noted,

> In some cases, sellers were observed advertising truthfully when trading with some buyers and trying to exploit others. For example, in one case a seller established a trading relationship with one favored buyer within which the seller always advertised truthfully and sold the goods at a reasonable price. When interacting with other buyers however, the seller tried to pass on low-quality goods as high-quality goods. When trying to sell a "lemon," the seller was very careful to shut out the favored buyer by making only private offers and only to the other three buyers. (p. 335)

The take-home point is that trust is fluid as there are often many "behind the scenes" considerations and deals that are made. From their review of experimental studies of trust in social exchange, Cook and Cooper (2005) conclude that trust may be either a consequence of cooperation or a precipitating factor. They also point out the value of experiments in their ability to precisely point out with greater precision than nonexperimental studies the conditions under which trust and other key factors such as emotion operate in social exchange. Last, Cook and Cooper suggest that study of the basis of trust should likely include research on reciprocity and looking at large levels of trust in social exchange at the macro level.

RECIPROCITY AND FAIRNESS

Given the seemingly important role that trust plays in social exchange and cooperation, insight into reciprocity and fairness is in order. Humans cooperate with strangers even though there is obviously little to be gained. One term used by social scientists to describe behaviors that are actively prosocial in the sense of consistent co-operation (positive reciprocity) with others and punishing persons (negative reciprocity) who do not cooperate is *strong reciprocity* (Gintis, 2000). This concept is used to try to explain why humans cooperate with others even though there is no relatedness (familial or friend). It is speculated that humans must have evolved this sense of sociality, and at some point "strong reciprocators" were particularly successful. Under traditional economic assumptions of exclusive self-interest in social exchange scenarios, it is hard to account for reciprocity behaviors that do not reveal any obvious short-term gain. Or is cooperation a form of self-interest that we recognize will reap benefits over the long term? Strict economic reasoning about the calculations of immediate costs and benefits does seem to hold for some people who, in the long run, may well have gained more by bypassing the immediate gain and discounting the future.

The concept of strong reciprocity has implications for basic research on the evolution of cooperation as well as practical implications for social justice issues. For example, Gintis, Henrich, Bowles, Boyd, and Fehr (2008) have examined these major implications in the form of public support for social welfare programs. In their analysis of survey data and focus groups regarding how Americans view welfare programs such as food stamps, there is less concern about the costs of the programs and greater concern for unfairness. They note that 70% of people in general and 71% of people on welfare believe that it is unfair to working people. The researchers also cite other studies that converge with these results. The conclusion of their analysis is that people support helping the less fortunate as long as they are perceived to deserve the support. It is not a matter of selfishness. If welfare program advocates could successfully demonstrate how welfare programs represent fairness and how welfare recipients are hard workers under difficult circumstances, they might possibly increase support for these programs.

Do humans have an evolved sense of fairness? Do they punish each other and themselves based on this principle? These are important questions with broad implications. Results from game theory trials reveal humans do indeed act on principles of fairness. Fehr and Gachter (2000b) have summarized results from multiple trials of the bargaining game as follows:

> Perhaps the most vivid game to demonstrate negatively reciprocal behavior is the ultimatum bargaining experiment. In this game, two subjects have to agree on the division of a fixed sum of money. Person A, the Proposer, can make exactly one proposal of how to divide the amount. Person B, the Responder, can accept or reject the proposed division. In the case of rejection, both receive nothing; in the case of acceptance, the proposal is implemented. A robust result in this experiment, across hundreds of trials, is proposals that give the Responder less than 30 percent of the available sum are rejected with a very high probability.... Apparently, Responders do not behave in a self-interest maximizing manner. In general, the motive indicated for the rejection of positive, yet "low," offers is that subjects view them as unfair. (p. 161)

Additional game experiments conducted by Fehr and Gachter (2000a) indicate that cooperators will punish or penalize "free riders" even if there is no direct gain, at least materially speaking, for the cooperator. Although it's possible that cooperators psychologically gain by punishing free riders as a form of retaliation, it seems more likely based on these studies that the results are driven by a sense of fair play. Fehr and Gachter suggest that free riders can decrease the likelihood or severity of penalty if they increase their level of cooperation. What is unclear is the nature of what a costly penalty is in real-world conditions. For example, one penalty might be ostracism from the group. Ostracism can be important, as shown by the effect of social approval as a reason to cooperate voluntarily (Hollander, 1990). Another penalty might be paying a steeper price for a needed good or service. One thought experiment is to think of what kinds of actions you have taken or witnessed when someone has been uncooperative in a formal setting like work or school, or in an informal setting like dinner with family or friends. In sum, these studies of reciprocity and cooperation provide a strong statement about the robustness of the sense of fairness that seems to be a fundamental part of what makes us human.

NEUROSCIENCE OF SOCIAL EXCHANGE AND COOPERATION

Key neural substrates underlying human behavior were discussed earlier in this book. Here we focus on studies that have examined the neuroscience of social exchanges, trust, and cooperation.

One potentially important neuropeptide hormone important for social exchanges is oxytocin. Oxytocin receptors are distributed throughout the brain, and studies in nonhuman mammals indicate that oxytocin is released during pair-bonding activities and is meant to aid animals in forming attachments with one another (Carter, 1998; Insel & Young, 2001; Uvnas-Moberg, 1998). Based on this physiological knowledge, Kosfeld, Heinrichs, Zak, Fischbacher, and Fehr (2005) hypothesized that oxytocin may facilitate trust among humans during social interactions. This study administered a single dose of intranasal oxytocin and a placebo to 58 randomized participants (29 in each group) during a game designed to test trusting behaviors. A double-blind design was used so researchers and participants did not know who received the oxytocin. In this way, they could not affect the outcome by behaving differently with those who received the oxytocin. Each game featured two participants, with one anonymously playing the trustee or the investor. Kosfeld et al. described the details of the game as follows:

> First, the investor has the option of choosing a costly trusting action by giving money to the trustee. If the investor transfers money, the total amount available for distribution between the two players increases but, initially, the trustee reaps the whole increase. The trustee is then informed about the investor's transfer and can honor the investor's trust by sharing the monetary increase generated by the investor's transfer. Thus, if the investor gives money to the trustee and the latter shares the proceeds of the transfer, both players end up with a higher monetary payoff. However, the trustee also has the option of violating the investor's trust. As sharing the proceeds is costly for the trustee, a selfish trustee will never honour the investor's trust because the investor and the trustee interact only once during the experiment. The investor is therefore caught in a dilemma: if he trusts and the trustee shares, the investor increases his payoff, but he is also subject to the risk that the trustee will abuse this trust. In the latter case, the investor is worse off than if he had not trusted at all and, adding insult to injury, the trustee has an unfair payoff advantage relative to the investor. (p. 673)

Results of the experiment showed that oxytocin has a significant effect on increasing trust. Specifically, 45% of those receiving oxytocin displayed maximum trust scores compared to 21% in the placebo group.

Although these results are impressive, critics could potentially note that oxytocin may not have actually served to increase trust among participants, but rather was helpful in terms of investors overcoming an aversion to risk. To this end, the researchers also tested both of these possibilities. An additional risk-only experiment was employed with no one to trust. Results of this experiment indicated that oxytocin had no effect on risk taking in the absence of a human relationship. Thus, trust seemed to be the mechanism of action that the oxytocin induced. Although those in the oxytocin group in the first experiment were more than twice as likely to increase their trust behavior compared to those in the placebo group, oxytocin did not uniformly increase trust in all research participants who received it.

Kosfeld et al. concluded that oxytocin plays a role in increasing prosocial behavior and speculated that oxytocin administration could help persons who have social phobias or conditions where individuals may be fearful or avoidant of social interactions. However, there are larger implications for the sphere of international relations. For example, could the administration of oxytocin to world leaders whose nations are in conflict with another, or have a history of conflict and therefore low trust, increase trust levels to the point that positive exchanges can begin?

Two studies have used brain imaging to investigate areas of the brain during an experimental game involving cooperation. The first study used fMRI technology in a prisoner's dilemma game between 36 adult women (Rilling et al., 2002). fMRI is useful because it can "see" into areas of the brain that are activated during a task. Players interacted via a networked computer that they controlled while in the scanner. Findings from the study showed that mutual cooperation during the game, whereby women avoided trying to one-up the other, was correlated with the activation of areas of the brain that involve rewards, such as the nucleus accumbens, caudate nucleus, and ventromedial frontal and orbitofrontal cortex. The researchers suggest that these activated areas indicate reinforcement derived from cooperation exhibited during the game scenario. In the second study, also using fMRI, 12 participants played both human and computer partners (36 iterations each) for monetary rewards in a simulated game. Participants were categorized as cooperators ($n = 7$) and noncooperators ($n = 5$) based on how many times they made a cooperative decision (defined as at least one third of the time). Cooperators had greater activation in the prefrontal cortex regions, which theoretically serve to delay reward, thus facilitating cooperative decisions rather than a short-term gain at another's expense. However, the activation was present only when playing the human and not when playing a computer, which had a fixed strategy of play.

POWER

Social exchanges often involve power differentials. This is basic to the nature of social exchange, as individuals and larger entities do not all have an equal amount of a given resource or quality that is of value. Examples can be money, food, water, shelter and building materials, physical attractiveness, humor, technical skills, and so forth. Differential levels of control of these resources create leverage. Needing something from someone or an entity provides that source with leverage and a certain degree of power unless one has something of equal or greater value to exchange. This occurs all the time in life, whether with friends, family members, or business acquaintances (primary exchange relationships). For instance, a social worker who is highly trained in cognitive behavioral therapy may experience a degree of leverage over her colleagues who are in need of further instruction or consultation on the technique. It also occurs at the group and organization levels, including nations around the world (secondary exchange relationships). Just think of the leverage and resulting power differentials that funding organizations such as the Bill & Melinda Gates Foundation have in terms of shaping the research and practice foci of social work and social development agencies. One can readily see why competition, cooperation, and conflict are part of the recipe of social exchange.

There are several ways to deal with power differentials besides acceptance and subordination in social exchange. Allan (2007) summarizes these strategies: "[obtain] a good or service that the other person does not have, find alternative sources to what you receive from the other person, get along without the good or service the other person controls, or you could attempt to force the person to give you what you need" (p. 360). In reality, these options are far more difficult to execute. Having a secondary option going into these exchanges is helpful, as anticipating that there will be a power differential may allow for greater maneuverability and thus lessen the impact of the power differential.

There are many instances in which power imbalances are obvious and sometimes necessary. In a workplace setting, it should be clear who is in a position of power. This power structure is necessary to ensure the proper functioning of most workplaces. But what about power imbalances that aren't so obvious? Many believe that there are power imbalances in our society that are structural, meaning that they are built into the fabric of our daily lives. Issues like racial profiling, salary inequality, and underfunded public school systems are some examples of what people consider to be structural power imbalances. These institutions perpetuate inequalities in our society that are less obvious on a daily basis than other power imbalances.

ALTRUISM

Robert Trivers (1971) defined *altruism* as "behavior that benefits another organism, not closely related, while being apparently detrimental to the organism performing the behavior" (p. 35). The classic example of altruistic behavior that Trivers provides is someone jumping into the water to save a stranger drowning in a river or stream. From a strict evolutionary-theory perspective, altruism is a major puzzle. Research into altruistic behavior has shown that altruism can fit into evolutionary explanations from the point of view that altruism is long-term self-interest. For instance, Trivers presented a model where natural selection can operate against a nonreciprocator. Some of the adaptations in what Trivers termed the *altruistic system* involved psychologically oriented traits and behaviors such as gratitude, suspicion, trust, aggression, sympathy, guilt, dislike, and a sense of friendship. In this perspective, humans are capable of having altruistic and cheating tendencies and situational contingencies as well as ecological settings selected for these tendencies. One of the reasons why altruistic behavior occurs is that over the long run, altruistic behavior

outweighs the benefit of nonaltruistic behavior. This does not mean that altruistic behavior is constant across the life course for each individual, as there are many times when we free-ride or do not reciprocate, but over the long haul this catches up with us. There is also variation in altruistic behavior, as some people are more or less altruistic. Given that humans rely on one another and are in effect interdependent to varying degrees, the number of encounters over the life course that will involve choices pertaining to altruistic or free-riding acts is immense. Trivers has listed some of the more common altruistic acts among humans, which include helping in times of danger (e.g., war, accidents), sharing food and water, helping the sick or injured or those who are disabled, and sharing knowledge and tools. Trivers also distinguishes between two forms of cheating in reciprocation. *Gross cheating* is the failure to give anything at all in return, and *subtle cheating* is always giving less than what was given. It is argued that selection processes will go against gross cheating, but the selection effect on short-term subtle cheating is not so clear, as under some situations a person can benefit from cheating and free riding. Altruistic acts can also be distinguished in terms of real or calculated (see Figure 9.3). *Real altruism* is behavior where there was no premeditated calculation of what might be received if the altruistic behavior is initiated, whereas *calculated altruism* can come about when there is premeditated calculation about receiving a benefit, such as a direct reciprocation or future considerations. At various times and in varying degrees, humans will typically engage in any one of these forms of altruism and reciprocation conditions (see Figure 9.4).

Despite the long-standing appeal of Trivers's framework of altruistic behavior, more recent experimental research has pointed to strong reciprocity, a previously discussed behavioral trait to which some persons are predisposed that does not fit well into these prior schemes. The reason why is that strong reciprocity is a tendency to cooperate *and punish* cheaters, even at a personal cost. Although experimental research has

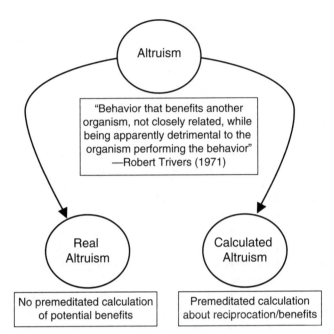

FIGURE 9.3 Trivers's Conceptualization of Altruism

	Gross or Subtle Cheating in Return	Equal or Greater Value in Return
Real Altruism	I	II
Calculated Altruism	III	IV

FIGURE 9.4 Possible Outcomes of Exchange Involving Real and Calculated Altruism and Gross and Subtle Cheating in Reciprocity

Source: Adapted from "The Evolution of Reciprocal Altruism," by R. L. Trivers, 1971, *The Quarterly Review of Biology, 46*, 35–57.

provided support for the strong-reciprocity construct, knowing why some individuals are strong reciprocators is important to understand as it has implications for human behavior theory and evolution generally. Gintis et al. (2003) have put forth a compelling explanation regarding the conditions under which strong reciprocity developed. They argue that in early human evolution, individuals with strong reciprocity could have affected populations of self-interested early humans and spread this trait, as the strong-reciprocity approach is stable over time. Although they acknowledge that altruism based on kinship and nonstrong reciprocity is an important factor, Gintis and his colleagues go further in arguing the importance of strong reciprocity (2003): "We do believe, however, that the evolutionary success of our species and the moral sentiments that have led people to value freedom, equality, and representative government are predicated upon strong reciprocity and related motivations that go beyond inclusive fitness and reciprocal altruism" (p. 154). Strong reciprocity theory is compatible with contemporary notions about gene–culture coevolution. Gintis (2000) has shown that strong reciprocity can emerge from basic reciprocal altruism under conditions of high threat, such as war or famine. Under these conditions, basic reciprocal altruism is not nearly as effective as strong reciprocity, where punishing others in the group who don't cooperate maintains the survivability of the group over and above standard exchanges. In dire times, persons who possess strong-reciprocity traits are more likely to contribute to the survival of the group even if they are a minority in that group. During difficult conditions, human groups that have a strong-reciprocity constituency are more likely to outperform or compete more favorably than another human group that is low on strong reciprocity. In turn, over time strong reciprocity becomes a trait that is selected for because of its contribution to survivability.

As Gintis et al. (2008) acknowledge, criticisms and alternative explanations with respect to the strong-reciprocity hypothesis have been put forth, and certainly much more is to be learned. One of the criticisms is simply that experimental evidence is not sufficient in itself on which to base a theory, and that humans have not evolved an adaptation such as strong reciprocity in real nongame settings—let alone conditions surrounding early human evolution, of which much is still unknown. There are too many other variables and not enough known about human evolutionary history to make these assertions based on repeated observations from game scenarios. Although this is a good point, Gintis et al. (2008) argue that humans are quite capable of discerning which people they will likely have future encounters with, and that in life we face repeated interactions with others and small groups. Strong reciprocity is every bit as viable in contemporary society as it was in ancestral environments.

One altruistic behavior, charitable giving, has been given studied attention as it can provide insight into why people give without receiving a particular good or resource in return. For example, many students pay large sums of money to attend elite private universities and then continue to give after graduation. In the past 10 years, numerous colleges and universities, including publicly affiliated universities, have conducted billion-dollar capital campaigns. Although at first glance givers in this situation do not receive a material return, schools do provide something in return to the giver: maintenance of social status. People often use the university they attended as a marker of status, and universities are in competition for students, faculty, and better facilities—a sort of academic arms race. Alumni of these universities often feel pressure to give, and often want to give so students who have fewer resources can receive scholarship support; however, the perceived value of one's degree is also diminished if competitor schools move ahead in the rankings.

In addition to giving to colleges and universities, an estimated 90% of Americans donate money to various charities (DellaVigna, List, & Malmendier, 2009). The overwhelming majority of people who benefit from these donations are strangers to the giver. But why should people do this? What are their motivations? And what do they receive in return? These are some of the questions that researchers into altruistic behavior attempt to address. According to DellaVigna et al. (2009), two major motivations drive people to donate to charities. The first is the positive feelings that givers experience; the second is the discomfort of saying no due to social pressures. In this second reason, people do not necessarily wish to give but do so anyway. These scholars tested this idea using a sample of nearly 8,000 households and a design that allowed them to distinguish whether donating enhanced or reduced well-being. Door-to-door solicitations with a flyer describing the time of solicitation were attached to some households' doorknobs (a relatively equal number of households did and did not receive a flyer). If DellaVigna et al.'s idea about social pressure were true, then this notice of solicitation should be met with a decrease in the number of households who open the door, thus avoiding the social pressure to give and providing evidence of the social pressure hypothesis. Study results supported their main idea of social pressure effects, as there was a 10 to 25% reduction in a person opening the door at these households. Of course, an alternative explanation is that people simply wish to not be bothered. However, results do suggest that social pressure plays a major role. DellaVigna et al. conclude that door-to-door fundraising campaigns are more likely to be successful if previous notice is not given, thereby allowing social pressure effects to operate.

Research into the cognitive neuroscience of charitable giving has yielded interesting results. Using fMRI scan technology, Moll et al. (2006) found that distinct areas of the brain were associated with decisions to donate to or to oppose certain societal causes in a sample of 19 adults. Results of the experiment revealed that the mesolimbic reward system was found to be generally involved in terms of reinforcement, but more specifically the areas of the brain that mediated social bonding and aversion—the subgenual area and the anterior prefrontal cortex—were activated in more complex altruistic decision making. Moll et al. point out that the subgenual area also plays a role in the release of oxytocin, which we learned earlier was associated with increases in trusting behaviors. In sum, this study is important not only because it shows that there is a neural basis for charitable donation, but also that the areas of the brain involved in reward, aversion, and attachment map to decision making with respect to societal causes.

Restorative Justice: A Form of Altruism?

One growing practice in the field of postconflict development is restorative justice. This practice can be explained as the act of bringing together victims and oppressors or aggressors so dialogue can take place. The focus is on the victims of the conflict, giving them an opportunity to voice their feelings about the experiences they had to live through because of the aggressors. The goal of restorative justice is to give the victims a chance to be heard and to provide a way for them to begin the healing process by receiving some form of justice (even if that means simply being listened to by their aggressors). This is important in promoting the peace-building process and avoiding future conflicts because of unresolved tension.

Can restorative justice, like charitable giving, be considered a form of altruism? For the aggressors, it takes an incredible amount of humility to listen to what their victims have to say about what they have put them through. And the reward for doing so is nothing but the hope to avoid further conflict someday. Why would individuals choose to put themselves through the process of being told how much they had affected others negatively without expecting anything in return? On the surface, it would seem that the only side benefiting from this practice is the victims. So why would the aggressors participate? What do they have to gain? Can this be considered altruism?

Race and Altruism

A possible moderator of altruistic behavior could be race or ethnicity, especially if the giver in the exchange harbors bigoted viewpoints. One interesting experimental setting in which to test the effects of racial identity on altruism is post-apartheid South Africa. This is exactly what Van der Merwe and Burns (2008) did, using the dictator game in a large sample of undergraduate students. In one condition, the surnames of the research participants were revealed so as to facilitate inferences about their racial identity, whereas in the other (control) condition, student surnames were not revealed. In the dictator game, participants reveal their behavior to the researcher based on a series of choices that have to be made. In this particular study, real money was used, which according to the researchers encourages participants to reveal their true behavior. Dictator game scenarios are nonreciprocal, meaning that resources are exchanged without expectation of any resources in return. Based on previous dictator game research, participants tend to give 10 to 25% of their resources, usually money. This finding itself is interesting as it indicates the range in amount of their resources that people are generally willing to give. Van der Merwe and Burns reported that White players tended to give larger offers than Black game players, but offers by White players tended to favor other Whites (insider bias), based on inferences made on surnames with respect to identity. Black players did not appear to make offers based on insider bias. The larger offers made by Whites could be because these students came from a background of higher SES compared to Black students. Although this study offers preliminary findings about the relationship between race and altruistic behavior, making generalizations from this study about South Africans or the role of racial identity in moderating altruistic behavior is premature. Other studies may come to entirely different conclusions.

Self-Report Measures of Altruism

Interestingly, there have been few attempts to develop a questionnaire or self-report measure that explicitly attempts to provide a scale of altruism. Such a measure would seem to be of value. In one of the earliest attempts, Rushton, Chrisjohn, and Fekken (1981) reported results on a 20-item self-report measure that attempted to assess the altruistic trait or personality. Example items included "I have donated blood," "I have given directions to a stranger," and "I have done volunteer work for a charity" with response options of *never*, *once*, *more than once*, *often*, and *very often*. They administered the measure to undergraduate students and used peer ratings as an attempt to validate the measure. Findings indicated correlations of moderate strength between self- and peer reports. The altruistic measure was also found to correlate significantly with other scales gauging moral judgment, empathy, and prosocial values. Later studies by other researchers (e.g., Krueger, Hicks, & McGue, 2001) have used this self-report measure in studying antisocial behaviors to identify the sources of these traits in individual personalities. Still others have formed altruism constructs using existing personality inventories such as the Five Factor Model of Personality (Ashton, Paunonen, Helmes, & Jackson, 1998).

Emotion Again

Emotion is an ancient system in mammals and has been hailed as an important mechanism by which people engage in direct altruistic behavior, such as helping someone who is hurting or in pain (de Waal, 2008). Humans are able to empathize because we have experienced pain, need, grief; human intervention comforts us; and we can readily see that in others. The ability to walk in other people's shoes and sense their viewpoints, need, and distress is known as *perspective taking*. Although there are a small percentage of humans that have functional deficits in their ability to empathize with others, in general the capacity to empathize is widespread—to varying degrees of course. De Waal (2008) distinguishes two kinds of empathy as it pertains to altruistic behavior (see Figure 9.5). The first is *sympathetic concern*, in which one feels the other's state of need and tries to make things better (i.e., consolation). As de Waal points out, consolation is common among humans and chimpanzees. The second is *cognitive empathy*, which involves appraisal of what caused the emotional state in the person and thoughts about amelioration. The former is more impulse driven, whereas the latter adds a rational element. De Waal (2008) summarizes

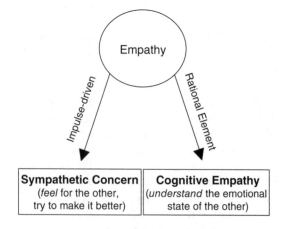

FIGURE 9.5 The Principal Components of Empathy

five key conclusions that can be made about the intersection of altruism and empathy:

1. An evolutionarily parsimonious account of directed altruism assumes similar motivational processes in humans and other animals.

2. Empathy, broadly defined, is an ancient capacity of humans.

3. Without the emotional engagement brought about by empathy, it is unclear what could motivate the extremely costly helping behavior occasionally observed in social animals.

4. Consistent with kin selection and reciprocal altruism theory, empathy favors familiar individuals and previous cooperators and is biased against previous defectors.

5. Combined with perspective-taking abilities, empathy's motivational autonomy opens the door to intentional altruism in a few large-brained species (p. 292).

EXPERT'S CORNER: PETER CORNING

Peter Corning, PhD, taught at Stanford University and currently serves as Director of the Institute for the Study of Complex Systems. He is the author of such books as *Nature's Magic: Synergy in Evolution and the Fate of Humankind* (2003) and *Holistic Darwinism: Synergy, Cybernetics, and the Bioeconomics of Evolution* (2005). His most recent book, *The Fair Society: The Science of Human Nature and the Pursuit of Social Justice* (2011), is not only pertinent to social exchange and cooperation, but is also fundamental to helping professions such as social work and public health.

Corning identifies major breakdowns in the economic system of the United States, such as the mortgage and housing debacle and health care (we spend far more than other nations with poor results), as examples of the flawed assumptions about human behavior under which American society operates. The results, according to Corning, are suboptimal (we can do much better) and simply unjust. Instead of continuing down the current road, Corning argues for a new vision of a "Fair Society" that moves beyond capitalism, socialism, and related hybrids.

The society that Corning envisions would be based on the growing knowledge of the nature–nurture foundations of human behavior, particularly those that relate to our many basic needs. Corning also highlights core human values such as fairness and altruism, which recent research has shown are fundamental components of human nature. As Corning describes it, "The Fair Society represents a new economic and political vision

(Continued)

Photo of Peter Corning
Courtesy of Peter Corning

that combines what I call 'biosocialism' (a basic needs guarantee that fulfills our prime directive) with what has been termed 'stakeholder capitalism' as well as appropriate social obligations (or reciprocities)" (p. xiii). Corning's "survival indicators," which provide a foundation for a basic-needs guarantee, include thermoregulation (body temperature), fresh water, adequate nutrition, waste elimination (individuals and communities), sleep, respiration, physical safety and health (including mental health), communications and information, reproduction and care of offspring, and social relationships. Taking care of these needs is the first step toward a fair society. For Corning, any social system must be rooted in a realistic understanding of human nature.

Based on the knowledge presented about fairness, social exchange, and cooperation in this chapter, Corning's ideas seem to have merit. Taking into account fairness and reciprocity as basic ingredients of human behavior is sensible. However, as Corning notes, implementing such a plan is a tremendous challenge.

EXCHANGE AND COOPERATION OVER THE LIFE COURSE

The majority of research results and convergent evidence strongly suggests that humans are wired for cooperation and are highly sensitive to exchange interaction, particularly basic fairness in the outcomes of these interactions.

Fetal Environment and Infancy

As discussed in previous chapters, biosocial development begins very early in life. Early prosocial development is intimately tied to social exchange and cooperation. Research on temperament suggests that some degree of variation is likely to exist with respect to exchange and cooperation. For example, in Chapter 7 we learned that children who at 6 months of age gaze at events that are frustrating to them, such as the removal of a toy, are more likely to be less cooperative at later ages; by contrast, infants who are able to shift their attention may be more cooperative. These findings on individual variation in temperament indicate there is likely to be individual variation in altruistic and cooperative behaviors as well. It is likely that maternal reactivity and behavior in response to cooperative and exchange-based behavior of infants will have an important effect

in moderating some preexisting behavioral tendencies. Parenting a child who shows early signs of aggression and a lack of cooperation requires skilled management. It would be interesting and fruitful if more game studies of exchange and cooperation incorporated data on temperament and personality into the simulations.

Childhood and Adolescence

Despite some difficulties that arise, most children are cooperative and have a developing sense of fairness that facilitates appropriate responses to social exchange situations and interactions. One of the ways children learn to cooperate is through play. Play involves give and take. As children age, they become less egocentric and realize others view things differently than they do (Kail & Cavanaugh, 2004). They also learn cooperation by watching others, such as parents and older siblings, cooperating with each other. Altruistic behavior can be readily observed when one child falls down and is hurt and another child shows concern and attempts to soothe him or her or do something that is helpful. Perspective taking and empathy building appears to help children learn concern for others and therefore increase the likelihood of altruistic behaviors (Kail & Cavanaugh, 2004). Can parents help children learn altruistic behavior? The answer appears to be yes. Parents can teach altruism by being altruistic with one another and other people (Bryant & Crockenberg, 1980; Eisenberg, Miller, Shell, McNalley, & Shea, 1991). Given the power of observational learning, parents who demonstrate altruistic behavior help to foster this behavior in their children.

Do humans develop a sense of fair play, and if so, when? According to Fehr, Bernhard, and Rockenbach (2008), children have a strong sense of fair play and aversion to inequality. This begins to develop between the ages of 3 and 8 years, with ages 3 and 4 showing relatively high levels of selfishness that diminishes substantially by ages 7 and 8. Fehr et al. conducted a number of experiments and found that 3- and 4-year-olds shared about 9% of the time, whereas 45% of 7- and 8-year-olds were willing to share, and 78% preferred egalitarian choices during the experimental conditions. Boys were more likely to demonstrate unequal sharing to those who were in-group versus those that were out-group, as compared to girls, who did not seem to differentiate between groups. Interestingly, children without siblings were more likely to share than children with siblings. This research suggests that equality instincts are part of the evolution of human social behavior, mainly because humans mostly evolved under conditions of small groups where egalitarianism was necessary for survival. That boys were more likely to show in-group versus out-group differences in sharing than girls is consistent with the notion that males are the ones who have historically borne the costs (injury and death) and benefits (status and new mates) of intergroup conflict and therefore might be more sensitive to keeping peace with outsiders while having less of a problem of inequality within their own group.

Sometimes compromise is not the best way to resolve a conflict. In most cases, what is really being sought is problem solving. Take the example of two siblings fighting over an orange. Using compromise as a strategy to resolve this conflict, the orange is cut in half and each sibling is given one half of the orange. However, upon speaking with both siblings, it becomes known that one sibling wants the orange for its peel, which she plans to use for a science experiment, and the other wants the orange for the fruit, which he plans to eat. Using cooperation, communication, and problem-solving abilities, a real resolution is found. One sibling is given the peel and the other the fruit, and both parties are able to walk away satisfied.

Most of the changes in altruistic behavior and cooperation continue to solidify in adolescence, although adolescents are more likely to expand outward in their social spheres, away from family, to spend more time with peers. Exchanges with peers gain greater importance during adolescence, and prosocial behavior exhibited during childhood portends successful adaptations during these years. In a classic study mentioned in Chapter 7, Caspi, Elder, and Bem (1987) examined longitudinal data spanning 30 years on boys and girls ages 8 to 10 years who had frequent temper outbursts. Did these outbursts inhibit successful cooperation later in life? Results showed that outbursts of childhood also emerged in cooperative settings such as work and school during adulthood.

Adulthood

Enduring effects for prosocial behaviors continue into adulthood. Successful adulthood depends on learning to cooperate with others and developing functional skills related to social exchange. One of the major influences is agreeableness, as measured by the Five Factor Model of Personality, often termed the Big Five, which was developed to assess personality functioning in adulthood (Costa & McCrae, 1992, 1997). According to this conceptualization, personality is composed of five major domains: Neuroticism, Extraversion, Openness to Experience, Agreeableness, and Conscientiousness. Although any of these domains can be associated with social exchange and cooperation tendencies, the facet of Agreeableness is most directly related. On the high end of the continuum, Agreeableness reflects traits such as acceptance and getting along with and caring about others, and on the low end includes distrust, impatience with others, and aggression in interpersonal encounters. Like the other domains, Agreeableness appears to be normally distributed within the population, at least in North American and European samples. Interestingly, little to no research has accrued on using Five Factor Model of Personality tests in game scenarios that assess exchange and altruistic behaviors.

SUMMARY

To ensure survival, humans are interdependent on one another. Exchange, cooperation, and altruism are critical ingredients that have allowed humans to flourish on the planet. These behaviors are found in every culture and seem to have evolved when humans lived in small groups, which was during the majority of human history. Much of the complexity of contemporary societies is based on the building blocks of social exchange and cooperation. The key concluding points of this chapter follow.

• The formal study of social exchange and cooperation is rooted in the evolution of social behavior. Intellectually it draws upon classical utilitarianism and the principles of a variety of disciplines. More recently, this field has seen great advancement due to the incorporation of game theory. An understanding of social exchange in its evolutionary and philosophical context permits a stronger appreciation of its fundamental nature in both practice and policy applications.

• Humans need to protect themselves and extract energy from an environment to survive. These driving forces propelled humans (as well as other primates and social animals) to form coalitions. Conditions such as these bring forth resource sharing. Sharing a resource, particularly when there is more than what one individual needs, can lead to a credit of sorts where the receiver owes the giver something.

• Social exchange involves emotions. Interactions and their outcomes are based on affection, fear, and anger. The outcomes of social exchanges elicit feelings such as contentment, excitement, and guilt. As Massey (2002) has pointed out, emotions were refined and used as social intelligence prior to a full development of rationality. Indeed, the vast majority of our time on earth as a species has involved the interplay of emotions and rationality, with emotions preceding the latter.

• Humans cooperate with strangers even when there is obviously little to be gained. Game experiments indicate that cooperators will punish or penalize free riders even if there is no direct gain for the cooperator. This is considered strong reciprocity, and studies of reciprocity and cooperation provide a strong statement about the robustness of the sense of fairness that seems to be a fundamental part of what makes us human.

• Social exchanges often involve differences in power. Individuals, groups, and nations do not possess equal amounts of resources or qualities such as money, water, materials, technologies, physical attractiveness, humor, and technical skills. Unless someone has something of equal or greater value to exchange, the control of such resources creates leverage and power differentials. This is part of why competition, cooperation, and conflict are part of social exchange processes.

• Altruism—behavior that benefits another person who is not closely related and where there is no apparent benefit—appears to outweigh nonaltruistic behavior over the long run.

• A substantial amount of empirical evidence and validation of social exchange and altruistic theories has come from using experimental games. The objective behind game theory and experiments is to uncover the reasons why people make the decisions they do. Researchers use all types of games to explore human behavior outcomes, but perhaps the most famous is the prisoner's dilemma, which is designed to achieve the best possible outcome for oneself in a very difficult situation.

KEY TERMS

Altruism

Calculated altruism

Cognitive empathy

Exchange context

Exchange process

Gross cheating

Perspective taking

Real altruism

Social exchange and cooperation

Strong reciprocity

Subtle cheating

Sympathetic concern

CHAPTER 10

SOCIAL NETWORKS AND PSYCHOSOCIAL RELATIONS

In his January 2012 State of the Union address, President Obama quoted Abraham Lincoln, saying that "government should do for people only what they cannot do better by themselves, and no more." President Obama followed by endorsing President Lincoln's sentiment. Since the dawn of America, citizens have sought care and support from four sources: (a) the state, (b) the family, (c) the labor market, and (d) the church. Of course, over the centuries our history reveals an uneven commitment from each of these in their collective responsibility to and provision of care to citizens. Other cultures have oriented to citizen care with great variation, some in less formal and less institutionalized ways. For example, Richard Sennett, in his book *Together* (2012), talks about the significance of the Chinese word *guanxi*, which represents an informal and intergenerational social bond that allows social and economic exchange to flow bidirectionally among people in a *guanxi* network, without shame or a formal contract (p. 135). In a *guanxi* network, there is simply and significantly an implicit "duty to cooperate." This chapter provides an overview of the construction, deconstruction, power, and influence of our social networks, from our most intimate relationships to our mainly institutional ones, with attention to the "webs of influence" we form across systems and across the life course, to understand how these social networks both facilitate and constrain human development.

DISTAL CONTEXT

Going It Alone?

Before turning to the social network literature, it is interesting to note that current and changing demographic trends in family formation and interpersonal connections are quickly capturing scholarly attention, as demographers and other social scientists scurry to understand, describe, and make projections about what they are seeing as a major hiccup in interpersonal structures. In his recent book, *Going Solo*, Klinenberg (2012) states that the majority of all Americans today are single; one out of seven adults lives alone. Single adults and childless couples are the most frequent type of residency status. The majority of single adults are between the ages of 35 and 64 (p. 4), and single women are the fastest growing sector of the house-buying market (p. 76). Klinenberg is careful to distinguish between being alone and loneliness, suggesting from the research that most people who choose to live alone are not necessarily lonely, and that the single life can often bring a sense of freedom, depending on circumstance. Social media, Klinenberg shows, are also responding readily to these demographic shifts, with websites such as SingleEdition.com, which provides a social media platform to discuss status-related discrimination for these increasingly common singletons. Other similar organizations have also sprung up over the past several decades, such as Single Mothers by Choice. Founded in 1981 by Jane Mattes, an LCSW, the group provides support and information to single mothers who choose motherhood despite lacking a partner or companion.

Although research indeed has demonstrated that pets can promote social interaction (Klinenberg, 2012), we are likely to conjecture what the future consequences of and opportunities for these single-by-choice relationships might be. And as we explore this question by examining the value and attendant challenges of forming and sustaining social relationships across the life course, we do so with an awareness that ultimately, it is not the quantity within a social network, but rather, as Bourdieu (1997) calls it, the opportunity for "conversion": being able to access and ultimately convert resources, skills, and abilities derived through social exchanges into social and economic advantage. For example, significant interpersonal relationships like marriage can produce positive psychological well-being for some people. Brooks (2011) cites one finding that suggests "being married produces the same psychic gain as earning $100,000 a year. According to another [finding], joining a group that meets even just once a month produces the same happiness gain as doubling your income" (p. 196). The burden and benefits of relationships must be examined, however, in the context of the larger socioenvironmental demands and resources within which an individual and/or family exists, and the entirety of context must be considered when we make assumptions about the value of particular social networks. For example, a young, unemployed married mother of two young children who is living in an economically stable but emotionally volatile home, characterized by unpredictable and infrequent bouts of domestic violence perpetrated by her husband, may experience significant ambivalence about leaving the relationship for many reasons, particularly fear of the economic vulnerability such a decision could bring to her and her children. To be sure, the context within which the costs and benefits of the social relationship occur does matter, and social workers should assess it to understand more fully the life choices clients confront.

Social relationships are developed across the life course. However, developmental researchers have focused significantly on those attachment bonds that develop at the very beginning of life, specifically the relationship in infancy between the newborn and his or her primary caregiver, typically the mother.

CASE STUDY 1: TYLER, DISCONNECTED AND STRUGGLING

Tyler is 18 years old. He knows he is legally able to continue to receive services through the child welfare system for 3 more years—but why would he? After all, he's been doing so for almost a decade. Like the majority of children in the foster care system, Tyler entered care as an early adolescent and has bounced around among different placements ever since. He knows he is not an easy kid, but he says every time he got comfortable in a house, someone tried to undermine his success by making him mad. Tyler's biological mother left the family when he was only 2 years old. Tyler's father, a laborer who was out of work at the time, was committed to Tyler's care, but over time could not keep up his meager earnings. So Tyler was sent to live with his paternal grandmother, Martha Jones.

Martha was well-meaning and had a heart of gold, but she also had chronic pain due to hip problems for which she had never received proper medical care. Over time, she too could not keep up with Tyler. And so Tyler landed in foster care at the age of 11, and has been in six different placements since then.

As is typical in most state-initiated permanency care plans, Tyler's social workers kept telling him the goal was for him to return home to live with his biological family. But that never worked out. Tyler remained in foster care until his 18th birthday when, determined to make his life work on his own terms, he moved in with his biological father. Unfortunately, that plan only lasted a month. Tyler and his father—who was now on permanent disability but, in Tyler's words, "had a full-time job drinking"—argued constantly, and Tyler would often find himself sleeping on a friend's couch. One day Tyler left for a friend's house and never returned to his father's home. Tyler's living patterns changed frequently over the course of the first year after his transition from care, to include living with four different friends, a cousin, a neighbor, and a great uncle. Although Tyler needed people to help *him*, he says that he has always dreamed of getting a job where *he* could help people. When he was very young, he dreamed of becoming a firefighter or police officer. More recently, at the advice of a high school teacher he admired, Tyler thought about a job in the health-care field. He wanted to become a certified nursing assistant because he had heard there was a 12-month program at a nearby community college where he could take evening classes and get a certificate. He said he would love to work at a hospital or in a nursing home with older adults, who, Tyler observed, always seemed to like him. So he signed up for the class, attended consistently, and did well for a while. But then he couldn't figure out how to cobble together enough money to pay his rent *and* the community college tuition; and so, despite doing well in his course of study, he never officially obtained the credentials he needed to be a certified nursing assistant. Determined to not waste more time, he was offered a job and he accepted the position right away. Today Tyler is an overnight stocker at Walmart, making $7.25 an hour. It's not the career path he was hoping for, and the shifts are unpredictable—sometimes he doesn't know his work schedule until the day before he is to report to the store—but he has a job and the way he sees it, "that's pretty good for now."

Critical Thinking Questions:

- Think about who the most important people are in your life—those on whom you can rely the most. How have you relied on them in the past? Currently?

- How have your own relational supports contributed to your educational, occupational, and self-development outcomes?

- As a social worker, how might we best promote interdependency and strong relational connections among aging-out foster youth? What relational supports do you think this population needs the most? Why? How does interdependency relate to independency or self-sufficiency?

ATTACHMENT: THE DEVELOPING SELF IN THE CONTEXT OF OTHERS

Theories of the developing self have a long history in psychology, and they vary in how they explain the influence and direction of how the very special social bond develops between infant and caregiver. Some theories have suggested the newborn is initially separate from the mother and attempts to bond during the first several months after birth; others argue that the mother and infant are bonded at first, and then undergo trials of separation in the first several months after birth. As interest in early attachment grew alongside empiricism in the social sciences in the early 20th century, formal attachment theories emerged from across the biological and social science disciplines. Arguably, Bowlby's attachment theory, and the important work of his student, Mary Ainsworth, and her student, Mary Main, hold prominence in the traditional developmental literature. As was presented in Chapter 3, Bowlby (1988) developed—and his colleagues empirically examined and refined—an infant–caregiver attachment classification system that ultimately categorized infants into four attachment domains: (a) *secure attachment* (acknowledges mother upon return, and confidently goes back to exploration); (b) *ambivalent attachment* (distressed from mother's separation, but not comforted when reunited); (c) *avoidant attachment* (infants are neither distressed nor comforted by the separation and return of their caregiver, but generally show little intimate involvement in the relationship); and (d) *disorganized attachment* (infants show inconsistent emotional and behavioral response to the separation and return of the primary caregiver; they may express confusion and hesitancy in response). The goal in infancy is to develop a secure internal working model from these early caregiving experiences that serves as a secure base for environmental exploration, and a template for future adult relationships.

More recently, neuroscientists and social scientists have expanded upon these earlier theories and their attendant empirical work, calling critical attention to the neurobiological processes implicated in early interpersonal relational experiences. The more recent field of interpersonal neurobiology examines the influence of early attachment processes on brain development, and has yielded important findings with pragmatic implications. Daniel Siegel (1999), one of the pioneers in the field of interpersonal neurobiology, and who has written extensively about the clinical value of neuroscientific findings, suggests that secure attachment is characterized by "attunement," which develops from contingent communication and accurate interpretation and response between parents and children. Attunement, which leads to secure attachment bonds, increases the release of the so-called attachment hormone, oxytocin, and is associated with intimate social bonds.

According to Louis Cozolino, relationships stimulate growth of glucocorticoid receptors in the amygdala, hippocampus, and HPA axis to decrease the imprint of stress on the brain and body. Attachment schemas are a type of implicit social memory that is experience dependent; they connect the orbitofrontal cortex and amygdala, and help regulate arousal, affect, and emotion. Negative attachment schemas are correlated with higher physical and emotional illness and decreased immune function (Cozolino, 2002). You might begin to see how the neurobiological literature is informing debate in the pediatric and parenting fields about what is considered optimal parenting practice. For example, you might wonder, given the importance of parent–infant contingent communication patterning on the developing brain and on infant self-regulation capacity, whether sleep-training advice that suggests letting babies "cry it out," so they learn to sleep on their own and self-soothe, still holds? What are the best ways to train a baby to sleep, given what we know about stress and attachment needs? How much stress is "too much" for the infant's developing brain?

Longitudinal studies show that early attachment relationships predict later socioemotional and educational outcomes. Sroufe, Egeland, Carlson, and Collins (2005) followed a cohort of individuals from in utero to adulthood. Secure attachment was associated with caregivers who were sensitive, communicative, and interactive with their infants. Study findings showed that reading and math scores in elementary school were associated with early-childhood secure attachment, and high school graduation could be predicted with 77% accuracy from early-childhood caregiver sensitivity scores (up to age 42 months). This important study convincingly suggests that the ability to develop and sustain relationships over the life course matters, and that early-childhood interactive experiences with caregivers tend to be some of the best predictors of later educational success and individual and interpersonal well-being. Early childhood attachment experiences offer an important foundation for later success across many different outcomes.

Synaptic development in the brain develops through early childhood experiences, solidifying neural paths that are strengthened with repetition. Neural pathways that are repeatedly activated, through experience-dependent learning processes, are retained and strengthened over time. Mirror neurons are mental processes that activate when watching or observing other people performing a physical act, even when the observer is not actively performing the same act. However, researchers have found distinctions in this phenomenon, in that such imitative behavior is processed only when the action is goal directed. Therefore, scientists believe that a function of these mirror neurons is to help interpret another human's behavioral intentions, and may serve as a foundation for empathy development and sociability. However, just as we would not expect that watching a basketball game would confer the same physiological workout as participating in an actual practice, we need to keep in mind the context and parameters that bound the usefulness of understanding the importance of mirror neurons. A person's mind may be primed via social relations to act in a certain way through observational behavior, but he or she will need circumstantial opportunities to "practice" and fully develop new, learned behaviors. We cannot substitute observation for participation, and we must understand the role of both in helping our clients work toward their goals and improve person–environment fit.

Environment and circumstance can affect opportunities for secure attachment. Children living in families characterized by active and chronic substance dependency experience severe attachment disruptions, resulting from chronic unpredictability in attunement behavior. Attachment disruptions in childhood, behaviorally expressed as incongruent attunement, can decrease opiate receptor density and thereby decrease the ability to effectively modulate pain while heightening sensitivity to painful emotions (Flores, 2004). Some scholars conceptualize chemical dependency itself as an attachment disorder (Flores, 2004), as drugs of abuse release the same hormones and neurotransmitters that human relationships do, and therefore, over time, may neurobiologically become the relational substitute for interpersonal human connections. Thus, drug-dependent individuals often characterize their relationship with drugs as a "love affair"—their only focus and insular object of desire. Similarly, Padykula and Conklin (2010) discuss the importance of several subsystem self-regulation capacities that facilitate adaptive response to environmental assaults predicated on subsystem organization and interdependency among self–other and self–other–environment transactions. These subsystem regulatory domains include physiology, emotion, cognition, interpersonal relatedness, sense of self, and behavior (p. 353). The contributory influence of each subsystem in organizing adaptive response to environmental stress can change over time and across the life course (see Figure 10.1).

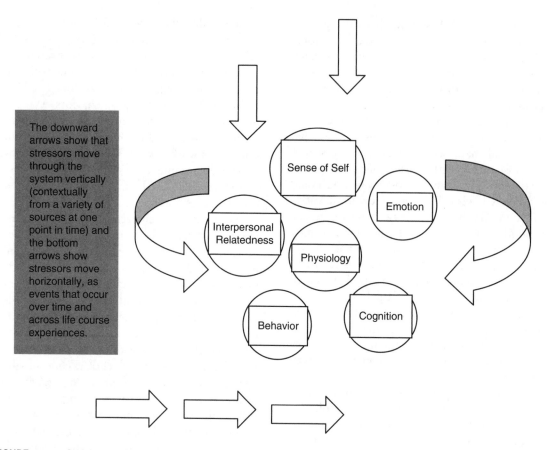

The downward arrows show that stressors move through the system vertically (contextually from a variety of sources at one point in time) and the bottom arrows show stressors move horizontally, as events that occur over time and across life course experiences.

Sense of Self

Emotion

Interpersonal Relatedness

Physiology

Behavior

Cognition

FIGURE 10.1   Self-System Regulatory Structures

CASE STUDY 2: JOEY, MARCHING INTO THE MIDDLE CLASS

The military is one of society's social institutions that can help youth from poor families move into the middle class through stable income and benefits, a predictable promotion structure, and promise of a retirement pension. Joey was one such young adult who was ready to have the military help him march into the middle class. Joey grew up in McDowell County, West Virginia. As a result of the decline in coal and steel industries, the social, economic, and educational risk conditions have dramatically increased for residents in McDowell County. And everyone there can tell you the same McDowell story. Most community insiders would say drug addiction is the worst of it all, whereas social scientist outsiders speculate that drug addiction is directly and indirectly related to the host of other ills that plague the community, such as high incarceration rates, joblessness, poor health and poor health-care access, a school dropout rate three times the national average, and the decaying institutional infrastructure and high truancy rates that go along with such a dropout rate. According to the *Washington Post* (Layton, 2011, http://www.highbeam.com/doc/1P2-30329377.html), McDowell County is one of the poorest areas in West Virginia, a county so entrenched in intergenerational poverty that its current social ills have garnered national political attention and social action. An action plan called the McDowell Initiative represents a collaboration among the American Federation of Teachers union and 40 other businesses and nonprofit partners, who have a common goal of helping McDowell County rise above its gripping poverty. The 5-year initiative commits to expanding wraparound services, such as drug treatment programs and health-care systems, and developing and promoting afterschool programs for county youth.

Joey knows all about McDowell County's social ills, and he had great ambition to get out. Joey knew he wanted to serve his country, as his great-grandfather and grandfather had before him, so right after his high school graduation, he enlisted in the U.S. Army. He was going to be part of something much bigger than McDowell County in every way, and he was going to be recognized for his talents. The military promised to take care of him, and one such promise was to support his continued education. His family in West Virginia could have never dreamed of financially supporting Joey's college education, but the military could, and so Joey enrolled. As a new recruit in the U.S. Army's Infantry branch, Joey set out for basic combat training at Fort Benning, Georgia. Basic training was easy for him. He will tell you that he has never minded people barking orders at him—he easily shuts it all out—and he was physically up for the challenge. But it was his first deployment that really affected him. He says he saw more than most people ever had or would back in his small, rural West Virginia hometown. He had friends in his platoon who were killed by IEDs; he himself narrowly escaped fatal sniper fire; and he began noticing that he tired more easily. His service as a soldier required constant vigilance, as he was always on alert trying to anticipate and avert the next impending crisis. He said it was the unpredictable and extreme changes that wore him out most—in his words, he was subjected to extreme mind-numbing boredom on the one hand, or fire, death, and crisis on the other. And worse, there was no real downtime because the boundaries between boredom and crisis were not clearly defined or predictable.

Joey has been deployed three times over the last 9 years, since starting college. As he puts it, "Most people who have done 9 years in college are called doctors or lawyers." He talks about how hard the frequent transitions from being a college student to soldier, and from soldier to college student, have been for him. On his most recent return, Joey was dealing with a new relational issue. A few days after handing in his final paper for one of his college courses, Joey said he would need permission to take the in-class exam another day because, as he told the instructor, the next day he would need to attend a memorial service for a fellow soldier who had taken his own life.

Critical Thinking Questions:

- Think about our social institutions. Do they function as gatekeepers to the American Dream? If so, how and for whom?

- Compare the functions of two social institutions. Pick one that you think facilitates access to opportunity for some groups or communities while restricting mobility for others. Pick another that you think offers more equitable opportunities. Compare and contrast the two.

SOCIAL RELATIONSHIPS ACROSS THE LIFE COURSE

Social networks are dynamic; thus, social capital benefits conferred through network relationships change over the life course. Change over time occurs both in the types of resources conferred through social networks (e.g., instrumental support, emotional support, tangible didactic advice, etc.), but also in the capacity to convert those resources to goods that benefit the individual, family, or community at a particular given position in the life course. An example is how the parental advice of taking a typing class in high school—seemingly irrelevant to the adolescent who does not see the immediate economic benefit of such a skill at the time—that may lead to a college work-study job transcribing interviews for a faculty research project, which in turn is essential to the student's ability to afford postsecondary education. Investment from *social capital* (e.g., parental advice, time, attention) at one point in the life course may lead to accumulation of *human capital* reserves (e.g., skills) that can be tapped later in life, and that yield new benefits when used at a later time. Think for a minute about what kinds of investments people made in earlier stages of your life course. Can you think of an example that may not have seemed to provide you an immediate benefit, but that was "converted" or paid off down the line in your life? How might your life have been different if those relational investments were made in different ways, at different times, or not at all?

In addition to differences across the life course in the distribution and convertability of social network benefits, the social convoy model (Kahn & Antonucci, 1980; Levitt, 1991) suggests that normative and nonnormative developmental changes across the life course are likely to change social network properties—how one's social network is structured—giving more or less importance to particular social relationships at various life course stages. For example, the family

typically serves as the primary socialization agent during early and middle childhood, whereas peers become an increasingly important source of influence in adolescence. Some scholars advocate focusing on the congruencies and incongruencies in socialization messages that are transmitted across social systems. For example, Spera and Matto (2007) provide a diagram of the contextual-congruence model of socialization, which depicts the child embedded within the family and situated in the center of a contextual web of relationships that carry information, ideas, norms, support, and resources to the child, directly and indirectly through the family. The bidirectional arrows show the flow of socialization messages and resources through the web, and the model suggests that optimal adaptation and goodness of child–environment fit will occur when there is consistency, rather than inconsistency, among the exchanges.

Early Childhood

Family is a primary socializing agent in the early years, and such socialization processes tend to last for a long time, even if the advice and support may not always be remembered in later years entirely as intended, as is illustrated by one emerging adult who told me, "My parents were very strict. They discouraged dating before marriage." Whereas the family is primary in these early years, school is an important secondary socializing space, and relationships to teachers and peers in the school context wield significant influence on developmental outcomes. Jennings and DiPrete (2010) examined how the relationship with teachers in the early elementary school years influenced children's development of social and behavioral skills, which tend to be most plastic in early childhood. Social and behavioral skills may impact the child's ability to make use of learning opportunities in the classroom and thereby indirectly influence academic gains, with teacher effectiveness related to academic gains (Nye, Konstantopoulos, & Hedges, 2004). Analyzing data from the ECLS-K cohort, Jennings and DiPrete found that noncognitive skills (social and behavioral) were related to academic achievement, and that teacher characteristics such as credentials and teaching experience were important in improving kindergartner's social and behavioral outcomes.

Adolescence

In adolescence, the influence of peers on behavior, attitudes, and time spent together is more important than the influence of parents. Special populations of adolescents may have unique social support needs to optimize development. For example, adolescents who have poor health are often situated in social networks where their network peers are disconnected from each other and where the adolescent resides at the periphery of the network (Cornwell, 2009). For adolescents, school is the primary socialization context with peers, and those individuals with chronic health conditions may experience decreased opportunities for interacting with peers due to hospitalizations, or increased stigma from peers resulting from physical limitations or physical differences that deviate from peer norms. Role strain in networks, where there are stressful interpersonal experiences or isolation from peer networks due to health or mental health conditions, can lead to smaller, weaker, and less supportive social networks over time for such youth. Haas, Schaefer, and Kornienko (2010) found that adolescents in poor health show smaller (in size) and weaker (in density) social networks than comparable youth without health problems. Given the importance of peers on school attachment and of school attachment on academic achievement, Haas et al. suggest that peer relations and social network relationships could be a point of intervention for those working with adolescents who have health problems.

School transitioning can also produce stress experiences that influence a peer's social network; an adolescent's social network can mitigate the effects of off-time educational transitions. For example, Langenkamp (2011) studied the effect of off-time educational transitions (transferring schools midyear or transitioning alone rather than with a cohort) in high school, and how that affects adolescent academic and social outcomes. Findings suggest that academic gains can be bolstered by strong social ties and participation in extracurricular activities for those adolescents making an off-time high school transition. Other studies have shown higher educational attachment for reintegrating military service personnel who have stronger social ties; in particular, small family size and high family income, along with strong information networks, have been shown to help veterans obtain necessary mental health treatment, and contribute to successful postsecondary educational attainment (Smith-Osborne, 2009).

Emerging Adulthood

In the emerging adulthood stage, unlike during adolescence, research shows that familial and romantic partner relationships are more important to happiness and well-being than quality of friendship relations (Walen & Lachman, 2000; Whisman, Sheldon, & Goering, 2000). Relationships with mothers were significantly related to emerging adults' well-being and happiness for those both with and without a romantic partner. By contrast, friendships receded in their importance to well-being only for emerging adults in romantic relationships, suggesting both continuity in specific parental influence across life course transitions (e.g., acquisition of a romantic partner) and change in peer influence on well-being after role transition.

Based on the encompassing work and support of the MacArthur Research Network on Transitions to Adulthood, and 500 interviews with emerging adults all over the country, Settersten and Ray (2010) demonstrated the dramatic importance of parent–child relationships and support in starting young adults on a trajectory of achievement, from settling and succeeding in college, obtaining a job, managing a first home, to starting a family of their own. They report that "strong, healthy relationships between parents and young adults are one of the most significant factors in determining whether young people succeed in early adulthood" (p. 176). Policies that support low-income families can, in turn, bolster young adults' life chances. For example, the most important housing policy is income support, as income is the largest predictor of housing insecurity (Pendall, Theodos, & Franks, 2012); with increased housing stability for low-income families, such families may be able to provide critical instrumental support to their young adult children, who are unable to afford to move into their own independent place of residence while seeking advanced education and training experiences.

Settersten and Ray's (2010) data reveal that without adequate and sustaining parental support, even small missteps emerging adults may make along the way can leave them mired in trajectories that do not match their aspirations. For example, they show that young adults who are first-generation college students often do not have the familial support to navigate through the higher educational system (e.g., selecting classes, filling out financial aid forms, etc.), and that they are at higher risk than young adults whose parents have college degrees to drop out of college or take longer to complete a degree. Connecting to mentors, particularly for this high-risk college student population, is critical to success. "In terms of civic engagement, what matters most about the college experience is not so much what it 'teaches' young people as what it connects them to in the future—the workplaces, schools, and community organizations they end up in" (Settersten & Ray, 2010, p. 165).

Bonding and bridging social capital connections in emerging adulthood is particularly salient for low-skill workers entering the labor market, as well as for employment advancement opportunities. Martinson (2010) describes community-based institutional partnerships (e.g., with community colleges and local businesses) as a viable method by which low-wage

workers can get on-site upgraded training experiences and credentialing for job advancement that matches employer needs. Given the inflexibility and often intense work and family demands that many low-wage young adults face, support beyond just education and credentialing is often needed, including tangible assistance such as child care availability and health care, and relational assistance such as career counseling or job coaching initiatives.

Middle Age

The decade-long MacArthur project on midlife, Midlife in the United States (MIDUS), conducted in the mid-1990s examined the positive experiences associated with midlife, finding that most happiness and well-being come from peer and familial relationships: "Everyone between 40 and 59 agreed that relations with others was the most important element of well-being, followed by feeling healthy, being able to enjoy oneself, and experiencing a sense of accomplishment and fulfillment" (in Cohen, 2012, p. 134). The longitudinal data suggest that, rather than being the tipping point for isolation and relational atrophy, social network relationships hold primacy in overall well-being and satisfaction in middle age.

Older Adulthood

Many studies specify that perceived emotional support is associated with improved health and longevity (Uchino, 2004). Social support is often increasingly important as we age and our social, physical, and instrumental needs rise. The risk of acquiring a functional limitation increases as we age, with some populations at greater risk for such impairment. In their population-based study of adults 60 years old and older, Louie and Ward (2011) examined functional limitations by education level, race/ethnicity, and poverty status, and found disparities in physical functioning across SES. Specifically, poverty was significantly associated with more functional limitations. As social workers, we should constantly assess both the actual and perceived value of older adult clients' social network, examining the structural properties (size, density, hierarchy of importance) as well as the types of resources exchanged (information, time, attention, emotional sense of belonging, companionship, etc.), and to understand how the network constellation fits with the older adult's needs.

SOCIAL NETWORKS: PEERS, FAMILY, AND COMMUNITY

Peers: The Influence of Your Friend's Friends' Friends

Brooks (2011) discusses "emergent systems" as interdependent and transactional; those for which the whole is greater than the sum of its parts, and in which people adopt habits and actions from unconscious cues to perpetuate and be consistent with derived system norms. According to this idea, because factors interact to create a condition for an outcome to occur, human socialization processes are influenced by the "web of influence" within which a child is situated. Our schools, neighborhoods, and other social institutions provide that context to which children are exposed and from which they absorb new cues. Peers are of particular influence to the developing child.

In his TED talk, Dr. Nicholas Christakis (2010) demonstrates the importance of patterns on the functional characteristics and properties of networks. He does so by way of an example comparing graphite and diamonds, both of which are made of the same element (carbon) but in different structural patterns that lead to very soft or very hard distinctive properties. So, too, is it true of human social network patterning, he says. Our respective spatial location or place in the social network (e.g., central or peripheral) will have a significant influence on our exposure and accessibility to the flow of goods (e.g., information, ideas, economic incentives,

disease, health, etc.) through the network. As Christakis says, "If your friends are obese, your risk of obesity is 45% higher. If your friend's friends are obese, your risk of obesity is 25% higher. If your friend's friend's friend, someone you probably don't even know, is obese, your risk of obesity is 10% higher. It's only when you get to your friend's friend's friend's friends that there's no longer a relationship between that person's body size and your own body size."

In Christakis's recent book, *Connected* (2009), authored with James Fowler, they discuss the science of social networks and the influence or spread they have on attitudes and behavior. Their empirical work suggests that the pattern of network ties is important because it influences network function. They discuss the term *homophily*, which they describe as the tendency to associate with people who are like us (e.g., drug addicted; like-minded in religious beliefs, etc.). They state that the average American has four close social contacts, but that it is not only the number of social contacts that can affect health, but also an individual's position or location in that network—being more central in a network makes a person more vulnerable to the currency that flows through it (i.e., disease, obesity, money, ideas, drugs, human capital skills, etc.). "Social networks, it turns out, tend to magnify whatever they are seeded with" (Christakis & Fowler, 2009, p. 31). They also discuss what they call *hyperdyadic spread* (or contagion), which they define as the social influence that spreads beyond an immediate dyad relationship, to friends of friends of friends. They suggest a "three-degree rule," by which three degrees of influence have the most impact on attitudes, feelings, and behaviors, and links beyond those three degrees may be more unstable and "decay." The authors' empirical work suggests that a person will have a 15% greater chance of being happy if their friend at one degree of separation is happy; two degrees = 10%, and three degrees = 6%. Each happy friend a person has increases that person's probability of being happy by 9%. Each unhappy friend decreases it by 7%. However, they state that friends' happiness effect on us only lasts about one year; then adaptations set in (p. 52). Their social network research suggests that behavioral-health prevention campaigns should target the core structure of networks rather than the periphery and target influential individuals within the network (Fowler, Dawes, & Christakis, 2009).

EXPERT'S CORNER: NICHOLAS A. CHRISTAKIS, MD, PHD, MPH

Nicholas A. Christakis directs the Human Nature Lab at Harvard University, is a Professor of Medical Sociology at Harvard Medical School, and is in the Faculty of Arts and Sciences. In 2009, he was named one of *Time* magazine's 100 most influential people in the world. Christakis is an expert in social networks and their influence on health and behavior. Christakis's research suggests that it is not only the material (information, disease, money, resources, etc.) that flows among social network members that makes a difference, but also the structure and pattern of the network ties that influences its members. Recently, Christakis and James Fowler, his long-term colleague at the University of California, San Diego, examined the influence of social networks on the spread of obesity over 3 decades. In an article that appeared in the *New England Journal of Medicine* in 2007, Christakis and Fowler examined a network of 12,067 people from the longitudinal Framingham Heart Study. Using body mass index > 30 as the obesity criterion, Christakis and Fowler found that spouse, sibling, and friend obesity patterns all contributed significantly to a person's increased risk of becoming obese himself or herself. In fact, they found that social distance among network ties matters, up to three degrees of separation; interestingly, however, geographic distance among social ties did not significantly influence risk. Obesity in mutual friendships (where the person considers the social tie a friend and vice versa) had the most impact on obesity risk. Specifically, they found if a person's mutual friend became obese, that person had a 171% increased risk of obesity himself or herself (p. 376). Risk of obesity in a person with a sibling who became obese was found to be 40% higher; risk related to a spouse who became obese was 37% higher. Christakis and Fowler observed that social ties may be related to network ties in three ways: (a) homophily—that people who have similar characteristics and behaviors tend to associate with each other; (b) confounding—that shared experiences and serendipitous circumstances cause simultaneous weight gain; and (c) induction—that behaviors among a person's social ties themselves influence the weight change, possibly through changes in social norms and attitudes

Photo of Nicholas A. Christakis (left) and James Fowler (right)
Courtesy of Nicholas A. Christakis

and/or behavioral exposures directly (p. 372). Their social network modeling provides evidence that social norms, and not just direct behavioral exposures, are a precipitating influence on obesity, given that geographic distance was not a significant factor and that norms may be preserved over distance, whereas direct behavioral exposure would not be sustained.

A video of Christakis's influential TED Talk on social networks as a superorganism, in which he further discusses this research, can be found at his website: http://www.HumanNatureLab.net.

Social media is a relational influence in children's lives. Social media platforms have been developed to engage youth and build community, like the Military Child Connect organization (https://www.militarykidsconnect.org), a social media community for children age 6 to 17 years from military families who have deployed parent(s). At the same time, criticism has been directed at social media platforms such as Facebook, charging that such electronic social networks contribute to a decrease in children's overall face-to-face sociability (Sennett, 2012). Other positive youth social spaces can come from formal social service programs that target at-risk youth and use prosocial youth mentors as supports for the target youth. For example, using the multidimensional risk and protective literature and a vulnerability–stress model to explain risk behavior in youth, Shelton (2009) describes a prevention program, Leadership, Education, Achievement, & Development (LEAD), a 14-week psychoeducational expressive arts program designed to mitigate the cumulative and deleterious effects of racism and discrimination on minority youth's mental health, which reduce their chances of engaging in prosocial productive behavior. The premise was that investing and leveraging local social networks could change the negative behavioral trajectory resulting from racial discrimination and neighborhood disadvantage, and could enhance adaptive capacity and resiliency. LEAD was implemented in three rural communities, with participating youth demonstrating increased self-esteem, enhanced behavioral control, and increased

resiliency at the end of the program. Youth who successfully completed the program were given the opportunity to participate in a peer training program and become a LEAD peer counselor, working with an adult mentor in the program with the target youth.

Peer supports used in formal and informal substance-dependency programs have also shown positive results. Burkey, Kim, and Breakey (2011) note the remarkably high rates of substance abuse in the homeless male population. As is well documented, substance abuse has a deleterious effect on social relationships, causing a pronounced increase in social isolation with continued use. Social networks and social capital contribute significantly to the chances of successful recovery for the population as a whole, but particularly for homeless males who are recovering from substance abuse. Burkey et al. interviewed men who had been staying at a Baltimore homeless shelter for an average of 6 to 12 months. The men shared that a primary source of recovery motivation for them came from the desire to restore broken family relationships, in some cases before the family member died. Mothers played a more significant role than other family members in the majority of the men's recovery stories. In addition, motivation to financially support and invest in their children's lives also provided recovery support for these men, even as they acknowledged that their own recovery must come first. Knowledge, information, and emotional support characterized by openness and identification were among the resources the men had gained from their recovery network and peer support relationships and that were of value to them in their recovery. They gained hope from their sponsors and from others who have walked through addiction and achieved recovery before them. They said they had respect for formal treatment providers who helped them take responsibility and, thereby, helped them increase control over life decisions that were compatible with their recovery goals. Importantly, they said the key was to avoid "outside distracting" relationships that might get in the way of their recovery. Therefore, family, peer, and formal treatment provider relationships were instrumental in their recovery trajectory.

In a study that examined what they called recovery capital, Laudet and White (2008) examined the extent to which peer supports and connections to a spiritual source might be influential at different stages of recovery from chemical dependency. "In the same way as substance dependence can affect all areas of functioning (e.g., social, mental, emotional, vocational), recovery from addiction is more than the absence of substance use in an otherwise unchanged life" (Laudet & White, 2008, p. 29). Laudet and White defined *recovery capital* as consisting of social support, spirituality, life meaning, religiousness, and 12-step affiliation. They examined four stages of recovery— (a) under 6 months, (b) 6 to 18 months, (c) 18 to 36 months, and (d) over 3 years—and looked at whether recovery capital, consisting of these five dimensions, facilitated sustained recovery, quality of life, and decreased stress levels over the course of one year (p. 31). Twelve-step involvement and life meaning were significant for long-term recovery gains. Also, for the early recovery group, 12-step involvement reduced stress levels, suggesting such involvement may help those in early recovery adjust to the instrumental and emotional demands of sobriety. Spirituality did tend to reduce stress levels at later intervals and related to higher quality of life scores for those with 18 months or more sobriety; religiosity was not a significant predictor.

Family: The Network of First and Last Resort

According to the National Alliance for Caregiving, 10 million people over age 50 are caring for aging parents, and two out of three informal family caregivers are women, many with their own children living with them. Providing family care can be challenging when it takes middle-age adults out of the labor force, which in turn poses financial risk to the sustainability of their own retirement savings. The emotional and financial burden can be tremendous; an Indiana University report recently found that informal caregivers save Medicare $375 billion a year (White, Caine, & Connelly, 2012). For example, a woman who is employed full time and living with a husband in his late 50s who has recently been diagnosed with early-onset Alzheimer's disease, and who also has her own mother living nearby, who herself has chronic health conditions that require daily functional assistance, will undoubtedly be challenged when making difficult decisions about her own career. If that same woman is living in financially fragile circumstances, her experienced stressors will be compounded.

Older adults caring for adult children with special needs is a subpopulation of family caregivers who present with unique challenges and needs. As children with special needs age out of the school system and child service programs, family members may find themselves struggling to meet these special caregiving needs, while also trying to plan to meet their own retirement needs and/or health challenges. The developmental demands and delights of children with special needs as they age out of childhood and enter into young adulthood can have emotional, interpersonal, financial, and physical consequences. Even as parents of such emerging adults may be elated at the growing independence, depending on the functional limitations, there may be daunting concerns about the continued provision of still-needed care for these young adults—and often these care responsibilities fall to the family. Long-term intensive caregiving for an adult child or grandchild with special needs can cause vulnerability and strain depending on the context and range of available supports.

For example, meet Maria. Maria is a 62-year-old grandmother of two children, both of whom are in their early 40s. She is also the grandmother of four grandchildren, one of whom, Jeffrey, has Down syndrome and is in his last year of high school. Maria has always been the family backbone—the caregiver of first and often last resort. Jeffrey now needs help transitioning into employment, and a community-run vocational program promises to offer him the specialized training he needs to get the unionized grocery clerk job at a supermarket. The problem is that the job is in the next town over. Maria will need to transport Jeffrey to the training program, and then to his job each day, because there is no public-access disability van service in their residential location.

And meet Karyn and Scott. Karyn is 54 years old and drives a school bus. Her husband, Scott, is 10 years older than Karyn, and had to stop working at the meat processing plant 5 years ago due to a work-related disability for which he was never compensated, and that has left him with extreme daily back pain. They have two grown children who no longer live with them, and they are currently living in a trailer with Scott's elderly mother who is bedridden with the severe physical sequelae of diabetes. The mother, Vera, is blind and not mobile. The family lives on $18,000 from disability and the wages from Karyn's bus job, which are $10.55 per hour.

In rural areas and small towns across the United States, particularly one-industry towns where that industry has collapsed, like Boydton, Virginia, and Pembroke, Illinois, many families are taking care of elderly family members who have chronic or terminal diseases and who lack public assistance. However, there are innovative programs that are striving to reach these families and ease caregiver burdens while increasing support. One example of such an innovation is the Pervasive Health Informatics

Technology laboratory at Indiana University, led by Dr. Kay Connelly. Dr. Connelly and her research team are devising ways to address caregiver strain by engaging community members, service providers, and other organizational leaders in using technology to help older adults, particularly vulnerable adults living in low-SES urban and rural communities, to age in place with assistive technology. Mobile devices and other tools can be used, for example, to organize and communicate important health information to providers from within the older adult's home.

In *The Accordion Family*, Newman (2012) offers compelling research that shows countries with weak welfare states tend to put families in the role of safety-net provider, with disproportionate numbers of parents in such countries supporting adult children, and for longer periods of time, particularly during economic downturns. Her research portrays a current demographic landscape that looks much different than it did a generation ago, one in which it takes longer to launch adult children due to extended educational requirements, credentials that often require unpaid internships, and the high cost of higher education and housing. Therefore, Newman says, we are seeing a consequence of this shift in delayed adulthood as young adults in their 30s and even early 40s find themselves returning to their parents' home to live while they try to make good on their future plans, becoming what Newman calls the "accordion family." As mentioned, Newman identifies this trend occurring most often in countries with the weakest welfare systems, such as the United States, Italy, and Spain; she has not found the accordion-family effect in stronger social welfare states such as Denmark and Sweden, where young people still tend to go out on their own, apart from their families of origin, at age 20. In addition, SES tends to make a difference in U.S. accordion family trends.

Higher income families often have the resources available to comfortably house their young adult (and in some cases approaching middle adult) children in their homes while they acquire the educational skills necessary to get a good job, but working poor families often do not have the resources to house nonworking young adults, who may be experienced as a drain on the family. Newman (2012) has found that in some of these families, the young adult typically may be required to contribute to the family household as a requirement for being able to stay there. For example, a 21-year-old mother and her 5-year-old son, who had searched for shelter for 6 months, found themselves sleeping at friends' houses and in cars during warmer months. The mother had already exhausted her welcome at the homes of family and relatives. She sought emergency shelter, but was told there were no spaces available. She finally found a one-bedroom apartment at a shelter and now attends a job training program during the day while her son is in school. The literature shows an increasing number of parents under age 24 seeking shelter; many have left their parents' households because they were evicted or the homes were too crowded with relatives. If youth are unable to financially contribute to the family, often they are asked to leave and find another place of residence (Newman, 2012).

In addition, working young adults who are single parents may find the structure and conditions of low-wage employment incompatible with adequately meeting their child care needs. For example, the schedules that single parents with one or more low-wage jobs have to weave together to provide financially for their families often require hardship hours of child care. Low-wage jobs may be characterized by sudden shift changes with little notice for child-care planning, and with parents often working multiple jobs over extended hours to keep the family financially afloat, children's care during off hours becomes a needed resource. At Happy Faces in northeast Washington, DC, parents can find 24-hour child care. Most of the parents who use the center are single or teen parents who are working multiple, part-time, low-wage shift-work jobs with irregular hours.

In many areas of the country, however, 24-hour child care is not available for such parents.

Williams (2010) has examined the interface between class and social networks, finding that lower SES families feature smaller, denser networks, whereas professional/managerial-class networks are more expansive but not as close, tend to be more widely distributed across a geographic location, and are characterized by large numbers of acquaintances and relationships among "friends of friends" that provide access to resources, jobs, and information. She notes that increases in education and social status tend to be related to increased network diversity and size, but not to density or closeness of network members (p. 169).

It is also true that the larger social context within which a child is reared will influence the opportunities and behavioral decisions he or she will make. "Often the school, the family background, peer groups, neighborhoods all provide cues to people about what their future prospects are going to be, and those cues influence decisions they'll make along the way—how vigilant to be about contraception, when to begin sexual relationships, and what to do if they become pregnant. All those decisions are different depending on the social world you're part of" (Furstenburg, cited in Settersten & Ray, 2010, p. 97). From the disproportionate burden of care, to the academic preparation opportunities parents can provide children, SES can make a difference in the developmental opportunities families can offer during childhood. For example, Hart and Risley (cited in Brooks, 2011, p. 106) found that 4-year-olds in poor families will have heard 32 million fewer total words than those from "professional" families, translating into 178 and 487 words per hour, respectively.

Community Connections: From Hull House to Facebook

Social workers today do not typically take up residence in the communities of their clients, to live, eat, sleep, and work alongside such families in shared communal residence in order to engage in arts and education together, or to observe the health and hygiene behaviors of those they study. Indeed, the Hull House community model of the early 20th century has given way to the virtual community of Facebook today. This deconstruction of the typical communal meeting place has evolved over time.

Sennett (2012) explains that in the 1800s, craftsmen at the closing of the day would engage in rituals to publicly demarcate, announce, and recognize each workshop craftsman and the contributions he made for collective betterment. Sennett argues that the structural relationships or "institutional bonds" within organizations have changed over the decades due to change in workforce employer–employee commitments, loyalties, and arrangements. In an interesting sociological examination of community in the South Side of Chicago, Sudhir Venkatesh (2000), a sociologist at Columbia University, chronicled the development and demise of Chicago's Robert Taylor Homes, a public housing experiment erected in 1962 and ultimately demolished in 2007. In their first year, the Homes were a veritablly well-functioning community space where its mixed-income residents shared bonds, trust, and support, and cooperated with one another to make their shared living space a thriving community. By 1965, 27,000 people resided in the housing complex. Despite the nonfunctional elevators, dense residential space, and lack of adequate outdoor play areas in the Robert Taylor Homes, the early years of its development saw residents coming together as neighbors in their efforts to build community and collectively respond to the challenges of living in their shared space.

To this end, they formed resident organizations and tenant associations. The "Mama's Mafia" was a formidable informal organization of support networks, composed of women who worked to decrease gang recruitment, increase building safety, and generally provide a sense of social control in and around the buildings.

Other formal tenant groups formed as well (e.g., Mothers on the Move Against Slums; Venkatesh, 2000, p. 31), and they worked closely with social services agencies. Informal peer groups provided child care, shared food, and loaned money. Support networks were formed according to residential place and space, by building and floor. Leadership of these organized networks became more identified and institutionalized as time went on. For instance, they established "elevator committees" of dedicated women who operated the dysfunctional elevators at heavy-use times to regulate the flow of activity, and "they created an overarching Citizens Committee of tenants and leaders in business, education, religion and law enforcement who would welcome the new Taylor Homes residents and integrate them into the fabric of the larger community. They helped to develop 'floor clubs' for tenants and selected individuals to be 'janitors' and 'special guards' who monitored traffic in lobbies" (p. 33). The Building Council had membership and specific roles, such as "floor captains," who were responsible for scheduling laundry times.

In her book, *True Wealth*, sociology professor Juliet Schor (2011) discusses how economic growth over the decades has served to undermine the necessity of labor and goods exchange among individuals within communities, leading to an erosion of social ties and mutually dependent exchanges that, in prior decades, collectively enhanced individual well-being. "Economies of reciprocity" have been replaced, she suggests, by an enormous expansion of individual time investment in work environments outside of the immediate community, resulting in weakened community connections. However, a focus on the social and economic benefits that come from increased community-level interactions has gained traction of late. In *The Great Reset*, Richard Florida (2011) suggests that revitalization efforts in declining cities will require a focus on human capital development via community-based bottom-up (ground level) initiatives that enhance citizen access to training and education, which in turn leads to skill development in areas of cultural and creative enterprise and professional occupational opportunities. Florida hypothesizes that human interaction is essential for the necessary idea exchange characteristic of the shifting knowledge-based economy that will drive innovation, growth, and subsequent economic revitalization. To Florida, economic growth and sustainability is driven by a focus on human capital rather than infrastructure or built-environment development (e.g., hotel construction). He suggests that economic growth and productivity—and, therefore, thriving cities—result from a clustering of the creative class and dense human spaces that maximize exchange of goods and ideas.

Health and well-being are related to social embeddedness in the community (Berkman & Glass, 2000). Social capital, defined as the collective capacity and interpersonal investment at a larger level, is related to health outcomes (Carlson & Chamberlain, 2003). The strength of an individual's formal and informal ties affects one's level of community attachment (Ryan, Agnitsch, Zhao, & Mullick, 2005). *Community attachment* consists of (a) belonging, (b) belief in having an impact on community, (c) belief that the community can meet personal needs, and (d) expression of emotional connections (McMillan & Chavis, 1986).

How does community help to meet personal needs? Pih, Hirose, and Mao (2012) found that in some low-wage Chinese immigrant communities, like the one they studied in California, families rely on interpersonal relationships to provide important information and social connections to employment opportunities, with

largely successful labor-market attachment outcomes. However, for the dissemination of health-care information, these interpersonal networks within their community are not often as helpful. The authors identified limited English proficiency as a significant barrier that reduced the bridging social-capital opportunities of key community members to be able to understand the majority community's health-care system and its resources, which decreased the informational support they could provide to the community's residents. Similarly, Hochhausen, Perry, and Le (2010) found a relationship between the number of years immigrants have been in the country and increased acculturation as measured by English usage, which was moderated by neighborhood concentration of Latinos. They found that the higher this concentration was, the lower the influence of years in country on acculturation. Therefore, living in highly concentrated Latino neighborhoods mitigates the influence that length of time in the United States has on increased acculturative English language utility.

Other examples of the impact of community embeddedness can be seen in recent news stories of military veterans struggling to find employment in their communities of origin upon their return from Iraq and Afghanistan. How can community supports be leveraged to help returning veterans, particularly those who may have visible or invisible wounds of war, transition successfully back into the community and into the civilian labor market? As a social worker, what kinds of reemployment workforce development strategies might be offered at the community level to facilitate successful employment outcomes for this special population?

SPOTLIGHT TOPIC: HARLEM CHILDREN'S ZONE

Geoffrey Canada grew up in the South Bronx, near the very streets to which he now brings his graduate-level Harvard education to change the intergenerational trajectories of Central Harlem families. The CEO of the Harlem Children's Zone since 1990, Geoffrey Canada is a dynamic leader committed to educational reform and providing a sustainable, relationally based web of supports and services to Harlem families from "cradle through college," to disrupt the cycle of generational poverty and to promote families' educational, occupational, and financial upward mobility. The focus of the HCZ is on the whole child, the whole family, and the whole community, with a commitment from birth through college, and across family generations.

Data show that Canada's programs work in providing positive outcome-based results, but they work in large part because of the success in relationship development and leadership that these programs require. Engaging and investing in families block by block; identifying key community leaders; and hiring, training, and supervising quality staff are requisites for the Zone's incredible success. Its internal organizational dynamics and relational experiences are directly correlated with the ability to provide the education and support to Harlem's families in need. A diagram at the HCZ website (http://www.hcz.org) depicts the integration of comprehensive services across the life course and across individual, family, and community systems.

The programs designed to address individual, family, and community needs across the pipeline includes a Baby College, which is a 9-week parenting workshop for parents with children ages 0 to 3 years, and which offers training in brain development, disciplinary techniques, and parenting support; and Harlem Gems, a pre-K program to improve school readiness and involve parents in understanding effective methods to enhance children's cognitive, emotional, and social skills. The HCZ also operates Promise Academy charter schools for elementary, middle, and high school students, using a lottery system for enrollment, and offers wraparound services such as medical, dental, and family programs to students and their families.

Other special HCZ programs include a monthly farmer's market where families can use vouchers to buy healthy foods; a fitness center that offers middle school youth karate and dance classes; a Fifth Grade Institute afterschool program that helps prepare students for middle school; Boys to Men Leadership and Girl Power youth social development programs; an Obesity Initiative; the HCZ Asthma Initiative to help families manage the disease and reduce illness-related emergency room visits; an afterschool arts and media literacy program; Investment Camp; an employment and technology center for teens and adults; and a College Success Office that provides assistance to HCZ students who attend college through "campus advisors."

For Reflection

Based on your understanding of the literature, what are the most important developmentally sensitive periods in which to intervene with clients living in disadvantaged communities? What interventions at this developmental period might be most effective? How can social workers best maximize developmental plasticity for residents living in impoverished neighborhoods?

CURRENT INNOVATIONS IN COMMUNITY BUILDING

At the community level, resiliency can be facilitated by collective enforcement of norms, providing opportunities for guidance, and identifying "community anchors" that provide stability and consistency. Mary's Center in Washington, D.C., is an example of an innovative, evidence-based holistic multiservice center that provides essential programs to the area's Latino community. Established in 1988 with an original focus on providing bilingual health services to pregnant women and their infants, Mary's

Center currently provides educational, physical and mental health, and other social service programs to underserved Latino populations and immigrants at multiple community sites. Specifically, their model is a social change model; integrated services include home visiting programs, teen afterschool programs and educational services for youth to help with college applications, parenting and job skill developing programs, and a child-care licensing program to help women who wish to operate child-care services in their homes.

For example, the mobile health unit "Mama & Baby Bus" conducts health screenings, testing, vaccinations, and dental services. Staff on the bus help families complete medical forms and assist with resource referrals. The focus, Mary's Center emphasizes, is not on the individual but the family-in-community, and the Center encourages neighbors and other family members or significant others to come with the client to program appointments and visits.

Permanent Supportive Housing models are also being developed and tested around the country. These provide permanent housing, social services, and health care to adults who have been homeless for a year or longer. The residents live together in an arrangement that maximizes the community of its residents. Colocating residents in the same building offers the opportunity to strengthen their support network among residents, rather than scattering them over different locations.

A movement toward collaborative consumption is growing in communities across the United States. Mobile technology, such as the proliferation of smartphones, is increasing access to a new kind of collaborative consumerism that contests traditional ownership of commodities such as toys, transportation, tools, and clothing (see the Tie Society rental company). The collaborative "sharing-through-renting movement" is picking up speed in many urban areas, where young people in particular are joining

for economic and environmental sustainability reasons.

A community focus is also gaining traction among people in their retirement years. These years are growing longer for some demographic groups, and the importance of finding meaningful service-oriented work, volunteer opportunities, and community engagement during these years and decades is of interest to many adults who are 65 years and older. In *The Big Shift: Navigating the New Stage Beyond Midlife*, Marc Freedman (2011) calls these "encore years," when people in the second half of life want to find work that matters. Encore careers are those that begin when traditional-life-course careers end; they offer older adults new occupational spaces to connect and mentor subsequent generations. Organizations like ReServe, developed in 2005, facilitate the match between older adults who have left their primary careers and are interested in engaging in service-oriented and industry-change opportunities so they can stay connected to people and communities. The opportunities capitalize on older adults' skills and experiences and offer part-time stipend-paid service positions for those looking to give back to their communities and to extend their work in new ways.

HIERARCHIES AND POWER

Economic models are increasingly being applied to understanding behavioral-health decision making. For example, Lessard (2007) suggests that social networks indirectly affect health decisions through their influence on skill development, attitudinal socialization, direct knowledge acquisition, and adoption of behavioral practices. Lessard, Contandriopoulous, and Beaulieu (2010) discuss Bourdieu's capital theory (Bourdieu, 1997) in application to health behaviors. Bourdieu identified four kinds of capital: (a) economic, (b) cultural (including embodied, or personal, capital; objectified capital, or technology, goods, and materials; and institutionalized capital, or degrees, skills, and knowledge), (c) social (e.g., group memberships, relational networks), and (d) symbolic (e.g., reputation, prestige). Lessard et al. (2010) suggest that, because these forms of capital are unequally distributed, are interdependent, and convey power to their holder, exploration of the access to and leverage of such power opportunities should be examined and ought to mark points of multilevel intervention.

In *Identity Economics*, Akerloff and Kranton (2010) more specifically focus on identity as a focal interest point within this capital framework. They suggest an emphasis on examining relational transactions, understanding how these transactions become institutionalized within a particular community, and how they serve to maintain community engagement and participation of its individuals. They discuss the importance of examining the cultural, symbolic, and economic gains and losses associated with particular community memberships, and how capital arrangements influence behavioral participation within each community. Moving to an identity economics perspective, Akerloff and Kranton (2010) would also suggest paying special attention to identity construction as a by-product of these interdependent transactions that lead to capital gains and losses and thus influence behavioral choice. If norms are immutable within certain identities (derived from the social context influence on their development), than there may be a necessary shift in focus, from trying to change behavior to identity change, with its attendant new related, requisite behaviors.

For example, a Black female in her early 50s who is in the contemplation stage of change (i.e., aware but not yet willing to commit to recovery behaviors) said, in talking about the recovery rooms, "It helps but it helps only when I want it to help. It hasn't stopped me from drinking, but it has made me aware of my drinking. For the better." Another client illustrated Akerloff and Kranton's principle of associating perceived utility with identity status gains and losses in order for behavioral shifting to occur, when she remarked, "I don't like that I have to say, 'Hi, I'm Janie and I'm an alcoholic.' What about just, 'Hi, I'm Janie'? Or 'Hi, I'm Janie and I'm a mother of two'? Or 'I'm Janie and I'm the grandmother of four'?" Perhaps Janie wants us to know that for her, her role as mother and grandmother holds significant value and contributes in positive ways to her identity, and is how she would like to be perceived by others through her introduction. As treatment providers, we might then ask, how do we assess and intervene to maximize the capital matrix and power of behavioral commitment in the recovery community, while diminishing the power capital forces on behavioral commitment within the addiction community? From a multilevel approach, we must focus on both *self-regulatory control* capacities and relational capital, and understand each domain's influence on behavioral decision making.

At a more global level, technological capital has become increasingly democratized, and has been used to shift the balance of power in governments around the world. Social media's ability to create perturbations in the power elite, giving voice to collectives of people far and wide, has been seen throughout the world, particularly in the Arab region since December 2010. Mansour (2012) reviewed the role of social networking sites in the recent revolutions in the Arab world, specifically in Tunisia, Egypt, and Libya. Social media sites were used to connect people, communicate information, and collaborate in protests. In particular, Facebook and Twitter helped people coordinate protests and disseminate news, and YouTube videos raised awareness of human rights violations and enhanced accessibility to the region from disparate geographic locations, which in turn helped mobilize the supportive base.

SUMMARY

The social networks within which we are embedded have a powerful influence on our behavior and life course development. Our earliest attachment experiences with our primary caregiver can set the template for how we form relationships at later developmental stages, and also shapes early brain development. But recent neurobiological research on brain plasticity shows that our neural pathways can be shaped and reshaped through interpersonal experiences throughout our lives.

- Warm, nurturing, responsive, attuned relationships are particularly important during infancy and early childhood, but such relationships can be cultivated and are important throughout the life course, and have the capacity to alter behavior at multiple stages of development.

- Research shows that it is not just the quantity of individuals in our social network that matters, but also the quality of the network, as well as our position or location within the network structure, that will determine its influence on us.

- Our ability to convert and use the resources available to us in our social networks also matters tremendously.

- Family demographics have changed over time, and family members are increasingly caring for younger and older generations simultaneously, or are feeling the strain of returning to a family-of-origin household as a young adult, due to delayed entry into first jobs.

- Virtual communities have grown over time and offer important opportunities, such as emotional support and exchange of information, ideas, and products.

- Child development researchers are also concerned that the proliferation of social media usage may curb the frequency of face-to-face interactions, particularly at developmentally sensitive times of childhood when socialization with peers is most important, and they suggest that paying attention to how screen time may influence other socioemotional developmental outcomes in children over time is critical.

KEY TERMS

Ambivalent attachment

Avoidant attachment

Community attachment

Disorganized attachment

Guanxi

Homophily

Human capital

Hyperdyadic spread

Relational capital

Secure attachment

Self-regulatory control

Social capital

CHAPTER 11

TECHNOLOGY

Technology is the way in which humans interact with the material world to meet their basic needs and increase well-being. Human beings need energy to survive, and thus energy needs to be extracted from the environment. Oil wells, coal mines, gas stations, farming, ranching, and fishing are all examples of activities that involve technologies used to meet the need for energy. As such, nearly everything humans do involves some form of technology. Satisfying basic biological needs such as food, water, energy, sex, and shelter are part and parcel of how a given society produces and reproduces itself within a particular ecological habitat. As Corning (2000) has written,

> The ground zero premise (so to speak) of the biological sciences is that survival and reproduction is the basic, continuing, and inescapable problem for all living organisms: life is at bottom a "survival enterprise." It follows that survival is the "paradigmatic problem" for human societies as well. (p. 41)

Developing and applying technology is one of the major ways that human societies and the individuals contained within them meet these basic survival needs (see Figure 11.1). Technology, because it constitutes the primary point of interaction between biology and culture, can be thought of as representing a social systems infrastructure (along with demographic patterns and the physical environment). *Infrastructure* refers to the aspects of society that involve meeting the biological needs necessary for survival. As such, meeting these needs revolves around production and reproduction. In other words, every human society has to produce for itself and reproduce its membership. This is because the survival of any society is predicated on meeting these basic needs, and technology is a major factor in this endeavor. Societal production consists of the technology and the practices human beings employ for expanding or limiting basic subsistence production, especially the production of food and other forms of energy, given the constraints and opportunities provided when a specific technology interacts with a specific habitat (Harris, 1979). *Reproduction* consists of the technology and practices employed by human beings for expanding, limiting, and maintaining population size (Harris, 1979). These two interact within a physical environment (more on the physical environment in Chapter 12). This chapter focuses on the role of technology in human behavior, especially at the macro level; the aggregate effects of technology in relation to daily life, including recent technologies such as the Internet and social media; and the implications technology has for social work.

DISTAL CONTEXT

Technology Systems Among Chimpanzees

One important matter to address with respect to demonstrating the significance of technology is to examine its use by other social mammals, such as chimpanzees. Next to humans, chimpanzees (*Pan troglodytes*) are the greatest tool users among all species. Tool use has been well documented among chimpanzees in Eastern and Western Africa (Boesch & Boesch, 1990; Nishida & Hiraiwa, 1982). Jane Goodall, the famous primatologist, was the first to scientifically

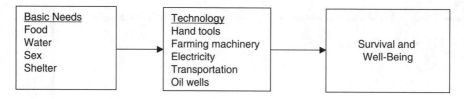

FIGURE 11.1 Relationship Between Basic Needs, Technology, and Survival

document tool use by chimpanzees in Tanzania (Goodall, 1964). Importantly, this use is mostly aimed at meeting subsistence needs (although tool use is often present in social interactions as well) and is not affected much by different habitats or environments. This suggests that tool use is fairly universal among chimpanzees.

In a 7-year study (2,000 hr of observation) of technology systems among chimpanzees in the Republic of Congo, Sanz and Morgan (2007) found 22 types of tool behavior, with half of those being commonly exhibited by most chimpanzees. These researchers categorized tool use into specific behaviors such as extracting, probing, wiping, scratching, and rubbing. The food sources chimps targeted most commonly

with tools were beehives and termite or ant nests, with the overwhelming majority of uses being to access termites using herbs and leaves, twigs, and branches. These tools were used for a number of purposes including dipping for ants, widening access to beehives, and pounding and breaking things open. Chimpanzees also use a leaf sponge to gather water. This process involves grabbing leaves from a water source, chewing them into a clump, and dipping them into the water. The clump of chewed leaves absorbs water that the chimpanzees squeeze out into their mouths. In sum, among mammals' tool kits, the chimpanzee tool kit is fairly large and complex (Sanz & Morgan, 2010) and likely the largest next to humans'.

CASE STUDY: MICRO AND MACRO INTERVENTIONS

New innovations are currently being developed using fMRI technology as a tool for training and retraining areas of the brain affected by environmental assaults, through a process called neurofeedback. Researchers like Frank Krueger at George Mason University's Krasnow Institute employ real-time fMRI techniques to help individuals (e.g., war veterans) learn to exercise control over brain response during a scanner task (see also Caria et al., 2010). Immediate neural feedback is given in vivo in the scanner, and individuals can see how areas of their brain respond when they employ various cognitive and emotional strategies. This kind of fMRI neurofeedback training may help individuals regulate brain regions for pain management and control emotions in response to stressful situations.

One example of a macro-level technological intervention in a developing market is the Urban Water Partners' (UWP) clean water project. Urban Water Partners is a social business, with a mission to solve social problems using sustainable business practices and new media technologies in developing markets. UWP's current project seeks to provide clean water to the 3.5 million residents of Dar es Salaam, Tanzania, where only 10% of the population has direct access to the city's water system, which doesn't even deliver clean, drinkable water. The rest of the population is left to purchase this unclean water from local water vendors who have a connection to the water supply. UWP leases water filters to these local water vendors so they can sell clean water to Dar es Salaam residents. Originally, slow sand filters were tried, but then the organization decided to use a more technologically advanced filtration system that uses activated carbon (similar to Brita filters) along with ultraviolet light. Tanzanian women, the traditional water providers for their families, service the filtration system on an ongoing basis. The project uses mobile technology to optimize water vendors' lease payment structure of the water filtration system through cell phone technology. The majority of people who will be using the products are unbanked and therefore do not have a bank account. These water vendors prepay by loading money on to a card-based account, and then their monthly lease payments are deducted from this card. Once their account balance drops below a predetermined threshold, the water vendor must reload money onto the card. In Tanzania most transactions are done in cash. Once people build up wealth and can open bank accounts, they will be transitioned to a different payment platform where they can pay directly from their bank account. An India-based app designer is developing the capability for water vendors to make their lease payments directly from their bank accounts through their cell phones. In addition to making filtration system lease payments, the mobile application will allow water vendors to connect to other water vendors, technicians, and the UWP organization via a message board for information sharing and social connection. A subsidized system and payment plan is available for those vendors who do not currently have a cell phone (Urban Water Partners, 2010).

Critical Thinking Questions:

- How can technology be used as an instrument of oppression or as a tool for empowerment? How can technology be used to open opportunities and at the same time increase socioeconomic equality?

- What micro- and macro-level social work interventions could use technology to improve the conditions of vulnerable populations nationally and/or globally?

- In your opinion, what are the most significant disciplines that the social work profession must collaborate with to successfully implement these ideas? What do you think is necessary to be able to engage effectively with these other disciplines?

TECHNOLOGY AND SOCIETY: MAJOR THEORETICAL FRAMEWORKS

Although technology is a major facet of every society (even nonhuman societies), in general, social scientists have often not made technology a central part of theories about human society and culture. A couple of notable exceptions can be found in the work of sociologist Gerhard Lenski (1966, 1970) and anthropologist Marvin Harris (1968, 1979, 1999).

Ecological–Evolutionary Typology

Lenski developed a typology of human societies known as *ecological-evolutionary typology* that diverged from previous attempts by emphasizing level of technology and physical environment. In *Power and Privilege* (1966), Lenski began to show how technology and physical environment are potent predictors of social inequality across different societies. Lenski believed that the greater a society's surplus was from technologies of subsistence, the greater the resulting inequality.

Perhaps Lenski's greatest achievement was the book *Human Societies*, which was first published in 1970 and has gone through 11 editions. This was a unique book in that it appealed to academics and researchers but was also used as a textbook in introductory undergraduate classes. For Lenski, the main evolutionary progression of societies was from hunter-gatherers to horticulturalists to agrarian societies and on to modern industrialization. Variation in the technological base in interaction with a given ecology is the prime mover in this progression.

Like other theories predicated on evolutionary principles, Lenski's work makes use of the concept of selection as a lever for societal change in two ways: via intrasocietal and intersocietal selection. *Intrasocietal selection* refers to how new elements are adopted or selected for within a society or culture (e.g., going from the horse and buggy to the automobile), whereas *intersocietal selection* refers to how whole cultures are extinguished by contact with a larger, more powerful society or culture. One of the classic examples of intersocietal selection is the decimation of Native American societies in the Americas following the influx of Europeans. Lenski is primarily concerned with large-scale aggregate change over time and the resulting social stratification, and not so much with the behavior of individuals. As such, the level of analysis is at the macro level. To understand social inequality, one must understand that it is tied to major changes in technology. To say that Lenski is interested in the big picture is an understatement.

Although Lenski's theory has great appeal and implications for understanding social change, one remaining question is: Has it been adequately tested? Analysis of cross-cultural data by Nielsen (2004) suggests that Lenski's typology does indeed predict many aspects of inequality across hunter-gatherer, horticulturalist, agrarian, and industrialized societies. In another study comparing the effects of technology to ideology in shaping the rest of society, Nolan and Lenski (1996) found that technology accounted for a greater share of variation in community size,

political organization, stratification and inequality, marital patterns, and premarital sex norms. Although not without its limitations, this study is consistent with materialist models of the evolution of human societies and social change. As with any theory or idea, empirical testing is crucial for establishing whether the theory is valid.

Cultural Materialism

Another major paradigm that places technology at the center of social change is *cultural materialism (CM)*. It asserts that the central issue in human behavior and evolution of human societies is the never-changing fact that humans universally must use their cultures (i.e., their ways of living including technology and institutions) to adapt to earthly (i.e., material) circumstances. CM is applicable to research activity and theory development throughout the social sciences. It has been largely developed, refined, and popularized by its most notable proponent, the late anthropologist Marvin Harris. Beginning with *The Rise of Anthropological Theory* (1968), Harris has continued to refine the paradigm (1979, 1994, 1999) and test it against a wide variety of cultural phenomena (1974, 1977, 1989). Although traditionally centered in anthropology, cultural materialism is relevant to any scientific field whose concerns are the similarities and differences in human social life. Broadly, CM embraces the comprehension of human beings in a global, comparative, and historical context. Although influenced by Marx, whom Harris (1979) believed to be the Darwin of the social sciences due to his identification of major mechanisms of societal evolution (e.g., cultural selection), CM nonetheless stands apart from Marxist approaches by cleaving their political ideological components and replacing them with a commitment to the scientific method and contemporary facts from the biopsychological and demographic sciences.

According to cultural materialists, subsistence and related technologies and reproduction (e.g., demographic patterns) are the major catalysts driving long-term societal change (more on demography in Chapter 12). As we previously alluded, the reason why technology is so important is that it directly facilitates the satisfaction of biologically and psychologically mandated survival mechanisms of human nature within a specific habitat. The interaction of factors rooted in natural and tangible processes provides the materialism to the overall strategy (e.g., Harris 1979, 1994).

Many investigators conduct research and build theory that is compatible with cultural materialist principles but either have never heard of or do not label themselves as cultural materialists. Nevertheless, prior research that is consistent with this approach includes theories and research findings from various topics such as general evolution (Leavitt, 1986; Sanderson, 1990) and world systems perspectives (Chase-Dunn & Hall, 1997); warfare and intergroup conflict (Balee, 1984; Ferguson, 1984, 1989; Harris, 1974); social stratification and ethnic relations (Abruzzi, 1982; Depres, 1975); demographic issues, migration, and settlement (Good, 1987; Harris & Ross, 1987); the rise of capitalism (Harris, 1977, 1999; Sanderson, 1990); expansion of cultural scale into larger, more differentiated units such as chiefdoms and the state (Kottak, 1972; Paulsen, 1981; Sanders & Price, 1968; Webster, 1985); and the study of leisure in society (Chick, 1988). These studies using a CM framework display the range of topics where cultural materialism can be applied.

At present, there has been no attempt to utilize a CM approach in social work. This book represents the first explicit rendering of this approach for social workers. Interestingly, previous studies in the field of applied anthropology using a CM perspective to focus on contemporary social problems related to international development or urban affairs either overlap or are consonant with social work concerns. These studies include efforts at reforestation projects in Haiti (Murray, 1980, 1995), attention to the causes of homelessness and poverty in New York City (Dehavenon, 1995), causes for the rise in

imprisonment (Sharff, 1995), and environmental pressures to steal water for survival (Price, 1995). Additionally, parallel concerns from behaviorist-oriented psychologists and psychiatrists should be noted regarding use of cultural materialism to integrate with and combine individual-level understanding within the behavior of larger social units (Biglan, 1988; Glenn, 1988; Vargas, 1985), and the extent of schizophrenia and other mental disorders within differing political economies (Warner, 1985).

Based on Lenski's and Harris's conceptual frameworks, we propose here that community and social development actions or macro-level intervention protocols that target or are in accord with changes in a society's technologies of subsistence will have more powerful and sustainable consequences than actions or intervention protocols that do not. From this viewpoint there are a number of questions that should be asked when implementing a project, such as:

- Has the project made use of technologies that could reduce costs over the long run?

- Have information technologies been fully exploited to the benefit of stakeholders?

- Has the project considered the climate and ecology (i.e., soils, temperature, vegetation, wind, solar, variability) and their sustainability?

- Has the project considered transportation routes and power requirements?

- Has the project considered land use capacity and potential?

- Has the project considered technologies related to subsistence and manufacturing?

- Can monetary or energy inputs into any of the above lead to positive feedback in the desired direction?

- What is the anticipated cultural response to such innovations and technologies? What are the potential barriers and opportunities that these responses might pose?

TECHNOLOGICAL DETERMINISM

In 1965, Gordon Moore (who later went on to cofound Intel) observed that the number of transistors on an integrated circuit was doubling each year. This observation, often heard repeatedly by techies at electronics stores, has become known as Moore's law, and represents the continued progress of computer technology and information technology, and perhaps technology in general. Despite the progress inherent in Moore's law, one cannot help but feel sometimes that there is an undercurrent of *technological determinism* at work. In some respects, the tail is wagging the dog. The general public seems to have tacitly accepted that technology is in control. Does social life really revolve entirely around technology? One way to answer the question is to perform a thought experiment. Think what your day is like when your computer, refrigerator, or (heaven forbid) your automobile is not operating. Do you experience distress? Most people would answer yes to that question for obvious reasons. We rely upon these technologies on a daily basis for our subsistence and pleasure. But is technology really in control? Did humans not invent and facilitate its proliferation? Certainly human agency has a strong role to play. After all, we turn on the power button. Although individuals can make decisions not to use these technologies, their livelihood and life chances would likely be at a disadvantage.

Individuals and larger entities such as corporations that are able to harness and market new technologies in many ways are in control. As Ceruzzi (2005) writes when discussing the ubiquity of e-mail:

> Microsoft Word has its flaws; most of us who use it, for example, have encountered instances where the font suddenly changes, randomly, for no apparent reason. Word is also a voracious consumer of memory, but thanks to Moore's law that does not matter. Attaching Word files to e-mail is simple and it works, and so the practice is ubiquitous. I compare it to the 4' 8½" railroad gauge, which experts say is slightly narrower than the optimum, in terms of engineering efficiency. That drawback is overshadowed by the virtue of being a standard. But remember that the encoding of text in Word is controlled by Microsoft, and Microsoft has the right to change the code according to its needs—not ours. (p. 592)

The dominance of technology is not a recent phenomenon, as each society and culture throughout human history, whether hunter-gatherer or agrarian, has made use of technologies that facilitated meeting basic needs (Harris, 1977). One way to enhance the use of technology and curtail some of its abuses is by better understanding its role in human affairs from a biosocial perspective.

According to Clark (2003), one of the major reasons for the success and proliferation of technology and especially tools that engage our thoughts, such as machines and computers, is that they complement the way in which the human brain is wired. Specifically, tools take advantage of the difficulty that humans have in remembering long tasks and act as scaffolds or external helpers that aid us in putting our thoughts into action. Because of the compatibility of tools in the life of humans, Clark refers to us and his book as *Natural Born Cyborgs*.

Technological Change

Meeting a nation's basic subsistence needs often involves technological change. *Diffusion* is the term usually used to describe the spread of technology within or between societies. One focused type of diffusion is *technology transfer*. The issue of technology transfer to underdeveloped regions from more advanced technological societies is an important component of the development agenda and meeting its goals of satisfying basic needs and reducing extreme forms of poverty and disease. The key is to reduce dependence and gain relative autonomy over natural resources (Hope, 1983). The Green Revolution in India provides an illustrative case in point. Although a highly complex nation, India, the second most populated country in the world, offers a useful case study in the implementation of sustainable and environmentally friendly agricultural technologies that represent considerable technological change. For generations, Indian farmers used local seeds and operated traditional wooden plows, carts, and waterwheels using energy provided by human and animal alike (Parayil, 1992). Following technology transfer in the 1960s, this system of technology for farming changed to high-yield modified seed varieties, fertilizers, pesticides, powered tool and pump machinery, and controlled irrigation (Parayil, 1992). The transformation, as is typical, was brought about by government, donor agencies (e.g., the Ford and Rockefeller Foundations), agricultural research firms, and Indian farmers and peasants. The effects of these technological changes were relatively immense. Production of cereal crops increased, and rural workers became employed with wages that reduced the gap between urban and rural Indians in areas where the technology transfer was successful (Parayil, 1992). Local farmers adapted to the new technologies and began favoring seeds that were more marketable and ecologically tolerant. In a sense, seeds and people were coevolving together. In areas where the technology transfer was less successful, it seemed land owners who had peasant farmers working for them calculated that the new system would be less favorable to them (Parayil, 1992). In most ways, this case study of technology transfer illustrates the importance of the cell to society framework that coordinates biological, technological, psychosocial, and larger cultural and ecological forces in an integrated fashion.

Technology Inside the Home

Although changes in technology alter the rest of society, one of the least studied settings of technological change is in the home (Cowan, 1976). Households are microenvironments that typically involve one or more persons but quite often whole families, and as such are an apt unit of analysis for investigating the effects of technology. Think of the average farm family in 1880 compared to the average urban family in 2010. Certainly, technology has played a major role in the changes between the two. In the former, women were more likely to stay home and tend to daily domestic duties, whereas in the latter women were more likely to go to a place of employment and sit in front of a computer screen all day. Besides the obvious differences in machinery and the use of electricity, social roles also changed due to preceding technological transformations. As Cowan (1976) pointed out, a clever way to assess these household changes is to examine the *Ladies' Home Journal*, a magazine that has been published since 1886. As a document of living history, this journal shows advertisements of household technology in use across long swaths of time. For example, candles changed to gaslights, which changed to electric bulbs. Cooking and cleaning machinery and products such as coal and wood stoves gave way to gas- and electric-powered devices, with small electrified appliances (e.g., blenders and toasters) becoming standard. Little systematic empirical knowledge is available on the psychosocial adaptations that these technological changes had on household members.

SPOTLIGHT TOPIC: THE AUTOMOBILE

Like other mammals, humans are perfectly willing to migrate in search of satisfying basic needs and a better life. Although Nicholas-Joseph Cugnot invented a steam-powered, three-wheeled device in 1760, the rise of the modern automobile can be traced directly to the invention of the four-stroke internal combustion piston engine in Germany by Nikolaus Otto in 1876 (Volti, 2004). Subsequently, Karl Benz, developed a three-wheeled motor vehicle in 1886 Volti, 2004). Bicycles were gaining in popularity during the latter half of the 19th century, and the bicycle is credited with spurring the development of the automobile. Henry Ford is credited with developing the standardization systems that would allow mass production of automobiles. These new technologies, which allowed humans to move freely about, were dependent on roads. Roads grew exponentially, and later interstate highways changed society in profound ways. Other forms of technology, goods, and services were able to diffuse to other towns and cities in an efficient manner. This fueled the growth of innumerable businesses, including the automobile industry, that were to employ large numbers of persons in single locations. The Industrial Revolution had the transportation complement it needed. In the United States, this led to greater urbanization and all of its attendant advantages and disadvantages.

Transportation is inextricably tied to employment and is an often overlooked aspect of helping individuals and families live more effective lives. Most people cannot walk to a place of employment. We are utterly dependent on transportation, including mass transit systems but in most cases the automobile. When our cars break down, stress ensues, and our life is miserable. This is particularly acute for the working poor who rely on transportation as a means to commute to opportunity. Many jobs have left the central cities, and reverse commutes out of the city are common. Although buses and trains can help, automobiles are still the most common and flexible means to commute. Most working-class households spend approximately 30% of their income on transportation (Roberto, 2008). In total, about four out of every five persons drives an automobile to their place of employment (Roberto, 2008). Quite simply, assessing clients' transportation issues is critical to helping them.

For Reflection

Think of the multiple ways in which you and others around you have become dependent on the automobile. How much time a year do you spend inside an automobile? In what ways is your life stressful when the automobile (or other primary mode of transportation you use most) is not working?

TECHNOLOGY AND ITS DISTRIBUTION IN A SOCIETY

Clearly, persons around the globe have increased their use of computer and information technology in its various forms. Given that technology is pervasive and fundamental to daily living, it follows that those who control it can gain power and financial rewards. It also follows that there are disparities in access to technology.

Power

Recent decades have witnessed the rise of a super-wealthy generation in the Information Age based on the control and proliferation of technology hardware and software. Just as in previous eras Andrew Carnegie and Cornelius Vanderbilt benefited from the rise of industrialization, Bill Gates and Steve Jobs have benefited from being at the forefront of Information Age technology. Control of technology facilitates the ability to control people, which can be defined as *power*. Outside of these extreme examples, what do we know about the intersection of power and technology? In a longitudinal study exploring the relationship between computer technology and power in an organization, Burkhardt and Brass (1990) found that early adopters of a new technology were able to increase their power and centrality within social networks inside that organization. Specifically, early adoption of technology was significantly and strongly correlated with facets of power. This finding suggests that adopting an innovation in technology before others provides the adopter with greater influence among individuals in organizations or groups. Early adopters were able to reduce uncertainty for others in the organization, and this in effect granted them power. One of the major shortcomings of this study, however, was the lack of an experimental control group; the only workers who could provide a comparison were those who were later adopters.

The power of early adoption of technology is a central feature of Jared Diamond's influential Pulitzer Prize–winning book, *Guns, Germs, and Steel* (1997), which described how technology (primarily with respect to weapons such as guns and steel), along with microbes against which native peoples possessed no immunity, played a major role in the European powers' conquest of the Americas. Because Europeans were closer to the major technological centers of steel and gun development, these cultures were able to adopt these advancements before they diffused throughout North and South America. Diamond's theory elegantly explains the disadvantage that native peoples had when encountering more technologically advanced peoples and the diseases they carried. It also explains why other parts of the globe were at a disadvantage due to geographic circumstances (more on this in Chapter 12).

Recently, technology has been used worldwide to intervene in political agendas and facilitate socio-political reform. For example, as noted in Chapter 10, social media was used to collectively mobilize constituencies in the recent revolutions in Egypt, Tunisia, and Libya. Shalhoub-Kevorkian (2011) also describes the use of digital technologies as tools of empowerment in Palestinian women's lives, employing "e-resistance" activism that opens access to the world beyond their confined conflict zone: "Women ... report that they use the Internet to obtain permits to cross physical boundaries, apply for school, look up medicines, search for lost relatives, get in touch with loved ones, and try to find a desired accessory, appliance, or piece of clothing" (p. 190). At the same time, Shalhoub-Kevorkian points out that such technological access can also create oppression through politically positioned surveillance systems that may be put in place in some public areas to restrict Internet access and control information retrieval and dissemination. And, of course, we need only look to the United States Congress to see how social media can be used as a tool for ruining political careers.

Gender, Race, and Computer Technology

The difference between major groups who possess Internet technology and those that have less access to it is often referred to as the *digital divide* (Norris, 2001). Although recent years have seen the divide narrow, Black adults use the Internet less than other groups even when education and income are controlled for (Jackson, Ervin, Gardner, & Schmitt, 2001b). Yet fundamental questions remain with respect to the differences in patterns of use between men and women, racial groups, and age ranges. In a study of middle school students with an average age of 12 years and who were sampled from 20 schools, Jackson et al. (2008) found that male students made greater use of video games than female students, who were more likely to use the computer and Internet for other activities. Black students were least likely to use the computer and the Internet. Importantly, this study found that length of time in computer and Internet use was predictive of academic performance, whereas video game playing was inversely associated with poor academic performance. Prior research with adults has shown that Black Americans are more likely to use the Internet for religious/spiritual content and jobs than other racial or ethnic groups (Spooner & Rainie, 2000). Research indicates that women's Internet use is driven by interpersonal relations and attempts to connect with others (Jackson, Ervin, Gardner, & Schmitt, 2001a). Jackson et al. recommend that community-based interventions target computer use for Black children early in their lives and make greater use of video games that incorporate learning materials.

In another study examining gender differences in computer and Internet use among college students in Germany, in which participants kept track of their usage via a daily diary, Imhof,

Vollmeyer, and Beierlein (2007) found comparable rates of Internet and computer usage among male and female students with respect to using technology for their studies. Men, however, were more likely to use the Internet for games, daily news, file sharing, and route planning. This study also examined technology self-efficacy and hypothesized that men would score higher. Contrary to the prediction, there were no significant score differences between males and female students on the technology self-efficacy measure.

Cross-National Comparisons

Most studies that have been conducted on various aspects of technology have involved samples from the United States. Few have examined cross-national differences between countries or differences in developed versus underdeveloped nations. Such studies would be crucial for establishing whether technology acceptance models are similar or different in various locations on the globe. Such models essentially state that individuals' perceptions of the usefulness and ease of use of a technology will govern actual usage. In a unique study that administered the same technology acceptance questionnaire to airline employees in Japan, Switzerland, and the United States, all of whom had access to the same sources of technology, Straub, Keil, and Brenner (1997) found that Japanese employees were different in their level of acceptance compared to Swiss and American employees. In particular, the technology acceptance model explained 10% of the variation in actual technology use among Swiss and U.S. employees but only 1% among Japanese employees. Why the different pattern? The study authors speculated that the collectivist orientation of Japanese employees, versus the individualist orientation of Swiss and American workers, was more likely to have cultural taboos toward assertiveness, and this may have accounted for the differences. Given the march of technology and greater global connectivity, knowledge of differential cross-cultural embrace of various technologies, and why they are or are not embraced, is useful for practitioners operating in these contexts to know.

EXPERT'S CORNER: NAZLI CHOUCRI

Nazli Choucri is Professor of Political Science at the Massachusetts Institute of Technology, Director of the Global System for Sustainable Development, and Associate Director of MIT's Technology and Development Program.

Photo of Nazli Choucri
Courtesy of MIT Political
Science Department

What is the future of cyberspace for relationships around the world? One often neglected area of political research is cyberpolitics, particularly in a global context. This is somewhat surprising given how cyberspace permeates our everyday lives. New technologies on the horizon and associated information systems bring many challenges for cross-national relations. Nazli Choucri's research is concerned with the politics of cyberspace and cybersecurity. Her most recent book, *Cyberpolitics in International Relations* (2012), investigates how cyberspace is shaping key aspects of international relations such as national security and basic institutions of government. Because cyberspace goes beyond the traditional boundaries found on a map, it is important to find out what impact this has on relations between nations. Choucri wrestles with ways to bring harmony to cyberspace and the global system. The end goal from a policy perspective is to identify where potential conflicts are likely to lie and where major sources of cooperation can be harnessed for the sustained betterment of the global community.

Choucri, consistent with the cell to society perspective, assigns priority to technology, population, and raw resources in her theorizing. These fundamentals act to undergird nations and their attendant institutions. In addition, these factors interact with natural environments. Choucri has applied her ideas to issues of conflict and war, sustainability of natural environments, and as mentioned previously, cyberpolitics. Although our understanding of the impact of cyberspace on the global community is still in its infancy, work by scholars such as Choucri shines some light on an otherwise unknown landscape.

COMPUTERS AND INFORMATION TECHNOLOGY

Although technology includes anything humans use to interact with the material world, we often think of computers when we think of technology. This is understandable, as computer and information technology dominate daily life. Most of us use a computer every day, and we have become dependent upon and in some cases addicted to them (more on this later). But have computers, and correspondingly the Internet, increased our well-being? Have they increased our intellectual capacity? Or, conversely, are computers making us stupid and unhappy? These are the primary questions that Carr (2010) attempts to answer. The major concept that is crucial to answering these questions is *neuroplasticity*. The idea is straightforward. Our experience in using computers causes changes (i.e., plasticity) in our brains. Carr believes that computers act as a sort of external brain for us, making our own less effective. Although many have speculated on the restructuring of our brains in the computer age, little empirical research has been conducted. Carr points to a 2008 brain-imaging study in which experienced and nonexperienced Internet users were compared as they performed Google searches. Results showed differences between the two groups. Experienced users showed significant activity in the prefrontal cortex area of the brain (areas of the brain involving problem solving and decision making). It took nonexperienced Internet users in this study less than a week of Internet surfing to achieve the same neural firing pattern as the experienced users. It is difficult to conclude from one study whether computer use is making us smarter. One of the problems is the disagreement over what constitutes being smart and happy. Importantly, what studies like these do suggest is that technology can affect our biology.

To date, no scientific investigations have shown that computer use interferes with our brain's ability to learn from non-computer sources, most notably, books. In a review of Carr's book in the *London Review of Books*, science writer Jim Holt (2011) takes stock and concludes that

> it's not that the web is making us less intelligent; if anything, the evidence suggests that it sharpens more cognitive skills than it dulls. It's not that the web is making us less happy; although there are certainly those who, like Carr, feel enslaved by its rhythms and cheated by the quality of its pleasures. It's that the web may be an enemy of creativity. (p. 12)

Holt may be correct about the downside of the Internet, but further research is needed to disentangle these effects.

The notion of computers having substantial effects on the human brain suggests a potentially important role for education. Certainly computers have become a staple tool in formal and informal education. However, one important question is whether computer-supported homework results in superior learning compared to traditional homework. Mendocino, Razzaq, and Hefferman (2009) attempted to answer this question in a study of 93 fifth-grade children using math homework. Four classrooms were employed, with two classrooms participating in the computer-supported homework with immediate feedback, and the other two classrooms performing traditional homework, meaning that these students did the homework with pencil and paper and received feedback on it the next day. Results showed that the fifth graders who did the computer-supported homework outperformed the traditional homework group. The effect size was 0.61, which corresponds to a medium effect. The key difference as to why the computer-supported homework was superior appears to be the immediate feedback received while doing the homework. Obviously, a teacher cannot go home with every student and give him or her feedback, but the computer can. Another explanation for this finding is that doing computer-supported homework was more of a novelty, and thus the fifth graders were more engaged. Perhaps repeating the homework condition a month later would result in the two groups being more similar in their performance. If follow-up studies reveal similar effects that favor computer-supported homework, then this represents a real opportunity for students to learn more in math—a subject that many students dislike or have trouble learning. Even if computers had to be purchased for this endeavor, the cost savings of raising math scores seemingly would justify it.

SOCIAL MEDIA

At its heart, social media technology is designed to enhance communication and information sharing. The diffusion of social media has been rapid. From a history-of-technology standpoint, social media is the latest in a long line of communication technologies. Older forms of communication such as the printing press also diffused rapidly (see Figure 11.2).

Social media consists of micro-technologies such as Twitter, MySpace, and Facebook. These applications have hundreds of millions of users. Although younger people are known to employ these technologies more than other age-groups, persons age 35 to 44 also use social media widely (Kaplan & Haenlein, 2010). Although social media seems like a recent craze, the idea and procedures for its use have been around for over 20 years, since the launch of Open Diary, around the same time the blog came into existence (Kaplan & Haenlein, 2010). However, the recent use of social media has been facilitated by increased access to high-speed Internet services (Moore's law at work again). Social media technology can be used for a wide variety of endeavors and organizations, for profit or nonprofit; we have barely scratched the surface of its potential. Kaplan and Haenlein (2010) offer five general recommendations for organizations who wish to use social media for their benefit:

1. Choose carefully—there are so many services, it's best to choose a few that are right for you (i.e., the organization).

2. Pick the application, or make your own.

3. Ensure activity alignment—consistent messaging rather than multiple messages across different channels.

4. Integrate your media plan—draw together social media with other communication used by the organization in a united front.

5. Provide access for all (but manage it)—social media technologies should be accessible to employees, but clearly defined rules governing their use should be put into action so it meets organizational objectives.

Social media technologies have also been used as a research tool. In a study designed to forecast box office revenues from movies, Asur and Huberman (2010) of Hewlett-Packard Laboratories designed a Twitter-based study extracting nearly 3 million tweets about 24 movies over a 3-month time span. They found that Twitter chatter was a stronger forecasting method of revenue than standard market-based analysis exemplified by the Hollywood Stock

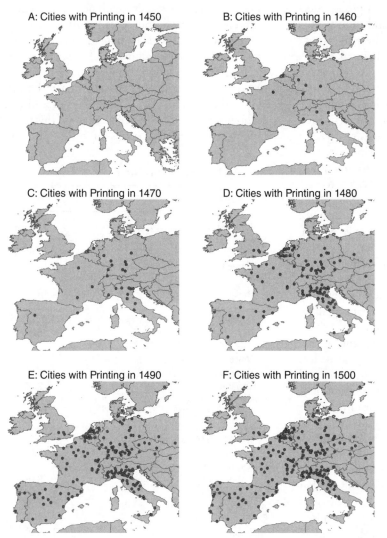

The Diffusion of the Movable Type Printing Press

A: Cities with Printing in 1450
B: Cities with Printing in 1460
C: Cities with Printing in 1470
D: Cities with Printing in 1480
E: Cities with Printing in 1490
F: Cities with Printing in 1500

FIGURE 11.2 The Diffusion of the Printing Press
Source: "Information Technology and Economic Change: The Impact of the Printing Press," by J. Dittmar, 2011, *The Quarterly Journal of Economics, 126*(3), 1133–1172. Retrieved from http://www.voxeu.org/index.php?q=node/6092. Copyright 2011 by Oxford University Press. Reproduced with permission of Oxford University Press.

Exchange. Essentially, tweet rate per movie (total number of tweets divided by hours) yielded a strong prediction, accounting for 80% of the variance in revenue. These results suggest that Twitter chatter can be used to forecast a number of important outcomes. The key, of course, is that the outcome needs to be something that people are willing to communicate about. Movies commonly attract tweets; many outcomes that are of interest to policy makers and social

service practitioners may not be of interest to a broad enough number of tweeters. Finding those outcomes that are of interest to such a user base may yield useful benefits.

In a very real sense, social media represents an online community. If social media is to achieve a useful social benefit, then finding ways for online communities to thrive is critical. Bishop (2007) has proposed a three-level conceptual framework for increasing participation in online communities that integrates the ecological and cognitive aspects of why people participate. Level 1 comprises desires and motivations that can be social, creative, or negative (e.g., vengeance). Level 2 includes individual cognitions (goals, plans, and other behavior-directive thoughts). Level 3 is direct contact with the environment and includes touch, visual, and auditory senses. At the base is environment, which provides the conditions and structures within which individuals operate. The principles that put this conceptual framework into operation are as follows: (a) Individuals are driven to satisfy a desire; (b) desire is limited by goals, plans, beliefs, interests, and other cognitive processes; and (c) environmental perceptions drive action. In effect, this framework reflects a general biosocial model where desire (biologically related), thought processes (brain related), and environment (physical and social) combine to determine behavior. Persuading individuals to participate in online communities therefore must take these major components into account. Presenting reasons that are consistent with desires and beliefs (e.g., doing so will have a positive outcome) and take the environment (e.g., family, community, and national cultures) in which the individual or group is operating within into account appears to be necessary. These facets are highly intertwined, so that one area may trigger action in another. For example, participating in an online community that is involved in Twitter campaigns that support nature conservation may tap a strong-enough belief that it triggers the corresponding desire to participate. However, if the individual resides in a family or community that derives its livelihood from deforestation or hunts endangered species for food or money, this factor could be strong enough to counteract belief and desire.

Who Tweets, Blogs, and Uses Facebook?

According to the Pew Research Center's Internet and American Life Project (Smith, 2011; see Table 11.1), approximately 13% of Internet users also use Twitter. Blacks and Hispanics are more likely than Whites to use Twitter,

as are people between the ages of 18 and 49 (vs. older age categories). Although no sex or income differences were found, people with a college degree were more likely than people who had only graduated from high school to use Twitter.

In addition to these demographic characteristics, it seems reasonable to ask what is known about the psychology of social media users. Although a large number of people use this technology, substantial portions of the population

Table 11.1   Who Uses Twitter?

Category	%
All Internet users	13.0
Sex	
Men	14.0
Women	11.0
Age	
18–29	18.0*
30–49	14.0*
50–64	8.0
65+	6.0
Race/ethnicity	
White, non-Hispanic	9.0
Black, non-Hispanic	25.0*
Hispanic	19.0*
Household income	
Less than $30,000	12.0
$30,000–$49,999	15.0
$50,000–$74,999	12.0
$75,000+	15.0
Education level	
High school grad	8.0
Some college	12.0
College+	16.0*
Geographic location	
Urban	15.0*
Suburban	14.0*
Rural	7.0

Note: Based on the percentage of Internet users within each group who use Twitter.

Source: The Pew Research Center's Internet & American Life Project, April 26–May 22, 2011 Spring Tracking Survey.

$N = 2,277$ adult Internet users, age 18 and older, including 755 cell phone interviews. Interviews were conducted in English and Spanish.

* indicates statistically significant difference between rows. Adapted from "13% of Online Adults Use Twitter," http://www.pewinternet.org/~/media//Files/Reports/2011/Twitter%20Update%202011.pdf

remain unimpressed with it, do not understand what its advantages are, or feel like it is just one more technological hassle. In a study of the personality and motivations associated with the use of Facebook, Ross et al. (2009) found that Facebook users were more likely to score higher on the personality facets of Extraversion and Openness to Experience using the well-researched Five Factor Model of Personality. However, Extraversion scores were not significantly related to the number of Facebook friends or time spent online. Because this study had a relatively small number of participants (<100) and utilized a sample of convenience (college undergraduates), findings should be considered preliminary. In an earlier study examining the personality predictors of blogging, also using the Five Factor Model, Guadagno, Okdie, and Eno (2008) found that higher scores on Openness to Experience and Neuroticism were predictive of blogging. The Neuroticism scores were stronger for women than men. Essentially, people who are more creative are also attracted to expressing themselves in other media, such as blogs. According to the authors, the findings on neuroticism (tendency toward worry and nervousness) suggest that persons, especially women, are reaching out to others as a means to blunt or assuage their anxieties and isolation. Guadagno et al. also point to other studies (e.g., Hamburger & Ben-Artzi, 2000) with similar results regarding neuroticism. This raises an important question: Does Internet use cause loneliness or are lonely people drawn to the Internet? In 2003, Amichai-Hamburger and Ben-Artzi attempted to answer this question and found evidence for that latter view. Specifically, neuroticism was significantly and positively correlated with loneliness, and loneliness was significantly and positively associated with Internet use.

THE DARK SIDE OF INTERNET AND COMPUTER USE

Is there a dark side to technology use? Can persons really become addicted to these technologies? Although the Internet has served a number of valuable functions and has facilitated many positive encounters, it is well documented that predators use the Internet to identify vulnerable people who can be manipulated for their gain. For more than a decade, media reports have highlighted cases of adult predators, who often have a lengthy history of sex-related crimes, taking advantage of children and adolescents (Wolak, Finkelhor, Mitchell, & Ybarra, 2008). The Internet enables someone to misrepresent themselves. For example, in a study comparing cyberspace and face-to-face relationships, Cornwell and Lundgren (2001) identified evidence of less commitment, less seriousness, less involvement, and overall greater misrepresentation in the cyberspace group. These findings are not very surprising, given that one can sit behind a computer and communicate just about anything about oneself without having to meet face to face.

Research on sexual solicitations and related forms of sexual harassment via the Internet suggests that there is substantial variation with respect to demographic characteristics. In a study of 1,500 adolescents in 2000 and a demographically similar sample of 1,500 adolescents in 2005 that queried these youth about sexual solicitations, unwanted pornography and harassment, and related events, Mitchell, Wolak, and Finkelhor (2007) found significant variation across age, sex, race and ethnicity, and levels of household income. Overall, 10% of 10- to 12-year-olds reported one of these events in 2000. By 2005, that number had dropped to 5%. Older adolescents reported a higher percentage in both years. Girls were more likely than boys to receive any kind of sexual solicitation over the Internet. In general, there was a decline in the reports of these events occurring from 2000 to 2005 except for low-income minority youth, who experienced an increase. These increases among low-income minority youth were associated with increased use of the Internet, which perhaps was a result of low-income groups being behind middle and upper-income groups with respect to Internet use. Mitchell et al. suggest targeted prevention efforts for these youth that can counter the effects of increased Internet speed, wider use of digital photography, and aggressive marketing of these materials by predators and merchants. Wolak et al. (2008) argue that online predators typically develop relationships over the Internet with youth and attempt to gain trust. Instead of approaching the problem as a lack of parental control, the adolescent should be directly targeted using prevention strategies that acknowledge that, from a developmental point of view, it is normal for adolescents to show interest in what they perceive to be a romantic relationship. Wolak et al. also point to studies (e.g., Livingstone, 2006; Yan, 2006) showing that children and adolescents are not particularly naïve about Internet use; by age 12, they are actually fairly savvy users. As they get older, however (e.g., 15–17 years), the risk heightens for *sexual victimization* because their Internet use is more complex, varied, and in effect more exploratory. As such, they have greater exposure. The development of avoidance skills when approached by adults online is recommended as a general preventive intervention.

Although drugs and alcohol come to mind when we think of addiction, *Internet addiction* has emerged as a behavioral addiction involving impulse-control problems. In an early study of 396 people defined as dependent users of the Internet, compared to a control group of 100 nondependent persons, Young (1998) found substantial differences in impairment including academic, relational, financial, and occupational problems. One of the major flaws, however, is that the dependent Internet users could very well have co-occurring problems, such as other impulse control problems (e.g., pathological gambling), psychiatric illnesses, or substance use disorders. Current thinking on the criteria of Internet addiction indicates similarity to other dependence syndromes involving preoccupation, inability to control impulses, and impairments in major life domains due to the compulsion to use the Internet (Shaw & Black, 2008). The best estimates of Internet addiction, according

to Shaw and Black, are that less than 1% of the population appears to meet these criteria. However, the prevalence is likely higher among certain age-groups, such as people in their 20s and 30s. As previously suggested, Internet addiction, like other behavioral health disorders, likely co-occurs with depression, anxiety, substance use disorders, and perhaps pathological gambling. There are few evidence-supported therapies for Internet addiction, but family therapy and treatments for other conditions could be adapted and prove useful (Shaw & Black, 2008). Given that adolescents and young adults appear to have the highest risk for a problematic relationship with the Internet, studying the types of psychiatric symptoms that are associated with this condition is useful for early prevention. In a 2-year study examining the predictive value of psychiatric symptoms in relation to Internet addiction among over 2,000 adolescents, Ko, Yen, Chen, Yeh, and Yen (2009) identified symptoms of depression, ADHD, social phobia, and hostility to predict the occurrence of Internet addiction. Specifically, ADHD was the strongest predictor; adolescents diagnosed with this condition were approximately twice as likely as those without ADHD to meet criteria for Internet addiction. Hostility and depressive symptoms were associated with 83% and 56% greater risk, respectively, of Internet addiction, and social phobia increased the risk by 36%. This study also found that men were twice as likely as women to be addicted to Internet use. There still remain several issues for Internet addiction as a clinical disorder for the fifth iteration of the *Diagnostic and Statistical Manual of Mental Disorders*. According to Block (2008), these issues include a firm grasp of its prevalence and measurement, associated cultural differences in its expression (although studies in Asia are similar to findings in the United States and Europe), and complications stemming from Internet addiction and co-occurring conditions. Furthermore, the evidence base regarding treatment interventions is weak. Despite the advances and acceptance of Internet addiction as a real phenomenon, little is known about other technological addictions.

INTEGRATING TECHNOLOGY INTO BEHAVIORAL INTERVENTIONS

Several technologies designed to track small changes in behaviors over time have been integrated into behavior analytics. These trials have largely been successful. In one study that assessed the use of an Internet-based technique for smoking abstinence and vouchers for reinforcement, Dallery and Glenn (2005) studied four heavy smokers over 4 weeks. Participants made Webcam videos of themselves twice per day and also provided a breath carbon monoxide (CO) sample. These materials were sent to a smoking clinic for evaluation. Study participants earned rewards for reductions in their breath CO content. Results showed that, compared to baseline levels, participants substantially reduced their smoke intake, and 75% of participants had sustained periods of smoking abstinence.

In another study, VanWormer (2004) evaluated the effects of pedometers with e-counseling for weight loss among three overweight adults. Pedometer steps and weight were both measured across the study period. Two of the three study participants increased the number of steps by 100% during the 6-month study and lost 5 and 6 pounds, respectively. Lack of physical activity is a major health issue, and employing technology to facilitate greater movement is critically important.

Two other movement-based studies have also showed positive results. First, Sigurdsson and Austin (2008) employed real-time visual feedback at computer workstations in an effort to improve posture and decrease problems associated with poor structural alignment. Eight study participants were assessed in a simulated work environment for three postural outcomes, each representing incremental postural improvement. Findings from this intervention showed great postural improvement. Overall, self-monitored posture with close and accurate assessment led to greater gains. Second, Van Houten, Hilton, Schulman, and Reagan (2011) examined the effect of a device designed to provide a sustained, 18-lb increase in accelerator-pedal resistance when six study drivers exceeded a specified speed limit without buckling their seatbelts. The force of the device was terminated once participants buckled up. Study results showed that this device achieved 100% compliance within 25 s.

TECHNOLOGY OVER THE LIFE COURSE

Technology is quite clearly ubiquitous. Its impact over the life course varies considerably as humans adapt to new innovations and older technologies are discarded. Because technology is interwoven with human life so thoroughly, it is difficult to comprehensively isolate technological effects on human development. We therefore highlight some of the major issues and impact of technology across major developmental periods.

Fetal Environment and Infancy

It is well known that many couples are unable to conceive due to fertility problems. Somewhat old estimates indicate that the number of couples seeking help for infertility is at least 2 million (Begley, 1995). There is little reason to believe that this figure has dramatically declined. Development and use of reproductive technologies has accelerated over the past two decades. Newman and Newman (2003) describe the major technological advancements in reproduction that have allowed couples to conceive. The oldest of these is artificial insemination. Essentially, sperm is collected and frozen, then injected directly into the uterus during ovulation. Fertility drugs are also popular. These drugs cause the release of multiple eggs, thus increasing the probability that one will become fertilized. In vitro fertilization is a technique where eggs are removed, and then sperm is added to them while they are in an incubator. This procedure has a higher success rate than artificial insemination and fertility drugs. Other less common techniques include intracytoplasmic sperm injection, gamete intrafallopian transfer, in vivo fertilization, and the use of a surrogate mother. Many of these reproductive technologies are controversial to some, and reproductive counseling is often helpful for couples experiencing fertility problems.

Early Childhood and Childhood

During this period, children learn the successful use of tools necessary for survival. For example, use of computer technology and writing accelerate. Young children use toasters and microwaves to cook and heat food and become handy with eating utensils such as knives, forks, and chopsticks. They are also able to operate drinking fountains and operate kitchen and bath equipment necessary for basic hygiene. They are able to put on seatbelts while in an automobile and use a wide variety of other safety equipment.

Children enjoy and benefit significantly from play. Technological advancements have had a tremendous impact on children's toys and games. Like other businesses, the toy industry has adapted to technological changes, and toys have changed as well (Cross, 1997). Toys were made of wood for hundreds of years, but with the discovery of electricity and the invention of the microcircuit, electronics-based toys and games have steadily replaced wooden ones. As circuits become smaller and less expensive to manufacture, toys have become more seemingly alive, with features such as voice activation and movement. Children's games have also become more interactive due to these same features. One might wonder, however, whether this serves as a substitute for human involvement in play with children. One might also ask whether future technological advancements could lead to nonhuman surrogate friends for children.

Adolescence

During adolescence the use of technology is, to a large extent, fully under way. In fact, adolescents are often first in the general population to master newer technologies. This seems particularly true for entertainment technology such as games, music, and communications. Troubled adolescents may turn to technology for help. For example, in a study of over 500 adolescents designed to explore use of the Internet for help-seeking behavior, Gould, Munfakh, Lubell, Kleinman, and Parker (2002) found that approximately 1 in 5 adolescents sought help on the Internet for emotional problems. Results indicated very little difference between boys and girls. Those adolescents who sought help were more likely to be impaired and have higher levels of depressive symptoms. With respect to service satisfaction, approximately 20% of adolescents who sought help in this study were dissatisfied with Internet resources, and 14% reported that the Internet resource helped them very much. It seems likely that adolescents who often experience emotional problems in silence will turn more and more to the Internet for help; therefore, having practical and effective resources available online is important.

Adolescents' use of technology (computer, television, phone, video game) may be causing health problems by reducing how much they sleep. Exploratory research by researchers in Philadelphia (Calamaro, Mason, & Ratcliffe, 2009) has shown that a sample of 12- to 18-year-olds who use communication technology at night also often consume caffeinated beverages at the same time, and this combination results in less sleep and associated sleepiness at school. The obvious implication is that greater monitoring by parents or caregivers—at least of caffeine use at night and cell phone use in bed—could improve adolescents' sleep length and next-day school performance.

Youth organizations like the Boys & Girls Clubs of America are making it their focus to offer state-of-the-art technology and requisite digital-literacy skill development for its members. For example, the Boys & Girls Club of America has developed "Club Tech" centers, which offer computers, software, and technology services, and a digital-literacy curriculum for youth. Boasting outreach to 1 million students a year, these centers offer members classes in photo illustration, filmmaking, music production, animation, robotics programming and gaming development (see http://www.myclubmylife.com/arts_tech/Pages/default.aspx).

Adulthood

Mastery of the technology related to subsistence occurs during adulthood. This does not mean that adults readily take to new technologies; just that technologies related to earning money are emphasized and accomplished. One of the downfalls of mastering a single or related set of technologies is that brain and motor functions often become highly specialized to that specific technology. Research on the cognitive aspects of technology among adults suggests that, as the expression goes, "if you don't use it you lose it." Using a nationally representative sample of adults, Tun and Lachman (2010) examined the effects of computer use on cognition among nearly 3,000 adults ages 32 to 84. After controlling for the effects of age, sex, education level, and health status, the researchers found that frequent computer use was associated with higher scores on tests of cognition. Individuals who used a computer frequently had better results on task-switching tests (which assessed components of executive control), even across the older age ranges. These effects were particularly strong for those with lower intellectual ability.

Because it has been recognized that age plays a role in adopting and using new technologies, attempts have been made to make technology more accessible to older people. This is particularly important as people live longer and will likely need to use complex technologies for longer periods of their lives. One approach is training programs designed specifically for older people. Empirical research suggests that both guided action training (doing a learning task with someone helping along the way) and guided attention training (exercised development of attention skills) yield benefits (Hickman, Rogers, & Fisk, 2007). Further advances will require more intensive research into neurofeedback and attention control systems in relation to learning, and the translation of these scientific findings into practical skills and techniques.

Another useful application of technology for older adults is the use of robotic pets in nursing or long-term care facilities. Although many of these facilities have employees who bring their dogs to work and allow residents to interact with them, older adults can benefit from more sustained time with and providing care to a pet to reduce loneliness and increase well-being. Because many of these facilities cannot allow residents to have real pets, robotic dogs are being used as a substitute. Preliminary findings suggest that they decrease feelings of loneliness (Banks, Willoughby, & Banks, 2008). The irony for older adults is that new technology serves to both isolate and help them.

SUMMARY

Technology is the universal way in which humans interact with their material world to meet their basic needs and increase well-being. Technology is therefore ubiquitous and involved in almost every human activity. Because of this, technology has played a major role in how societies have evolved over time. Even though technology is passed between groups through a process

of diffusion, some societies have had greater access than others to particular technologies and have therefore been able to develop at a more rapid pace.

- Major theoretical frameworks that place technology at center stage in understanding human society and culture are Lenski's evolutionary-ecological framework and cultural materialism.

• In current times, computer technology has had a large effect on social behavior via communication platforms such as e-mail, blogs, and social media such as Facebook or Twitter. Technology is heavily intertwined with the life course, and mastery of these tools is a critical part of successful adaptation.

• When technology fails, lives are greatly affected. This is because humans use technology to survive, and this fact should not be lost on social workers who work in direct practice, in community practice, or at policy-making levels.

KEY TERMS

Cultural materialism (CM)

Diffusion

Ecological-evolutionary typology

Internet addiction

Intersocietal selection

Intrasocietal selection

Neuroplasticity

Power

Sexual victimization

Technological change

Technological determinism

Technology

Technology transfer

CHAPTER 12

THE PHYSICAL ENVIRONMENT

In the previous two chapters we examined the fundamental roles of technology and demography and how these core infrastructural domains serve to meet the basic needs of a society. In this chapter we examine the third component of a social system's infrastructure, the physical environment. The physical environment refers to the natural environment and the built environment. It should be noted that the term *ecology* is often used interchangeably with these forms of environment. Both forms of environment shape and are shaped by the behavior of humans in myriad ways. Technology and demography are highly intertwined with the physical environment and often vary in accord with changes in that environment. Future chapters will continue to deepen the triadic relations of technology, demography, and physical environment by examining the role of political and economic institutions and ideology. Knowledge of the interaction between humans and the physical environment is an interdisciplinary field of study that, although naturally involving geography, also includes biology, environmental psychology, architecture and design engineering, public health, anthropology, social work, and sociology. The *interconnectivity* of humans within the physical environment, both in the long and short run, is the major theme of this chapter. It delineates specific effects of the natural and built environments and the associated spatial determinants that influence the pursuit of satisfying basic needs and well-being by individuals and collectives.

DISTAL CONTEXT

Geographic Origins of Inequalities

In Chapter 11, we noted the work of Jared Diamond and his seminal work *Guns, Germs, and Steel* (1997) with respect to the role that technological advances played in facilitating the conquest of the Americas by Europeans. But why did Europeans have this advanced technology to begin with and the native peoples of the Americas did not? According to Diamond's theory, much of this can be explained by geography.

Axis Orientations

The planet Earth has two major axis orientations that run north to south in the Americas and Africa and east to west across Eurasia. These orientations facilitated the spread of innovations across the globe. That the axis across Eurasia runs east to west is crucial. Food production from crops and livestock, and the associated technologies and organization needed for larger, more complex societies, were able to spread along the same latitude much more easily given relatively similar climate features. North–south axes are constrained by climate changes that greatly affect crops and livestock that are not adapted for survival in different temperate zones (e.g., this is why you don't see palm trees growing in Canada). Thus, agricultural practices and livestock production that proved successful, along with other technologies, were able to spread east toward India and China and west toward Europe and North Africa. These areas were in effect catapulted ahead of areas that did not benefit from this process of diffusion. As populations were increasing rapidly, cities were forming, and ships were being built along this east–west axis, many other parts of the globe were carrying on with a relatively static subsistence technology. For Diamond, these geographic determinants represent *ultimate factors*, whereas political organization and specific technologies, such as guns and steel, represent *proximal factors*. In terms of theorizing about human behavior, proximal factors are those things or variables that are closer to the outcome (inequality) than the ultimate factor. The ultimate factor, however, gives rise to the proximal factor in the chain of causation. When theorizing about human behavior, it is often useful to distinguish between ultimate and proximal factors for a particular outcome.

In an additional example of geography perhaps being an ultimate factor in determining the technological and developmental lag of sub-Saharan Africa, Harris (1989) writes:

> In A.D. 500, the feudal kingdoms of West Africa—Ghana, Mali, and Sanghay—strongly resembled the feudal kingdoms of Europe except for the fact that Africans were cut off by the Sahara from the heritage of technology and engineering that Rome had bequeathed to Europe. Subsequently, the great desert inhibited the southward flow of Arabic influences that did so much to revitalize European science and commerce. While the people that lived in the Mediterranean basin carried out their trade and warfare on ships and became maritime powers, their dark-skinned counterparts south of the Sahara were mainly concerned with crossing the desert and lacked any motivation for maritime adventures. So when the first Portuguese ships arrived off the Guinea coast in the fifteenth century, they were able to seize the ports and seal the fate of Africa for the next 500 years. (pp. 118–119)

Although attempting to explain differences between world societies based on geography is noteworthy, one of the criticisms of this approach (and the work of Diamond and Harris) is that it ignores the inequalities that exist within a culture. In many cases, there is greater variation within a geographically bound region than between geographic regions. As with any theory or factor, one cannot expect it to explain everything.

CASE STUDY: COMMUNITY TYPES

Chinni and Gimpel (2010) empirically identified 12 community types out of the 3,141 counties that comprise the United States of America: boom towns, campus and careers, emptying nests, evangelical epicenters, immigration nation, industrial metropolis, military bastions, minority central, monied burbs, Mormon outposts, service worker centers, and tractor country. The researchers describe trends in political affiliation, population density, education, income, labor market, immigration patterns, and religious affiliation and religiosity that characterize and distinguish these 12 communities. These community types offer varying permutations of housing stock, school quality, tax base, political representation, and transit and commuting options to their residents. Their data suggest that a family's position within a community type will partly determine their life choices, opportunities, and constraints. As social workers explore the fit of individuals and families within a community, it is important for them to understand the community context—and how, for example, job opportunities in a particular locale might interact with family roles and dynamics—to successfully assess and intervene with our clients.

One example of how real lives interface with and move in and out of these community types can be found in our introduction to the Lopez family, part of a military bastion community. Julianne Lopez is a 20-something Army wife and mother of a 1-year-old girl, Lila, and a 3-year-old boy, Elonzo. Lila was born 6 weeks early and had considerable heart conditions at birth, though they were not recognized until after delivery at the local military hospital during a routine postnatal checkup. Her heart conditions required immediate attention, and Lila ended up in the NICU for 4 months with catheterizations and other surgeries during that time. When Lila was finally able to go home, she required nursing assistance and was on a heart monitor at all times. The monitor would go off at various times of day and night, often not indicating distress, but at other times necessitating a call to the paramedic and late-night hospitalization. Julianne's doctors told her that she was not to leave the house with her infant, which made grocery shopping and other daily routines and errands challenging.

Julianne's husband, Marcos, also in his early 20s, has been in the Army for several years and was away in training when Lila was born. Since Lila's birth, he has been a strong support for Julianne and seems to always bring much-needed optimism in times of greatest despair. However, Julianne and Marcos just got orders of his impending deployment. Marcos is still unsure of his exact deployment location, but he does know he will be away for at least a year. Living in base housing, Lila knows that she has a supportive military community all around her; but having just recently moved to the community from several states away, she does not feel this support yet. Indeed, adjustment to a new state, a new city, and new housing, away from biological family, while caring for a daughter with serious medical challenges and a 3-year-old son, has all been quite overwhelming for Julianne. At times she does not know how she is going to cope with raising her daughter and son, but she is determined to do her best. She is worried about the quality of health care in her community and wants to learn more about the military's family support services that might be of assistance to her. Right now, she is not quite sure how to navigate the community's services, and feels increasingly isolated and worried about the opportunities that will be available for her and her family.

Critical Thinking Questions:

- How does community context matter to families? What do you think are the *most* important contextual characteristics for enhancing family well-being overall?

- As a social worker working in the Lopezes' community, what are some of the most important community-level interventions you think would be necessary to help the Lopez family?

- Imagine that the Lopez family was situated in one of the other 11 community types that Chinni and Gimpel discuss. Would you view their situation differently? The same?

GEOGRAPHY AND ECONOMICS INTERSECT

Gross domestic product (GDP) is a measure of the market value of goods and services a given nation produces in a given time period. It is a proxy economic indicator of standard of living, and represents the nation's sum of consumption, investment, government expenditures, and total net exports. Not surprisingly, GDP varies greatly around the globe (see Figures 12.1 and 12.2). As Gallup, Sachs, and Mellinger (1999) point

FIGURE 12.1 Gross Domestic Product in Global Perspective

Source: The Willis Group. (n.d.). GDP-based global diversification. Retrieved from http://www.thewillisgroup.net/global.html.

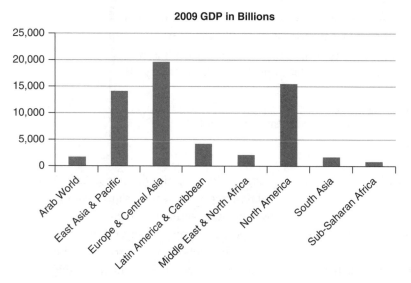

FIGURE 12.2 2009 GDP in Current U.S. Dollars

Source: World Bank. (n.d.). GDP (current US$). Data retrieved from http://data.worldbank.org/indicator/NY.GDP.MKTP.CD

out, nations in tropical regions of the globe are substantially poorer, and countries in higher latitudes are wealthier. In addition, nations that are landlocked tend to have a lower GDP, with the exception of landlocked countries in Europe. However, no landlocked nations on any other continent are among the higher income group. It also appears that the disparity in wealth between some continents has been growing. For example, according to Madison (1995), Western Europe had 2.9 times the GDP of Africa in 1820, which grew to a factor of 13.2 in 1992, an increase of approximately 350%.

In a study by Eaton and Kortum (2002) that examined some of the basic geographic factors involved in wealth and trade, findings indicated that trade diminishes with distance, and prices for goods are greatest among places farthest apart. Geographic distance and ease of diffusion also play a major role in the spread of new technologies around the globe, which seemingly further compounds the disparity in economic gain. This seems to reflect common sense, as distance creates a cost for the migration of goods and services and the negotiations involved in trade. If location matters so much, are some nations simply cursed by it? In attempting to answer this question, Ghosh and Wolf (2000) found that global location does indeed have an effect on the flow of capital to emerging markets. However, the moderators of this effect have not been fully explored. Although Ghosh and Wolf speculate that the correlation between distance and reduced capital flow could be accidental, evidence from previously mentioned sources seems to argue against that explanation. This does not mean, however, that nations that do not have geography on their side cannot improve their GDP. Other factors, such as technology, demography, and institutional strength and leadership could have a positive impact on economic growth.

DIFFUSION OF RELIGION AROUND THE GLOBE

The major religions of the world have spread around the globe and have had a major impact on regional cultures. Monotheistic (single-god) religions such as Christianity and Islam spread from similar origins. One major reason for this global reach is that these religions, as well as others, are universalizing religions, meaning that their practitioners attempt to convert others. Another reason is migration, in which followers take their religion with them. Christianity, the largest religion in terms of membership, has spread the most thoroughly around the globe, followed by Islam, which has been remarkably successful in its global diffusion. Buddhism and Hinduism have been less successful, being mostly practiced in South and East Asia. Although there are large-scale global patterns in the spread of religion, and religion has had a profound effect on shaping various nations, many countries and religions are heterogeneous in how the religion is expressed. For example, the United States, despite its diversity, is generally regarded as a Christian nation because of the large numbers of persons who claim membership in one of many Christian faiths. However, in the geographic distribution of Christians in the United States, the Southeast contains more Baptists than New England, which is largely Roman Catholic (Fouberg, Murphy, & de Blij, 2009). Further regional differences show that the upper Midwest is extensively Lutheran, and Utah and contiguous areas are Mormon (Fouberg et al., 2009). These geographic religious patterns have associated political institutions and views on important social issues that persons in the helping professions should not ignore. Chapter 14 will devote in-depth attention to the role of religion and other symbolic-ideational factors in human behavior.

ECOSYSTEMS THEORY

One of the major theoretical frameworks in which the physical environment is central is *ecosystems theory*. Although more of a perspective than a specific theory, the ecosystems approach can be traced back to the theoretical writings of British social philosopher Herbert Spencer (1820–1903), and later to the Chicago School of American sociology. Spencer compared human societies to biological organisms, in that adaptation and dependence on the environment were crucial to understanding both societal development and evolution. For Spencer, social intervention would interrupt the natural processes of society and do more harm than good (Leighninger, 1978). The highly influential Chicago School was housed at the University of Chicago. These sociologists, most notably Robert E. Park, Clifford Shaw, and Henry D. McKay, utilized the city of Chicago as a living laboratory to investigate social ecological processes. These researchers found that within and between areas of shifting housing and manufacturing, distinctive neighborhoods and subcultures arose (Abbott, 1997). These investigators, who mainly operated in between the two world wars, took the ideas bequeathed to them by the armchair theorists of 19th-century Europe such as Spencer and sought to collect data, empirically test the ecological effects of urbanization, and further these ecological concepts.

The ecological perspective approach (also called the *ecological systems theory approach* or the *ecological-developmental perspective*) is prominent in developmental science, and the work of Bronfenbrenner (1979) is often cited as a major conceptualization that defined levels of analysis (i.e., micro, meso, and macro) across the human life course. Systems perspectives are prevalent in social work, including the ecosystems approach and general systems theory. Although variations occur between approaches, they all tend to emphasize a holistic view of individuals, institutions, structures, and natural habitats in an interactive and adaptive framework (Meyer, 1983, 1988, 1993). The ecological perspective in social work is fashioned from knowledge drawn from anthropology, psychology, sociology, and other social science disciplines that deal with human ecology. The ecological systems approach is arguably the preeminent general viewpoint in social work (Wakefield, 1996a, b). In social work, some of the major proponents in the ecological tradition are Germain and Gitterman (1980), Meyer (1983, 1988, 1993), and Siporin (1980). Essentially, the

ecological viewpoint can be seen as a heuristic device from which to analyze the everyday transactions individuals have across many layers of social interaction. A *heuristic device* is the use of an abstract or artificial construct to enhance the investigation of some phenomenon of interest. Germain (1994) provided a synthesis that incorporates biopsychosocial theorizing with an emphasis on "social pollutions" such as poverty and oppression along with a stress-coping perspective. The problem with this conceptualization is the awkwardness of the term *pollutions* and the fact that it can refer to just about everything.

As expected from such a broad and generic systems framework, the range of issues in social work to which the ecosystems framework has been applied is vast. This includes studies that investigate the causal context of incest (Taubman, 1984) and violence toward women (Heise, 1998), adolescent treatment interventions for delinquency (Northey, Primer, & Christensen, 1997), homeless youth (Bronstein, 1996), preventing school dropouts (Dupper, 1993), and improving school social worker performance (Early, 1992). There have also been a notable number of studies focusing on international settings and culture-specific research. These include case studies on how empowerment proceeds among poor rural women in South Africa (Gray & Bernstein, 1994), urban Black men's adaptations toward the presentation of self (Holman, 1997), tests of Taiwanese adolescents' general well-being (Chang, 1998), externalizing behaviors among Black youth (Mason, Cauce, Gonzales, Hiraga, & Grove, 1994), child labor exploitation in Nigeria (Wilson-Oyerlaran, 1989), and racial comparisons of quality of life (DeFrances, 1996). In addition, treatment of Black women and their families in community crisis centers (Ligon, 1997) and in the context of dementia (Monahan, 1993) have been explored. What is unclear is the extent to which this perspective yields empirically valid results over and above other perspectives.

Additionally, there are works of a more theoretical nature that address conceptual integration of the ecological perspective (Gilgun, 1996;

Mattaini, 1990; Park, 1996). There are also essays that advocate the ecosystems theory as a macro-level unifying paradigm and to enhance casework practice (Allen-Meares & Lane, 1987) as well as intervention principles (Pardeck, 1996).

Mainly due to social work's systems orientation, the ecosystems perspective has been generally well received in the discipline. However, there are problems with this approach. In a two-part article, Wakefield (1996a, 1996b) analyzed the arguments for the utility of ecosystems theory for both its clinical and conceptual applications. With respect to clinical usefulness, Wakefield (1996a, b) considered its comprehensiveness, its integrative abilities, and its role as a counter to individual-level reductionism. He found these arguments to be invalid and the usefulness for the clinician to be an "illusion." As far as its conceptual utility, Wakefield examined three arguments centered on coherence, identification to social work, and heuristic insight. He also found these arguments wanting and concluded that social work does not need a generic theory, just interventions and domain-specific theories.

Although we agree that generic perspectives such as the ecosystems approach are typically not useful to direct-practice clinicians, and that specific theories generated from the perspective have not been adequately tested, some remain useful for understanding the sweep of human behavior. After all, this book is guided by a cell to society perspective that we developed to surmount some of the limitations in extant perspectives such as the ecosystems approach, which are largely derivative and less refined than more prominent perspectives in other fields. In summary, the ecosystems approach has a long history in the social sciences in various forms, and at times has been highly regarded in the social work profession. It has found its way into multiple textbooks and has been applied to numerous substantive issues. It purports to place behavior and events into a larger context of interrelated patterns that touch or interface with social processes and the physical environment.

These processes are thought to be mutually interdependent and necessary to understand before effective interventions can occur.

STEWARD'S CULTURAL ECOLOGY

One specific theoretical perspective, cultural ecology, has been influential across the many fields studying human–ecology interactions. *Cultural ecology*, as pioneered by anthropologist Julian Steward (1955), sought to unravel the extent to which human adaptations to environmental circumstances required specific kinds of human behaviors. As Moran (2010) outlined, the methodological component of cultural ecology consisted of (a) analyzing the relationship between subsistence systems and environment, (b) analyzing the behavior patterns entailed in a given subsistence technology, and (c) determining the extent to which the behavior pattern entailed in a given subsistence system affects other aspects of a society or culture.

Steward clearly recognized that persons of any society must meet the basic needs of obtaining food, water, and shelter, and therefore how these needs are met directly impacts the physical environment. The meeting of basic needs in contemporary societies typically occurs via the mechanism of employment or business ventures (even illegal ones) and is connected to the physical environment in various ways. For example, employment in the information sector, working for a small company or large corporation, occurs within the built environment of an office building, usually in a city, which in turn lies within a natural environment. The construction of the office is dependent upon materials such as wood (from trees), concrete (from sand and water), and steel (from iron ore, coal, and other metals), and technologies such as electricity and metallurgy. Individuals' behavior in these office settings is not isolated from changes in the ecology of the physical environment. How the behavior of whole populations of individuals, or *aggregates* as they are commonly termed, is governed by political and economic institutions (more on this in Chapter 13), and how the behavior of individuals influences institutions, is also an integral part of this broad set of interactions. It is important to point out that despite using abstractions such as human–environment interactions and cultural ecology, these concepts are built up out of the behavior of individuals adapting to a particular set of circumstances. Although the cultural ecological approach has been around for over 50 years, in many ways it is still in its infancy and has perhaps taken on greater relevance as the issue of sustainability has come to the forefront (Moran, 2010).

The work of Steward (1955) and other cultural ecologists can be used in practical ways. One such way is to derive checklists consisting of questions to consider when to involve the physical environment in helping communities. Some of the major questions are as follows:

- Has the project considered the climate and ecology (i.e., soils, temperature, vegetation, wind, solar, variability) and their sustainability?

- Has the supply and utilization of water been considered?

- What is the spatial distribution of household resources?

- Has the project considered transportation routes and power requirements?

- Has the project considered land use capacity and associated technologies?

CLIMATE

Although it may seem obvious that climate impacts human behavior, most people have not considered the many ways in which this occurs. Cultures such as the Inuit, Inupiat, and Yupik that have adapted to extreme climates provide a useful illustration. These groups, often termed Eskimos (considered a pejorative term by native peoples), are cultures that reside mostly in Canada, near and above the Arctic Circle, an area of the globe where the climate is bitterly cold and survival is difficult (Forman & Burch, 1988; Stern & Stevenson, 2006). They are primarily hunters and fishers who consume a very high-fat diet from the blubber in such prey as seals, walruses, and caribou (Forman & Burch, 1988; Stern & Stevenson, 2006). These fats help to provide warmth. Although high in fat, the blubber from these animals is rich in omega-3 fatty acids, which are healthy fats that, among other things, are cardioprotective (Stern & Stevenson, 2006). These Arctic cultures tend to live in small groups and villages, not in cities. Almost every aspect of their behavior, even rituals, is tied directly or indirectly to the climate in which they have adapted.

Climate can even affect one's mood. A common example of this is *seasonal affective disorder (SAD)*. SAD occurs during the fall and winter when there is reduced sunlight, and involves symptoms of depression such as a loss of energy, greater irritability, weight gain, and social withdrawal (Mayo Clinic, 2011). Individuals living in some areas of the United States where there are fewer sunny days, such as Seattle or Pittsburgh, are more likely to experience SAD than individuals residing in Phoenix or other American cities with an abundance of sunlight. One of the treatments for SAD is light therapy. Although rare, some people experience the symptoms of SAD during spring and summer (Mayo Clinic, 2011). Taking a large-scale view, one of the major reasons why climate directly affects human societies across the globe is that changes in climate affect transportation, soils and vegetation, deforestation, supply and utilization of water, and natural disasters. These effects are costly in economic terms but also with respect to health and well-being (Kunkel, Pielke, & Changnon, 1999).

Esteemed sources have argued that the climate is the most important issue of the 21st century. The prestigious British medical journal *The Lancet* has commissioned a report from experts at the Institute for Global Health at University College, London, to delineate the major climatic issues for the readership. The conclusions from this report are that the interaction of climate and health is highly complex and conversely, complex solutions likely will be necessary (Costello et al., 2009). Unfortunately, the report also found that most organizations do not possess the capacity to solve these types of complex problems because most do not have the necessary range of interdisciplinary knowledge and associated technical ability. The report specifies several challenges that include (a) addressing humans' lack of knowledge regarding how best to respond; (b) creating health systems in impoverished areas of the globe where climate will impact people the most; (c) using technologies that will increase food output and water treatment and storage, and that will enhance early warning systems that better identify climate changes in micro environments than those currently employed; and (d) developing the political institutions necessary to create the conditions for low-carbon-output living. In sum, confronting the effects of weather is inescapable. Recognition and development of broad and nuanced solutions that take advantage of available expertise, political organization, and technology to help individuals and groups of people survive and thrive in the face of climate adversity will be a major challenge.

NATURAL DISASTERS

To many, natural disasters (e.g., earthquakes, floods, windstorms, extreme temperature events) represent the ultimate clash between humans and their physical environment. They attract immense attention from the news media, and in many respects are a wake-up call that we are at the mercy of rapid and severe changes in earth and weather. Natural disasters are truly multidimensional in their impact. They alter the landscape; destroy buildings; injure people physically, emotionally, and cognitively; are expensive; and stretch governmental and nonprofit aid resources.

The death toll from the havoc that natural disasters wreak varies dramatically across countries.

In a study of the role of geography, income, and institutions in disaster fatalities, Kahn (2005) reported that between 1980 and 2002, India had 14 earthquakes that caused more than 32,000 deaths, whereas the United States had 8 earthquakes that resulted in 143 deaths. Why are earthquakes in India so much more deadly? Using data on natural disasters from 73 nations over a 22-year period, Kahn tested the effect of national wealth and geography in determining the death toll. After controlling for the severity of the earthquake and natural disaster, the data showed that wealthier nations experienced fewer deaths than poorer nations. One of the major reasons is that wealthier nations are able to enforce building codes so that the built environment can withstand greater shock and resistance, thus reducing fatalities. Another reason is emergency responsiveness. Wealthier nations have higher quality emergency organizations, which also reduces the death toll. Wealthier nations also have better weather-tracking technology and thus are forewarned to a greater degree. Kahn also found that geography makes a big difference. Nations that have higher elevations are significantly less likely to experience natural disasters that result in high death tolls. Politically, nations that are less democratic also experience more natural disaster fatalities than more democratic nations. Interestingly, Africa experienced fewer natural disasters than Asia, the Americas, and Europe.

Natural disasters obviously cause people to experience tremendous stress. Yet little is known about how disaster-related stress varies within a disaster area. This is important to know, as this can guide counseling and mental health services for victims of disasters more effectively. In a study of the geography of stress following Hurricane Katrina, Curtis, Mills, and Leitner (2007) were part of a team that provided *geospatial analysis* services to the emergency and disaster relief efforts following hurricane Katrina. According to Curtis et al., site (defined as proximity to the disaster) and situation (social context of the community) are the key factors that determine vulnerability to stress. Mapping the geography of stress resulted in five geospatial stress categories: (a) experiencing the storm, (b) evacuation and relocation stress, (c) pre-Katrina stress, (d) pre-Katrina health outcomes, and (e) rebound and recovery potential. Because levels of PTSD appear to vary with disaster severity and how close one is to the experience, geospatial mapping can suggest the locations of residents most likely to experience symptoms of PTSD. Reported suicide attempts or addresses of people involved in stress-related events known to public health officials can be mapped as well to create a geography of stress. Disaster readiness is therefore an important aspect of ameliorating mental health problems. In the case of New Orleans, Curtis et al. also report that large numbers of people did not flee, which possibly reduced the experience of stress. This is partly because in coastal areas such as New Orleans, reports of severe storms and hurricanes are relatively common, and many people weigh the costs and hassles of evacuation against the probability of a storm missing the city, which has happened many times in the past. An additional reason why so many people did not leave is that many in New Orleans cannot afford to own a motor vehicle. In sum, geospatial analysis can be a useful tool from which to direct services in disaster areas where stress loads are their highest.

Hurricane Katrina also pointed out the important connections between natural disasters, race, and poverty. New Orleans developed at the intersection of several major sources of water: the Gulf of Mexico, the Mississippi River, and Lake Pontchartrain. Its original settlements developed along higher ground, but New Orleans continued to grow below sea level, so extensive levee building was needed to protect the city as much as possible. Migrations of mostly impoverished Blacks from rural areas looking for employment in the city took place throughout the 20th century, but as time passed, Whites moved to the suburban areas, which also were generally located on higher ground. Public housing was built in the city (and not in the most desirable areas) during the 1950s and 1960s as a means to handle the large number of poor Black residents

(Cutter, 2006). Thus, social vulnerability converged with topography (low-lying areas were cut off) and climate. Although a rare event, a major hurricane hitting a major city has enormous consequences, and disaster personnel are often poorly trained for the mass evacuations and devastation of physical structures that follow.

The extent to which the consequences of Hurricane Katrina could be blamed on a mix of racism, classism, and just poor planning is debatable (Elliott & Pais, 2006). However, these factors are clearly intertwined, as preliminary research has pointed out (Elliott & Pais, 2006). The continued legacy of structured inequality, particularly in urban areas, coupled with severe natural disasters beyond human control (such as hurricanes), brings to the surface a number of issues of racism. One of these is the media depiction of the storm's aftermath. In their research on media coverage, Sommers, Apfelbaum, Dukes, Toosi, and Wang (2006) found that media disproportionately focused on crime and violence committed by Black survivors and far less on the search for food and adequate shelter. Public administrative policies have also been found to be discriminatory based on research by Stivers (2007). These policies are particularly pernicious if they became entrenched over decades.

URBAN ECOLOGY

The need to study urban ecology is pressing today, but will become even more so in the future as humanity increasingly congregates in cities. In 1900, it was estimated that approximately 10% of people worldwide lived in cities; now that number is over 50% and growing (United Nations Population Division, 2005). As mentioned, to a large degree the ecosystems perspective had its origins in early 20th-century Chicago through the studies of several notable social scientists. More recent attempts at understanding the ecology of the city are being pursued as an integrative science utilizing biology, social components, and the city's physical features. A case in point is the Baltimore Ecosystem Study, conducted by a multidisciplinary team. Pickett et al. (2008) built their study around three primary questions:

1. How do the spatial structures of the socioeconomic, ecological, and physical features of an urban area relate to one another, and how do they change through time?

2. What are the fluxes of energy, of matter, and of human, built, and social capital in an urban system; how do they relate to one another; and how do they change over the long term?

3. How can people develop and use an understanding of the metropolis as an ecological system to improve the quality of their environment, and to reduce pollution to downstream air- and watersheds? (p. 140)

As we can readily see, these research questions intersect and involve a number of specialized fields. The major social findings that have resulted from the pursuit of these three questions indicate several expected and unexpected findings on the social and bioenvironmental aspects of the urban system. Among these unexpected findings, variations in SES and ethnicity were not found to affect viewpoints on environmental problems. In other words, people from across the whole spectrum have concerns about the environment. Also contrary to popular discourse, Whites in this study were more likely to live near toxic waste sites than people of color. Bioenvironmental findings show that the urban ecology has a diverse and thriving set of flora (plants) and fauna (animal life) that exceeded researchers' expectations. For example, they were able to identify rare plants, exotic beetles, and well over 100 native bird species. Lawns and trees can have an effect on neighborhood stability by displaying investment and commitment to home ownership. Overall, this study shows that common assumptions about urban ecology are not typically true.

Knowledge gleaned from urban ecology has been influential in discovering the spatial determinants of city residents' health and well-being.

Spatial simply refers to location and distribution in space or geographic boundary. It is well established empirically and through common sense that low levels of physical activity are associated with greater obesity rates and poor health. Thus, studies examining how different ecological conditions can modify these relationships are potentially important. In one large-scale study involving over 100,000 participants that investigated the degree to which sprawl (urban spread across counties) influences physical activity and major health outcomes, Ewing, Schmid, Killingsworth, Zlot, and Raudenbush (2003) revealed that increases in county-level sprawl are associated with less walking and higher body weight and blood pressure. However, although the effect was statistically significant, its magnitude was small. Despite the small effect, if it impacts a large number of people, then the consequences become larger in scope. The findings suggest that if sprawl is left unchecked, it will continue to contribute to poor health outcomes via the mechanism of reduced physical activity. Sprawl creates distance between people and the material goods and services they need to survive. As such, it diminishes their ability to walk to a food market, school, or visit friends.

Other spatial characteristics affect health, too. In their analysis of health disparities (differences in health outcomes among groups) in the city of Detroit, Schulz, Williams, Israel, and Lempert (2002) suggest that the spatial organization of racial segregation is a cause of health disparities, and that eliminating or reducing segregation is necessary to close the gap. These authors argue that segregation not only influences access to the material wealth that facilitates health services, but also damages one's health directly. Although it is quite plausible that segregation is associated with poor health outcomes among minority citizens, there are potentially other explanations that need to be ruled out before this hypothesized relationship can be considered causal.

Neighborhood problems and public safety concerns independently impact health outcomes. One of the means by which this occurs is reduced mobility and exercise. As is well established in the health literature, exercise and physical movement are associated with reduced weight, which in turn improves cardiovascular health and overall well-being. In a multiethnic atherosclerosis study, Escheverria, Diez-Roux, Shea, Borrell, and Jackson (2008) found that people exercised more and smoke and drank less in neighborhoods experiencing fewer problems such as dilapidated buildings and higher crime rates.

The impact of place on health has led to an emerging new field, public health geography, which seeks to locate, explain, and intervene in public spaces to benefit their residents' health. Health-geography approaches can help in many ways. According to Dummer (2008), these include analyzing geographic accessibility of healthy foods; mapping infectious diseases; analysis of geographic clusters of deaths or cancers; air pollution and mortality; the effect of green or natural spaces on indicators of health and well-being; and access to hospitals, medical clinics, and physicians. In terms of scale, these concerns can extend beyond cities and metropolitan areas to entire nations around the globe. Global concerns are especially pressing as some researchers (McMichael, Nyong, & Corvalan, 2008) have found that environmental degradation (e.g., deforestation and environmental contaminants) leads to poor health outcomes because soil and water health are important drivers in any food supply and hygiene system. The exhaustion of natural resources and biodiversity are real concerns not just for their own sake but also because of the direct pressures they place on local populations.

One important principle to keep in mind when reasoning about the relationship between ecology and human behavior is the *ecological fallacy*. This occurs when we make inferences about specific individuals based on aggregate patterns or data. For example, if the data show that a particular neighborhood has the highest rates of sexually transmitted disease in the city, one cannot assume that a specific person from that neighborhood has such a disease. The inherent variation in any pattern of data about large numbers of people makes it difficult to conclude that one specific person is part of the pattern. So what's the use of generalizing from aggregate data? Despite the pitfalls of the ecological fallacy, it is helpful to generalize about phenomena even though they may not apply to everyone. For example, smoking has been strongly associated with lung cancer, but although not everyone who smokes will get lung cancer, it is useful to know that smoking increases the probability of developing it.

BUILT ENVIRONMENT

The *built environment* refers to homes, office buildings, roads, and other features humans have constructed. There has been a surge of interest in the effects of the built environment, mainly regarding health-related behaviors but also how they influence office workers' productivity and well-being.

Growing research on the relationship between the built environment and health behaviors such as diet and exercise has been steadily accumulating over the past 15 years (Berrigan & McKinnon, 2008). In a national study comparing overweight and physical activity across major locations and neighborhoods for a sample of over 20,000 adolescents, Nelson et al. (2006) revealed that compared to adolescents in newer suburban neighborhoods, those who resided in rural working-class, near-urban, and mixed-race urban areas were more likely to be overweight even when controlling for the effects of age, SES, and race/ethnicity. Interestingly, compared to adolescents living in newer suburbs, youth in older suburbs were more likely to be physically active. These study findings indicate that sprawl is not necessarily harmful as adolescents living in the newer suburban areas, farther outside of the urban core, were not the least physically active youth in the sample. The researchers conclude that place effect is more complex than previously believed, and older conceptualizations involving simple urban–rural or urban–suburban comparisons do not capture the complexity of the built environment and surrounding social ecology. One of the reasons for this complexity is that these areas were built in different times, and urban planners have since changed their design orientations accordingly. For example, the new urbanism design movement has recognized the importance of walking and cycling, and has integrated them into newer planned communities that facilitate greater physical activity (Handy, Boarnet, Ewing, & Killingsworth, 2002).

Studies of the built environment on alcohol use have also been conducted. Using random-digit dialing procedures among people living in New York City, Bernstein, Galea, Ahem, Tracy, and Vlahov (2007) sought to examine the relationship between neighborhood characteristics such as building conditions and home structural problems (e.g., peeling paint, leaks) and alcohol use, including heavy use (defined as five or more drinks in one sitting) in the past 30 days. Results from this investigation of 1,355 individuals across the city showed that living in a housing unit with peeling paint or plaster and leaks was associated with greater likelihood of using any alcohol in the past 30 days. External building conditions were not just associated with alcohol use but with heavy drinking. Specifically, residents living in buildings that had window and external stairway problems were twice as likely to drink heavily as those living in buildings without these problems. As with reports of any alcohol use, persons reporting heavy drinking were also more likely to reside in locations experiencing peeling paint and plaster and leaks. Note that these results controlled for the effects of age, neighborhood and household income, race, and sex. Bernstein et al. speculate that people living in these conditions are also more likely to experience heightened overall levels of stress and increased stress on both the cardiovascular and central nervous systems, and are therefore using alcohol as a means to alleviate stress and in effect self-medicate.

Based on the speculative effects of built environment on stress and despair, it seems logical to examine the relationship between built environment and mental health. Although little research has accrued in this area, Evans (2003) reviewed studies of the direct relationship between built environment and mental health and has drawn several important conclusions. With respect to direct effects, high-rise housing was associated with increased psychological distress in low-income mothers across multiple studies. Second, findings consistently show that housing quality is associated with psychological distress. Third, multiple studies suggest that physical and social neighborhood attributes are associated with poorer cognitive development in children. Fourth, the number of people in a residence (residential density) was associated across several surveys and laboratory studies with negative mood and distress but not psychiatric disorders. Additional studies suggest that the built environment affects indirect pathways such as social support and personal control, which are directly related to mental health problems.

Rural Ecology

Much less is known about the ecology of rural life compared to its urban counterpart. One reason for this is the accelerating trend of humans living in and migrating to cities. Another is that most researchers work and live in cities. As expected, there are common misconceptions about rural ecology and social life compared to beliefs about urban ecology. One such comparison involves poverty. Although we tend to think of the poor as being trapped in cities, rural areas have higher rates of poverty than metropolitan areas (Weber, 2007).

Just as cities are diverse, so are rural areas. Therefore, generalizations about rural areas based on one region may or may not hold for other rural areas. One such generalization about rural behavior and ecology compared to urban settings is that rural people tend to be directly tied to their natural habitat, compared to urban residents, who are seen as more directly tied to the built environment. Although there have been debates regarding the relative benefits of urban versus rural living, having closer access to natural habitats may confer several benefits to rural people. One area of benefit may be cognitive. In a set of experiments, Berman, Jonides, and Kaplan (2008) found that natural environments were less stressful and more relaxing mainly because urban environments require greater directed attention (top-down cognitive processes), whereas natural environments elicit bottom-up, non–goal-directed attention that allows top-down systems a chance to rest. Another example is the research finding that rural environments moderated the genetic susceptibility to substance use and anti-social behavior among a sample of 17-year-old twins. As we learned in Chapter 2, the twin design allows researchers to see the effects of genes, shared environments (those the twins have in common), and nonshared environments (those the twins do not have in common). Using the Minnesota Twin Family Study, an ongoing study of over 1,000 twins, Legrand, Keyes, McGue, Iacono, and Krueger (2008) showed that living in a rural residence reduced the genetic propensity to engage in externalizing behaviors (alcohol and drug use, oppositional-defiant and conduct problems) compared to adolescents residing in urban environments. The researchers suggest that compared to adolescents living in urban areas, behavior of rural adolescents is shaped to a larger extent by shared environmental influences such as family and community.

SPOTLIGHT TOPIC: SENSE OF PLACE

It seems logical that humans would form strong emotional attachments to places, whether those are physical environments such as natural landscapes or built environments such as a house. One reason for this is that many powerful emotions are associated with a given place. For example, people are often reluctant to sell homes in which they have lived for long periods of time because so many life events, such as raising a family, took place within them. Positive or negative emotions derived from life events or key social relationships are therefore linked to the physical environments in which they occurred.

Although empirical studies on place identity and sense of place are few, a study by White, Virden, and van Riper (2008) examined the effect of prior experience with an outdoor recreation place among 351 visitors and found that prior experience with the recreation area was significantly associated with greater place identity via increased concern for the environmental and depreciative behavior in that location. This study suggests that more frequent contact with a place (especially positive) tends to result in increased concern and sensitivity for that location.

As Williams and Stewart (1998) have discussed, the concept of a sense of place offers a way for ecosystems policy and management practitioners to take advantage of the attachments people form with places. Many people invest these attachments with near-spiritual and symbolic meaning. While many such attachments are positive and instill feelings of pride, other places can be seen by some as symbols of oppression. Williams and Stewart offer the example of Mount Rushmore, an amazing feat of outdoor sculpture that depicts Presidents Washington, Jefferson, Lincoln, and Theodore Roosevelt. Many Americans admire the exploits of these leaders, but many (although seemingly fewer) view them as exploiters, and they are symbols of oppression to some Native American groups.

Williams and Stewart suggest that ecosystem managers learn and make use of the names for local places that are common among people in that area. Maintaining these local place names shows concern for tradition and respect for a community. They also suggest that managers understand the politics of places. There may be locations in specific communities that, to outside planners, appear to hold no particular landscape or architectural significance, yet they may be the site of an event of importance to that community. Individuals who work with communities will likely achieve better results if they take into account sense-of-place attachments instead of ignoring the emotional power that people associate with locations.

For Reflection

Think of the places that evoke strong emotions for you. Why have you developed either a strong attachment or aversion to these places?

The micro analogue to the larger macro ecological processes that we have discussed thus far is the specific setting in which humans interact. Two good example of micro ecological settings are jails and prisons.

THE EFFECT OF SETTING: JAILS AND PRISONS

A popular book in criminological circles, *The Jail* (1985) by John Irwin—a former prisoner himself—describes the built environment of the jail and the effect that this micro setting has on inmates. Irwin employed a research technique known as participant observation. Irwin essentially explored major themes based on his time observing jail procedures and interviewing 100 men charged with felonies and 100 prisoners charged with misdemeanors in a municipal jail. According to Irwin, jails mostly constitute people who are offensive to others rather than dangerous criminals. Irwin refers to these offensive persons as "rabble." For Irwin, jails serve a basic function of controlling or managing the rabble. The rabble is composed of persons who are poor, detached and displaced, perhaps mentally ill and homeless—essentially, the "leftovers" that society does not know what to do with but must contain and control. However, Irwin's own data (p. 19) on the felony sample reveals 14 burglaries, 12 assaults, 9 robberies, 2 rape charges, and numerous other crimes, which seemingly undermines Irwin's assertion that people in jail are largely not criminals.

The micro ecology in Irwin's study suggests that jail demoralizes and degrades people.

During arrest and booking an individual loses autonomy. Jail cells easily become crowded. Some prisoners are drunk, sick, or bleeding, and many smell bad. The toilet and sink are open to view. Following booking, prisoners are assigned to cells, or "tanks." Capacity of these tanks varies across cities, but in Irwin's study in San Francisco, the tank held up to 20 men. The physical environment is cramped, quarters are Spartan, and every act is watched. Each new prisoner arrives in a tank where some men have been living for several months. Consequently, these tank veterans possess a greater claim to the space. As Irwin describes, "He is moving into foreign territory, much of it claimed by the residents. If he is stranger to the jail setting, he will lack knowledge needed to interpret local interactions, and he will not understand the vast repertoire of taken-for-granted responses used by most of the locals in their daily rounds" (p. 60). Under these micro settings, new prisoners must adapt to having little power. However, these experiences vary between prisoners. Some who have a strong reputation on the street and/or who have experienced the jail before are in a better position to shield themselves from the negative aspects of the jail environment.

One of the classic studies of the effects of prison ecology and social roles on individual behavior is the Stanford Prison Experiment, which occurred in 1971. The person most associated with this study is lead researcher and Stanford University social psychologist Philip Zimbardo. Zimbardo has revisited this famous experiment in an attempt to understand how well we know ourselves and each other in a more recent book, *The Lucifer Effect* (2007). Zimbardo seeks to understand the conditions under which good people do evil things to others. The perspective that frames Zimbardo's analysis is the *situationist perspective*, which means that factors external to the individual that are components of a given situation contribute strongly to particular behavior. In this particular case the situation is functioning as a guard, inmate, or superintendent inside a prison. The situationist perspective contrasts with the *dispositional perspective*, which assigns greater weight to factors inside of an individual, such as traits or thought processes.

The Stanford Prison Experiment took place in a basement of the psychology building at Stanford University and attempted to simulate the situational social roles and ecology of a prison. Consultants were hired to help make the location as realistic as possible. Regular office doors were removed and bars were added. A small area or "hole" was constructed to simulate solitary confinement. All events were videotaped and recorded. Interestingly, Zimbardo performed the role of the prison superintendent, and 24 research volunteers (students who were paid $15 per day) were randomly assigned roles as guards and inmates. Participants assigned to be inmates were arrested by county police and taken from their homes to what they thought was the county jail. Each prisoner (i.e., volunteer) was strip-searched and deloused using chemical spray. This procedure was meant to be a degradation ritual. Prisoners were given uniforms with identification numbers and ankle chained. Participants who were guards were told to do whatever was necessary to maintain law and order within the prison— within reason. Guards had khaki uniforms, wore sunglasses, carried billy clubs borrowed from police, and worked three 8-hour shifts. In terms of punishment, guards began to require pushups.

There were no major incidents on the first day. However, on the second day the prisoners rebelled and barricaded themselves inside of a cell. The guards retrieved fire extinguishers and sprayed the prisoners, stripped them, and took the leader of the rebellion to solitary confinement. Guards also began to psychologically confuse prisoners to better control them by placing the worst behaved prisoners in the good cells and the best behaved prisoners in solitary confinement. Prisoners began to not trust one another. They were forced to urinate and defecate in a bucket. By Day 2 some prisoners began to cry and scream. The guards thought it was a ploy and ignored it. In keeping the situation as real as possible, friends and family were allowed to visit, but the prison was cleaned up, as were the prisoners (who were also given a large meal), and pleasant music was played for the visitors. Following additional humiliation and a planned prison escape, this resulted in more abuse from the guards. At one point, when one of the prisoners was crying, the superintendent (Zimbardo) has to tell him that this was not real, that he was a psychologist, and this was a research study.

On the evening of Day 5, Zimbardo realized that the study had to be ended. Although it was planned to run for 2 weeks, it ended on Day 6, as too much abuse, sadism, and emotional distress had accumulated. Not surprisingly, the Stanford Prison Experiment has served as an example of why research studies need close scrutiny by institutional review boards and why ethics are a critical component of study design.

Other unique studies have taken place in prison settings. For example, Fournier, Geller, and Fortney (2007) designed a study to test the effect of human–animal interactions on criminal behavior, progress in treatment, and social skills development in a sample of 48 male inmates. The authors argue that new interventions are needed for the prison setting given that the vast majority (perhaps 95%) will be released and because the prison environment is antisocial. One relatively new intervention involves caregiving and training of pets for service and adoption.

There are theoretical reasons why caregiving and training of animals may be helpful to inmates. One is that providing care to an animal that is entirely dependent upon a human may increase empathy and discipline. In their study, Fournier et al. studied the effects of dog training by inmates in a minimum-security correctional facility over an 8- to 10-week study period. Inmates were instructed beforehand in dog training techniques. The dogs lived with the inmate for the study period and were later adopted by people in the community. To participate in the study, inmates could have no history of animal abuse or domestic violence. The outcomes tested were treatment engagement in the prison's therapeutic community, social skills, and behavioral infractions. Posttest results revealed increases in treatment engagement, reductions in infractions, and higher levels of self-reported sensitivity and emotional control. In sum, inmates who participated appeared to benefit. However, there are several cautions to keep in mind before concluding that human–animal interaction programs are effective. One issue is there was no true control group for comparison. Inmates in the study did differ from the general prison population, calling into question the validity of this type of program being beneficial for the more typical prison inmate. Despite these limitations, there is a near endless supply of dogs who need human interaction and ultimately a functional home, and testing human–animal interactions in a unique ecological setting (i.e., prison) is potentially useful.

OFFICE SPACES AND PRODUCTIVITY

In Western industrialized nations, and even in developing countries, a substantial proportion of the population earns its living by working in an office space of some kind. As is well known, people spend a large amount of their lives in these spaces. Leaman and Bordass (2005) estimated that office space can affect productivity by as much as 20% positively or negatively, depending on the office space. As such, the design of office spaces is important. The conventional view of office space is that there are two types: traditional and open plan. The open-plan office design has supplanted traditional spaces because it was thought that they would enhance communication and therefore productivity (Brookes & Kaplan, 1972). Another reason, however, was that more people can be put in a building with an open-plan approach, which reduces costs due to fewer interior walls. One of the drawbacks with open-plan office spaces is that workers lack psychological privacy (Brookes & Kaplan, 1972; Kupritz, 1998). There is no ready escape from other people, and to many employees (especially introverts) is overstimulating. Another problem is ambient noise, because there are no walls to block the sound waves. Workers often report that they wish office noise could be reduced (Leaman & Bordass, 2005).

One of the most important considerations for workers and designers regarding office spaces are windows. People clearly prefer windows in their workspaces. But what if this is not possible? Can other features reduce the dissatisfaction of working in a windowless environment? In a study of the adaptations to windowless offices, Heerwagen and Orians (1986) surveyed five windowless and windowed office buildings on the campus of the University of Washington. The final study sample comprised 37 spaces with windows and 38 without. The windowless spaces had 195 décor items, compared to 82 in the windowed spaces. This result was statistically significant, even assuming that windowed offices would have three available walls for décor compared to four in the windowless spaces. The content of the décor items in the windowless spaces showed a greater use of landscape and natural scenery. These findings suggest that workers do indeed engage in adaptive behaviors aimed at making their workspaces seem more natural.

If workers adapt their spaces to draw in more of the outdoors, then it seems possible that interior plants may increase worker productivity and reduce stress. Lohr, Pearson-Mims, & Goodwin (1996) attempted to test the effects of plants on people in interior spaces. A computer laboratory with 24 workstations was the setting for the experiment, which involved 96 undergraduate volunteers. A computer program was used to assess volunteers' productivity and induce stress in them. Measures of blood pressure, pulse, and emotional state were used. Volunteers worked at the computer stations with plants randomly placed in the room: on the floor, hanging, and on shelves. Volunteers who worked in the room with plants reported greater levels of attention, but pulse readings were not different. However, there were significant differences in blood pressure reading with volunteers in the room with plants showing reduced systolic blood pressure during stressful tasks. Thus, plants had a moderating influence.

Given advances in technology and the cost of adding windows to existing walls, could plasma screens function as a surrogate for access to the outdoors? In a unique study, Kahn et al. (2008) tested the effect that plasma screens playing natural scenery in an office space had, compared to just a wall and having a window. Ninety study participants were divided into three conditions (30 per condition): office space with 50-inch plasma screen, windowless office space, and office space with a window. Assessments included heart rate and looking behavior, which was measured using cameras. Results indicated that heart rate recovery was significantly better in the room with the window. Interestingly, there was little difference between the space with the plasma screen and the windowless office. Looking outside the window was a common behavior that decreased heart rate. It appeared that study participants were unconsciously looking out the window to reduce their heart rate. Looking at the plasma screen did not have this same effect, and it was no better than looking at a wall. In terms of restorative behavior, this study suggests windows to the outside world are necessary and plasma screens depicting a natural environment are not a surrogate.

TOOLS FOR SPATIAL ANALYSIS

Geographic navigation technologies have become increasingly common in new automobiles, and people commonly use onboard navigation systems to reach their desired destinations. Advances in technology related mainly to satellite imaging have permitted the development of a number of tools that can be used for spatial analysis by people in the helping professions. Importantly, the physical environment can be linked to individuals' behavior. Those involved in community-based practice and social development projects often find geographic information systems (GIS) to be quite useful. In general, these systems are computer software packages in which neighborhood data are entered into the software program to facilitate spatial analysis. For example, it is quite common for police departments using GIS to assess crime "hot spots" to better allocate police officers to those locations (e.g., Andreson, 2006). Human services professionals can assess needs in much the same way. This offers a functional method to increase the efficiency of an organization given finite resources.

Almost any form of data collection can be tied to a location (i.e., geocoding). As such, if you interview a resident and have their location, you can begin to build a database, where further information collected in interviews or administrative records can then be tied to that location. The interplay of location and data can then be analyzed to reveal important patterns depending on the goals of the organization. Phenomena such as employment, child abuse, drug sales, housing and homelessness, domestic violence, and many other issues can be better understood and ameliorated. Thus, GIS software allows for behavior to be connected to a spatial pattern. Another important use of GIS is in the area of public health. Disease outbreaks, for example, can be mapped and charted, and changes in the progress of the disease as well as any spatial effects can be assessed, thus improving the success of interventions. GIS technology can be used not only for urban problems and health but also for studying larger land-use options including erosion, flora, and sprawl (Jensen, 2007; McCoy, 2005).

CASE STUDY: COMMUNITY DEVELOPMENT AND YOUTH GANGS

Another poignant example of the interrelationship between the social and physical environments can be found in Gregory Boyle's book, *Tattoos on the Heart* (2010). Boyle is a Jesuit priest who for 2 decades has worked with gang members in Los Angeles, California. He has taken his ministry to prisons, jails, juvenile detention centers, and the streets. At the start of his community development efforts he successfully opened an alternative school, Dolores Mission Alternative, and began to focus on job placement for incarcerated youth who were returning to their communities. Later, he engaged a Hollywood agent to buy a store that became the original Homeboy Bakery, which has, decades later, become Homeboy Industries. Homeboy Industries includes Homeboy Bakery, Homegirl Café, Homeboy Maintenance, Homeboy/Homegirl Merchandising, and Homeboy Silkscreen, where gang members from the community work together to bake, create, and sell products. According to Father Boyle, of the 86,000 gang members and 1,100 gangs in LA, he estimates he has worked with approximately 1,000 members per month from 800 gangs, offering job placement services and tattoo removal, mental health counseling, case management, and legal services. Father Boyle sees his commitment as "part worksite and part therapeutic community," but certainly it is economic development within a built environment. In the details of his book, Father Boyle invites a deep and wide range of emotional responses from his readers, as he tells the stories of lives transformed through building relationships at the individual, family, community, and institutional levels.

Social work cannot work alone in its attempts to change the trajectories and life chances of vulnerable populations living in distressed communities. Interdisciplinary collaborations with urban planners, other social scientists, and the business community are necessary. Community volunteer organizations that partner with corporations can significantly change social interactions and shape residents' behavior in high-risk physical environments. For example, Planters Grove, a newly developed 5,000-square-foot park in Northeast Washington, D.C., is a project that grew out of President Obama's America's Great Outdoors initiative, and represents a partnership between the Planters nut company and the Corps Network, a national community-volunteer mobilization network, who worked together to develop a safe and clean peanut-shaped park in an area once besmirched with drug activity and crime. In the past 10 years, volunteers have transformed the space by cleaning up trash, removing abandoned cars, and initiating a youth-run farmer's market. These efforts have driven out the brazen drug activity and open-air heroin markets that once controlled the open space (Wu, 2011).

Critical Thinking Questions:

- Do you think the *physical* environment has more of an impact on community development, or does the *social* environment have more of an impact? Why?

- How do physical and social environments interrelate to influence developmental outcomes of community residents?

- How can social institutions be leveraged to enhance the biosocial outcomes and life chances of residents living in distressed communities?

SPATIAL EFFECTS AND VARIATION OVER THE LIFE COURSE

Although it is not surprising that there is geographic variation in human behavior, it is important to map the spatial distribution of important behaviors and social outcomes. Taking spatial effects into account not only allows us to assess which areas need more help, but also furthers our understanding of what causes a given phenomenon. Although we have already seen how spatial and ecological conditions affect human behavior throughout the life course, we now highlight some spatial effects on specific stages.

Fetal Environment and Infancy

Infant mortality rate is a powerful indicator of the economic and overall well-being of a given location. As part of their KIDS COUNT child well-being data collections occurring every year since 1990, the Annie E. Casey Foundation has included data on U.S. infant mortality in their child well-being index (see O'Hare & Lee, 2007). Their findings show that states such as New Hampshire, Vermont, Minnesota, New Jersey, and North Dakota rank near the top, whereas New Mexico, West Virginia, Alabama, Louisiana, and Mississippi rank at the bottom. Statistical analyses indicate that population characteristics such as race/ethnicity, and economic measures such as employment-to-population ratio, predict much of the variation in child well-being across states.

In a unique study that examined the role of relative poverty (e.g., comparisons to others in a population) versus absolute poverty (e.g., minimal standards for attaining food and shelter) on infant mortality rates across 16 nations with advanced economies (the United States and 15 European nations), Messner, Raffalovich, and Sutton (2010) found that relative poverty was the stronger predictor. In turn, relative poverty and infant mortality rates were a strong predictor of homicide rates. In general, finding ways to reduce infant mortality rates is part and parcel of improving the material well-being of cities, states, and nations.

Early Childhood and Childhood

Research indicates that decay or disintegration occurring in a neighborhood causes residents to be less involved and end up staying away from others. Massey and Denton (1993) argue that the process of social disintegration weakens the control and guardianship over the behavior of community members. This process then leads to less and less involvement, and therefore weaker controls and supervision. Although there is individual variation in response to neighborhood conditions, one can see how this condition would lead to reduced supervision of children and perhaps even reduced contact between children, thereby limiting a number of important factors involved in socialization and positive interactions with others. Conversely, one could see how resident involvement in their community and people freely interacting with one another can enhance the experiences of children in these situations. Research has revealed that children residing in more stressful conditions, like a neighborhood experiencing social disintegration, show higher levels of cortisol (a biomarker for stress) compared to children residing in stronger neighborhoods (Lupien, King, Meaney, & McEwen, 2000). Human services professionals working with families in beleaguered neighborhoods should be aware of these effects on children.

Adolescence

Achieving healthy sexual development during adolescence is important for later romantic and intimate relationships, self-confidence, and identity. Understanding the larger global trends in adolescent sexual development provides perspective to helping professionals. This knowledge also has important policy implications as approximately 50% of the world's population is under the age of 25 (United Nations World Youth Report, 2007). Although most adolescents initiate sexual behavior that is functionally adaptive, many engage in risky and harmful sexual behavior.

A review of global patterns by Koyama, Corliss, and Santelli (2009) with respect to key indicators of adolescent sexual functioning reports a number of important findings. Some of the factors associated with risky sexual behavior that seem to operate globally are disadvantage and dysfunction in the adolescent years, sexual norms and attitudes, and connections with adults or groups who frown upon risky sexual behaviors, whereas some of the protective factors include increased formal education and avoidance of alcohol and drugs. Their review also points out that contraceptive practices vary worldwide, with youth from sub-Saharan Africa, for example, being more likely to use condoms as opposed to more modern technologies. Importantly, these scholars also note in their review that there is variation even among developing nations, such as 20% of men in Malawi reporting condom use, compared to 47% of men in Ghana. Also,

teen pregnancy is lower in developing countries in Asia and Southeast Asia than in nations in sub-Saharan Africa, the Caribbean, and Latin America. Studies of efforts such as abstinence-only intervention have been shown in randomized experiments to have little benefit in reducing the number of partners, condom use, and increasing the age of sexual initiation (Kirby, 2007).

Adulthood and Older Adulthood

Although proper nutrition is important across the entire life course, older persons, particularly those with chronic health conditions, who are poor, or who live alone, often have a difficult time maintaining adequate nutrition. Decreased intake of important nutrients and calories furthers cognitive decline and exacerbates existing chronic health problems such as diabetes and hypertension (U.S. Department of Health and Human Services, 2005; Woo, 2000). One neglected factor involved in poor nutrition and food insecurity among older people is the food environment. In a study of over 1,000 adults in rural Texas, public health researchers Sharkey, Dean, and Johnson (2011) found that 18.6% of older adults reported food insecurity, defined as running out of food and not having enough money to buy more. Community characteristics were important predictors of food insecurity in this study. Specifically, measures of community integration pertaining to involvement of residents, and positive perceptions of the physical state of the community, were associated with decreased risk of food insecurity even after controlling for the effect of education and income level. Community features seem to matter for a number of problems that affect older people, including food insecurity, because of the way they influence residents' behavior in such communities. Less is known about the effects of geographically bound communities (such as those that are isolated) on behavior in countries other than the United States and less developed countries in particular. There are likely useful lessons to be learned about how different individuals respond to differences in physical environments from a global perspective.

EXPERT'S CORNER: CLAUDIA COULTON, CASE WESTERN RESERVE UNIVERSITY

There has been a growing realization that place matters with respect to many social work outcomes, but the science of neighborhoods vis-à-vis the behavior of individuals is really in its infancy. Over her career as a social work scholar, Claudia Coulton has emphasized the role of one aspect of place, the local community, as a means to disadvantaged populations. Coulton codirects the Center on Urban Poverty and Community Development in the Mandel School of Applied Social Sciences, and is particularly interested in community change and urban poverty. Coulton is an early pioneer in the use of GIS to study neighborhood change and the geographic concentration of poverty. Some of the major projects that Coulton has been instrumental in developing are the Northeast Ohio Community and Neighborhood Data for Organizing (NEO CANDO), a web-based data storehouse for information on neighborhood indicators and property information. One of the key aspects of intervening in communities and developing functional policies for neighborhoods is having adequate data that can be examined to assess what is needed for a given action and its likely outcomes. Consistent with the importance of having useful, location-specific community data that is meaningful to residents of those neighborhoods, Coulton is also a founding member of the National Neighborhood Indicators Partnership. In many ways, these neighborhood data-collection strategies are similar to collecting information on one's health so that a diagnosis can be made and informed treatment (i.e., policies) can be implemented. Coulton, Chan, and Mikelbank's (2011) recent work investigated how residents in neighborhoods perceive and specifically map their own communities. This is important because if planners and community organizers rely on externally imposed spatial boundaries that do not fit with the perceptions of the residents who actually live in these neighborhoods, programs' impact may be lessened. Complementing residents' perception with externally derived data may increase the overall chances that neighborhood initiatives will be successfully evaluated.

Photo of Claudia Coulton
Photo by Richard Cole, on behalf of Case Western Reserve University

SUMMARY

The physical environment, composed of natural and built environments, forms an ecological setting to which humans adapt but that they also shape. Several key points stand out with respect to human behavior and the physical environment:

• Physical features of the planet such as mountains, rivers, and deserts have powerful ultimate effects on shaping the trajectories of different cultures. For example, the planet Earth is composed of two major axis orientations that run north–south in the Americas and Africa but east–west across Eurasia. These orientations facilitate the spread of innovations and technologies across the globe that, according to Jared Diamond, have resulted in inequalities because some cultures had a substantial head start.

• Individuals in every society must meet the basic needs of obtaining food, water, and shelter; therefore, the methods by which people meet these needs have a direct impact on the physical environment.

• Climate influences mood and how we live our everyday lives, and produces events such as natural disasters that can be truly multidimensional in their devastation. Disasters affect some individuals and societies to a greater degree than others.

• More people are living in cities than at any time in human history—over 50% of the world population and growing. Studies of urban ecology suggest that humans not only are affected by urban settings (both indoor and outdoor), but cities are also affected by specific individuals who reside in a given area (selection effect). The spatial characteristics of urban, suburban, and rural settings are associated with mental and physical health.

• Extreme environments, such as those found in prisons and jails or deserts, are associated with extreme behaviors.

• Spatial location affects life course trajectories. For example, residing in certain states is associated with higher levels of infant mortality and other deleterious outcomes.

• Although the precise causal mechanisms are difficult to pin down, the effects of neighborhoods are complex, influencing some people differently than others and at different ages, with some displaying heightened stress levels.

KEY TERMS

Built environment

Cultural ecology

Dispositional perspective

Ecological fallacy

Ecological systems theory

Ecology

Ecosystems theory

Geospatial analysis

Interconnectivity

Proximal factors

Seasonal affective disorder

Situationist perspective

Ultimate factors

CHAPTER 13

INSTITUTIONS

Formal and informal *institutions* use rules and customs to organize and structure activities that attempt to meet the needs of a given society. In some respects they are analogous to what the skeletal system does for the human body. Institutions are formed and aggregated from individual behavioral choices that are influenced by a nexus of biosocial factors examined previously in this book, comprising individual behavior, micro-level exchange, cooperation, and social network processes. Institutions are also built upon the technological, demographic, and environmental needs of a society, and in turn they influence changes in these spheres as well (see Figure 13.1). Institutions are a result of greater social complexity and scale and are used as a means to solve problems that technology, population, and environment impose. Combined, these interactions have important effects on the ways in which societal institutions are expressed. This chapter describes the major institutions of human societies and considers the constraints they place on human behavior. Although people do make choices, they operate under varying political-economic and institutional contexts, and this chapter illustrates the roles these large-scale macro structures have on human behavior within a cell to society framework.

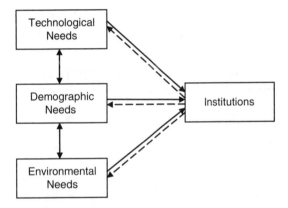

FIGURE 13.1 Relationship Between Institutions and the Technological, Demographic, and Environmental Needs of a Society

CASE STUDY: THE OVERTHROW OF INSTITUTIONS: REVOLUTION AND THE ARAB SPRING

As demonstrated throughout Chapter 13, institutions are an unavoidable and necessary part of modern society. As mentioned at its start, institutions become embedded into society and can become very difficult to change or alter. Although it may be difficult to change institutions that exhibit negative behaviors, such as exploiting oppressed populations or certain groups of people, it is still possible to do so. Under a democratic system of government, there is an assumption that change is possible by altering the very system in which the institutions are housed by voting, protesting, or lobbying, among other ways.

In some cases, options that are supposedly available to us turn out not to be so readily available. It may therefore be more difficult to manage major institutional change peacefully. This was clearly demonstrated in the events of the recent Arab Spring, in which people in several Arab countries, beginning in North Africa and moving into the Middle East, mobilized to hold massive protests and, in some cases, start a civil war to overthrow their governments. The institutions these countries had in place, which had not been altered in decades and greatly exploited large majorities of the population, needed to be changed. With limited means to enact those changes, the people turned to revolution, as they have done historically in many nations when change is necessary but not easily obtained.

Critical Thinking Questions:

- In American history, what incidences of major institutional change can you identify?
- In your own life history, have you experienced any institutional change, whether as a passive observer or an active participant?
- As a social worker, what role do you believe you will play in institutional change? Why is this type of change important?

BACKGROUND AND DISTAL CONTEXT

Institutions

Hodgson (2006) defined *institutions* as "systems of established and prevalent social rules that structure social interactions" (p. 2). Thus, institutions influence human behavior via regulating, facilitating, and coordinating functions. The rules and norms that make this possible are transmitted through social interaction and social learning. There are many examples of institutions including employment, credit, energy regulation, law and social control, education, physical and mental health, government, corporate, military, and religious. Institutions impose constraints on human behavior but also facilitate action, particularly on a large scale. For example, the federal government uses military institutions to conduct war, which is a large-scale operation. Strict hierarchies and rules serve to tightly control the behavior of soldiers. Other large-scale institutional operations that have powerful effects on individual and collective behavior include income taxation, laws (e.g., traffic, contracts, employment), and elementary and secondary schools.

Although democracy is a large political and social institution, it is expressed by the behavior of individuals and smaller groups acting within an institutional framework. As Lawrence and Suddaby (2006) note, "Democracy, for instance, resides in the acts of polling, campaigning, and related activities that people do as citizens of a democratic society, rather than describing some emergent property of the society that is separate from those practices" (p. 220). This also suggests that change can occur from the ground up via individual and group behavior.

Even though institutions are composed of individuals, they possess enormous power. This is because once the rules and norms for how the institution operates are entrenched, it becomes very difficult to overcome the force of their traditions. In a study of the power of institutions compared to geography and trade with other countries, it was institutional presence that predicted income across nations, over and above geography and trade (Rodrik, Subramanian, & Trebbi, 2002). Institutions tend to become crystallized and stable—so much so, that over time their rules and norms become part of the thought and behavior of individuals who become habituated to them (Hodgson, 2006). This process of habituation to the rules and authority of institutions provides a strong behavior-regulating function that is not easily altered. And because many institutions are large, they do not change very quickly. Institutions are like an aircraft carrier—not as nimble in their ability to change course as, for instance, a speedboat. When institutions do change dramatically, the effects reverberate and alter the behavior of other institutions and individuals who are intertwined with their trajectory. Much like the course of an aircraft carrier, institutional change is smoother when it is gradual.

Given that institutions survive for long periods, they develop their own cultures and language that members of the institutions readily understand. Much of the language pertains to terminology that reflects the technical aspects of what the institution actually does. This is not to state that each institution is unique, as they share aspects and have many things in common. Institutions acculturate individuals to their rules and rituals and socialize new employees. So what does changing an institutional culture entail? Most instances of institutional change involve an attempt at altering the formal rules of the given institution along with its associated norms and shared meanings (Morgan, 1997). Cultural aspects of an institution (i.e., institutional culture) are thought to play a significant role in the trajectory and stability of an institution. However, it is not clear what the relationship is between institutional culture and other components of an institution. In a study of 27 countries designed to examine the relations between cultural dimensions on family-owned firms (which are very common in some countries), Chakrabarty (2009) hypothesized that the greater the collectivist culture was in a nation, the more family-owned firms there would be, and the greater the influence of such firms would be. Results showed that national culture does have an effect on family ownership patterns, but that the effect is greatly diminished if an institution has strong regulatory functions, such as clear systematic rules and norms. In other words, the effects of national culture on a nation's family-owned firms are stronger when standard organizational rules and norms are weak or nonexistent.

Delivery of effective services to persons in need may depend to some extent on organizational culture. In a study of therapist turnover, program sustainability, and its organizational predictors in 100 mental health clinics across the United States, Glisson et al. (2008) found that clinic culture profiles explained the lion's share of variance in sustainability. Simply put, the clinics with the best organizational culture—measured in terms of organizational flexibility, professional proficiency, and openness to innovation—were able to sustain their programs approximately twice as long as clinics with weaker cultures. Further, organizational structure and climate significantly predicted therapist turnover. Study findings specifically suggest that therapists' cultural norms and expectations are important for program sustainability, and that their perceptions of their work environment (e.g., stress) were associated with turnover. Overall, the cultural context of organizations can affect workers' morale at various levels of an organization in both positive (e.g., engaged and motivated) and negative (e.g., stressed and disengaged) ways.

Given the importance of organizational culture, it would seem advantageous to find ways to diagnose problems in organizations just as one does in individuals and to implement effective change strategies. Cameron and Quinn (1999) argue that institutional values, vision, and beliefs are the most critically important aspects for long-term success. Organizations that are able to develop a distinctive culture and carefully nurture and manage it will have stability. This does not mean that effective organizations never change, but according to Cameron and Quinn, successful adaptability depends to a large extent on organizational culture. They describe a diagnostic instrument, the Organizational Culture Assessment Instrument (OCAI), designed to measure and profile an organization's culture. The OCAI assesses four dimensions or culture types: hierarchy, market, clan, and adhocracy). Several organizational profiling systems are available, and most have been tested in for-profit organizations. It is not clear whether these types of profiling systems can be used at a larger institutional level (e.g., the federal government) and what the interaction effects of bureaucracy on organizational culture might be.

Workplace Culture

As mentioned earlier in this section, workplaces are institutions. They are probably the institutions with which people are most familiar, and the ones with which they spend the majority of their time. It has been said—and in many cases this is true—that Americans spend more time at their job than they do with their spouses. That being said, the culture of a workplace can have a tremendous impact on how the workplace functions, the level of turnover, and overall employee happiness and productiveness. When people are not happy where they work, or not passionate for or motivated by their workplace, they are less likely to be as productive as they possibly can be.

In a study conducted by Marshall (1986) in a Central Scotland tavern, it was shown that the workplace culture there resulted in high employee satisfaction, despite the poor treatment employees received. In this study, the roughly 30 employees of the tavern worked long, hard hours under difficult conditions for low wages. However, they all displayed satisfaction with their employment. Marshall argues that the culture of this particular workplace, where employees worked so directly with a clientele that was enjoying leisure time, was highly reflective of clients' mood. In other words, because their clientele was enjoying leisure time, the staff felt as though they were enjoying that time with them, despite the fact that they were working. The lines between employee and client were somewhat blurred within the culture of that workplace, and therefore, despite working conditions that would generally produce low employee satisfaction, the opposite was found to be true at this establishment.

Evolution of Institutions and Social Organization

From an evolutionary point of view, how do institutions emerge? Given that institutions are a natural part of human social life, it is worthwhile to assess how they have evolved. Examining the roots of institutions involves understanding the behavior of primates because they represent a close approximation of early humans. Although humans differ in substantial ways from other primates, we still share many of the propensities and characteristics as a social species, albeit in more complex forms. Demonstrating the links between primate and human social behavior is illuminating as it provides insights into the origins of human social behavior. With respect to organization and institutions, it is reasonable to investigate what is known about the major features of primate social organization. Anthropologists Anthony Di Fiore and Drew Rendall (1994) provide an analysis of the major features of the primate social system. Primate social organization is driven by dispersal patterns (migrations around food foraging), mating patterns, intragroup and intergroup sexual relations, and investment in reproduction. The community structures of primates vary considerably, as Di Fiore and Rendall point out, "from the solitary foraging lorises (*Perodictus*), to the cohesive troop of gorillas (*Gorilla*), to the flexible parties of chimpanzees (*Pan*), to the multilevel societies of some terrestrial baboons (*Papio and Theropithecus*)" (p. 9941). Just as with humans, the structures of these primates interact within and adapt to specific ecological habitats.

Much of the structure in primate social organization revolves around rank within a dominance hierarchy. Neuro-endocrinologist Robert Sapolsky has studied the effects of rank with the social structure on the physical health of primates (see Figure 13.2). These poor health effects are not only due to injury during a dominance-imposing encounter but also are a result of stress hormones such as glucocorticoids secreted by the adrenal glands. Although such secretion is normal for

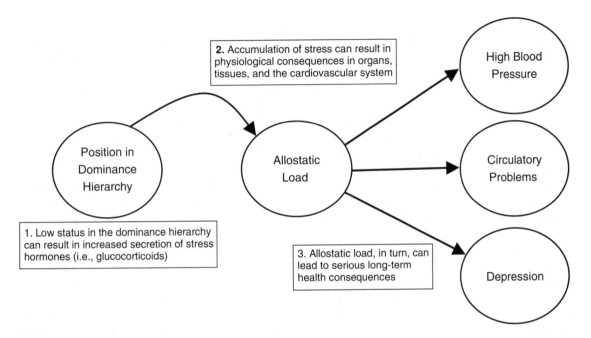

FIGURE 13.2 Sapolsky's Model of the Relationship Between Stress, Allostatic Load, and Negative Health Consequences

acute stress, when it occurs due to chronic stress and physiological mobilization, it begins to wear down the body. Research on humans has shown that this condition, often termed *allostatic load*, has deleterious consequences such as high blood pressure, circulatory problems stemming from platelet aggregation, depression, and fatigue (McEwen, 2000; McEwen & Stellar, 1993; McGowan et al., 2009).

Sapolsky (2005) examined which ranks are most stressful and harmful to health. One way that rank causes harm is through access to resources. Dominant primates, especially males, use aggression to ensure greater access to food and breeding. Sapolsky (2005) points out that they also use aggression to maintain the particular hierarchy. As such, lower rank members are reminded of their position in the hierarchy through psychological and physical intimidation. However, the stress is not always highest on low-ranking members. Sometimes, such as during periods of upheaval in the social hierarchy, the highest ranking primate experiences the greatest

levels of stress. This is because it takes a toll on the body to constantly stay in the top rank via frequent fighting. During stable periods, however, subordinate members typically experience the greatest stress among primates. Coping mechanisms that subordinate members use include grooming and forming coalitions. Another method Sapolsky identified is avoidance, which varies based on the ecological setting of the primate group. Sapolsky believes studies like these shed light on understanding the physical health of humans in different socioeconomic strata. It also seems valuable to examine stress levels and mental functioning in human organizations based on where a worker is in the management structure.

Even though there are some fundamental similarities between primate social organization and human social structure, understanding the roots of human institutions represents a significant leap in complexity. Mathematician H. Peyton Young (2001) has argued that institutions emerge from the strategies of individual decision makers. In the rudimentary form of this process, an individual takes an action based on information of what has happened in the past, which is an expectation. This action becomes a precedent that begins to influence other individual behaviors. If we begin to enlarge the scope of these decisions and behaviors, and a large number of individual actors also base their actions on expectations and precedent, shared norms take shape. Young argues that random events and unpredictable behaviors that are outside the norm represent mutations in this dynamic system. Thus, this process comprises both stable and dynamic elements. In the long run, individual actors do not know the result of their decisions. Therefore, the evolutionary paths of these collective actions are not predictable in any sort of absolute sense, although probabilities can be estimated. Young provides an example from computer technology within a given social network:

> If most people own IBMs it is advantageous to own an IBM; if most people own Macs, it is more desirable to own a Mac. The reason is that the more popular a given model is, the more software will be created for it, and the easier it will be to share programs with others. (p. 13)

Of course, this does not explain why IBMs became more popular in the first place. One explanation that is consistent with Young's theory is that the IBM computers came first and therefore had the precedent advantage from which to influence an exponentially large number of users, and as such has a greater likelihood of achieving an institutionalized sort of effect.

It appears then that institutions and individual behavior are tightly intertwined. Although it can be said that individual behavior and institutional behavior have coevolved over time, each influencing the other, a full understanding of this relationship has yet to be elucidated. Bowles, Choi, and Hopfensitz (2002) draw on simulation research, a form of research that attempts to imitate a real-life scenario over and over again to better understand it, to argue that individuals' behaviors that are costly but that benefit the group are the result of social institutions that act to limit within-group competition and conflict. Because humans have lived in groups for thousands of years, institutions extend the need to advance group interests over and above the individual. Institutions based in customs that increase survival such as resource sharing (e.g., food and technology) are likely to persist for a long time, and the formalization of rules around these customs (e.g., laws against stealing food) increase their power. Bowles et al. argue further that institutions that are successful are replicated and spread, just as individual traits that are successful are passed along both genetically and via social learning.

SPOTLIGHT TOPIC: BUREAUCRACY

In their modern rational incarnation, institutions become bureaucratized. Bureaucracy is a form of social organization characterized by rules and tasks. Notable German social theorist Max Weber (1864–1920) wrote a classic analysis of bureaucracy in which he identified six of its major characteristics in the modern age.

The first of these are laws and regulations. These consist of fixed official duties in a bounded jurisdiction and the administrative authority to carry them out. Bureaucratic authority is present in both governmental (local, state, and federal) and corporate structures, although government is known more for using the term *bureau*. Second, they possess hierarchies. Hierarchies facilitate the top-down movement and execution of rules and commands throughout a given structure. They are universal components of social organization. Bottom-up appeals occur but are carried out via a prescribed set of informal and informal rules. Third, written documents are a major feature of bureaucracies. These documents contain the codified aspect of rules and regulations. Fourth, specialized training and development of a specific expertise is explicitly assumed throughout the organization. Fifth, full commitment of time is demanded of officials in bureaucracies. Sixth, stable rules predominate, and learning these rules is itself a specialized task, particularly in large, complex bureaucracies.

Weber pointed out that officials in bureaucracies achieve higher social esteem or status when there is also an associated expertise that is in demand in a given society, and when the officials came from upper socioeconomic means. The relative status of an official is lessened in societies where demand for experts is low and organizations and institutions are new and have not been firmly established by the force of habit. Weber also pointed out that bureaucracies, due to the highly rationalized functions of rules and regulations, which are designed to increase efficiency, become an "iron cage" that is rigid, overly formalized, and lack the agility to adapt. This has resulted in the negative connotation often associated with the term *bureaucracy*. As such, the irony of bureaucracies is that they often become the very problem they were designed to address.

People in the helping professions will be affected by various components of bureaucracy, and having a fuller understanding of their characteristics can help not only to identify areas where its harmful consequences can be lessened, but also to appreciate their wider context that can impinge on their work.

For Reflection

Think of the schools that you are attending now or have attended in the past, and attempt to identify the bureaucratic processes that helped and hindered student development and learning. Which rules and regulations were helpful and which ones were harmful?

PROXIMAL MECHANISMS

Hierarchies

Much like those of other primates, human social structure is hierarchical. However, the hierarchy can range from simple to complex, depending on the size of the structure. It is hard to imagine an institution or social structure of any kind that doesn't have a hierarchy. After all, doesn't someone need to take the lead when there are groups of people with tasks that need to be accomplished? Hierarchies do lend themselves to power differentials among individuals and groups based on political and economic resources. Thus, one outcome of hierarchies in complex societies is social stratification based on status and resources, which often go hand in hand.

Social Stratification

Ever since the agrarian revolution, which allowed human groups to settle and store food surpluses, which in turn facilitated population growth and the rise of bureaucracy, human societies became stratified to varying degrees based on material goods (including property and ownership of technologies), currency (i.e., money), and status. The value of goods, currency, and status became more and more meaningful as humans groups grew to include larger levels of social organization. The distribution and access to goods and currency is less even in larger social units, and differences between individuals can become more pronounced. Differences in clusters of individuals based on goods and currency have direct effects on status and rank. Such differentiation creates long-standing differences, resulting in classes of persons in a process known as *social stratification*. According to esteemed archaeologist Colin Renfrew (2007), the end of prehistory and beginning of modern world history began as money, first documented in Turkey over 2,000 years ago, began to flourish as the primary standardized method of exchange. Renfrew argues that money (at least in its paper form) has little value in itself, but instead represents value reflected in material goods or labor. As such, the symbol provides a potent source of status and prestige because of its ability to obtain and control important goods and services.

It is often common for people to purchase more than what they can afford and to display these possessions, something Thorstein Veblen (1857–1929) termed *conspicuous consumption* in his classic work, *The Theory of the Leisure Class* (1899/1934). According to Veblen, individuals emulate the upper or leisure classes because of an innate need to feel superior to others. Taking a long-term view, anthropologist Marvin Harris (1989) has argued that prestige and status were important rewards for leaders and "headmen" of early chiefdoms and states, and provided them symbols of power to maintain order and have the influence necessary to improve well-being of the culture. However, as it turns out, Veblen's leisure class was not universal, as research among hunter-gatherers indicates that they often spend less time satisfying basic needs and, overall, work less than contemporary Westerners (Harris, 1989). Prestige and power do seem to involve, in symbolic form, displays of wealth that provides evidence of superiority. It's not surprising that people in stratified societies would perhaps want to emulate upper classes by purchasing and displaying symbols of wealth that are associated with greater rank and status.

Research on the effects of economic inequality and individual status suggests that in countries where there is greater economic inequality (e.g., the United States), individuals tend to engage in behavior that is meant to increase how they see themselves compared to the average person. This tendency to view oneself as superior is known by psychologists as *self-perception enhancement* (Loughnan et al., 2011). In countries with greater economic equality (e.g., Japan), self-perception enhancement thinking is less common. In a unique study spanning five continents and 15 nations, Loughnan et al. surveyed 1,625 young-adult university students, asking them how much of a given trait they possessed compared to the average student. Data from these surveys were then compared with data about each nation's level of individualism, collectivism, and views of hierarchy. Results indicated that across all 15 nations, individuals believed they possessed more desirable traits than the average person. Consistent with the theory, however, the effect varied by level of national economic equality; people in nations with greater economic inequality demonstrating more self-perception enhancement responses. These effects were more powerful than the effect of individualism and collectivism levels.

Although income inequality exists even in socialist nations, the key question is whether and to what extent income inequality affects the happiness and well-being of individuals. In an important study that attempted to intersect the fields of economics and psychology, Oishi, Kesibir, and Diener (2011) examined the relationship between income inequality and happiness in the United States from 1972 to 2008 using national survey data from over 50,000 respondents. Results from this study showed that Americans were happier when income inequality was less; as income inequality increased in the United States, average levels of happiness decreased. However, the relationship between income inequality and happiness operated through or was explained by perceived fairness and trust. In other words, when income inequality increases, people tend to trust each other a little less but also perceive that there is less fairness. This in turn works to decrease general happiness. One of the major limitations of this study, as the authors point out, is that happiness, trust, and perceived fairness were each measured by only a single question, which raises questions over the validity of the study's findings. Future studies of this interesting topic should therefore attempt to measure these factors in greater detail. Although it is easy to conclude from this study that if we want to increase happiness, we should develop policies that reduce income inequality, it can also be concluded that advocating for policies that increase trust and fairness among citizens would more directly increase happiness.

Economic stratification based on income and status results in what is known as *social class*. Social class is an institution in that it is fairly stable over time and has powerful regulating effects. Researchers and social workers often use the term *socioeconomic status* (SES) to denote the conjoint effects of status and income (see Table 13.1). Another aspect of social class that goes beyond income (which is usually measured in the form of an annual salary) is assets. Property, for example, is not counted as annual income but is an important asset that often contributes to one's status. Gold, jewelry, and savings bonds are other assets that are items of value that can be used to enhance well-being and buffer risks associated with salary fluctuations and life events such as losing one's job. Therefore, wealth is not merely a reflection of one's income but also of one's assets.

In terms of social status there are two major forms, *ascribed* and *achieved*. *Ascribed status* is assigned based on some characteristic or set of attributes over which an individual has no control. Some examples of ascribed status are race/ethnicity, gender, physical attractiveness, developmental disability, and residence. In contrast to ascribed status, *achieved status* is based on an individual's actions. Achieved status can be viewed positively or negatively. For example, being a physician is generally viewed as higher status than being a custodial worker or administrative assistant, and much higher than being a burglar or other felon. Status facilitates how one is viewed and, not surprisingly, greater options in life tend to be open to persons who have more of it. Stigma is often attached to the various statuses, which works to unfairly decrease social acceptance of these individuals and often their own self-worth. Some nations ascribe greater weight to one's position in the social strata and in many contexts these can become fixed.

The Caste System in India

In America, most people value the idea of equality and individual freedoms. Although there is a class system in place in this country, we like to pride ourselves on the idea of the American Dream: the concept that, regardless of a person's background, anyone in this country can improve their social status by taking advantage of our capitalist economic system. Despite issues such as institutional racism and gender bias, many Americans and citizens of other countries still believe in this concept and do not view America as a country with a fixed hierarchy.

Table 13.1   Thompson and Hickey Model of Social Class Characteristics in the United States

Upper class (1%)	Top-level executives, celebrities, heirs; income of $500,000+ common.
Upper middle class (15%)	Highly educated (often with graduate degrees) professionals and managers with household incomes varying from the high five-figure range to commonly above $100,000.
Lower middle class (32%)	Semiprofessionals and craftsmen with some work autonomy; typically some college education.
Working class (32%)	Clerical, pink-, and blue-collar workers, often with low job security; common household incomes below $30,000. High school education.
Lower class (14%–20%)	Those who occupy poorly paid positions or rely on government transfers. Some high school education.

Source: Adapted from *Society in Focus*, by W. Thompson & J. Hickey, 2005, Boston, MA: Pearson, Allyn & Bacon.

In some parts of the world and within some communities, however, there are social class systems that are clearly defined and, for the most part, permanent. Within the ecclesiastical structures of the Roman Catholic Church, for example, there is a very clear and strict hierarchy that trumps notions of equality. Although female members of religious communities (nuns) and laypeople of both sexes have important roles to play within the Church community, only male priests can carry out particular sacred rituals and serve in high-ranking leadership roles.

One of the most blatant and well-known instances of social hierarchy is India's caste system, a system of social stratification that has existed for over 1,000 years. Having its roots in the Hindu faith, the caste system divides each person in Indian society into a particular caste along the spectrum of a social ladder. On the top rung of the ladder are the *brahmins*, and at the bottom are the *dalit*, known internationally as the "untouchables." Despite modern attempts to eliminate the caste system, this bottom class historically has been treated as subhuman, segregated from the rest of the population, abused, and prevented from ever moving out of their social position.

Within this caste system, people are born into the social class they will belong to for the rest of their lives. It is believed that the class you are born into is a result of the karma you accrued in your last life. If you accrued good karma in your past life, you were born into a higher caste, and vice versa. Moving out of your caste historically has not been an option. You are in the class you are in as a result of your karma, and all you can do is try to accrue better karma in this life and hope for a better slot in the next one.

The modern Indian constitution makes the caste system illegal. However, the social structure the system has established is still reflected in modern Indian society. Much like the experience of Blacks in our own country, it will likely be a long, hard struggle for the untouchables and India's other lower classes to create a more equitable and accepting society.

Energy Regulation

Every society that has ever existed has had to extract energy from the environment to meet its basic survival needs. As delineated in previous chapters, the intersection of technology, physical environment, and population is a major engine in driving societal change, and energy in various forms is the fuel. Humans use social institutions and organizations to govern and regulate energy development and distribution. This is no small task as humans' global energy use is increasing as population increases. Large sums of capital surround energy regulation and control of resources, and to a large extent energy production is closely aligned with political and military goals such as protection of oil reserves in the Middle East. In this way energy regulation involves nongovernmental, profit-making corporations and government agencies (e.g., the U.S. Department of Energy). Profit is the primary goal of energy corporations, and this is why using traditional energy sources such as oil and coal are good for the energy business. However, governmental energy regulation seeks to protect workers and the environment from excessive corporate intrusion and human error driven by the pursuit of capital. The relationship between corporations and governments regarding energy is complex because corporations employ

Table 13.2 Examples of Energy Sources and Industries Reliant Upon Government Energy Regulation

Solar and wind technologies	Road transportation
Food manufacturing	Trail transportation
Textile manufacturing	Water transportation
Chemical manufacturing	Air transportation
Metals manufacturing	Rail transportation
Machinery manufacturing	Fossil fuel reserves
Lumber manufacturing	Crude oil
Electrical manufacturing	Coal
Crop production	Natural gas
Farmlands	Livestock production
Geothermal heat	Mineral resources
Hydroelectric power	

and provide a livelihood for a large number of individuals and their families. Although the corporate-government relationship is complex, government corruption among policy makers or agency officials in both developing and wealthier Western nations weakens local oversight of energy projects and results in costly environmental degradation and loss of confidence in government (e.g., Fredriksson, Neumayer, Damania, & Gates, 2005; Fredriksson & Svensson, 2003; Goel & Nelson, 2010; López & Mitra, 2000; Shleifer & Vishny, 1993). The push for alternative energy sources that are less environmentally harmful (i.e., green technologies) is a growth industry and represents an important evolved adaption at the societal level. Table 13.2 displays the range of energy sources and domains reliant upon energy policy such as transportation and manufacturing.

Two of the key questions that energy institutions must confront in carrying out various projects are (a) has the project considered the leadership structures that will administer key aspects of energy goals, and (b) has the project considered regulatory procedures (e.g., laws), both governmental and nongovernmental?

EXAMPLE: CONFLICT AND ENERGY

SPOTLIGHT TOPIC: ENERGY SHARING

In the Israeli–Palestinian conflict, one of the major areas of tension is the sharing of energy. In such a small, largely arid space, there is a constant struggle over resources (mainly water) that are limited and must be shared across a large population. On a hill in the West Bank, there is a Palestinian-owned plot of land, surrounded by Israeli settlements on the adjacent hills. As hills are strategically important places for Israelis to build settlements in the West Bank, the Israelis were eager to obtain this land from its Palestinian owners. These owners, however, were not so readily willing to give up this land, and a conflict quickly arose.

Unlike most Palestinian landowners, the owners of this property had registered the land and had papers supporting their ownership of it. The conflict was brought to the court system where, 10 years later, it is still being fought. One of the tactics used by the Israelis to attempt to force the Palestinians off of the property was to cut off their electricity and water supply. The Palestinian owners, after applying for grant funding from a German NGO, managed to make the entire plot, which includes several structures, solar powered. They also began using wells that had been drilled prior to the existence of running-water systems. The Palestinian owners now pride themselves on not only being able to find a solution to their problems—and, therefore, being able to continue fighting for their land—but also on their complete reliance on solar energy, and they see themselves as a model for other communities to use this healthy energy alternative. To learn more about this Palestinian property, which has formed into an education and awareness NGO, please visit http://www.tentofnations.org.

Law and Social Control

Another major institution is law and its social control functions. This includes crime and the criminal justice system, which involves the behavior of individuals who encounter the system (clients, defendants, probationers, inmates, prisoners, parolees, and offenders), law enforcement, courts, and the juvenile and adult correctional system. In its simplest form, crime is a behavior that violates a law. Although some behaviors can be socially abnormal or annoying, if there is no law that designates them a crime, then the behavior (assuming it is detected) does not enter the institutions of law and social control.

There has been a tremendous increase in incarceration over the last several decades. For example, the number of individuals incarcerated in state and federal prisons increased from approximately 300,000 in 1980 to more than 1.5 million in 2008 (James & Glaze, 2006). Similar trends have been observed in the juvenile justice system as more youth become involved in it. These increases have naturally caused justice system budgets and expenditures to also increase. One consequence that the helping professions must confront is that the number of individuals reentering society from prisons and jails has risen. It is estimated that more than 740,000 individuals reenter society each year from state or federal prisons (Sabol, West, & Cooper, 2009). According to the U.S. Bureau of Justice Statistics and a number of studies, reincarceration rates among these offenders are often over 50% and approximately two thirds are rearrested (Langan & Levin, 2002), with recidivism rates being highest for young offenders (Krisberg & Howell, 1998; Mears & Travis, 2004). Studies have found that many offenders face a greater multitude of adjustment problems (Dembo & Schmeidler, 2003; Petersilia, 2003), including lack of education and a history of sexual and physical abuse and neglect (Cuomo, Sarachiapione, Massimo, Mancini, & Roy, 2008; Dembo, Schmeidler, Nini-gough, & Manning, 1998) and high levels of mental health and substance abuse problems (James & Glaze, 2006; Mumola & Karberg, 2006).

Like people in other institutions, those in the juvenile justice system make a substantial number of decisions when processing cases. Vaughn, Pettus-Davis, and Shook (2012) have described and provided an overview of the process for youth who encounter the juvenile justice system. The point of contact is usually the arrest of the juvenile, although young people can also be referred to the court by other actors, either for status offenses (e.g., truancy or incorrigibility) or serious offenses such as assault or property theft. Although states differ with regard to how offenses are handled, once an arrest is made and a youth is referred to the court, a decision needs to be made about whether to divert the case out of the system or file a formal charge in the juvenile court. A variety of actors can be involved in this decision, including law enforcement (e.g., police and prosecutors), intake officers, victims, and the youth and their parents. Typically, a number of criteria, such as the number of prior contacts with the juvenile justice system and offense history, are considered in the decision-making process.

If the decision is made to proceed with filing a charge, a youth may be held in a secure detention facility. This is usually determined by a hearing in which a juvenile court judge deems the detention to be in the best interest of the community. The majority of charges are filed in the juvenile court, but some states can choose to charge a youth in the adult criminal court if the offense is deemed serious enough. Some states allow the prosecutor to make this determination. In this situation, states employ a judicial waiver mechanism, in which the prosecutor files a motion for transfer and a judge makes a determination. In juvenile court, the state must prove beyond a reasonable doubt that the youth committed the offense. Many cases are handled through a plea agreement, others are dismissed by a juvenile court judge for lack of evidence, and still others are handled informally, where a youth agrees to specific sanctions in lieu of a formal charge. If a juvenile is adjudicated as delinquent, a disposition hearing is held and the judge decides whether to order probation or send the juvenile to a residential treatment (public or private) facility, where schooling continues but the youth are in a secured environment. These decisions can be multidimensional, involving combinations of probation, weekend confinement, drug abuse counseling, and restitution to the victim. Clearly in this process, many of the rules and regulations and much of the hierarchy of bureaucracy are at work.

JUVENILE JUSTICE THROUGH SUPREME COURT DECISIONS

In two rulings the Supreme Court made sweeping changes to the juvenile justice system, intended to protect minors from some of the punishments adults are eligible to receive and to recognize the developmental differences between minors and adults. The first is *Roper v. Simmons*, a 2005 case in which Christopher Simmons, who participated in the brutal murder of a woman in her 50s when he was 17 years old, asked the court to reverse his death penalty sentence. The case made its way to the Supreme Court, where the decision was made that anyone under the age of 18 cannot receive the death penalty (prior to the case, the age was 16).

The second ruling is *Graham v. Florida*, a 2010 case that made it unconstitutional to sentence a minor to a sentence of life without the chance of parole for nonhomicide offenses. Both of these cases reflect the values of social work, which recognize that minors are developmentally different than adults and therefore should be treated differently. It also reflects a belief that minors are more amendable than adults—they can more easily be rehabilitated and grow into adults who do not commit these types of crimes. Of course, this is a hotly debated subject; there are many different opinions about what type of punishment minors should receive for their crimes and what, exactly, the definition of justice means when applied to minors.

Leadership

There is little doubt that leaders make a difference, but do large organizations and structures reflect their chief executive? Does it matter what the leader's characteristics are for achieving organizational outcomes? These are questions that affect not only major institutions but also smaller human service agencies, where many social workers are employed. In a study designed to assess the connections between CEOs and organizational outcomes, Berson, Oreg, and Dvir (2008) collected data from 26 CEOs, 71 company vice presidents, and 185 organizational members. These researchers hypothesized that CEOs' values (self-directedness, security, and benevolence) would impact organizational culture and in turn would be associated with tangible outcomes such as efficiency, bureaucratic functioning, and satisfaction. Study results yielded three major findings: (a) Self-directedness was positively associated with innovation, which in turn was associated with increased sales; (b) security was associated with bureaucratic functioning, which in turn was positively associated with efficiency; and (c) benevolence was associated with support, which in turn was positively associated with increased satisfaction. These results suggest that, at least in the case of private-sector organizations, organizational leadership is reflected in organizational culture and outcomes.

Long ago, Max Weber (1922/1968) argued that leaders were effective if they had legitimate authority. What this means is that people must believe in their leader, in their skills, talents, and power. If people do not believe in the legitimate authority of a given leader, then they may need to be coerced to act. Coercion is costly to maintain. It is far better for people to buy into and believe in the authority of a leader, as then they will be more likely to work and act in accord with leadership goals. Weber identified three types of authority: (a) *charismatic authority*, defined by special (even supernatural) qualities; (b) *traditional authority*, characterized by the past, stability, and the force of tradition; and (c) *rational legal authority*, exemplified by procedural and regulatory correctness and order. According to Weber, charismatic authority was the only form of leadership that could result in major changes in society. Persons such as Gandhi and Martin Luther King were charismatic leaders. However, charismatic leaders can also be evil despots such as Adolf Hitler.

IMPACT OF ECONOMIC INSTITUTIONS ON HUMAN BEHAVIOR

In many ways economic institutions are the backbone of contemporary societies. Although the economic system might seem complex and confusing, the actions of economic institutions trickle down through society to influence human behavior. Economic institutions, and their role in human behavior, are best understood in the context of specific examples. In the United States, major economic institutions include the Federal Reserve (the Fed), the Internal Revenue Service (IRS), and the Federal Deposit Insurance Corporation (FDIC). Economic institutions affecting the international economic system include the International Monetary Fund (IMF) and the World Trade Organization (WTO).

The *Federal Reserve* serves as the central bank of the United States and includes its headquarters in Washington, D.C., and 12 regional banks throughout the country. The primary function of the Fed is "to oversee the banking system and regulate the quantity of money in the economy" (Mankiw, 2007, p. 464), but how does either function impact human behavior? First, the Fed cares for the health of the banking system and affixes regulations on banks to ensure proper functioning. One basic regulation that the Fed imposes is reserve requirements, which are "regulations on the minimum amount of reserves that banks must hold against deposits" (Mankiw, 2007, p. 470). For example, if Gina puts $100,000 in a savings account at the Bank of St. Louis, that bank can then use Gina's money to make a loan for Juan to buy a house. If the Fed has a minimum reserve requirement of 10%, then 10% of the value of Gina's account, or $10,000, cannot be made available for the loan. This requirement limits the amount of money that banks can lend, which in turn limits the amount of money that Juan can spend on a house. If the Fed were to require banks to hold only

5% of deposited funds, then Juan can receive an additional $5,000 to spend on his house.

Additionally, the Fed determines the amount of money that is available in the economy. If the Fed adds currency into the economy, more money will be in circulation and inflation will increase. Inflation is the commonly used term to describe a situation in the economy when there is an overall increase in prices. When prices increase, goods and services tend to become more expensive, which in turn reduces the demand for those goods and services. The buying power of consumers will also decrease if inflation rises too much. For example, if prices rise by 5% in 2011, but Melissa's salary only increases by 1%, she will be unable to buy as many goods as she bought in 2010. Melissa's spending patterns will be forced to change if she does not want to end up in debt.

Furthermore, the Fed dictates the federal funds rate, which is the rate that banks charge to borrow money from one another. If the Fed decreases the federal funds rate, interest rates as a whole will decrease. The Fed lowers interest rates, which jump-starts economic growth by decreasing the cost of borrowing. In an economy of low interest rates, consumers are enticed to make large purchases, such as a house or car, because the cost to repay money borrowed for these purchases is less expensive. Although the work of the Fed occurs behind closed doors in Washington, D.C., its actions have indirect impact on the decisions and behaviors of consumers.

Another economic institution that affects human behavior is the *Internal Revenue Service*, a government agency historically feared by many citizens who associate it with making them pay taxes. Although it does have this function, various tax credits that the IRS offers—including the retirement savings credit for funding Individual Retirement Accounts (IRAs), the child care credit, and the tax credit for first-time home buyers—influence behavior in myriad ways. For example, the retirement savings credit may motivate someone to invest additional money in an

IRA; the child care credit may influence one's decision as to whether child care is affordable; and the home-buyers' credit may influence the decision to buy a house. Tax credits enforced by the IRS also influence the behavior of businesses, which has an indirect impact on human behavior. Credits such as the Low Income Housing Tax Credit (LIHTC) and the Work Opportunity Tax Credit (WOTC) facilitate tax breaks for housing developers that build affordable housing units aimed toward low-income households. Along with increasing housing options for such households, the LIHTC has also been found to decrease crime in low-income areas (Freedman & Owens, 2011). The WOTC provides subsidies to businesses for hiring individuals from various groups who have consistently faced significant barriers to obtaining gainful employment (United States Department of Labor, 2011). Preliminary research has found increased employment opportunities in the short run for individuals within the target groups, along with a 9% increase in wages (Hamersma, 2008). Increased wages facilitate saving and satisfaction of basic needs under less economic stress.

The third major economic institution impacting human behavior is the *Federal Deposit Insurance Corporation*, which was created to stabilize and build the confidence of the people in the financial sector (Federal Deposit Insurance Corporation, 2009). The function of the FDIC most familiar to people is insuring bank deposits of up to $250,000. The FDIC was created during the Great Depression, when a lack of confidence in the banking system was widespread and bank runs (people pulling their money out in a panic) were rampant. With the FDIC insurance in place, deposit holders knew that their savings would not be lost. This insurance has made bank runs unheard of in the United States today and provides deposit holders with an additional incentive to keep their funds in the banking system. Banks lend these increased funds out to others, which facilitates investment in the economic system.

Since the FDIC's inception in 1934, no depositor has lost their money as a result of a bank failure (Federal Deposit Insurance Corporation, 2009).

In addition to these domestic economic institutions, international economic institutions also indirectly impact human behavior through interactions with individual countries. Such institutions include the *International Monetary Fund (IMF)* and the *World Trade Organization (WTO)*. The most observable function of the IMF is its provision of loans to countries in the midst of economic instabilities. Although one may imagine that IMF bailouts only go to developing countries with unstable governments, developed countries have also been recipients of IMF bailouts, specifically Greece and Ireland in recent years. The IMF does not simply hand out money to struggling countries and then let them decide how to use it. Rather, to increase control over its use, the IMF attaches stipulations to the loans and creates plans for the country not only for how to use the funds but also how to manage itself. IMF loans have a domestic austerity program attached to them, forcing the recipient country to cut back on spending and increase taxes in the midst of economic crisis (Stiglitz, 2002). A country can get an IMF bailout in the midst of economic instability when it lacks the free capital necessary to pay its debt. Although the bailout allows the country to pay its bills, increased government spending is also needed to jump-start the economy (e.g., stimulus), but the terms of the bailout do not allow the government to follow this course of action. Instead, government spending will decrease and taxes will increase to make up for the shortfall, further inhibiting economic growth as consumers give more of their money to the government rather than putting it back into the economic system in the form of consuming goods and services. Thus, the population is limited on how they can spend income, and the government services the people receive are also limited. This could include a decrease in unemployment insurance or other social services for which the population might have a greater need during a recession. This state of affairs could affect the general well-being of the populace and perhaps serve as a potent stressor that activates underlying vulnerability to environmental stress.

The WTO concerns itself with rules and regulations of commerce between nations, and its members account for 97% of world trade (World Trade Organization, 2011). Its most visible function is its role as a facilitator in trade negotiations between countries, which include imposing sanctions such as quotas and tariffs that interrupt the natural flow of trade. Quotas dictate how much of a particular good (e.g., oil) can pass a country's borders, with import

quotas limiting the amount that can be brought in from another country and export quotas limiting the amount that can leave the country. Tariffs are taxes placed on an imported good. To eliminate the use of international trade in political interactions, the WTO enforces the Most Favored Nation principle, which simply means that a favor granted to one WTO member extends to all members. For example, if the United States wants to get on good terms with China, they might increase the import quota on Chinese silk so that U.S. consumers can purchase more silk from China than any other country. Under the Most Favored Nation principle, however, the increased amount of silk that U.S. consumers can buy from China must apply to all of the United States's trading partners. The

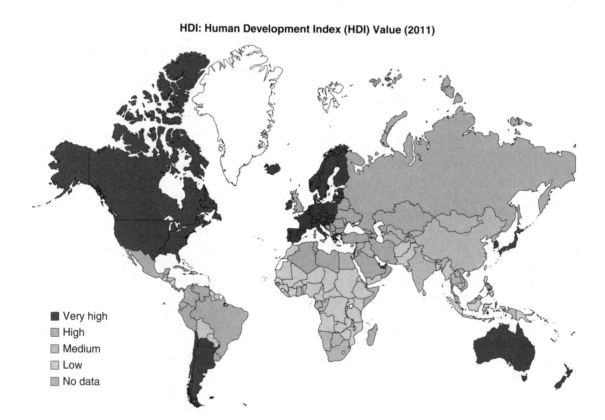

HDI: Human Development Index (HDI) Value (2011)

- Very high
- High
- Medium
- Low
- No data

FIGURE 13.3   Human Development in Global Perspective

Source: United Nations Development Programme, *Human Development Report*, International Human Development Indicators (2011).

principle has helped reduce quotas and tariffs, as countries must match their lowest quotas and tariffs for all trading partners. This directly impacts the spending behavior of consumers, as the price of international goods will decrease and give consumers additional choices between products.

Governments use economic institutions to increase their control. Whether it is in the form of managing the banking system, interest rates, inflation, IRA investment, or employment, the actions of these institutions directly impact people's everyday decisions. As such, they demonstrate how the macro level is built from the behavior of individuals and how macro-level changes (i.e., the broader context) in turn affects individuals' cognitive decision making, mood, and behavior.

Macro-level economic changes can and do impact our biology, for instance via physiological stress fueled by economic downturns (e.g., rapid increases in the price of gasoline or rent) and the added mental burden of surviving and maintaining well-being in the face of change.

As one would expect, development across nations is varied. Many assessments of cross-national development are based merely on economic growth. However, attempts have been made more recently to capture human development within the context of human capabilities and a broader array of indicators. Figure 13.3 displays nations in terms of scores on the Human Development Index (HDI). As can be readily deduced, high development scores are associated with economic activity and wealth.

EXPERT'S CORNER: MICHAEL SHERRADEN, BENJAMIN E. YOUNGDAHL PROFESSOR OF SOCIAL DEVELOPMENT, WASHINGTON UNIVERSITY IN ST. LOUIS

Michael Sherraden is the founder and director of the Center for Social Development at the George Warren Brown School of Social Work, Washington University in St Louis. Sherraden has garnered tremendous attention for his work on asset development. In his seminal book, *Assets and the Poor: A New American Welfare Policy* (1991), Sherraden makes the case for a shift to Individual Development Accounts (IDAs), which are matched savings by federal or state governments to enable low-income families to save and accumulate assets. Withdrawals of IDA deposits would be matched if they are used for such things as home ownership, postsecondary education, or some sort of microenter-prise. IDAs place emphasis on savings as a social policy for helping poor families. Because poor people often do not have pension plans or are unable to participate to any significant degree in 401(k) or similar plans, IDAs can fill this gap. People on the left and the right of the political spectrum have both supported this approach.

Sherraden has been successful in gaining widespread support for IDAs. For example, IDAs have been adopted in federal legislation in more than 40 states and in many other countries. One IDA program in Seoul, South Korea, "Hope Development Accounts," received a United Nations Public Service Award in 2010. His current research includes an experimental test of IDAs for children at birth in Oklahoma, and a study of savings among youth in Colombia, Ghana, Kenya, and Nepal. Sherraden was listed on *Time* magazine's 100 most influential people in the world for 2010.

(Continued)

Photo of Michael Sherraden
Kevin Lowder, WUSTL Photos

Persons with IDAs report that they feel more hopeful about the future and more in control of their lives. Of course, this is true of people who save in general. The goal of the IDA movement is to have them become institutionalized. Sherraden and colleagues have been committed to careful empirical evaluations of IDA experiments. Overall, results suggest that poor people can save just like everyone else. However, savings performance is not the same for all persons with IDAs. Some do not save, whereas others save more than expected. Ongoing research is attempting to identify some of the moderators and mediators of savings performance and the long-term effects of accumulated assets over the life course. Regardless of the empirical outcomes, it can be argued that IDAs should be implemented from the standpoint of fairness and opportunity.

INSTITUTIONS OVER THE LIFE COURSE

Several major institutional sectors such as economic (via poverty), political (e.g., the military), and educational affect us in direct and indirect ways over the life course. Educational institutions are unique in that they are a powerful source of socialization. Children become part of this institution early on and have substantial and sustained contact over important periods of the life course. The relationships between these major sectors and the life course are highlighted next. Keep in mind that the causal relationships between institutions and periods of the life course have not been fully elucidated. More research into the biosocial relationships underlying the associations between institutions and key life-course outcomes is needed.

Fetal Environment and Infancy

Poverty, defined as a lack of income that interrupts the ability to meet basic needs, has been found to be associated with low birth weight, greater exposure to lead poisoning, general poor health, mortality, and hospitalizations (see Brooks-Gunn & Duncan, 1997). Other effects have also been documented, including developmental delay and learning disabilities, with both twice as likely to occur among poor children. More recent research by Naiman et al.

(2009), using a large sample of Australian families, has shown that both chronic and episodic poverty reduces levels of cognitive development, and that children who were in poverty from birth to 14 years have even worse cognitive delays.

Unsurprisingly, poverty is closely linked with education. Mothers with lower levels of education have a more difficult time with infant care for a number of reasons, including lack of resources and reduced ability to solve problems (e.g., Ross & Murowsky, 1989). A landmark and unprecedented study, the National Children's Study, is underway that will recruit pregnant women and study the multidimensional aspects of life-course development from womb through childhood in numerous study sites. It ultimately will involve over 100,000 children across the United States in order to fully understand the role of socioeconomic, environmental, medical, biological, and psychological factors in development (The National Children's Study, Eunice Kennedy Shriver National Institute of Child Health and Human Development).

Childhood and Adolescence

In a study reviewing the findings from major longitudinal studies, Brooks-Gunn and Duncan (1997) found that a host of outcomes for children and adolescents are associated with poverty. Lack of achievement in school (i.e., grade repetition, dropping out, suspension) is more likely among children and adolescents residing in poverty. Poor children are also much more likely to experience hunger. Female teenagers who experience poverty are three times more likely to have children without being married. Perhaps most surprising, nearly 50% of all children have resided in a household that received food stamps at some moment in time (Rank & Hirschl, 2009).

Household income and assets facilitate greater access by children and adolescents either to schools and educational opportunities that are perceived to be of a higher quality or, at least, to contact with a social network that enhances future earnings. For example, wealthier families can send their children to college preparatory schools and summer experiences (e.g., science camps) that increase their odds of later success. Wealthier households benefit from residing in areas where other people have similar opportunities and expectations about education and economic success. Conversely, children and adolescents living in poverty may only experience lower expectations in their surroundings.

Another important influence across the life course comes from the military, which affects several million families in the United States alone (ICF International, n.d.). Children from military families experience tremendous upheaval stemming from frequent moves and the sudden deployment of a parent. Chandra and colleagues (2010) found that youth in military families experienced greater emotional problems such as anxiety than those in more nationally representative samples. Girls and older youth reported significantly greater peer, school, and family difficulties as well. Findings also showed that longer deployment times resulted in higher levels of reported difficulties. In another study of 169 families that assessed internalizing (e.g., depression) and externalizing (e.g., aggression) in children with a deployed parent compared to children without a deployed parent, Chartrand, Frank, White, and Shope (2008) found that children of deployed parents had significantly higher mean levels of externalizing behaviors. In the same study, spouses of deployed service personnel

reported significantly greater depression. Some children respond differently to deployment, and those who adapt in a positive manner are thought to be resilient and less vulnerable to family disruption. Research on the effects of deployment on military families is relatively new, and future studies will need to be conducted to determine what specific interventions or types of aid can help children and adolescents during these times of rapid change.

Adulthood

Adults who were poor as children have been found to be 90% more likely to be unemployed in early adulthood (Brooks-Gunn & Duncan, 1997). Adults living in poverty are also at heightened risk for domestic violence and are more likely to report a fear of going outside the home at night. In general, family income has substantial yet selective effects. For example, the effects can be stronger for life outcomes related to achievement rather than emotional development. It also appears that the timing of poverty is important, with stronger effects found for children who have experienced poverty during preschool years versus adolescence. Turrell, Lynch, Leite, Raghunathan, and Kaplan (2007) studied the effect of socioeconomic conditions over the life course in a sample of over 6,000 people age 17 to 94, and found that by middle and older adulthood, mortality and functional limitations such as difficulty in lifting, kneeling, crouching, and stooping were associated with cumulative socioeconomic burden experienced in childhood. Additional testing on cumulative socioeconomic burden and disadvantage indicates that education is related to behavioral risk, which in turn increases health risk (Dupre, 2008). Although some mechanisms have been suggested, such as resilience and coping, what these and other studies often are unable to reveal is the precise links that connect socioeconomic conditions to these outcomes.

As with children, military service can impact adult family members greatly. Among American combat veterans, PTSD is not an uncommon occurrence. In addition to adjustment problems related to depression and daily functioning, veterans afflicted with PTSD often report marital and parenting problems (Goff, Crow, Reisbig, & Hamilton, 2007; Samper, Taft, King, & King, 2004; Sayers, Farrow, Ross, & Oslin, 2009). Because military service affects the entire family unit, the needs of children and caregivers both need to be assessed in total.

Although institutions impact behavior, it is also true that individuals have an influence on institutions. For example, older people tend to vote at relatively high rates. Leaders in political organizations and institutions are aware of this, particularly as the population as a whole is aging. Older people are more likely to volunteer in community organizations such as hospitals, schools, and charitable organizations. There are many opportunities for individuals to influence economic and political institutions over the life course. Some involve peaceful protests that spark collective movements demanding change, whereas others involve donating time and money to specific causes. Interestingly, very little scientific research has accrued on ways in which individuals can affect institutions. Although advocacy is often a part of what social workers do, not much evidence-based scientific research is available to guide these efforts.

SUMMARY

Institutions use rules and customs to organize and structure human activities. Institutions are powerful largely because they carry the force of tradition. Despite their power, institutions are influenced by their interface with biology, technology, demographic factors, and the physical environment. Importantly, institutions have resulted from greater social complexity and are necessary to solve large-scale problems. Although seemingly abstract, institutions, it must be kept in mind, are composed of individual actors, and they are aggregated from the many behavioral choices that are selected for over time. The key summary points of this chapter are listed hereafter.

- Modern societies have numerous institutions in common, including those involved in education, labor, the economy, energy regulation, criminal justice, physical and mental health, corporations, the military, and religion. These institutions impose constraints on human behavior but also facilitate action, particularly on a large scale.

- Institutions survive for long periods of time. As such, they develop their own cultures of shared meanings and identity, including specific language, to which their members become socialized. Much of the enculturation process involves learning the rules and norms of the institution and the terminology that enables technical functions to be carried out. Institutional change usually involves alterations in rules or functions.

- The evolutionary roots of human institutions can be found in primate social organization. Geared toward optimizing survival, these organizations, just like human institutions, must interact and adapt within a specific ecological habitat. Much of the structure in primate social organization revolves around rank within a dominance hierarchy. Rank-driven features also characterize human institutions.

- Since human groups settled and formed civilizations, the rise of institutions facilitated stratification based on material goods (including property and ownership of technologies), currency (i.e., money), and status. The process of social differentiation tends to create long-standing differences resulting in classes of persons. Status and prestige are associated with these class differences. Often people purchase more than they can afford in order to emulate persons in the upper classes and symbolically demonstrate their superiority.

• Every human society that has existed has needed to extract energy from the environment to meet its basic survival needs. Human beings use institutions to govern and regulate energy extraction and delivery. Large sums of capital and natural resources surround energy use, and to a large extent energy is closely aligned with political and economic institutions, both governmental and corporate.

• The impact of economic institutions on daily life is enormous. In the United States, major economic institutions include the Federal Reserve, the Internal Revenue Service, and the Federal Deposit Insurance Corporation. Economic institutions impacting the international economic system include the International Monetary Fund and the World Trade Organization. These institutions are good examples of how contextual relationships with economic institutions can affect our well-being.

• During the life course, several major institutions, such as the education system and the military, affect our behavior in direct and indirect ways. These institutions are powerful sources of socialization. They can affect our biological, psychological, and social development. Although seemingly a unidirectional effect, individual actors can and do influence changes in these institutions.

KEY TERMS

Achieved status

Allostatic load

Ascribed status

Charismatic authority

Conspicuous consumption

Federal Deposit Insurance Corporation (FDIC)

Federal Reserve

Institution

International Monetary Fund (IMF)

Rational legal authority

Self-perception enhancements

Social stratification

Traditional authority

World Trade Organization

CHAPTER 14

BELIEF SYSTEMS AND IDEOLOGY

Belief systems and *ideology* are universal ways that humans conceptualize their world. Ideology matters because it influences worldviews, shaping individuals' perceptions of human behavior and how best to intervene in positive ways in those behaviors. The ideals that constitute a given ideology are heavily intertwined with belief. One major example is political ideologies, which prescribe a set of ideas about how the world should be viewed and how humans should behave in it. Ideologies are therefore self-justifying. Adherents to a particular political ideology such as *liberalism* or *conservatism* often have strong beliefs regarding these ideals. Ideologies are often abstract, but their believers apply them to everyday events such as how one lives their life and behaves around others. In this way they become codified as rules for living. It is common for those in powerful positions to use ideology to sway the masses and maintain control. This view of ideology is often associated with classical Marxist thought, in which the impact of the dominant ideology of a ruling class leads to a situation of false consciousness: People in the nonruling class adhere to an ideology that is essentially not in their best interests. However, ideologies are distributed widely, and groups across economic strata often adhere to particular ideologies. Ideology is also influenced by technology, the physical environment, institutions, and our biology. As such, ideology and belief systems are associated with the same biosocial constraints as the other major sectors of the cell-to-society perspective. Although ideology and belief systems are learned through socialization and social interactions over the life course, accumulating

evidence indicates that humans are predisposed to believe in particular ways or to select certain ideologies.

This chapter considers the individual and collective commitments to various forms of ideology that weigh heavily on human behavior and social life (see Table 14.1). The origins and expressions of ideologies from a biological, psychological, and social perspective have important short- and long-term effects. Belief systems and ideologies influence how individuals view the world around them and how they view themselves; ultimately, they have the power to shape people's developmental trajectories across the lifespan. Key concepts such as the intersection of culture, belief, and ideology; confirmatory bias; and individual and social change within the context of these ideologies will be explored.

Table 14.1 Examples of Ideological and Symbolic Variables

Art forms (aesthetics)	Electronic media	Class ideologies
Music	Print media	Educational values and ideologies
Sports	Literature	Taboos
Recreational activities		Marketing and advertising
		Magic
Folklore		Religious practice and ideologies
Superstitions		
Myths	Political ideologies	Racial and ethnic ideologies
Rituals	Ethical ideologies	Culture concept

Source: Adapted and expanded from Harris (1979).

CASE STUDY: WESTBORO BAPTIST CHURCH

As will be discussed in this chapter, belonging to a group is a defining characteristic of culture as well as being human. Human beings want to feel socially connected and that they are a part of something. There are many benefits to be gained from being a part of a group, including fulfilling the desire to be part of a group, protection from nature and rival groups, a sense of support and security, and shared common values. The chapter also will discuss the tendency of groups to put their own needs and desires ahead of those of other groups. In our modern society, what happens when a group expresses desires that are so different from the rest of mainstream society that they become incredibly alienated and isolated?

An example of this is the Westboro Baptist Church, a Topeka, Kansas–based congregation of about 100 members, mostly family members of the church's founder, Fred Phelps. This congregation has what many perceive to be a severely conservative, right-wing ideology that specifically targets homosexuals and what they see as America's tolerance for the LGBTQ community and homosexual acts in general. The tactics this group uses to advance its position have made them a national sensation, and landed them in a lawsuit that reached the Supreme Court (which they won). The church uses funerals of soldiers killed in Iraq and Afghanistan as platforms to protest their view of America as a nation of sinners. While families and friends are mourning their loss, members of the church stand nearby, holding signs bearing statements such as, "Thank God for 9/11," "Pray for More Dead Soldiers," "God Hates Fags," "God Hates America," and "Thank God for IEDs" (the type of bombs popular with Iraqi and Afghan insurgents that are largely responsible for these soldiers' deaths).

Most Americans, whether Democrat or Republican, deplore the Westboro Baptist Church's ideology and their actions. One such person was Albert Snyder, a man whose son's funeral the church protested. Snyder sued the church in a case that made its way to the Supreme Court where, as mentioned, the church won the case on First Amendment free-speech grounds. Snyder's argument cited his right to privacy in a time of mourning, but the court did not find that argument to trump the church's right to freedom of speech.

Critical Thinking Questions:

- Do you feel that the Supreme Court's decision was right?

- As part of a modern democratic society, should we be completely open and accepting of all group practices and ideologies, even when they are drastically different from ours? What if they are harmful to the rest of society?

- At what point do we put the needs of the majority group above the desires of a minority group or ideology? Should we ever do that?

DISTAL CONTEXT

Evolution and Symbols

One of the major paths by which ideology becomes expressed is through symbols. Humans use symbols to transmit knowledge about a given culture's ways of doing things. Symbols can range from such things as color to hand gestures to articles of clothing. The key is that symbols are signifiers of something. For example, in American and other cultures, people are taught that seeing the color red while driving from place to place signifies "stop." Thus, there is a shared meaning around symbols that facilitates their sustainability.

The archaeological record from the Upper Paleolithic, a period in prehistory tens of thousands of years ago, suggests that the use of figurative (cave drawings of animals) and non-figurative (shapes) symbols was widespread and an important part of early human culture (Chase & Dibble, 1987). Of course, words themselves are powerful symbols that can be used to express complex ideas. Given the importance of verbal and written communication, it is safe to say that the development of language greatly enhanced the use of symbols (Schepartz, 1993). Complex language development is seen as one of the major areas that are uniquely human (Schepartz, 1993). Little is known about the use of symbols before the Upper Paleolithic period. Early proto-humans may have used symbols to communicate with one another, but the archaeological record is scarce. It seems useful to investigate whether primates such as chimpanzees make use of symbols. Although chimpanzees in captivity appear to be able to learn how to use rudimentary symbols beyond communication gestures, vocalizations, and facial expressions, their symbol use in the wild is very basic, such as using tools for display (Whiten et al., 1999). Overall, humans universally use symbols, and although this usage is very old (i.e., tens of thousands of years), there is scant evidence linking its rise across major periods of prehistory (e.g., Lower to Middle to Upper Paleolithic).

PATRIOTISM AND NATIONALISM

Patriotism, or love for or devotion to one's country, is a major form of ideology. Although there is nothing wrong with being proud of one's country, stronger forms of patriotism inhibit constructive criticism. Identification and affection toward one's country has a positive impact on subjective well-being (Reeskens & Wright, 2011). Being satisfied with the larger context of nation enhances pride and confidence. Just think of the healthy pride people might feel in watching their country's athletes compete in the Olympic Games, or when learning that their country has contributed to a humanitarian crisis. However, extreme devotion manifest as hyper-patriotism can lead to or be used to justify extreme acts such as the Oklahoma City bombing, which killed numerous people. Like many concepts, national pride and patriotism mean different things to different people, and behavior associated with these feelings is diverse. For example, Reeskens and Wright (2011) separated two forms of *nationalism*, civic (pride in nation) and ethnic (pride in racial/ethnic grouping), and found significantly different results for predicting subjective well-being in a large sample of over 40,000 people from 31 countries. Specifically, these researchers found that higher levels of civic nationalism are associated with greater subjective well-being, and higher levels of ethnic nationalism are associated with lower levels of subjective well-being. However, national pride was associated with heightened subjective well-being, even among people reporting high ethnic nationalism. In other words, those who take pride in their nation tend to perceive themselves and the world around them more positively than do individuals whose nationalism is based primarily upon pride in their nation's racial or ethnic identity. Overall, people who reported high levels of civic nationalism were also the happiest. One wonders, though, whether positive people who tend to be happy anyway are also more likely to also have positive views about their nation as well, and thus have high civic nationalism. In other words, civic nationalism would not be the cause, but would be a byproduct of a positive worldview.

One of the more interesting patriotic phenomena is the rally-'round -the-flag effect. Classic examples are the behavior of Americans following the Japanese attack on Pearl Harbor and the attacks of September 11, 2001. Surges in flag buying, support for political leaders (especially the president), and generally nationalistic displays followed these events. These behaviors are a result of threatening situations emanating from outside the nation. At face value, this is consistent with the us-and-them notion that taps group survival instincts. It is also consistent with a theory known as terror-management theory, which posits that self-preservation behavior is the most important driver of human behavior when the threat of destruction is possible (Cohen & Solomon, 2011). According to this theory, the awareness of death in these scenarios is managed by allegiance to cultural worldviews that mitigate thoughts and feelings of terror. In the face of grave danger, people reach out to the ideas that hold them together to cope with the overwhelming fear of the moment. These worldviews often are political and, as we have learned thus far, carry with them specific symbols such as the nation's flag. Another viewpoint, elaborated by Lambert, Schott, and Scherer (2011), asserts that the rally-'round-the-flag effect stems more from an emotion-based anger response than from security and instability. In this framework, nations are just like individuals who come under attack and become angry but in this case the anger is not individual but collective. Lambert et al. suggest in their explanation that positive events, such as national accomplishments like military victories or achievements in the Olympic Games, are less powerful than negative events such as a terrorist attack or even verbal denigration from a rival nation. The reason is simply because the latter examples are more likely to produce a stronger emotional reaction in the form of anger.

One of the major driving symbols of patriotism and nationalism is the flag. There are certainly other symbols that represent national pride, but flags are formal symbols that all nations use. Mainly through the use of color and patterns, flags are designed to embody in some way the identity and culture of the people residing in that nation. But does exposure to a powerful symbol such as a flag really possess the ability to alter thought and behavior in any significant way? Carter, Ferguson, and Hassin (2011) set out to answer this question in a series of experiments. The first experiment tested whether a single exposure would shift people in a politically conservative direction. An online survey was administered to 396 adults who were primed with the American flag. In social science or experimental research, *priming* refers to a process in which exposing individuals to a certain stimulus (the flag) is designed to influence their responses to a subsequent stimulus (survey questions). Results showed that exposure to the flag shifted people to a conservative political behavior by voting for a Republican presidential candidate. The effect was small but statistically significant. Study participants in the flag-priming condition also reported higher levels of warmth toward Republican candidates and greater mistreatment of Republican candidates by the media, compared to reports from the control group.

Carter et al.'s (2011) second experiment replicated findings from the first by demonstrating a shift toward a conservative worldview in the flag-primed group. Overall, people self-identifying as Democrats and Republicans had shifted toward Republicanism in the flag-exposure condition. This effect lasted for the 8-month span of the study. Why the shift toward Republicanism? The authors speculated that, at least in their study samples, people perceived the American flag as having a stronger association with the Republican Party and conservative values in general. The researchers noted that their sample was more Democratic and liberal, and thus exposure to the flag shifted them more toward the center. Also, it should be emphasized that the shift was small in magnitude. Exposure to the flag did not radically alter individuals' views, but it did change them in relatively slight but significant ways. Despite these caveats, this study is important because it speaks to the power of symbols such as flags, inasmuch as it reveals that they have the potential to cause changes in political behavior.

The implications for the helping professions such as social work are that symbols represent powerful sources of identity and, in turn, influence behavior. As noted, the power of political symbols such as the flag or other national icons should not be underestimated. Social workers do well to appreciate and respect the ways that such symbols inform the identities of clients and their communities, but also to be mindful of how such symbols can be used to shape political ideology and behavior. Within clinical practice, therapists and case managers can enhance their practice by listening carefully for the ways that national, cultural, religious, or other symbols contribute to developmental mastery or pathology in the lives of their clients. At the level of community practice, social workers can collaborate with communities to identify symbols that have the power to bring neighbors and local groups together for common goals or projects. Likewise, at the macro level of practice, advocacy efforts can potentially be of benefit by using evocative symbols to arouse support for various social or political causes designed to help vulnerable populations.

For social work and other helping professions, symbols such as the American flag represent powerful sources of identity to some people, and as part of professionals' respect for different views, they should not be underestimated. The preceding discussion also shows that symbols can be used to change political behavior. Thus, advocacy efforts can potentially be of greater benefit by using symbols to arouse support for various causes that help vulnerable populations.

Political Ideology and Cognition

Although there is substantial variation in thought and behavior among major groupings based on dimensions of political ideology, social scientists have noted interesting differences in patterns of cognition among these groups. For example, psychological studies have found that with respect to decision making, conservatives tend to be more structured and determined and possess a lower tolerance for disorder, whereas liberals seem to tolerate complexity and nuance and are more open to novelty (Jost, Glaser, Kruglanski, & Sulloway, 2003). Previous work suggests that these tendencies can be assessed by a general self-regulatory feature of conflict awareness. This refers to how humans gauge strife around them. Jost et al. also found that liberals are more sensitive to response conflict and conservatives are more likely to persist in a habitual response pattern. Amodio, Jost, Master, and Yee (2007) attempted to pin down these political ideological tendencies into specific neurocognitive functioning. These researchers measured political conservatism and liberalism by use of a validated self-report scale ranging from *extremely liberal* (−5) to *extremely conservative* (+5) in a sample of 43 adult participants. The neurocognitive measures used primarily tapped activity in the anterior cingulate cortex, an area of the brain that plays a role in rational cognitive and emotional functioning, by using the Go/No Go task. The Go/No Go task assesses responsiveness to complex and conflicting information and is thus a measure of response control or, more broadly, self-regulation. Specifically, the Go/No Go task engages participants to respond in a habitual pattern in the Go situation, then at some point the No Go stimulus appears, requesting that the response be withheld. Study results showed that the tendency toward liberalism is associated with significantly greater conflict-related neural activity compared to conservatism. As the study authors state, "The association suggests that a more conservative orientation is related to greater persistence in a habitual response pattern, despite signals that this response pattern should change" (p. 1247). Replication of these study findings is needed because the sample size was not drawn from a representative population. Further, it would be interesting to examine whether these findings would hold in samples from other countries. Nevertheless, these preliminary findings point to interesting neurocognitive differences that appear to vary along the political spectrum and, more generally, that suggest ideology may be shaped by factors far more primal than reason or logic.

Interestingly, these personality facets, like personality in general, are moderately heritable (Bouchard, 2004; Bouchard & McGue, 2003), suggesting that people are predisposed to some degree to be a member of a certain political party, or at least to have an orientation to a particular political worldview. This does not mean that a predisposition or neurocognitive test performance automatically leads to a particular ideological commitment such as political liberalism or conservatism. However, studies such as these are important because they deepen popular notions about political ideology affiliation, which have tended to cast causes for ideological orientation into simplistic family and class environment origins. Note also that ideologies serve a unique counterbalancing purpose. For example, political conservatives often seek to preserve traditional ways of doing things and provide a check on too much or overly rapid change. Social workers need to be careful when categorizing people into dichotomies such as liberal or conservative as there is substantial variation within these categories and they are probably best understood as continuums.

RELIGIOUS IDEOLOGY

Religious ideologies are similar to political ideologies in that they prescribe ways for their adherents to view and operate in the world. It has often been stated that religion serves as a moral compass for human beings. Like all ideologies, they are simply to be believed in and not tested in any empirical sense, although religious and political organizations use data from various faiths, such as surveying their membership, to reach important decisions. Religion certainly plays an important role in people's lives all over

the world; thus social workers and other helping professionals need to have a deeper understanding of religious ideology and its impact on human behavior.

In recent decades, practitioners in multiple fields have shown intense interest in religiosity and belief systems. Studies from an evolutionary point of view have suggested that religion is an adaptation and that the forces of natural selection may have "wired" humans to believe and attempt to interact, often by way of prayer and ritual, with supernatural beings (Sanderson, 2008). But why is religion adaptive in an evolutionary sense? Sanderson offers several reasons (see Figure 14.1). The first is that people in ancestral environments had a universal appreciation for shamans, who were spiritual leaders who could lead a given culture or social group in their contact with the supernatural world for the benefit of the group. Second, religion in general has been associated with better health and overall well-being. Third, religion is procreative and, as such, religious people tend to leave behind more offspring than nonreligious people. Fourth, most religions offer people a benevolent god who promises salvation or paradise in an afterlife.

Although religion is a powerful belief system and shaper of worldviews, it also has the function of social identity. The ties that a particular religious system binds on human behavior are strong. For example, most religious communities also have some system of religious education, such as Catholic elementary and high schools for Roman Catholic children. Children from the religious community attend school together, parents are drawn together for a combination of school and religious activities, and social relationships emerge between children and their families. Thus, religious identity forms a strong shared experience. For many people, the social rewards of belonging to a group, more than the religious practices themselves, are the compelling reason for religiosity (Ysseldyk, Matheson, & Anisman, 2010). Additionally, social identity in the form of religious affiliation can be thought

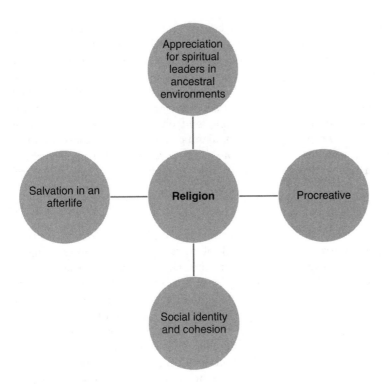

FIGURE 14.1 Adaptive Functions of Religion

of as a way of self-enhancement by distinguishing oneself within a group that is unique or different from other groups, depending on the particular religious sect. The social identity viewpoint of religious membership may be particularly true in contexts such as the United States where religious affiliation is generally high relative to places such as Western Europe. Given the important role of social connectedness and support in predicting well-being, social identity may be one of the reasons why religiosity is associated with greater psychological health (Haslam et al., 2009).

Graham and Haidt (2010) also argue that religiosity is more than just people's beliefs and rituals. According to these scholars, being part of a tightly knit community increases functional attachments to other people and their sense of belonging. Being part of such a community of believers with largely shared ideals, and being happier due to this sense of belonging, also leads to greater charitable giving. This

contrasts with the view that religious people are charitable because it is one of the major principles of their faith. This perspective also matches aforementioned evolutionary theories on the adaptive functionality of religiosity, based on the many positive social benefits that believers accrue.

Despite the positive aspects of religiosity just mentioned (better health and well-being, social connectedness, and greater charitable giving), several research-based findings suggest that religiosity can have a dark side. Because religious groups have such a strong in-group orientation, people outside of the group often are not well tolerated. Thus, intolerance in the form of racial prejudice is one of the major downsides of many religious groups. Hall, Matz, and Wood (2010) conducted a meta-analysis to examined the link between religiosity and racial prejudice. A meta-analysis is a "study of studies" in that it attempts to identify and systematically analyze a group of similar studies in order to determine the net findings of an area of research.) Hall et al. identified 55 published and unpublished studies from 1964 to 2008 with data that allowed them to assess the size of the effect with respect to the association between religiosity and prejudice. Although more recent studies (those after 1986) showed a decline in this association, overall results showed that religiosity was indeed correlated with greater racial prejudice. Interestingly, self-identified agnostics (neither believing nor disbelieving that there is a god) were the only group to be racially tolerant.

The theory behind these findings is that strong religious-group identification works in ways that make nonbelievers members of a so-called out group. Strong in-group identification with respect to nationalism and political ideology also tends to cause members to perceive of outsiders in less positive ways than in-group members. The racial-prejudice connection comes into play because, at least in the United States, religiosity is often practiced within racial and ethnic groups. Therefore, outsiders are often of another racial/ethnic group. Furthermore, other meta-analytic reviews have showed that religiosity is also associated with greater respect for tradition (Saraglou, Delpierre, & Dernelle, 2004). As such, these tendencies suggest that in-group within-race religious ideology predisposes members to view nonmembers, particularly those of other racial and ethnic groups, with some degree of suspicion and prejudice. As with all research studies, this does not mean that all members behave in this manner. Based on this theory, it seems likely that greater racial integration across religious congregations would decrease the level of racial prejudice among religious people in the United States. Social workers will no doubt encounter and work with clients who are moderate or fundamentalist in their religious beliefs and commitments, and who will likely have different views with respect to various out-group religions and associated racial and ethnic groups. Learning to be effective in these encounters is another important facet of cultural competence.

EXPERT'S CORNER: JONATHAN HAIDT

Jonathan Haidt is a social psychologist at the New York University Stern School of Business. He is author of *The Righteous Mind: Why Good People Are Divided by Politics and Religion* (2012), a work that attempts to reveal why conservatives and liberals have a difficult time understanding each other and often think of each other as opponents, or worse, enemies. It is not uncommon for both conservatives and liberals to believe their positions are righteous and often a matter of good versus evil. Under these conditions, the adversarial nature of politics makes accomplishing tasks for the benefit of society quite difficult.

Haidt sheds new light on this phenomenon by viewing conservative and liberal philosophies as a sort of yin and yang, with each ideology needing the other. Haidt sees these views as having arisen under evolutionary conditions. As such, they are formed from complex interactions between the human genome and ancestral environments, which are then molded by culture and socially transmitted. The reason why it is so difficult to understand the "other side" is the strong human propensity to use ideologies and worldview to increase group solidarity and cooperation, which was a necessary part of survival in ancestral environments where humans evolved as a prey species, and which still may be operating today (see Hart & Sussman, 2005).

Photo of Jonathan Haidt
Photo by Daniel Addison

Haidt uses data from several questionnaires that people from all over the world have completed (which can be accessed at http://www.yourmorals.org). One of these assesses six moral foundations and impulses: care/harm, fairness/cheating, loyalty/betrayal, liberty/oppression, authority/subversion, and sanctity/degradation. Sample questions might ask users to consider how relevant something is when deciding whether or not it is right or wrong, such as "whether or not someone showed a lack of respect for authority" or "whether or not someone cared for someone weak or vulnerable." Other questions use a different format (using a scale ranging from *strongly disagree* to *strongly agree*) and ask users to respond to statements such as "It can never be right to kill a human being," "If I were a soldier and disagreed with my commanding officer's orders, I would obey anyway because that is my duty," and "I would call some acts wrong on the grounds that they are unnatural." Results suggest that liberals feel strongly about care/harm and fairness/cheating issues but much less about the others. In contrast, conservatives and most people across the world care about all of these items at roughly equal levels. However, because this is a web-based survey that anyone can fill out, the sample is not necessarily representative of people from around the globe.

Finding ways for humans to overcome our in-group and self-driven decision making—even though it is often functional—to include intergroup cooperation across ideologies is critical for solving current and future problems that will likely cut across borders. Haidt's work is often lauded as a major breakthrough. Although no easy task, a deeper understanding such as the one Haidt provides likely will be useful toward this end.

Religious and Spiritual Evidence-Based Practices

Given that a substantial proportion of the population is religious, it seems important to know whether specific religious and spiritually based interventions are effective. These interventions, though diverse, incorporate general and specific religious values and beliefs into the therapy session. In an extensive and systematic review of studies assessing the efficacy of religious and spiritual interventions for mental health problems, Hook, Worthington, Davis, Jennings, and Gartner (2010) identified several helpful therapies. Two of the more efficacious were Christian accommodative cognitive therapy for depression and 12-step programs for alcohol dependence recovery. (Christian accommodative cognitive therapy is similar to standard cognitive therapy but uses biblical teachings and ideas in guided imagery and restructuring of thoughts.) Importantly, for both treatments, the gains or benefits derived from participation in a particular intervention persisted during follow-up of 3, 6, and even 12 months. Other interventions such as Christian devotional meditation for anxiety were deemed possibly efficacious but more empirical study is needed to confirm helpfulness. In general, religious and spiritual interventions have attained positive results but only in limited testing. Although they demonstrated efficacy, these interventions were not superior to secular and established interventions. Hook et al. conclude that the decision to use these interventions should be based on client preferences and the skill and comfort of the practitioner. What is not clear about religious and spiritual therapies is the mechanism by which they change behavior. Theoretically, the reason why these interventions may be effective is cultural congruence, which means that a stronger match is made between the client's worldview and the treatment. A stronger match, again theoretically, should be linked to higher levels of engagement in the treatment and thus a greater likelihood of success.

Throughout most of its history, the United States has been a predominantly Christian nation. However, one of the fastest growing religious groups in America is Islam, with estimates ranging from 2 to 8 million Muslims (Hodge, 2005). Helping professionals typically have had little exposure to Islamic communities. A key question to ask is whether current treatments are congruent with the Islamic worldview to the extent that they can be helpful? Hodge and Nadir (2008) tackled this question by examining the major principles of psychoanalytic, group, cognitive, and strengths-based approaches vis-à-vis Islamic beliefs. These researchers also attempted to modify existing treatment statements in these approaches for Muslims. Results indicated that psychoanalytic and group-based treatments may not be as congruent or adaptable for Muslims as strengths-based or cognitive therapies. Psychoanalytic psychotherapy is very individualistic, and Muslims tend to be community oriented; and group treatments would need to take place only with other Muslims of the same sex. Although cognitive approaches are individualistic, "I" statements can be modified to include Allah. As Hodge and Nadir show in a straightforward manner, one way for Muslims to express self-control and the change principle could be:

> "*Allah* (God) gave us free will, including the ability to control our *nafs* (self). In addition, Allah has also given us many opportunities to practice self-control through fasting during Ramadan and weekly *sunna* (traditional) fasting on Mondays and Thursdays. These are ways, with the help of Allah, we can enhance our self-discipline and change for the better."

Another example for the principle of accepting responsibility goes as follows: "Although facing difficulties is often challenging, Islam reminds us to persevere through adversity. No one else will bear our burdens for us. Each of us is responsible for our action and the path we choose." As shown here, many traditional therapies, in this case cognitive treatment, can be adapted for use with Muslim populations. This is also likely true for other faith communities as well. Despite the promise of these modifications, there is much heterogeneity within these religions. Not all Muslims are alike, just as not all Christians are the same. Another limitation is that these modifications have not been extensively tested under controlled conditions, and their real-world effectiveness, although promising, still has not been established.

RACE, GENDER, AND CLASS IDEOLOGIES

Given the tendency for humans to be members of groups, and the tendency for groups to place their needs ahead of other groups, it is no surprise that major categories such as race, gender, and class are associated with particular ideologies reflecting the needs and goals of those categories. This does not mean that all of society is involved in intergroup conflict, as large numbers of people are happy to transcend these categories and rise above their own experiences. Further, there is substantial variation within these categories, such that members of one racial group may be more alike than people in other racial groups. In effect, there is often greater ingroup variation than between-group variation. This is because categories such as race and gender in particular are biosocially based and comprise enormous complexity. Although the study of race, gender, and class ideologies is vast, and a comprehensive coverage would require several volumes, it is important to highlight some of the major viewpoints and empirical findings that can shed light on the biosocial nexus of human behavior and the helping professions.

One of the first ideas to understand is that of *intersectionality*. This viewpoint holds that race, gender, and class are not to be considered separately, as these phenomena invariably intersect (see Figure 14.2) and are difficult to study in isolation (Collins, 2000). Oppressive ideologies

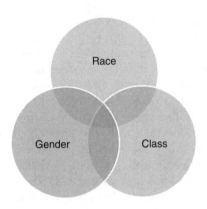

FIGURE 14.2 The Intersectionality of Race, Class, and Gender

that have evolved about race, for example, are modified by input from gender and class. Major institutional components such as legal, political, and economic bureaucracies are likely influenced by particular ideologies (e.g., the wisdom of the free market), which in turn affect specific individuals and their behavioral options through the behavior of the overall institution. However, it should not be overlooked that larger aggregates such as institutions are composed of individuals.

Race- and gender-based ideological orientations certainly vary in their intensity, ranging from overt hatred and subjugation to nationalist agendas based in these orientations. Some nationalist agendas, which often arise in the context of oppression, create antagonism toward other groups even though their primary intent is to uplift a given group. For example, Davis and Brown (2002) studied research participants who endorsed a Black Nationalist ideology and found that adherents tended to have a "greater disaffection toward Whites, but not toward gays, black conservatives, lesbians, middle-class blacks, or feminists" (p. 239). Extreme ideological positions are more closely linked to fanaticism; for example, the Aryan ideological theories of Adolf Hitler and the Nazis. Both superiority and threat are common ingredients in extreme ideologies. In the case of extreme ideologies,

superiority refers to the belief that one's group is morally, intellectually, or biologically superior to another group or to all others. *Threat* refers to the identification of a particular enemy or ideology that is perceived as having the capacity to undermine one's ideology or well-being. However, many race, gender, and class ideologies elevate one group over others. If one group holds a major advantage in social and economic power, it may implement an extreme ideology with oppressive results. Both multiculturalist and assimilationist ideologies attempt to surmount this limitation.

One of the major questions that confronts helping professionals is whether we should recognize differences across racial, gender, and class categories or transcend these categories and opt for a transcendent universal view of humans. Both sides often make sophisticated arguments. Research suggests that pluralistic ideologies such as multiculturalism, which acknowledges and honors the unique differences of particular groups, are associated with lower levels of bias among the majority group (Verkuyten, 2005; Wolsko, Park, & Judd, 2006) and are beneficial for minority-group members as well (Plaut, Thomas, & Goren, 2009). Why this is the case is described by Plaut et al. (2009), who contrast multiculturalism with approaches that attempt to obviate difference: "Paradoxically, emphasizing minimization of group differences reinforces majority dominance and minority marginalization" (p. 445). What is not clear is the precise mechanism by which this happens and under what circumstances it occurs. Another study (Hehman et al., 2012) looked at assimilationist and pluralist views among college students at a historically Black college (HBC) where Black students were the majority and a university where White students were the overwhelming majority. Interestingly, both dominant racial and ethnic groups on their respective campuses endorsed assimilationist views, while minority students (Whites at the HBC and Blacks at the non-HBC) endorsed pluralist views. This research suggests that assimilationist or pluralist viewpoints are more of a function of majority–minority group dynamics rather than race or ethnicity. Those in the majority or dominant position feel that the minority group should adopt their ways of doing things.

Can humans be deft enough to minimize differences, yet still recognize and appreciate them? We seem capable of recognizing that there are differences, and beliefs and ideologies associated with these categories are not only interesting to learn but are often important to people and can be used to better engage and help. Yet as we have learned throughout this book, the biosocial principles that underlie survival and well-being are common to all humans. This viewpoint, however, is not at odds with pluralistic ideologies. It seems that pan-human science-based views about commonality can be incorporated into standard multicultural ideas and training.

Sexism, which can be defined as an ideology that promotes superiority of men or women at the expense of the other, is a global issue seemingly tied to male-dominance hierarchies. But is sexism associated with social and economic inequality around the world? Brandt (2011) attempted to answer this question using data on sexism and inequality from 57 nations, including such diverse countries as Norway, Andorra, Ethiopia, Trinidad and Tobago, Australia, Uruguay, Mexico, Zambia, Cyprus, Morocco, India, Vietnam, Japan, and the United States. Results showed that in 56 of 57 nations (Vietnam was the exception), men were more likely than women to report attitudes reflecting a sexist ideology. In general, less developed nations had more sexist attitudes. The largest effects in sexist attitudes were found in Morocco and Bulgaria. Furthermore, and perhaps more importantly, higher levels of sexism predicted lower levels of equality.

Effective Race-, Gender-, and Class-Based Practices

One concept that appears to be gaining strength in the creation of effective practices with minority groups is cultural sensitivity, sometimes termed *congruence* (Sue & Sue, 2008). What these practices aspire to do is incorporate norms, beliefs, and values common to a minority population into social and psychotherapeutic interventions. Theoretically, effectiveness is increased because these practices move toward reflecting the cultural norms of a given population (Wolf, 1978). Consistent with this line of thinking, minority-group members often endorse somewhat different cultural values (Marin, 1993) compared to the majority group. One of the major shortcomings of culturally sensitive practices is their relatively weak empirical base. Although there are exceptions, many theories of human behavior as they relate to effective practices along the race, gender, and class continuum are untested or poorly tested. When tested empirically, the behavior-change mechanism is often not clear. Despite this state of affairs, several meta-analyses have been conducted to take stock of the small but emerging base of studies. Three meta-analyses were conducted on the effects of culturally sensitive interventions (CSIs) in reducing high-risk behaviors among Black youth (Jackson, Hodge, & Vaughn, 2010), externalizing (acting out) with Latino youth (Hodge, Jackson, & Vaughn, 2010), and behavioral health among minority youth in general (Hodge, Jackson, & Vaughn, 2010). Results for CSIs with Black youth indicated that these interventions have a statistically significant and moderate effect in reducing high-risk behaviors such as violence, substance use, delinquency, and risky sex compared to youth not participating in CSIs. Effects for using CSIs for externalizing behaviors among Latino youth were small but in the beneficial direction. Last, results from 10 studies on CSIs for substance use among minority youth in general showed small effects for alcohol use and larger but moderate effects for marijuana use. In sum, although none of these findings are definitive and they should be viewed as preliminary in nature, the results do suggest using CSIs with these cultural groups is promising. Using CSIs presents practitioners with both an opportunity and a responsibility. Practitioners must be able to employ these interventions skillfully; otherwise more standard evidence-based practices for these outcomes should be used. Finding ways to enhance CSIs and test their effects is likely to gain greater importance in future practice contexts, particularly those where there are large or growing numbers of minority youth.

Additional practices have been identified to enhance the effectiveness of interventions with diverse populations. For example, Sue and Sue (2008) have identified a conceptual framework for interaction that first takes into account group-specific worldviews. In the United States this includes five broad categories: European American, Black, Latino, Native American, and Asian American. This can be broadened to include age, gender, class, sexuality, and disability status. Although it is important to learn about group affiliations and identities associated with these categories, it is equally important not to reify these categories as fixed ways of viewing other people. There is tremendous variation within each category. They serve as a starting point or shortcut to help make sense of a massive amount of variation. What should guide learning about these categories? According to Sue and Sue (2008), the primary areas where competence should be increased begin with awareness, which leads to knowledge, which can then translate into concrete skills. For example, compared to European Americans, many cultural groups such as Latinos place a stronger value on collective, interdependent relational styles (e.g., family or *familismo*) versus personal autonomy as embodied in rugged individualism. However, as some members of a minority cultural group begin to acculturate (often via increasing SES), these traditional worldviews can change (Lopez-Class, Castro, & Ramirez, 2011). Next, the focus of intervention needs to be specified. Although individual behavior is a common target of intervention, other aggregated units of behavior are also targets, including organizations, neighborhoods, cities, and nations. People in the helping professions potentially have much to

Age
Developmental **D**isabilities
Religion
Ethnicity/Race
Socioeconomic Status
Sexual Orientation
Indigenous Heritage
National Identity
Gender

FIGURE 14.3 Acronym for the Complex Identities of Individuals in Diverse Societies

offer in terms of relating to others at a nation-to-nation level. Unfortunately, there has been little systematic study of evidence-based culturally competent practices at the global level. It is likely that with the implementation of such practices, many past hostilities could have been averted.

Practitioners are often overwhelmed by the sheer volume of categories with which people have become affiliated. This is understandable, and this is likely to become more complex as increased cultural contact and intercultural marriages and new family formations create new identity designations. Sommers-Flanagan and Sommers-Flanagan (2009) describe a useful acronym for clinical interviewing, which was originated by Hays (2008), known as ADDRESSING: Age, Developmental Disabilities, Religion, Ethnicity/race, Socioeconomic status, Sexual orientation, Indigenous heritage, National identity, and Gender (see Figure 14.3). Individuals obviously identify with one or more of these domains; however, some may be more salient than others. This acronym can also be used for work with communities as it provides a way to orient a practitioner or policy maker with their basic demographic variations.

WHAT IS CULTURE?

Culture is a commonly invoked term in the helping professions, as is *cultural competence*, but both have failed to systematically answer the question of what culture actually is. Anthropologists disagree over its definition as well. Some definitions emphasize the ideals and symbols that are intrinsically important to a group of people. Others assert that culture is composed of socially transmitted behavior and thought, whereas still others are completely holistic, in that they use culture as an umbrella term that essentially includes features from all of these definitions (Harris, 1999). Most practitioners know very little about the concept, often using it as a synonym for ethnicity or what people receive when they visit an art museum or attend a musical performance. In short, because culture seems to be an important concept, we ought to use it in a way that advances the research and knowledge base to increase the well-being of others.

The rationale for examining the uses and definitions of culture rests upon a simple premise: Concepts predispose the direction of practice and inquiry. Our ideas about the world give rise to certain assumptions about how to understand our place in it. These ideas or concepts shape practice and policy context. The direction of where to look to substantiate our notions is intrinsic to both scholarship and practice. As Hatch (1973) points out, "Arguments over the meaning of abstract terms like culture have an immediate bearing on the understanding of concrete facts" (p. 12). Ideas developed in the Western tradition about what culture is have orchestrated not only how existing research is to be interpreted, but also how questions are to be formed and new information is to be gathered. In this way, one's answers are predetermined by one's questions.

Another aspect of examining the history of ideas is revealed by the tendency of ideas in the social sciences (including social work) to linger. Why do ideas seem to recur so persistently? Seemingly because those ideas reflect a cherished belief system or worldview, are stated over and over and passed across generations, and are unverified or unverifiable, and are therefore not discredited. In both the physical and social sciences, practitioners obstinately adhere to old ideas and old ways of explaining things until the empirical evidence against them has become so overwhelming as to make them untenable (at least in their current form). In the physical sciences, because of the nature of the subject matter, the persistence of ideas has not been as marked as it has been in the social sciences and helping professions. It is especially difficult to falsify or verify ideas in the social sciences, and consequently, many of them have persisted because little evidence against them has been presented. In addition, the phenomenon of confirmatory bias is more common in the behavioral and social sciences, as described later.

Why is understanding the culture concept important for social workers? The answer is that culture is a major aspect of how people live their lives and clients vary in their cultural values and commitments. The strategy we take is to examine the culture concept from the viewpoint of a scientist and the scientific method, which is designed to test research hypotheses by means of systematic observation, measurement, and experimentation. Science serves social work practice by making it credible, professional, and evidence based. Specifically, the perspective we employ here centers upon a viewpoint of the scientific research process as twofold. Science consists of both conceptual and empirical aims. Conceptual aims relate to implicit or explicit worldviews and assumptions, which occur prior to empirical discovery. Conceptual aims often are neglected either consciously or unconsciously; they generally lie beneath the surface of empirical aims. These conceptual frameworks, maps, blueprints, or paradigms play a crucial role in science-based practices. Empirical aims seek to gather facts or data and link them to concepts that advance the hand-in-hand process of research and practice.

Comparison and evaluations of concepts can be performed based on criteria such as logical structure, scope, parsimony, and their validity based on empirical testing. This is as much a part of the scientific research process as the comparison and evaluation of various data collections, such as needs assessments and client backgrounds. Because concepts can occur prior to empirical products, they can be analyzed and assessed prior to fact collection and interpretation. For this to occur, it is necessary to render one's assumptions and paradigm commitments explicit and open to criticism. In other words, before gathering any data or testing any hypotheses, the self-reflective scientist must make a clear-eyed assessment of the ideas and assumptions that inform the entire process.

One might ask the question at this point: Is science just another form of ideology? The answer is yes, but with one important caveat that distinguishes science from other forms of ideology. The key difference is that science is committed to falsification and open scrutiny, and knowledge gained under its auspices is tentative and open to revision. Science as an ideology contrasts sharply with all other ideologies, which are not open to being wrong and by their very nature are not committed to empirical testing.

SPOTLIGHT TOPIC: CULTURAL NEUROSCIENCE

As knowledge about one of the greatest complexities in science—the human brain—takes shape, new intersections between neuroscience and the behavioral and social sciences are being formed. One such intersection is an emerging field known as cultural neuroscience (CN). This field seeks to understand the bidirectional influences that culture and the human brain have on each other. Put more specifically by Chiao et al. (2010), "How do cultural traits (e.g., values, beliefs, practices) shape neurobiology (e.g., genetic and neural processes) and behavior and how do neurobiological mechanisms (e.g., genetic and neural processes) facilitate the emergence and transmission of cultural traits?" (p. 1). Thus, the scope and applicability of CN is vast.

Research on the CN paradigm conjointly uses tools such as brain imaging (e.g., fMRI), molecular genetics, and culturally adapted questionnaires to study the interactions between cultural dimensions such as individualism–collectivism, class-based status and areas of the brain involved in thought and feeling, and the gene involved in coding proteins that make up these neural substrates. One of the foremost CN researchers, Joan Chiao, has executed a number of fascinating studies with her colleagues. For example, in a sample of young adults from the United States and Japan, Chiao and fellow researchers (2008) in these two nations examined the neurological underpinnings of cultural values infused in individualistic (self) and collectivistic (self within context) worldviews, and found that activity within the medial prefrontal cortex (an area involved with self-awareness) was associated with the extent to which a person was individualistic or collectivistic. In another study, Chiao and Blizinsky (2010) examined the prevalence of 5-*HTTLPR* short-allele genetic polymorphism, a genetic risk marker for depression and mood problems, across 29 nations. Findings showed that there was a higher prevalence of the genetic variant found among nations possessing a more collectivist cultural orientation (e.g., East Asia). However, individuals in these countries with the short allele were less apt to possess an anxiety or mood disorder, seemingly as a result of increased collectivistic cultural values. One conclusion was that cultural values appeared to modify the risk associated with a genetic susceptibility.

Although CN is still in its infancy, findings at this stage suggest that cultural values do indeed strongly influence adaptations that result in genomic variations that influence important neural substrates that, in turn, reinforce cultural values. Understanding the biosocial diversity in cultural traits extends the value of appreciating diversity in general—a value that social workers embrace. However, translating CN findings into specific practice applications may take considerable time.

For Reflection

Think about the strengths and weaknesses of individualistic and collectivist cultural orientations. In what ways have they shaped public policies with respect to social welfare, the environment, and crime and justice?

A BRIEF HISTORY OF THE CULTURE CONCEPT

Culture is a term that lends itself to a multitude of definitions. The essential feature that underlies the various concepts of culture is that people learn culture. Beyond this notion, there is little consensus on the term and use of the concept, even in anthropology. In 1952, American anthropologists Alfred Kroeber and Clyde Kluckhohn published a list of 160 different definitions of culture. Bodley (1994) condensed these definitions into the following eight areas: topical, historical, behavioral, normative, functional, mental, structural, and symbolic. Bodley's categories, as well as those from sociology or cultural studies fields, can be further simplified into two general areas: the *symbolic-ideational* and the *materialist-behaviorist*. Typically, the more humanities-oriented fields of study embrace the symbolic-ideational concept, which would include aesthetic expressions found in art and architecture. This is true of many anthropological and sociological accounts as well. In 1958, Alfred Kroeber and sociologist Talcott Parsons decided to limit the culture concept to the symbolic-ideational realm—the domain of values, beliefs, and other meaningful factors (Harris, 1980). They assumed two important things: first, that ideas guide behavior but not the other way around; and second, that they were self-appointed spokespersons for their respective disciplines. This commitment to the symbolic/ideational-only culture concept reflected the ascendancy of functionalist viewpoints about the world, which essentially regard features

of human behavior as functionally contributing to society (see Harris, 1980). In other words, functionalists believe that what people do must serve some larger function. Functionalism seemingly has not been a particularly useful theory for social work practice or other helping professions.

Because the notion of culture has been around for quite a long time, it is interesting that very little systematic analysis of the concept has taken place prior to the Enlightenment. Although Herodotus is often called the father of anthropology, most modern works on the culture concept begin with the Enlightenment. The primary reason for this is the culture concept in Western discourse is rarely explicitly rendered. In these early writings, the concept itself is vague and implicit and must be extracted from the works of previous scholars. Terms such as *human nature*, *civilization*, *custom*, and *manners* are representative of the early concept of culture. In fact, as Kroeber and Kluckhohn (1952) have pointed out, the word *culture* derives itself from ancient Latin, meaning "cultivation" or "nurture." Although social workers use the term *culture*, a deeper understanding of its origins within social work and other helping fields would be an important contribution toward helping them move beyond using definitions derived from other fields.

THE CULTURE CONCEPT IN CLASSICAL ANTIQUITY

The culture concept has been identified in the West as being associated with the historical writing of *Herodotus* (484–425 B.C.E.; Darnell 1974; Hodgen, 1964; Pandian, 1985). Herodotus was a Greek member of an Ionian tribe and a prodigious traveler who inquired into both the differences and similarities of peoples. He observed, wrote, and carried on regular discourse with the peoples with whom he came into contact. Herodotus utilized the culture concept as pertaining to manners and customs embodied in such basic social institutions as marriage, religious rituals, death rites, food habits, and language (Hodgen, 1964). In his use of informants, Herodotus was an early precursor of the ethnographic method, which calls for the ethnographer to be immersed into a culture to understand it from the inside out.

Although the Greco-Roman tradition typically emphasized both similarity and difference, which continued through the Renaissance and into today, one notable exception to that practice was the work of *Thucydides* (Pandian, 1985). An Athenian, Thucydides (460–c. 399 B.C.E.) focused exclusively on the culture of the Greeks. The culture concept to Thucydides was essentially a development process that evolved in one continuous direction. Culture was something that grows slow and steady and exemplifies the natural history of change. For Thucydides, the culture concept was like a child inevitably reaching adult status. This is a biological analogy, in which culture is identified as an organism.

The early *Greek Sophists* (450–300 B.C.E.) believed that humans possessed no core instincts but did possess rationality. Physiological constants such as needs, drives, and aversions were not part of their concept of human nature. Sophists believed that the construction of institutions was necessary for humans to minimize strife. Culture was what humans created by reasoning and interacting with a social and physical environment. This concept of culture can be effectively called an eco-mentalist formulation, because the rational faculties of the mind work in cooperation with a given habitat. Although this was an interesting early postulate, its weakness was the deficiency of not taking into account the

facts of the early historical record, which were not as available as they are today. The Sophists maintained that culture could be understood and studied through reason alone.

The march of culture understood as progressive and orderly change was furthered by Lucretius (99–55 B.C.E.) in *De Rerum Natura* (*On the Nature of the Universe;* 1913). Lucretius had a materialistic, scientific bent and was an early evolutionist. His three stages of Stone, Bronze, and Iron made a case for specific developmental phases in human civilization. Lucretius was an early functionalist, in that he posited the origin of institutions as meeting needs and their duration as being tied to their usefulness. The Lucretian culture concept, albeit in crude form, is psychogenetic, evolutionist, and materialist, and is linked to the idea of progress. Table 14.2 highlights key components of the culture

Table 14.2 Major Historical Conceptualizations of the Idea of Culture

Classical Antiquity

Herodotus	Culture as both thought and behavior
	Material conditions emphasized
Thucydides	Heavy usage of biological analogy
	Idea of progress
	Biosocial method/human nature
Early Greek Sophists	Early rationalists
	Eco-mentalism (reasoning in conjunction with social habitat)
Lucretius	Early evolutionist
	Functionalist
	Materialist/behaviorist

Medieval and Renaissance Periods

Ibn Khaldun	Early science of culture
	Materialist/evolutionist
Age of Discovery	Early taxonomy
	Manners and customs
	Lifestyles/rituals
Machiavelli	Human nature causation
	Drives, wants, needs, conflict
	Institutions for order and control
Hobbes	Human nature causation
	Fear, conflict
	Institutions for order and stability

concepts in classical antiquity and the medieval/ Renaissance periods.

Medieval and Renaissance Periods

The Islamic scholar *Ibn Khaldun* (1332–1406) devoted much of his life to developing a science of culture based upon a universal history (Darnell, 1974). Khaldun traveled extensively in the Islamic world and described Bedouin lifestyles. Khaldun sought to determine the laws of history via reason. In this sense, Khaldun attempted a scientific approach to history. Although his work was only rediscovered in the early 19th century, his contribution can be seen as a linkage between classical antiquity and the Renaissance formulations of culture. Khaldun's approach to the concept of culture consisted of three major components: (a) There are general laws that are discoverable, (b) subsistence and lines of descent were the foundation for understanding the character of a group, and (c) culture evolves through a series of progressive stages. Although Khaldun's scholarship appears to have been of minimal influence, probably owing to its home in the Islamic world, it was in many ways ahead of its time.

The concept of culture during the European rebirth of interest in classical learning known as the Renaissance was influenced both internally by the renewed focus on learning and reason and externally by discoveries during the age of exploration, which brought diverse human traditions into contact with one another. Issues of cultural diversity are indeed very old. This was a time when those who collected customs and manners confronted a series of unavoidable questions (Hodgen, 1964). These questions included: What was a custom? How was it to be described and classified? How does knowing about these things allow people to get along better with each other?

As Margaret Hodgen states in *Early Anthropology in the Sixteenth and Seventeenth Centuries* (1964), "Unless the cultural themes, categories, orders or structures were perceived, unless they and their logical subordinate elements were made

flesh in familiar words, ideas or images, manners and customs remained curious indeed" (p. 165). Conceptually, therefore, Renaissance "cultural collections" need the organizational framework of science to order customs into understandable ways of living (i.e., culture).

Both *Machiavelli's* and *Hobbes's* concepts of culture were born out of a perceived, almost excessive need for order and stability. Machiavelli and Hobbes believed that the goal of any arrangement of human systems ought to focus on creating the systemic qualities that bring out control and security. These ideas, along with other important issues, were expressed by Machiavelli in *The Prince* (1995) and by Hobbes in *Leviathan* (1994). Both authors' assumptions about human nature directly influenced the culture concept in these formulations. Machiavelli believed that human desires and appetites are greater in proportion to the means by which they can ever be satisfied. Hobbes believed the sensations of fear and insecurity to be the essence of human nature. Interestingly, Hobbes and Machiavelli developed differing assumptions of human nature, but both led to similar conclusions with regard to controlling and securing those basic inner drives. This linkage between human nature and culture harkens back to early Greek formulations of the biosocial method. In natural scientific language, this approach essentially recognizes a biological organism interacting with a specific habitat. Both nature and environment are necessary for understanding the outcome of events.

What is most interesting is the strong emphasis on the interaction between biology and environment in the conceptualizations of culture. Although these ideas were not empirically tested, in many ways they were consistent with a science-of-culture viewpoint. In several respects this contrasts with 20th-century ideas about culture; these ideas seemingly restrict their use to less material (i.e., how people live their daily lives) and more transient conceptualizations, which seem to have less value for the advancement of evidence-based practice as it intersects with culture. Herodotus, Lucretius, Khaldun, and others were certainly more scientific or concerned with general biosocial processes. Lucretius and Khaldun were early pioneers on the trail of the "laws" of history and sociocultural evolution. In this sense, it would seem that this historical survey of the culture concept shows any progress in the ideas to have been a myth. Furthermore, contemporary culture concepts in the social sciences, when gauged against these criteria, are less impressive than the best pre-Enlightenment thought. One could argue that the culture concept has regressed rather than progressed.

PRACTICE IMPLICATIONS

In summary, it is important to reemphasize the implicit nature of the culture concept in the Western intellectual tradition. This acknowledgement leads to an important recommendation for contemporary social work: At the outset, scholars and practitioners alike ought to render explicitly the meaning of culture they will use in their work. This is especially imperative given the multitude of meanings, either indirect or direct, that culture can have. In addition, it may be beneficial to speak of culture as part of a biosocial system. This is because culture is interactively entangled in a web of biosocially based human relationships. Although the concept of culture is being more commonly invoked as central to a fuller understanding in major practice domains such as mental health and social service delivery, there has been relatively little systematic analysis of various definitions of this concept and their resulting empirical implications. For example, various ideas about culture can be formally applied to issues of causation, diagnostics, acculturation, treatment, and access to services. Applications across the range of practice issues can vary by specific model of culture employed. How practitioners and researchers conceptualize culture is not without significant ramifications. The import of very narrow approaches to culture may be especially appealing to practitioners in a wide variety of settings and provide clinically useful information about diagnostics, acculturation, treatment, and help-seeking behaviors. Evolutionary approaches to culture shed light on the aggregate features of mental health issues and could be of particular relevance to policy makers. Given the heterogeneity of conceptualizations of culture, it is critical that researchers and practitioners who employ the construct make explicit their usage of the term. Both symbolic-ideational and evolutionary-materialist approaches and their specified models can be useful to social work practitioners and scholars depending on the problem at hand.

THE PROBLEM OF CONFIRMATORY BIAS

Commitment to a particular ideology or belief system carries with it a common tendency to seek out evidence that nourishes that particular belief or worldview and to ignore or attack evidence that is not consistent or supportive. This tendency is known as *confirmatory bias*. Confirmatory bias hampers reasoning and results in widespread distortions that can result in tremendous harm. Although confirmatory bias is sometimes explicit and intentional, most of the time individuals are not fully aware that they are practicing it (Nickerson, 1998). According to Nickerson, there are two general forms of confirmatory bias, motivated and unmotivated. Motivated forms of confirmatory bias occur when individuals select or interpret evidence a certain way when the issue matters to them, sometimes dearly. For example, imagine a social worker or social work researcher who desperately clings to deep-seated beliefs that "anyone who works hard can get ahead" despite mounting practice in the empirical research to the contrary. Such an individual may look for information that lends support to their beliefs and systematically ignore evidence that potentially undermines their convictions. Unmotivated confirmatory bias occurs when we unconsciously select or interpret evidence that lends support or credibility to our ideas, but we are unaware of this bias and perhaps even believe we are being unbiased. Experiments have shown that we are far more biased than we think (Nickerson, 1998).

Previously mentioned cultural categories are highly prone to confirmatory bias via reification. Categories are often used because they simplify complexity and facilitate communication about a given phenomenon. Reification happens when we think the categories are the actual reality. When we learn about something that is compelling to us, we often interpret the world in accordance with that view. Susceptibility to confirmatory bias appears to be tied to ways we have developed to produce comfort. This is why, when we are presented with unfamiliar or alternative evidence that refutes our views, we often have an emotional reaction to it. Often the magnitude of this emotional reaction to contrary views or evidence reflects our degree of bias. Consequently, our typical response is to seek evidence or confirmation that our cherished ideas are indeed "correct," even though this new evidence is incorrect despite its seeming logic or inherent persuasiveness. The discomfort that stems from having our views questioned has been termed *cognitive dissonance* (Festinger, 1957), which is the experience of holding thoughts or opinions based on opposite or near-opposite conditions or information.

Confirmatory bias is a major hurdle in the effort to build an evidence-based science of helping. Although pure objectivity is likely impossible, high levels of bias hurts the credibility of research findings and damages practitioners' and policy makers' confidence in the decisions they make. This is especially difficult in the helping professions, where there are a number of highly politicized views. The downside of value-based professions like social work is that the values themselves are not subject to falsification. Putting aside personal biases is not easy, but subjecting one's work to the peer review of experts has been one way to reduce bias. Another useful way is to get in the habit of taking the other side and attacking your own ideas or asking others to do so. Explicitly biased professions and organizations undermine the confidence of the public at large. Despite this, people tend to agree or disagree with empirically based results to the extent that they confirm their own views, and attribute contradictory findings to the ideological positions of those making the claims (MacCoun & Paletz, 2009). There is no easy solution to the many problems of confirmatory bias, as it seems to be a durable aspect of human reasoning.

CASE STUDY: CULTURAL AWARENESS

As a social worker, you will likely work with a diverse population of clients, which is one of the reasons why the NASW and most universities stress the importance of cultural competence or, using a more modern and popular term, cultural awareness (meaning the ability to be aware of cultural differences while not assuming that every individual from that culture will exhibit the same characteristics). What happens when cultural values or ideologies clash?

In her book *The Spirit Catches You and You Fall Down* (1997), Anne Fadiman tells the story of a young Hmong girl with epilepsy and her family who migrated from Laos to the United States. She discusses the relationship between the family's cultural ideology, which viewed the young girl's epilepsy as a positive thing (Hmong culture believes that having seizures makes you more in touch with the spiritual world), and the Western medical system, which viewed it as a very negative thing. These types of issues occur frequently, and it is often the job of the social worker to find an appropriate middle ground that is respectful of both cultural ideologies.

It is not always the clients who have different cultural ideologies. As a social work intern at a very reputable hospital in Northern Virginia, I witnessed a different type of clash of cultural ideologies. Several doctors in the hospital were refusing to sign off on very old and/or ill patients' DNR (do not resuscitate) forms because of their religious beliefs, which valued life no matter what. The doctors felt that signing these forms was a way of facilitating a person's death, which they saw as counter to their religious beliefs. The patients and their families, however, felt that they had made a decision based on their own cultural beliefs and their desires and that they had a right to die if that was what they chose.

Critical Thinking Questions:

- Who is "right" in a case like this?
- As a social worker, how do you approach an issue like this?

BELIEF SYSTEMS AND IDEOLOGY OVER THE LIFE COURSE

As children we believe in things strongly; although we are curious, we lack the rational skepticism that we are capable of later in life. For example, most children believe in the existence of Santa Claus and most adults do not. It is also easy to tell children fantastic stories and have them believe that made-up entities possess a real material existence. Even adults do not possess enough skepticism to counteract the belief in what Michael Shermer (1998) calls "weird things." We are all guilty of having believed in things that later proved to be false. Often we do so because they make us feel good or content. In short, we become emotionally attached to them. According to Shermer, believing in weird things has dangerous consequences for humanity, such as Aryan superiority or Holocaust denial. Although some unfounded beliefs such as alien abduction may seem harmless, they do cause unnecessary anxiety and divert our energy away from real-world solutions to earthly problems. Systematic empirical research on belief systems and ideology over the life course, particularly during certain periods, is relatively scant. However, it is important to highlight and discuss those few studies that do exist because

they are germane to ideas and practices about helping others.

Childhood

There are many child-development myths that lack empirical scientific support. Mercer (2010) has researched many of these, including the beliefs that vaccines cause autism, kids will be smarter if they listen to Mozart, sugar causes hyperactivity, learning styles are based on being left- or right-brain dominant, and playing with matches will cause children to evince serious pathology later in life. Despite their lack of empirical support, many of these beliefs about child development continue. One very controversial belief directly relevant to social work practitioners, use of corporal punishment in disciplining children, is discussed in the Adulthood section. Studies about ideology and beliefs systems from the child's point of view are not extensive. However, several studies are relevant to practitioner knowledge about these systems in childhood.

Children typically like to interact with and make friends with other children who are like them. This includes age, race, gender, and ethnic background. However, research by Kinzler, Corriveau, and Harris (2011) shows that children also prefer to make friends with children who have similar accents—so much so that accent is more important than race. Specifically, their research found that White children preferred Black children who had a native accent over White children with a foreign accent.

Does ideology have a role to play for children living under adverse circumstances? This notion was tested by Punamaki (1996) among 385 Israeli girls and boys living under conditions of political violence. Punamaki hypothesized that ideological commitment, defined as patriotism, a negative and defiant view of the enemy, and glorifying war, would protect the mental health of children in these conditions. Results supported this hypothesis as higher levels of ideological commitment were associated with decreased anxiety and depression. Theoretically, ideological commitment provides people with meaning, understanding, and perhaps justification (e.g., the enemy is wrong and evil) for the events around them and helps to provide the resolve to endure.

In school, children are often exposed to activities and field trips that increase their appreciation and concern for animals and the natural environment. The extent to which children's worldviews about the natural environment are shaped over time depends upon good measurement. Manoli, Johnson, and Dunlap (2007) studied worldviews about the natural environment among 10- to 12-year-old children. The measure employed, the New Ecological Paradigm scale, assessed factors such as rights of nature, ecological crisis, and human exceptionalism. Results showed that 85.2% of children thought that plants and animals have as much right to live as people do, 66.9% of children reported that when people mess with nature it has bad results, and 79.7% of children believed that people must still obey the laws of nature. Interestingly, 23.7% of children thought there were too many people on earth. Relatively small changes were found in these responses over time. Many children do develop fairly strong worldviews about the environment; however, given the measurement limitations, it is largely unknown how these views change

across generations. These types of studies also indicate that children can develop empathy for nonhuman entities.

Adolescence

Peer groups are obviously an important component of adolescent social life. They typically form based on shared features such as gender and ethnicity, but they also form around common interests like music and sports. The dynamics of interaction in peer groups often involve social dominance. Some adolescents assert themselves and push group behavior in varying directions. With respect to gender, adolescence is a time when gender-specific ideologies flower and begin to crystallize. Boys and girls tend to adopt gender-based ideological expectations into their behavioral repertoire (e.g., toughness and higher risk tolerance for boys and greater nurturance sensitivity and physical attractiveness among girls). In a study of testosterone and social dominance in relationships among 599 adolescents in Belgium, Vermeesh, Tsjoen, Kaufman, Vincke, and Van Houtte (2010) found that testosterone was directly linked to dominance among adolescent girls but not boys. Instead, among boys ideology about masculine identity norms was a key driver of dominance. Studies such as these are important because they show how social interaction variables are influenced by hormones and prevailing ideologies.

Ideology expresses itself in many ways during adolescence. Specifically, prejudiced ideas emerge and often change rapidly. For example, Poteat and Anderson (2012) studied changes in prejudice toward gay and lesbians between the ages of 12 and 18 and found that boys reported greater prejudice at age 12 than did girls. Level of prejudice toward gay people decreased over time among girls but not among boys. Both boys and girls reported decreases in levels of prejudice toward lesbians over time. However, these researchers point out there was substantial heterogeneity in prejudice beliefs, which were to some extent associated with social dominance ideology, measured as the degree to which adolescents supported hierarchies between groups in society. Simply put, gender is an important predictor of prejudiced ideas among adolescents, but important social factors also shape how male and female adolescents view those around them.

Adolescents who are members of minority groups often find that their racial and ethnic heritage and the cultural values associated with them help to buffer them from the pressures of majority or prevailing norms, of which they do not feel they are completely a part. Minority adolescents learn about and perceive inequalities and adapt to them in various ways. One important adaptation is, as developmental psychologist Laura Berk (2007) states, to "react to years of shattered self-esteem, school failure, and barriers to success in the mainstream by defining themselves in contrast to majority values" (p. 404). Sometimes these oppositional cultural adaptations are functional, but at other times they are not, such as in extreme cases when receiving good grades in school is viewed as "acting White." It is important for adolescents to feel proud of their cultural heritage, and it only becomes unhealthy when that pride leads to the denigration of other groups in society.

One of the cultural values that some adolescent rely on is religious traditions. Numerous studies have documented the fact that American adolescents are overwhelmingly religious, and that this religiosity has important consequences for their development, especially in terms of their involvement in various problem behaviors (Koenig, King, & Carson, 2012). We know that more than four out of five American adolescents report believing in God and identifying with a religious tradition, and that more than half of all young Americans routinely attend religious services and affirm that they do so without coercion (Smith, 2005). As such, helping professionals need to be aware that religious tradition can be an important source of positive change when working with troubled adolescents.

Adulthood

Adulthood is a large swath of time. Ideologies and beliefs change from early adulthood to old age. With respect to politics, people often who are left of center earlier in adulthood find as they reach middle adulthood that they have moved to the right of the political spectrum. Often this is thought to be a result of having children and changing lifestyles. Compared to early adulthood, older people often become more religious as well. Are these "settling in" effects following the relatively newfound independence of early adulthood the major reason? The empirical literature on this question is correlational, and it has not been scientifically established that this is in any way a fixed pattern of behavior.

Another ideology with potent effects that begins early and seemingly solidifies in adulthood is masculinity. Several models have been developed to attempt to assess and measure masculinity. Four of these stand out according to Abreu, Goodyear, Campos, and Newcomb (2000), and they consist of (a) "No Sissy Stuff" (hide emotions and do not show any strong affinities for "feminine" behavior), (b) "The Big Wheel" (earning money for the family and being respected and revered), (c) "The Sturdy Oak" (tough and confident and standing tall in difficult times), and (d) "Give 'Em Hell" (aggression and risk taking). Research suggests that these models vary across cultures, with Latinos most likely to endorse these traditional masculinity values (Abreu et al., 2000). Although it is widely held that these models are social constructions, they do have a strong biological basis and there is also an evolutionary basis for them. For example, aggression, risk taking, earning something of value, toughness, and confidence are all traits that may have been particularly important in ancestral environments. Males with these combinations of traits may have had a selection advantage in terms of procreation.

One of the more controversial ideological debates germane to child welfare is corporal punishment. Those who oppose it believe that any physical punishment (e.g., spanking) of a child is wrong under all circumstances, whereas others believe that so-called physical correction in some situations and in some cultural contexts is expected and useful for instilling discipline and teaching right and wrong. Research on these beliefs has linked them to various political and religious systems. Supporters of corporal punishment are more likely to be religious fundamentalists and evangelicals (Ellison & Bradshaw, 2009). Religious views trump the person's specific period of adulthood on these views, suggesting that it is the belief system rather than an older value system driving the results.

Is corporal punishment really harmful to children? The tentative answer seems to be yes and no, depending to a great extent on a person's cultural and religious background. For children in White middle-class families in North America, the answer is more likely to be yes (Deater-Deckard & Dodge, 1997). The key determinant of harm appears to involve expectations. For example, children in a cultural context where physical correction is commonplace view corporal punishment differently, and to some extent believe that it shows profound concern for keeping children on the straight and narrow path.

SUMMARY

Belief systems and ideology are important shapers of human behavior. Some of the major ideological systems covered in this chapter were political and religious ideologies and belief systems; the role of culture, gender, and ethnic ideologies; and the problem of confirmatory bias in human affairs. Interestingly, there is mounting evidence that suggests that humans are predisposed to believe or adopt ideologies in particular ways. The key summary points of this chapter are listed as follows:

• The archaeological record and contemporary research on primates indicate that humans have always manipulated symbols and expressed their worldviews in cosmological and artistic ways. Many of these worldviews become belief systems that were linked to survival. Shared meanings around these beliefs and symbols likely were as adaptive for early humans as they are today.

• Patriotism and nationalism are two forms of ideology that are associated with conflict between groups and cultures. Pride in one's background is healthy, but pride without the ability or willingness to constructively critique is detrimental. Groups and entire nations often

rally around certain symbols such as flags as a way to close ranks against a common enemy, real or perceived.

• Religious ideologies are similar to other ideologies in that they prescribe ways to view and operate in the material world. Religion certainly plays an important role in the lives of people around the world for many reasons, including social identity. Social workers and other helping professionals therefore need to have a deeper understanding of religious ideology and its impact on human behavior.

• Humans are group oriented and groups have a strong tendency to place their own needs ahead of those of other groups. Therefore, it is not surprising that major categories such as race, gender, and class are associated with specific ideologies. Sometimes group ideologies come into conflict. Many people, however, are able to transcend group identity and see others' circumstances. It is always important to remember that there is typically substantial variation within these categories; members of one group may be more alike than members of other groups.

• Culture is a common term in the helping professions, and conceptualizations of culture vary. These conceptualizations matter because we tend to act on how we view something. A historical analysis of the culture concept suggests that many older views of this concept were more scientific in nature than they are today. Given the fuzziness and general heterogeneity of definitions of culture, it may make sense for practitioners and researchers to make their usage of the term explicit.

• Humans tend to seek out arguments or evidence that nourishes their particular belief or worldview, and they ignore or attack arguments or evidence that is not consistent or supportive of them. This phenomenon is known as confirmatory bias. Confirmatory bias is a major impediment to sound reasoning and can result in widespread distortions. As such, the common phenomenon of not subjecting ideas about the world and how best to help others (whether policies or direct services) to scientific scrutiny can result in significant harm to others.

• During the life course, ideologies and belief systems, including myths, affect our behavior in myriad ways. Ideologies and belief systems are important components of socialization and how we view the world. Ideologies also affect the way in which we view socialization.

KEY TERMS

Confirmatory bias

Conservatism

Culture

Greek Sophists

Herodotus

Hobbes

Ibn Khaldun

Ideology

Intersectionality

Liberalism

Machiavelli

Materialist-behaviorist

Nationalism

Patriotism

Religious ideology

Symbolic-ideational

Thucydides

GLOSSARY

Achieved status   Social status assigned based on actions of an individual, such as profession.

Action stage   Stage of change characterized by actual behavioral changes and observable commitment to making progress toward goals.

Adaptation   The ability to adjust to changes in the environment and handle stress in a healthy, effective, and prosocial way.

Adaptive phenotypic plasticity   The capacity of genetic factors to support a range of phenotypes or behaviors depending on the environmental context in which they occurred.

Affect   The manner in which an individual presents their emotions.

Affect specificity   The child's ability to make distinctions among emotions that are similar or have the same valence, such as understanding the differences between fear and anger.

Agreeableness   Personality dimension in the Five Factor Model of Personality that refers to the kinds of interactions a person has along a continuum from compassion to antagonism.

Alexithymia   A condition characterized by an inability to articulate one's emotional experiences.

Alleles   Variants of a single gene.

Allostatic load   The wear and tear on the body and brain resulting from chronic over- or underarousal of the stress response system.

Altruism   Behavior benefiting another organism while being detrimental to the organism performing the behavior.

Ambivalent (insecure) attachment   Attachment that occurs in approximately 10% of children, who display closeness to their parent and are not able to separate from them after reuniting following a brief separation (stressor).

Ambiverts   Medium scorers on the Extraversion dimension of the Five Factor Model of Personality who are more moderate in activity and enthusiasm and prefer a balance of privacy and the company of others.

Amygdala   Part of the brain's limbic system that processes fear and other emotional responses.

Antisocial personality disorder   A personality disorder characterized by a pervasive pattern of disregard for and violation of the rights of others.

Ascribed status   Social status assigned based on some characteristic or set of attributes that an individual has no control over, including race/ethnicity, gender, visual attractiveness, developmental disability, and residence.

Attachment theory   The enduring affective bond between child and caregiver (usually parents) that is importantly related to child development and the ability of the child to adapt to and overcome stress across the life course.

Attention-deficit/hyperactivity disorder (ADHD)   A disorder characterized by inattention, impulsivity, hyperactivity, and related deficits.

Attentional control   The ability to focus on environmental demands in the face of distractions, irrelevant information, and habitual or overlearned behaviors.

Avoidant personality disorder   A personality disorder characterized by a pervasive pattern of social inhibition, feelings of inadequacy, and hypersensitivity to negative evaluation.

Basic emotions   Universally expressed emotions (anger, disgust, fear, happiness, sadness, and surprise) found across cultures and epochs and theorized to be hardwired into the brain's circuits by evolution.

Behavioral disinhibition   A general behavioral tendency characterized by failure to inhibit antisocial behaviors because of susceptibility to emotional impulses and rewards.

Behavioral parent training   A behavioral modification program based on learning theory that teaches parents to identify and manipulate the causes and consequences of behavior. It is commonly used for children with deficits in executive functioning and conduct problems.

Behaviorism Environmental input shapes behavior of the organism. Many of these environmental inputs involve social learning via reinforcement. Thus, development is a sum of learning experiences based on specific environmental conditions.

Borderline personality disorder A personality disorder characterized by a pervasive pattern of instability of interpersonal relationships, self-image, affect, and marked impulsivity.

Built environment Homes, office buildings, roads, and other constructions built by humans.

Calculated altruism Premeditated calculation about receiving a benefit for altruistic behavior.

Central dogma of molecular biology Describes the process by which DNA is transcribed and then translated during protein synthesis.

Charismatic authority Authority defined by special (even supernatural) qualities.

Choleric In the classical four-humors temperament model, a person who was angry and irritable with a predominance of yellow bile.

Cluster A personality disorders Personality disorders that are viewed as odd or eccentric.

Cluster B personality disorders Personality disorders that are viewed as dramatic or emotional.

Cluster C personality disorders Personality disorders that are viewed as anxious or fearful.

Codon Three adjacent mRNA nucleotides that contain the message for a specific amino acid.

Cognitive empathy Appraisal of what caused the other person's emotional state and thoughts about how to ameliorate it (rationally driven).

Cognitive perspective Focused attention on the frame of reference or schemas (thought patterns) that humans are born with; we need to have this structure to process information from our external environment.

Cold executive functions Executive functions that relate to cognitive processes.

Community attachment Consists of: (a) belonging, (b) belief in having an impact on community, (c) belief that the community can meet personal needs, and (d) expression of emotional connections.

Compassion fatigue A state of tension and preoccupation with the suffering of those being helped to the degree that it is traumatizing for the helper.

Complementary base pairing The principle of nucleotide pairing in which A always bonds with T and G always bonds with C.

Concept formation The ability to begin tasks and devise problem-solving strategies.

Confirmatory bias Tendency to seek out evidence that nourishes one's own belief or worldview and ignore/attack evidence that is not consistent or supportive; hampers reasoning and results in widespread distortions; high levels of confirmatory bias hurts the credibility of research findings and confidence in the decision making of practitioners and policy makers.

Conscientiousness Personality dimension in the Five Factor Model of Personality that captures the degree of organization, persistence, control, and motivation in goal-directed behavior.

Conservative ideology Political ideology that tends to be more structured and determined and possesses a lower tolerance for disorder.

Conspicuous consumption Individuals purchase and display symbols of wealth to fulfill their need to feel superior to others.

Contemplation stage Stage of change where clients have increased awareness of a problem but are still not ready to make a commitment to change.

Core consciousness Results from the integration of new sensory information with a subjective sense of self to create a conscious self-representation.

Corrective attachment therapy An intervention that seeks to provide the conditions of secure attachment to children and adolescents who engage in aggressive and antisocial forms of behavior.

Culture Ideals and symbols intrinsically important to a group of people; socially transmitted behavior and thought.

Cultural ecology The extent to which humans adapt to environmental circumstances requires specific kinds of behaviors by humans; the impact of their meeting basic needs on the physical environment.

Cultural materialism Societal change arises from subsistence technologies and reproduction; technology facilitates the satisfaction of biologically and psychologically mandated human survival mechanisms.

Deduction Taking an idea or theory about something and gathering data to assess the theory's validity.

Dependent personality disorder A personality disorder characterized by a pervasive and excessive need to be taken care of, which leads to submissive and clinging behavior and fears of separation.

Determination stage Stage of change where ambivalence favors action; typically clients in this stage are ready to make a change within the next month.

Dialectical behavior therapy (DBT) A cognitive behavioral treatment that helps patients to validate their feelings and experiences while changing their emotional expression and behavior responses to environmental stimuli that had previously produced conflicts.

Diathesis-stress model People who are at genetic risk for some disorder or condition are most sensitive to the stressors created by environmental risk.

Differentiation Change toward greater complexity in system.

Difficult children Temperamental children who are prone to conduct problems, aversive interactions, and externalizing conditions.

Disorganized attachment Characterized by a breakdown in the attachment process, where the child lacks a consistent strategy for organizing responses to needs for comfort and security during periods of distress.

Dispositional perspective Internal factors of an individual, such as traits or thought processes, that contribute strongly to a particular behavior.

Distress The aversive, negative emotional state resulting from stress exposure.

DNA Contains the blueprint or code for making proteins and enzymes and regulating how and when they are made.

Easy children Well-adjusted children with positive temperament profiles.

Ecological-evolutionary typology Societal change arises from the interaction of two different ecologies with varying levels of technologies.

Ecological fallacy Inferences about specific individuals based on aggregate patterns or data; helpful for making generalizations about a phenomenon but dangerous when one assumes it applies to everyone.

Ecological systems theory The individual interacts with multiple levels of the environment (i.e., micro, meso, macro) to influence behavior and development across time in complex ways.

Ecology The physical environment, composed of both the natural environment and the built environment.

Ecosystems theory Adaptation and dependence on the environment is crucial to understanding societal development or evolution; this theory analyzes the everyday transactions of individuals across many layers of social interaction.

Effortful control The subordination of a dominant or prepotent impulse in favor of a subdominant but socially appropriate one; in Rothbart's model, the general sense of self-control, including attention control, inhibitory control, perceptual sensitivity, and low-intensity pleasure.

Emotion A person's attempt to establish, maintain, or change the relation between the person and his or her changing circumstances on matters that are of significance to that person.

Emotional acceptance The value-free acknowledgment of emotions without experiencing negative reactions to those emotions, if appropriate.

Emotional awareness The understanding of one's emotions, how they relate to one's behavior, and how both phenomena affect others.

Emotional competence The achievement of self-efficacy (competence) during social interactions that often create emotional challenges.

Emotional control The modulation of emotional responses to the environment.

Emotional reappraisal The strategy of changing one's interpretation of situations that may elicit strong/negative emotion in a way that reduces the emotional experience.

Emotional security theory Theory that suggests that parental discord (e.g., arguing, fighting, engaging in destructive behavior) increases children's vulnerability to psychopathology by disrupting the sense of safety, security, and protection that children receive from parents.

Emotional self-efficacy The final point for emotional competence, where an individual is comfortable with his or her emotional experience.

Emotional suppression The strategy of inhibiting the behavioral (usually facial) expression of one's emotional experience.

Emotional versatility The use of and access to a variety of emotional regulation strategies that individuals utilize to control their emotions to achieve behavioral goals.

Empathizing Baron-Cohen's idea that the female brain is wired to infer the mental states of others and respond in emotional ways.

Empathy The capacity to vicariously experience the emotions, feelings, or thoughts of other people.

Equifinality Many different means to achieve the same end.

Exchange context   The way in which emotions are displayed is dependent upon emotion norms, which are derived out of social interactions and guided by scripts or prescribed ways of displaying emotions based on prevailing norms.

Exchange outcomes   One's frequency and nature of social exchange are impacted by the way in which the individual displays emotions.

Exchange process   Emotions help to convey information within or between individuals. Within an individual, based on one's emotional reaction, individuals infer something about themselves and their environment. Between individuals, one's display of emotions allows others to understand their internal reactions or disposition.

Executive functions   An umbrella term that is meant to characterize the interrelated cluster of higher order cognitive functions that help individuals modulate their emotional and behavioral responses to the environment through problem solving, planning, attention, verbal reasoning, and related tasks.

Expanded consciousness   Occurs when integrated self-representation is modified to include past memories.

Explicit memories   The memories that are available to us at a cognitively conscious level.

Extraversion (and surgency)   The tendency to approach stimuli in an excitatory as opposed to inhibitory way.

Extraversion (and personality)   Personality dimension in the Five Factor Model of Personality that refers to the quantity and intensity of preferred interpersonal interactions, activity level, need for stimulation, and capacity for joy.

Extraverts   High scorers on the Extraversion dimension of the Five Factor Model of Personality, who are outgoing, energetic, and enjoy being around other people.

Federal Reserve (The Fed)   Regulates the U.S. banking system and determines the amount of money in the economy.

Federal Deposit Insurance Corporation   Insures U.S. bank deposits up to $250,000, thereby increasing consumer confidence in the banking sector.

Five Factor Model of Personality   A structural model of personality that contains five dimensions: Openness to Experience, Conscientiousness, Extraversion, Agreeableness, and Neuroticism.

Fluency   Intensity of emotions.

Fluid intelligence   Logical reasoning and analysis, which tends to decrease in efficiency and processing speed as we age.

Frequency   Repetition of emotions.

Galen   The leading Greco-Roman scholar who developed the four-humors temperament model.

Gene   A distinct section of DNA in a cell's chromosome that contains the codes for producing specific proteins involved in brain and bodily functions.

Genetic drift   Genetic evolution that is random and neutral.

Genetic polymorphisms   Genes with different forms within a population.

Genome   The complete genetic map of an organism.

Geospatial analysis   Mapping of disaster-related stress within a disaster area; helps direct services to places affected by the disaster where stress loads are at their highest.

Goodness of fit   The match between child temperament and parenting strategies that produces the best opportunities for prosocial development and behavior.

Greek Sophists   Greek philosophers believing that the construction of institutions was necessary for humans to minimize strife and that culture was created by humans through reasoning and interacting with a social and physical environment; maintained that through reason alone, culture could be understood and studied.

Gross cheating   Failure to give anything at all in return.

Happiness   A state of well-being characterized by high positive emotion and low negative emotion.

Harm avoidance   A heritable tendency of intense avoidant or inhibitory responses to stimuli.

Heritability (h^2)   A population statistic indicating the proportion of variance in a phenotypic (or outcome) trait in a population that is attributable to genetic factors.

Herodotus   Greek historian who utilized the culture concept as pertaining to manners and customs embodied in basic social institutions such as marriage, religious rituals, death rites, food habits, and language.

High reactive   In Kagan's work, this term describes children with high activity levels and who respond with distress to unfamiliar stimuli, including other people and social situations.

Histrionic personality disorder A personality disorder characterized by a pervasive pattern of excessive emotionality and attention seeking.

Homeostasis The state of internal balance without psychological or physiological disturbance.

Homophily The tendency to associate with people who are like ourselves.

Hostile attribution bias The tendency to believe that others have hostile intentions toward them.

Hot executive functions Executive functions that relate to affective/emotional processes.

Human capital Skills and knowledge an individual has acquired.

Hyperdyadic spread The social influence that spreads beyond an immediate dyad relationship, to friends of friends of friends.

Hypothalamic-pituitary-adrenal (HPA) axis The major neurological-endocrine response system to stress.

Ibn Khaldun Islamic scholar describing the three primary components of culture to be: 1) there are general laws that are discoverable; 2) subsistence and lines of descent are the foundation to understand a group's character; and 3) culture evolves through a series of progressive stages.

Ideology Universal ways that humans conceptualize their world; rules of living applied to everyday events such as how one lives one's life and behaves around others.

Implicit memories The memories that reside at a nonverbal level of awareness.

Induction To observe facts and form a theory capable of explaining or making sense of our observations.

Inhibitory control The ability to modulate unwanted thoughts, emotions, and actions and stop one's behavior.

Inputs Flows of energy (i.e., stimuli) into a person or system.

Insecure (ambivalent) attachment Attachment that occurs in approximately 10% of children, who display closeness to their parent and are not able to separate from them after reuniting following a brief separation (stressor).

Insecure/avoidant attachment Attachment that occurs in about 20% of children where they ignore or avoid their parent after reuniting with them following a brief separation (stressor).

Institution Systems of established and prevalent social rules that structure social interactions.

Interconnectivity Concept whereby all parts of a system interact with and rely upon one another since they occupy the same system; in regards to human behavior, specifically, humans must interact with factors such as technology and the physical environment due to their existence in the same system.

Interdependence Mutual reliance between actors in a system and habitat.

Interface The point of interaction or change target.

International Monetary Fund (IMF) Provides bailouts and economic austerity plans for countries on the verge of bankruptcy.

Internet addiction Individuals lacking impulse-control and are dependent upon constant Internet usage.

Intersectionality Race, gender, and class are not to be considered separately, as these are difficult to study in isolation from one another.

Intersocietal selection The extinction of whole cultures through contact with larger, more powerful societies.

Intrasocietal selection How new elements are adopted or selected for within a society.

Introverts Low scorers on the Extraversion dimension of the Five Factor Model of Personality, who are generally reserved, serious, and prefer to be alone or with only close friends.

Liberal ideology Political ideology that tends to tolerate complexity and nuance and is more open to novelty.

Limbic system Area of the brain that is involved in producing emotion and storing emotional memory.

Low reactive In Kagan's work, this term describes children who display lower levels of motor activity and minimal distress to novelty.

Machiavelli Italian historian discussing the idea that human desires and appetites are greater in proportion to the means by which they can ever be satisfied, human nature causes culture, and institutions were created by humans to maintain order and control.

Maintenance stage Change of stage where clients try to sustain desired results and actively maintain a focus on doing what they need to do to stay on track with their goals and with the changes they have already made.

Maladaptive behavior Negative responses to stress, such as rumination.

Materialist-behaviorist Concept of culture that includes the objects created by humans and the way individuals act as defined by their culture.

Melancholic In the classical four-humors temperament model, a person described as moody and anxious with a predominance of black bile.

Mendelian disorder An inherited condition caused by a single genetic mutation.

Mental flexibility or set shifting The ability to move from one stimulus to another as environmental circumstances demand.

Mesolimbic reward system Brain circuit that provides positive reinforcement for eating, drinking, sex, and other functions that are basic to survival and rooted in our evolutionary past.

Motivational enhancement therapy (MET) Evidence-based practices commonly used in practice to shore up client motivation in a relational, collaborative manner. It focuses on the FRAMES model: providing *Feedback* to the client; helping clients take *Responsibility* for change; offering *Advice* and encouragement; compiling, with the client, a *Menu* of options for change; using *Empathic* rapport; and working to *Support* client self-efficacy.

Motivational interviewing (MI) Evidence-based practices commonly used in practice to shore up client motivation in a relational, collaborative manner; relies on client autonomy in treatment decision making, and invites clients to explore perceived discrepancies between their own values, goals, and problem behaviors.

Multifactorial phenotypes Phenomena caused by genes, environments, and their interaction.

Multifinality One starting point leading to many outcomes.

Multiple intelligences Intelligence is comprised of seven core intelligences of the human mind, including: linguistic (words/language); logical-mathematical (logic and numbers); musical (rhythm, music, sound); bodily-kinesthetic (movement); spatial-visual (images, finding one's way through physical environment); interpersonal (relationships with others and knowing others' emotions); and intrapersonal (self-awareness).

Multisystemic therapy (MST) An intensive family- and community-based treatment that addresses the multiple needs of serious, violent, and chronic juvenile delinquents.

Narcissistic personality disorder A personality disorder characterized by a pervasive pattern of grandiosity in fantasy and behavior, need for admiration, and lack of empathy.

Nationalism Strong identification of a group of individuals with a nation; can be further classified into civic nationalism (pride in nation) and ethnic nationalism (pride in ethnic/racial group).

Natural selection Characteristics that facilitate the survival and reproductive success of an organism persist, whereas characteristics that do not facilitate the survival of the species desist.

Negative affectivity The frequency of negative mood based upon experiencing negative emotions.

Neural substrates Brain pathways that are the result of genetic expression and that give rise to behavioral variance.

Neuroplasticity The brain's capacity to grow and change over the life course; allows social workers to intervene at all points in a person's development to help strengthen and build skills that enhance functional capacity and well-being.

Neuropsychological deficits Brain-based deficits in social cognitive processes that are risk factors for conduct problems and related maladaptive behaviors, such as problems with school, relationships, and work, and unhealthy habits.

Neuroticism Personality dimension that refers to the chronic level of emotional adjustment and instability.

Nonshared environment (e^2) A source of environmental variation that relates to circumstances unique to the individual even within the same family.

Novelty seeking The heritable tendency of frequent exploratory activity and intense feelings of joy/satisfaction in response to novel or appetitive stimuli.

Nucleotides (base pairs) Adenine, thymine, guanine, and cytosine.

Obsessive-compulsive personality disorder A personality disorder characterized by a pervasive pattern of preoccupation with orderliness, perfectionism, and mental and interpersonal control at the expense of flexibility, openness, and efficiency.

Openness to Experience Personality dimension from the Five Factor Model of Personality that involves the appreciation and seeking of experiences.

Outputs Flow of energy out of a person or system.

Oxytocin A hormone and neurotransmitter that plays an important role in social behavior and is involved in the regulation of stress.

Paranoid personality disorder A disorder characterized by a pervasive pattern of distrust and suspiciousness of others such that their motives are interpreted as malevolent.

Patriotism Love for or devotion to one's country.

Performance monitoring The ability to self-evaluate one's work or performance.

Persistence The capacity to persevere in spite of obstacles or blockage of goals.

Personality The relatively consistent and stable ways that an individual behaves, thinks, and feels.

Personality disorder An enduring pattern of inner experience and behavior that deviates markedly from the expectations of the individual's culture.

Perspective taking The ability to get into another person's shoes and sense his or her viewpoint, needs, and distress.

Phlegmatic In the classical four-humors temperament model, a person who was slow to arousal, with a predominance of phlegm.

Planning The ability to manage current and future-oriented task demands.

Pleiotropic Individual genes that are associated with multiple phenotypes.

Polygenic A trait or behavior caused by many genes.

Posttranscriptional modification Also known as the editing phase of RNA production because sections of nonuseful or "junk" RNA called introns are cut out and sections of useful RNA called exons are spliced together.

Posttranslational modification Stage of protein synthesis that could be thought of as the "final assembly" stage, in which the polypeptide chain folds on itself to take a three-dimensional form.

Power The ability to influence the behavior of others.

Preconscious processing Information that can be retrieved with effortful attention that suppresses the distracters that mask conscious awareness.

Precontemplation stage Stage of change where clients exhibit no intention to change behavior anytime soon and demonstrate limited awareness of the problem.

Prefrontal cortex Area of the frontal lobe that is involved in a range of processes that deal with modulating emotional signals and regulating behavior.

Proximal factors Those things or variables, such as political organizations or technologies, that are closest to or immediately causing an outcome.

Pseudoscience Use of persuasion and misinformation in support of cherished claims; characterized by a lack of empirical testing, rigorous external review, and self-correction.

Psychodynamic theory Posits that development takes place in a series of discrete stages driven by innate sexual impulses and early experiences.

Rational legal authority Authority exemplified by procedural, legal, and regulatory correctness and order.

Real altruism Behavior where there was no premeditated calculation of what might be received if altruistic behavior is initiated.

Real-time fMRI Provides clients with in-scanner visual feedback on how their brains change in response to the application of specific treatment techniques or strategies learned in the treatment sessions.

Referential specificity The understanding that emotional expressions are specifically directed toward objects in the environment (e.g., other people) and not randomly directed.

Relational capital Inherent value of the relationships between residents and other stakeholders within a community.

Religious ideology Prescribed ways of viewing and operating in the world based on religious grounding; are to be believed in and not tested in any empirical sense.

Resilience The process whereby individuals are able to successfully adapt despite considerable environmental stress.

Reward dependence The behavioral maintenance involving conditioned responses to reward and the avoidance of punishment.

Sanguine In the classical four-humors temperament model, a person who was described as cheerful, spirited, and good natured with a predominance of blood.

Schizoid personality disorder A disorder characterized by a pervasive pattern of detachment from social relationships and restricted range of emotional expression in interpersonal settings.

Schizotypal personality disorder A personality disorder characterized by a pervasive pattern of social and interpersonal deficits marked by acute discomfort with and reduced capacity for close relationships, cognitive or perceptual distortions, and eccentricities in behavior.

Science   A way of knowing about the world that is based on empiricism and testing.

Seasonal affective disorder   Occurs during fall and winter when there is reduced sunlight; involves symptoms of depression.

Secondary traumatic stress   Situation where practitioners display symptoms of chronic stress exposure due to their chronic interaction with people in need.

Secure attachment   Normative attachment response that occurs in approximately 70% of children; secure attachment means that children feel that their emotional needs will be met by their caregivers/parents because their parents have been responsive previously.

Self-control   The capacity to inhibit an inappropriate behavioral response.

Self-perception enhancements   Individual behavior wherein one views oneself as superior to the average person.

Self-regulatory control   Ability to regulate one's behavior and refrain from responding to cognitive impulses.

Set-point hypothesis   A concept that suggests that genetic and environmental factors produce a baseline level of a specific emotional response to which people will return after specific events.

Severe mood dysregulation (SMD)   A disorder characterized by abnormal mood involving irritability, anger, and/or sadness that is noticeable to others and present most of the time.

Sexual victimization   Adolescents between the ages of 15 and 17 are at a heightened risk for sexual solicitations and related forms of sexual harassment through the Internet.

Shared environment (c^2)   Common environmental exposure that usually relates to within-family characteristics.

Situationist perspective   Factors external to the individual that are components of a given situation contribute strongly to a particular behavior.

Slow-to-warm children   Cautious, perhaps inhibited but still largely prosocial children.

Social capital   Value of relationships formed within residents of a community.

Social exchange and cooperation   Way in which humans primarily interact with another to meet and optimize their well-being.

Social information processing theory   Theory that suggests there are individual differences in the ways that people read or encode, interpret, respond, and evaluate social contexts and interactions.

Social stratification   Process wherein differences between groups divide people into classes.

Social support   Material and emotional support that is provided to help others.

Stress   A challenge, change, or threat to an individual's internal feeling of balance and well-being.

Stressors   The events, people, places, or situations that cause stress.

Strong reciprocity   Tendency to cooperate with strangers and punish cheaters, even at a personal cost.

Structural model of personality   A systematic way to conceptualize and measure essential personality traits.

Subliminal processing   Undetectable even with focused attention.

Subtle cheating   Always giving less than what was given.

Symbolic-ideational   Concept of culture that includes the domain of values, beliefs, and other meaningful factors.

Sympathetic concern   The state in which one feels another's state of need and tries to make things better (impulse driven).

Sympathetic nervous system   System that controls the response to stress and initiates the fight or flight responses to it.

Systemizing   Baron-Cohen's idea that the male brain is wired to analyze input-operation-output relations and inferring rules that govern such systems. An extreme male brain is seen in autism.

Technological change   Overall process whereby new technologies are invented or current technologies are innovated and defused across societies.

Technological determinism   The control of technology over daily lives and societal development as a whole.

Technology   The way in which humans interact with the material world to meet their basic needs and increase their well-being.

Technology transfer   Focused type of diffusion wherein technology is spread from higher to less advanced societies.

Temperament The stable, largely inborn tendency with which an individual experiences the environment and regulates his or her responses to the environment.

Thomas, Alexander Scholar who, with Stella Chess, resurrected the scientific study of temperament in the mid-20th century.

Thucydides Greek historian likening culture to the development of a child into an adult, in which culture grow slow and steady and exemplifies the natural history of change.

Tools of the Mind Curriculum that targets inhibitory control, working memory, and cognitive flexibility among at-risk preschool children.

Traditional authority Authority characterized by past and stability and the force of tradition.

Transactions Exchange of information and behavioral interactions between people and others in the environment.

Transcription The copying stage where RNA is synthesized from a single strand of DNA.

Transdisciplinary Joining together and transcendence of disciplines toward a common understanding of complex phenomena.

Translation Process whereby a triplet of nucleotides, known as a codon, of messenger RNA (mRNA) enters a reading frame in the ribosome, where a molecule of transfer RNA (tRNA) with the complimentary triplet of nucleotides, known as an anticodon, binds to the codon; the amino acid carried by the tRNA attaches to the polypeptide chain, which is a series of amino acids linked together.

Transportation Process whereby mRNA leaves the cell nucleus, enters the cytoplasm, and attaches to a ribosome; the ribosome is basically a protein factory where polypeptide chains (series of amino acids that are linked together) are produced.

Triune brain hypothesis MacLean's model, in which the limbic system was referred to as the paleomammalian component of the brain: phylogenetically younger than the reptilian brain, which controls the most basic instinctual behaviors involved in the survival of the species, and older than the neomammalian brain, which controls the most evolutionarily advanced, and thus human, behaviors, centering on language, cognition, and executive functioning.

Ultimate factors Higher-level, indirect variables, such as geographic determinants, that cause an outcome.

Updating The ability to constantly monitor and rapidly add or delete information from working memory.

Valence A concept that captures how good or bad, attractive or aversive a specific emotion is.

Working memory The ability to maintain mental representations in active memory and manipulate them for behavioral purposes.

World Trade Organization Regulates commerce between countries; facilitator during trade negotiations to decrease the usage of tariffs and quotas that interrupt trade.

REFERENCES

PREFACE

Bowles, S., Choi, J. K., & Hopfensitz, A. (2002). The co-evolution of individual behaviors and social institutions. *Journal of Theoretical Biology, 223,* 135–147.

Fuentes, A. (2009). A new synthesis: Resituating approaches to the evolution of human behavior. *Anthropology Today, 25*(3), 12–17.

Magnarella, P. (1993). *Human materialism: A model of sociocultual systems and a strategy for analysis.* Gainesville, FL: University Press of Florida.

Spear, L. P. (2010). *The behavioral neuroscience of adolescence.* New York, NY: Norton.

Turrell, G., Lynch, J. W., Leite, C., Raghunathan, T., & Kaplan, G. A. (2007). Socioeconomic disadvantage in childhood and across the life course and all-cause mortality and physical function in adulthood: Evidence from the Alameda County Study. *Journal of Epidemiology and Community Health, 61,* 723–730.

CHAPTER 1

Birdsell, J. B. (1999). Mitosis, meiosis, and the origins of genetic variability. In R. W. Sussman (Ed.), *The biological basis of human behavior: A critical review* (pp. 12–18). Upper Saddle River, NJ: Prentice Hall.

Brekke, J. S. (2012). Shaping a science of social work. *Research on Social Work Practice, 22*(5), 445–464.

Brekke, J. S., & Barrio, C. (1997). Cross-ethnic symptom differences in schizophrenia: The impact of culture and minority status. *Schizophrenia Bulletin, 23,* 305–316.

Brekke J. S., Kay, D., Kee, K., & Green, M. F. (2005). Biosocial pathways to functional outcome in schizophrenia. *Schizophrenia Research, 80,* 213–225.

Caspi, A., & Moffitt, T. E. (2006). Gene-environment interactions in psychiatry: Joining forces with neuroscience. *Nature Review: Neuroscience, 7,* 583–590.

Cicchetti, D., & Blender, J. A. (2004). A multiple-levels-of-analysis approach to the study of developmental processes in maltreated children. *Proceedings of the National Academy of Sciences, 101,* 17325–17326.

Cloninger, C. R. (1999). A new conceptual paradigm from genetics and psychobiology for the science of mental health. *Australian and New Zealand Journal of Psychiatry, 33,* 174–186.

Cloninger, C. R. (2004). *Feeling good: The science of well-being.* New York, NY: Oxford University Press.

Cloninger, C. R., Svrakic, D. M., & Pryzbeck, T. R. (1993). A psychobiological model of temperament and character. *Archives of General Psychiatry, 50,* 975–989.

Cloninger, C. R., Svrakic, D. M., & Svrakic, N. M. (1997). Role of personality self-organization in development of mental order and disorder. *Development and Psychopathology, 9,* 881–906.

de Waal, F. B. M. (1995). Bonobo sex and society: The behavior of a close relative challenges assumptions about male supremacy in human evolution. *Scientific American, 272,* 82–88.

Galea, S., Riddle, M., & Kaplan, G. A. (2010). Causal thinking and complex system approaches in epidemiology. *International Journal of Epidemiology, 39,* 97–106.

Gambrill, E. (2012). *Propaganda in the helping professions.* New York, NY: Oxford University Press.

Glass, T. A., & McAtee, M. J. (2008). Behavioral science at the crossroads in public health: Extending horizons, envisioning the future. *Social Science and Medicine, 62,* 1650–1671.

Gould, S. J. (2003). *The hedgehog, the fox, and the magister's pox: Mending the gap between science and the humanities.* New York, NY: Random House.

Greenspan, R. J. (1999). Understanding the genetic construction of behavior. In R. W. Sussman (Ed.),

The biological basis of human behavior: A critical review (pp. 19–25). Upper Saddle River, NJ: Prentice Hall.

Harris, M. (1974). *Cows, pigs, wars and witches: The riddles of culture*. New York, NY: Random House.

Harris, M. (1979). *Cultural materialism: The struggle for a science of culture*. New York, NY: Random House.

Harris, M. (1999). *Theories of culture in postmodern times*. Walnut Creek, CA: AltaMira.

Kirk, S. A., & Reid, W. J. (2002). *Science and social work: A critical appraisal*. New York, NY: Columbia University Press.

Kolb, B. (1999). Neuroanatomy and development overview. In N. A. Fox, L. A. Leavitt, & J. G. Warhol (Eds.), *The role of early experience in infant development* (pp. 5–14). Calverton, NY: Johnson & Johnson Pediatric Institute.

Laub, J. H. (2006). Edwin H. Sutherland and the Michael Adler report: Searching for the soul of criminology seventy years later. *Criminology, 44*, 235–258.

Lewin, K. (1936). *Principles of topographic psychology*. New York, NY: McGraw-Hill.

Lohr, J. M., Devilly, G., Lilienfeld, S. O., & Olatunji, B. O. (2006). First do no harm, and then do some good: Science and professional responsibility in the response to disaster and trauma. *The Behavior Therapist, 29*, 131–135.

MacLean, P. D. (1990). *The triune brain in evolution: Role in paleocerebral functions*. New York, NY: Plenum.

Makgoba, M. W. (2002). Politics, the media, and science in HIV/AIDS: The peril of pseudoscience. *Vaccine, 20*, 1899–1904.

Massey, D. S. (2002). A brief history of human society: The origin and role of emotion in social life. *American Sociological Review, 67*, 1–29.

Matsumoto, D. (2007). Culture, context, and behavior. *Journal of Personality, 75*, 1–35.

Mayr, E. (1976). *Evolution and the diversity of life*. Cambridge, MA: Belknap Press of Harvard University Press.

Meadows, D. H. (2008). *Thinking in systems: A primer*. White River Junction, VT: Chelsea Green.

National Institute of Neurological Disorders and Stroke. (2012, December 20). Amyotrophic Lateral Sclerosis (ALS) fact sheet (NIH Publication No. 12–916). Retrieved from www.ninds.nih.gov/disorders/amyotrophiclateralsclerosis/detail_ALS.htm

Peck, S. C. (2007). TEMPEST in a gallimaufry: Applying multilevel systems theory to person-in-context research. *Journal of Personality, 75*, 1127–1156.

Roberts, N., Andersen, D., Deal, R., Garet, M., & Shaffer, W. (1983). *Introduction to computer simulation*. Reading, MA: Addison-Wesley.

Sagan, C. (1997). *The demon-haunted world: Science as a candle in the dark*. New York, NY: Ballantine Books.

Sanderson, S. (1990). *Social evolutionism: A critical history*. Oxford, England: Basil Blackwell.

Schlegel, A., & Barry, H. (1991). *Adolescence: An anthropological inquiry*. New York, NY: Free Press.

Senge, P. M., Kleiner, A., Roberts, C., Ross, R. B., & Smith, B. J. (1994). *The fifth discipline fieldbook*. New York, NY: Currency and Doubleday.

Sussman, R. W. (1999). The myth of man the hunter/man the killer and the evolution of human morality. In R. W. Sussman (Ed.), *The biological basis of human behavior: A critical review* (pp. 19–25). Upper Saddle River, NJ: Prentice Hall.

Thelen, E., & Smith, L. B. (1998). Dynamic systems theories. In W. Damon & R. M. Lerner (Eds.), *Handbook of child psychology: Volume 1: Theoretical models of human development* (5th ed., pp. 563–634). New York, NY: Wiley.

Vaughn, M. G. (2007). Biosocial dynamics: A transdisciplinary approach to violence. In M. DeLisi & P. J. Conis (Eds.), *Violent offenders: Theory, research, public policy, & practice* (pp. 63–77). Burlington, MA: Jones & Bartlett.

Wilson, E. O. (1975). *Sociobiology: The new synthesis*. Cambridge, MA: Harvard University Press.

Wilson, E. O. (2012). *The social conquest of earth*. New York, NY: Norton.

Wright, J. P., Dietrich, K., Tis, M. D., Hornung, R. W., Wessel, S. D., Lanphear, B. P., . . . Rae, M. N. (2008). Association of prenatal and childhood lead concentrations with criminal arrests in early adulthood. *PLoS Medicine, 5*, 732–740.

CHAPTER 2

Ahmed, F. (2010). Tales of adversity. *Nature, 468*, S20.

Arseneault, L., Cannon, M., Fisher, H. L., Polanczyk, G., Moffitt, T. E., & Caspi, A. (2011). Childhood trauma and children's emerging psychotic symptoms: A genetically sensitive longitudinal cohort study. *American Journal of Psychiatry, 168,* 65–72.

Auerbach, J. G., Benjamin, J., Faroy, M., Geller, V., & Ebstein, R. (2001). DRD4 related to infant attention and information processing: A developmental link to ADHD? *Psychiatric Genetics, 11,* 31–35.

Auerbach, J. G., Landau, R., Berger, A., Arbelle, S., Faroy, M., & Karplus, M. (2005). Neonatal behavior in infants at familial risk for ADHD. *Infant Behavior & Development, 28,* 220–224.

Balog, D. (Ed.). (2006). *The Dana sourcebook of brain science: Resources for teachers and students* (4th ed.). New York, NY: Dana Press.

Barkley, R. A., Smith, K. M., Fischer, M., & Navia, B. (2006). An examination of the behavioral and neuropsychological correlates of three ADHD candidate gene polymorphisms (DRD4 7+, DBH Taq1 A2, and DAT1 40 bp VNTR) in hyperactive and normal children followed to adulthood. *American Journal of Medical Genetics B Neuropsychiatric Genetics, 141,* 487–498.

Baron-Cohen, S. (2011). *The science of evil: On empathy and the origins of cruelty.* New York, NY: Basic Books.

Beaver, K. M., DeLisi, M., Vaughn, M. G., & Barnes, J. C. (2010). MAOA genotype is associated with gang membership and weapon use. *Comprehensive Psychiatry, 51,* 130–134.

Bevilacqua, L., Doly, S., Kaprio, J., Yuan, Q., Tikkanen, R., Paunio, T., . . . Goldman, D. (2010). A population-specific HTR2B stop codon predisposes to severe impulsivity. *Nature, 468,* 1061–1068.

Bowcock, A. M., Kidd, J. R., Mountain, J. L., Hebert, J. M., Carotenuto, L., & Cavalli-Sforza, L. L. (1991). Drift, admixture, and selection in human evolution: A study with DNA polymorphisms. *Proceedings of the National Academy of Sciences of the United States of America, 88,* 839–843.

Burmeister, M., McInnis, M. G., & Zöllner, S. (2008). Psychiatric genetics: Progress amid controversy. *Nature Reviews Genetics, 9,* 527–540.

Cannon, T. D., & Keller, M. C. (2006). Endophenotypes in the genetic analyses of mental disorders. *Annual Review of Clinical Psychology, 2,* 267–290.

Carey, G. (2003). *Human genetics for the social sciences.* Thousand Oaks, CA: Sage.

Casey, B. J., Jones, R. M., & Hare, T. A. (2008). The adolescent brain. *Annals of the New York Academy of Sciences, 1124,* 111–126.

Caspi, A., Langley, K., Milne, B., Moffitt, T. E., O'Donovan, M., Owen, M. J., . . . Thapar, A. (2008). A replicated molecular genetic basis for subtyping antisocial behavior in children with attention-deficit/hyperactivity disorder. *Archives of General Psychiatry, 65,* 203–210.

Caspi, A., McClay, J., Moffitt, T. E., Mill, J., Martin, J., Craig, I. W., . . . Poulton, R. (2002). Role of genotype in the cycle of violence in maltreated children. *Science, 297,* 851–854.

Chen, J., Lipska, B. K., Halim, N., Ma, Q. D., Matsumoto, M., Melhem, S., . . . Weinberger, D. R. (2004). Functional analysis of genetic variation in catechol-O-methyltransferase (COMT): Effects on mRNA, proteins, and enzyme activity in postmortem human brain. *American Journal of Human Genetics, 75,* 807–821.

Chiang, M.-C., Barysheva, M., Shattuck, D. W., Lee, A. D., Madsen, S. K., Avedissian, C., . . . Thompson, P. M. (2009). Genetics of brain fiber architecture and intellectual performance. *Journal of Neuroscience, 29,* 2212–2224.

Churchland, P. S. (2011). *Braintrust: What neuroscience tells us about morality.* Princeton, NJ: Princeton University Press.

Crick, F. (1970). Central dogma of molecular biology. *Nature, 227,* 561–563.

Dagher, A., & Robbins, T. W. (2009). Personality, addiction, dopamine: Insights from Parkinson's Disease. *Neuron, 61,* 502–510.

Day, J. J., & Sweatt, J. D. (2010). DNA methylation and memory formation. *Nature Neuroscience, 13,* 1319–1323.

DeLisi, M., Wright, J. P., Vaughn, M. G., & Beaver, K. M. (2010). Nature and nurture by definition means both: A response to Males. *Journal of Adolescent Research, 25,* 24–30.

Esposito-Smythers, C., Spirito, A., Rizzo, C., McGeary, J. E., & Knopik, V. S. (2009). Associations of the DRD2 *TaqIA* polymorphism with impulsivity and substance use: Preliminary results from a clinical sample of adolescents. *Pharmacology Biochemistry and Behavior, 93,* 306–312.

Ferguson, C. J. (2010). Genetic contributions to antisocial personality and behavior (APB): A meta-analytic review (1996–2006) from an evolutionary perspective. *Journal of Social Psychology, 150,* 160–180.

Fine, C. (2010). *Delusions of gender: How our minds, society, and neurosexism create difference*. New York, NY: Norton.

Frazetto, G., Di Lorenzo, G., Carola, V., Proletti, L., Sokolowska, E., Siracusano, A., . . . Troisi, A. (2007). Early trauma and increased risk for physical aggression during adulthood: The moderating role of MAOA genotype. *PLoS One*, *2*(5), e486.

Hur, Y., & Bouchard, T. J., Jr. (1997). The genetic correlation between impulsivity and sensation seeking traits. *Behavior Genetics*, *27*, 455–463.

Jacobs, B. L., & Azmitia, E. C. (1992). Structure and function of the brain serotonin system. *Physiological Reviews*, *72*, 165–229.

Jordan-Young, R. M. (2010). *Brain storm: The flaws in the science of sex differences*. Cambridge, MA: Harvard University Press.

Kendler, K. S., & Prescott, C. A. (2006). *Genes, environment, and psychopathology: Understanding the causes of psychiatric and substance use disorders*. New York, NY: Guilford Press.

Kim-Cohen, J., Moffitt, T. E., Caspi, A., & Taylor, A. (2004). Genetic and environmental processes in young children's resilience and vulnerability to socioeconomic deprivation. *Child Development*, *75*, 651–668.

Kimura, M. (1968). Evolutionary rate at the molecular level. *Nature*, *217*, 624–626.

Kochanska, G., Philibert, R. A., & Barry, R. A. (2009). Interplay of genes and early mother-child relationship in the development of self-regulation from toddler to preschool age. *Journal of Child Psychology and Psychiatry*, *50*, 1331–1338.

Lander, E. S. (2011). Initial impact of the sequencing of the human genome. *Nature*, *470*, 187–197.

Langley, K., Fowler, T. A., Grady, D. L., Moyzis, R. K., Holmans, P. A., van den Bree, M. B. H., . . . Thapar, A. (2009). Molecular genetic contribution to the developmental course of attention-deficit hyperactivity disorder. *European Child and Adolescent Psychiatry*, *18*, 26–32.

Lederbogen, F., Kirsch, P., Haddad, L., Streit, F., Tost, H., Schuch, P., . . . Meyer-Lindenberg, A. (2011). City living and urban upbringing affect neural social stress processing in humans. *Nature*, *474*, 498–501.

Li, D., Sham, P. C., Owen, M. J., & He, L. (2006). Meta-analysis shows significant association between dopamine system genes and ADHD. *Human Molecular Genetics*, *15*, 2276–2284.

Ma, D. K., Marchetto, M. C., Guo, J. U., Ming, G., Gage, F. H., & Song, H. (2010). Epigenetic choreographers of neurogenesis in the adult mammalian brain. *Nature Neuroscience*, *13*, 1338–1344.

Males, M. (2009). Does the adolescent brain make risk taking inevitable? A skeptical appraisal. *Journal of Adolescent Research*, *24*, 3–20.

Mason, D. A., & Frick, P. J. (1994). The heritability of antisocial behavior: A meta-analysis of twin and adoption studies. *Journal of Psychopathology and Behavioral Assessment*, *16*, 301–323.

Meyer-Lindenberg, A., & Weinberger, D. R. (2006). Intermediate phenotypes and genetic mechanisms of psychiatric disorders. *Nature Reviews Neuroscience*, *7*, 818–827.

Miles, D. R., & Carey, G. (1997). Genetic and environmental architecture of human aggression. *Journal of Personality and Social Psychology*, *72*, 207–217.

Moffitt, T. E. (2005). Genetic and environmental influences on antisocial behaviors: Evidence from behavioral genetic research. *Advances in Genetics*, *55*, 41–104.

Munafò, M. R., Yalcin, B., Willis-Owen, S. A., & Flint, J. (2008). Association of the DRD4 gene and approach-related personality traits: Meta-analysis and new data. *Biological Psychiatry*, *63*, 197–206.

National Human Genome Research Institute. (2011). *A guide to your genome*. Washington, DC: National Institutes of Health, National Human Genome Research Institute.

Nyman, E. S., Ogdie, M. N., Loukola, A., Varilo, T., Taanila, A., Hurtig, T., . . . Peltonen, L. (2007). ADHD candidate gene study in a population-based birth cohort: Association with DBH and DRD2. *Journal of the American Academy of Child and Adolescent Psychiatry*, *46*, 1614–1621.

Plomin, R., & Caspi, A. (1998). DNA and personality. *European Journal of Personality*, *12*, 387–407.

Plomin, R., Owen, M. J., & McGuffin, P. (1994). The genetic basis of complex human behaviors. *Science*, *264*, 1733–1739.

Potts, M., & Hayden, T. (2008). *Sex and war: How biology explains warfare and terrorism and offers a path to a safer world*. Dallas, TX: BenBella.

Prom-Wormley, E. C., Eaves, L. J., Foley, D. L., Gardner, C. O., Archer, K. J., Wormley, B. K., . . . Silberg, J. L. (2009). Monoamine oxidase A and childhood adversity as risk factors for conduct problems in females. *Psychological Medicine*, *39*, 579–590.

Raine, A., Meloy, J. R., Bihrle, S., Stoddard, J., La-Casse, L., & Buchsbaum, M. S. (1998). Reduced prefrontal and increased subcortical brain functioning assessed using positron emission tomography in predatory and affective murderers. *Behavioral Sciences and the Law*, *16*, 319–332.

Rhee, S. H., & Waldman, I. D. (2002). Genetic and environmental influences on antisocial behavior: A meta-analysis of twin and adoption studies. *Psychological Bulletin*, *128*, 490–529.

Roper v. Simmons, 543 U.S. 551 (2005).

Rubia, A., Halari, R., Smith, A. B., Mohammed, M., Scott, S., Giampietro, V., ... Brammer, M. J. (2008). Dissociated functional brain abnormalities of inhibition in boys with pure conduct disorder and in boys with pure ADHD. *American Journal of Psychiatry*, *165*, 889–897.

Seeyave, D. M., Coleman, S., Appugliese, D., Corwyn, R. F., Bradley, R. H., Davidson, N. S., ... Lumeng, J. C. (2009). Ability to delay gratification at age 4 years and risk of overweight at age 11 years. *Archives of Pediatrics & Adolescent Medicine*, *163*, 303–308.

The 1000 Genomes Project Consortium. (2010). A map of human genome variation from population-scale sequencing. *Nature*, *467*, 1061–1073.

Tucker-Drob, E. M., Rhemtulla, M., Harden, K. P., Turkheimer, E., & Fask, D. (2011). Emergence of a gene × socioeconomic status interaction on infant mental ability between 10 months and 2 years. *Psychological Science*, *22*, 125–133.

van Goozen, S. H. M., Fairchild, G., Snock, H., & Harold, G. T. (2007). The evidence for a neurobiological model of childhood antisocial behavior. *Psychological Bulletin*, *133*, 149–182.

Vinkhuyzen, A. A. E., van der Sluis, S., Posthuman, D., & Boomsma, D. I. (2009). The heritability of aptitude and exceptional talent across different domains in adolescents and young adults. *Behavior Genetics*, *39*(4), 380–392.

Watson, J. D. (1996). *The double helix: A personal account of the discovery of the structure of DNA*. New York, NY: Touchstone Books. (Original work published 1968.)

White, M. J., Morris, C. P., Lawford, B. R., & Young, R. McD. (2008). Behavioral phenotype of impulsivity related to the ANKK1 gene are independent of an acute stressor. *Behavioral and Brain Functions*, *4*, 54.

Wright, J. P., Dietrich, K. N., Ris, M. D., Hornung, R. W., Wessel, S. D., Lanphear, B. P., ... Rae, M. N. (2008) Association of prenatal and childhood blood lead concentrations with criminal arrests in early adulthood. *PLoS Medicine*, *5*(5): e101. doi:10.1371/journal.pmed.0050101.

CHAPTER 3

American Psychiatric Association. (2000). *Diagnostic and statistical manual of mental disorders* (4th ed., Text Rev.). Washington, DC: Author.

Anderson, T., & Davis, C. (2011). Evidence-based practice with families of chronically ill children: A critical literature review. *Journal of Evidence-Based Social Work*, *8*, 416–425.

Bakermans-Kranenburg, M. J., van Ijzendoorn, M. H., & Juffer, F. (2003). Less is more: Meta-analyses of sensitivity and attachment interventions in early childhood. *Psychological Bulletin*, *129*, 195–215.

Biringen, Z., Altenhoffen, S., Aberle, J., Baker, M., Brosal, A., Bennett, S., ... Swaim, R. (2012). Emotional availability, attachment, and intervention in center-based child care for infants and toddlers. *Development and Psychopathology*, *24*, 23–34.

Bowlby, J. (1951). Maternal care and mental health. *Bulletin of the World Health Organization*, *3*, 355–534.

Bowlby, J. (1969). *Attachment and loss: Volume 1. Attachment*. New York, NY: Basic Books.

Bowlby, J. (1973). *Attachment and loss. Volume 2. Separation: Anxiety and anger*. New York, NY: Basic Books.

Bowlby, J. (1980). *Attachment and loss: Volume 3. Loss: Sadness and depression*. New York, NY: Basic Books.

Bride, B. E., Jones, J. L., & Macmaster, S. A. (2007). Correlates of secondary traumatic stress in child protective services workers. *Journal of Evidence-Based Social Work*, *4*, 69–80.

Camara, M., & Calvete, E. (2012). Early maladaptive schemas as moderators of the impact of stressful events on anxiety and depression in university students. *Journal of Psychopathology and Behavioral Assessment*, *34*, 58–58.

Chen, F. S., Kumsta, R., von Dawans, B., Monakhov, M., Ebstein, R. P., & Heinrichs, M. (2011). Common oxytocin receptor gene (OXTR) polymorphism and social support interact to reduce stress in humans. *Proceedings of the National Academy of Sciences of the United States of America, 108,* 19937–19942.

Cohen, S., & Wills, T. A. (1985). Stress, social support, and the buffering hypothesis. *Psychological Bulletin, 98,* 310–357.

Coleman, D. (2005). Trauma and incarcerated youth. *Journal of Evidence-Based Social Work, 2,* 113–124.

Cornwell, B. (2003). The dynamic properties of social support: Decay, growth, and staticity, and their effects on adolescent depression. *Social Forces, 81,* 953–978.

Coull, C., & Morris, P. G. (2011). The clinical effectiveness of CBT-based guided self-help interventions for anxiety and depressive disorders: A systematic review. *Psychological Medicine, 41,* 2239–2252.

Davies, P. T., & Cummings, E. M. (1994). Marital conflict and child adjustment: An emotional security hypothesis. *Psychological Bulletin, 116,* 387–411.

Del Giudice, M., Ellis, B. J., & Shirtcliff, E. A. (2011). The adaptive calibration model of stress reactivity. *Neuroscience and Biobehavioral Reviews, 35,* 1562–1592.

Derzon, J. H. (2010). The correspondence of family features with problem, aggressive, criminal, and violent behavior: A meta-analysis. *Journal of Experimental Criminology, 6,* 263–292.

Dougherty, L. R., Klein, D. N., Rose, S., & Laptook, R. S. (2011). HPA axis reactivity in the preschool-age offspring of depressed parents: Moderation by early parenting. *Psychological Science, 22,* 650–658.

Ellis, B. J., & Boyce, W. T. (2008). Biological sensitivity to context. *Current Directions in Psychological Science, 17,* 183–187.

El-Sheikh, M., & Erath, S. A. (2011). Family conflict, autonomic nervous system functioning, and child adaptation: State of the science and future directions. *Development and Psychopathology, 23,* 703–721.

Gillespie, C. F., & Nemeroff, C. B. (2007). Corticotropin-releasing factor and psychobiology of early-life stress. *Current Directions in Psychological Science, 16,* 85–89.

Gray, J. A. (1982). *The neuropsychology of anxiety: An enquiry into the functions of the septo-hippocampal system.* New York, NY: Oxford University Press.

Hodge, D. R., Jackson, K. F., & Vaughn, M. G. (2010). Culturally sensitive interventions for health related behaviors among Latino youth: A meta-analytic review. *Children and Youth Services Review, 32,* 1331–1337.

Hölzel, B. K., Lazar, S. W., Gard, T., Schuman-Olivier, Z., Vago, D. R., & Ott, U. (2011). How does mindfulness meditation work? Proposing mechanisms of action from a conceptual and neural perspective. *Perspectives on Psychological Science, 6,* 537–559.

Howe, D. (2006). Disabled children, parent–child interaction and attachment. *Child and Family Social Work, 11,* 95–106.

Injeyan, M. C., Shuman, C., Shugar, A., Chitayat, D., Atenafu, E. G., & Kaiser, A. (2011). Personality traits associated with genetic counselor compassion fatigue: The roles of dispositional optimism and locus of control. *Journal of Genetic Counseling, 20,* 526–540.

Kobak, R., Cassidy, J., Lyons-Ruth, K., & Ziv, Y. (2006). Attachment, stress, and psychopathology: A developmental pathways model. In D. Cicchetti & D. J. Cohen (Eds.), *Developmental psychopathology: Volume 1. Theory and method* (2nd ed., pp. 333–369). Hoboken, NJ: Wiley.

Korte, S. M., Koolhaas, J. M., Wingfield, J. C., & McEwen, B. S. (2005). The Darwinian concept of stress: Benefits of allostasis and costs of allostatic load and the trade-offs in health and disease. *Neuroscience and Biobehavioral Reviews, 29,* 3–38.

Krämer, M., Seefeldt, W. L., Heinrichs, N., Tuschen-Caffier, B., Schmitz, J., Wolf, O. T., & Blechert, J. (2012). Subjective, autonomic, and endocrine reactivity during social stress in children with social phobia. *Journal of Abnormal Child Psychology, 40,* 95–104.

Levy, T. M., & Orlans, M. (2000). Attachment disorder as an antecedent to violence and antisocial patterns in children. In T. M. Levy (Ed.), *Handbook of attachment interventions* (pp. 1–26). San Diego, CA: Academic Press/Elsevier.

Littrell, J. (2009). Expression of emotion: When it causes trauma and when it helps. *Journal of Evidence-Based Social Work, 6,* 300–320.

Mather, M., & Lighthall, N. R. (2012). Risk and reward are processed differently in decisions made under stress. *Current Directions in Psychological Science, 21,* 36–41.

McEwen, B. S. (2007). Physiology and neurobiology of stress and adaptation: Central role of the brain. *Physiological Reviews, 87,* 874–904.

Mead, H. K., Beauchaine, T. P., & Shannon, K. E. (2010). Neurobiological adaptations to violence across development. *Development and Psychopathology, 22*, 1–22.

Miller, G. E., Chen, E., Fok, A. K., Walker, H., Lim, A., Nicholls, E. F., ... Kobor, M. S. (2009). Low early-life social class leaves a biological residue manifested by decreased glucocorticoid and increased proinflammatory signaling. *Proceedings of the National Academy of Sciences of the United States of America, 106*, 14716–14721.

Miller, G. E., Lachman, M. E., Chen, E., Gruenewald, T. L., Karlamangla, A. S., & Seeman, T. E. (2011). Pathways to resilience: Maternal nurturance as a buffer against the effects of childhood poverty on metabolic syndrome at midlife. *Psychological Science, 22*, 1591–1599.

Moffitt, T. E., Caspi, A., Rutter, M., & Silva, P. A. (2001). *Sex differences in antisocial behavior: Conduct disorder, delinquency, and violence in the Dunedin Longitudinal Study.* New York, NY: Cambridge University Press.

Moore, G. A. (2009). Infants' and mothers' vagal reactivity in response to anger. *Journal of Child Psychology and Psychiatry, 50*, 1392–1400.

Nebbitt, V. E., Lombe, M., Yu, M., Vaughn, M. G., & Stokes, C. (2012). Ecological correlates of substance use in African American adolescents living in public housing communities: Assessing the moderating effects of social cohesion. *Children and Youth Services Review, 34*, 338–347.

Ouellet-Morin, I., Odgers, C. L., Danese, A., Bowes, L., Shakoor, S., Papadopoulos, A. S., ... Arseneault, L. (2011). Blunted cortisol responses to stress signal social and behavioral problems among maltreated/bullied 12-year-old children. *Biological Psychiatry, 70*, 1016–1023.

Ozer, E. J., Best, S. R., Lipsey, T. L., & Weiss, D. S. (2003). Predictors of PTSD and symptoms in adults: A meta-analysis. *Psychological Bulletin, 129*, 52–73.

Pluess, M., Velders, F. P., Belsky, J., van Ijzendoorn, M. H., Bakermans-Kranenburg, M. J., Jaddoe, V. W., ... Tiemeier, H. (2011). Serotonin transporter polymorphism moderates effects of prenatal maternal anxiety on infant negative emotionality. *Biological Psychiatry, 69*, 520–525.

Polanczyk, G., Caspi, A., Williams, B., Price, T. S., Danese, A., Sugden, K., ... Moffitt, T. E. (2009). Protective effect of CRHR1 gene variants on the development of adult depression following childhood maltreatment. *Archives of General Psychiatry, 66*, 978–985.

Prati, G., & Pietrantoni, L. (2009). Optimism, social support, and coping strategies as factors contributing to posttraumatic growth. *Journal of Loss and Trauma, 14*, 364–388.

Roberts, A. L., Gilman, S. E., Breslau, J., Breslau, N., & Koenen, K. C. (2011). Race/ethnic differences in exposure to traumatic events, development of PTSD, and treatment-seeking for PTSD in the United States. *Psychological Medicine, 41*, 71–83.

Rodrigues, S. M., Saslow, L. R., Garcia, N., John, O. P., & Keltner, D. (2009). Oxytocin receptor genetic variation relates to empathy and stress reactivity in humans. *Proceedings of the National Academy of Sciences of the United States of America, 106*, 21437–21441.

Rood, L., Roelofs, J., Bogels, S. M., & Arntz, A. (2012). The effects of experimentally induced rumination, positive appraisal, acceptance, and distancing when thinking about a stressful event on affect states in adolescents. *Journal of Abnormal Child Psychology, 40*, 73–84.

Rutter, M. (2010). Child and adolescent psychiatry: Past scientific achievements and challenges for the future. *European Child and Adolescent Psychiatry, 19*, 689–703.

Seery, M. D. (2011). Resilience: A silver lining to experiencing adverse life events? *Current Directions in Psychological Science, 20*, 390–394.

Shecory, M. (2012). Attachment styles, coping strategies, and romantic feelings among battered women in shelters. *International Journal of Offender Therapy and Comparative Criminology*, doi:10.1177/0306624X11434917.

Sturge-Apple, M. L., Davies, P. T., Martin, M. J., Cicchetti, D., & Hentges, R. F. (2012). An examination of the impact of harsh parenting contexts on children's adaptation within an evolutionary framework. *Developmental Psychology*, doi:10.1037/a0026908.

Susman, E. J. (2006). Psychobiology of persistent antisocial behavior: Stress, early vulnerabilities and the attenuation hypothesis. *Neuroscience and Biobehavioral Reviews, 30*, 376–389.

Tyuse, S. W., Hong, P. P., & Stretch, J. J. (2010). Evaluation of an intensive in-home family treatment program to prevent out-of-home placement. *Journal of Evidence-Based Social Work, 7*, 200–218.

van Goozen, S. H. M., Fairchild, G., Snock, H., & Harold, G. T. (2007). The evidence for a neurobiological model of childhood antisocial behavior. *Psychological Bulletin, 133*, 149–182.

van Ijzendoorn, M. H., Schuengel, C., & Bakermans-Kranenburg, M. J. (1999). Disorganized attachment in early childhood: Meta-analysis of precursors, concomitants, and sequelae. *Development and Psychopathology, 11*, 225–249.

Vaske, J., Newsome, J., & Wright, J. P. (2012). Interaction of serotonin transporter linked polymorphic region and childhood neglect on criminal behavior and substance use for males and females. *Development and Psychopathology, 24*, 181–193.

Williams, K. D., & Nida, S. A. (2011). Ostracism: Consequences and coping. *Current Directions in Psychological Science, 21*, 71–75.

Wright, J. P., Cullen, F. T., & Miller, J. T. (2001). Family social capital and delinquent involvement. *Journal of Criminal Justice, 29*, 1–9.

CHAPTER 4

Ackerman, D. (2004). *An alchemy of mind: The marvel and mystery of the brain*. New York, NY: Scribner.

Baumgartner, T., Fischbacher, U., Feierabend, A., Lutz, K., & Fehr, E. (2009). The neural circuitry of a broken promise. *Neuron, 64*, 756–770.

Borduin, C. M., & Schaeffer, C. M. (2001). Multisystemic treatment of juvenile sex offenders: A progress report. *Journal of Psychology and Human Sexuality, 13*, 25–42.

Bradley, R., Henderson, K., & Monfore, D. A. (2004). A national perspective on children with emotional disorders. *Behavioral Disorders, 29*, 211–223.

Burns, B. J., Schoenwald, S. K., Burchard, J. D., Faw, L., & Santos, A. B. (2000). Comprehensive community-based interventions for youth with severe emotional disorders: Multisystemic Therapy and the wraparound process. *Journal of Child and Family Studies, 9*, 283–314.

Canli, T., Ferri, J., & Duman, E. A. (2009). Genetics of emotion regulation. *Neuroscience, 164*, 43–54.

Crick, N. R., & Dodge, K. A. (1994). A review and reformulation of social information processing mechanisms in children's social adjustment. *Psychological Bulletin, 115*, 74–101.

Crick, N. R., & Dodge, K. A. (1996). Social information-processing mechanisms on reactive and proactive aggression. *Child Development, 67*, 993–1002.

Darwin, C. (2005). *The expression of emotion in man and animals*. New York, NY: D. Appleton. (Original work published 1872.)

Davidson, R. J. (2001). Toward a biology of personality and emotion. *Annals of the New York Academy of Sciences, 935*, 191–207.

Davidson, R. J. (2003). Affective neuroscience and psychophysiology: Toward a synthesis. *Psychophysiology, 40*, 655–665.

Davidson, R. J., Putnam, K. M., & Larson, C. L. (2000). Dysfunction in the neural circuitry of emotion regulation: A possible prelude to violence. *Science, 289*, 591–594.

DeLisi, M. (2011). The limbic system and crime. In K. M. Beaver & A. Walsh (Eds.), *The Ashgate research companion to biosocial theories of crime* (pp. 167–180). Burlington, VT: Ashgate.

Dolan, R. J. (2002). Emotion, cognition, and behavior. *Science, 298*, 1191–1194.

Ekman, P. (1992). An argument for basic emotions. *Cognition and Emotion, 6*, 169–200.

Fullam, R. S., McKie, S., & Dolan, M. C. (2009). Psychopathic traits and deception: Functional magnetic resonance imaging study. *British Journal of Psychiatry, 194*, 229–235.

Gospic, K., Mohlin, E., Fransson, P., Petrovic, P., Johannesson, M., & Ingvar, M. (2011). Limbic justice: Amygdala involvement in immediate rejection in the Ultimatum Game. *PLoS Biology, 9*, e1001054. doi:10.1371/journal.pbio.1001054

Graham, J. R., & Shier, M. L. (2010). The social work profession and subjective well-being: The impact of a profession on overall subjective well-being. *British Journal of Social Work, 40*, 1553–1572.

Gruber, J. (2011). Can feeling too good be bad? Positive emotion persistence (PEP) in bipolar disorder. *Current Directions in Psychological Science, 20*, 217–221.

Gruber, J., Mauss, I. B., & Tamir, M. (2011). A dark side of happiness? How, when, and why happiness is not always good. *Perspectives on Psychological Science, 6*, 222–233.

Henggeler, S. W., Mihalic, S. F., Rone, L., Thomas, C., & Timmons-Mitchell, J. (1998). *MST: Blueprints for violence prevention*, Book 6. Boulder,

CO: Center for the Study and Prevention of Violence, Institute of Behavioral Sciences, University of Colorado.

Hertel, P. T., & Mathews, A. (2011). Cognitive bias modifications: Past perspectives, current findings, and future applications. *Perspectives on Psychological Science, 6*, 521–536.

Hill, S. E., DelPriore, D. J., & Vaughn, P. W. (2011). The cognitive consequences of envy: Attention, memory, and self-regulatory depletion. *Journal of Personality and Social Psychology, 101*, 653–666.

Kagan, J. (1994). *The nature of the child: Tenth anniversary edition*. New York, NY: Basic Books.

Kang, J. (2012). Pathways from social support to service use among caregivers at risk of child maltreatment. *Children and Youth Services Review, 34*, 933–939.

Kendler, K. S., Eaves, L. J., Loken, E. K., Pedersen, N. L., Middeldorp, C. M., Reynolds, C., ... Gardner, C. O. (2011). The impact of environmental experiences on symptoms of anxiety and depression across the life span. *Psychological Science, 22*, 1343–1352.

Kochanska, G., & Murray, K. T. (2000). Mother-child mutually responsive orientation and conscience development: From toddler to early school age. *Child Development, 71*, 417–431.

Kosfeld, M., Heinrichs, M., Zak, P. J., Fischbacher, U., & Fehr, E. (2005). Oxytocin increases trust in humans. *Nature, 435*, 673–676.

Kret, M. E., & De Gelder, B. (2012). Sex differences in processing emotional signals of others. *Neuropsychologia, 50*, 1211–1221.

Lee, V., & Hoaken, P. N. S. (2007). Cognition, emotion, and neurobiological development: Mediating the relation between maltreatment and aggression. *Child Maltreatment, 12*, 281–298.

Lindsey, M. A., Gilreath, T. D., Thompson, R., Graham, J. C., Hawley, K. M., Weisbart, C., ... Kotch, J. B. (2012). Influence of caregiver network support and caregiver psychopathology on child mental health need and service use in the LONGSCAN study. *Children and Youth Services Review, 34*, 924–932.

Lochman, J. E., & Dodge, K. A. (1994). Social-cognitive processes of severely violent, moderately aggressive, and nonaggressive boys. *Journal of Consulting and Clinical Psychology, 62*, 366–374.

Meier, B. P., Robinson, M. D., & Wilkowski, B. M. (2006). Turning the other cheek: Agreeableness and the regulation of aggression-related primes. *Psychological Science, 17*, 136–142.

Moffitt, T. E. (1993). Adolescence-limited and life-course-persistent antisocial behavior: A developmental taxonomy. *Psychological Review, 100*, 674–701.

Munson, M. R., Scott, L. D., Jr., Smalling, S. E., Kim, H., & Floersch, J. E. (2011). Former system youth with mental health needs: Routes to adult mental health care, insight, emotions, and mistrust. *Children and Youth Services Review, 33*, 2261–2266.

Patrick, C. J., Fowles, D. C., & Krueger, R. F. (2009). Triarchic conceptualization of psychopathy: Developmental origins of disinhibition, boldness, and meanness. *Development and Psychopathology, 21*, 913–938.

Roberton, T., Daffern, M., & Bucks, R. S. (2012). Emotion regulation and aggression. *Aggression and Violent Behavior, 17*, 72–82.

Saarni, C. (1999). *The development of emotional competence*. New York, NY: Guilford Press.

Saarni, C., Campos, J. J., Camras, L. A., & Witherington, D. (2006). Emotional development: Action, communication, and understanding. In N. Eisenberg (Ed.), *Handbook of child psychology, Volume 3: Social, emotional, and personality development* (6th ed., pp. 226–299). Hoboken, NJ: Wiley.

Simpson, J. A., Collins, W. A., & Salvatore, J. E. (2011). The impact of early interpersonal experience on adult romantic relationship functioning: Recent findings from the Minnesota Longitudinal Study of Risk and Adaptation. *Current Directions in Psychological Science, 20*, 355–359.

Sonuga-Barke, E. J. S., Oades, R. D., Psychogiou, L., Chen, W., Franke, B., Buitelaar, J., ... Faraone, S. V. (2009). Dopamine and serotonin transporter genotypes moderate sensitivity to maternal expressed emotion: The case of conduct and emotional problems in ADHD. *Journal of Child Psychology and Psychiatry, 50*, 1052–1063.

Tambs, K., Czajkowsky, N., Røysamb, E., Neale, M. C., Reichborn-Kjennerud, T., Aggen, S. H., ... Kendler, K. S. (2009). Structure of genetic and environmental risk factors for dimensional representations of DSM-IV anxiety disorders. *British Journal of Psychiatry, 195*, 301–307.

Taylor, A., & Kim-Cohen, J. (2007). Meta-analysis of gene-environment interactions in developmental psychopathology. *Development and Psychopathology, 19*, 1029–1037.

Thompson, R. (2010). Maltreatment and mental health care: Focusing on neglect. *Psychiatric Services, 61,* 96.

Thompson, R., Lindsey, M., English, D., Hawley, K., Lambert, S., & Browne, D. (2007). The influence of family environment on mental health need and service use among vulnerable children. *Child Welfare, 86,* 57–74.

Tsai, J., Ying, Y., & Lee, P. (2000). The meaning of "being Chinese" and "being American": Variation among Chinese-American youth adults. *Journal of Cross-Cultural Psychology, 31,* 302–332.

Vaughn, M. G., & Howard, M. O. (2004). Adolescent substance abuse treatment: A synthesis of controlled evaluations. *Research on Social Work Practice, 14,* 325–335.

Vaughn, M. G., Howard, M. O., Foster, K. A., Dayton, M. K., & Zelner, J. L. (2005). Substance use in a state population of incarcerated juvenile offenders. *Journal of Evidence-Based Social Work, 2,* 155–173.

Viding, E., Jones, A. P., Frick, P. J., Moffitt, T. E., & Plomin, R. (2008). Heritability of antisocial behavior at 9: Do callous-unemotional traits matter? *Developmental Science, 11,* 17–22.

Volkow, N. D., Tomasi, D., Wang, G., Fowler, J. S., Telang, F., Goldstein, R. Z., ... Alexoff, D. (2011). Positive emotionality is associated with baseline metabolism in orbitofrontal cortex and in regions of the default network. *Molecular Psychiatry, 16,* 818–825.

Wakschlag, L. S., Kistner, E. O., Pine, D. S., Biesecker, G., Pickett, K. E., Skol, A. D., ... Cooke, E. H. (2010). Interaction of prenatal exposure to cigarettes and MAOA genotype in pathways to youth antisocial behavior. *Molecular Psychiatry, 15,* 928–937.

Watson, D., & Clark, L. A. (1984). Negative affectivity: The disposition to experience aversive emotional states. *Psychological Bulletin, 96,* 465–490.

Watson, D., Clark, L. A., & Tellegen, A. (1988). Development and validation of the brief measure of positive and negative affect: The PANAS scales. *Journal of Personality and Social Psychology, 54,* 1063–1070.

Whittle, S., Yücel, M., Yap, M. B. H., & Allen, N. B. (2011). Sex differences in the neural correlates of emotion: Evidence from neuroimaging. *Biological Psychology, 87,* 319–333.

Zahn-Waxler, C. (1991). The case for empathy: A developmental review. *Psychological Inquiry, 2,* 155–158.

CHAPTER 5

American Psychiatric Association. (2000). *Diagnostic and statistical manual of mental disorders* (4th ed., Text Rev.). Washington, DC: Author.

Auerbach, J. G., Landau, R., Berger, A., Arbelle, S., Faroy, M., & Karplus, M. (2005). Neonatal behavior in infants at familial risk for ADHD. *Infant Behavior & Development, 28,* 220–224.

Ayduk, Ö., Mischel, W., & Downey, G. (2002). Attentional mechanisms linking rejection to hostile reactivity: The role of hot versus cool focus. *Psychological Science, 13,* 443–448.

Barkley, R. A. (1997a). *ADHD and the nature of self-control.* New York, NY: Guilford Press.

Barkley, R. A. (1997b). Behavioral inhibition, sustained attention, and executive functions: Constructing a unifying theory of ADHD. *Psychological Bulletin, 121,* 65–94.

Barkley, R. A. (2001). The executive functions and self-regulation: An evolutionary neuropsychological perspective. *Neuropsychology Review, 11,* 1–29.

Barkley, R. A. (2012). *Executive functions: What they are, how they work, and why they evolved.* New York, NY: Guilford Press.

Baron-Cohen, S. (2003). *The essential difference: Men, women, and the extreme male brain.* New York, NY: Penguin Books.

Baron-Cohen, S., Knickmeyer, R. C., & Belmonte, M. K. (2005). Sex differences in the brain: Implications for explaining autism. *Science, 310,* 819–823.

Beaver, K. M., Vaughn, M. G., DeLisi, M., & Higgins, G. E. (2010). The biosocial correlates of neuropsychological deficits: Results from the National Longitudinal Study of Adolescent Health. *International Journal of Offender Therapy and Comparative Criminology, 56,* 878–894.

Beaver, K. M., Wright, J. P., & DeLisi, M. (2007). Self-control as an executive function: Reformulating Gottfredson and Hirschi's parental socialization thesis. *Criminal Justice and Behavior, 34,* 1345–1361.

Berkman, E. T., Falk, E. B., & Lieberman, M. D. (2011). In the trenches of real-world self-control: Neural correlates and breaking the link between craving and smoking. *Psychological Science, 22,* 498–506.

Bernardi, S., Faraone, S. V., Cortese, S., Kerridge, B. T., Pallanti, S., Wang, S., & Blanco, C. (2012). The lifetime impact of ADHD: Results from the National Epidemiologic Survey on Alcohol and Related Conditions (NESARC). *Psychological Medicine, 42,* 875–887.

Chronis, A. M., Chacko, A., Fabiano, G. A., Wymbs, B. T., & Pelham, W. E., Jr. (2004). Enhancements to the behavioral parent training paradigm for families of children with ADHD: Review and future directions. *Clinical Child and Family Psychology Review, 7,* 1–27.

Cohen, J. R., Asarnow, R. F., Sabb, F. W., Bilder, R. M., Bookheimer, S. Y., Knowlton, B. J., & Poldrack, R. A. (2010). A unique adolescent response to reward prediction errors. *Nature Neuroscience, 13,* 669–671.

Coolidge, F. L., & Wynn, T. (2001). Executive functions of the frontal lobes and the evolutionary ascendancy of Homo sapiens. *Cambridge Archaeological Journal, 11,* 255–260.

Corcoran, J., & Dattalo, P. (2006). Parent involvement in treatment for ADHD: A meta-analysis of the published studies. *Research on Social Work Practice, 16,* 561–570.

Coyle, T. R., Pillow, D. R., Snyder, A. C., & Kochunov, P. (2011). Processing speed mediates the development of general intelligence (g) in adolescence. *Psychological Science, 22,* 1265–1269.

DeLisi, M., Vaughn, M. G., Beaver, K. M., Wexler, J., Barth, A. E., & Fletcher, J. M. (2011). Fledgling psychopathy in the classroom: ADHD subtypes, psychopathy, and reading comprehension in a community sample of adolescents. *Youth Violence and Juvenile Justice, 9,* 43–58.

DeLisi, M., Vaughn, M. G., Beaver, K. M., & Wright, J. P. (2010). The Hannibal Lecter myth: Psychopathy and verbal intelligence in the MacArthur Violence Risk Assessment Study. *Journal of Psychopathology and Behavioral Assessment, 32,* 169–177.

Diamond, A., Barnett, W. S., Thomas, J., & Munro, S. (2007). Preschool program improves cognitive control. *Science, 318,* 1387–1388.

Diamond, A., & Lee, K. (2011). Interventions shown to aid executive function in children 4 to 12 years old. *Science, 333,* 959–964.

Franklin, C., Kim, J. S., & Tripodi, S. J. (2009). A meta-analysis of published school social work practice studies: 1980–2007. *Research on Social Work Practice, 19,* 667–677.

Friedman, N. P., Miyake, A., Young, S. E., DeFries, J. C., Corley, R. P., & Hewitt, J. K. (2008). Individual differences in executive functions are almost entirely genetic in origin. *Journal of Experimental Psychology: General, 137,* 201–225.

Glatz, T., Stattin, H., & Kerr, M. (2011). Parents' reactions to youths' hyperactivity, impulsivity, and attention problems. *Journal of Abnormal Child Psychology, 39,* 1125–1135.

Gyurak, A., & Ayduk, Ö. (2007). Defensive physiological reactions to rejection: The effect of self-esteem and attentional control on startle responses. *Psychological Science, 18,* 886–892.

Himelstein, S., Hastings, A., Shapiro, S., & Heery, M. (2012). A qualitative investigation of the experience of a mindfulness-based intervention with incarcerated adolescents. *Child and Adolescent Mental Health, 17*(4), 231–237.

Houben, K., Wiers, R. W., & Jansen, A. (2011). Getting a grip on drinking behavior: Training working memory to reduce alcohol abuse. *Psychological Science, 22,* 968–975.

Kalbfleisch, M. L., & Loughan, A. R. (2012). Impact of IQ discrepancy on executive function in high-functioning autism: Insight into twice exceptionality. *Journal of Autism and Developmental Disorders, 42,* 390–400.

Kopp, C. B. (2002). Commentary: The codevelopments of attention and emotion regulation. *Infancy, 3,* 199–208.

Krueger, R. F., Hicks, B. M., Patrick, C. J., Carlson, S. R., Iacono, W. G., & McGue, M. (2002). Etiologic connections among substance dependence, antisocial behavior, and personality: Modeling the externalizing spectrum. *Journal of Abnormal Psychology, 111,* 411–424.

Lahey, B. B., Van Hulle, C. A., Rathouz, P. J., Rodgers, J. L., D'Onofrio, B. M., & Waldman, I. D. (2009). Are oppositional-defiant and hyperactive-inattentive symptoms developmental precursors to conduct problems in late childhood? Genetic and environmental links. *Journal of Abnormal Child Psychology, 37,* 45–58.

Lutz, A., Slagter, H. A., Rawlings, N. B., Francis, A. D., Greischar, L. L., & Davidson, R. J. (2009). Mental training enhances attentional stability: Neural and behavioral evidence. *The Journal of Neuroscience, 29,* 13418–13427.

Matto, H. C. (2002). Investigating the validity of the draw-a-person: screening procedure for emotional disturbance: A measurement validation study with high-risk youth. *Psychological Assessment, 14,* 221–225.

Matto, H. C., Naglieri, J. A., & Clausen, C. (2005). Validity of the draw-a-person: screening procedure for emotional disturbance (DAP:SPED) in strengths-based assessment. *Research on Social Work Practice, 15,* 41–46.

Matto, H. C., Strolin, J. S., & Mogro-Wilson, C. (2008). A pilot study of a dual processing substance user treatment intervention with adults. *Substance Use & Misuse, 43,* 285–294.

Matto, H. C., & Strolin-Goltzman, J. (2010). Integrating social neuroscience and social work: Innovations for advancing practice-based research. *Social Work, 55,* 147–156.

Meier, S., & Sprenger, C. D. (2012). Time discounting predicts creditworthiness. *Psychological Science, 23,* 56–58.

Morgan, A. B., & Lilienfeld, S. O. (2000). A meta-analytic review of the relation between antisocial behavior and neuropsychological measures of executive function. *Clinical Psychology Review, 20,* 113–136.

Moreno, S., Bialystok, E., Barac, R., Schellenberg, E. G., Cepeda, N. J., & Chau, T. (2011). Short-term music training enhances verbal intelligence and executive functions. *Psychological Science, 22,* 1425–1433.

Moses, T., & Kirk, S. A. (2006). Social workers' attitudes about psychotropic drug treatment with youths. *Social Work, 51,* 211–222.

Munakata, Y., Snyder, H. R., & Chatham, C. H. (2012). Developing cognitive control: Three key transitions. *Current Directions in Psychological Science, 21,* 71–77.

Nordgren, L. F., & Chou, E. Y. (2011). The push and pull of temptation: The bidirectional influence of temptation on self-control. *Psychological Science, 22,* 1386–1390.

Odgers, C. L., Milne, B. J., Caspi, A., Crump, R., Poulton, R., & Moffitt, T. E. (2007). Predicting prognosis for the conduct-problem boy: Can family history help? *Journal of the American Academy of Child and Adolescent Psychiatry, 46,* 1240–1249.

Ogilvie, J. M., Stewart, A. L., Chan, R. C. K., & Shum, D. H. K. (2011). Neuropsychological measures of executive function and antisocial behavior: A meta-analysis. *Criminology, 49,* 1063–1107.

Ozonoff, S., Pennington, B. F., & Rogers, S. J. (1991). Executive function deficits in high-functioning autistic individuals: Relationship to theory of mind. *Journal of Child Psychology and Psychiatry, 32,* 1081–1105.

Paloyelis, Y., Asherson, P., Mehta, M. A., Faraone, S. V., & Kuntsi, J. (2010). DAT1 and COMT effects on delay discounting and trait impulsivity in male adolescents with ADHD and healthy controls. *Neuropsychopharmacology, 35,* 2414–2426.

Parasuraman, R. (2011). Neuroergonomics: Brain, cognition, and performance at work. *Current Directions in Psychological Science, 20,* 181–186.

Pollatsek, A., Romoser, M. R. E., & Fisher, D. L. (2012). Identifying and remediating failures of selective attention in older drivers. *Current Directions in Psychological Science, 21,* 3–7.

Rindermann, H., & Thompson, J. (2011). Cognitive capitalism: The effect of cognitive ability on wealth, as mediated through scientific achievement and economic freedom. *Psychological Science, 22,* 754–763.

Rubia, K. (2011). "Cool" inferior frontostriatal dysfunction in ADHD versus "hot" ventromedial orbitofrontal-limbic dysfunction in conduct disorder: A review. *Biological Psychiatry, 69,* e69–e87.

Séguin, J. R. (2004). Neurocognitive elements of antisocial behavior: Relevance of an orbitofrontal cortex account. *Brain and Cognition, 55,* 185–197.

Unsworth, N., Miller, J. D., Lakey, C. E., Young, D. L., Meeks, J. T., Campbell, W. K., & Goodie, A. S. (2009). Exploring the relations among executive functions, fluid intelligence, and personality. *Journal of Individual Differences, 30,* 194–200.

Vinogradov, S., Fisher, M., & de Villers-Sidani, E. (2012). Cognitive training for impaired neural systems in neuropsychiatric illness. *Neuropsychopharmacology, 37,* 43–76.

Volkow, N. D., & Baler, R. D. (2012). To stop or not to stop? *Science, 335,* 546–548.

Willcutt, E. G., Doyle, A. E., Nigg, J. T., Faraone, S. V., & Pennington, B. F. (2005). Validity of the executive function theory of ADHD: A meta-analytic review. *Biological Psychiatry, 57,* 1336–1346.

Young, S. E., Stallings, M. C., Corley, R. P., Krauter, K. S., & Hewitt, J. K. (2000). Genetic and environmental influences on behavioral disinhibition.

American Journal of Medical Genetics (Neuropsychiatric Genetics), 96, 684–695.

CHAPTER 6

Allport, G. W. (1961). *Pattern and growth in personality.* New York, NY: Henry Holt.

Arikha, N. (2007). *Passions and tempers: A history of the humours.* New York, NY: Harper/Perennial.

Auerbach, J. G., Benjamin, J., Faroy, M., Geller, V., & Ebstein, R. (2001). DRD4 related to infant attention and information processing: A developmental link to ADHD? *Psychiatric Genetics*, 11, 31–35.

Auerbach, J. G., Landau, R., Berger, A., Arbelle, S., Faroy, M., & Karplus, M. (2005). Neonatal behavior in infants at familial risk for ADHD. *Infant Behavior & Development*, 28, 220–224.

Bates, J. E. (1989). Concepts and measures of temperament. In G. A. Kohnstamm, J. E. Bates, & M. K. Rothbart (Eds.), *Temperament in childhood* (pp. 3–26). Oxford, England: Wiley.

Beaver, K. M., DeLisi, M., Vaughn, M. G., & Wright, J. P. (2010). The intersection of genes and neuropsychological deficits in the prediction of adolescent delinquency and low self-control. *International Journal of Offender Therapy and Comparative Criminology*, 54, 22–42.

Beaver, K. M., Wright, J. P., & DeLisi, M. (2007). Self-control as an executive function: Reformulating Gottfredson and Hirschi's parental socialization thesis. *Criminal Justice and Behavior*, 34, 1345–1361.

Benson, N., Oakland, T., & Shermis, M. (2009). Cross-national invariance of children's temperament. *Journal of Psychoeducational Assessment*, 27, 3–16.

Blair, J., Mitchell, D., & Blair, K. (2005). *The psychopath: Emotion and the brain.* Malden, MA: Blackwell.

Blatny, M., Jelinek, M., & Osecka, T. (2007). Assertive toddler, self-efficacious adult: Child temperament predicts personality over forty years. *Personality and Individual Differences*, 43, 2127–2136.

Bouchard, T. J., & Loehlin, J. C. (2001). Genes, evolution, and personality. *Behavior Genetics*, 31, 243–273.

Buckingham, R. M. (2002). Extraversion, neuroticism, and the four temperaments of antiquity: An investigation of physiological reactivity. *Personality and Individual Differences*, 32, 225–246.

Buss, A. H., & Plomin, R. (1975). *A temperament theory of personality development.* New York, NY: Wiley.

Campbell, S. B. (1994). Hard-to-manage preschool boys: Externalizing behavior, social competence, and family context at two-year follow-up. *Journal of Abnormal Child Psychology*, 22, 147–166.

Campbell, S. B., & Ewing, L. J. (1990). Follow-up of hard-to-manage preschoolers: Adjustment at age 9 and predictors of continuing symptoms. *Journal of Child Psychology and Psychiatry*, 31, 871–889.

Caspi, A. (2000). The child is father of the man: Personality continuities from childhood to adulthood. *Journal of Personality and Social Psychology*, 78, 158–172.

Caspi, A., Elder, G. H., & Bem, D. J. (1987). Moving against the world: Life-course patterns of explosive children. *Developmental Psychology*, 23, 308–313.

Caspi, A., Henry, B., McGee, R. O., Moffitt, T. E., & Silva, P. A. (1995). Temperamental origins of child and adolescent behavior problems: From age 3 to age 15. *Child Development*, 66, 55–68.

Caspi, A., Moffitt, T. E., Newman, D. L., & Silva, P. A. (1996). Behavioral observations at age 3 years predict adult psychiatric disorders: Longitudinal evidence from a birth cohort. *Archives of General Psychiatry*, 53, 1033–1039.

Caspi, A., & Silva, P. A. (1995). Temperamental qualities at age 3 predict personality traits in young adulthood: Longitudinal evidence from a birth cohort. *Child Development*, 66, 486–498.

Chess, S., & Thomas, A. (1996). *Temperament: Theory and practice.* Philadelphia, PA: Brunner/Mazel.

Chess, S., & Thomas, A. (1999). *Goodness of fit: Clinical applications from infancy through adult life.* Philadelphia, PA: Brunner/Mazel.

Cloninger, C. R. (1987). A systematic method for clinical description and classification of personality variants. *Archives of General Psychiatry*, 44, 573–588.

Cloninger, C. R., Svrakic, D. M., & Przybeck, T. R. (1993). A psychobiological model of temperament and character. *Archives of General Psychiatry*, 50, 975–990.

Crockenberg, S. C., Leerkes, E. M., & Barrig Jo, P. S. (2008). Predicting aggressive behavior in the third year from infant reactivity and regulation as moderated by maternal behavior. *Development and Psychopathology*, 20, 37–54.

Cuijpers, P., Smit, F., Penninx, B. W., de Graaf, R., ten Have, M., & Beekman, A. T. (2010). Economic costs of neuroticism: A population-based study. *Archives of General Psychiatry, 67*, 1086–1093.

Davidson, R. J. (2001). Toward a biology of personality and emotion. *Annals of the New York Academy of Sciences, 935*, 191–207.

Davidson, R. J. (2003). Affective neuroscience and psychophysiology: Toward a synthesis. *Psychophysiology, 40*, 655–665.

Davidson, R. J., Putnam, K. M., & Larson, C. L. (2000). Dysfunction in the neural circuitry of emotion regulation: A possible prelude to violence. *Science, 289*, 591–594.

DeLisi, M. (2009). Psychopathy is the unified theory of crime. *Youth Violence and Juvenile Justice, 7*, 256–273.

DeLisi, M., Umphress, Z. R., & Vaughn, M. G. (2009). The criminology of the amygdala. *Criminal Justice and Behavior, 36*, 1231–1242.

DeLisi, M., & Vaughn, M. G. (2011). The importance of neuropsychological deficits relating to self-control and temperament to the prevention of serious antisocial behavior. *International Journal of Child, Youth and Family Studies, 1 & 2*, 12–35.

Derryberry, D., & Rothbart, M. K. (1988). Arousal, affect, and attention as components of temperament. *Journal of Personality and Social Psychology, 55*, 958–966.

DiPietro, J. A., Ghera, M. M., & Costigan, K. A. (2008). Prenatal origins of temperamental reactivity. *Early Human Development, 84*, 569–575.

DiPietro, J. A., Hodgson, D. M., Costigan, K. A., & Johnson, T. R. B. (1996). Fetal antecedents of infant temperament. *Child Development, 67*, 2568–2583.

Emde, R. N., Plomin, R., Robinson, J., Corley, R., DeFries, J., Fulker, D. W., ... Zahn-Wexler, C. (1992). Temperament, emotion, and cognition at fourteen months: The MacArthur Longitudinal Twin Study. *Child Development, 63*, 1437–1455.

Gartstein, M. A., & Rothbart, M. K. (2003). Studying infant temperament via the Revised Infant Behavior Questionnaire. *Infant Behavior & Development, 26*, 64–86.

Goldsmith, H. H., Lemery, K. S., Buss, K. A., & Campos, J. J. (1999). Genetic analyses of focal aspects of infant temperament. *Developmental Psychology, 35*, 972–985.

Gray, J. A. (1982). *The neuropsychology of anxiety: An enquiry into the functions of the septo-hippocampal system*. New York, NY: Oxford University Press.

Hare, R. D., & Neumann, C. S. (2008). Psychopathy as a clinical and empirical construct. *Annual Review of Clinical Psychology, 4*, 217–246.

Heath, A. C., Cloninger, C. R., & Martin, N. G. (1994). Testing a model for the genetic structure of personality: A comparison of the personality systems of Cloninger and Eysenck. *Journal of Personality and Social Psychology, 66*, 762–775.

Hill, A. L., Degnan, K. A., Calkins, S. D., & Keane, S. P. (2006). Profiles of externalizing behavior problems for boys and girls across preschool: The roles of emotion regulation and inattention. *Developmental Psychology, 42*, 913–928.

Hirshfeld-Becker, D., Biederman, J., Faraone, S. V., Violette, H., Wrightsman, J., & Rosenbaum, J. F. (2002). Temperamental correlates of disruptive behavior disorders in young children: Preliminary findings. *Biological Psychiatry, 50*, 563–574.

Ilott, N., Saudino, K. J., Wood, A., & Asherson, P. (2010). A genetic study of ADHD and activity level in infancy. *Genes, Brain, and Behavior, 9*, 296–304.

Jong, J., Kao, T., Lee, L., Huang, H.-H., Lo, P-T., & Wang, H-C. (2010). Can temperament be understood at birth? The relationship between neonatal pain cry and their temperament: A preliminary study. *Infant Behavior and Development, 33*(3), 266–272.

Kagan, J. (1998). *Galen's prophecy: Temperament in human nature*. Boulder, CO: Westview.

Kagan, J. (2003). Biology, context, and developmental inquiry. *Annual Review of Psychology, 54*, 1–23.

Kagan, J. (2010). *The temperamental thread: How genes, culture, time, and luck make us who we are*. New York: Dana Press.

Kagan, J., Reznick, J. S., & Snidman, N. (1988). Biological bases of childhood shyness. *Science, 240*, 167–171.

Kagan, J., & Snidman, N. (2004). *The long shadow of temperament*. Cambridge, MA: Belknap/Harvard University Press.

Kant, I. (1974). *Anthropology from a pragmatic point of view*. The Hague, Netherlands: Martinus Nijhoff. (Original work published 1798.)

Keane, S. P., & Calkins, S. D. (2004). Predicting kindergarten peer social status from toddler and preschool problem behavior. *Journal of Abnormal Child Psychology, 32*, 409–423.

Keenan, K., & Wakschlag, L. S. (2000). More than the terrible twos: The nature and severity of behavior problems in clinic-referred preschool children. *Journal of Abnormal Child Psychology, 28,* 33–46.

Kochanska, G. (1997). Multiple pathways to conscience for children with different temperaments: From toddlerhood to age 5. *Developmental Psychology, 33,* 228–240.

Kochanska, G., Aksan, N., Knaack, A., & Rhines, H. M. (2004). Maternal parenting and children's conscience: Early security as moderator. *Child Development, 75,* 1229–1242.

Kochanska, G., Barry, R. A., Aksan, N., & Boldt, L. J. (2008). A developmental model of maternal and child contributions to disruptive conduct: The first six years. *Journal of Child Psychology and Psychiatry, 49,* 1220–1227.

Kochanska, G., DeVet, K., Goldman, M., Murray, K., & Putnam, S. P. (1994). Maternal reports of conscience development and temperament in young children. *Child Development, 65,* 852–868.

Kochanska, G., & Murray, K. T. (2000). Mother-child mutually responsive orientation and conscience development: From toddler to early school age. *Child Development, 71,* 417–431.

Krueger, R. F. (1999). The structure of common mental disorders. *Archives of General Psychiatry, 56,* 921–926.

Lahey, B. B., Van Hulle, C. A., Keenan, K., Rathouz, P. J., D'Onofrio, B. M., Rodgers, J. L., & Waldman, I. D. (2008). Temperament and parenting during the first year of life predict future child conduct problems. *Journal of Abnormal Child Psychology, 36,* 1139–1158.

Loeber, R. (1991). Antisocial behavior: More enduring than changeable? *Journal of the American Academy of Child and Adolescent Psychiatry, 30,* 393–397.

Lynam, D. R., & Widiger, T. A. (2007). Using a general model of personality to identify the basic elements of psychopathy. *Journal of Personality Disorders, 21,* 160–178.

MacLean, P. D. (1949). Psychosomatic disease and the visceral brain: Recent developments bearing on the Papez theory of emotion. *Psychosomatic Medicine, 11,* 338–353.

MacLean, P. D. (1955). The limbic system (visceral brain) and emotional behavior. *Archives of Neurology and Psychiatry, 73,* 130–134.

MacLean, P. D. (1990). *The triune brain in evolution: Role in paleocerebral functions.* New York, NY: Plenum.

Marysko, M., Finke, P., Wiebel, A., Resch, F., & Moehler, E. (2009). Can mothers predict childhood behavioral inhibition in early infancy? *Child and Adolescent Mental Health, 15,* 91–96.

McCrae, R. R., Costa, P. T., Jr., Ostendorf, F., Angleitner, A., Hrebickova, M., Avia, M. D., . . . Smith, P. B. (2000). Nature over nurture: Temperament, personality, and life span development. *Journal of Personality and Social Psychology, 78,* 173–186.

Moffitt, T. E., Arseneault, L., Belsky, D., Dickson, N., Hancox, R. J., . . . Caspi, A. (2011). A gradient of childhood self-control predicts health, wealth, and public safety. *Proceedings of the National Academy of Sciences of the United States of America, 108,* 2693–2698.

Morgan, A. B., & Lilienfeld, S. O. (2000). A meta-analytic review of the relation between antisocial behavior and neuropsychological measures of executive function. *Clinical Psychology Review, 20,* 113–136.

Mullineaux, P. Y., Deater-Deckard, K., Petrill, S. A., Thompson, L. A., & DeThorne, L. S. (2009). Temperament in middle childhood: A behavioral genetic analysis of fathers' and mothers' reports. *Journal of Research in Personality, 43,* 737–746.

Munafò, M. R., Yalcin, B., Willis-Owen, S. A., & Flint, J. (2008). Association of the DRD4 gene and approach-related personality traits: Meta-analysis and new data. *Biological Psychiatry, 63,* 197–206.

Neppl, T. K., Donnellan, M. B., Scaramella, L. V., Widaman, K. F., Spilman, S. K., Ontai, L. L., & Conger, R. D. (2010). Differential stability of temperament and personality from toddlerhood to middle adulthood. *Journal of Research in Personality, 44,* 386–396.

Oldehinkel, A. J., Hartman, C. A., De Winter, A. F., Veenstra, R., & Ormel, J. (2004). Temperament profiles associated with internalizing and externalizing problems in preadolescence. *Development and Psychopathology, 16,* 421–440.

Papez, J. W. (1937). A proposed mechanism of motion. *Archives of Neurology and Psychiatry, 38,* 725–743.

Pfeifer, M., Goldsmith, H. H., Davidson, R. J., & Rickman, M. (2002). Continuity and change in inhibited and uninhibited children. *Child Development, 73,* 1474–1485.

Plomin, R. (1990). The role of inheritance in behavior. *Science, 248*, 183–188.

Raine, A., Moffitt, T. E., Caspi, A., Loeber, R., Stouthamer-Loeber, M., & Lynam, D. (2005). Neurocognitive impairments in boys on the life-course persistent antisocial path. *Journal of Abnormal Psychology, 114*, 38–49.

Raine, A., Reynolds, C., Venables, P. H., Mednick, S. A., & Farrington, D. P. (1998). Fearlessness, stimulation-seeking, and large body size at age 3 years as early predispositions to childhood aggression at age 11 years. *Archives of General Psychiatry, 55*, 745–751.

Ratchford, M., & Beaver, K. M. (2009). Neuropsychological deficits, low self-control, and delinquent involvement: Toward a biosocial explanation of delinquency. *Criminal Justice and Behavior, 36*, 147–162.

Rothbart, M. K. (1981). The measurement of temperament in infancy. *Child Development, 52*, 569–578.

Rothbart, M. K. (2007). Temperament, development, and personality. *Current Directions in Psychological Science, 16*, 207–212.

Rothbart, M. K. (2011). *Becoming who we are: Temperament and personality in development*. New York, NY: Guilford Press.

Rothbart, M. K., Ahadi, S. A., & Evans, D. E. (2000). Temperament and personality: Origins and outcomes. *Journal of Personality and Social Psychology, 78*, 122–135.

Santucci, A. K., Silk, J. S., Shaw, D. S., Gentzler, A., Fox, N. A., & Kovacs, M. (2008). Vagal tone and temperament as predictors of emotion regulation strategies in young children. *Developmental Psychobiology, 50*, 205–216.

Schwartz, C. E., Kunwar, P. S., Greve, D. N., Moran, L. R., Viner, J. C., Covino, J. M., . . . Wallace, S. R. (2010). Structural differences in adult orbital and ventromedial prefrontal cortex predicted by infant temperament at 4 months of age. *Archives of General Psychiatry, 67*, 78–84.

Schwartz, C. E., Wright, C. I., Shin, L. M., Kagan, J., & Rauch, S. L. (2003). Inhibited and uninhibited infants "grown up": Adult amygdalar response to novelty. *Science, 300*, 1952–1953.

Sentse, M., Veenstra, R., Lindenberg, S., Verhulst, F. C., & Ormel, J. (2009). Buffers and risks in temperament and family for early adolescent psychopathology: Generic, conditional, or domain-specific effects? The TRAILS study. *Developmental Psychology, 45*, 419–430.

Sheese, B. E., Rothbart, M. K., Posner, M. I., White, L. K., & Fraundorf, S. H. (2008). Executive attention and self-regulation in infancy. *Infant Behavior and Development, 31*, 501–510.

Stelmack, R. M., & Stalikas, A. (1991). Galen and the humour theory of temperament. *Personality and Individual Differences, 12*, 255–263.

Stifter, C. A., Putnam, S., & Jahromi, L. (2008). Exuberant and inhibited toddlers: Stability of temperament and risk for problem behavior. *Development and Psychopathology, 20*, 401–421.

Tangney, J. P., Baumeister, R. F., & Boone, A. L. (2004). High self-control predicts good adjustment, less pathology, better grades, and interpersonal success. *Journal of Personality, 72*, 271–324.

Terracciano, A., Lockenhoff, C. E., Zonderman, A. B., Ferruci, L., & Costa, P. T., Jr. (2008). Personality predictors of longevity: Activity, emotional stability, and conscientiousness. *Psychosomatic Medicine, 70*, 621–627.

Thomas, A., & Chess, S. (1977). *Temperament and development*. New York, NY: Brunner/Mazel.

Thomas, A., Chess, S., Birch, H. G., Hertzig, M. E., & Korn, S. (1963). *Behavioral individuality in early childhood*. New York: New York University Press.

van den Akker, A. L., Dekovic, M., Prinzie, P., & Asscher, J. J. (2010). Toddlers' temperament profiles: Stability and relations to negative and positive parenting. *Journal of Abnormal Child Psychology, 38*, 485–495.

van Goozen, S. H. M., Fairchild, G., Snock, H., & Harold, G. T. (2007). The evidence for a neurobiological model of childhood antisocial behavior. *Psychological Bulletin, 133*, 149–182.

Vaughn, M. G., DeLisi, M., Beaver, K. M., & Wright, J. P. (2009). Identifying latent classes of behavioral risk based on early childhood manifestations of self-control. *Youth Violence and Juvenile Justice, 7*, 16–31.

Vazsonyi, A. T., & Huang, L. (2010). Where self-control comes from: On the development of self-control and its relationship to deviance over time. *Developmental Psychology, 46*, 245–257.

Walters, G. D. (2011). Childhood temperament: Dimensions or types? *Personality and Individual Differences, 50*, 1168–1173.

Whittle, S., Allen, N. B., Lubman, D. I., & Yücel, M. (2006). The neurobiological basis of temperament:

Towards a better understanding of psychopathology. *Neuroscience and Biobehavioral Reviews, 30,* 511–525.

Yang, Y., Glenn, A. L., & Raine, A. (2008). Brain abnormalities in antisocial individuals: Implications for the law. *Behavioral Sciences and the Law, 26,* 65–83.

CHAPTER 7

Acker, G. M. (1999). The impact of clients' mental illness on social workers' job satisfaction and burnout. *Health & Social Work, 24,* 112–120.

Allport, G. W. (1961). *Pattern and growth in personality.* New York, NY: Holt, Rinehart and Winston.

American Psychiatric Association. (2000). *Diagnostic and statistical manual of mental disorders* (4th ed., Text Rev.). Washington, DC: Author.

Anderson, S. W., Aksan, N., Kochanska, G., Damasio, H., Wisnowski, J., & Afifi, A. (2007). The earliest behavioral expression of focal damage to human prefrontal cortex. *Cortex, 43,* 806–816.

Arnett, J. J. (1996). Sensation seeking, aggressiveness, and adolescent reckless behavior. *Personality and Individual Differences, 20,* 693–702.

Bakker, A. B., Van Der Zee, K. I., Lewig, K. A., & Dollard, M. F. (2006). The relationship between the Big Five personality factors and burnout: A study among volunteer counselors. *The Journal of Social Psychology, 146,* 31–50.

Barak, M. E., Nissly, J. A., & Levin, A. (2001). Antecedents to retention and turnover among child welfare, social work, and other human service employees: What can we learn from past research? A review and meta-analysis. *Social Service Review, 75,* 625–661.

Barrett, B., & Byford, S. (2012). Costs and outcomes of an intervention program for offenders with personality disorders. *British Journal of Psychiatry, 200,* 336–341.

Bartlett, C. P., & Anderson, C. A. (2012). Direct and indirect relations between the Big 5 personality traits and aggressive and violent behavior. *Personality and Individual Differences, 52,* 870–875.

Ben-Zur, H., & Michael, K. (2007). Burnout, social support, and coping at work among social workers, psychologists, and nurses: The role of challenge/control appraisals. *Social Work in Health Care, 45,* 63–82.

Blatny, M., Jelinek, M., & Osecka, T. (2007). Assertive toddler, self-efficacious adult: Child temperament predicts personality over forty years. *Personality and Individual Differences, 43,* 2127–2136.

Bogg, T., & Roberts, B. W. (2004). Conscientiousness and health-related behaviors: A meta-analysis of the leading behavioral contributors to morality. *Psychological Bulletin, 130,* 887–919.

Bouchard, T. J., & Loehlin, J. C. (2001). Genes, evolution, and personality. *Behavior Genetics, 31,* 243–273.

Boyce, C. J., & Wood, A. M. (2011). Personality prior to disability determines adaptation: Agreeable individuals recover lost life satisfaction faster and more completely. *Psychological Science, 22,* 1397–1402.

Caspi, A., Elder, G. H., & Bem, D. J. (1987). Moving against the world: Life-course patterns of explosive children. *Developmental Psychology, 23,* 308–313.

Chapman, B. P., Fiscella, K., Kawachi, I., & Duberstein, P. B. (2010). Personality, socioeconomic status, and all-cause mortality in the United States. *American Journal of Epidemiology, 171,* 83–92.

Costa, P. T., Jr., & McCrae, R. R. (1985). *NEO Personality Inventory manual.* Odessa, FL: Psychological Assessment Resources.

Costa, P. T., Jr., & McCrae, R. R. (1992). *Revised NEO Personality Inventory (NEO-PI-R) and NEO Five-Factor Inventory (NEO-FFI) professional manual.* Odessa, FL: Psychological Assessment Resources.

Damasio, A. R. (1994). *Descartes' error: Emotion, reason, and the human brain.* New York, NY: Grosset/Putnam.

Del Giudice, M., Booth, T., & Irwing, P. (2012). The distance between Mars and Venus: Measuring global sex differences in personality. *PLoS One, 7,* e29265.

De Pauw, S. S. W., & Mervielde, I. (2010). Temperament, personality and developmental psychopathology: A review based on the conceptual dimensions underlying childhood traits. *Child Psychiatry and Human Development, 41,* 313–329.

Digman, J. M. (2002). Historical antecedents of the Five-Factor Model. In P. T. Costa, Jr., & T. A. Widiger (Eds.), *Personality disorders and the five-factor model of personality* (2nd ed., pp. 17–22). Washington, DC: American Psychological Association.

Donnellan, M. B., Trzesniewski, K. H., Robins, R. W., Moffitt, T. E., & Caspi, A. (2005). Low self-esteem is related to aggression, antisocial behavior, and delinquency. *Psychological Science, 16,* 328–335.

Edmonds, G. W., Bogg, T., & Roberts, B. W. (2009). Are personality and behavioral measures of impulse control convergent or distinct predictors of health behaviors? *Journal of Research in Personality, 43,* 806–814.

Furnham, A., & Trickey, G. (2011). Sex differences in the dark side traits. *Personality and Individual Differences, 50,* 517–522.

Goodman, A., Joyce, R., & Smith, J. P. (2011). The long shadow cast by childhood physical and mental problems on adult life. *Proceedings of the National Academy of Sciences of the United States of America, 108,* 6032–6037.

Heath, A. C., Cloninger, C. R., & Martin, N. G. (1994). Testing a model for the genetic structure of personality: A comparison of the personality systems of Cloninger and Eysenck. *Journal of Personality and Social Psychology, 66,* 762–775.

Houts, R. M., Caspi, A., Pianta, R. C., Arseneault, L., & Moffitt, T. E. (2010). The challenging pupil in the classroom: The effect of the child on the teacher. *Psychological Science, 21,* 1802–1810.

Jackson, J. J., Thoemmes, F., Jonkmann, K., Lüdtke, O., & Trautwein, U. (2012). Military training and personality trait development: Does the military make the man, or does the man make the military? *Psychological Science, 23,* 270–277.

Jones, S. E., Miller, J. D., & Lynam, D. R. (2011). Personality, antisocial behavior, and aggression: A meta-analytic review. *Journal of Criminal Justice, 39,* 329–337.

Kagan, J., Reznick, J. S., & Snidman, N. (1988). Biological bases of childhood shyness. *Science, 240,* 167–171.

Kandler, C., Bleidorm, W., Riemann, R., Angleitner, A., & Spinath, F. M. (2012). Life events as environmental states and genetic traits and the role of personality: A longitudinal twin study. *Behavior Genetics, 42,* 57–72.

Kendler, K. S., Aggen, S. H., & Patrick, C. J. (2012). A multivariate twin study of DSM-IV criteria for antisocial personality disorder. *Biological Psychiatry, 71,* 247–253.

Kendler, K. S., & Prescott, C. A. (2006). *Genes, environment, and psychopathology: Understanding the causes of psychiatric and substance use disorders.* New York, NY: Guilford Press.

McAdams, D. P., & Olson, B. D. (2010). Personality development: Continuity and change over the life course. *Annual Review of Psychology, 61,* 517–542.

McCrae, R. R., & Costa, P. T., Jr. (2010). The five factor theory of personality. In O. P. John, R. W. Robins, & L. A. Pervin (Eds.), *Handbook of personality: Theory and research* (3rd ed., pp. 159–181). New York, NY: Guilford Press.

Miller, J. D., & Lynam, D. R. (2001). Structural models of personality and their relation to antisocial behavior: A meta-analytic review. *Criminology, 39,* 765–798.

Moffitt, T. E. (1993). Adolescence-limited and life-course-persistent antisocial behavior: A developmental taxonomy. *Psychological Review, 100,* 674–701.

Newhill, C. E., Mulvey, E. P., & Pilkonis, P. A. (2004). Initial development of a measure of emotional dysregulation for individuals with Cluster B personality disorders. *Research on Social Work Practice, 14,* 443–449.

Newhill, C. E., Vaughn, M. G., & DeLisi, M. (2010). Psychopathy scores reveal heterogeneity among patients with borderline personality disorder. *Journal of Forensic Psychiatry and Psychology, 21,* 202–220.

Oldehinkel, A. J., Hartman, C. A., De Winter, A. F., Veenstra, R., & Ormel, J. (2004). Temperament profiles associated with internalizing and externalizing problems in preadolescence. *Development and Psychopathology, 16,* 421–440.

Petitclerc, A., Boivin, M., Dionne, G., Pérusse, D., & Tremblay, R. E. (2011). Genetic and environmental etiology of disregard for rules. *Behavior Genetics, 41,* 192–200.

Plomin, R. (1990). The role of inheritance in behavior. *Science, 248,* 183–188.

Prinzie, P., Stams, G. J. J. M., Dekovic, M., Reijntjes, A. H. A., & Belsky, J. (2009). The relations between parents' Big Five personality factors and parenting: A meta-analytic review. *Journal of Personality and Social Psychology, 97,* 351–362.

Roberts, B. W., Harms, P. D., Caspi, A., & Moffitt, T. E. (2007). Predicting the counterproductive employee in a child-to-adult prospective study. *Journal of Applied Psychology, 92,* 1427–1436.

Samuel, D. B., & Widiger, T. A. (2008). A meta-analytic review of the relationships between the Five-Factor model and DSM-IV-TR personality disorders: A facet level analysis. *Clinical Psychology Review, 28,* 1326–1342.

Schwartz, C. E., Wright, C. I., Shin, L. M., Kagan, J., & Rauch, S. L. (2003). Inhibited and uninhibited infants "grown up": Adult amygdalar response to novelty. *Science, 300,* 1952–1953.

Sentse, M., Veenstra, R., Lindenberg, S., Verhulst, F. C., & Ormel, J. (2009). Buffers and risks in temperament and family for early adolescent psychopathology: Generic, conditional, or domain-specific effects? The TRAILS study. *Developmental Psychology, 45,* 419–430.

Siever, L. J., & Weinstein, L. N. (2009). The neurobiology of personality disorders: Implications for psychoanalysis. *Journal of the American Psychoanalytic Association, 57,* 361–398.

Spengler, M., Gottschling, J., & Spinath, F. M. (2012). Personality in childhood: A longitudinal behavior genetic approach. *Personality and Individual Differences, 53*(4), 411–416.

Terracciano, A., Löckenhoff, C. E., Crum, R. M., Bienvenu, J., & Costa, P. T., Jr. (2008). Five-Factor model and personality profiles of drug users. *BMC Psychiatry, 8*(22), doi:10.1186/1471-244X-8-22.

Terracciano, A., Löckenhoff, C. E., Zonderman, A. B., Ferrucci, L., & Costa, P. T., Jr. (2008). Personality predictors of longevity: Activity, emotional stability, and conscientiousness. *Psychosomatic Medicine, 70,* 621–627.

Thomaes, S., Bushman, B. J., Stegge, H., & Olthof, T. (2008). Trumping shame by blasts of noise: Narcissism, self-esteem, shame, and aggression in young adolescents. *Child Development, 79,* 1792–1801.

Ting, L. (2011). Depressive symptoms in a sample of social work students and reasons preventing students from using mental health services: An exploratory study. *Journal of Social Work Education, 47,* 253–268.

Twenge, J. M., & Campbell, W. K. (2003). "Isn't it fun to get the respect that we're going to deserve?" Narcissism, social rejection, and aggression. *Personality and Social Psychology Bulletin, 29,* 261–272.

Vaughn, M. G., Fu, Q., Beaver, K. M., DeLisi, M., Perron, B., & Howard, M. (2010). Are personality disorders associated with social welfare burden in the United States? *Journal of Personality Disorders, 24,* 709–720.

Vaughn, M. G., & Perron, B. E. (2011). Substance use careers and antisocial behavior: A biosocial life-course perspective. In M. DeLisi & K. M. Beaver (Eds.), *Criminological theory: A life-course approach* (pp. 109–120). Sudbury, MA: Jones & Bartlett.

Verheul, R., Van Den Bosch, L. M. C., Koeter, M. W. J., De Ridder, M. A. J., Stijnen, T., & Van Den Brink, W. (2003). Dialectical behavior therapy for women with borderline personality disorder: 12-month, randomized clinical trial in The Netherlands. *British Journal of Psychiatry, 182,* 135–140.

Zellars, K. L., Perrewe, P. L., & Hochwarter, W. A. (2000). Burnout in health care: The role of the five factors of personality. *Journal of Applied Social Psychology, 30,* 1570–1598.

CHAPTER 8

Aamodt, S., & Wang, S. (2011). *Welcome to your child's brain: How the mind grows from conception to college.* New York, NY: Bloomsbury.

Blakemore, S., den Ouden, H., Choudhury, S., & Frith, C. (2007). Adolescent development of the neural circuitry for thinking about intentions. *Social Cognitive and Affective Neuroscience, 2,* 130–139.

Bodrova, E., & Leong, D. J. (2007). *Tools of the mind: The Vygotskian approach to early childhood education.* Boston, MA: Allyn & Bacon.

Brewer, J. A., & Potenza, M. N. (2008). The neurobiology and genetics of impulse control disorders: Relationships to drug addictions. *Biochemical Pharmacology, 75,* 63–75.

Carter, R. (2010). *Mapping the mind: Revised and updated edition.* Berkeley: University of California Press.

Charney, D. S. (2004). Psychobiological mechanisms of resilience and vulnerability: Implications for successful adaptation to extreme stress. *American Journal of Psychiatry, 161,* 195–216.

Childress, A. R., Ehrman, R. N., Wang, Z., Li, Y., Sciortino, N., Hakun, J., Jens, W., Suh, J., . . . O'Brien, C. P. (2008). Prelude to passion: Limbic activation by "unseen" drug and sexual cues. *PLoS ONE, 3*(1). doi:10.1371/journal. pone.0001506

Cozolino, L. (2002). *The neuroscience of psychotherapy: Building and rebuilding the human brain.* New York, NY: Norton Books.

Damasio, A., & Meyer, D. E. (2009). Consciousness: An overview of the phenomenon and of its possible neural basis. In S. Laureys & G. Tononi (Eds.), *The neurobiology of consciousness: Cognitive neuroscience and neuropathology* (pp. 3–14). London, England: Elsevier.

Dehaene, S., & Changeux, J.-P. (2011). Experimental and theoretical approaches to conscious processing. *Neuron, 70,* 200–227.

Di Chiara, G. (2002). Nucleus accumbens shell and core dopamine: Differential role in behavior and addiction. *Behavior Brain Research, 137,* 75–114.

Di Chiara, G., & Bassareo, V. (2007). Reward system and addiction: What dopamine does and doesn't do. *Current Opinion in Pharmacology, 7,* 69–76.

Duggan, P., & Wiggins, O. (2012). 12-year-old charged with murder of toddler. *The Washington Post,* July 5th.

Fishman, T. C. (2010). *Shock of gray: The aging of the world's population and how it pits young against old, child against parent, worker against boss, company against rival, and nation against nation.* New York, NY: Scribner.

Fjell, A. M., & Walhovd, K. B. (2012). Neuroimaging results impose new views on Alzheimer's disease—The role of amyloid revised. *Molecular Neurobiology, 45,* 153–172.

Francis, R. C. (2011). *Epi-genetics: The ultimate mystery of inheritance.* New York, NY: Norton.

Gardner, H. (1983). *Frames of mind: The theory of multiple intelligences.* New York, NY: Basic Books.

Gardner, H. (2006). *Multiple intelligences: New horizons in theory and practice.* New York, NY: Basic Books.

Gardner, H. (2009). *Five minds for the future.* Boston, MA: Harvard Business School Press.

Grüsser, S. M., Wrase, J., Klein, S., Hermann, D., Smolka, M. N., Ruf, M., . . . Heinz, A. (2004). Cue-induced activation of the striatum and medial prefrontal cortex is associated with subsequent relapse in abstinent alcoholics. *Psychopharmacology, 175,* 296–302.

Heinz, A., Siessmeier, T., Wrase, J., Hermann, D., Klein, S., Grüsser, S. M., . . . Bartenstein, P. (2004). Correlation between dopamine D-2 receptors in the ventral striatum and central processing of alcohol cues and craving. *American Journal of Psychiatry, 16,* 1783–1789.

Hester, R., & Garavan, H. (2009). Neural mechanisms underlying drug-related cue distraction in active cocaine users. *Pharmacology, Biochemistry and Behavior, 93,* 270–277.

Houben, K., Schoenmakers, T. M., & Wiers, R. W. (2010). I didn't feel like drinking but I don't know why: The effects of evaluative conditioning on alcohol-related attitudes, craving and behavior. *Addictive Behaviors, 35,* 1161–1163.

Kahneman, D. (2011). *Thinking, fast and slow.* New York, NY: Farrar, Straus & Giroux.

Knudsen, E. I., Heckman, J. J., Cameron, J. L, & Shonkoff, J. P. (2006). Economic, neurobiological and behavioral perspectives on building America's future workforce. *Proceedings of the National Academy of Sciences of the United States of America, 103,* 10155–10162.

Krueger, F., Barbey, A. K., McCabe, K., Strenziok, M., Zamboni, G., Solomon, J., Raymont, V., & Grafman, J. (2009). The neural bases of key competencies of emotional intelligence. *Proceedings of the National Academy of Sciences, 106*(52), 22486–22491.

Krueger, F., Pardini, M., Huey, E. D., Raymont, V., Solomon, J., Lipsky, R. H., Hodgkinson, C. A., Goldman, D., & Grafman, J. (2011). The role of the Met66 brain-derived neurotrophic factor allele in the recovery of executive functioning after combat-related traumatic brain injury. *The Journal of Neuroscience, 31*(2), 598–606.

Kunkle, F. (2012, February 4). Fairfax County focusing on neediest in more modest affordable housing program. *The Washington Post.* Retrieved from www.washingtonpost.com/local/dc-politics/fairfax -county-focusing-on-neediest-in-more-modest-aff ordable-housing-program/2012/02/01/gIQABYw CqQ_story.html

LeDoux, J. (2002). *Synaptic self: How our brains become who we are.* New York, NY: Penguin Group.

Levesque, J., Joanette, Y., Mensour, B., Beaudoin, G., Leroux, J. M., Bourgouin, P., & Beauregard, M. (2004). Neural basis of emotional self-regulation in childhood. *Neuroscience, 129,* 361–369.

Matto, H. C., Strolin-Goltzman, J., Hadjiyane, M., Kost, M., Minter, J., & Wiley, J. (in press). Clinical trial of an innovative dual-processing group therapy relapse prevention protocol conducted in a community-based setting. *Journal of Groups in Addiction and Recovery, 8*(4).

Miller, W. R., & Rollnick, S. (2002). *Motivational interviewing: Preparing people for change.* New York, NY: Guilford Press.

Milton, A. L., Lee, J. L, Butler, V. J., Gardner, R., & Everitt, B. J. (2008). Intra-amygdala and systemic antagonism of NMDA receptors prevents the reconsolidation of drug-associated memory and impairs subsequently both novel and previously acquired drug-seeking behaviors. *Journal of Neuroscience, 28,* 8230–8237.

Myrick, H., Anton, R. F., Li, X. B., Henderson, S., Drobes, D., Voronin, K., & George, M. S. (2004). Differential brain activity in alcoholics and social drinkers to alcohol cues: Relationship to craving. *Neuropsychopharmacology, 29,* 393–402.

Noble, K. G., Tottenham, N., & Casey, B. J. (2005). Neuroscience perspectives on disparities in school readiness and cognitive achievement. *School Readiness: Closing Racial and Ethnic Gaps, 15,* 71–89.

Ochsner, K. N., Bunge, S. A., Gross, J. J., & Gabrieli, J. D. E. (2002). Rethinking feelings: An fMRI study of the cognitive regulation of emotion. *Journal of Cognitive Neuroscience, 14,* 1215–1229.

Perlman, S. B., & Pelphrey, K. A. (2011). Developing connections for affective regulation: Age-related changes in emotional brain connectivity. *Journal of Experimental Child Psychology, 108,* 607–620.

Pessiglione, M., Schmidt, L., Draganski, B., Kalisch, R., Lau, H., Dolan, R. J., & Frith, C. D. (2007). How the brain translates money into force: A neuroimaging study of subliminal motivation. *Science, 316,* 904–906.

Prochaska, J. O., & DiClemente, C. C. (2005). The transtheoretical approach. In J. C. Norcross & M. R. Goldfried (Eds.), *Handbook of psychotherapy integration* (pp. 147–171). New York, NY: New York University Press.

Rooke, S. E., & Hine, D. W. (2011). Dual process account of adolescent and adult binge drinking. *Addictive Behaviors, 36,* 341–346.

Sapolsky, R. M. (2005). The influence of social hierarchy on primate health. *Science, 308,* 648–652.

Scarborough, M. K., Lewis, C. M., & Kulkarni, S. (2010). Enhancing adolescent brain development through goal-setting activities. *Social Work, 55,* 276–278.

Siegel, D. J. (1999). The developing mind: Toward a neurobiology of interpersonal experience. New York, NY: Guilford Press.

Sinha, R., & Li, C. S. (2007). Imaging stress-and cue-induced drug and alcohol craving: Association with relapse and clinical implications. *Drug & Alcohol Review, 26*(1), 25–31.

Slovic, P., Finucane, M. L., Peters, E., & MacGregor, D. G. (2002). The affect heuristic. In T. Gilovich, D. Griffin, & D. Kahneman (Eds.), *Heuristics and biases: The psychology of intuitive judgment* (pp. 397–420). New York, NY: Cambridge University Press.

Tapert, S. F., Brown, G. G., Baratta, M. V., & Brown, S. A. (2004). FMRI BOLD response to alcohol stimuli in alcohol dependent young women. *Addictive Behaviors, 29,* 33–50.

Uhl, G. R. (2008). "Higher order" addiction molecular genetics: Convergent data from genome-wide associations in humans and mice. *Biochemical Pharmacology, 75,* 98–111.

Volkow, N. D., Fowler, J. S., & Wang, G. J. (2004). The addicted human brain viewed in the light of imaging studies: Brain circuits and treatment strategies. *Neuropharmacology, 47,* 3–13.

Whoriskey, P. (2012, February 19). U.S. manufacturing sees shortage of skilled factory workers. *The Washington Post.* Retrieved from http://articles.washingtonpost.com/2012-02-19/business/35444240_1_factory-workers-laid-off-workers-jobs

Wiers, R. W., Rinck, M., Kordts, R., Houben, K., & Strack, F. (2010). Retraining automatic action tendencies to approach alcohol in hazardous alcohol drinkers. *Addiction, 105,* 279–287.

Wrase, J., Grüsser, S. M., Klein, S., Diener, C., Hermann, D., Flor, H., . . . Heinz, A. (2002). Development of alcohol-associated cues and cue-induced brain activation in alcoholics. *European Psychiatry: The Journal of the Association of European Psychiatrists, 17,* 287–291.

Wrase, J., Schlagenhauf, F., Kienast, T., Wustenberg, T., Bermpohl, F., Kahnt, T., . . . Heinz, A. (2007). Dysfunction of reward processing correlates with alcohol craving in detoxified alcoholics. *NeuroImage, 35,* 787–794.

Zink, C. F., Tong, Y., Chen, Q., Bassett, D. S., Stein, J. L., & Meyer-Lindenberg, A. (2008). Know your place: Neural processing of social hierarchy in humans. *Neuron, 58,* 273–283.

CHAPTER 9

Allan, K. (2007). *The social lens: An invitation to social and sociological theory.* Thousand Oaks, CA: Pine Forge Press.

Ashton, M. C., Paunonen, S. V., Helmes, E., & Jackson, D. N. (1998). Kin altruism, reciprocal altruism, and the Big Five personality factors. *Evolution and Human Behavior, 9,* 243–255.

Axelrod, R., & Hamilton, W. D. (1981). The evolution of cooperation. *Science, 211,* 1390–1396.

Barash, D. P. (2003). *The survival game: How game theory explains the biology of cooperation and competition.* New York, NY: Times Books.

Bryant, B. K., & Crockenberg, S. (1980). Correlates and dimensions of prosocial behavior: A study of female siblings with their mothers. *Child Development, 51,* 529–544.

Camerer, C. F. (2003). *Behavioral game theory: Experiments in strategic interactions.* Princeton, NJ: Princeton University Press.

Carter, C. S. (1998). Neuroendocrine perspectives on social attachment and love. *Psychoneuroendocrinology, 23,* 779–818.

Caspi, A., Elder, G. H., & Bem, D. J. (1987). Moving against the world: Life-course patterns of explosive children. *Developmental Psychology, 23,* 308–313.

Cook, K. S., & Cooper, R. M. (2005). Experimental studies of cooperation, trust, and social exchange. In L. Ostrom & J. Walker (Eds.), *Trust and reciprocity: Interdisciplinary lessons for experimental research* (pp. 209–244). New York, NY: Russell Sage Foundation.

Cosmides, L., Barrett, H. C., & Tooby, J. (2010). Adaptive specializations, social exchange, and the evolution of human intelligence. *Proceedings of the National Academy of Sciences, 107,* 9007–9014.

Cosmides, L., & Tooby, J. (1989). Evolutionary psychology and the generation of culture, Part II. Case study: A computational theory of social exchange. *Ethnology and Sociobiology, 10,* 51–97.

Cosmides, L., & Tooby, J. (1992). Cognitive adaptations for social exchange. In J. Barkow, L. Cosmides, & J. Tooby (Eds.), *The adapted mind: Evolutionary psychology and the generation of culture* (pp. 163–228). New York, NY: Oxford University Press.

Costa, P. T., Jr., & McCrae, R. R. (1992). *Revised NEO Personality Inventory (NEO-PI-R) and NEO Five-Factor Inventory (NEO-FFI) manual.* Odessa, FL: Psychological Assessment Resources.

Costa, P. T., Jr., & McCrae, R. R. (1997). Longitudinal stability of adult personality. In R. Hogan, J. Johnson, & S. Briggs (Eds.), *Handbook of personality psychology* (pp. 269–292). San Diego, CA: Academic Press.

DellaVigna, S., List, J. A., & Malmendier, U. (2009, October). *Testing for altruism and social pressure in charitable giving.* [Unpublished monograph.] Chicago, IL: University of Chicago.

de Waal, F. B. M. (2008). Putting the altruism back into altruism: The evolution of empathy. *Annual Review of Psychology, 59,* 279–300.

Eisenberg, N., Miller, P. A., Shell, R., McNalley, S., & Shea, C. (1991). Prosocial development in adolescence: A longitudinal study. *Developmental Psychology, 27,* 849–857.

Fehr, E., Bernhard, H., & Rockenbach, B. (2008). Egalitarianism in young children. *Nature, 454,* 1079–1083.

Fehr, E., & Gachter, S. (2000a). Cooperation and punishment in public goods experiments. *The American Economic Review, 90,* 980–994.

Fehr, E., & Gachter, S. (2000b). Fairness and retaliation: The economics of reciprocity. *Journal of Economic Perspectives, 14,* 159–181.

Fuentes, A. (2009). A new synthesis: Resituating approaches to the evolution of human behavior. *Anthropology Today, 25,* 12–17.

Gintis, H. (2000). Strong reciprocity and human sociality. *Journal of Theoretical Biology, 206,* 169–179.

Gintis, H., Bowles, S., Boyd, R., & Fehr, E. (2003). Explaining altruistic behavior in humans. *Evolution and Human Behavior, 24,* 153–172.

Gintis, H., Henrich, J., Bowles, S., Boyd, R., & Fehr, E. (2008). Strong reciprocity and the roots of human morality. *Social Justice Research, 21,* 241–253.

Harris, M. (1989). *Our kind.* New York, NY: Harper & Row.

Heise, D. R. (1966). Social status, attitudes and word connotations. *Sociological Inquiry, 36,* 227–239.

Hollander, H. (1990). A social exchange approach to voluntary cooperation. *The American Economic Review, 80,* 1157–1167.

Homans, G. C. (1958). Social behavior as exchange. *American Journal of Sociology, 63,* 597–606.

Insel, T. R., & Young, L. J. (2001). The neurobiology of attachment. *Nature Reviews. Neuroscience, 2,* 129–136.

Kail, R. V., & Cavanaugh, J. C. (2004). *Human development: A life-span view* (3rd ed.). Belmont, CA: Wadsworth

Kollock, P. (1994). The emergence of exchange structures: An experimental study of uncertainty, commitment, and trust. *American Journal of Sociology, 100,* 313–345.

Kosfeld, M., Heinrichs, M., Zak, P. J., Fischbacher, U., & Fehr, E. (2005). Oxytocin increases trust in humans. *Nature, 435,* 673–676.

Krueger, R. F., Hicks, B. M., & McGue, M. (2001). Altruism and antisocial behavior: Independent tendencies, unique personality correlates, distinct etiologies. *Psychological Science, 12*, 397–402.

Lawler, E. J., & Yoon, J. (1996). Commitment in exchange relations. Test of a theory of relational cohesion. *American Sociological Review, 61*, 89–108.

Lawler, E. J., & Thye, S. R. (1999). Bringing emotions into social exchange theory. *Annual Review of Sociology, 25*, 217–244.

LeDoux, J. (1996). *The emotional brain: The mysterious underpinnings of emotional life.* New York, NY: Simon & Schuster.

Lindstrom, L. (1984). Doctor, lawyer, wise man, priest: Big-men and knowledge in Melanesia. *Man, 19*, 291–309.

Massey, D. S. (2002). A brief history of human society: The origin and role of emotion in social life. *American Sociological Review, 67*, 1–29.

Moll, J., Krueger, F., Zahn, R., Pardini, M., de Oliveira-Souza, R., & Grafman, J. (2006). Human fronto-mesolimbic networks guide decisions about charitable donation. *Proceedings of the National Academy of Sciences, 103*, 15623–15628.

Nowak, M. A. (2006). Five rules for the evolution of cooperation. *Science, 314*, 1560–1563.

Rilling, J. K., Gutman, D. A., Zeh, T. R., Pagnoni, G., Berns, G. S., Kilts, C. D. (2002). A neural basis for social cooperation. *Neuron, 35*, 395–405.

Roscoe, P. B. (1988). From big-men to the state. A processual approach to circumscription theory. *American Behavioral Scientist, 31*, 472–483.

Rushton, J. P., Chrisjohn, R. D., & Fekken, G. C. (1981). The altruistic personality and the self-report altruism scale. *Personality and Individual Differences, 2*, 293–303.

Sahlins, M. (1972). *Stone age economics.* Chicago, IL: Aldine Press.

Trivers, R. L. (1971). The evolution of reciprocal altruism. *The Quarterly Review of Biology, 46*, 35–57.

Uvnas-Moberg, K. (1998). Oxytocin may mediate the benefits of positive social interaction and emotions. *Psychoneuroendocrinology, 23*, 819–835.

van der Merwe, W. G., & Burns, J. (2008). What's in a name? Racial identity and altruism in post-apartheid South Africa (Working Paper No. 24). Retrieved from University of Cape Town, Southern Africa Labour and Development Research Unit website: www.saldru.uct.ac.za/home/index .php?/component/option,com_docman/Itemid,32/ gid,252/task,doc_download/

Zafirovski, M. (2005). Social exchange theory under scrutiny: A positive critique of its economic-behaviorist formulations. *Electronic Journal of Sociology.* Retrieved from www.sociology.org/content/ 2005/tier2/SETheory.pdf

CHAPTER 10

Akerloff, G., & Kranton, R. (2010). *Identity economics.* Princeton, NJ: Princeton University Press.

Berkman, L. F., & Glass, T. (2000). Social integration, social networks, social support, & health. In L. F. Berkman & I. Kawachi (Eds.), *Social epidemiology.* Cambridge, MA: Oxford University Press.

Bourdieu, P. (1997) The Forms of Capital, in: A. Halsey, H. Lauder, P. Brown & A. Stuart Wells (Eds.) *Education: Culture, Economy and Society*, Oxford: Oxford University Press.

Bowlby, J. (1988). *A secure base.* New York, NY: Basic Books.

Brooks, D. (2011). *The social animal.* New York, NY: Random House.

Burkey, M. D., Kim, Y. A., & Breakey, W. R. (2011). The role of social ties in recovery in a population of homeless substance abusers. *Addictive Disorders & Their Treatment, 10*(1), 14–20.

Carlson, E. D., & Chamberlain, R. M. (2003). Social capital, health, and health disparities. *Journal of Nursing Scholarship, 35*, 325–331.

Christakis, N. A. (2010, May). *The hidden influence of social networks* [Video file]. Retrieved from www .ted.com/talks/nicholas_christakis_the_hidden_in fluence_of_social_networks.html

Christakis, N. A. & Fowler, J. H. (2007). The spread of obesity in a large social network over 32 years. *The New England Journal of Medicine, 357*, 370–379.

Christakis, N. A., & Fowler, J. H. (2009). *Connected.* New York, NY: Little, Brown & Co.

Cohen, P. (2012). *In our prime.* New York, NY: Scribner.

Cornwell, B. (2009). Good health and the bridging of structural holes. *Social Networks, 31*, 92–103.

Cozolino, L. (2002). *The neuroscience of psychotherapy: Building and rebuilding the human brain.* New York, NY: Norton.

Flores, P. (2004). *Addiction as an attachment disorder*. New York, NY: Jason Aronson.

Florida, R. (2011). *The great reset*. New York, NY: HarperCollins.

Fowler, J. H., Dawes, C. T., & Christakis, N. A. (2009). Model of genetic variation in human social networks. *Proceedings of the National Academy of Sciences, 106*(6), 1720–1724.

Freedman, M. (2011). *The big shift: Navigating the new stage beyond midlife*. New York, NY: PublicAffairs.

Haas, S. A., Schaefer, D. R., & Kornienko, O. (2010). Health and the structure of adolescent social networks. *Journal of Health and Social Behavior, 51*(4), 424–439.

Hochhausen, L., Perry, D. F., & Le, H. N. (2010). Neighborhood context and acculturation among Central American immigrants. *Journal of Immigrant Minority Health, 12*, 806–809.

Jennings, J. L., & DiPrete, T. A. (2010). Teacher effects on social and behavioral skills in early elementary school. *Sociology of Education, 83*(2), 135–159.

Kahn, R. L., & Antonucci, T. C. (1980). Convoys over the life course: Attachment, roles and social support. In P. Bakes & O. Brim (Eds.), *Life span development and behavior* (Vol. 3, pp. 253–286). San Diego, CA: Academic Press.

Klinenberg, E. (2012). *Going solo: The extraordinary rise and surprising appeal of living alone*. New York, NY: Penguin Press.

Langenkamp, A. G. (2011). Effects of educational transitions on students' academic trajectory: A life course perspective. *Sociological Perspectives, 54*(4), 497–520.

Laudet, A. B., & White, W. L. (2008). Recovery capital as prospective predictor of sustained recovery, life satisfaction, and stress among former polysubstance users. *Substance Use & Misuse, 43*, 27–54.

Layton, L. (2011, December 15). Teachers union leads effort that aims to turn around West Virginia school system. *The Washington Post*. Retrieved from www.washingtonpost.com/local/education/teachers-union-leads-effort-that-aims-to-turn-aro und-west-virginia-school-system/2011/12/14/gIQ A5pxywO_story.html

Lessard, C. (2007). Complexity and reflexivity: Two important issues for economic evaluation in health care. *Social Science & Medicine, 64*(8), 1754–1765.

Lessard, C., Contandriopoulous, A.-P., & Beaulieu, M.-D. (2010). The role (or not) of economic evaluation at the micro level: Can Bourdieu's theory provide a way forward for clinical decision-making? *Social Science & Medicine, 70*, 1948–1956.

Levitt, M. J. (1991). Attachment and close relationships: A life-span perspective. In J. L. Gewirtz & W. M. Kurtines (Eds.), *Intersections with attachment* (pp. 183–205). Hillsdale, NJ: Lawrence Erlbaum Associates.

Louie, G. H., & Ward, M. M. (2011). Socioeconomic and ethnic differences in disease burden and disparities in physical function in older adults. *American Journal of Public Health, 101*(7), 1322–1329.

Mansour, E. (2012). The role of social networking sites (SNSs) in the January 25th revolution in Egypt. *Library Review, 61*(2), 128–159.

Martinson, K. (2010). *Partnering with employers to promote job advancement for low-skill individuals*. Washington, DC: National Institute for Literacy.

McMillan, D. W., & Chavis, D. M. (1986). Sense of community: A definition & theory. *Journal of Community Psychology, 14*, 6–23.

Newman, K. S. (2012). *The accordion family*. Boston, MA: Beacon Press.

Nye, B., Konstantopoulos, S., & Hedges, L. V. (2004). How large are teacher effects? *Educational Evaluation and Policy Analysis, 26*, 237–257.

Padykula, N. L., & Conklin, P. (2010). The self regulation model of attachment trauma and addiction. *Clinical Social Work Journal, 38*, 351–360.

Pendall, R., Theodos, B., & Franks, K. (2012). *The built environment and household vulnerability in a regional context*. Washington, DC: Urban Institute.

Pih, K., Hirose, A., & Mao, K. R. (2012). The invisible unattended: Low-wage Chinese immigrant workers, health care, and social capital in Southern California's San Gabriel Valley. *Sociological Inquiry, 82*(2), 236–256.

Ryan, V., Agnitsch, K., Zhao, L., & Mullick, R. (2005). Making sense of voluntary participation: A theoretical synthesis. *Rural Sociology, 70*, 287–313.

Schor, J. B. (2011). *True wealth*. New York, NY: Penguin Books.

Sennett, R. (2012). *Together: The rituals, pleasures and politics of cooperation*. New Haven, CT: Yale University Press.

Settersten, R., & Ray, B. E. (2010). *Not quite adults*. New York, NY: Bantam Books.

Shelton, D. (2009). Leadership, education, achievement, and development: A nursing intervention for prevention of youthful offending behavior. *Journal of the American Psychiatric Nurses Association*, *14*, 429–441.

Siegel, D. (1999). *The developing mind*. New York, NY: Guilford Press.

Smith-Osborne, A. (2009). Mental health risk and social ecological variables associated with educational attainment for Gulf War veterans: Implications for veterans returning to civilian life. *American Journal of Community Psychology*, *44*, 327–337.

Spera, C., & Matto, H. C. (2007). A contextual-congruence model of socialization. *Families in Society*, *88*(4), 551–560.

Sroufe, A., Egeland, B., Carlson, E., & Collins, A. (2005). *The development of the person: The Minnesota study of risk and adaptation from birth to adulthood*. New York, NY: Guilford Press.

Uchino, B. N. (2004). *Social support and physical health: Understanding the health consequences of relationships*. New Haven, CT: Yale University Press.

Venkatesh, S. A. (2000). *American project*. Cambridge, MA: Harvard University Press.

Walen, H. R., & Lachman, M. E. (2000). Social support and strain from partner, family and friends: Costs and benefits for men and women in adulthood. *Journal of Social and Personal Relationships*, *17*, 5–30.

Whisman, M. A., Sheldon, C. T., & Goering, P. (2000). Psychiatric disorders and dissatisfaction with social relationships: Does type of relationship matter? *Journal of Abnormal Psychology*, *109*, 803–808.

White, G., Caine, K., & Connelly, K. (2012). SOLACE project. Pervasive Health Information Technologies Lab, Indiana University and Clemson University. Retrieved from www.iu.edu/~phitlab/indiana/?page_id=88

Williams, J. C. (2010). *Reshaping the work-family debate*. Cambridge, MA: Harvard University Press.

CHAPTER 11

Abruzzi, W. (1982). Ecological theory and ethnic differentiation among human populations. *Current Anthropology*, *23*, 13–32.

Amichai-Hamburger, Y., & Ben-Artzi, E. (2003). Loneliness and Internet use. *Computers in Human Behavior*, *19*, 71–80.

Asur, S., & Huberman, B. A. (2010). Predicting the future with social media. Retrieved from www.hpl.hp.com/research/scl/papers/socialmedia/socialmedia.pdf

Balee, W. (1984). The ecology of ancient Tupi warfare. In B. Ferguson (Ed.), *Warfare, culture and environment* (pp. 241–265). Orlando, FL: Academic.

Banks, M. R., Willoughby, L. M., & Banks, W. A. (2008). Animal-assisted therapy and loneliness in nursing homes: Use of robotic versus living dogs. *Journal of the American Medical Directors Association*, *9*, 173–177.

Begley, S. (1995, September 2). The baby myth. *Newsweek*, 38–41.

Biglan, A. (1988). Behavior analysis and the larger context. *Behavior Analysis*, *23*, 25–32.

Bishop, J. (2007). Increasing participation in online communities: A framework for human-computer interaction. *Computers in Human Behavior*, *23*, 1881–1893.

Block, J. J. (2008). Issues for DSM-V: Internet addiction. *American Journal of Psychiatry*, *165*, 306–307.

Boesch, C., & Boesch, H. (1990). Tool use and tool making in wild chimpanzees. *Folia Primatology*, *54*, 86–99.

Burkhardt, M. E., & Brass, D. J. (1990). Changing patterns or patterns of change: The effects of a change in technology on social network structure and power. *Administrative Science Quarterly*, *35*, 104–127.

Calamaro, C. J., Mason, T. B. A., & Ratcliffe, S. J. (2009). Adolescents living the 24/7 lifestyle: Effects of caffeine and technology on sleep duration and daytime functioning. *Pediatrics*, *123*(6), 1005–1010.

Caria, A., Sitaram, R., Veit, R., Begliomini, C., & Birbaumer, N. (2010). Volitional control of anterior insula activity modulates the response to aversive stimuli. A real-time functional magnetic resonance study. *Biological Psychiatry*, *68*, 425–432.

Carr, N. (2010). *The shallows: How the Internet is changing the way we think, read, and remember*. Conshohocken, PA: Atlantic.

Ceruzzi, P. E. (2005). Moore's law and technological determinism: Reflections on the history of technology. *Technology and Culture*, *46*, 584–593.

Chase-Dunn, C., & Hall, T. D. (1997). *Rise and demise: Comparing world-systems*. Boulder, CO: Westview Press.

Chick, G. (1988). Science, materialism and the quest for anthropology of leisure: A rejoinder. *Leisure Sciences, 20*, 229–242.

Choucri, N. (2012). *Cyberpolitics in international relations*. Boston, MA: MIT Press.

Clark, A. (2003). *Natural born cyborgs*. New York, NY: Oxford University Press.

Corning, P. A. (2000). Biological adaptation in human societies: A "basic needs" approach. *Journal of Bioeconomics, 2*, 41–86.

Cornwell, B., & Lundgren, D. C. (2001). Love on the Internet: Involvement and misrepresentation in romantic relationships in cyberspace vs realspace. *Computers in Human Behavior, 17*, 197–211.

Cowan, R. S. (1976). The "industrialized revolution" in the home: Household technology and social change in the 20th century. *Technology and Culture, 17*, 1–23.

Cross, G. (1997). *Kids' stuff: Toys and the changing world of American childhood*. Boston, MA: Harvard University Press.

Dallery, J., & Glenn, I. M. (2005). Effects of an Internet-based voucher reinforcement program for smoking abstinence: A feasibility study. *Journal of Applied Behavior Analysis, 38*, 349–357.

Dehavenon, A. L. (1995). A cultural materialist approach to the causes of hunger and homelessness in New York City. In M. Murphy & M. Margolis (Eds.), *Science, materialism and the study of culture* (pp. 111–131). Gainesville: University Press of Florida.

Depres, L. (1975). Ethnicity and resource competition in Guyanese society. In L. Depres (Ed.), *Ethnicity and resource competition in plural societies* (pp. 87–117). The Hague, Netherlands: Mouton.

Diamond, J. (1997). *Guns, germs, and steel*. New York, NY: Norton.

Ferguson, B. (1984). Introduction: Studying war. In B. Ferguson (Ed.), *Warfare, culture and environment* (pp. 1–61). Orlando, FL: Academic.

Ferguson, B. (1989). Game wars? Ecology and conflict in Amazonia. *Journal of Anthropological Research, 45*, 149–206.

Glenn, S. (1988). Contingencies and metacontingencies: Towards a synthesis of behavior analysis and cultural materialism. *The Behavior Analyst, 11*, 161–179.

Good, K. (1987). Limiting factors in Amazonian ecology. In M. Harris & E. Ross (Eds.), *Food and evolution: Toward a theory of human food habits* (pp. 407–426). Philadelphia, PA: Temple University Press.

Goodall, J. (1964). Tool-using and aimed throwing in a community of free living chimpanzees. *Nature, 201*, 1264–1266.

Gould, M. S., Munfakh, J. L., Lubell, K., Kleinman, M., & Parker, S. (2002). Seeking help from the Internet during adolescence. *Journal of the American Academy of Child and Adolescent Psychiatry, 41*(10), 1182–1189.

Guadagno, R. E., Okdie, B. M., & Eno, C. A. (2008). Who blogs? Personality predictors of blogging. *Computers in Human Behavior, 24*, 1993–2004.

Hamburger, Y. A., & Ben-Artzi, E. (2000). The relationship between extraversion and neuroticism and the different uses of the Internet. *Computers in Human Behavior, 16*, 441–449.

Harris, M. (1968). *The rise of anthropological theory: A history of theories of culture*. New York, NY: Thomas Crowell.

Harris, M. (1974). *Cows, pigs, wars and witches: The riddles of culture*. New York, NY: Random House.

Harris, M. (1977). *Cannibals and kings: The origins of cultures*. New York, NY: Random House.

Harris, M. (1979). *Cultural materialism*. New York, NY: Random House.

Harris, M. (1989). *Our kind*. New York, NY: Harper & Row.

Harris, M. (1994). Cultural materialism is alive and well and won't go away until something better comes along. In Robert Borofsky (Ed.), *Assessing cultural anthropology* (pp. 62–76). New York, NY: McGraw-Hill.

Harris, M. (1999). *Theories of culture in postmodern times*. Walnut Creek, CA: AltaMira Press.

Harris, M., & Ross, E. (1987). (Eds.). *Food and evolution: Toward a theory of human food habits*. Philadelphia, PA: Temple University Press.

Hickman, J. M., Rogers, W. A., & Fisk, A. D. (2007). Training older adults to use new technology. *Journal of Gerontology: Psychology and Social Science, 62*(1), 77–84.

Holt, J. (2011). Smarter, happier and more productive. *London Review of Books, 33*, 9–12.

Hope, K. R. (1983). Basic needs and technology: Transfer issues in the "new international economic order." *American Journal of Economics and Sociology, 42*, 393–403.

Imhof, M., Vollmeyer, R., & Beierlein, C. (2007). Computer use and the gender gap: The issue of access, use, motivation, and performance. *Computers in Human Behavior*, *23*, 2823–2837.

Jackson, L. A., Ervin, K. S., Gardner, P. D., & Schmitt, N. (2001a). Gender and the Internet: Women communicating and men searching. *Sex Roles*, *44*, 363–380.

Jackson, L. A., Ervin, K. S., Gardner, P. D., & Schmitt, N. (2001b). The racial digital divide: Motivational, affective, and cognitive correlates of Internet use. *Journal of Applied Social Psychology*, *31*, 2019–2046.

Jackson, L. A., Zhoa, Y., Kolenic, A., Fitzgerald, H. E., Harold, R., & Von Eye, A. (2008). Race, gender, and information technology use: The new digital divide. *Cyberpsychology and Behavior*, *11*, 437–442.

Kaplan, A. M., & Haenlein, M. (2010). Users of the world, unite! The challenges and opportunities of social media. *Business Horizons*, *53*, 59–68.

Ko, C.-H., Yen, J.-Y., Chen, C.-S., Yeh, Y.-C., & Yen, C.-F. (2009). Predictive values of psychiatric symptoms for Internet addiction in adolescents: A 2-year prospective study. *Archives of Pediatrics & Adolescent Medicine*, *163*, 937–43.

Kottak, C. R. (1972). Ecological variables in the origin and evolution of African states: The Buganda example. *Comparative Studies in Society and History*, *14*, 351–380.

Leavitt, G. (1986). Ideology and the materialist model of general evolution. *Social Forces*, *65*, 525–553.

Lenski, G. (1966). *Power and privilege*. Chapel Hill: University of North Carolina Press.

Lenski, G. (1970). *Human societies: A macro-level introduction to sociology*. New York, NY: McGraw-Hill.

Livingstone, S. (2006). Drawing conclusions from new media research: Reflections and puzzles regarding children's experience of the Internet. *The Information Society*, *22*, 219–230.

Malagodi, E. (1986). On radicalizing behaviorism: A call for cultural analysis. *The Behavior Analyst*, *9*, 1–18.

Mendocino, M., Razzaq, L., & Hefferman, N. T. (2009). A comparison of traditional homework to computer-supported homework. *Journal of Research on Technology in Education*, *41*, 331–358.

Mitchell, K. J., Wolak, J., & Finkelhor, D. (2007). Trends in youth reports of sexual solicitations, harassment and unwanted exposure to pornography on the Internet. *The Journal of Adolescent Health*, *40*(2), 116–26.

Moore, G. E. (1965). Cramming more components onto integrated circuits. *Electronics*, *19*, 114–117.

Murray, G. F. (1995). Peasants, projects, and anthropological models: Fragile causal chains and crooked causal arrows. In M. Murphy & M. Margolis (Eds.), *Science, materialism, and the study of culture*. Gainesville, FL: University Press of Florida.

Newman, B. M., & Newman, P. F. (2003). *Development through life: A psychosocial approach*. New York, NY: Wadsworth Press.

Nielsen, F. (2004). The ecological-evolutionary typology of human societies and the evolution of social inequality. *Sociological Theory*, *22*, 292–314.

Nishida, T., & Hiraiwa, M. (1982). Natural history of a tool-using behavior by wild chimpanzees in feeding upon wood-boring ants. *Journal of Human Evolution*, *11*, 73–99.

Nolan, P., & Lenski, G. (1996). Technology, ideology, and societal development. *Sociological Perspectives*, *39*, 23–38.

Norris, P. (2001). *Digital divide: Civic engagement, information poverty, and the Internet worldwide*. New York, NY: Cambridge University Press.

Parayil, G. (1992). The green revolution in India: A case study of technological change. *Technology and Culture*, *33*, 737–756.

Paulsen, A. (1981). The archaeology of the absurd: Comments on cultural materialism, split inheritance, and the expansion of ancient Peruvian empires. *American Antiquity*, *46*, 31–47.

Price, D. H. (1995). Water theft in Egypt's Fayoum Oasis: Emics, etics and the illegal. In M. Murphy & M. Margolis (Eds.), *Science, materialism, and the study of culture* (pp. 96–110). Gainesville, FL: University Press of Florida.

Roberto, E. (2008). *Commuting to opportunity: The working poor and commuting in the United States* (pp. 1–20). Washington, DC: Metropolitan Policy Program, Brookings Institute.

Ross, C., Orr, E. S., Sisic, M., Arseneault, J. M., Simmering, M. G., & Orr, R. R. (2009). Personality and motivations associated with Facebook use. *Computers in Human Behavior*, *25*(2), 578–586.

Sanders, W. T., & Price, B. (1968). *Mesoamerica: The evolution of a civilization*. New York, NY: Random House.

Sanderson, S. (1990). *Social evolutionism: A critical history*. Oxford, England: Basil Blackwell.

Sanz, C., & Morgan, D. (2007). Chimpanzee tool technology in the Goualougo Triangle, Republic of Congo. *Journal of Human Evolution, 52*, 420–433.

Sanz, C., & Morgan, D. (2010). Complexity of chimpanzee tool using behaviors. In E. V. Lonsdorf, S. R. Ross, & T. Matsuzawa (Eds.), *The mind of the chimpanzee: Ecological and experimental perspectives* (pp. 127–140). Chicago, IL: University of Chicago Press.

Shalhoub-Kevorkian, N. (2011). E-resistance among Palestinian women: Coping in conflict-ridden areas. *Social Service Review, 85*(2), 179–204.

Sharff, J. W. (1995). We are all chickens for the colonel: A cultural materialist view of prisons. In M. Murphy & M. Margolis (Eds.), *Science, materialism and the study of culture* (pp. 132–158). Gainesville, FL: University Press of Florida.

Shaw, M., & Black, D. W. (2008). Internet addiction: Definition, assessment, epidemiology, and clinical management. *CNS Drugs, 22*(5), 353–365.

Sigurdsson, S. O., & Austin, J. (2008). Using real-time visual feedback to improve posture at computer workstations. *Journal of Applied Behavior Analysis, 41*, 365–375.

Smith, A. (2011, June 1). *13% of online adults use Twitter.* Retrieved from Pew Internet & American Life Project website: www.pewinternet.org/~/media//Files/Reports/2011/Twitter%20Update%202011.pdf

Spooner, T., & Rainie, L. (2000). *African-Americans and the Internet.* Retrieved from Pew Internet and American Life Project website: www.pewinternet.org/~/media//Files/Reports/2000/PIP_African_Americans_Report.pdf.pdf

Straub, D., Keil, M., & Brenner, W. (1997). Testing the technology acceptance model across cultures: A three country study. *Information and Management, 33*, 1–11.

Tun, P. A, & Lachman, M. E. (2010). The association between computer use and cognition across adulthood: Use it so you won't lose it? *Psychology and Aging, 25*(3), 560–568.

Urban Water Partners. (2010). *Urban Water Partners building clean water communities.* Cambridge, MA: Urban Water Partners, Harvard Business School.

Van Houten, R., Hilton, B., Schulman, R., & Reagan, I. (2011). Using accelerator pedal force to increase seat belt use of service vehicle drivers. *Journal of Applied Behavior Analysis, 44*, 41–49.

VanWormer, J. J. (2004). Pedometers and brief e-counseling: Increasing physical activity for overweight adults. *Journal of Applied Behavior Analysis, 37*, 421–425.

Vargas, E. (1985). Cultural contingencies: A review of Marvin Harris's Cannibals and Kings. *Journal of the Experimental Analysis of Behavior, 43*, 419–428.

Volti, R. (2004). *Cars and culture: The life story of a technology.* Westport, CT and London, England: Greenwood Press.

Warner, R. (1985). *Recovery from schizophrenia: Psychiatry and schizophrenia.* Boston, MA: Routledge & Kegan Paul.

Webster, D. (1985). Surplus, labor, and stress in late classic Maya society. *Journal of Anthropological Research, 41*, 375–399.

Wolak, J., Finkelhor, D., Mitchell, K., & Ybarra, M. (2008). Online "predators" and their victims: Myths, realities and implications for prevention and treatment. *American Psychologist, 63*, 111–128.

Yan, Z. (2006). What influences children's and adolescents' understanding of the complexity of the Internet? *Developmental Psychology, 42*, 1–11.

Young, K. S. (1998). Internet addiction: The emergence of a new clinical disorder. *CyberPsychology & Behavior, 1*, 237–244.

CHAPTER 12

Abbott, A. (1997). Of time and space: The contemporary relevance of the Chicago School. *Social Forces, 75*(4), 1149–1182.

Allen-Meares, P., & Lane, B. A. (1987). Grounding social work practice in theory: Ecosystems. *Social Casework, 68*, 515–521.

Andreson, M. A. (2006). Crime measures and the spatial analysis of criminal activity. *British Journal of Criminology, 46*, 258–285.

Berman, M. G., Jonides, J., & Kaplan, S. (2008). The cognitive benefits of interacting with nature. *Psychological Science, 19*(12), 1207–1212.

Bernstein, K. T., Galea, S., Ahern, J., Tracy, M., & Vlahov, D. (2007). The built environment and alcohol consumption in urban neighborhoods. *Drug and alcohol dependence, 91*(2–3), 244–252.

Berrigan, D., & McKinnon, R. A. (2008). Built environment and health. *Preventive Medicine, 47*, 239–240.

Boyle, G. (2010). *Tattoos on the heart: The power of boundless compassion*. New York, NY: Free Press.

Bronfenbrenner, U. (1979). *The ecology of human development: Experiments by nature and design*. Cambridge, MA: Harvard University Press.

Bronstein, L. R. (1996). Intervening with homeless youths: Direct practice without blaming the victim. *Child and Adolescent Social Work Journal*, *13*(2), 127–138.

Brookes, M. J., & Kaplan, A. (1972). The office environment: Space planning and affective behavior. *Human Factors and Ergonomics in Manufacturing*, *14*(5), 373–391.

Chang, P.-C. (1998). General well-being among Taiwanese early adolescents: A developmental-ecological approach. *Dissertation Abstracts International*, *59*(66), 2677.

Chinni, D., & Gimpel, J. (2010). *Our patchwork nation*. New York, NY: Gotham Books.

Costello, A., Abbas, M., Allen, A., et al. (2009). Managing the health effects of climate change. *Lancet 373*, 1693–1733.

Coulton, C. J., Chan, T., & Mikelbank, K. (2011). Finding place in community change initiatives: Using GIS to uncover resident perceptions of their neighborhoods. *Journal of Community Practice*. *19*, 10–28.

Curtis, A., Mills, J. W., & Leitner, M. (2007). Katrina and vulnerability: The geography of stress. *Journal of Health Care for the Poor and Underserved*, *18*, 315–330.

Cutter, S. L. (2006, June 11). *The geography of social vulnerability: Race, class, and catastrophe*. Retrieved from http://understandingkatrina.ssrc.org/Cutter/

DeFrances, C. J. (1996). The effects of racial ecological segregation on quality of life: A comparison of middle-class Blacks and middle-class Whites. *Urban Affairs Review*, *31*(6), 799–809.

Diamond, J. (1997). *Guns, germs, and steel*. New York, NY: Norton.

Dummer, T. J. B. (2008). Health geography: Supporting public health policy and planning. *Canadian Medical Association Journal*, *178*, 1–6.

Dupper, D. R. (1993). Preventing school dropouts: Guidelines for school social work practice. *Social Work in Education*, *15*, 141–149.

Early, B. P. (1992). An ecological–exchange model of social work consultation within the work group of the school. *Social Work in Education*, *14*(4), 207–214.

Eaton, J., & Kortum, S. (2002). Technology, geography, and trade. *Econometrica*, *70*(5), 1741–1779.

Elliott, J. R., & Pais, J. (2006). Race, class, and Hurricane Katrina: Social differences in human responses to disaster. *Social Science Research*, *35*, 295–321.

Escheverria, S., Diez-Roux, A. V., Shea, S., Borrell, L. N., & Jackson, S. (2008). Associations of neighborhood problems and neighborhood social cohesion with mental health and health behaviors: The multi-ethnic study of atherosclerosis. *Home & Place*, *14*, 853–865.

Evans, G. W. (2003). The built environment and mental health. *Journal of Urban Health*, *80*, 536–555.

Ewing, R., Schmid, T., Killingsworth, R., Zlot, A., & Raudenbush, S. (2003). Relationship between urban sprawl and physical activity, obesity, and morbidity. *American Journal of Health Promotion*, *18*(1), 47–57.

Forman, W., & Burch, E. S. (1988). *The Eskimos*. Norman, OK: University of Oklahoma Press.

Fouberg, E. H., Murphy, A. B., & de Blij, H. J. (2009). *Human geography: People, place, and culture*. Malden, MA: Wiley.

Fournier, A. K., Geller, E. S., & Fortney, E. V. (2007). Human-animal interaction in a prison setting: Impact on criminal behavior, treatment progress, and social skills. *Behavior and Social Issues*, *16*, 89–105.

Gallup, J. L., Sachs, J. D., & Mellinger, A. (1999). Geography and economic development. *Harvard University Center for International Development Working Papers*, *1*, 1–57.

Germain, C. B. (1991). *Human behavior in the social environment: An ecological view*. New York, NY: Columbia University Press.

Germain, C. B. (1994). Human behavior and the social environment. In F. G. Reamer (Ed.), *The foundations of social work knowledge* (pp. 88–121). New York, NY: Columbia University Press.

Germain, C. B., & Gitterman, A. (1980). *The life model of social work practice*. New York, NY: Columbia University Press.

Ghosh, S., & Wolf, H. (2000). Is there a curse of location? Spatial determinants of capital flows to emerging markets. In S. Edwards (Ed.), *Capital flows and the emerging economies: Theory, evidence, and controversies* (pp. 137–158). Chicago, IL: University of Chicago Press.

Gilgun, J. F. (1996). Human development and adversity in ecological perspective, part one: A conceptual framework. *Families in Society, 77*(7), 395–402.

Gray, M., & Bernstein, A. (1994). Pavement people and informal communities: Lessons for social work. *International Social Work, 37*(2), 149–163.

Handy, S. L., Boarnet, M. G., Ewing, R., & Killingsworth, R. E. (2002). How the built environment affects physical activity: Views from urban planning. *American Journal of Preventive Medicine, 23*, 64–73.

Harris, M. (1989). *Our kind.* New York, NY: Harper & Row.

Heerwagen, J. H., & Orians, G. H. (1986). Adaptations to windowlessness: A study of the use of visual décor in windowed and windowless offices. *Environment and Behavior, 18*(5), 623–639.

Heise, L. L (1998). Violence against women: An integrated ecological framework. *Violence Against Women, 4*(3), 262–290.

Holman, W. D. (1997). The "gangsta" persona: A case study from an ecosystems perspective. *Smith College Studies in Social Work, 67*(3), 487–501.

Irwin, J. (1985). *The jail: Managing the underclass in American society.* Berkeley, CA: University of California Press.

Jensen, J. (2007). *Remote sensing of the environment: An earth resource perspective.* Upper Saddle River, NJ: Prentice Hall.

Kahn, M. E. (2005). The death toll from natural disasters: The role of income, geography, and institutions. *Review of Economics and Statistics, 87*(2), 271–284.

Kahn, P. E., Friedman, B., Gill, B., Hagman, J., Severson, R. L., Freier, N. G., Feldman, E. N.,... Stolyar, A. (2008). A plasma display window? The shifting baseline problem in a technologically mediated natural world. *Journal of Environmental Psychology, 28*, 192–199.

Kirby, D. (2007). *Emerging answers 2007: Research findings on programs to reduce teen pregnancy and sexually transmitted diseases.* Washington, DC: The National Campaign to Prevent Teen and Unplanned Pregnancy.

Koyama, A., Corliss, H. L., & Santelli, J. S. (2009). Global lessons on healthy adolescent sexual development. *Current Opinion in Pediatrics. 21*, 444–449.

Kunkel, K. E., Pielke, R. A., & Changnon, S. A. (1999). Temporal fluctuations in weather and climate extremes that cause economic and human

health impacts: A review. *Bulletin of the American Meteorological Society, 80*(6), 1077–1098.

Kupritz, V. W. (1998). Privacy in the work place: The impact of building design. *Journal of Environmental Psychology, 18* (4), 341–356.

Leaman, A., & Bordass, W. (2005). *Productivity in buildings: The killer variables.* Retrieved from the Usable Buildings Trust website: www.usable buildings.co.uk/Pages/Unprotected/KVChicago Apr05.pdf

Legrand, L. N., Keyes, M., McGue, M., Iacono, W. G., & Krueger, R. F. (2008). Rural environments reduce the genetic influence on adolescent substance use and rule-breaking behavior. *Psychological Medicine, 38*, 1341–1350.

Leighninger, R. D. (1978). Systems theory. *Journal of Sociology and Social Welfare, 5*(4), 446–480.

Ligon, J. (1997). Brief crisis stabilization of an African American woman: Integrating cultural and ecological approaches. *Journal of Multicultural Social Work, 6*(3–4), 111–122.

Lohr, V. L., Pearson-Mims, C. H., & Goodwin, G. K. (1996). Interior plants may improve worker productivity and reduce stress in a windowless environment. *Journal of Environmental Horticulture, 14*(2), 96–100.

Lupien, S. J., King, S., Meaney, M. J., & McEwen, B. S. (2000). Child's stress hormone levels correlate with mother's socioeconomic status and depressive state. *Biological Psychiatry, 48*(10), 976–980.

Madison, A. (1995). *Monitoring the world economy, 1820–1992.* Paris: Organisation for Economic Co-operation and Development.

Mason, C. A., Cauce, A. M., Gonzales, N., Hiraga, Y., & Grove, K. (1994). An ecological model of externalizing behaviors in African-American adolescents: No family is an island. *Journal of Research on Adolescence, 4*(4), 639–655.

Massey, D., & Denton, N. (1993). *American apartheid: Segregation and the making of the underclass.* Cambridge, MA: Harvard University Press.

Mattaini, M. A. (1990). Contextual behavior analysis in the assessment process. *Families in Society, 71*(4), 236–245.

Mayo Clinic (2011, September 22). *Seasonal affective disorder.* Retrieved from www.mayoclinic.com/health/seasonal-affective-disorder/DS00195

McCoy, R. M. (2005). *Field methods in remote sensing.* New York, NY: Guilford Press.

McMichael, A. J., Nyong, A., & Corvalan, C. (2008). Global environmental change and health: Impacts, inequalities, and the health sector. *British Medical Journal*, *336*, 191–194.

Messner, S. E., Raffalovich, L. E., & Sutton, G. M. (2010). Poverty, infant mortality, and homicide rates in cross national perspective: Assessments of criterion and construct validity. *Criminology*, *48* (2), 509–538.

Meyer, C. H. (1983). *Clinical social work in the eco-systems perspective*. New York, NY: Columbia University Press.

Meyer, C. H. (1988). The eco-systems perspective. In R. A. Dorfman (Ed.), *Paradigms of clinical social work*. New York, NY: Brunner-Mazel.

Meyer, C. H. (1993). *Assessment in social work practice*. New York, NY: Columbia University Press.

Monahan, D. J. (1993). Assessment of dementia patients and their families: An ecological–family centered approach. *Health and Social Work*, *18*(2), 141–149.

Moran, E. F. (2010). *Environmental social science*. Malden, MA: Wiley-Blackwell.

Nelson M., & Gordon-Larsen, P. (2006). Physical activity and sedentary behavior patterns are associated with selected adolescent health risk behaviors. *Pediatrics*, *117*, 1281–1692.

Northey, W. F., Primer, V., & Christensen, L. (1997). Promoting justice in the delivery of services to juvenile delinquents: The ecosystemic natural wrap-around model. *Child and Adolescent Social Work Journal*, *14*(1), 5–22.

O'Hare, W., & Lee, M. (2007). *Factors affecting state differences in child well-being*. Baltimore, MD: Working paper, Kids Count Series, The Annie E. Casey Foundation. Retrieved from www.aecf.org/ KnowledgeCenter/Publications.aspx?pubguid=% 7BCF4C070F-E74C-4B0D-B876-C433CF100C C3%7D

Pardeck, J. T. (1996). An ecological approach for social work intervention. *Family Therapy*, *23*(3), 189–198.

Park, K. M. (1996). The personal is ecological: Environmentalism of social work. *Social Work*, *41*(3), 320–323.

Pickett, S. T. A, Cadenasso, M. L., Grove, J. M., Groffman, P. M., Band, L. E., Boone, C. G., ... Wilson, M. A. (2008). Beyond urban legends: An emerging framework of urban ecology, as illustrated by the Baltimore Ecosystem Study. *BioScience*, *58*(2), 139–150.

Schulz, A. J., Williams, D. R., Israel, B. A, & Lempert, L. B. (2002). Racial and spatial relations as fundamental determinants of health in Detroit. *The Milbank Quarterly*, *80*(4), 677–707.

Sharkey, J. R., Johnson, C. M., & Dean, W. R. (2011). Nativity is associated with sugar-sweetened beverage and fast-food meal consumption among Mexican-origin women in Texas border colonias, *Nutrition Journal*, *30*, 101.

Siporin, M. (1980). Ecological systems theory in social work. *Journal of Sociology and Social Welfare*, *7*(4), 507–532.

Sommers, S. R., Apfelbaum, E. P., Dukes, K. N., Toosi, N., & Wang, E. J. (2006). Race and media coverage of hurricane Katrina: Analysis, implications, and future research questions. *Analyses of Social Issues and Public Policy*, *6*, 39–55.

Stern, P. R., & Stevenson, L. (2006). *Critical Inuit studies: An anthology of contemporary Arctic ethnography*. Lincoln, NE: University of Nebraska Press.

Steward, J. (1955). *The theory of culture change*. Urbana, IL: The University of Illinois Press.

Stivers, C. (2007). "So poor and so Black": Hurricane Katrina, public administration, and the issue of race. *Public Administration Review*, *47*(Issue Supplement), 48–56.

Taubman, S. (1984). Incest in context. *Social Work*, *29*(1), 35–40.

United Nations Population Division. (2005). *World urbanization prospects: The 2005 revision*. New York, NY: The United Nations.

United Nations World Youth Report. (2007). *Young people's transition to adulthood: Progress and challenges*. New York, NY: United Nations.

U.S. Department of Health and Human Services, U.S. Department of Agriculture. (2005). *Dietary Guidelines for America—6th edition*. Washington, DC: U.S. Government Printing Office.

Wakefield, J. (1996a). Does social work need the eco-systems perspective? Part one. Is the perspective clinically useful? *Social Service Review*, *70*, 1–32.

Wakefield, J. (1996b). Does social work need the eco-systems perspective? Part two. Is the perspective clinically useful? *Social Service Review*, *70*, 183–214.

Weber, B. (2007). Rural poverty: Why should states care and what can state policy do? *The Journal of Regional Analysis and Policy*, *37*, 48–52.

White, D. D., Virden, R. J., & van Riper, C. J. (2008). Effects of place identity, place dependence, and experience-use history on perceptions of recreation impacts in a natural setting. *Environmental Management, 42*(4), 647–657.

Williams, D. R., & Stewart, S. I. (1998). Sense of place: An elusive concept that is finding a home in ecosystem management. *Journal of Forestry, 96*, 18–23.

The Willis Group. (n.d.). *GDP-based global diversification*. Retrieved from www.thewillisgroup.net/global.html

Wilson-Oyelaran, E. B. (1989). The ecological model and the study of child abuse in Nigeria. *Child Abuse and Neglect, 13*(3), 379–387.

Woo, J. (2000). Relationships among diet, physical activity, and other lifestyle factors and debilitating diseases in the elderly. *European Journal of Clinical Nutrition, 54*(3), S143–S147.

World Bank. (n.d.). *GDP*. Data retrieved from http://data.worldbank.org/indicator/NY.GDP.MKTP.CD

Wu, J. Q. (2011, July 13). At Planters Grove, it's 'Needle Park' no more. *The Washington Post*. Retrieved from www.highbeam.com/doc/1P2-29140248.html

Zimbardo, P. (2007). *The Lucifer effect: Understanding how good people turn evil*. New York, NY: Random House.

CHAPTER 13

Berson, Y., Oreg, S., & Dvir, T. (2008). CEO values, organizational culture and firm outcomes. *Journal of Organizational Behavior, 29*, 615–633.

Bowles, S., Choi, J. K., & Hopfensitz, A. (2002). The co-evolution of individual behaviors and social institutions. *Journal of Theoretical Biology, 223*, 135–147.

Brooks-Gunn, J., & Duncan, G. J. (1997). The effects of poverty on children. *The Future of Children, 7*, 55–71.

Cameron, K. S., & Quinn, R. E. (1999). *Diagnosing and changing organizational culture*. Upper Saddle River, NJ: Prentice Hall.

Chakrabarty, S. (2009). The influence of national culture and institutional voids on family ownership of large firms: A country level empirical study. *Journal of International Management, 15*, 32–45.

Chandra, A., Lara-Cinisoma, S., Jaycox, L. H., Tanielian, T., Burns, R. M., Ruder, T., & Han, B. (2010). Children on the homefront: The experience of children from military families. *Pediatrics, 125*, 16–25.

Chartrand, M. M., Frank, D. A., White, L. F., & Shope, T. R. (2008). Effect of parents' wartime deployment on the behavior of young children in military families. *Archives of Pediatric and Adolescent Medicine, 162*, 1009–1014.

Cuomo, C., Sarachiapone, M., Massimo, D. G., Mancini, M., & Roy, A. (2008). Aggression, impulsivity, personality traits, and childhood trauma of prisoners with substance abuse and addiction. *The American Journal of Drug and Alcohol Abuse, 34*, 339–345.

Dembo, R., & Schmeidler, J. (2003). A classification of high-risk youths. *Crime and Delinquency, 49*, 201–230.

Dembo, R., Schmeidler, J., Nini-gough, B., & Manning, D. (1998). Sociodemographic, delinquency abuse history and psychosocial functioning differences among juvenile offenders or various ages. *Journal of Child and Adolescent Substance Abuse, 8*, 63–78.

Di Fiore, A., & Rendall, D. (1994). Evolution of social organization: A reappraisal for primates by using phylogenetic methods. *Proceedings of the National Academy of Sciences, 91*, 9941–9945.

Dupre, M. E. (2008). Educational differences in health risks and illness over the life course: A test of cumulative disadvantage theory. *Social Science Research, 37*, 1253–1266.

Federal Deposit Insurance Corporation. (2009). *FDIC mission, vision, and values*. Retrieved from www.fdic.gov/about/mission

Fredriksson, P. G., Neumayer, E., Damania, R., & Gates, S. (2005). Environmentalism, democracy, and pollution control. *Journal of Environmental Economics and Management, 49*, 343–365.

Fredriksson, P. G., & Svensson, J. (2003). Political instability, corruption and policy formation: The case of environmental policy. *Journal of Public Economics, 87*, 1383–1405.

Freedman, M., & Owens, E. G. (2011). Low income housing development and crime. *Journal of Urban Economics, 70*, 115–131.

Glisson, C., Schoenwald, S. K., Kelleher, K., Landsverk, J., Hoagwood, K. E., Mayberg, S., &

Green, P. (2008). Therapist turnover and new program sustainability in mental health clinics as a function of organizational culture, climate, and service structure. *Administrative Policy and Mental Health, 35*, 124–133.

Goel, R. K., & Nelson, M. A. (2010). Causes of corruption: History, geography, and government. *Journal of Policy Modeling, 32*, 433–447.

Goff, B. S., Crow, J. R., Reisbig, A. M., & Hamilton, S. (2007). The impact of individual trauma symptoms of deployed soldiers on relationship satisfaction. *Journal of Family Psychology, 21*, 344–353.

Hamersma, S. (2008). The effects of an employer subsidy on employment outcomes: A study of the work opportunity and welfare-to-work tax credits. *Journal of Policy Analysis & Management, 27*(3), 498–520.

Harris, M. (1989). *Our kind*. New York, NY: Harper & Row.

Hodgson, G. M. (2006). What are institutions? *Journal of Economic Issues, XL*, 1–25.

ICF International. (n.d.). *Demographics 2007 profile of the military community*. Washington, DC: Office of the Deputy Under Secretary of Defense (Military Community and Family Policy). Retrieved from www.militaryonesource.mil/12038/MOS/Reports/2007%20Demographics.pdf

James, D. J., & Glaze, L. E. (2006). *Mental health problems of prison and jail inmates* (NCJ 213600). Washington, DC: Bureau of Justice Statistics. Retrieved from http://bjs.ojp.usdoj.gov/index.cfm?ty=pbdetail&iid=789

Krisberg, K., & Howell, J. C. (1998). The impact of the juvenile justice system and prospects for graduated sanctions in a comprehensive strategy. In R. Loeber & D. P. Farrington (Eds.), *Serious & violent juvenile offenders: Risk factors and successful interventions* (pp. 346–366). Thousand Oaks, CA: Sage.

Langan, P. A., & Levin, D. J. (2002). *Recidivism of prisoners released in 1994*. (NCJ 193427). Washington, DC: Bureau of Justice Statistics. Retrieved from http://bjs.ojp.usdoj.gov/index.cfm?ty=pbdetail&iid=1134

Lawrence, T. B., & Suddaby, R. (2006). Institutions and institutional work. In S. R. Clegg, C. Hardy, T. B. Lawrence, & W. R. Nord (Eds.), *Handbook of organization studies* (2nd ed., pp. 215–254). London, England: Sage.

López, R., & Mitra, S. (2000), Corruption, pollution and the Kuznets environment curve. *Journal of Environmental Economics and Management, 40*(2), 137–150.

Loughnan, S., Kuppens, P., Allik, J., Balazs, K., de Lemus, S., Dumont, K., . . . Haslam, N. (2011). Economic inequality is linked to biased self-perception. *Psychological Science, 22*, 1254–1258.

Mankiw, N. G. (2007). *Essentials of economics* (4th ed.). Mason, OH: Thomson South-Western.

Marshall, G. (1986). The workplace culture of a licensed restaurant. *Theory, Culture, and Society, 3*, 33–47.

McEwen, B. S. (2000). Allostasis and allostatic load: Implications for neuropsychopharmacology. *Neuropsychopharmacology, 22*, 108–124.

McEwen, B. S., & Stellar, E. (1993). Stress and the individual: Mechanisms leading to disease. *Archives of Internal Medicine, 153*, 2093–2101.

McGowan, P. O., Sasaki, A., D'Alessio, A. C., Dymov, S., Labonté, B., Szyf, M., . . . Meaney, M. J. (2009). Epigenetic regulation of the glucocorticoid receptor in human brain associates with childhood abuse. *Nature Neuroscience, 12*(3), 342–348.

Mears, D. P., & Travis, J. (2004). Youth development and reentry. *Youth Violence and Juvenile Justice, 2*, 3–20.

Morgan, G. (1997). *Images of organization* (2nd ed.). Thousand Oaks, CA: Sage.

Mumola, C. J. & Karberg, J. C. (2006). *Drug use and dependence state and federal prisoners*, 2004. (NCJ 213530). Washington, DC: Bureau of Justice Statistics. Retrieved from http://bjs.ojp.usdoj.gov/index.cfm?ty=pbdetail&iid=778

Naiman, K. M., Hayatbakhsh, M. R., Heron, M. A., Bor, W., O'Callaghan, M. J., & Williams, G. M. (2009). The impact of episodic and chronic poverty on child cognitive development. *Journal of Pediatrics, 154*, 284–289.

The National Children's Study. (2012, April 2). Eunice Kennedy Shriver National Institute of Child Health and Human Development, National Institutes of Health. Retrieved from www.nationalchildrensstudy.gov/Pages/default.aspx

Oishi, S., Kesibir, S., & Diener, E. (2011). Income inequality and happiness. *Psychological Science, 22*, 1095–1100.

Petersilia, J. (2003). *When prisoners come home: Parole and prisoner reentry*. New York, NY: Oxford University Press.

Rank, M. R., & Hirschl, T. A. (2009). Estimating the risk of food stamp use and impoverishment during childhood. *Archives of Pediatrics and Adolescent Medicine, 163*, 994–999.

Renfrew, C. (2007). *Prehistory: The making of the human mind*. New York, NY: Random House.

Rodrik, D., Subramanian, A., & Trebbi, F. (2002, October). Institutions rule: The primacy of institutions over geography and integration into economic development (National Bureau of Economic Research Working Paper 9305). Retrieved from the National Bureau of Economic Research website: www.nber.org/papers/w9305.pdf?new_window=1

Ross, C. E., & Murowsky, J. (1989). Explaining the social patterns of depression: Control and problem solving—or support and talking. *Journal of Health and Social Behavior, 30*, 206–209.

Sabol, W. J., West, H. C., & Cooper, M. (2009). Prisoners in 2008. (NCJ 228417). Washington DC: Bureau of Justice Statistics. Retrieved from http://bjs.ojp.usdoj.gov/index.cfm?ty=pbdetail&iid=1763

Samper, R. E., Taft, C. T., King, D. W., & King, L. A. (2004). Posttraumatic stress disorder symptoms and parenting satisfaction among a national sample of male Vietnam veterans. *Journal of Traumatic Stress, 17*, 311–315.

Sapolsky, R. M. (2005). The influence of social hierarchy on primate health. *Science, 308*, 648–652.

Sayers, S. L., Farrow, V. A., Ross, J., & Oslin, D. W. (2009). Family problems among recently returned military veterans referred for a mental health evaluation. *Journal of Clinical Psychiatry, 70*, 163–170.

Sherraden, M. (1991). *Assets and the poor: A new American welfare policy*. Armonk, NY: M.E. Sharpe.

Shleifer, A., & Vishny, R. W. (1993). Corruption. *Quarterly Journal of Economics, 108*(3), 599–617.

Stiglitz, Joseph. (2002). *Globalization and its discontents*. New York, NY: Norton.

Thompson, W., & Hickey, J. (2005). *Society in focus*. Boston, MA: Allyn & Bacon.

Turrell, G., Lynch, J. W., Leite, C., Raghunathan, T., & Kaplan, G. A. (2007). Socioeconomic disadvantage in childhood and across the life course and all-cause mortality and physical function in adulthood: Evidence from the Alameda County Study. *Journal of Epidemiology and Community Health, 61*, 723–730.

United Nations Development Programme (2011). *Human Development Report*, International Human Development Indicators. United Nations, New York.

United States Department of Labor. (2011). *Work opportunity tax credit*. Retrieved from www.doleta.gov/business/incentives/opptax/

Vaughn, M. G., Pettus-Davis, C., & Shook, J. J. (2012). *Conducting research in criminal and juvenile justice settings*. New York: NY: Oxford University Press.

Veblen, T. (1934). *Theory of the leisure class*. New York, NY: Modern Library. (Original work published 1899.)

Weber, M. (1968). *Economy and society: An outline of interpretive sociology*. New York, NY: Bedminster Press. (Original work published 1922.)

World Trade Organization. (2011). *What is the WTO?* Retrieved from http://wto.org/english/thewto_e/whatis_e/whatis_e.htm

Young, H. P. (2001). *Individual strategy and social structure: An evolutionary theory of institutions*. Princeton, NJ: Princeton University Press.

CHAPTER 14

Abreu, J. M., Goodyear, R. K., Campos, A., & Newcomb, M. D. (2000). Ethnic belonging and traditional masculinity ideology among African Americans, European Americans, and Latinos. *Psychology of Men and Masculinity, 1*, 75–86.

Amodio, D. M., Jost, J. T., Master, S. L., & Yee, C. M. (2007). Neurocognitive correlates of liberalism and conservatism. *Nature Neuroscience, 10*, 1246–1247.

Berk, L. E. (2007). *Development through the lifespan* (4th ed.). Boston, MA: Allyn & Bacon.

Bodley, J. H. (1994). *Cultural anthropology: Tribes, states and the global system*. Mountain View, CA: Mayfield.

Bouchard, T. J. (2004). Genetic influence on human psychological traits: A survey. *Current Directions in Psychological Science, 13*, 148–151.

Bouchard, T. J., & McGue, M. (2003). Genetic and environmental influences on human psychological differences. *Journal of Neurobiology, 54*, 4–45.

Brandt, M. J. (2011). Sexism and gender inequality across 57 societies. *Psychological Science, 22*, 1413–1418.

Carter, T. J., Ferguson, M. J., & Hassin, R. R. (2011). A single exposure to the American flag shifts support toward Republicanism up to 8 months later. *Psychological Science, 22*, 1011–1018.

Chase, P. G., & Dibble, H. L. (1987). Middle Paleolithic symbolism: A review of current evidence and interpretations. *Journal of Anthropological Archeology, 6*, 263–296.

Chiao, J. Y., & Blizinsky, K. D. (2010). Culture-gene coevolution of individualism-collectivism and the serotonin transporter gene (5-HTTLPR). *Proceedings of the Royal Society B: Biological Sciences, 277*(1681), 529–37.

Chiao, J. Y., Harada, T., Komeda, H., Li, Z., Mano, Y., Saito, D., et al. (2008). Neural basis of individualistic and collectivistic views of self. *Human Brain Mapping*, doi: 10.1002/hbm.20707.

Chiao, J. Y., Hariri, A. R., Harada, T., Mano, Y., Sadato, N., Parrish, T. B., & Iidaka, T. (2010). Theory and methods in cultural neuroscience. *Social Cognitive and Affective Neuroscience, 5*, 356–361.

Cohen, F., & Solomon, S. (2011). The politics of mortal terror. *Current Directions in Psychological Science, 20*, 316–320.

Collins, P. H. (2000). *Black feminist thought* (2nd ed.). New York, NY: Routledge.

Darnell, R. (1974). *Readings in the history of anthropology*. New York, NY: Harper & Row.

Davis, D. W., & Brown, R. E. (2002). The antipathy of black nationalism: Behavioral and attitudinal implications of an African-American ideology. *American Journal of Political Science, 46*, 239–253.

Deater-Deckard, K., & Dodge, K. A. (1997). Externalizing behavior problems and discipline revisited: Nonlinear effects and variation by culture, context, and gender. *Psychological Inquiry, 8*, 161–175.

Ellison, C. G., & Bradshaw, M. (2009). Religious beliefs, sociopolitical ideology, and attitudes toward corporal punishment. *Journal of Family Issues, 30*, 320–340.

Fadiman, A. (1997). *The spirit catches you and you fall down*. New York, NY: Farrar, Straus and Giroux.

Festinger, L. (1957). *A theory of cognitive dissonance*. Stanford, CA: Stanford University Press.

Graham, J., & Haidt, J. (2010). Beyond beliefs: Religions bind individuals into moral communities. *Personality and Social Psychology Review, 14*, 140–150.

Haidt, J. (2012). *The righteous mind: Why good people are divided by politics and religion*. New York, NY: Pantheon.

Hall, D. L., Matz, D. C., & Wood, W. (2010). Why don't we practice what we preach? A meta-analytic review of religious racism. *Personality and Social Psychology Review, 14*, 126–139.

Harris, M. (1979). *Cultural materialism: The struggle for a science of culture*. New York, NY: Random House.

Harris, M. (1980). History and ideological significance of the separation of social and cultural anthropology. In E. Ross (Ed.), *Beyond the myths of culture: Essays in cultural materialism* (pp. 391–407). New York, NY: Academic.

Harris, M. (1999). *Theories of culture in postmodern times*. Walnut Creek, CA: Alta Mina.

Hart, D. L., & Sussman, R. W. (2005). *Man the hunted: Primates, predators, and human evolution*. New York, NY: Perseus.

Haslam, S. A., Jetten, J., Postmes, T., & Haslam, C. (2009). Social identity, health, and well-being: An emerging agenda for applied psychology. *Applied Psychology: An International Review, 58*, 1–23.

Hatch, E. (1973). *Theories of man and vulture*. New York, NY: Columbia University Press.

Hays, P. A. (2008). *Addressing cultural complexities in practice: Assessment, diagnosis, and therapy* (2nd ed.). Washington, DC: American Psychological Association.

Hehman, E., Gaertner, S. L., Dovidio, J. F., Mania, E. W., Guerra, R., Wilson, D. C., & Friel, B. M. (2012). Group status drives majority and minority integration preferences. *Psychological Science, 23*, 46–52.

Hobbes, T. (1994). *Leviathan*. London: Hackett.

Hodge, D. R. (2005). Social work and the house of Islam: Orienting practitioners to the beliefs and values of Muslims in the United States. *Social Work, 50*, 162–173.

Hodge, D. R., & Nadir, A. (2008). Moving toward cultural competent practice with Muslims: Modifying cognitive therapy with Islamic tenets. *Social Work, 53*, 31–41.

Hodge, D. & Jackson, K., & Vaughn, M. G. (2010). Culturally sensitive interventions for health related behaviors among Latino youth: A meta-analytic review. *Children and Youth Services Review, 82*, 1331–1337.

Hodge, D. & Jackson, K., & Vaughn, M. G. (2010). Culturally sensitive interventions and health and behavioral health youth outcomes: A meta-analytic review. *Social Work in Health Care, 49*, 401–423.

Hodgen, M. T. (1964). *Early anthropology in the sixteenth and seventeenth centuries*. Philadelphia, PA: University of Philadelphia Press.

Hook, J. N., Worthington, E. L., Jr., Davis, D. E., Jennings, D. J. II, & Gartner, A. L. (2010). Empirically supported religious and spiritual therapies. *Journal of Clinical Psychology, 66*, 46–72.

Jackson, K., Hodge, D., & Vaughn, M. (2010). A meta-analysis of culturally sensitive interventions designed to reduce high-risk behaviors among African American youth. *Journal of Social Service Research, 36*, 163–173

Jost, J. T., Glaser, J., Kruglanski, A. W., & Sulloway, F. J. (2003). Political conservatism and motivated social cognition. *Psychological Bulletin, 129*, 339–375.

Kinzler, K. D., Corriveau, K. H., & Harris, P. L (2011). Children's selective trust in native-accented speakers. *Developmental Science, 14*, 106–111.

Koenig, H. G., King, D., & Carson, V. B. (2012). *Handbook of religion and health* (2nd ed.). New York, NY: Oxford University Press.

Kroeber, A. L., & Kluckhohn, C. (1952). *Culture: A critical review of concepts and definitions*. Cambridge, MA: Harvard University Press.

Kroeber, A. L., & Parsons, T. (1958). The concept of culture and of social systems. *American Sociological Review, 23*, 582–583.

Lambert, A. J., Schott, J. P., & Scherer, L. (2011). Threat, politics, and attitudes: Toward a greater understanding of rally-'round-the-flag effects. *Current Directions in Psychological Science, 20*, 343–348.

Lopez-Class, M., Castro, F. G., & Ramirez, A. G. (2011). Conceptions of acculturation: A review and statement of critical issues. *Social Science and Medicine, 72*, 1555–1562.

Lucretius. (1913). *De rerum natura*. (H. A. J. Munro, Trans.). London, England: G. Bell.

MacCoun, R. J., & Paletz, S. (2009). Citizens' perceptions of ideological bias in research on public policy controversies. *Political Psychology, 30*, 43–65.

Machiavelli, N. (1995). *The prince*. London, England: Hackett.

Manoli, C. C., Johnson, B., & Dunlap, R. E. (2007). Assessing children's environmental world views: Modifying and validating the new ecological paradigm scale for use with children. *Journal of Environmental Education, 38*, 3–12.

Marin, G. (1993). Defining culturally appropriate community interventions: Hispanics as a case study. *Journal of Community Psychology, 21*, 149–161.

Mercer, J. (2010). *Child development: Myths and misunderstandings*. Thousand Oaks, CA: Sage.

Nickerson, L. (1998). Confirmation bias: A ubiquitous phenomenon in many guises. *Review of General Psychology, 2*, 175–220.

Pandian, J. (1985). *Anthropology and the western tradition*. Prospect Heights, IL: Waveland Press.

Plaut, V. C., Thomas, K. M., & Goren, M. J. (2009). Is multiculturalism or color blindness better for minorities? *Psychological Science, 20*, 444–446.

Poteat, V. P., & Anderson, C. J. (2012). Developmental changes in sexual prejudice from early to late adolescence: The effects of gender, race, and ideology on different patterns of change. *Developmental Psychology, 48*, 1403–1415.

Punamaki, R. (1996). Can ideological commitment protect children's psychosocial well-being in situations of political violence? *Child Development, 67*, 55–69.

Reeskens, T., & Wright, M. (2011). Subjective well-being and national satisfaction: Taking seriously the "proud of what?" question. *Psychological Science, 22*, 1460–1462.

Sanderson, S. K. (2008). Adaptation, evolution, and religion. *Religion, 38*, 141–156.

Saraglou, V., Delpierre, V., & Dernelle, R. (2004). Values and religiosity: A meta-analysis using Schwartz's model. *Personality and Individual Differences, 37*, 721–734.

Schepartz, L. A. (1993). Language and modern human origins. *Yearbook of Physical Anthropology, 36*, 91–126.

Shermer, M. (1998). *Why people believe weird things: Pseudoscience, superstition, and other confusions of our time*. New York, NY: W. H. Freeman.

Smith, C. (2005). *Soul-searching: The religious and spiritual lives of American teenagers*. New York, NY: Oxford University Press.

Sommers-Flanagan, J., & Sommers-Flanagan, R. (2009). *Clinical interviewing* (4th ed.). Hoboken, NJ: Wiley.

Sue, D., & Sue, D. (2008). *Counseling the culturally diverse: Theory and practice* (5th ed.). Hoboken, NJ: Wiley.

Verkuyten, M. (2005). Ethnic group identification and group evaluation among minority and majority groups: Testing the multiculturalism hypothesis.

Journal of Personality and Social Psychology, 88, 121–138.

Vermeesh, H., Tsjoen, G., Kaufman, J. M., Vincke, J., & Van Houtte, M. (2010). Gender ideology, same-sex peer group affiliation and the relationship between testosterone and dominance in adolescent boys and girls. *Journal of Biosocial Science, 42*, 463–475.

Whiten, A. G., McGrew, W. C., Nishida, T., Reynolds, V., Sugiyama, Y., Tutin, C. E. G., … Boesch, C. (1999). Culture in chimpanzees. *Nature, 399*, 682–685.

Wolf, M. (1978). Social validity: The case for subjective measurement. *Journal of Applied Behavior Analysis, 11*(2), 203–214.

Wolsko, C., Park, B., & Judd, C. M. (2006). Considering the tower of Babel: Correlates of assimilation and multiculturalism among ethnic minority and majority groups in the United States. *Social Justice Research, 19*, 277–306.

Ysseldyk, R., Matheson, K., & Anisman, H. (2010). Religiosity as identity? Toward an understanding of religion from a social identity perspective. *Personality and Social Psychology Review 14*, 60–71.

AUTHOR INDEX

SUBJECT INDEX

Page numbers followed by *f* indicate a figure; Those followed by *t* indicate a table.